52
Fifty Two Sales Meetings

ALBERT R. TEICHNER

F.R.I., CMR, R.I.(B.C.), (Retired), CRES

TRAFFORD
USA ▪ Canada ▪ UK ▪ Ireland

© Copyright 2007 Albert R. Teichner.
All rights reserved. No part of this publication may be reproduced, stored in a retrieval system, or transmitted, in any form or by any means, electronic, mechanical, photocopying, recording, or otherwise, without the written prior permission of the author.

Note for Librarians: A cataloguing record for this book is available from Library and Archives Canada at www.collectionscanada.ca/amicus/index-e.html
ISBN 1-4120-7806-7

Printed in Victoria, BC, Canada. Printed on paper with minimum 30% recycled fibre.
Trafford's print shop runs on "green energy" from solar, wind and other environmentally-friendly power sources.

TRAFFORD
PUBLISHING

Offices in Canada, USA, Ireland and UK

Book sales for North America and international:
Trafford Publishing, 6E–2333 Government St.,
Victoria, BC V8T 4P4 CANADA
phone 250 383 6864 (toll-free 1 888 232 4444)
fax 250 383 6804; email to orders@trafford.com

Book sales in Europe:
Trafford Publishing (UK) Limited, 9 Park End Street, 2nd Floor
Oxford, UK OX1 1HH UNITED KINGDOM
phone +44 (0)1865 722 113 (local rate 0845 230 9601)
facsimile +44 (0)1865 722 868; info.uk@trafford.com

Order online at:
trafford.com/05-2703

10 9 8 7 6 5 4 3

This book is dedicated to my dear wife Shirley

as my heartfelt thanks for her many years of patience, love, support and encouragement while I was busy selling real estate and/or working as a Manager

CONTENTS

(I) PREFACE 15

(II) FOR SALES MANAGERS AND THOSE WHO WANT TO BECOME ONE

    (a) The changing role for the Real Estate Sales Manager. 20

    (b) Components of a well-run Sales Meeting. 24

(III) 52 SALES MEETINGS

(A) GROUND RULES and SKILLS to HELP a Salesperson to SUCCEED

<u>Sales Meeting # 01</u>

BACK TO BASICS - PART I

Physical requirements. 28
    Office equipment, tools, car, real estate forms, VISUAL CREDIBILITY, personal appearance

BACK TO BASICS - PART II

Psychological requirements. 33
    What do consumers want from a Real Estate Agent?
    - The Realtor should be patient, attentive and trustworthy
    - He should have empathy, communication and negotiation skills

<u>Sales Meeting # 02</u>

GOAL SETTING 39

    Short term and long term goals
    Goals should be realistic, attainable, clearly defined and worthwhile

<u>Sales Meeting # 03</u>

Essay on BEING ORGANIZED, PLANNING, TIME MANAGEMENT And On How To Stay Focused 41

    Self-discipline
    Weekly Activity Record

(B) GUIDELINES FOR DEALING WITH PEOPLE

Sales Meeting # 04

THOUGHTS on EFFECTIVE VERBAL COMMUNICATION 47

"Communicating" means the transfer of a thought or an abstract concept in the form of a mental picture.

Sales Meeting # 05

BODY LANGUAGE

    Part I: The senses of sight, smell, hearing and touch 53
                Poise check

    Part II: Body posture. Signals from the face, eyes, ...57
                mouth and hand gestures

Sales Meeting # 06

EMPATHY, The Manager and The Salesperson 62

Empathy (not to be confused with "sympathy") is a triumph in communication.
How to acquire and practice it.

(C) LISTINGS ARE YOUR "STOCK ON THE SHELF"

Sales Meeting # 07

Winning strategies for PROSPECTING 75

How to overcome the fear of rejection.
Sources for prospecting.

Sales Meeting # 08

OBTAINING LISTINGS 86

Sources where to find listings.
How many listing should you carry?

Sales Meeting # 09

FOR SALE BY OWNER

    Part I - Psychological aspects of dealing successfully with a FSBO. 86

    Part II - A professional Realtor's SERVICES and EXPERIENCE can 93
               solve a FSBO's problems.

Index

Sales Meeting # 10

"Operation Grasshopper"..................107

A concentrated listing EFFORT to be made in fall to ensure that you will survive in the real estate business during the difficult winter months. This can also be in the form of an Office Listing Contest.

(D) OUT IN THE FIELD

Sales Meeting # 11

Preparation for a LISTING APPOINTMENT..................110

First contact, research and personal preparation to meet the Customer.

Sales Meeting # 12

The LISTING APPOINTMENT

Part I   -   The importance of making a good 1st impression..............115
              The house inspection with the Seller.
              The Listing Work Sheet.

Part II   -   The ACTUAL Listing PRESENTATION....................125
              Follow-up courtesy letters to the Sellers:
              - "THANK YOU for listing with me"
              - Letter of "regret" in case you didn't get the listing.
              - PAMPHLET "How long will it take to sell your house?"

Part III   -   Analyzing the difference between the Selling Salesperson........137
              (Buyer's Agent) and the Listing Salesperson and their
              respective problems.

Sales Meeting # 13

THE AGENCY DISCLOSURE...................139

Fiduciary Duties, Informed Consent, the Agency Relationship.

Sales Meeting # 14

ABOUT the VULNERABILITY of the PRINCIPAL

Part I   -   The Principal's vicarious liability plus case law............148

Part II   -   The Principal's (Seller's) obligations and duties..........151

Part III   -   Information about a TRANSACTION BROKER..........155

Sales Meeting # 15
The Property Condition Disclosure Statement
   Part I   -   Health, safety, legal and environmental matters. **158**

   Part II -   Case law. **167**

Sales Meeting # 16
DEFECTS (PATENT AND LATENT) **171**

Sales Meeting # 17
A FEW THOUGHTS ABOUT FIXTURES AND CHATTELS **179**
   "What stays with the house" ADDENDUM to the Contract of Purchase and Sale.

Sales Meeting # 18
ABOUT EXISTING AND NEW FINANCING **184**
   The "Mortgage Information Request" Sheet

Sales Meeting # 19
FAIR MARKET VALUE AND SALEABILITY **192**
   What factors will determine the Sale Price?
   The importance of "Showability"
   What influences "saleability?"

Sales Meeting # 20
REASONS for OVERPRICING a property **202**
CONSEQUENCES of overpricing a property **209**

Sales Meeting # 21
SUGGESTED GUIDELINES TO DETERMINE **THE VALUE OF RAW ACREAGE** BEFORE IT IS SUBDIVIDED INTO RESIDENTIAL LOTS **217**

Sales Meeting # 22
(a) Confidential Report to be kept in the Listing File:
   "ACTIVITY Check List" for the marketing of a property **220**

(b) Reports to be shared with the Sellers:
   - **PAMPHLET:** "Helpful suggestions to show your property to its
                 best advantage. How to hold a GARAGE SALE." **225**

- "Activity Record" 227
- "Monthly Statistical Market Activity Report" 229
- "Advertising Record" 230
- "Record of Showings" (with Buyers' comments) 231

<u>Sales Meeting # 23</u>
SERVICING a LISTING
Step by step description of this service.
Part I   - Obligations of a Realtor. Working with skill and diligence when selling houses, strata properties, apartments, mobile homes etc. **232**

Part II - How to promote your new listing **240**
- by creating excitement and
- by making it the "Centre of Influence"
- The value of other Realtors' opinion about the saleability of the property (Office and MLS Tours).

<u>Sales Meeting # 24</u>
ADVERTISING 245
A FEW MORE THOUGHTS ABOUT ADVERTISING 256
ADVERTISING LEAD LINES 260

<u>Sales Meeting # 25</u>
HOW TO HOLD A PRODUCTIVE "OPEN HOUSE" 269
Open House "Guest Register"

<u>Sales Meeting # 26</u>
SHOWING PROPERTIES IS AN ART 277
Lining up the "Tour of Homes."
Methods of showing houses.
The actual showing of a property.
"Educating" the Buyer to recognize real estate "facts."

<u>Sales Meeting # 27</u>
REPRESENTATIONS 283
- "Puffing"
- Innocent misrepresentation
- Negligent misrepresentation
- Fraudulent misrepresentation
- Case law

Sales Meeting # 28
SHOULD YOUR CLIENT BUY FIRST OR SELL FIRST?........289
    Advantages, risks and disadvantages

Sales Meeting # 29
The "SUBJECT TO THE SALE OF THE BUYER'S PROPERTY" clause AND THE "TIME CLAUSE."........293

Sales Meeting # 30
OVERCOMING OBJECTIONS
    Overcoming objections is the icing on the cake of a sale.

Part I   - Preparation, strategic psychology: dealing with the Clients' personalities........299

Part II   - The pitfalls of dealing with sundry "advisers" "Waiting" (with a decision) has its hazards........309

Part III   - Objections can be healthy "Buying Signals" Greed, fear, benefits and advantages........318

Part IV   - Recognizing the Death Knell (when you are wasting your time)........323

Part V   - Summary of Standard Objections to enable you to prepare your own good answers........326

Part VI   - How to overcome 27 obstacles when trying for a listing All of the answers are here - be prepared for the next time........329

Sales Meeting # 31
CLOSING TECHNIQUES

Part I   - A few initial thoughts about closing techniques........342

Part II   - Bringing home the bacon through gentle persuasion........344

Part III   - Important considerations and strategies........352

(E) THE JOB ISN'T DONE UNTIL THE PAPERWORK IS DONE.

Sales Meeting # 32
The Contract of Purchase and Sale........361

Index

Sales Meeting # 33

The "SUBJECT-to" CLAUSE

Part I   -   The 3 categories of "subject-to" clauses
Case law. 366

Part II   -   Third Party approval clause
"Whim and Fancy" clause. 374

Sales Meeting # 34

The DEPOSIT. 378

The reasons for a deposit.
If there is no deposit.
Staggered deposits.
Refundable v. Non-refundable deposits.
The Trust Account.
Deposits paid to somebody else other than the Real Estate Company (what is a "stakeholder?")
Deposits exceeding the commission.

Sales Meeting # 35

The LIMITED DUAL AGENCY 387

Sales Meeting # 36

The Presentation of Offers.

Part I   -   Presenting an offer like a Pro. 392

Part II   -   How to become a Master Negotiator. 399

Part III   -   Reasons why a Selling Salesperson (Buyer's Agent) should be able to present his own offer to the Seller. 407

Sales Meeting # 37

THE PERILS OF REVOKING A COUNTER OFFER. 410

How a revocation can go wrong and how a house can be sold to 2 different Buyers simultaneously.
Case law.

Sales Meeting # 38

Commission cutting and selling bonus. 417
The Commission Agreement.

Sales Meeting # 39

AFTER SALE SERVICE **423**

   Courtesy "Closing Letter" to the Sellers.
   Pamphlet: "Things to do and people to notify when moving."

Sales Meeting # 40

Conveyancing instructions **428**

   Getting along with lawyers. 435

(F) POSSIBLE PITFALLS.

Sales Meeting # 41

Selling a rented property **438**
Selling a property with unauthorized accommodation. **444**
Selling renovated properties and owner built houses **449**

Sales Meeting # 42

How to AVOID a law suit. 453

Sales Meeting # 43

When a DEAL GOES SOUR **458**

   Survival strategies.
   **A Realtor's right to commission when the transaction
   is not completed.** **461**

(G) YOUR MENTAL HEALTH

Sales Meeting # 44

Dealing with DISAPPOINTMENTS. **464**

   Shock, disbelief, anger, anxiety, the "laying-of-blame," low self-esteem.
   **DAMAGE CONTROL: How to face Failure Experiences with
   COURAGE and OPTIMISM.**

Sales Meeting # 45

Are you living in a citadel of S-T-R-E-S-S ? **473**

   Battle fatigue.
   Intelligent coping behaviour to keep stress at bay.

Index

Sales Meeting # 46

HOW to SNAP OUT of a SLUMP

    Part I   -   Concise and practical help how to put out the fires.. . . . . **477**

    Part II   -   About polishing up your enthusiasm and maintaining a Positive Mental Attitude. **484**

    Part III   -   Analysis of what a Negative Mental Attitude is. **490**

Sales Meeting # 47

How to keep busy and sell in a SLOW MARKET **495**

(H) YOUR PHYSICAL HEALTH

Sales Meeting # 48

About the PERSONAL SAFETY of Realtors **498**
Footnotes on your ACHING FEET **503**

(I) ON THE HOME FRONT

Sales Meeting # 49

    Part I   -   **Realtors, marriage and divorce** **507**

    Part II   -   **A few thoughts about the MEANING of a "marriage"** **513**

Sales Meeting # 50

Common sense tips on money matters **515**

    Monthly House Rental Contract.

(J) SUNDRY

Sales Meeting # 51

At the beginning of a NEW YEAR

    - Thoughts for the New Year **523**
    - Worthwhile New Year's Resolutions **526**
    - More New Year's Resolutions and 12 ways how to keep them **528**

Sales Meeting # 52

"Vigilantibus non dormientibus scripta est lex"
(The law is written for the wide-awake ... not for the sleepy) 531

CASE LAW of interest TO REALTORS:

(I) BEFORE YOU GO TO COURT.

(II) CLOSING ARGUMENTS which have been used successfully when a Real Estate Company sued for commission in Small Claims Court.

(III) DISCUSSION AND CASE LAW with Highlights of a Realtor's RIGHT to COMMISSION.
- (a) Based on the Listing Contract **(effective cause of sale)**.
- (b) Based on the concept of **"the unbroken chain of events."**
- (c) On the basis of **"QUANTUM MERUIT."**
- (d) On the principles of **"UNJUST ENRICHMENT."**
- (e) A Realtor's right to commission when the transaction is not completed (expanded version).

(IV) **Other issues**
- (a) The duties of an Agent.
- (b) Listing price, Market Value, The "Righteous Price," Appraisals.
- (c) Allegations of **Breach of Fiduciary Duty:**
   - **"Standard of Care"**
   - **"Professional Negligence"**
- (d) Failure to remove a "subject-to" clause.
- (e) The credibility of witnesses in Court.

Preface

To give you some confidence in my book, here are a few words

About me:
I was (and still am in my private life) a "bookish" person in love with opera, classical music and good books. All of my friends and relatives thought that I had taken leave of my senses when I decided to quit my secure job as a Clerk at the railway in order to enter the real estate business. Years later I found out that many of them had made bets how long I would last in real estate sales. My mother-in-law, that kind soul, gave me the longest - 6 months. So how did I survive in this business for over 35 years? The answer is simple: starting with day one I knew that I would have to learn the business thoroughly, that I had to work hard and for long hours and that I needed an iron determination to succeed.

About my credentials:
After successfully completing the Salesmen's Pre-Licensing Course, I entered the real estate business on October 26, 1962. I got my first listing on the same day: it was a FSBO on a busy street. My surprised boss instructed everybody at the office not to tell me that this property had been for sale on and off for about 10 years. The Sellers' asking price was always one step ahead of the market. Another thing which I had not been aware of was the fact that real estate sales in Vancouver usually died towards the end of November because nobody wanted to move over the year-end holidays. Real estate activity wouldn't resume until the weather improved sometime in January. All of this meant that I had started in real estate at the worst possible time of the year. However in my ignorance I carried on enthusiastically, got calls from my sign (the overpriced listing on the busy street), turned some of the callers into listings and made 3 sales before Christmas of that year.
In the following year - in 1963 - I was the 4th Top Selling Salesman in the Vancouver Real Estate Board.
In 1964 I was the No. 1 Top Listing Salesman in the Vancouver Real Estate Board and in 1965 I was No. 2.
I completed the 3 year Diploma Course in Real Estate at the University of British Columbia and graduated on Sept. 9, 1966 (I won the "Blane, Fullerton and White" prize for being the Top Student).
On September 30, 1966 I became a "Fellow" of the Real Estate Institute of Canada ("F.R.I." designation).
On November 1, 1966 I became a member of the Real Estate Institute of B.C. ("R.I.[B.C.]" designation).
On September 19, 1967 I achieved "Millionaire" Status in the MLS Medallion Club of the Vancouver Real Estate Board. I had sold $ 1,000,000 worth of real estate in 5 years. At that time the selling prices of the residential properties which I handled ranged between $ 8,000 and $ 20,000.
In 1982 and 1983 I was the Top Producing Sales Associate in British Columbia for

Century 21 and one of the 21 Top Century 21 producers across Canada. I also received 2 of the coveted "Centurion Awards."

In due course I became a 17 year member of the MLS Medallion Club.

For about 5 years I worked as the Manager of a 10 salesmen office specializing in commercial sales. As a side line I did mortgage appraisals for several banks and my boss and I also developed land and built new houses.

After my boss retired, I went back selling. During the 9 years immediately preceding my retirement (on April 30, 1998) I managed a 120-plus salespersons office.

During my career I trained many a successful salesperson.

For a long time people urged me that I should write a book because it would be a shame if all of my accumulated knowledge and experience would be lost. Well, here it is. It is a labour of love.

About my book.

Like many other Realtors I was often hungry for **survival information in a CONCISE and straight forward manner.** One of the reasons why I gave up reading books on real estate sales was because I often had to wade through pages and pages of anecdotal and self-celebratory reminiscences before I would find a measly kernel of useful revelation. I used to highlight the sentences which were important and meaningful to me, so that I wouldn't have to go back and reread everything time and again. Often I was frustrated because I was longing for belly-filling steak and potatoes fare and got only a diet of fluffy pastry.

For these reasons I tried to write a different kind of book. You will see that some of it is in the form of a text book, with **certain important items** appearing **in fat print,** so that its lessons can be **ABSORBED and RETAINED EASIER.**

I also tried to write this book with common sense and down-to-earth detail. From my school days I remember that my history teacher only taught the "glorious aspects" of history plus a lot of dates which we had to memorize and promptly forgot after the examination. When he, for example said that "Alexander the Great" had conquered a large portion of Asia, I wondered silently: by himself? Didn't he have at least a few spear carriers and a cook with him? Did he walk all the way or did he ride a horse? (For those of you who might be interested: Alexander's battle steed was called "Bucephalus," which means "Oxhead," because he had an unusually large head. Eventually the horse died in battle and Alexander allegedly wept at its funeral). You see, this is what I mean with spicing up a dry subject with some interesting details. Don't be apprehensive, this is the one and only history lesson which you will find in this book.

I wrote this book based on

(a) **my personal experience and knowledge accumulated over 35 rewarding years in the real estate business.** Much of this experience and knowledge was obtained by trial and error in "The SCHOOL of HARD KNOCKS" or, if you prefer a more dramatic expression: experience gained through **"sweat, blood and tears."**

- Yes, there was a LOT of sweat over the years!
- There was also some blood, namely on the occasion when I was descending a dark basement staircase. The light bulb at the bottom of the stairs was out. The staircase made a curve (which I didn't know about and didn't see in the dark), I missed a step and fell like a sack of potatoes. When I landed on the concrete basement floor the "shatter-proof" lenses in my glasses broke and cut up my face. I also hurt my wrist and shoulder.
- On that occasion I was tempted to shed a few tears out of sheer frustration. Not because of my injuries, but because I had to cancel my next appointment and instead ended up in the Emergency Ward to get stitched up.

(b) Pages and pages of **extensive handwritten notes** which I took while attending **countless sales seminars and lectures and a few conventions**. For some unknown reason I never seemed to have written down the dates when these seminars were held nor the individual lecturers' names. Looking back I can only assume that I was always too preoccupied with the subject matter of the lectures. For that reason and to my profound regret I am now unable to give personal and individual recognition to those deserving educators. Thank you, Ladies and Gentlemen, whoever you were.

My philosophy for attending seminars always was that
- if you want to stay in the forefront, then you must never stop learning. I attended lectures and seminars right up to my retirement.
- It was worth attending seminars as long as I managed to pick up at least **"ONE NEW IDEA" which would eventually put some money in my pocket.**
- **Knowledge is portable** and
- nobody can take it away from me.
- **Knowledge will make my job easier** and consequently
- I would earn more money which in turn will improve my family's quality of life.

(c) I also used to be an avid reader of all educational bulletins and reports issued by
- The Vancouver Real Estate Board (as it was then called) now The Real Estate Board of Greater Vancouver,
- The Westminster County Real Estate Board which became the Fraser Valley Real Estate Board,
- the Real Estate Council of B.C. and
- the Real Estate Errors and Omission Insurance Corporation.

When I retired I donated all of my accumulated material to the archives of the 2 local real estate boards. And now you have seen above some of **the "text book" format** which I have mentioned before.

In my opinion CASE LAW is an easy and practical way to
- teach about "AGENCY" and
- to learn how to stay out of Court. Law suits are not only expensive, but also very unproductive and time consuming for Realtors; they are also hard on the nerves.

The law cases which are mentioned in my book I have obtained from:

(a) the Law Library of the B.C. Supreme Court in New Westminster, B.C. My heartfelt thanks to the kind librarians for their generous assistance.
(b) The Internet (the Canadian Legal Information Institute. www.courts.gov.bc.ca and scroll down to CLII).
(c) Over the years I have learned a lot from reading BCREA's "Legally Speaking" publication written by the distinguished lawyer Mr. Gerry Neely, BA, LL.B.

The title of my book is "52 Sales Meetings" because I thought that I would provide one year's worth of sales meetings to hard pressed Managers who don't know what to talk about on a Monday morning. You are getting good value, because some of the chapters actually consist of several parts.

After I had finished the book I realized that it will also be a good **REFRESHER COURSE for seasoned salespersons and a valuable TRAINING GUIDE for new salespersons.** When I was putting on the finishing touches on this book, my 8 year old grandson TRAVIS decided that he would become a Realtor, just like his grandfather used to be. I do hope that he will read my book when he gets his license.

Each chapter of my book is designed to be **a self-contained and complete unit by itself.** This resulted occasionally in an inadvertent overlapping of (a portion of) a certain subject matter. Whenever that was necessary, I tried to fashion the overlapping portion in a new and interesting way:
- possibly from a different view point or
- by elaborating on various salient points which had previously only been touched on.

For the purposes of this book
- I have used the male gender when I had to refer to or describe a person. For those who object, I will use in future an English unisexual pronoun, as soon as somebody is able to come up with one.
- The word "Realtor" is used in the sense of a "real estate practitioner" or a "salesperson."
- As much as possible, I have tried to be politically correct by e.g. referring to a "chairPERSON" instead of a "chairMAN." But I draw the line at the designation of a "chair." I may be old-fashioned, but a "chair" in my mind is still a piece of furniture.

DISCLAIMER:
3 things should be understood explicitly:
(1) At no time was I or am I giving "legal advice" of any kind whatsoever. E.g.
    - whenever I had to become "technical" (e.g. "revocation")
    - or referred to law cases and the lessons learned from them
    - or the contents of Chapter (Sales Meeting) # 52.

    I am merely relaying information which any member of the public can obtain by visiting a Law Library.
(2) The information about sales techniques and how to conduct business are merely suggestions. **Take** (adopt) **what you like and feel comfortable with, discard the rest**. We are all different persons with different personalities. Some of the things which worked for me may not work for you. I have found that out when I tried to follow some of the things which I had been taught during various seminars.

    Because I was not comfortable with a certain recommended sales technique, I came across as "pushy" and I ended up with a spectacular failure (e.g. didn't get the listing).
(3) I have prepared this book with great care and to the best of my knowledge and ability, but assume no liability.

Cordially yours,

Albert R. Teichner,
F.R.I., CMR, R.I.(B.C.)(Retired), CRES
Delta, B.C.,

March 25, 2005.

Albert passed away January 15th, 2007 with his family at his side.

The Changing Role Of The Real Estate Sales Manager

Good Sales Managers have always been a scarce commodity.
(1) If they are young and ambitious, then they will sooner or later strike out on their own (and take a portion of the sales staff with them).
(2) If they are older persons then they will eventually retire.
(3) Gone are the old-style Managers who preferred to rely on the "command-and-control-over-people" concept. Salespersons often suspected that their work diaries featured pictures of their favourite dictators as centrefolds.
(4) Gone are also the Managers who were so set in their ways, that they were unwilling to change and/or keep up with the many changes which the real estate business has experienced in the last decade or so.

In the "good old days" the work of a Manager used to consist of:
- planning and organizing
- leading and supervising
- and possibly some socializing.

In the last few years management has become an art, a way of life or better still, a life-long learning process that cannot be learned anymore by reading books or by watching a video or by attending some seminar. Nowadays, management has to be learned "in the trenches" through "hands-on" experience; not so much by way of battlefield triumphs, but by the less glamorous and more monotonous day-to-day dealings with the Salespersons.

ON DEALING WITH SALESPERSONS.

Under no circumstances should a Manager "lord it" over his Salespersons; the Manager should not add to the Salesperson's discomfort, but make his problems more tolerable. If a Salesperson comes to the Manager with a problem (and the Manager should consider himself lucky that he still does), then it is no longer good enough to bark out a 30 second "instant solution" to the problem. INSTEAD the Manager should:
- drop everything that he has been doing
- put his pen down
- quit fiddling with the computer
- if necessary put all calls (except for emergencies) on hold
- clear his mind of everything
- look the Salesperson into his eyes and
- be there 110% for the Salesperson.
- Then listen to the problem and analyze it with him in detail, discuss the options and consequences so that he will learn not only for this one time, but also for future occasions. As an added bonus this will free the Manager from having to rehash with that Salesperson time after time the same old thing over and over again.

The principle of the above-mentioned is as follows: if you give a person food, then he will eat TODAY. But if you teach him how to plant, grow, harvest, prepare and cook food, then he will eat for a lifetime.

By continuously coaching and training his Salespersons, the Manager will be REWARDED with
- unswerving loyalty and
- increased production.

About "New Year" Resolutions.
At the beginning of a new year, Managers bravely talk about "setting attainable goals" and they develop heroically optimistic "sales strategies" all of it "in writing," of course. This is designed to increase production and enhance the bottom line for everybody: the Sales Staff, the Company and the Manager. After a while, when the routine drudgery of every day life and business pressures take over, many a Manager comes to realize that the road to hell is paved with good intentions. For "practical" reasons they start taking a few short cuts and by summer time it is back to the same old rut of yesteryear. So for "the New Year" Managers may wish to try something different, something revolutionary and at the same time something quite simple:
RESOLVE
- **that you will merely do what you are supposed to be doing,**
- **but that you will stick to it without fail ALL YEAR LONG.**

ON EFFECTIVE LEADERSHIP.
You are entrusted with the overall direction and management of your customer-driven business.

As a Manager you have 3 types of customers:
(a) "The Clients" (being the "Public" - Buyers and Sellers).
(b) Your Sales Staff.
(c) Your Clerical Support Staff.

A real estate company's most valuable assets are not furniture and computers, but PEOPLE:
- your real estate SALESPERSONS
- and the clerical SUPPORT STAFF.

Managers should ask themselves the following questions:
(a) Have I mastered the necessary psychological elements of PEOPLE-CENTRED SERVICE?
(b) Am I truly interested in solving my Clients' (sales staff) individual and particular business problems?
(c) Am I paying UNDIVIDED attention when they come to me for help or do I

continue to fiddle with my computer? Do I continue (hunched over the desk) to read letters and let the person sitting across from me admire the bald spot on top of my head?

(d) Am I an inspiration to MY Clients by setting a good example? (e.g. working hard, no "extended" lunch hours, readily available and willing to help?)

ON SALES MEETINGS.

There should be weekly Sales Meetings.

These meetings are the glue which will hold things together.

They should resemble a family gathering around the dinner table.

(a) Always **start** the meeting **on time**.
(b) Other than quoting interest rates and sales statistics, keep it interesting and **have something constructive to say:** serve healthy and satisfying intellectual food.
(c) Don't just "lecture" (monologue) - encourage audience participation (this will keep them awake and give you some feedback).
(d) The basic secret of an accomplished speaker is to finish before the audience's attention span runs out.
Therefore:
- "stand up"
- "speak up"
- and don't forget to "shut up."

ON MISTAKES.

Many mistakes and errors are avoidable.

Mistakes are made as a result of:
- overconfidence
- carelessness
- time pressure
- being indifferent or too lazy to acquire FACTS or KNOWLEDGE to enable one to THINK ACCURATELY. Do you really prefer to act on OPINIONS created by GUESSWORK or SNAP-JUDGMENTS?

On the other hand don't become paralyzed into inaction by the fear of making a mistake. Everybody makes mistakes.

The sign of a GOOD MANAGER is
- how quickly and efficiently he will repair the mistake and
- how he will manage to minimize its fallout or ripple effect.

ON INTELLECTUAL DEVELOPMENT and ON EDUCATION.

(a) It is delusionary to think that at the present time you and your sales staff know everything that all of you need to know now and in the future.
(b) Do you and some of your staff lack up-to-date education in the latest developments

and as a result don't have the requisite skills and attributes necessary for survival in this highly competitive business? In this respect, we are not just talking about "technology."

(c) Are you encouraging and motivating your salespersons to enhance their understanding of our difficult and continuously changing business? How to avoid legal pitfalls and cope with problems your salespeople will encounter while out in the field? (e.g. How to deal with the presentation of multiple offers, uncooperative competitors, disappointments, rejections etc.).

ON COMPLAINTS.

A complaint is a person's communication to you that something has gone wrong in your business relationship.
- Do you see a VALID complaint from a member of the public or one of your salespersons as a nuisance to be ignored?
- Are you in the habit of taking care of such an unhappy person promptly and graciously?

ON YOUR LIFE AND FUTURE.

(a) Have you developed for yourself and discussed with your individual salespersons an INVESTMENT PROGRAM (with an Annual Dollar Objective) to achieve FINANCIAL INDEPENDENCE?

(b) Is it your goal to give your family at home AND at work a relatively worry-free and good life?

(c) Do you periodically take time out to enjoy with them (at home and at work) the wondrous journey of life?
- Will a family picnic with your loved ones result in happy memories?
- Will an annual office barbecue cement relations and increase "Loyalty?"

ON YOUR DIET.

Volumes have been written about the importance of a proper diet. Unfortunately all these instructions don't take into account your emotional status when you are eating. Eating bland and uninteresting low fat diet food is no good when you are upset and your stomach is churning from "pressure." It may be better not to eat when you are agitated rather than devouring chocolate or guzzling a beer.

Components Of A Well-Run Sales Meeting

Managers!
- Are you puzzled why the sales meetings in your office have lately been suffering from poor attendance?
- Do you get a nagging feeling that the few who do attend seem to sit there listlessly as if they were waiting for the torture to end?
- Have you been "winging it" because of a lack of preparation?

Salespersons!
- Are you suffering from the "Boring-Sales-Meetings-Blues?"
- Do you have to endure a dull and seemingly endless monologue by your Manager who
  - appears to be in love with the sound of his voice
  - but otherwise has no discernable subject to talk about?
- Do you find that you are finished listening before he is finished talking?

Everybody!
Do you find that your sales meetings have become counterproductive because they resemble a depressing "Coffee Klatsch" gathering where people with mug-in-hand rehash their "Weltschmerz?" (Universal Lament of what went wrong lately).

Here are a few suggestions to make a SALES MEETING more PROFITABLE and INTERESTING for all:

(1) Managers should learn to **treat a Sales Meeting like a business transaction**. In exchange for the salespersons getting out of their beds and coming to the office he has to offer them something **Valuable, Useful and Essential**. A brief definition of "V.U.E." is:
   (a) Anything that has at least a 50/50 chance of making everybody some **money**.
   (b) Anything that has at least a 50/50 chance of enabling them **to stay out of trouble** (the Courts, Business Practices and Arbitration Committees, ethical conduct, cooperation with other Realtors etc.)
   (c) **Technology training:** review of money making products and/or programs, which will make a salesperson's life easier, his work more efficient and are at the same time income tax deductible.
(2) **Time is a precious commodity for everybody.** Therefore meetings should start on time and end on time. Ideally they should be no longer than one hour. Managers simply have to remember that "The mind cannot absorb what the seat cannot endure." Therefore, the watch word of the day is to "stand up, speak up and don't forget to shut up."
(3) **Sales Meetings are business meetings.** Therefore logic demands that at least 90% of the time be allotted for the serious discussion of important or significant issues concerning real estate. Everything else is socializing.

Don't misunderstand me: there is nothing wrong with socializing at the right time and in the right place.

E.g. the office picnic, the Christmas Party etc.

Because of the resulting liability, most Company Policies frown on the consumption of alcoholic beverages on office premises even "after hours."

(4) The Manager should be sensitive to the fact that probably there is a wide range of diversities in his group.
- One of them is the **generation gap**. It is no secret that each generation has a different outlook on life and different priorities (e.g. baby boomers or the sceptical "Generation X").
- There may also be a cross-section of different educational and social backgrounds.
- No doubt there is often a significant difference in various persons' **financial positions** (e.g. a retired person with a good pension income is not under the same pressure to produce as a person who is supporting a growing family).

(5) In spite of the afore-mentioned differences, every item on the AGENDA of the sales meeting should be of interest to most (preferably to all) of the attendees. This, no doubt, will represent a serious challenge to the Manager.

(6) As a direct consequence of the above it should be a given that **the various items selected for the Agenda must be carefully prepared well in advance**.

(7) The subject matter(s) of the meeting should be announced or communicated to the entire sales staff several days BEFORE the meeting. E.g. a notice tacked onto the Office Bulletin Board, onto the back door leading to the parking lot and [no snickering please] onto the washroom doors - I can assure you that it works!

(8) The crude "Ra-Ra" sessions of yesteryear may no longer appeal to today's more sophisticated salespersons. In order for everybody to leave the meeting energized and with a burning desire and/or firm will of succeeding, **meetings should have an OBJECTIVE**. The most obvious objective is to INSPIRE and MOTIVATE the Realtors in your office. And how can this be done convincingly and elegantly? By explaining to them in simple, plain language

(a) What you want to accomplish for THEM (NOTE: if THEY prosper then the company also will prosper).
(b) How long it will take and
(c) how to achieve it.

In case anybody is wondering about "item (c)" ("How to achieve it"), it can be accomplished by teaching
(a) the cultivation of the WILL (becoming mentally strong, being methodically organized, the discipline to work).
(b) The development of the MIND (accumulating knowledge and experience, learning to deal successfully with different situations including adversities).
(c) The education of the HEART (work ethics: putting the Client's interests

and welfare ahead of your own; dealing fairly with your competitors; sharing generously your time and experience with others).
   (d) Teaching **PERSEVERANCE** which is another name for **SUCCESS**. God gives nothing to those who keep their arms crossed. You also have to get off your knees if you want to have your prayers answered.
(9) Ideally nobody should become bored or disinterested during a meeting. The only way to capture and hold everybody's interest is to **get everybody** (or at least most of them) INVOLVED **in the meeting**.
   - Instead of a monologue by the Manager
   - there should be dialogue between the staff and the Manager.
   - Preferably there should be a lively, spontaneous, informed and for everybody **USEFUL exchange of ideas**. But be careful that one enthusiastic soul in the crowd does not end up dominating or monopolizing the meeting. The Manager cannot afford the luxury of loosing control.
(10) **Important elements of a Sales Meeting are:**
   (a) **"Need-to-know" Information** (e.g. latest changes in mortgage interest rates).
   (b) **Education** geared to the experience level of the entire group. If there is too much diversity between members of the group then the training may have to be split up between beginners and more seasoned staff.
   (c) **The atmosphere of the meeting** should be inviting and relaxed. The Manager does not have to act like the Grim Reaper. A little funny joke (in good taste) dropped unexpectedly here or there (especially at the beginning of the meeting) will break the ice. (Search for jokes on the internet under www.google.com; some of the lawyers' and Realtors' jokes are really hilarious).
   (d) **The program of the meeting** should not only be entertaining but it should also be reasonably fast paced and filled with practical, common sense ideas.

In some ways the Manager conducting a meeting is like a stage director or better still, like the conductor of a symphony orchestra. A symphony orchestra produces gorgeous music partly because of the virtuosity of the individual musicians, but mostly because the Maestro (title of an outstanding conductor) is able to fuse the efforts of all musicians into a cohesive unit while at the same time he sets the pace and encourages every single member to give his best effort for the common good.
As a good leader a Manager will similarly - through his actions and words - endeavour to focus the talents and energies of his workforce into a symphony of success.

It has been said that leadership is about getting things done through others. I would like to take it one step further by saying that true leadership is to bring Realtors past their own self-imposed limitations of their present potential.

To achieve this goal the Manager
- must know his job,
- he must know his business,

- he must know his people and
- he must show respect for the people who work for him.

And one of the best ways of doing the latter is to conduct outstanding sales meetings. It should come as no surprise that the dividends from good Sales Meetings will be glorious:
- Loyalty and
- mutual trust,
- staff cohesion and
- increased production.

Thus in the end EVERYBODY will win.

Back To Basics - Part I
(Physical Requirements)

Athletes prepare themselves for competitions
- by having the right equipment, special clothing, the right type of shoes etc.
- and by training diligently for a long time.

Similarly, Realtors have to prepare themselves physically and psychologically if they wish to be successful in the real estate business.

1) The right EQUIPMENT.
  (a) A decent **briefcase** which is large enough for your individual purposes. Some Realtors have 2 or more briefcases. E.g.
    - one set up for listing presentations containing a tape measure, Listing Contracts, presentation forms etc.
    - one set up for preparing offers with a calculator, Contracts for Purchase and Sale, addendum forms etc.
  (b) Office equipment:
    - 2 to 3 ballpoint pens. There is nothing so embarrassing as trying to complete a listing contract or an offer and your ballpoint pen runs dry and you don't have another one.
    - You also need scratch pads, paper clips, a stapler, scotch tape, envelopes etc.
    - In your home office you should have an adequate computer with which you are able to contact the Real Estate Board's computer system.
  (c) Tools:
    - a measuring tape and a small ruler.
    - A flashlight (to avoid various hazards [e.g. a pothole] while walking in the dark along a strange driveway. Sometimes it is difficult to find a light switch in a dark basement).
    - Lock box(es) and a lock box key.
    - A hammer and screw driver (preferably one where different types of bits are stored in the handle).
    - A camera, a cassette tape recorder (or a notebook), a calculator, a pager and cell phone, a lap top computer.
    - A mortgage amortization book (or a mortgage calculator).
    - An address book together with a list of important phone numbers.
    - Local street maps.
    - In the glove compartment of your car a small container with coins for parking meters.
    - An adequate supply of **business cards**.
    - A WORK DIARY into which you should record all of your appointments. This will not only remind you of your next week's appointments, but it

will be an invaluable asset for the time when the income tax people will audit you. Rest assured, that you will be audited at least once during your working life as a Realtor. VERY IMPORTANT: for income tax purposes (business expense deduction of your car mileage) you should log your daily car mileage into your work diary.
- A box in which you will keep your office and business expense invoices for the entire year. These are needed for your periodic GST Reports and your annual income tax preparation.

(d) A reliable car:
- with a full tank of gas. You should always fill up when the tank is half empty, because you never know what will come up during the day. One also seems to get better mileage on the first half tank of gas.
- The car should be regularly serviced.
- The windshield and windows must be clean to give good visibility (especially at night or in inclement weather).
- The interior of the car should be clean:
  - no garbage, pop bottles etc. on the floor or
  - sundry stuff cluttering up the seats.
- Deodorant spray to ensure that the car's interior smells fresh.
- A clean piece of cloth to wipe fogged up windows.
- A roll of paper towels (to wipe hands etc.)
- In areas where there are severe winters, you should carry a small shovel, a bucket of sand, chains etc. in case you get stuck somewhere.
- A spare set of car keys (in case you lock yourself out).
- Discuss with an income tax accountant the pros and cons of "leasing" v. "owning" a car, office furniture.
- Whatever car you drive, it should have 4 doors and be adequately roomy to accommodate several people.
- If you sell Million Dollar properties you may wish to drive a high-end luxury car (to fit in with the social station of your Clients). There may be some income tax implications.
- If you sell properties in the low(er) end of the market you may find that your Clients could resent (or envy) your luxury car.

(e) Real Estate Forms:
Listing Contracts (MLS and exclusive)
Listing amendment forms (for price changes, extensions)
Property Condition Disclosure Statement: residential, strata, farm & acreage.
"Working with a Realtor" pamphlet.
Contract of Purchase and Sale.
Limited Dual Agency form.
Addendum forms (with and without printed clauses).
Amendment forms (for subject removals).
Exclusive Buyer's Agency Contract.

Fee Agreements (in case of selling unlisted property or if there is a variation in the amount of the commission).

(f) Signs:
"For sale" signs.
"Open House" arrows and "House for Sale" arrows.
(Clean regularly your stake signs. Yardarm signs are maintained by the service company which puts the signs up and takes them down again).
Stickers: "Sold," "Shown by appointment only," "MLS," "Exclusive," "Reduced" etc.

(g) Promotional Handouts (optional):
Small gifts displaying your and your Company's names and phone numbers: ballpoint pens, scratch pads, coffee mugs, fridge magnets etc.

2) YOUR PERSONAL APPEARANCE.
We live in a visual culture and the diet and workout craze have hit hard everywhere. Many people are obsessed with their body-fat percentages. Are Realtors expected to live only on Diet Food or sea weeds? As people come in all shapes and sizes, the question is why should it be almost a stigma if one is overweight? Why should one's "anatomy" become his "destiny" in the real estate business?
Will KNOWLEDGE and EXPERIENCE and HARD WORK get upstaged in a welter of eye candy and theatrical distractions?
In our culture we also seem to be obsessed with "eternal youth." Well, all of us will invariably GROW OLD(er). The secret is to do it well: an older person who dresses and acts his/her age will make a gentil impression.

Regardless of what the diet-gurus say ... the only important question is: "WHAT does the PUBLIC WANT?"

As far as "looks" are concerned, the public wants ...

"VISUAL CREDIBILITY."

(a) In old real estate books this chapter used to be called "Dress for Success." This is partly outdated. Whoever you are at whatever station in life, dress so that you look
- APPEALING,
- BELIEVABLE
- and LIKEABLE.

For the public it is important that the Realtor should be
- confidence inspiring,
- neat and clean,
- polite and pleasant,
- knowledgeable and well-spoken (not the MOST words - just the

RIGHT ones)
- and a hard worker.

For better or for worse, the prospective Customer will invariably form an opinion of the Realtor during the first few minutes of their meeting.

There is no 2nd chance for a first impression. If a Realtor shows up for his first meeting with a Customer in an untidy and/or sloppy condition, then such Customer will think the following: "Seeing that he can't be bothered with his appearance, what are his WORK HABITS going to be like?"

(b) Generally good quality clothes will last longer with proper maintenance.
- Clothing should be tailored for the comfortable proportions of YOUR body.
- The idea is to make a "business-like appearance."
- "Appearance" also **includes personal hygiene** (clean hair, clean finger nails, no bad breath or bad body odours).

FOR MEN, a Realtor's "uniform" means:
- a neatly pressed suit, preferably in a neutral or subdued colour. Nothing "flashy" but on the other hand you don't have to look like you are going to a funeral.
- Well-kept polished shoes.
- A clean shirt (no worn-out collar or cuffs) and
- a matching elegantly self-defining necktie.
- A suit jacket commands authority, a sports jacket is more informal/casual.

WOMEN generally know how to dress well. Many women prefer "Chic Simple" as their dress code.

For example some may choose a stylish navy suit, white cotton blouse, highlighted by a coloured scarf, pearl earrings. A belt or handbag may match the shoes, the lipstick will match the overall impression.

Women generally also know which colours suit them best: knowing THAT - it is hard to go wrong. Favourable colours are also easy to accessorize and may be seasonless.

Make-up should be age appropriate and suitable for the occasion. (You meet the Clients on business and not for an evening at the opera).

(c) All Realtors should wear comfortable shoes, because they have to walk a lot.
(d) Here are a number of general "DON'Ts":
- You don't have to be a fashion plate and walk around in Armani suits (unless you are selling multi-million Dollar properties).
- Don't be too "in" (latest, on-the-cutting-edge fashion) or too "out" (hopelessly outdated).
- Don't wear clothes that:
  - make you look awkward or
  - that you are not comfortable in or
  - that restrict your mobility.

- Don't arrive in a cloud of cigarette smoke.
- Don't arrive with alcohol on your breath.

(e) Some "Don'ts" for MEN:
- Generally speaking men should try not to take their jackets off, especially if they wear a short sleeved shirt. However, if it is brutally hot, ask the Clients first for permission to take off your jacket. This little polite gesture will greatly impress them and most likely they will not refuse.
- If you merely loosen your neck tie then you may look like you have been on a bender.
- "Business casual" does not mean T-shirts with a logo on your chest, running shoes and dirty jeans .
- Wear cowboy boots only if you sell farm properties.
- No shorts (unless you sell safari properties).
- Don't wear any underwear, shirts or socks which wouldn't pass the "sniff test."

(f) Here are a few simple rules for the LADIES. Please keep in mind that "MRS." Client could become "uncomfortable" with what you are wearing:
- Nothing too tight or clingy.
- Nothing too short ("short shorts" or riding-up skirt).
- Nothing too sheer or too transparent.
- No low (plunging) necklines.
- No extensively exposed midriffs.

To summarize:

The paramount objective of all of this is that at the end of the day
- the Clients should only REMEMBER what the Realtor "SAID."
- The Clients should NOT remember your scuffed, worn-out shoes, your wrinkled clothes with missing buttons, your body odour and/or your bad breath.

Back To Basics - Part II
(**Psychological requirements**)

What else do CONSUMERS ("The Public") want?

(1) They want the Realtor to **establish** RAPPORT with them.
How does a Realtor "establish rapport" with a Client?
The Realtor has to be "sensitive" (experienced, alert and smart) enough to **effectively gain EMPATHY with the Client.**
"Empathy" is NOT "sympathy."

SYMPATHY merely means
- **agreeing** with the Client's concerns.
- The Realtor **emotionally identifies** himself with the Client's concerns.

This is counterproductive in the negotiation process, because in that case both the Client and the Realtor will end up frozen in inactivity.

EMPATHY means **understanding** the Client's concerns in 5 ways: the Realtor must not only
a) understand **the literal meaning of the words**, which the Client is speaking, but
b) he must also try to **comprehend the Client's thinking and feelings** behind his words.
c) Furthermore, with time and a lot of practice, the Realtor will learn to ANTICIPATE when
   - **a problem is "swimming just below the surface"** and
   - **stops a Client** from making a decision.
d) In order to find out what stops a Client from making a decision and to move him from Point A to Point B, the Realtor must know how to **intellectually** step into the Client's shoes.
e) The Realtor must learn how to **encourage and to make it easy** for the Client to **voice his concerns readily, openly and explicitly.**

(2) The actual act of ESTABLISHING RAPPORT is partly done by the SPOKEN WORD and partly by BODY LANGUAGE.

THE SPOKEN WORD:
a) To get the Clients in a relaxed frame of mind, create a pleasant atmosphere by starting your conversation "socially": spend a few minutes talking about neutral subjects like the weather, mutual friends etc. Under no circumstances discuss politics or religion. Your speaking pattern should be non-demanding, calm and matter-of-fact.
b) Don't forget that you are there on business. Therefore don't discuss the weather, sports etc. **ad infinitum (forever).**

c) When you get down to business make sure that
   - the immediate surroundings are free from any distractions (TV and radio, pets wanting attention, noisy children).
   - Before you begin to speak about business, look directly at the person and make sure that you have his/her undivided attention.

BODY LANGUAGE:

The Realtor must become an expert in observing the Client's body language and at the same time he must learn how to unobtrusively allow the Client to observe HIS (the Realtor's) body language. To put the Client at ease, the Realtor should recognize what type of personality the Client is. Generally people's personalities range from being an **extrovert** to an **introvert** and all shades in between these 2 extremes. If a Client is more of an introvert (soft spoken, somewhat shy and reserved) then it is usually fatal if the Realtor is loud voiced and acts like a boisterous bull in a china shop. By no means does this mean that the Realtor has to be a chameleon to mirror the Client's personality: that would not only be wrong, but also demeaning and phony. He just has to be **creatively sensitive** enough NOT to be the exact opposite of the Client.

(3) Another trait which Clients expect from a Realtor is
TRUSTWORTHINESS.
The Realtor **must EARN** the Client's trust through
- promptness (never be late and keep them waiting).
- Politeness and good manners
- and "follow-through": **keep your promises** - The Watchword is: **"Promise less and keep more."**
- The Realtor must also be THOROUGH:
  He should pay attention to all details to make sure that there are no "rough edges" and that nothing will "fall through the cracks." Mistakes can turn out to be expensive for everybody.

(4) The Realtor must be ATTENTIVE:
During the time of their business association, **the Client must feel that he is the most important person in the Realtor's (business) life.**
Amongst other things the Realtor must be a GOOD LISTENER and find out WHAT MOTIVATES the Client.
An old real estate saying goes something like this:
"When talking to a Realtor, Buyers give their Specifications for a home; but when it comes to buying, they buy their Motivations."
Some dominant motivations are:
- Love: security and comfort for the family.
- The need for privacy.
- Health.

- Financial considerations (wanting to take advantage of low mortgage interest rates; having to sell because of foreclosure proceedings).
- Time factors (sudden job transfers; school year).
- Leisure and recreation.
- Prestige (job promotion, entertaining).
- Fear (of loosing out on a bargain or of ending up on the street).

(5) The Realtor must be HARD WORKING.
The 3 key words are:
- PRODUCT KNOWLEDGE,
- PROMOTION and
- DILIGENCE. Through the Realtor's diligent service the Clients will have the satisfaction of knowing that they are getting good value for their money. E.g.:

A Listing Broker must not only
- know all and everything about the property he is trying to sell (product knowledge, "doing his homework"),
- but he must do everything possible to emphasize the advantages and benefits of the property (this is where "selling" comes in).

In order to find the right house for his Clients, **a Buyer's Agent** should
- pour over listings,
- go on office and MLS Tours in order to familiarize himself with what is available on the market and
- finally he should preview all houses with a critical eye before showing them to his Clients (to make sure that they are suitable).

(6) A Realtor must also be PATIENT because buying and selling can be very stressful for people. A Realtor should always remember that the Client is probably more frustrated and stressed out than he is. Instead of arguing or being condescending, the Realtor should stay calm, patient and helpfully matter-of-fact. By doing all of this the Realtor will **create an appearance of "CARING"** which will help to cement further the "establishing-rapport" process.

(7) Another service which a Realtor can offer to his Client is (real estate) PROBLEM SOLVING. This generally means getting a bigger or smaller house, selling quickly in case of a transfer, getting the highest possible price (resulting in a satisfactory "net equity Dollar amount"), getting the most house value for his Dollars spent.

When solving a problem, the Realtor must control the situation and tactfully, but firmly guide it to the desired resolution.

a) Sometimes it is easy for a Client to get off on a tangent, which could deteriorate into an argument. This must be avoided at all cost.

b) All problems must be clearly defined in order to be able to find the right solution.
c) The Realtor should suggest several alternatives and then he should explore each one of them with the Client.

By discussing various ideas, an acceptable solution may be found. (E.g. "If you, Mr. Client, will accept this solution, what do you think would be the positive and negative results for you?")

d) Sometimes problems (objections) can be eliminated by offering the Client some sort of increased reward or benefit. (E.g.: "Mr. and Mrs. Buyer. If you accept this counter offer then we will not need to look at anymore houses").
e) The Realtor should NEVER get involved in the Clients' PERSONAL problems. E.g. in case of a divorce, taking one side or the other. The Realtor is not a social worker.

(8) A Realtor must also continuously hone his COMMUNICATION SKILLS so that he will increase his ability to explain complicated things in a simple and understandable way.

This is best done as follows:
a) In order to find out what troubles the Client and exactly what he wants and needs to know, the Realtor must LISTEN CAREFULLY. In case of doubt, he must clarify what the Client wants.
b) The Realtor must avoid to generalize (e.g. "this should be ok").
c) The Realtor should answer all questions
   - directly
   - concisely (don't be long winded)
   - and factually (let the facts speak for themselves).
d) **Technical information** must be given
   - in such a language that the Client will understand it.
   - In such a manner that the Client will easily remember it.
   - Avoid complicated technical lingo and industry buzz-words.
   - Allow enough time for the information to be absorbed.
e) Never argue with a Client or tell him what he can't do. Even if you win the argument - you are bound to loose in the long run.

(9) Throughout his entire working life, a Realtor should make a concentrated effort to LEARN continuously until the day he retires from the business.
The reason for learning is:
   - to gain EXPERIENCE.
   - With increased experience the Realtor will attain INCREASED CONFIDENCE in himself.

- With increased experience and increased confidence the Realtor will be able to offer to his Clients a HIGHER QUALITY OF SERVICE.
- All of this in turn will result in an INCREASE in SALES and consequently in INCREASED EARNINGS for the Realtor.

Instead of yesteryear's "safe" role-playing back at the office (where he has nothing to loose, because he is playing to the sympathetic eyes and ears of his Manager and fellow Realtors), GAINING VALUABLE EXPERIENCE is best done
- by PRACTICING in the field and
- by talking to actual prospective Buyers and Sellers.
- You will learn faster from your mistakes (in the field the stakes are high and you are liable to loose a commission).
- If you fail (and you will occasionally), don't forget to pick yourself up and start all over again.
- NEVER GIVE UP!

(10) And finally, the Realtor must also have a good working knowledge of NEGOTIATION SKILLS.

A simplified definition of "negotiating" is:
- to change another person's mind.
- To convince another person of something.
- To resolve differences on the way to closing a sale.

Prerequisites for good negotiation skills are:
a) The Realtor must have confidence in himself. This means that he must not only know what he is doing, but he must be able to work and do his job without continuous, immediate supervision.
b) The Realtor must be able to be CREATIVE to come up quickly and independently with different solutions to problems as they arise. (He must be able to "think on his feet").
c) The Realtor cannot afford to be "set in his ways," namely to do things only in a certain way; he must be open-minded to change and changing situations.
d) A skilful negotiator will be alert to verbal and non-verbal cues (CAUTION: body language can be easily misinterpreted by an inexperienced Realtor).
e) If there are more than one client, a sensitive negotiator will quickly endeavour to discover
- who is the motivating force (in the family),
- who is the dominant decision maker and
- to whom he should direct the LARGER portion of his conversation to. (It would be a grave mistake to simply disregard the other less prominent party).

Goal Setting

Much has been written about setting goals. E.g.:

- GOALS are only a WISH until you write them down.
- Goals should be **evaluated** daily/weekly/monthly for the purpose of CHARTING YOUR PROGRESS. (Always remember that too much analysis of what "should/could have been" may turn into a frustrating paralysis-by-analysis).
- Vividly VISUALIZE your goals frequently.
- Ardently DESIRE achieving your goals.
- You should set goals for **different areas in your life:**

(1) Business career and Financial independence, security, retirement.

Briefly, there are

(a) **short term goals:** "This week I am going to get a listing"
(b) **long term goals:** "This year I want to make $ 60,000."
   - Be specific and break it down into components: in order to achieve my goal of $ 60,000 a year, I have to produce $ 5,000 a month in commissions.
   - Set yourself a DEADLINE: In order to earn on the average $ 5,000 a month, I must
   - make at least 1 sale a month and/or
   - get 3 new listings each month (because not every listing may sell).
   - Based on past experience I must make 20 prospecting phone calls to get 1 listing. Therefore, my goal for the month is to make at least 60 prospecting attempts.
   - If each prospecting call takes about 10 minutes, then
   I have to spend 600 minutes (or 10 hours) on the phone this month.
   This month has 30 days; 600 minutes divided by 30 days = 20 minutes. I have to phone canvass each day for 20 minutes.

You must have a total commitment to make a daily effort to reach your short term goals. Don't play the "blame game":
- the economy is not right, there is lots of unemployment.
- The interest rates are too high
- Nobody will be home because it is hot and they are down at the beach; this month people are away on holidays etc.
- Fate is against me.
- He is lucky and I am not.

LONG TERM (big) goals are achieved by successfully linking together a number of smaller goals.

Generally speaking, goals have to be
(a) **Realistic and attainable** for your current stage of development in the business. A new salesperson should not try to measure himself against an experienced Top Producer. That is a good way to become frustrated.
(b) **Clearly and well defined.**
Ambiguous goals (e.g. "I want to get rich") are merely a futile search for an elusive and/or nebulous dream.
Because there are no guidelines, they are time wasters.
(c) Goals must also be **worthwhile and useful**, otherwise you will not keep them.
(d) Goals must be **"workable."**
- Find out what worked for you last year and what didn't.
- On hand of that **evaluate your strengths** and **weaknesses**.
- Determine in what areas you need IMPROVEMENT and then
- set a goal to alleviate that situation. ("Work" towards improving yourself).

HOW TO ACHIEVE YOUR GOALS.

After you have established realistic, attainable, well defined and useful goals, the next step is IMPLEMENTATION. Simply put YOU have TO DO SOMETHING about your newly minted goals.

We all know that the road to hell is paved with good intentions. Therefore, it is important to stop procrastinating and to get the ball rolling. This is best achieved by getting out of your warm bed or comfortable chair and MEET with and SPEAK to PEOPLE.

(2) Your FAMILY.
You cannot afford to fail on the home front.
(a) **Schedule your day** so that you can spend some quality time with your wife and children (e.g. a common meal = supper time).
(b) **COMMUNICATE with them.** Instead of talking about real estate at the dinner table, LISTEN to what has happened during THEIR day. Children have the habit of growing up very fast. One day you may suddenly wake up to the fact that you have lost out on a lot of good and important things. Regrettably you cannot turn back the clock.
(c) **Go on a holiday with them;** preferably without your pager. Your cellular phone should be used only in an emergency (flat tire etc.).
(d) Spend some time alone with your wife (after the kids have gone to bed). Communicate with her; she may be starved for adult conversation. Take her out to a nice dinner. Surprise her by sending her flowers. Get away for a romantic weekend.

(3) Your HEALTH.
One of your most important assets is your health. One of your top goals should be to look after your health.

If you haven't got health, you've got NOTHING. It is as simple as that.

The "Number 1" threat to a Realtor's health is STRESS.

The "Number 2" threat to a Realtor's health is FRUSTRATION which often expresses itself in ANGER. (Please don't vent your frustrations and anger on your loved-ones).

If you are not PROACTIVELY trying to counter these threats, then they will result in ILLNESS (which is your body's way of going on strike): upset stomach, ulcers, headaches, nervous facial twitches etc.

SET A GOAL that you must LEARN HOW to "soothe the savage beast."
Here are a few suggestions:

(a) **Listen to soothing music** in your car instead of listening to educational tapes.
(b) **Learn relaxation techniques** like self-hypnosis or Tai Chi
(c) Learn how to say "NO":
   - Don't take on more work than you can handle.
   - Don't deal with people who upset or abuse you.
(d) Learn how to relieve anger:
   - Some people go to the golf driving range and whack a few golf balls.
   - Others express their anger in temper tantrums. If you prefer to do the latter, then do it in private so you don't make a spectacle of yourself:
   - punch a pillow in your basement
   - "get it off your chest" in some place where nobody can hear you: scream your head off or lament as loudly as you wish about the unfair thing which has happened to you.
   - Tears can give genuine relief.
(e) Learn that eventually you must be "done with it."
   It is a truly WORTHWHILE goal to get rid of excess baggage like continuous and unrelenting anger, debilitating frustration and searing guilt.

Essay On Being Organized, Planning, Time Management And How To Stay Focused

In this chapter we are going to talk about
- what to do when there is nothing to do otherwise also known as "planning"
- and "time management."

Basically you have to establish
- where you are NOW
- where you want to GO TO
- and HOW you are going to get there.

All of these GO TOGETHER hand-in-hand. A good **Work Diary** or **Weekly Planner** will be helpful to keep you on track.

It takes a lot of DISCIPLINE to stick to your "planned" day. A Realtor has the luxury of choosing his own hours and days when he wants to work. On those days when he does decide to work there are some basic requirements he should stick to:

(1) **Get out of bed** (Don't laugh it is easier said than done!)
   (a) If you have worked late the night before and have nothing scheduled for that morning, then by all means you are entitled to sleep in.
   (b) Otherwise it is preferable that you get out of bed at a regular time,
   (c) which should fit in with your regular work schedule.
   (d) The expression of "getting out of bed" is meant to be also a metaphor for STARTING to WORK.
(2) **"Report to work"**: (unless you have an in-house office or work area from where you can conduct business without interruptions and distractions) you must get out of the house and go to the office (your "work environment").
(3) Even bringing your body to the office is no guarantee that you will "START WORKING" (preferably at a regular time so that you get yourself into a routine).
(4) Because a Realtor is not required to punch a time clock, all of this is very difficult to do "consistently."
(5) Only iron SELF-DISCIPLINE will make you a Master of Your Time and Work.

WHERE YOU ARE NOW:
Here are some incentives which may inspire a Realtor to work:
- Check your bank account.
- Check your bills.
- Check your cash-flow.
- Check to see how close you are to achieving your financial goals (your children's university tuition fees, a clear title house, comfortable retirement).

- Check how much or how little you know about your business.

WHERE YOU WANT TO GO TO:
- To get out of debt.
- To achieve the security of financial independence. E.g. "Clear-Title-Living" is heaven on earth!
- Decide if you want to remain an average producer or become a Top Salesperson.

HOW YOU ARE GOING TO GET THERE:
(I) Think positive.
Your BRAIN is a powerful machine which can either make or break you: NEGATIVE THOUGHTS will produce habitually NEGATIVE TALK and eventually all of it will lead you to a MISERABLE LIFE.

Instead it is far better to think about POSITIVE THINGS you can actually do, namely STAYING FOCUSED on the job at hand: Because
- YOU are the ONLY person responsible for taking the initiative
- and only YOU CAN make things happen,

(II) Therefore, make a COMMITMENT to yourself and to your FAMILY that you will:
   (1) "WORK"
   (2) "CONSTRUCTIVELY"
   (3) "PERSISTENTLY"
   (4) and "RELENTLESSLY"
   (5) "for … hours a day"
   (6) "… days a week."

The following are definitions of the words contained in the above statement:

(1) "WORK" in real estate means:
   - Inspecting properties to familiarize yourself with what is on the market: MLS Tours, Office Tours.
   - Choose and inspect EVERY DAY the most saleable listing of the day; (you can find it by checking new [or latest] listings on the computer).
   - Showing properties to prospective Buyers.
   - "Follow-up" whenever one of your listing has been shown. This means that you should phone the Realtor who has shown your listing and find out what his Client's reaction was (why he didn't make an offer on the property); then pass this information on to your Seller. This will be of great assistance to you on the day when you will present an offer on your listing.
   - Prospecting and canvassing for a listing.
   - Reviewing the saleability of your current listings (price reductions).
   - Write the following sentence on a piece of paper and then hang it up in your

work area:

"Price will remedy all defects."

This simply means that if it is cheap enough, then somebody will buy it regardless of what condition the house is in or where it is located.

- Extending the expiry dates of your listings.
- Writing and polishing ads.
- Preparing flyers and hand-out sheets.
- Holding an "Open House."
- Keep in touch with former Clients.
- Plan what you will do on the next day.
- **Learn something:**
- Attend your Office Sales Meetings.
- Attend seminars, lectures and conventions.
- Improve your telephone techniques.
- Improve your prospecting dialogue.
- Improve your listing presentation,
- Hone your communication skills.
- Read up on "body language."
- Improve your offer presentation.
- Improve your closing techniques.
- Learn to overcome objections.
- Keep up to date on the latest LEGAL ISSUES: this will save you a lot of heartache, wasted time, money and needless excitement caused by an unnecessary and/or avoidable law suit. Always remember: even if the Judge rules that you are innocent, in the end it is only the lawyers who will be ahead financially.
- Learn about computers. Although computers will never replace Realtors, it has been said that Realtors WITH computers will eventually replace those without.

The above list is by no means exhaustive, but hopefully you will get the idea. Drinking coffee, idle chatter in the office etc. might be a nice break, but it is not "work."

Another thing which you might consider learning is MORAL EDUCATION: This is
- the education of the HEART,
- the cultivation of the WILL,
- and the development of the MIND.

(2) "CONSTRUCTIVELY" means
   (a) doing something which **has at least a 50/50 chance of putting some money into your pocket during the next 30 days.**

It is a total waste of time and gas money to drive an unmotivated "lookeeloo" aimlessly around to show him houses. This endeavour is similar to trying to teach a turkey to fly by marching it up and down a runway at the local airport.

- (b) Working CONSTRUCTIVELY also means doing your job (especially your **paperwork**) RIGHT **the first time around**. It is not only a waste of time but also frustrating to have to go back and to revisit and to redo the same thing over and over again. Remember: the job isn't done until the paperwork is done.

- (c) Get into the habit of double-checking everything for accuracy and clarity.

(3) "PERSISTENTLY" means "I will never give up."

(4) "RELENTLESSLY" means "Anything is possible if I put my mind to it and want it badly enough."

(5) "… HOURS a day": A Realtor is an Independent Business Person. It is his privilege to chose the number of hours he is willing to work during a day. There is the morning shift, the afternoon shift, the evening shift and the split shift (you work for a couple of hours in the morning, take the afternoon off and work again in the evening). On some days you may be working only 2 or 3 hours; on others you could be working for 12 or more hours.

(6) "… days a WEEK": same as with the HOURS, a Realtor has the choice to coast or to loaf or to work himself into the ground 365 days a year. A sensible compromise is, of course, somewhere in between these extremes.

PLANNING and TIME MANAGEMENT.

(1) Don't go overboard in planning your day by allotting something for every waking minute. Invariably you will fall behind your schedule and this will lead to frustration.
Instead **remain flexible** and make a time allowance for
- unexpected emergencies (e.g. a flat tire),
- delays (e.g. encountering heavy traffic when driving to an appointment),
- disappointments (e.g. when the Buyers don't show up).
- Interruptions (e.g. every office has a "friendly time waster" who likes to "visit and chat").

(2) PROCRASTINATION.
Procrastination is to postpone something for tomorrow, which you should have done last year.
Almost everybody procrastinates sooner or later.
Many do nothing, because they fear making a mistake. In Real Estate Sales, **the**

problem of doing nothing is that it produces nothing WORTHWHILE:
- no commissions, no sales awards, no prestige, no better quality life for you and your family.
- On the other hand it does produce cash-flow problems, increased financial pressure, worries etc.
- Avoid procrastination: **it is the ONE TIME WASTER over which you have control.**

(3) Your TIME is an important ASSET.
Don't let anybody (and that includes yourself) waste your precious time: e.g.
   (a) The phone is a business tool. Avoid
   - unnecessary phone calls.
   - Unnecessarily long phone calls.
   - Instead of socializing on the phone, find a polite exit excuse so you can get off the phone without insulting the other person by abruptly ending the conservation.

   (b) Make an appointment before you meet somebody.

   (c) Phone ahead and make sure that they will be there.

   (d) Qualify and constantly requalify all of your Clients: Buyers as well as Sellers. Drop them if they are wasting your precious time.

   (e) The tool for the efficient use of time is called PRIORITIZING. Divide your time for tasks which are
   - crucially important
   - important
   - not too important
   - of no value.

   It should be self-evident what must be done first.

   (f) Another time waster is "WORRY."
   Worry is the most useless of all emotions. Regardless of how much you worry about something, it will not change anything. **Worry is totally concerned with negative thoughts** and can lead to serious illness.
   If something seriously worries you, the ONLY ANTIDOTE is to take action. Of course, you must also learn to accept that some things cannot be changed (they are beyond your powers to change it. E.g. Government policy on interest rates; the weather etc.)

WEEKLY ACTIVITY SHEET for the period of _____

What is the best use of your time	Mon	Tues	Wed	Thur	Fri	Sat	Sun
Sales Meeting							
Inspecting properties							
Office and MLS tours							
Prospecting							
• In person							
• by telephone							
For Sale by Owner							
Listing presentation							
Write/polish ads							
Report to Seller							
Price reduction							
Listing extension							
Presenting an offer							
Showing properties							
Open House							
Contact former clients							
Mailouts							
Planning your next day							
Self development							

What did you ACCOMPLISH this week?_____
What are you grateful for this week?_____
What did you plan to do that you didn't do?_____
_____
What needs improvement?_____
What do you have to concentrate on during next week?_____
_____

Thoughts On Effective Communication

The invention of the printing press has brought a proliferation of books to the common man and through them he has been invited to feast at the table of knowledge. As a direct consequence he has gained a vastly expanded vocabulary!
Because he is nowadays preoccupied by saturation TV the modern common man (after completion of his basic schooling), has often largely stopped reading valuable books. As a consequence of that his arsenal of words is no longer in excess of his needs.

Intellectual activities of present-day Realtors must have at its centre:
- LEARNING the trade
- **keeping up with changes** and
- the art of COMMUNICATION.

A Realtor's COMMUNICATION SKILLS are one of his most important assets in the performance of his work. Therefore, it is essential that the Realtor should not only DEVELOP, but also CONTINUOUSLY UPGRADE and HONE his communication skills. Mutual understanding between himself and his Clients will promote more constructive and positive outcomes of his efforts.

"**Communicating**" basically **means the transfer of thought or an abstract concept in the form of a mental picture by the Communicator to a Recipient.**

The **success or clarity** of this transfer (which is actually a cooperative transaction between 2 or more parties) depends on
(a) the SKILL of the Communicator and
(b) the ABILITY of the Recipient(s) to translate (in their minds) what they hear (and NOT what they **think** they hear).

The 2-way goal in communication is:
- First for the **Realtor to understand the Client**.
  The more the Realtor is able to understand the Client's point of view, his problems and concerns etc. the easier it is for the Realtor to arrive at a solution which is satisfactory to both.
- 2nd for the **Client to understand the Realtor**.
  When the Client makes assumptions about what the Realtor has said, it should be understood that these assumptions are most likely "coloured" by the Client's background, life experiences etc. For that reason it is of great importance that the Realtor should be able to communicate with a great degree of clarity.

Good COMMUNICATION SKILLS will
(a) enhance the Realtor's listening ability and
(b) as a result will increase his understanding of the Client

(c) which in turn **will build trust** in the business relationship between him and the Client.
(d) As a consequence of good communications the Realtor's **effectiveness to close MORE transactions with LESS problems will be enhanced.**
(e) In fact the Realtor will **catch problems BEFORE they arise.**
Costly and time consuming law suits and disciplinary hearings can be avoided.
(f) The opposite is also true:
Lack of communication or insufficient or unsatisfactory communication will erode trust in the relationship between the Client and the Realtor.
(g) To procrastinate, to wait or ignore problems has the potential of turning into a crisis.
(h) **BEFORE a law suit is filed** or a disciplinary complaint is made, the Realtor will usually get a phone call from the complaining party. The Realtor should be:
- a good listener
- he should sound sympathetic
- making excuses or to apologize may be misunderstood as him accepting liability.
- **the best route is to OFFER to SEARCH FOR WAYS TO SOLVE THE PROBLEM and/or to find a way to settle the matter.**

Communication between 2 or more persons can be either **verbal or non-verbal (body language). In reality it is often a combination of both.**

In VERBAL communication we rely on the sense of HEARING: In order to succeed, **Realtors must learn the art of speaking:**

WORDS are signals or codes which trigger **INTERPRETATIONS in** (are INTERPRETED by) the **Recipient's MIND** based on the Recipient's accumulated past life experiences, education, sophistication etc.

(1) **When the Realtors speaks** and the Client listens, then
   (a) **the SOUNDS of the Realtor's VOICE are important:**
   - tone, inflection and strength of voice: loud, low, audible, inaudible;
   - keep the **pitch (tone)** of your voice low; try to use a tone of voice that you would like people to use with you.
   - RAISING the volume may indicate aggression.
   - LOWERING the volume suggests sharing and confidentiality
   - **the inflection and strength of the voice:** speak warmly and confidently in an easy-going and pleasant manner e.g. about the extent of services which you are offering.
   - **The clarity of pronunciation** will help to eliminate some misunderstandings and enhance comprehension. **Pronounce individual words clearly.** Use short and simple sentences.

- **Eloquence:** knowledge of the subject matter will enable the Realtor to speak confidently and with authority.
- **The fluency of speech:** no hesitations, pauses or awkward "uh's" or "oh's."
- **The speed of speech:**
- should preferably **match** the *Client's* **ability to absorb what is said** (otherwise his mind will wander).
- speaking slower and with a deeper voice **indicates conviction.**
- if you increase the speed of your speech somewhat, it may **create excitement.**

There is nothing wrong with being assertive; but at all costs **AVOID making the impression that you are arrogant or overpowering.**

- **A COLD or CASUAL voice** may suggest that the speaker is not emotionally involved:
- he is either bored with what he is doing or
- he is merely "going through the exercise" by reciting the memorized words of a canned sales talk.
- Or else that he is only interested in himself (and his real estate commission) and is indifferent about the welfare of his Clients.

(b) **IT IS IMPORTANT to be at eye level with the person you are talking to,** especially with an elderly person or those who are hard of hearing (they may be lip-reading).

(c) **If your Clients don't immediately understand you, then resist the temptation of "lecturing" them by:**
- speaking louder
- or raising the voice pitch by an octave
- or speeding up your speech.
- On the other hand don't speak patronizingly or condescendingly slow (because it will be resented by the Client as "preaching").

(d) Communicators have to take the trouble of **finding the RIGHT WORDS to CLEARLY and EFFECTIVELY express their thoughts.** The right words could mean **simple but POWERFULLY DESCRIPTIVE words and phrases.** As only quality counts, the right words are also not necessarily the "most words."

(2) **When the Client speaks** and the Realtor listens, then the Realtor should realize that the Client may not be as able or proficient or willing to express his thoughts as he, the trained professional might be. Therefore, the Realtor must learn to not only LISTEN CAREFULLY to what is being said, but also to try to **INTERPRET the real meaning** of what the Client wants to or appears to be saying.

Based on past experiences, Realtors are no doubt aware that the following can happen:

(a) **The Realtor will be misunderstood by the Client.** There are many reasons for this:

- The Client will pay attention only to what has the **greatest MEANING and VALUE and EMOTIONAL SIGNIFICANCE to HIM ... "here and now."**
- The Realtor has made the mistaken assumption that his Client is interested in what he (the Realtor) is saying.
- The Client prejudged (jumped to the conclusion) that what the Realtor is going to talk about is NOT interesting and of little value to him (the Client). (E.g. the Realty company's standing on the stock market or its association with a big international company; in the Client's mind none of these have any immediate bearing on how much he will get for his property).
- The Client's mind tends to wander impatiently when the Realtor's **speed of speech is considerably slower than the Client's ability to hear and absorb what is said**. How the Client listens and pays attention determines the level of reception (and consequently of the degree of successful communication).

What can the Realtor do when he is consistently having trouble being understood by the Client:
- **he should be PATIENT** because people with different levels of sophistication may need different amounts of time to process the offered information. **Above all a bottomless supply of patience can take the edge off difficult moments.**
- He should try to think about the complexity of what he is saying.
- Can it be said more simply?
- Have you used too many words and too technical words?
- Have you employed abstract concepts which are too onerous for the Client to understand?
- Can you be more concrete?
- Try to demonstrate VISUALLY what you are saying: people do absorb information not only with their ears, but also with their eyes. (e.g. the use of a "flip chart" during a listing presentation).
- If everything else fails, try other forms of communication:
    - Visual aids (the use of a calculator to establish the Seller's "net sale proceeds"; "advantages" and "disadvantages" summarized on a sheet of paper)
    - professionalism and composure
    - tolerance and yes, some humility (don't brag about your expensive car or computer: instead of impressing the Client it will only serve to antagonize him).

(b) **Reasons why a Realtor may misunderstand his Client.**

- The Realtor is not listening "effectively." The Client will more or less try to say

what is on his mind; his concerns and problems will be voiced as "objections" which could either be feared or are unwelcome by the Realtor.
- The Realtor is not willing to let the Client finish talking about his concerns; instead he discontinues paying attention to what the Client is trying to say and jumps to a premature conclusion.

When the Realtor has trouble understanding the Client then:
- he should listen more actively and carefully to what the Client is trying to say.
- He should try to focus on words and phrases that make sense to him.
- He should respond to the emotional tone of the speaker's voice and body language.
- Even if the Realtor cannot decipher all of the meaning of what the Client is trying to convey, the Realtor may be able to recognize a plethora of feelings: concern, worry, joy, anger, frustration, resignation. **These could serve as valuable directional beacons to guide his next move.**
- If the Realtor still does not understand, then he should apologize and ask the Client to repeat it: this lets him or her know that the Realtor cares and is anxious to communicate to everybody's mutual satisfaction.

From all of the above it should be obvious that **to successfully communicate** with a person can be a terribly difficult task. Nevertheless it is possible to explain complicated things by making an extra effort of literally "painting" the right mental images in the right circumstances.

Ways to build TRUST with a Client:
(Trust will often make the Realtor's task much simpler)
(a) The Realtor should begin the conversation with orienting information, e.g.
- identify yourself (if you haven't done so already)
- establish your authority ("I have been selling real estate for ... years")
- create a relaxed atmosphere (possibly by addressing the Client by name)
- Try a calm, gentle, matter-of-fact approach
- Always remember that YOU are in control of the direction of the conversation and therefore it is YOU who can set the mood for the interaction. Your relaxed manner may even be contagious!
- Some humour and cheerfulness may result in a non-demanding and non-threatening approach.
- By beginning your conversation socially (common ground: hobbies, children etc.) you may win the Client's trust easier.

(b) The Realtor should ensure that the Client has understood what has been said to him. How can the Realtor check up on this?
- The Realtor should **pause periodically and thus allow plenty of time for the information to be understood and absorbed by the Client.**
  This may require some tact and patience on the Realtor's part. To verify that

the Recipient/Client is still with you, test him periodically by asking simple questions that require a choice of a "yes/no" answer, rather than an open-ended question. E.g. instead of saying: "What kind of counter-offer do you want to make?" you might give choices: "Do you want $ 200,000 or did you have $210,000 in mind?"

- By getting the Client's FEEDBACK. By asking the appropriate questions the Realtor can verify if like-minded communication has been achieved.

(c) The Realtor should use familiar words and concrete terms in order to ensure that the Recipient/Client understands abstract concepts. Don't say that "the Seller is under a previous contract"; instead inform your Buyer that the Seller has already accepted a conditional offer and that "we are the first back-up offer and thus next in line."

(d) The Client should be able to rely and count on the Realtor at all times.

(e) The Realtor must absolutely keep his word under all circumstances.

(f) The Client will see this as an expression of RESPECT.

AND FINALLY HERE ARE A FEW THINGS WHICH YOU SHOULDN'T DO:

(a) Are you more interested in showing off your eloquence, wit and wisdom rather than listening to what your Clients want, need and can afford? God gave you one mouth and 2 ears: this alone should **tell you that careful listening is not only an excellent CLOSING TOOL, but also a TIME-SAVING DEVICE.**

(b) For heaven's sake, don't argue with your Client. You may win the battle (the argument), but you will lose the war (the listing or sale).

(c) Don't be bossy or controlling when you try to explain what it is you propose to do. Few of us like to be bossed around, so don't order a Client around or tell him what he or she can't do.

(d) And finally there is the matter of the wrong words at the wrong time and in the wrong place: to discuss taboo subjects like politics and religion may convince your client to communicate you out the door empty handed.

Body Language - Part I

BODY LANGUAGE is a continuous and silent flow of information and communication from one party to the other. By OBSERVING and INTERPRETING the body language of your conversation partner, you can increase your UNDERSTANDING of how that person is feeling.

Of course, the same applies in reverse: a Realtor who is concerned with being successful must be aware that in turn HIS OWN body language is also giving off powerful signals. Therefore at all times and whatever you do … try to project the thought: **"I am here to assist and serve you"**; and don't forget to smile pleasantly and act confidently.

Some of the **basic components of NON-VERBAL communication** are:

(1) **The sense of SIGHT** allows human beings to see people, objects and animals and to experience colour, brightness and darkness. The observation of body language is a continuous and silent flow of information and communication from one party to the other. By observing and interpreting the body language of your conversation partner you can increase your understanding of how that person is feeling. An important area of body language is your FACIAL EXPRESSION and YOUR EYES.

(2) **The sense of SMELL** differentiates between pleasing sensations and unpleasant ones. Beware of your personal space. Poking your face into the face of your Client may involve the risk of making a lasting impression with your breath. Alternatively a heavy dose of perfume or deodorant cannot mask the odours emanating from an unwashed body.

(3) **The sense of TOUCH** can tell us what is hot or cold, smooth or rough. In touch, the degree of physical contact can also be enlightening, e.g. **a limp handshake** can create the negative impression of indifference or lack of self-esteem. The opposite of the limp handshake is **the crushingly firm handshake** which resembles the grip of death by the Grim Reaper; this can not only hurt the recipient but may also give the impression of aggression.

Grabbing, touching or hugging somebody impulsively may be misunderstood or resented.

(1) **All of these SENSES combine to STIMULATE our brain into making OBSERVATIONS.**
(2) Next we then **INTERPRET what our senses have communicated to us and then we form some sort of OPINION based on past filed-away experiences.**

PERCEPTION is a complex and continuous process and is often practiced unconsciously. Due to our own prejudices, faults or motives there are unfortunately some pitfalls which can be avoided by using a little common sense:

- For obvious reasons, care should be taken not to jump to hasty conclusions (**snap judgements**). E.g. if somebody crosses their arms over their chest, it might be done for comfort rather than confrontation.
- Mistakenly **projecting** onto others some of our own faults or motives. This goes hand in hand with **prejudice** which is often based on unfortunate past experiences or erroneous teachings.

(3) The next step in this development is **our REACTION to the situation**. Our response will be governed by what we perceive and how we interpret it. On an emotional level, a certain amount of **EMPATHY** with the other party is decisive for interpersonal reaction and relations.

(4) And finally, our brains will file away everything that has taken place in a given situation and keep a record for future reference. **We are accumulating EXPERIENCE for future feedback.**

Non-verbal communication is a two-edged sword and is practiced unconsciously. Therefore the Realtor should be aware that **the signals which HE is giving off can also be recognized and consciously interpreted by the CLIENT.** The Client in turn will project his own motivations and personality traits onto the Realtor, regardless of how inaccurate some of these perceptions may be.
Thus communication for the Realtor depends not only on what he is saying and how he is saying it, but also on HIS own BODY LANGUAGE.

Amongst other things a smart Realtor will keep the following in mind:

(a) care should be taken that **the Realtor does NOT appear to be STARING intently** at the client for the obviously sole purpose of "reading" and "evaluating" the prospective Client. If the process of observation of the Client's body language is too painfully apparent, then the other party will become selfconscious, upset or mad all of which is counter productive to the free flow of information.

(b) **A stone-faced Realtor** trying intently to hide his activity of scrutinizing the Client could come across as an uncaring cold fish. This will not increase the Realtor's credibility.

(c) A politically correct but **permanently frozen grin** on the Realtor's face while he is mechanically rattling off poorly memorized lines (e.g. open-ended questions) does NOT make the Realtor appear to be "sincere." In the contrary, he will give the impression of being phony or pushy. Why run the risk of alienating the Client by "playing a role?"

(d) A "canned sales talk" requires a superb actor who can - after many years of practice - recite his lines "naturally." In order to **give the appearance of speaking** "spontaneously" he must be able to mentally rewrite the script while he is speaking, in order to adapt what he is saying to an ever-changing scenario.

CAUTION: While the Client is talking to you, you will create a NEGATIVE IMPRESSION if you:
- continue what you have been doing (e.g. fiddling with your computer, concentrate on shuffling papers, filing away letters, putting stuff into the desk drawers etc.)
- roll your eyes or look intently somewhere else
- bend over your desk and start doodling and let the other party talk to the top of your head. As your conversation partner is admiring your bald spot, he will eventually get the idea that you are totally disinterested in what he is saying.
- The same effect can be achieved by leaning back in your chair, unbuttoning your jacket, hooking both thumbs under your suspenders and tilting your head back so that you can study the intricacies of the ceiling.
- With droopy eyes resting your chin on the knuckles of both hands.
- Yawning repeatedly and extensively
- after discreetly nodding off with open eyes - waking up with a start during a break or lull in the conversation. This will indicate that you haven't been paying attention and are lost at sea.

The following means that you are IMPATIENT (and maybe somewhat frustrated) and want to get on with it:

- nodding continuously and impatiently
- **tapping** with your foot on the floor
- **drumming** with your fingers on the table
- looking at your watch and checking the time repeatedly
- continuously clicking your ballpoint pen
- **rattling your keys or jiggling the coins in your pocket**
- puffing your cheeks and exhaling noisily
- clenching your jaws or gnawing with your teeth
- an old cliche says that scratching your head indicates puzzlement. Whereas scratching may feel good, it can in fact be very distracting. Dandruff may dislodge and fall on your shoulders (which may be about eye level of the other party). Dandruff will become painfully obvious if you wear dark clothing.

You are in trouble and the interview may be finished ... when the CLIENT
- leans back and exchanges meaningful glances with his/her partner
- when one or both Clients stand up and walk away from the table for no apparent reason.

The public has - for better or worse - **a preconceived idea of how a Realtor should look**. The Realtor **must make from head to toe a total confidence-building impression:**

- personal appearance including his wardrobe,
- visual characteristics (body language),
- wholesome cleanliness (smell),
- personal habits (**good manners and emotions under control**).
- **acts with confidence**
- **talks with authority.**

A TALL ORDER, indeed!

POISE CHECK:

Now close your eyes and picture honestly what your Client will see when you stand before him.

Does your total appearance and the impression you will create give cause for him to think that he can safely entrust the sale of his biggest financial asset (namely his home) to you?

Or are you a person who betrays his insecurity by giving hesitant and evasive answers and who through his body language and untidy wardrobe appears to be just scraping by?

Your Clients will rationalize in the same way as you are: they will play it safe and go with the person that - in their minds - looks and acts like a professional.

UNDERSTANDING your Clients' body language as well as being conscious of your own can make the difference between concluding successfully a sale (or obtaining a listing) or going home empty handed.

Body Language - Part II

OVERALL BODY POSTURE and STANCE.

Try to **STAND comfortably and evenly balanced on both feet.** Don't shift repeatedly your weight from one foot to the other; it might give the impression that you are uneasy or insecure.

On the other hand **don't just stand there rigidly like a stone statue.**

If the occasion warrants it, move with purpose but **avoid sudden, jerky movements which may startle your client.** Sudden unexpected rapid movements (e.g. getting up and pacing back and forth) may also suggest that you are nervous or aggressive which in turn will subconsciously activate the client's defense mechanism. Many a sale has been lost this way.

When SITTING
- hold your body erect,
- face the customer squarely,
- stop whatever you have been doing and
- **make eye contact.**

This will tell your client that he has your full and undivided attention.

From various movements of your body you can communicate to your client **THE DEGREE of INTEREST YOU HAVE in what he is saying:**
- leaning your torso slightly forward **indicates interest**.
- nodding occasionally is a good **silent indication of agreement**.
- To encourage someone to keep on talking or to elaborate more on a topic, nodding can be combined with prodding words like "go on" or "I see" or "yes …?"

The following may indicate that you are **concentrating on what you are hearing:**
- taking off your glasses and placing them in front of you,
- pinching or rubbing the bridge of your nose with your thumb and index finger,
- stroking your chin with your thumb and index finger
- both of your hands form a steeple close to your nose
- resting your chin lightly on the knuckles of ONE hand while looking questioningly at the customer
- tugging at an ear while maintaining eye contact.

HOW TO HOLD YOUR HEAD.

Hold your head proudly (but not arrogantly) erect. At the same time try not to create the impression that you are suffering from a stiff neck.

- Resting your chin in the palm of your hand may indicate that you are pensive (or else that you are trying to hide your double chin).
- Various instances of "nodding" have been mentioned previously.
- Shaking the head from one side to the other means a silent "no," disagreement or disapproval.
- Tilting the head to one side can mean intent listening and increased interest.
- Tilting your head could also indicate that you are pondering a point which the other person has just made; or that you are not quite in agreement with the other side's position.

An important area of body language is your **FACIAL EXPRESSION**. Without you realizing it, it is quite possible that during a - for YOU uninteresting - stretch of the conversation a blank or bored expression can creep over your face. If you want to avoid "check mate," then keep alert somehow.

THE EYES.

It has been said that the **EYES** are the mirrors of the soul. When you are addressing a customer, always look him into his eyes; if you don't, then you run the risk of appearing as shifty or that you have something to hide.

On the other hand try to avoid "hypnotizing" the other party by **staring into his eyes relentlessly and piercingly over a long period of time.** This will make your conversation partner uneasy; he may also resent it that you appear to be "staring him down." This situation would be reminiscent of a hunter with a rifle zeroing in on an animal for the kill.

For a brief relief, shift your gaze from one person to another or briefly look down to the papers in front of you. At any rate confine your gaze to something or someone in the immediate vicinity of your conversation partners. But don't look out the window.

A **blank look, droopy or unfocused eyes with a faraway gaze** will tell your opposite that you are daydreaming instead of paying attention to what he is saying.

THE MOUTH.

The mouth serves not only to pronounce your words, but is a dead giveaway of how you are feeling:

A small, confident smile on your slightly parted lips means that you are **relaxed**. As your customer is often tense (because he is emotionally involved and worried about making a costly financial mistake), a smile will help putting him at ease.

A relaxed and pleasant (not arrogantly overconfident) smile will say that you are no threat, that you have nothing to hide and that you know what you are doing.

When it is appropriate and the occasion calls for it, then you may be able to broaden your smile.

A tense mouth with lips compressed so tightly that they are drained of their natural colour will make you appear as grim, to some even as forbidding. It will indicate that YOU are
- under some sort of pressure,
- unsure what to do next,
- that you may be ruthlessly determined to bulldoze this deal through regardless of how they (the customers) feel about it

THE EYE BROWS.

Somehow the eyes and the eye brows seem to work in concert.
- Wrinkling or pulling the eye brows together in a frown will express concern;
- surprise is suggested by a sudden raising of one of the eye brows.
- if you frown frequently, you may end up with a permanent furrow between the eye brows. To some this may add "character" to your face; to others it may merely mean that you frown a lot.

HAND GESTURES.

Some people talk by waving their arms and using their hands to such an extent, that they would be unable to communicate effectively in the dark. Even when they are on the phone, they appear to be conducting an orchestra. Have you ever observed people talking on a cell phone? One hand - frozen in a permanent cramp - will clutch the little instrument awkwardly while simultaneously trying to drill it into the owner's head. While he is fiercely goose-stepping back and forth, his body may be rocking forward and backward to some inaudible music. Simultaneously the free other arm and hand will slice through the air with vicious karate chops emphasizing certain conversation points.

Hand gestures CAN distract from a conversation.

THE FOLLOWING IS COUNTER PRODUCTIVE:
- Smashing a tight fist resoundingly into the open palm of the other hand when trying to make a point, will come across as an ill tempered overpowering command.
- Stabbing the air with or pointing a rigidly extended index finger (with the hand closed into a tight fist) into somebody's face at close range is not only rude, but also may make the customer angry.

WHAT IS ACCEPTABLE:
An open flat hand with the palm up or out in a slow and gentle movement may serve a graceful way of making a point.

ABOUT TOUCHING.
In North American society it is not quite acceptable to touch a stranger spontaneously, even if it is done in a non-threatening manner and merely on the hand, wrist or elbow. Other **unwelcome advances to relative strangers** which could be misunderstood or resented are:
- slapping somebody resoundingly on the back,
- hugging him for no reason and
- putting your arm around his shoulders
- grabbing his/her hand spontaneously and forgetting to let go. This can be especially embarrassing and/or of questionable taste if the grabber and grabbed are of different genders.
- Mussing up a little boy's short-cropped hair might be fine and a gesture of friendly familiarity; but doing the same thing to a little girl's carefully braided hair will neither be appreciated by her nor by her mother.

ABOUT YOUR PERSONAL SPACE.

The distance between you and the other person depends largely on the social circumstances of the situation you find yourself in. Being close to a family member or a romantic partner is obviously ok.

On the other hand poking your face into the face of a stranger or standing too close to a stranger may be uncomfortable or embarrassing. That is why people in a fully loaded elevator tend to shrink into the corners or look uneasily at the ceiling.

The distance between you and a customer should be such that:
- the proximity of your respective bodies should be neither threatening nor embarrassing to either one of you
- but close enough for a confidential discussion; that is why it is better to sit around a kitchen or dining room table.
- To present an offer across the distance of a living room is awkward because the distance is too great; you may have to jump up several times and go over to your client and bend over him or her to explain something or to point to a certain part on a document.
- **Ideally the distance between yourself and the others should** be safe and comfortable enough so that you don't appear to be invading their "private space" but at the same time close enough so that you can communicate with them effectively.

ABOUT PERSONAL GROOMING

When dealing with "proximity," the sense of SMELL comes in. If you stand too close to somebody, your body odour will become noticeable. If you regularly take care of yourself, then there will be no problem.

A heavy dose of perfume or deodorant cannot mask the odours emanating from an unwashed body. You will merely stink of a repulsive combination of perspiration and heavy perfume.

When using a deodorant or body cologne, make sure that it is not overpowering; "less" and "discreet" is better. When selecting a perfume or deodorant, seek and obtain the opinions of friends and relatives which one seems to be the most appropriate one for you. Sometimes the same perfume on different bodies seems to have a slightly different smell from one person to another.

Clothes should be regularly cleaned, because they can give off a scent of their own; e.g. tobacco, certain spicy foods, heavy perspiration over a long period of time. This can defeat the good impression of your daily personal hygiene.

Bad breath.
Care should be taken to avoid things which can make a "lasting" impression, even if it is relatively temporary.
Bad breath may come from
(1) stomach acids: if you are nervous acidy stomach juices may cause bad breath; either see your doctor or there are various kinds of mouth wash or sprays available.
(2) Bad breath sometimes also emanates from rotting teeth or lack of mouth hygiene.
(3) Bad breath can also come from something which you may have just consumed:
   (a) **Immediately before you go on an appointment**: Don't eat raw onions, chili or foods prepared with a heavy dose of garlic or currie. Your "culinary" breath may not be appreciated by the customer.
   (b) **In your car (just before you go into the customer's house):**
   - to have a furtive swig from a bottle of cheap plonk will not put fire into your belly, but alcohol on your breath.
   - to smoke a cigarette hastily in the confines of your car (with the windows rolled up because it is cold outside) will result in your clothes soaking up the tobacco smell. The smell from the cigarette smoke will be not only on your breath, but it will surround you with an invisible cloud of intensive and repulsive stench. You will reek of cold and biting tobacco stench.

In either case the customer doesn't have to be a rocket scientist to conclude that you have just "fortified" yourself in order to steady your nerves.

Understanding body language must become part of your working arsenal.

Empathy, The Manager And The Salesperson

Empathy is not to be confused with **sympathy**, which - according to Webster's Dictionary - is compassion or commiseration. **Sympathy is an emotional issue** during which your feelings correspond to those which another person experiences.

On the other hand **empathy is part of and a triumph in communication**. Although it takes a lot of time and effort to learn and master empathy, it can be done. You don't have to have a talent for it, although it helps. A Sales Manager should endeavour to make empathy a part of his management skills, because he will find it helpful in his dealings with his sales staff. As a leader he should strive to become aware of his sales and clerical staff's thoughts and feelings and their perspective on certain things; in the end this may be important for business success (the bottom line). Depending on how well a Manager knows his people, he can possibly anticipate the reactions of the staff to new initiatives, which in turn may help avoid unnecessary conflict (upheaval). By using empathy, a Manager may be able to quickly get to the heart of the matter, which in turn may save time spent on unnecessary (wrong) issues. Trying to calm things down again may further involve a lot of unnecessarily wasted nerves, effort and precious time.

If a Manager does not use empathy, then he will block communication, which sadly in turn may end up in a communication shutdown between himself and his staff:
- His sales persons might feel frustrated and helpless;
- no doubt this will negatively effect productivity.
- People will quit coming to him ("what's the use, he doesn't listen anyway") and
- the Manager in turn may end up feeling isolated
- while he simultaneously generates anger and hurt in his subordinates and associates.

So **how does a Manager go about acquiring and/or practicing empathy?**

(1) When one of your salespersons comes to talk to you, then **quit doing whatever you have been doing and concentrate totally on him:**
   - Quit shuffling papers around on your desk,
   - quit fiddling with your computer;
   - put your ballpoint down and don't doodle.
   - Ask your secretary to hold all of your calls (no interruptions except for emergencies).
   - Lean back and look him in the eyes (non-threateningly).

Your salesperson will have the satisfaction of knowing that he has your undivided attention. At the same time he hopefully will realize how precious your time is and he will keep it short.

(2) Whereas **it is important to establish facts,** don't grill or interrogate the other person relentlessly. You are neither a policeman drilling a stubborn criminal, nor a lawyer cross-examining somebody in court. **Guide the conversation by asking interested questions which should yield informative answers.**

(3) Keep your voice calm and even. Adopt a non-threatening posture.

(4) **Develop your LISTENING skills.**
It takes discipline and a concerted effort to REALLY listen. Take time to notice the other person's:
 (a) real, implicit message of what he is actually trying to say. Not everybody has the gift of the gab; not everybody can express himself eloquently. **Make a determined effort to understand what the other person is trying to communicate to you.**
 (b) Don't shut your ears to another person's view point.
 (c) **Don't be impatient** and jump to hasty conclusions or make a premature decision before the other party has finished talking.

(5) **Develop your OBSERVATION skills:**
 (a) Observe the other person's body language.
 (b) Notice what his facial expression is (agitation: tight lips, twitching around the mouth and eyes, pale or flushed red cheeks etc.)

(6) It is of utmost importance that the Manager understands **what motivates his people.** Realize and know what is going on in the office and the market place (self-awareness).

(7) **Don't patronize** by saying: "It's not a big deal" or "He didn't mean it" or "Forget it, on to the next deal." This will not solve the problem.

(8) For a hands-on "take-charge" Manager it requires real discipline to resist the urge to fix a problem by giving orders or unsolicited advice. Remember the old story: You will feed a person for one day if you give him a fish to eat. You will feed him a life time if you teach him how to fish.

(9) It is also **important to convey** (or to communicate) to the other person **that you have understood** what he is trying to say. But always be honest and tell the truth. It is phony and insincere to say: "I feel your pain."

(10) Instead of stammering and searching for compassionate and to-the-point words, **learn to have a good and expressive vocabulary addressing and expressing emotions.** If necessary rehearse the words and expressions until they become ingrained and part of your usual vocabulary.

The rewards for your efforts to have empathy will be great.

(a) Your associates and employees will feel more important, more trusted and more appreciated.
(b) They also will become happier, more loyal and productive;
(c) all of this will be reflected in the company's bottom line (profitability).

Exercising empathy may involve a certain amount of risk (of looking foolish) and/or subsequent discomfort of making a mistake while trying to "guess" how people feel. But this will correct itself with time during which the Manager will gain increased experience in how to "read" people.

Incidentally "reading" people is also very important for all Salespersons in their dealings with clients, the public and their fellow salespersons (both in the office, as well as the competition).

Winning Strategies For Prospecting

"Prospecting" is necessary
- if you want to stay in real estate sales
- if you want to avoid the ups and downs of commission income.

"Prospecting" should be a continuous, daily and never-ending task and procedure; and yes, it is not only tedious work but also a lot of "blood, sweat and tears."

"Prospecting" involves talking constantly to many people.

"Prospecting" requires that you get into a **daily routine**.

The most difficult thing about prospecting daily is to **make the first call or to make the first attempt.**

The best time to prospect is when you are fresh and have **the most energy**. At the end of your work day you may be physically and mentally exhausted.

The OBJECTIVE of prospecting is to obtain new business (either a Buyer or a Seller). This is best achieved by talking to
- one of the decision makers
- and by finding out what their real estate interests, needs and expectations are.

Understand that prospecting is **a numbers game.** Sooner or later somebody will say "yes." **You can improve the odds by developing**
- **the habit of daily** prospecting (it is difficult to procrastinate if you have an established daily routine) and
- by honing **your verbal and mental skills.**

2 reasons WHY many Realtors try to AVOID prospecting.

1) Because of their fear of **personal rejection.**

HOW TO OVERCOME THIS FEAR:
You must be mentally strong: this doesn't mean that you have to love daily rejection. It simply means that you should look at the situation objectively:
(a) If somebody says "no" just thank him politely and move on to the next one. There are always more fish in the ocean.
(b) His "no" could not have been a personal rejection, because both of you are strangers to each other. He merely indicated that he didn't want to do business at this time.
(c) It would be a shame, if you are willing to let a total stranger dictate what happens in your life (namely how much or how little business you will conduct).

(d) Are you willing to let your fear of rejection **negatively impact** on your present and future financial well being?
(e) If this fear of rejection is going to defeat you, then ask yourself bluntly: "If I am unable to overcome this fear, then how much of my potential financial earnings, security and independence is it going to cost me? Is it really worth it?"

2) The principle of **DELAYED GRATIFICATION**.

If your boss would pay you $ 5.00 for each call you are making then you would be on the phone night and day and wouldn't worry about personal rejection.
In real life you are prospecting for yourself. When you do eventually connect, then in due course you will earn a big, fat commission. If you devide the commission amount by the number of hours you have spent prospecting and selling the listing, then you will most likely find that you have earned more than $ 5.00 for each time you dialled the phone. Thus your pay day is delayed until the deal is completed.

Therefore, if you love
- the feeling of success
- financial security
- independence
- and a good life

then you have to learn to become "strong-at-heart" and you must be willing to pay the price. This means that you must be willing to "stick with it."

When you are prospecting, then you should understand that
(a) The best you can hope for is a chance of getting your foot into the door; and then the real "selling" starts.
(b) It is not possible to get a written contract (listing or sale) over the phone.
(c) You have to learn to be patient because due to human nature
- many people need time to make a decision
- and they have to feel comfortable with that decision.
(d) If they don't want to list or buy today, they may want to do so sometime in the future; therefore, keep a record of them and don't forget to follow up periodically.

Prospecting can be done in many ways and forms but **basically it comes down to talking to people either**
(A) in person
(B) or by telephone.
(C) Other ways of prospecting are:
- flyers delivered by bulk mail,
- newsletters containing interesting real estate statistics, trends, mortgage rates etc.
- researching municipal records for absentee landlords,
- the internet (sites serving your local area),

- "listings wanted" ads in the newspaper,
- enquiries generated from
  - your own "for sale" signs,
  - your newspaper ads promoting the sale of a specific listing
- institutional advertising (TV ads, billboards, shopping carts, bus benches etc.)

(A) Prospecting (or canvassing) in person.

General considerations:
- Be careful of your personal appearance, neatness and cleanliness (including bad breath).
- Try to smile pleasantly whenever possible or warranted
- Try to keep your face free from grim and hard expressions (e.g. tight lips, avoid frowning).
- Make sure that your vocabulary, grammar and enunciation are pleasing, appropriate and adequate.
- Make sure that
  - your sentences are short
  - your ideas are clear, intelligent and practical
- be aware that the other party is talking to you only by his gracious consent and not as a result of your aggressiveness.

Sources for business and avenues for prospecting.

(1) For many people "real estate" is an interesting and fascinating subject. They like to talk about it - especially with someone who knows more about it than they do. Therefore, **everyone you meet, see or talk** with throughout your daily travels may be a potential customer or alternatively he may lead you to some business (referral). Any type of social contact: barbershop, gas station, a party, restaurant, auction sale etc.

(2) **Farming**.
This can be either
(a) contacting homeowners within a certain geographic area
(b) maintaining contact with
- former Clients (Buyers and Sellers)
- Lawyers and Notaries Public
- accountants,
- bank managers,
- ministers,
- personnel managers,
- insurance agents
- past business associates

- merchants (hardware and paint store, carpet store)
- contractors and builders
- subtrades (painters, carpenters, electricians)
- hotel and motel desk clerks
- mailman and newspaper carriers
- storage companies
- (unlicensed) sales staff of big condominium contractors (one of their prospective buyers may have to sell his house first before he can buy the condo).

(3) **Open House**.
- Prospective Sellers come to an Open House in order to check out comparable values.
- Prospective Buyers come to see if the house is suitable for them (they also may have a house to sell).

(4) **Centre of Influence**.
   (a) If you have a **new listing then** you should canvass the immediate neighbourhood and ask the following questions:
   - "Do you know of somebody who may want to live here?"
   - "Are YOU interested in selling? I can work both houses simultaneously."
   - "Do you know of somebody in the neighbourhood who might be thinking of selling?"
   - If nobody is home, drop off a "Just Listed" card.
   Write down the address; back at the office look up the owner's name and phone number in the Criss/Cross Directory, so that you can follow up by phone later on.
   (b) **After you have sold the house**, you should canvass the neighbourhood again; this time around you can report "SUCCESS" and somebody who has seen your "sold" sign might get the urge to move. If nobody is home drop off a "Just sold" card ("introducing your new neighbour").
   Same follow up procedure as above.

(5) **Creative canvassing**.
   (a) While you are driving around, you might see
   - a man painting his house. Stop your car, get out and talk to him: he might be fixing up the house and getting it ready to sell.
   - a small house with a tricycle or some toys on the front lawn or in the driveway. These people have a growing family and might need more space (a bigger house with more bedrooms and bathrooms).
   (b) Pick out the nicest and best kept house on the block; this owner has been there for a long time and knows everybody in the neighbourhood. Ask the owner:

- "Did anybody in the vicinity have his house for sale during the last year and it didn't sell?"
- "Do you know of anybody in the neighbourhood who is considering selling?"

(6) **"For Sale By Owner" signs**.

Reasons why people are trying to sell without a Realtor:
(a) they want to "save the commission" or are willing/able to pay only a reduced commission because they have no or little equity.
(b) Fear:
- they had a bad experience in the past (the house didn't sell).
- Or they know of somebody who has had a bad experience with a Realtor.
(c) Lack of motivation:
- they are "in no hurry to sell"
- they are merely "testing the market" (translation: they will sell if a sucker comes along who is willing to pay their inflated asking price).
(d) It is a Seller's Market and there are many willing buyers around who are competing against each other.
- they think that they are terrific salespersons and can sell it themselves.

Suggested dialogue:
"Good morning. My name is ... and I am with ... Realty. I am canvassing this area because we have several **qualified buyers who want to locate in this area**. Would you cooperate with a Realtor to get your house sold?
May I come in to inspect the house to see if it is suitable for my buyers? (I don't want to waste your time and mine).

To build RAPPORT you should ask questions during the walk-through.
- Questions will prolong the conversation.
- By asking questions you **will gain information** (hopes, needs, expectations) about the Seller **which you can use later** (to get the listing).
- By asking the right "guiding" questions, the Seller may discover **the benefits of dealing with you.**
- Let the Seller do most of the talking and you LISTEN.
- The more the Seller talks, the better he will like you.

Questions which you could ask casually during the walk-through:
- How long have you owned this house?
- Why are you selling?
- How soon will you have to move?
- What are you asking for your house?
- How did you arrive at this price?

- What methods do you use to market your house? (Most likely he has none other then the sign on his front lawn).
- Are all of your showings by appointment and only to pre-qualified buyers? (Most likely he is admitting any and all lookeeloos who are knocking on his front door).
- Why did you decide to sell yourself and not list with a Realtor?
- Where are you moving to?
- When do you have to move?

NOTE: **The higher the Seller's motivation is,** the **lower will be his asking price** and **the better are your chances of listing the house.**

(7) **Personal contacts.**
  (a) Clubs or organizations which you belong to: Chamber of Commerce, fraternal organization, sports club, social club.
  (b) Let everybody know that you are in real estate: relatives, friends, neighbours, acquaintances.

(8) **"For Rent" signs.**
The owner may have no luck renting out the house. Or else he may be fed up dealing with tenants.

(9) **Vacant properties.**
Find out who the owner is and then find out why the house is vacant.

(10) **Neglected properties.**
The property may be neglected because
  (a) of a bad tenant.
  (b) or else due to old age or failing health the owners are no longer able to keep it up. They want to move to an apartment, but have been procrastinating.
  (c) The owners cannot afford the house (other debts, high mortgage payments, unemployment, high taxes etc.)

(11) **Door-to-door cold canvassing.**

Disadvantages:
- Nobody is home.
- You may ring the door bell at an inconvenient time for the owner.
- The wife is home alone and doesn't want to open the door to an uninvited stranger.
- You are able to cover only a limited territory before you are tired and have sore legs and feet.
- The weather (hot, blazing sun, cold, windy, rain)

Advantages:
- It can yield a "virgin" listing (the house had never been listed before).
- The exercise (walking, stair climbing) will put you in a better physical shape. (Lose some weight).
- You can also canvass at random: every 2nd, 3rd or 4th house.

(B) **Prospecting by TELEPHONE.**

General considerations:
(1) The telephone is not only an important and convenient business tool, but it will also save you a lot of time.
(2) Before starting to canvass by phone, you should
- **clear your mind** of all personal and business worries
- and **concentrate on the task at hand.**
(3) Common courtesy requires that while you are speaking on the telephone you should not
  (a) **eat, drink or chew gum**. The other party will not appreciate having to listen to the sounds of gulping liquid or smacking lips.
  (b) **you should also not smoke**. The other party may be offended by having to listen to you taking a deep satisfying drag from your cigarette and then exhaling noisily into the telephone.
(4) Do not use a speaker phone (because there might be an annoying echo making conversation difficult).
(5) Try to make a good "first impression" so that the prospect should feel comfortable with you. You should appear as
- helpful
- confident and
- competent.
(6) To achieve that goal you should start by holding the telephone properly:
- speak directly into the mouthpiece.
- Your lips should be close to the mouthpiece.

  This will allow the other party to hear you well.
(7) Speak in a relaxed manner which is normal for you.
(8) **Put a smile into your voice.**
  (a) In order to achieve this keep a small mirror in front of you and watch your face: it is impossible to sound grumpy if you are smiling pleasantly.
  (b) If you sound happy and alert then the other party may think that you are a helpful person who is sincere and service oriented.
  (c) The most pleasant sounding voice is achieved by a **forward placement of the voice.**
  (d) Try to get rid of speech patterns and habits which are unnatural, twisted, guttural or with poorly placed tone or pitch.
(9) **Don't mumble**: pronounce your words properly and carefully.

(10) **Don't speak too fast or too slow.**
- When you speak too fast you will sound like you are in a hurry or else you may be difficult to understand.
- If you speak too slow, then your conversation partner's mind is liable to wander or else he will become impatient: he may interrupt you and ask that you get to the point.

(11) **Don't speak too loud or too low.**
- If you speak too loud you might appear as aggressive or angry.
- If you speak too softly the other party may
  - have difficulty hearing you or
  - think that you are shy or uncertain and don't know what you are doing.

(12) **Vary the pitch in your voice** so that you don't sound monotonous.

(13) **Sell the sizzle and not the steak**. Don't talk too much - get to the point, because the other person may have a **short attention span**.

(14) Have a plan and know what you want to accomplish.

When you start prospecting by phone, you should concentrate on 3 things because they are the **sole representation of your personality over the phone**:

(a) **Your WORDS.**

Rather than fumbling for words, it is important that you know what you are going to say. Develop, practice and fine tune **"a script."** A well thought out and a thoroughly rehearsed "script" will provide **a good guide to follow**. If you so choose, you can still be "spontaneous" by making small variations to suit the occasion.

(b) **Your VOICE.**

Concentrate on the **tone of your voice**. Your voice should demonstrate **warmth and enthusiasm** (see above).

Try to avoid tenseness and nervousness in your voice.

Don't prejudge the customer by the sound of his voice

(c) **Good MANNERS.**
- Introduce yourself by giving your full name, the Realty's name and the purpose of your call.
- Be patient and attentive: listen carefully to what the other person has to say.
- Disarm discourtesy with studied courtesy.
- Be quick to praise
- Be slow to criticize (e.g. your competition).
- Don't loose your temper or make satirical comments.
- Resist to be drawn into an argument or controversy.
- Don't be overconfident (cock-sure), self-important, all-knowing or impatient.
- End the call on a positive note: "Thank you for giving me your time."
- Let the other party hang up first. It will make him feel good (he will be under the illusion of having been "in control").

Prospecting by TELEPHONE can be either:

(a) **Cold canvassing**
- expired multiple listings (refer to the Privacy Act and local real estate board rules)
- expired exclusive listings (refer to the Privacy Act and local real estate board rules)

  Important question to ask in the above 2 cases:
  "Mr. Seller, what do you think is the reason why your house didn't sell the last time around?"
- For Sale by Owner ads
- Telephone/addresses Directory

  You will very likely fail if you ask: "Mr. Homeowner, are you interested in selling your house?" There is no attempt in establishing communication with the prospect. Chances are that he will simply say "No" and hang up on you. Instead try the following:

  Before he can reject you:
  - **Capture and hold his attention**
  - by offering some benefit to him:
    - **ask him if he needs a bigger or smaller house.**
    - **ask him if he wants a newer house.**
    - **a house closer to transportation, schools and shopping etc.**

(b) **Prospects calling on one of your listed properties.**
  A good number of people who will call you could have a house for sale. Enquiries could be generated by your
  - signs or
  - ads in the newspaper.

In these cases the customer wants as much information as possible while avoiding to have to commit himself to you by giving you his name and phone number. The caller is concerned that
- you will hound him forever if he gives you his name and phone number
- you will high pressure him if he doesn't like the house.

Modern technology has solved the problem of obtaining the caller's name and phone number: new phones have "call display" (the telephone shows the caller's name and phone number).

On the other hand the Realtor wants to establish a rapport with the caller in order to turn him into a prospective buyer or seller.
To reconcile these opposing goals, try to (before giving out the address, price etc.)
- prolong the conversation by concentrating on "product benefits" and "customer needs."

- Try to gain the caller's trust by offering him a benefit:
  - "You know, Mr. Caller, house hunting by newspaper is very time consuming and can be frustrating. If you have circled any other ads, I could perhaps help you out."
  - "Driving around is inefficient, because sometimes there is no "For Sale" sign outside."
  - "Seeing only the outside of a house could be misleading, because the inside might be surprisingly attractive and suitable for your needs."

Advantages of phone canvassing:
- The homeowner might feel more relaxed if he/she isn't confronted face-to-face by a difficult to get rid of stranger (you) standing on his door step.
- The prospect's guard may be down, because he knows that he can get rid of you by simply hanging up.
- Both of you can arrange to meet or speak again at a more convenient time.
- You can cover more territory with less physical effort.
- You can contact more prospects in less time.
- You can work in comfort: sitting in an air-conditioned office, the coffee pot or a pop machine is available, a bathroom is nearby (don't laugh, for many of us this is important).
- The contact with the prospect is swift and to the point.

Disadvantages of phone canvassing:
- Because you can cover more prospects, the possibility of more rejections exists.

Obtaining Listings

The Reader must have heard many times before that LISTINGS are the "life blood of a Realtor" and the "backbone of the industry." There should be no doubt that "to LIST" is a very important part of SELLING real estate.

**There are 2 types of approaches for a Realtor's endeavour:
REACTIVE and ACTIVE.**

I) **In REACTIVE selling** the salesperson waits patiently for a LEAD (Buyer or Seller) to appear from somewhere; e.g. from an ad call or a call from one of his "For Sale" signs. A prospective Customer may come to one of his Open Houses. Then there is the "FLOOR DAY" where the Realtor sits in the comfort of an airconditioned office and waits for somebody to either walk in or phone in.

II) **In ACTIVE selling,** you start from scratch: it is **"self-disciplined LEGwork"** instead of comfortable "SITTING-down-and-waiting-for-something-to-happen-work."
"YOU" TAKE THE INITIATIVE and "YOU" ACT by locating new business: that is where securing listings comes in. Although creating new opportunities takes courage (by overcoming the fear of rejection) and nose-to-the-grindstone type of work, **it brings with it many advantages:**
(1) It costs you nothing but some **EFFORT.**
(2) It puts the **"merchandise on the shelf"** meaning that you have something to sell.
(3) It gives you **a degree of security:** you have a written contract with the Seller and regardless of who sells it, you are assured of getting the Listing portion of the commission.
(4) The mere possession of several listings of your own will make you **feel good:**
- the satisfaction of **accomplishment**
- the **pride** of ownership
- the **expectation/anticipation** of future earnings: with some work and luck you will receive a commission in due course.
(5) A good listing is "sold subject to finding a Buyer."
The knowledge that you "have an iron in the fire" should take some of the **financial pressure off your shoulders.**
(6) This in turn will give you the courage and impetus to proceed to bigger and better things (e.g. get more listings).
(7) As soon as you have a saleable listing, **every salesperson in your area will work for you** …for FREE! (The Selling Broker gets paid only IF and WHEN YOU get paid).
(8) In fact all of these **other salespersons will be competing with each** other to

sell your listing and thus **put money into YOUR pocket**.
(9) Once the property is sold, the owner will most likely have to buy again. He becomes **a built-in Buyer**. He already knows you better than any other salesperson and as he trusts you, chances are that he will buy another house through you. More money into your pocket!
(10) Your signs and ads can and will attract more Customers (Potential Buyers and Sellers will call you).
(11) And all the time you are free to go out and get more listings.
(12) The more saleable LISTINGS you acquire and have, the better your business and the higher your income will be.
(13) With all of this activity going on, you are bound to feel excited and your spirits will be way up. Because other Realtors will keep you busy with offers, there simply will be no time to commiserate about high interest rates, how bad business generally is etc.
(14) You will be surprised to notice that the hours and days will fly by in a rush because you are always "on the go".
(15) **SUCCESS will BOOST your CONFIDENCE. With time you will gain EXPERIENCE which in turn will make conducting business easier for you.** What a glorious life! It is almost like you had a license to print money!
(16) As properties are selling ambitious Realtors must constantly replenish and maintain a new and fresh stock of properties to sell.
(17) Alert salespersons will develop a "nose" for listings and will look constantly for properties with **"Qualified Sellers."** ("Qualified" means that they have a good reason for selling).
(18) By working only with **qualified Clients** you will enjoy the freedom from the aggravation of having to work with marginal Clients!
If a Realtor wants to be successful then he cannot afford the luxury of wasting his precious time on badly overpriced properties where the owner repeatedly refuses to face reality and refuses to reduce his asking price to Market Value.
(19) The pleasant feeling of working mostly with happy and satisfied Clients will generate in the Realtor a positive mental attitude.
(20) A steady stream of commission cheques will result in financial peace of mind, domestic tranquility and a raised living standard.

III) There is no secret formula of how to get listings.
Each Realtor must DEVELOP HIS OWN PERSONAL AND INDIVIDUAL STYLE.
Here are some basic considerations:

(a) CONSISTENCY: this means that **you must canvass for a listing WITHOUT FAIL EVERY DAY** (e.g. 2 or 3 a day). No sudden spurts of phoning 50 expiries for 4 days and then nothing for the next month.

(b) **HAVE A DAILY PLAN, GOAL OR PROGRAM:** Every day regardless of how busy you are, you shouldn't go to bed before you have made at least ONE try at getting a listing. This doesn't mean that you should phone somebody at midnight after you have put in a long day; but you can address a few flyers which you will mail the next morning on the way to the office.
ALTERNATIVELY, double your prospecting on the next day in order to catch up… and **do it first thing in the morning** before you get sidetracked by or involved in something else.

(c) **PERSISTENCE:** once you have found a prospective listing don't give up after the owner has initially said "no." This is one of the few exceptions where "No" could mean "maybe" and "maybe" can mean "yes." Avoid high pressure, but **keep in touch with the owner until you get the listing** or he has listed with somebody else.
In that case it is still not a failure because you already know the house, have an idea what the owner will take and it should be an excellent house to show to your current Buyers.

IN ADDITION: if you are gracious about the fact that the owner has listed with somebody else instead of with you, the owner
- might feel a little guilty and may refer some other business to you.
- OR if the house doesn't sell with the other Realtor he may end up listing with you the next time around and most likely he will do it at the more realistic price which you had suggested to him in the first place.

(d) You must continuously polish and improve **YOUR LISTING PRESENTATION** until it is perfect. Confidentially: it will never be perfect, but with increased experience you will be able to smooth over various "rough spots" and eliminate many of the basic "kinks and glitches."

(e) **USING THE RIGHT WORDS is psychologically important**.
Many Realtors are obsessed with the word "LISTING" and don't seem to realize that **the owner doesn't want to "LIST" - he wants to "SELL."**
"SELLING" to the OWNER means:
- ACTION,
- SHOWINGS,
- **BUYERS who make OFFERS.**
- The SATISFACTION **of a sale and**
- **being able to continue with his future plans**.

"LISTING" to the OWNER means:
- to tie himself up and
- possibly be stuck with a Realtor (who might turn out to be a dud, who doesn't advertise his house, who refuses to hold "Open Houses," who is lazy or who

has very little experience and who has little or no ambition to improve himself; in other words, who is not a "go-getter").
- As a result of having chosen the wrong person to sell his property
  - there will be no action and no showings
  - resulting in no offers, disappointment and a waste of HIS (the owner's) time.

So INSTEAD OF "listing" a house, the Realtor should use euphemisms like
- **"putting the house on the market,"**
- **exposing the house in the market place.**
- Tell him **HOW** you will **"market his house"** or
- suggest that **"WE should sell it."** By using the word **"WE"** you identify yourself with the Seller which may plant the following thought into his mind:
  - both of you are **on the SAME TEAM,**
  - both of you are going to **PULL IN THE SAME DIRECTION,**
  - both of you have **the same GOAL** which is to **SELL.**

Explain to the Seller that a "LISTING" is merely his written authorization for you to MARKET his house and be of assistance when he gets an offer. Other than that a "listing" costs you nothing but money and work and **will result in a commission for you ONLY if and when the property SELLS. Therefore you are VITALLY interested in the fact that the listing should SELL.**

IV) "LISTING" v. "SELLING."

Some Realtors mistakenly claim that they have "no talent" to get listings. The good news is that THE ART OF LISTING CAN BE LEARNED by anybody with some effort and diligence.

On the other hand it is true, that some Realtors **prefer** to work with Buyers and many are very successful at it. After all, it is the SELLING Broker who sets things into motion to eventually make the cash register ring. But it is a hard life. In spite of assurances of "loyalty" a Buyer's Agent can't afford to let his roaming Client out of sight for a minute. To be 100% safe the Realtor must literally camp on the Buyer's doorstep until he has bought.

How many times has a Realtor shown Buyers houses all day long, bought them lunch, put up with badly behaved children and finally in the late afternoon with everybody being totally exhausted they all went home. When the Realtor phoned the Buyers on the next morning, he found out to his dismay that - on the way home - they had driven by an "Open House," gone in "out of curiosity" and bought that house on the spot last night. This sort of disappointment can be very upsetting: lost opportunity to earn a commission, expense (gas, lunch) plus the aggravation of having wasted time and work.

It is also true that there is such a thing as a **"Buyer's Contract,"** whereby the Buyer promises in writing to be loyal to you and to buy only through you. The pitfall is that many Buyers are reluctant to sign such a document and even if they do sign it, how are you going to enforce it if they renege? Are you going to sue them for a commission which you could have earned if they had kept their word? Will your lawyer's fees exceed the amount of your commission? How about the aggravation, wasted time and bad public relations of such a law suit?

It is a fact of life, that in the past, present and the foreseeable future, Buyers have been, are and will remain a footloose commodity. It is human nature.

V) **SOURCES where to find listings:**

(A) **Prospecting**:
GROUND RULE: **Computers may be able to generate leads, but the more PEOPLE "YOU TALK to," the better are your chances of obtaining a listing.**
(1) For Sale by Owner ADS
(2) For Sale by Owner SIGNS
(3) Expired Multiple Listings***
(4) Expired Exclusive Listings***
*** Everybody seems to pounce on an expired listing the day after it runs out. Some Sellers will relist right away. Some of them may not.

BACKCHECKING means keeping track of those expired listings where the owners have decided to take a rest and wait for a while. Sooner or later they will relist.
(a) Set up some sort of filing system whereby you can periodically contact them to enquire if they are still interested in selling and when;
(b) make a note of each contact date and of what was said during that interview.
(c) Make a determined effort to CULTIVATE those prospective Sellers **by selling them on the benefits of dealing with you** and your Company.

FORECHECKING:
CAUTION: "Forechecking" is the deliberate act of contacting a Seller before the current listing on his property has expired for the SOLE purpose of:
(a) either persuading/encouraging the owner to cancel the current listing (if he is dissatisfied with the work of his present Listing Broker) OR
(b) alternatively to ingratiate oneself with the owner in order to ensure that he will list with you AFTER his current listing has expired.
(c) In both cases the contact is initiated by the Realtor and is considered to be unethical.

Whereas some people have become accomplished Grand Masters in getting their surreptitious message across to a disgruntled Seller, this manoeuvre is deliberately undermining the business relationship of your fellow Realtor with his Clients. It can and will cause a lot of dissention and hard feelings. No doubt, your local Real Estate

Board has detailed guidelines in this respect which the Reader may wish to consult.

(5) **Have an effective program to keep in touch with former clients.** Contact them at least 4 times a year.
- They are a good source for LEADS and REFERRALS.
- At some future date former Buyers will become SELLERS.

(6) Whenever you take a listing or sell a house CANVASS the neighbourhood (the surrounding houses in a 2 or 3 block radius). **Make the newly listed house your CENTRE OF INFLUENCE and parlay it into another listing or sale.**
  (a) If you are canvassing after taking a new listing ask the person on whose door you have just knocked
  - **if they have a friend or relative** who wants to live nearby (this could result in a ready made Buyer).
  - Or maybe they know of **a neighbour who has a friend or relative** who wants to live in the area. There is always somebody on a block who knows almost everything about anybody in the vicinity.
  - **This can produce a motivated BUYER.**
  (b) In ALL cases ("just listed" and "just sold") also ask the following 3 questions:
  - Have YOU been thinking of selling?
  - Do YOU need a bigger/smaller house?
  - Have YOU heard of anybody around here who is thinking of selling? People often know what their neighbours intend to do.

(7) If nobody is home, leave a "Just Listed" or "Just Sold" flyer.

(8) Direct mail and flyers to your "**FARM AREA**."

(9) Weather permitting **door-to-door cold canvassing** in various areas.

(10) In inclement weather **cold canvassing by phone** (from the Directory). **COLD CANVASSING has the potential of producing "VIRGIN LISTINGS"** (houses which hadn't been listed before).
CAUTION: Cold canvassing day in and day out for hours on end may result in battle fatigue. In order to avoid the loss of enthusiasm it may be preferable to vary one's endeavour: try something else for a change of pace.

(11) **CULTIVATE CONTACTS WITH**
  (a) bank managers, credit union managers, lawyers and your mailman (yes! Your Letter Carrier knows what is going on in the neighbourhood and who is moving!); they can be excellent sources for listings, e.g. foreclosures, divorces, transfers etc.

(b) Personnel Officers of large corporations, the Armed Forces, RCMP etc. for employee transfers.
(c) Moving companies, Accountants and Insurance Agents,
(d) CULTIVATE **REFERRALS from REALTORS** in other towns (you may meet these Realtors during a convention or conference).
(e) Approach UNLICENSED SALES STAFF of large condominium projects for REFERRALS. These can be a source for "Empty Nesters" who are **"downsizing" and who may have a house to sell before they can buy the condo.**

(12) Offer your assistance to an out-of-the-area Realtor who has a listing in your area and who has a long way to drive to show the house. This may result in a co-listing. OR make an arrangement with the Manager of another branch office of your Company to attend one of their Sales Meetings; introduce yourself to the sales staff at the meeting and offer your help for showings/listings in your area (co-listing or referrals).

(13) LEADS from relatives, friends, acquaintances and former customers are usually high-quality leads.

(14) **Rented houses:** ask the tenants if they would be interested in buying the house which they are currently renting. This can be done with a low downpayment and you will arrange financing for them for the balance.
The tenants will have the following advantages:
- they already know the house
- they won't have to move
- by buying they will accumulate equity instead of subsidising the Landlord
- there will be no more rent increases; the monthly mortgage payments stay the same during the term of the mortgage.

(15) **Contact absentee landlords:**
- they may have rented out the house because they were unable to sell it in the past.
- They may NOW need the CASH from their equity.
- They may be fed up with the work and responsibility associated with renting out a house.
- They may be fed up dealing with difficult tenants.

(16) **"House for rent" ads or signs:**
- the owner may be fed up with trying to find another suitable tenant.
- This time around the owner may have no luck finding a suitable tenant for his vacant house.

(17) **Neglected and vacant properties.**
   In the case of a neglected property, the owner may be physically or financially unable to keep it up.

(18) **Divorce.**
   The house may be tied up in litigation which could be resolved by the sale of the house (and the subsequent division of the sale proceeds).

(19) **Builders of new houses.**
   Tell them how your services can benefit them:
   - your Company may take the Buyer's house in trade,
   - you can sell the Buyer's house quickly through MLS.
   - It doesn't pay for a Builder to tie down his own sales force for the last 2 or 3 houses in a subdivision.

(20) (a) **Legal notices of foreclosure** (some Court records giving the names of the litigants are often available on a public computer in the vestibule of the Court House).
   (b) Houses coming up for **Municipal Tax Sale** (if the owner is in tax arrears).

(21) Check **the bulletin boards** in supermarkets, laundromats, drug stores for tell-tale ads; tack up your own business card on those bulletin boards.

(22) Watch the newspapers for births, marriages, promotions and transfer announcements.
   A successful Realtor knows that **it is always PEOPLE** and not property **that will provide the key to listing and selling** real estate. Therefore study not only the property, but also **study the Sellers**. If you are interested in securing LISTINGS then ANYTHING effecting a change in people's HOUSING NEEDS will and can effect YOU.

(23) **The Estate Sale:**
   CAUTION:
   "Ambulance chasing" often creates an unfavourable reaction; e.g. to contact a widow before her late husband is buried is in very poor taste. Unless the house is in Joint Tenancy, it cannot be sold anyway until the estate is settled.
   To list an "estate sale" requires extreme delicacy and tact and is best achieved if contact is made through a 3rd party (e.g. a mutual friend). Also the widow may not want to move right away.

(24) **"Bird dogs":** check with your local Real Estate Board and Government licensing agency if the payment of a referral fee or the gift of anything of value (e.g. dinner for 2) to an unlicensed person is legally allowed in your area or not.

- e.g. car salesman, insurance salesman, barber, mailman;
- the sales staff in the local paint and hardware store: anytime somebody buys several gallons of paint, it might indicate that they are fixing up the house prior to putting it on the market.

(25) **Yard and garage sales:** clearing out old stuff is often the prelude to listing the house.

(26) Prospective customers who come to one of **your "OPEN HOUSES"** may have to sell their house first before they can buy; this is more in the league of a "chance meeting," sometimes the lead turns out to be good, sometimes their house is already listed.

(27) Leads obtained during your **Floor Day**.
Prospective customers (Buyers or Sellers) may either phone in or walk into the office during your office duty time.

(28) Leads obtained through **newspaper ads**: either
- institutional advertising of your Company OR
- somebody calls you on one of your regular ads (to promote the sale of one of your listed houses and he has to sell his house first before he can buy).

(B) Be ALERT for listing OPPORTUNITIES:

(29) You may hear of somebody thinking of selling during a conversation or at a chance meeting.

(30) If somebody calls you on one of your "For Sale" or "Sold" signs, explore tactfully if they are renting now or if they need to sell their house first before they can buy.

(31) TV ads (for weekend Open Houses)

(32) **Your personal sphere of influence:** leads could come from friends and acquaintances, clubs, associations, Chamber of Commerce, church, night school, auctions, fraternal organizations.

(33) When you drive somewhere, don't always go there via busy streets or direct routes. Instead drive on some side streets and **be on the lookout for tell-tale signs**:
  (a) if somebody is painting the outside of his house or fixing up the yard he may be getting the place ready to sell.
  (b) If there are tricycles, children's bicycles and/or toys on the front lawn of a small no basement house - they may soon need a bigger house with more bedrooms.

(34) CAUTION: Don't harness your children into becoming your walking real estate commercials or your unwitting "real estate promoters or ambassadors" by making them to hand out your flyers at school, on Sports Day etc. On the other hand your children should not be ashamed to let people **casually** know how you are earning your living.

VI) HOW MANY CURRENT LISTINGS SHOULD A REALTOR CARRY?

That will depend on the individual and will vary from person to person, depending on his comfort level and on how hard he wants to work.

(a) Some Realtors feel that they are better off carrying a **FEW GOOD listings**, which they can market intensively and turn over quickly. These Realtors can give their clients individual attention and often will "**double-end**" their own listings (sell it themselves). A good way of getting repeat business and referrals from satisfied Clients.

(b) Others prefer to work "the law of average" by acquiring **a larger number of mediocre-quality listings** and hope that other Realtors will bring an offer. These Realtors will have some expiries and occasionally a dissatisfied Seller. In spite of some ups and downs, a Realtor should be able to make a reasonably good living.

(c) Others still will play the numbers game: **they will list anything under the sun at any price**, as long as they get the listing. A few listings will sell, many will not. Because of the large number of listings they carry these Realtors are unable to give individual attention to their Sellers; in fact they may even have difficulty remembering the names of their Clients. Because of the many For Sale signs which they have out, these Realtors will create (in the mind of the public) the appearance (illusion) of a highly active Realtor. However, if nothing or very few properties sell the public may sooner or later notice the lack of "sold" signs. For a Realtor this type of activity can result in an abundance of complaints, requests for cancellations and most likely in a cash-flow problem.

VII) If you find that "**listings are hard to get**" then do the following:

    (a) **Don't panic.**
    (b) **Spend less.**
    (c) **Investigate your working method**: are you doing everything necessary? Should you try a new approach? E.g. switch from cold canvassing to phoning expiries or FSBO.
    (d) **Work a little harder and a little longer**
    (e) **LEARN TO USE YOUR IMAGINATION** to come up with more listing sources (leave your business card on some chairs at an auction sale).
    (f) If necessary talk to your Manager, an experienced fellow Realtor or your spouse for some new ideas.

(g) **Don't quit.**
(h) Finally remember that Old Realtors never die - they just become "LISTLESS" and eventually may "go out of commission."

"For Sale By Owner"- Part I
Psychological aspects of dealing successfully with a FSBO.

Everybody loves a bargain. What many of us don't realize is that a bargain is not measured by how little you pay for something, but by what you achieve and get in return. The FSBO and especially an Internet-savvy consumer has specific reasons why he is trying to sell a property himself.

These reasons are:
- the confidence that he can do it himself
- and by doing so **he will save money.**
- As a result their ATTITUDE **towards Realtors will be a tough challenge**.

To meet this challenge, the Realtor must first find out what the FSBO is THINKING:

1) Why doesn't a FSBO trust Realtors? **Why is he apprehensive, suspicious and/or weary?**
   (a) Maybe he has heard some "bad things" about Realtors from relatives, neighbours or friends.
   (b) Maybe he doesn't want to pay a commission. Why? Because to him it appears that the Realtor is out to take a part of his NET EQUITY. What the average FSBO doesn't realize is
      - that any prospective Buyer will also deduct a commission (from the asking price) when he makes an offer,
      - because in the Buyer's mind the FSBO is not paying (and "saving" himself) a commission by not dealing with a Realtor.
   (c) Possibly the FSBO thinks that he will not get good value for the money he has to pay for a commission. E.g. his hard earned money will go to a lazy windbag who will just place a sign on the front lawn and wait for Buyers to come.

2) **Why would a FSBO be angry or resentful?**
   (a) Possibly he has been burned or disappointed by a Realtor on a previous occasion.
   (b) Did the FSBO have his house listed before and it didn't sell? **Ask him why he thinks that it didn't sell.**
   (c) Or there may have been some unresolved problems or "rough edges" on a previous deal in the past.

3) **Why would a FSBO be defiant?**
   (a) Does the FSBO Seller have a BIG EGO?
   (b) Is he cocky and overconfident?
   (c) Does he think that he doesn't need a Realtor because he is perfectly capable of selling the house himself?
   (d) Are those the reasons why he doesn't WANT a Realtor?

Having considered the above challenges, the Realtor can now successfully guard himself against any emotional hurts caused by (thoughtless) rejections and at the same time prepare a successful strategy how to convince the FSBO to deal with him.

In order to improve his chances of success and to eventually get PAID, the Realtor must be:

(1) PARTICULAR, selective, picky and choosy with whom he is dealing.
   (a) The FSBO Seller is extra difficult to deal with because it might be the first time around for him. The entire process of selling a house is new, somewhat frightening and full of surprises and later on frustrations for him.
   (b) Grab the bull by the horns and ask the FSBO
      - why he is reluctant to deal with a Realtor,
      - what his opinion is of Realtors (and keep your temper under control when you hear his answer).
      - There will be many objections to overcome but **at least you will then know what the problems are which you will have to deal with**.
   (c) Sometimes a FSBO will hesitate to make a decision. Actually this means that he has (at least subconsciously) **made a decision NOT TO MAKE ANY DECISIONS**.
   (d) Try to motive him to do something or take action.
   (e) Be aware that the more visibly you are trying to manipulate him, the more stubbornly resistant he can become.
   (f) Forewarned is forearmed. There is a distinct possibility of much abuse:
      - the Seller is **unreasonable** because he has
         - a poor (low) motivation to sell
         - the asking price is too high (and he knows it!)
         - He is "high maintenance": like a primadonna or an expensive mistress he continuously makes unreasonable demands, e.g. weekly advertising in all newspapers.
         NOTE: many "high maintenance" Sellers either
         - don't care what they are doing to you
         - or they are under the erroneous impression that they are "LOW maintenance"
         - or they think that the type of service they demand from you is merely "NORMAL" and/or "average."
   (g) Finally the FSBO may downright reject you and thereby inflict an emotional hurt on you. Remember that he is a potential stranger to you and **his rejection is therefore nothing "personal."** In the grand scheme of things in your life his petty rejection is meaningless and therefore should not be hurtful.

(1) HOW TO BE SELECTIVE and why you should choose not to work with a difficult FSBO:

(a) Life is too short to deal with and waste your precious time on such a person.
(b) A lot of abuse will sap your physical and mental strength.
(c) You can do more business somewhere else with less effort.
   Always remember that **a MOTIVATED SELLER will be very cooperative** and open to your suggestions (on the price etc.) because HE HAS TO SELL.
(d) To protect himself from hurt and/or bad experiences, the Realtor should make it a game when he is dealing with a FSBO:
   - it is a numbers game and you will not be able to list all of them. So do your best, but under the circumstances don't expect too much. With that attitude you could be surprisingly successful in listing FSBOs.
   - If no listing results then don't look at it as a "failure," but consider it to be a valuable LEARNING EXPERIENCE which will enable you to HONE YOUR SKILLS (so you don't make the same mistakes the next time around).
   - BE CHOOSY and deal only with those who **"HAVE" to sell**, and NOT with those who "want" to sell.

(2) The Realtor must be PATIENT:
If you are not patient and pounce on them too early and too hard, then it will back fire on you; it will be counter-productive. Occasionally the FSBO has to go through the entire cycle of frustration, before he realizes that he cannot do it himself.

(a) The Realtor must patiently OUTWAIT the FSBO Seller. To satisfy himself the FSBO Seller must first have a good run at selling the house himself.
(b) The length of time required to satisfy himself and for him to come to the conclusion that he needs help will VARY with each individual. It could be as short as a few days, on the other hand some FSBO are perennial Sellers.
(c) **The higher the motivation to sell, the shorter the time period which they will waste on being a FSBO.**
(d) The Realtor must be able to sit back and wait and let the FSBO make all of the usual mistakes (people phone, make an appointment and then they don't show up; Buyers with poor credit but a big mouth are unable to arrange the necessary financing).
(e) Resist your urge to offer help: they have chosen not to use your services or insight. They must find out that experience is gained in the School of Hard Knocks.
(f) To demonstrate your goodwill you can offer them a list of SAFETY TIPS when dealing with the public. For example:

SECURITY GUIDELINES **for owners who are showing their homes themselves:**
- Confirm every appointment by calling back the potential customer.
- Ask for ID; are the "Buyers" there to look at the home or are they possibly "casing the joint?"
- Get Buyers to sign a visitors' log or guest book: name, address and phone number. Even if the Buyers give phony information, it will at least impress on

them that the Seller is CAREFUL.
- A woman with little children should never show a house to several strangers if she is alone and by herself in the house.
- Never let strangers wander around your house by themselves. Watch every move they are making.
- When the owner is escorting people through the house he should never lead in front of them; he should always follow them so that he can keep an eye on them.
- All visitors should enter and leave through one door only. If they exit through the basement door by themselves then the Seller has lost control over them.
- If too many people show up all at once, the owner should ask some of them to wait outside for the "next tour" of the house.
- The owner should always carry a cell phone with him with a single button "911" programming.
- For security reasons he should phone a neighbour or friend just before and just after a showing.
- The owner should not show the house after sunset (because the Buyer will invariably want to see it in daylight).
- He should hide all valuables (jewellery, cash, credit cards, keys) and prescription drugs. Unfortunately nowadays prescription drugs and cartons of cigarettes seem to be big (illegal) business.
- The owner should never let strangers know when he is going to be out of the house: e.g. "I work the night shift"; "I leave for work at 4:30 p.m. and will be at work within half an hour."
- The FSBO should not leave a message on the answering machine saying that he is not at home; instead he should say that he can't come to the phone right now.
- After an "Open House" the owner should check that all windows and doors are locked.

PLEASE NOTE THAT SOME OF THESE PRECAUTIONS SHOULD ALSO BE OF INTEREST TO REALTORS WHO ARE HOLDING AN "OPEN HOUSE."

(3) The Realtor must be PERSISTENT.
- Never give up on a well-motivated FSBO.
- If the FSBO is well motivated, your time required to be patient and persistent is shorter.
- Keep in touch with the FSBO on a regular basis; ask for the progress they are making (it will show that you care).
- Commiserate with their disappointments but don't gloat over their failures and frustrations.
- Let them know that you are only a phone call away.
- When the right time comes and the FSBO

- is at the end of his rope and
- he understands the reality of what selling real estate is all about then
- STEP IN DECISIVELY and TAKE CHARGE AGGRESSIVELY. (Flavoured with some caution so not to hurt his feelings).

(4) **About getting PAID.**
After all of this effort and energy and time spent on the FSBO, make sure that you get paid by drawing up a listing contract or a commission agreement (FEE AGREEMENT FOR THE SALE OF UNLISTED PROPERTY).

(5) **A brief SUMMARY of a Realtor's ATTITUDE when dealing with a FSBO.**
The Realtor should know that he is dealing with a tough person who is deliberately blind to the wonderful services a Realtor can offer. All because he doesn't want to pay a commission.

So what does the average Realtor do? Instead of concentrating on the FSBO's ATTITUDE (see previous remarks) the Realtor is like a work horse with BLINDERS on who is pulling a heavy cart with his head bent to the ground. Thus the average Realtor sticks to his OWN AGENDA:
- on the door steps (wrong place)
- he tells the owner (wrong time)
- all the things which can go wrong for a FSBO (wrong subject matter) and then
- proceeds to give a brief, but dynamic, take-no-prisoner listing presentation.
- Hello! The front door steps are neither the place nor the time to give any kind of listing presentation.

What the Realtor should do instead:
(1) The first step is to get the foot in the door.
(2) The 2nd step is to make sure that the owner doesn't slam the door on your foot. **Peek his interest** by having a SOLD sticker protruding coyly from your binder or make sure that he sees your old briefcase which has a "SOLD" sticker glued across it. This should be an old, well-worn briefcase which you use only for listing presentations and which contains everything you need in connection with the listing of a property. Your new, deluxe briefcase is reserved for writing and presenting offers.
(3) Once inside the door, you talk only about
- SELLING the house (which is the FSBO's sole interest)
- and your marketing efforts (what YOU are going to do to SELL his house).
- Thus in the FSBO's eyes YOU are different, because all of the other Realtors only talked about LISTING (they act like the horse with the blinders).
- Of course, eventually you also will need a "listing," but merely as the FSBO's AUTHORITY so that you can set into motion your marketing efforts. (E.g. you cannot very well advertise his house without being authorized in writing to do so. Your boss will not spend the money for the ad without a listing

"authorising" you to advertise).
(4) **Win their trust**: admit that you have the self-interest of needing to earn a commission to support your family. You are not there as a saint willing to work for free.
(5) Split the commission into 2 portions:
Selling portion: if you were to bring him a Buyer who is willing to buy his house, is he willing to pay you a SELLING COMMISSION of 2.5% or 3.5%?
If yes, then the only problem to be solved is the LISTING PORTION of the commission. This is needed for the promotion of the property (advertising, signs etc.)
(6) The Realtor may give a SECURITY list to the FSBO (see above) as a gesture of goodwill.
(7) Never discuss price until you have a commitment to get the listing. If you quote a suggested Listing Price and it is too low for him, it will give the FSBO only another excuse why he shouldn't list his property with you.
(8) **Never leave your Market Analysis behind with the owners.**
It is your intellectual property, the product of your hard work. He can have a copy when he lists with you.
Many a Realtor has the bad habit of leaving his CMA behind with a FSBO. A CMA is the product of hard work and has value. Why teach the FSBO that he gets something for free?
(9) **Never offer to do work for free**: e.g.
- publishing an ad in the paper at your expense
- or help him to write an ad,
- or holding an "Open House" for him,
- or to lend him your Open House arrows (especially if they have your Company's name on them),
- or to put their house on your website (that would be unfair to all of your other Clients who have listed with you).
(10) Instead of being manipulative the Realtor should explain straightforward the facts of real estate life.
- The Realtor can SAVE him precious TIME.
- The Realtor can SAVE him MONEY.
- In fact the Realtor can put MORE money into the owner's pocket than he (the owner) can:
  - It is only possible to obtain TOP PRICE if the property is exposed to the MAXIMUM number of BUYERS.
  - Through the efforts of a Realtor, MORE EXPOSURE can be achieved;
  - more Buyers means more DEMAND and in the end a BETTER PRICE.
- Convince them that you will keep your word: that you can and will do what you are promising them.
- Elaborate on your marketing efforts.
- Build trust and a mutually comfortable business relationship (if you want to become his friend, do it later AFTER the sale has been made).

- Generally deal from a position of strength: you are willing to share with them
  - your knowledge of the market.
  - Your experience of dealing with Buyers.
  - You will protect the Sellers from legal problems: e.g. selling "as is - where is" is no substitute for the Seller's obligation of disclosing known latent defects.

    All buyers are entitled to receive complete information about everything which will significantly affect their buying decision and future use of and enjoyment while living in the house (e.g. Legally Non-Conforming Zoning).
  - Your skills (practical solutions to problems).
  - Your hard work (good value for the money which they will pay as commission).

"For Sale By Owner" - Part II
How a professional Realtor can solve a FSBO's problems.

One of the definitions of being "terminally naive" is the belief that somebody would undertake to sell his house himself
- for "the learning experience" or
- "to meet the challenge."

It is no secret nor should it come as a surprise that the one and only reason why any owner would embark on the arduous and onerous task of selling his house as a FSBO is to SAVE THE COMMISSION. Because of this monetary reason, Realtors who are trying to list a FSBO are often in for a real battle.

The following are some **helpful basic considerations:**

(1) **LOGIC** makes people **THINK** and **EMOTIONS** make people **ACT.**
(2) **FSBO's do need help:** some may not realize it and many will not admit it.
(3) Sometimes a FSBO sign turns out to be nothing more than **a cry for help.** The owner will list with the first Realtor who is courageous enough to knock on his door.
(4) FOR THE SELLER the undertaking of selling his (or any) house is
- most likely "the first time around" and
- therefore **there is a lot that he doesn't know about.**

(5) FOR THE REALTOR to sell a house might be
- boring routine,
- but he shouldn't take anything for granted.

(6) **IN ORDER FOR A REALTOR TO SUCCEED**
   (a) the owner must **not** be **lectured** in a detached manner with abrupt words and in a patronizing tone of voice.
   (b) Instead, **information must be SHARED** in a friendly and confident manner with courteous words showing that you care and are genuinely concerned to **earn the Owners' trust.**
   (c) Be sure to address yourself to both husband and wife and maintain eye contact with both of them. Nobody should feel left out, because such an omission may offend that person.
   (d) If one of the owners is not home then don't expect the party which you have talked to
   - to do your job and
   - to repeat accurately and convincingly your sales talk to the absent one.
   - **You will have to repeat everything again in the evening when both of them are home.**

(7) **And WHAT WILL the Realtor SHARE with them?**
   (a) the potential perils and disadvantages of a do-it-yourself-venture and
   (b) the advantages, expertise, benefits and service which a Realtor can offer.

(c) Speak normally and use your own words. Memorized formulas will come across like an artificial "spiel."
(d) Remember the old adage that **"SELLING" is telling the truth attractively.**

Problems which a FSBO may encounter and how a professional REALTOR can solve them.

(1) **The TRIBULATIONS and PITFALLS of DIRECT NEGOTIATIONS. The average Buyer is reluctant TO DEAL DIRECTLY with the OWNER because:**
   (a) politeness doesn't allow the uttering of critical remarks;
   (b) or he may be timid and is hesitant to voice his concerns or
   (c) to voice any objections because he doesn't want to put the owner into a position of having to defend his home or having to justify his asking price.
   (d) All of the above will result in **many UNREVEALED and UNSPOKEN objections and UNRESOLVED concerns** which in turn can result in a lost sale.
   (e) Many Buyers find it embarrassing to negotiate (haggle) over the price directly with the owner for **fear of insulting him** or of **provoking an unpleasant confrontation.** As a result Buyers often make a few pleasant and non-committal remarks and depart, never to be seen or heard of again.

WHAT THE REALTOR CAN OFFER:
On the other hand **Buyers will have no scruples to criticize the house to a Realtor who** is trained to allay all concerns and overcome objections. The Realtor is viewed as a not-emotionally-involved middleman: it is easy to haggle with him, because for one it is not his home and also "negotiating" is part of his job.

(2) **A sale can also be lost because of a clash of personalities.** (The Sellers' and Buyers' "PERSONALITIES" MAY CONFLICT).

The Seller may be a methodically plodding Conservative (with a capital "C"). Such a person likes being able to sleep in peace at night. In order to ensure that he feels safe, he may need somebody who will hold his hand. Instead of unforeseen bad surprises he prefers that everything progresses smoothly along a predictable path.

The Buyer may be a confused dreamer or a happy-go-lucky risk taker who enjoys flying by the seat of his pants. He is willing to explore untested approaches and new avenues: "To buy FSBO? Why not? I'll put the minimum downpayment on my VISA and for the rest I will get a mortgage from somewhere."

One party may make an unguarded remark or do something which doesn't quite agree with the other person who will promptly take offence or exception. The next thing you know is that the deal is gone out of the window.

WHAT THE REALTOR CAN OFFER:
The Realtor will tactfully avoid any pitfalls, smooth over diplomatically sundry personality conflicts and skilfully bring about the successful conclusion of a sale.

(3) FOR THE OWNER the concept of "SAVING THE COMMISSION" can turn out to be an expensive illusion.
   (a) In the process of shopping around, prospective Buyers learn what Market Value is. They cannot be fooled and if the owner is asking too much, they will recognize it.
   (b) The main attraction for a prospective Buyer to deal with a FSBO is, that he expects to get a better deal than on a house which is listed with a Realtor (where the commission is built into the Listed Price).
   (c) The Buyer is fully aware that the Seller is trying to save the commission and expects "a bargain" in the form of a corresponding reduction in the selling price
   (d) An aggressive Buyer who is not shy to negotiate directly with the owner, is also a "Bargain Hunter" and often a "Tough Negotiator": he will try to undercut the Seller's "already-without-commission" Asking Price.
   (e) As the Seller usually doesn't have the necessary experience and negotiating skills, he may - (in his anxiety not to loose the sale) accept a "low-ball offer" which the savvy Buyer never intended or even expected to be accepted.
   (f) **The making of such a low-ball offer was MERELY a TEST by the Buyer**
      - designed to **reduce** the Sellers' high expectations (to bring him down to reality)
      - and to **elicit** (on hand of the Sellers' counter offer) **how low a price** the Seller might or is willing to accept.

WHAT THE REALTOR CAN OFFER:
Had the Seller BEEN REPRESENTED BY A REALTOR, it is entirely feasible to assume that this sort of debacle could have been avoided and in the end the Seller would have "netted" more money even after paying a commission.

(4) **THE OWNER is "NOT FAMILIAR with the Market."** The real estate market can be constant or fluctuate upwards or spiral downwards. An owner getting second hand or slightly distorted information through the media, neighbours, friends or relatives may miss the boat:
   (a) **In a rapidly dropping market** he could always be one step behind in his valuation and miss out on a sale because he is still clinging to an outdated price. (This happens often).
   (b) **In a rapidly rising market** he (theoretically) may miss out and undersell his house. (This happens seldom).
   (c) **SELLER's MARKET v. BUYER's MARKET.**

FOR AN OWNER it is **EASY TO SELL** in a **SELLER's MARKET** where many Buyers and speculators compete with each other for the relatively limited number of houses which are for sale.

In a BUYER's MARKET however, there are many properties on the market competing against each other for the attention of a low number of Buyers. **Such Buyers are**
- **very PRICE SENSITIVE,**
- **they have all the time in the world to be SELECTIVE,**
- **they will COMPARE what is available**
- **and do some tough NEGOTIATING in order to get the best possible deal.**

WHAT THE REALTOR CAN OFFER:
ONLY A REALTOR who is daily and actively involved in the real estate market, can make accurate and up-to-date judgments about values and advise the owner about the current state of the market. He also has the required knowledge, experience, negotiation skills and will use proven closing techniques to bring about positive results.

(5) **THE OWNER is "UNCERTAIN what the MARKET VALUE of his house is."**
  (a) Because an **owner does not have a clear idea and OBJECTIVE KNOWLEDGE** of what similar houses in his area are selling for, it is difficult for him to put the right price tag on his home.
  (b) He may get misinformation from his neighbour who just sold. "I got the price I wanted" is an ambiguous statement. As the neighbour doesn't disclose his actual selling price (because he is embarrassed what he actually accepted in comparison with what he had originally listed for), all the enquiring future Seller has to go by is the rumoured Listing Price. He assumes that the neighbour either got that or something close to it. Woefully **the undisclosed real selling price could be quite a bit lower.**
  (c) Then there are the conflicting suggestions from a horde of well-meaning flat-wallet friends and relatives who intone in unison: "I wouldn't sell this beautiful house for less than …."
  (d) As the owner is also emotionally involved and maybe a little greedy, he will most likely overprice his house.
  (e) If the price is unrealistically high Buyers will not even look less alone deal on the house. Precious time will be wasted in the marketing of the house. Naturally the owner will be reluctant to reduce the Asking Price of his own volition. The reason is that each time he reduces his price, he thinks that he is "loosing" money (translation: obtaining less net equity. That "portion" actually never really existed).
  It may require the fictitious "sacrifice" of several price reductions before the property becomes saleable and by that time the owner may be bitter about the whole thing.

WHAT THE REALTOR CAN OFFER:
A REALTOR CAN prepare a Comparative Market Analysis based on recent sales of similar houses in the area and will suggest a realistic Asking Price.

The owner will be able to start off on the right foot: the house can be sold in the shortest period of time and with the least amount of inconvenience to him.

(6) **"The stumbling block of a thorough HOME INSPECTION."**
AN OWNER LACKS SELLING EXPERIENCE and is not properly trained to demonstrate the true highlights of the house.
  (a) When he shows the Buyers around he will mistakenly think that his "Memories in the house" have market value.
  (b) Little does he realize what the Buyers think of his selfmade remodelling and various "improvements" which often are of lesser than professional workmanship.
  (c) On the other hand some details which may appear to be of no or little importance to him are sure of great interest to the Buyers. For fear of offending the Seller or intruding on his privacy many Buyers are reluctant to open closet doors and inspect kitchen cupboards and bathroom cabinets. Afterwards they will fret: "I wish we could have seen how big the closets are. I wonder if all of our clothes will fit into them." Homemakers especially are interested in these sort of details. Not being able to inspect freely a little thing like a closet or sundry storage space can dampen interest which in turn will contribute to loosing a sale.

WHAT THE REALTOR CAN OFFER:
THE REALTOR IS an emotionally detached go-between and this sort of awkward feeling does not arise in his presence. He is not only trained to show the home professionally and efficiently, but he will also elaborate on its many benefits and advantages. Furthermore, the Realtor will deal tactfully with the Buyers' concerns and objections and will try to reduce to a minimum the bad impressions created by any drawbacks.

(7) **THE OWNER HAS "The problem with the FOLLOW-UP."**
  If the Seller asks potential Buyers for their names and phone number in order to be able to contact them again later on, he will inadvertently make the impression that he is "anxious to sell." This impression is compounded when and if he does phone them back a few days later.

WHAT THE REALTOR CAN OFFER:
On the other hand, it is not unusual for A REALTOR to ask for the Buyer's name and phone number.

It is more or less **expected** of him **to call the Clients back** to find out what their reaction to the house is and to enquire if they are interested in making an offer. That is no sign of weakness on his or for that matter on anybody else's part; it is merely his job to follow up.

(8) **FSBO means "Embarking on an EMOTIONAL ROLLER COASTER."**
Every owner is proud of his home; direct one-on-one contact with the Buyers can become irritating, frustrating and stressful if the Seller takes negative comments or the continuous rejection of his home personally and they often do.
They ask themselves: "Why doesn't anybody make me an offer? Don't they like our home?"

WHAT THE REALTOR CAN OFFER:
A REALTOR IS a 3rd party and is not emotionally involved as far as the property is concerned. Fault-finding with the house isn't offensive to him because it is not his house; he may recognize (excessive) "fault-finding" as a ploy by the Buyer to bring the price down. As an "outsider" he is able to conduct negotiations more objectively and skilfully.

(9) **THE OWNER will experience a "DISTURBING LACK OF PRIVACY."**
The moment an owner puts his home-made sign on the front lawn he has, in effect, started a round-the-clock "Open House" for any and all persons who will knock on his door and who want to gain admittance to his house.
(a) People will drop in at any time and on any day - usually unannounced.
(b) They may be the perfect Buyer or perhaps a "lookeeloo," a trifler, a shopper or a dreamer with "champagne taste on beer money." It also could be somebody looking for decorating ideas.
(c) While he is at work, his wife might have to face alone various prying strangers all of whom she is reluctant to turn away for fear of them being perhaps "good buyers" after all.
(d) In order not to miss out on a Buyer, somebody will have to be home at all times.
(e) Those who come to look - are they **MORE "suspects" THAN "qualified prospects?"**
As all of these people trek through the FSBO house and dirty his clean carpets, **the only thing the FSBO can be sure of is just 2 things:**
• that they could read his sign and
• that they were capable of ringing his doorbell.
OTHER THAN THAT he doesn't know what kind of house they need and how much of a house they can afford.
As he cannot greet them at the door with: "This is a 2 bedroom house with an unfinished basement and I want $ 210,000 for it," **they will take up a lot of his time and patience - often for nothing.**

WHAT THE REALTOR CAN OFFER:
A professional real estate sign often has a sticker on it which says: **"Shown by appointment only."** If somebody drives by and likes the outside of the house, they will write down the Realtor's name and phone number and call him. As the Realtor

works on a commission-basis, he cannot afford to waste his (and consequently anybody else's) time:

(a) The Realtor will make sure that the Buyer needs and is interested in this specific type of house.
(b) The Realtor will prequalify the Buyer to ensure that he can afford it financially.
(c) The Realtor will arrange for a showing by appointment at a time convenient and agreeable to everybody.

(10) **AN OWNER WILL RUN THE RISK that the public might be "Judging the book by its cover."** Sometimes people drive by a house and like the area, but are not too impressed with the outside of the house. With a FSBO sign they will be reluctant to speak to the owner IN PERSON and will keep on driving.

WHAT THE REALTOR CAN OFFER:
(a) **If there is a REAL ESTATE BROKER's sign out front,** chances are that they will write down his phone number and call him if for no other reason than out of curiosity about the price. Remember that they like the area and the call costs them nothing. At this stage the Buyer is "anonymous" (not face-to-face with anybody) and therefore in total control of the situation: By merely hanging up the phone he can easily terminate his conversation with the Realtor.
(b) However during this short window of opportunity an alert and savvy Realtor may realize that e.g. the exterior of the house is the problem.
(c) He will immediately proceed to inform the Buyers of the interior value and other benefits of the house. This is called "selling." Beauty is only skin deep; many other things are more important. Often an "ugly duckling" can and will be sold through the skilful handling of the situation by a trained professional.

(11) **THE OWNER's problem with "FINANCING."**
   (a) It is awkward for the owner to ask a prospect outright if he can afford the house.
   (b) The miffed prospect in turn will be reluctant to reveal his financial status (debts, income and ability to qualify for a mortgage).
   (c) **The Buyer may also have endless questions:** "How much downpayment? What will my monthly payments be? How much less will they be with a bigger downpayment? What prepayment privileges will I have? Where can I get the best deal?" etc.
   (d) How does the FSBO Seller know for sure if and when and that his Buyer has actually applied for his new financing somewhere?
   (e) Has the Buyer made his "best effort" to obtain a mortgage? Or is he using his failure to get financing as an excuse to get out of the deal?
   (f) Will the Lending Institution notify the Seller when their appraiser is coming and when everything is approved?

(g) Who keeps track of the fire insurance binder with loss payable firstly to the Lender?

WHAT THE REALTOR CAN OFFER:
(a) **A REALTOR cannot afford to waste his time** by showing houses to people which they cannot afford to buy. **He will bring only prequalified Buyers.**
(b) **After the sale is made,** the Realtor will make sure that the Buyer applies for his new financing in a timely fashion and that he has all the documentation required for such application. (Proof of earnings etc.)
(c) He will arrange for the inspection by the bank's appraiser, keep track of the approval process and finally
(d) he will notify the Seller when the loan is approved (at which time the "subject to financing" clause will be removed in writing).
(e) A good Realtor can also save the Seller some money in the refinancing; e.g. the buyer might need a larger loan amount than what the existing mortgage is. Many lending institutions might be persuaded to waive or at least reduce the prepayment penalty on the Seller's old mortgage,
- if the Buyer agrees to refinance through them and
- if the new loan amount is higher than the old mortgage was and
- if the current interest rate is higher than the rate was on the existing (to be discharged) mortgage.
(f) Real estate companies have often an **in-house Mortgage Broker** who will be able to get the Buyer a favourable loan quicker and easier than if the Buyer were to shop around. Making the rounds from one bank to another can be very time consuming, confusing and frustrating. Mortgage Brokers are able to submit the Buyer's requirements and qualifications to several lending institutions simultaneously; after reviewing the details submitted, several of them may make an offer to finance; the Mortgage Broker can then discuss the various options with the Buyer who will be able to choose one of them.

(12) **THE COST OF SUNDRY EXPENSES.**
 (I) **The SIGN.**
  A self-made stick-it-into-the-ground **"House for sale by owner" sign** may cost only a few Dollars and the expense for it is negligible; but what about the "looks?" (aesthetic impression).

WHAT THE REALTOR CAN OFFER:
(a) **A REALTOR has a professionally manufactured sign designed for maximum visibility and NAME recognition.**
(b) In many cases it is a nationally recognized For Sale sign. The sign is the same across the country and will be easily identified by out of town buyers.

 (II) **The PROMOTION.**
  (a) DOES THE OWNER know how to **write an effective AD** which

grabs the attention of the reader by emphasizing the key selling features of the house?

(b) Also the owner is advertising only one house, namely his. By necessity, his promotion is limited and will result in a limited number of prospective buyers.

WHAT THE REALTOR CAN OFFER:
(a) Realtors too have to pay for their ads. In order to get maximum returns for their business costs (which are their investments in doing business) they will hone their ad writing skills.
(b) They routinely advertise many different homes and will attract more Buyers than a single owner can. One of these Buyers may have called on the ad for another house, only to end up being switched to this house.

(III) **There is another cost the owner will have to face: it is his "TIME COMMITMENT."**

Once he has an ad in the paper, he will become a slave to it by tending to stay at home in order to answer all incoming calls. The FSBO will become a prisoner in his own house because many people don't like to talk to a recording or leave a message on an answering machine.

WHAT THE REALTOR CAN OFFER:
(a) **REALTORS HAVE** a switchboard operator at the office. After hours there is a professional answering service (with a live human being speaking), they have pagers, cellular phones etc. They are unlikely to miss any calls.
(b) **REALTORS HAVE ACCESS** to the Multiple Listing Service through which they promote their listings to all other Realtors in the area.
(c) **REALTORS** are able to place their listings on **"The Internet."** By logging on a certain site Buyers in a different part of the country can see a picture and peruse details of the house without ever leaving the comfort of their home. This is cross-country promotion.
(d) SUCCESSFUL REALTORS ALSO HAVE **a large and constantly updated and self-renewing pool of prospective Buyers** from which they can select ready, willing and qualified Buyers for a particular type of house.

(13) **The "TIMING" Factor.**

(A) IF A SELLER is transferred and has only a limited amount of time to sell and wastes a good portion thereof before listing with a Realtor, then the Realtor may not have enough time to market the house properly and bring about a sale before the owner has to move out.
This will result in the following:
(a) A vacant house, even if it is cleaned up and redecorated, may be more difficult

to sell than one with furniture in it. Empty houses also tend to smell (stale air, musty odour).
(b) Constantly closed drapes can attract the dual problems of break-ins and vandalism.
(c) A vacant house is a continuing expense: mortgage payments, heat and light, insurance, upkeep etc.

(B) **IF AN OWNER fails** to sell his house himself, he will eventually list it with a Realtor. Buyers have the habit of asking: "How long has this house been on the market?" If the house has been for sale for a long time, then it becomes " market stale." People will say: "What? Is this house still for sale? What's wrong with it?"
Consequently the following problems will be encountered:
(a) Buyers will become more suspicious that "there is something wrong with the house." By this they express their fear of hidden serious defects which will be costly to repair.
(b) There will be more objections which will have to be overcome and as a result the house will be tougher to sell.
(c) Suspicious Buyers will be reluctant to make an offer and will prefer to wait and see if the owner will come down some more in his price.
(d) In the end the sale price could well be lower than the owner could have realized, if he would have hired a Realtor to start with.

(14) **Considerations about "THE FUTURE" and "CREDIBILITY."**

It is a fact that in the case of a resale (used) house the owner is not obliged to and will not give any guarantees or warranties should something go wrong after the Buyer has taken possession. (On new construction Builders usually give some sort of guarantee for a limited period of time).
Many Buyers are of the opinion that all the owner is interested in is to sell his house. Once the owner has moved away, he will loose all interest in them and the house and all personal contact will cease. Therefore, statements made by the Sellers are often taken more or less with a grain of salt.

WHAT THE REALTOR CAN OFFER:
A REALTOR HAS powerful incentives to conduct himself in a prudent and business like manner, because
(a) he is not moving away and will continue to be locally available
(b) he has a legal duty to tell the truth,
(c) and he has an ethical obligation to deal fairly (which includes the making of all necessary disclosures).
(d) He also has **a future interest** in a satisfied Buyer for a source of referrals and leads and
(e) some day the Buyer will hopefully turn into a built-in Seller who will list with him.

(15) **The Buyer's immediate "ABILITY to buy."**
>AN OWNER MAY encounter a Buyer who will have to sell his own house first before he is in a position to buy the FSBO house. Usually all such an owner can say to his Buyer is: "I hope that you will be able to sell your house quickly. Come back and see me when you are ready to deal."

WHAT THE REALTOR CAN OFFER:
A REALTOR MAY have
>(a) a ready-made Buyer on hand for the Buyer's house or else
>(b) he could attempt a "trade," some sort of "guaranteed purchase plan" or "bridge financing."
>(c) He could also list the Buyer's house on Multiple Listing and
>(d) promote the Buyer's house in the customary way.

(16) **"Potential legal pitfalls."**
>(A) **"The consequences of tying up the house":**
>>AN OWNER MAY come across a Buyer who requires an unrealistically long time for removing some sort of "subject-to" clause. As one or both are inexperienced, there will not be adequate safeguards for the Seller (e.g. a 72-hour "escape clause" in case another acceptable offer materializes). Thus the owner can tie up his house (and effectively take it off the market) for an unnecessarily long period of time, during which the market could change.
>>
>>In the worst case scenario:
>>(a) The Seller's house will have reduced or interrupted market exposure.
>>(b) During this time the market value of his home could go down further due to an increasing oversupply of homes and a decrease in demand. (There are fewer Buyers around).
>>(c) And finally, after tying up the house for several months, the Buyer may - for various reasons - never consummate the sale.

WHAT THE REALTOR CAN OFFER:
(a) A Realtor is conversant with escape clauses and will as a matter of routine **insert into any contract** - with the appropriate wording - **a protection clause which requires that the Buyer must remove within a specified period of time all "subject-to" clauses** should another subsequent acceptable offer materialize.
In the meantime, the marketing of the house continues without any interruption until such time when the first Buyer has removed all subject-to clauses.
(b) Back-up offers can be entertained.
(c) In case another acceptable offer materializes, notice will be served on the first Buyer to remove all subject-to clauses within the specified time or else to step aside. **Thus the Seller will have a sale one way or another.**

(B) **"The preparation of the Contract of Purchase and Sale."**

AN OWNER (or Buyer) can have the Sale Contract drawn up by a Notary Public or a Lawyer; this, however, could entail additional expenses (legal fees) which one or both of them may want to avoid. If the Buyer's lawyer draws up a contract, it may contain clauses favouring his Client (the Buyer) which may not necessarily be agreeable to the Seller or be in his best interest.

Of course, Buyer and Seller can get together in spontaneous solidarity and take out a piece of paper and write some sort of agreement. The danger with this is that such an agreement can contain clauses or terms which could make the contract unenforceable (void for uncertainty) or risky or unfair to one party or the other.

WHAT THE REALTOR CAN OFFER:
(a) In his Prelicensing Course and in subsequent seminars the Realtor has learned to draft an enforceable contract.
(b) Realtors have many opportunities to upgrade their professional skills to keep themselves constantly up-to-date.
(c) There is no extra charge or expense for the Realtor's work of drafting the contract or removing "subject" clauses.

(C) **"Liability."**

AN OWNER MAY attract legal liability by the inadvertent non-disclosure of existing easements or Right-of-Ways. E.g. if the Buyer wanted to build a pool or garage in the backyard he may find that he is not able to do so because of an undisclosed easement.

No doubt, the information about the previously undisclosed easement or Right-of-Way will come up at the time of the signing of documents in the lawyer's office. By that time moving vans have been ordered; on the strength of his FSBO sale the Seller may have bought another house.

The Buyer has incurred costs for the mortgage appraisal, survey certificate and legal fees. If the sale collapses at this point - and it can - then there can be a lot more than just frazzled nerves.

WHAT THE REALTOR CAN OFFER:
A REALTOR WILL HAVE access (either through his office or his local Real Estate Board) to a **TITLE SEARCH** which will show any and all financial encumbrances and non-financial charges against the property. Easements and Right-of-Ways will have to be disclosed to all serious Buyers.

FURTHERMORE **AN OWNER MAY incur a legal liability by the deliberate concealment of certain latent defects.** (e.g. freshly painted basement floor to hide water marks in a leaky basement; drywall installed to hide a crooked and crumbling basement wall. A leaky roof, dryrot etc.)

WHAT THE REALTOR CAN OFFER:

A REALTOR WILL suggest - for their Buyers' protection - to have a home inspection done by a qualified expert.

CAUTION: If the Realtor recommends only one inspector and there is subsequently something wrong (which the inspector failed to mention in his report), then the Realtor in turn could attract some legal liability. The safe thing is to submit to the Buyer a list with the names of SEVERAL inspectors. The Buyer then can choose with which one he wants to do business with after taking the following considerations into account:

(a) what are the inspector's qualifications and experience?
(b) Exactly what will his report include and what it will not include.
(c) Any contract with the inspector should be read carefully before it is signed.

IN A NUTSHELL

SUMMARY FOR SELLERS

A SELLER who wonders how to sell his house without loosing his mind, here is a brief **SUMMARY of hazards which he can encounter without a Professional Realtor guiding him.**

Undecided sightseers and
sundry neighbourly tourists
looking for decorating ideas.
Unqualified buyers and
prying strangers asking
endless questions and
wasting a lot of time.
The constantly ringing
door bell and telephone
will exchange privacy for
irritating, unkind and critical remarks.
In the end the frustrated owner may
finally receive a low-ball offer.
Unfamiliar terms,
fine print confusion and
unnecessary legal aggravation,
can lead to communication failures,
missed opportunities and lost sales.

ON THE OTHER HAND A REALTOR

knows his business and will
work hard for his Client
in order to earn his trust.
He knows where and how to find a Buyer,

he is a skilful negotiator and
will protect his Client from
legal entanglements.
He is emotionally detached
and will tie up all loose ends.
He will get paid his hard-earned
commission only if and when
and after the property is sold.

SUMMARY FOR REALTORS

In the end the problem with a FSBO all boils down to a very simple formula:

The FSBO's unspoken question to the Realtor is this:
"What can YOU do for ME that no one else (including myself) can do?"

The Realtor who can answer this question **masterfully** will be able to list a FSBO **successfully**.

"Operation Grasshopper"

A concentrated LISTING EFFORT in fall to ensure that you survive successfully the long and harsh winter months.

THE FABLE.

Once upon a time there was a happy-go-lucky grasshopper. He didn't have a care in the world, it was summer, the sun was shining warmly and there was plenty to eat and drink in the meadow where he lived. Life was easy and he lived for the day. He continuously partied with the other animals which ventured forth from the surrounding forest. When one day the rays of the sun became weaker the grasshopper noticed that some of the other animals didn't visit him as frequently as they used to. First it was the rabbits. When he asked Mr. Rabbit why he and his family didn't come to his celebrations, he was told that they were busy building a warm nest and were storing food for the coming winter months. Then it was Mr. and Mrs. Bear and their droll offspring who absented themselves. Their excuse was that they had to hunt to fatten themselves up, so that they could hibernate in their cave through the winter months. "Ah!" the grasshopper said without a care, "Winter, whatever that means is a long way off" and he kept on dancing in the meadow during the lazy late-summer days. When one fine day the birds started flying South, he reassured himself that there was no reason yet to panic and he continued basking and dancing in the golden rays of the sun. That night a cold wind blew over the meadow and the grasshopper, clinging to a swaying blade of grass, woke up shivering. But when the next morning brought radiant sunshine again, he ignored all warning signs and reverted to his carefree life style. Then one day the sun was hidden by clouds and it was pelting cold rain. When the grasshopper tried to find shelter he found that the big leaves had suddenly wilted and shrivelled up. There was no place to stay warm and dry. To his surprise, it also became more difficult to find food. By this time most of the animals had disappeared from the meadow and finally he was left by himself. "No need to get upset," he told himself "things will work out, they always do." After a while, even finding a little food became a problem and for the first time in his life he experienced hunger. When the cold rain continued, food became so scarce that he was starving. On the day when the first snow fell, Mr. Rabbit decided to venture out of his nest to look around. He was sad when he came across the lifeless body of the grasshopper. "I wonder," he mused, "how did that poor grasshopper perish? Did he starve to death or did he first succumb to the cold weather?."

What does this story have to do with us Realtors? Well the winter months are coming and you should prepare yourselves for them. With the onset of inclement weather many of the Buyers will disappear. On the other hand a listing contract signed by the Seller will ensure that you have something to fall back on.

Surely all of you must have heard at least a thousand times that "Listings are the lifeblood of this business." In September it is still relatively easy to get listings. On the other hand the closer we get to the end of the year, the more you are liable to hear: "We don't want to put our house for sale before the holidays. Call us after the first of the year."

Therefore each year on September 1st …
"OPERATION GRASSHOPPER" should swing into action.

(1) **"Operation Grasshopper" is an intensive listing effort** to ensure that you can stay in the real estate business during the difficult winter months.
(2) During this massive LISTING spree you should continue to work only with **red hot Buyers.** Marginal Buyers should be put on the back burner in favour of your listing efforts. Or else you can refer them to somebody else and hopefully earn a referral fee.
(3) Whenever possible the listing should expire sometime in January of the next year. That way you will
   - have something to advertise and attract a Buyer. There always seem to be some anxious out-of-town Buyers around at the end of the year. Or perhaps you may receive a call from somebody who is idly reading the newspaper over the holidays and your ad caught his eyes.
   - A "Grasshopper Listing" has a better chance of selling during a period of time when there is a small(er) selection of homes on the market. Most of the Sellers who were merely "testing the market" would have taken their houses off the market by this time.
(4) The long listing term will also give you plenty of time for price adjustments.
(5) One way of overcoming the Seller's resistance against a 4 months listing is
   (a) by pointing out to him that if his listing expires "before the Holidays" he may be flooded with annoying phone calls from Realtors calling on "expired listings."
   (b) Besides, the objective is to "sell" and hopefully the property would be sold long before the listing will expire.
   (c) Wouldn't it be exciting to sell and celebrate Christmas in a new home?
   (d) For Sellers who don't want to move before the holidays, we would ask for a long possession date.
   (e) The plan is to sell in October or November and then buy something from somebody who has a good reason to sell or is desperate to sell. Everybody would then move in January or February.
(6) Sales Managers may consider running a LISTING CONTEST until the middle of December. Instead of one huge prize to be given out to one salesperson at the end of the contest it may be preferable that everybody should win something.
   (a) At each sales meeting each Realtor who has turned in a listing during the previous week should be individually "recognized" and receive a small token gift (e.g. a ballpoint pen or a mug with the Company logo on it or a Company T-shirt).
   (b) Also that salesperson's business card should go into a barrel for the "big draw" at the end of the contest.
   (c) The more business cards a salesperson has accumulated in the barrel, the better will be his chances of winning "the big prize."
   (d) The draw for the big prize could take place during the Office Christmas Party.

(e) The idea is to create an atmosphere of excitement in the office which will translate into increased friendly competition and satisfying production.

(f) To increase the sense of excitement the various handout prizes and the "big prize" could be attractively displayed in the Manager's Office.

(g) Increased production will in turn raise the morale in the office. Nobody will have the inclination or the time to cry the winter blues because everybody will be busy making money. In short this Listing Contest will be an all around "win/win situation."

(6) The ultimate purpose of any listing is that the property should sell. So what if all of your hard-earned "Grasshopper" listings should sell by the end of December.

(a) In due course the commissions from these sales will end up in your bank account.

(b) What a wonderful way of ending up the old year and starting off the new one. The "Grasshopper" commissions will give you financial peace of mind.

(c) Enjoy your well earned rest over the holidays in the company of your loved ones and friends.

(d) If you are forced to start the New Year with no listings then it is no disaster. Your pocket full of "Grasshopper money" should inspire you to go out and list or sell something in the New Year.

So what is it going to be come September 1st? Are you going to continue dancing in the meadow like the grasshopper or …?

Preparation For A Listing Appointment

Athletes train strenuously for a competition.

Before a play opens actors rehearse their lines, practice stage movements and experiment around with make-up.

For many years Opera singers study languages and take singing lessons before they can go on stage and perform. Even after they have become accomplished singers they still warm up their vocal chords by vocalizing for an hour before curtain time.

What does the average Realtor do before a listing appointment?
- He probably goes to a listing appointment cold turkey;
- Occasionally he is late for the appointment because he left his home or the office too late or else he can't find the house in the dark.
- He shows up in a wrinkled suit and may smell of perspiration; his bad breath (from nervous stomach acid) is enough to bowl over an ox.
- Often he is totally unprepared for the questions which the owners will ask him (e.g. what the neighbour's house down the road recently sold for).
- He will ad lib about "market value" while scribbling a few figures on the back of a crumpled business card.

And then he will be surprised and will feel rejected if the owner refuses to list with him.

A listing appointment is a JOB INTERVIEW where several thousands of Dollars of commission income are at stake. Logic says that if you want to be successful in getting the job it is important to be **well prepared** in all aspects.

1) **DURING THE FIRST CONTACT YOU CAN IMPROVE YOUR ODDS OF SUCCESS BY CAREFULLY SETTING THE STAGE FOR THE APPOINTMENT.**

    If you talk to a Seller about when to "come over and give us a price for our house," you should realize that this is a potential invitation for a listing appointment. Therefore:
    - make sure that **all registered owners will also be there;** you can get an enforceable listing contract only when all of the registered owners will sign it.
    - Make the appointment to meet with them for a time AFTER the children will have gone to bed. This will ensure that you have the Customers' **undivided attention.**

2) **THE RESEARCH:**

    a) Check on the office computer:
    - **If the property is currently listed for sale.** If it is, then it is unethical to presolicit an existing listing. Phone the owner and ascertain the current status of his listing: he may have just recently obtained a cancellation which hasn't

yet been processed by the Real Estate Board's MLS service.
- Verify if the listing is expired or if it has been extended.
- Print out a copy of the last listing on this property. It will give you some useful ideas, e.g. the wording in the "remarks" column, the last asking price etc.
- The Board's computer program will most likely have a **"historical menu"** from which you will be able to determine
    - WHEN the current owners have bought the house and
    - WHAT PRICE THEY have PAID for it at that time.
- A printout of the **Municipal Statistics** will give you
    - the legal description,
    - the current gross taxes and
    - the current assessment figures for the land and building.
- Also the names of all registered owners.

b) **Phone the Tax Department** of the **Municipal Hall** and verify
- if all taxes are paid in full and
- if all utility charges for water, sewer and garbage collection are up to date.
- **Various other departments** (e.g. "Engineering") of the Municipality will be able to give you information about the following:
- if the sanitary sewer is connected to the house or not.
  If there is no sanitary sewer, then find out the location of the septic tank and anything else they can tell you about it (e.g. health inspections). Alternatively find out where the nearest sanitary sewer connection is and obtain an estimate of what it would cost to bring it up to the property line. A Plumber will be able to give you an estimate of what it would cost to connect the house to the sanitary sewer (from the property line to the house).
- The Building Dept. or "Permits" will be able to give you the date when the final occupancy permit has been issued (this will give you the age of the house). If there is no occupancy permit, then the age can be deduced from the date of the water connection.

c) From the legal description you should be able to **get the lot size from the legal maps in your office. The maps will also show any easements or Right-of-Ways.**

d) **DURING DAYLIGHT HOURS drive by the house** you hope to list.
This will give you the following information:
- you will gain an approximate idea of how long it will take for you to drive from the office or your home to this house. (This will ensure that you will not be late).
- When you arrive for your listing appointment, you will be able to locate and **recognize the house in the dark.**
- A visual exterior inspection of the house should give you an idea of the approximate floor area, if it has a basement or not; all of which should be helpful for your preparation of a CMA (Comparative Market Analysis).

e) While you are in the area, note any other houses in the immediate neighbourhood which are currently for sale or which have been recently sold (the "sold" sign is still up).

f) Investigate any FSBO's in the area.
g) Back at the office run off a copy of the listings of:
   - all houses in the vicinity which are currently listed: **these are your "competition."** Find out from the Listing Salespersons what sort of action they have had on their listings.
   - All houses which have been **recently sold** in the area.
   These are EVIDENCE OF VALUE.

   This exercise is important because it will enable you to talk intelligently with the Sellers when they bring up the subject of their neighbours' houses which are for sale; or when they start talking about the fantastic prices which some of those houses allegedly sold for.
h) Prepare a CMA. Some Realtors prefer a 2-stage listing appointment, whereby they arrange to view the inside of the house in the afternoon, before the evening's presentation.

3) **THE SALESPERSON's PREPARATION.**

a) As you may be at this appointment till late it is best to call on the customer **WELL RESTED.** If you continuously YAWN during your presentation you are liable to turn the Sellers off. You might be justifiably tired from working hard all day, but customers don't look at it that way: this is THEIR time and you are talking about THEIR house which is most likely their biggest financial asset: for these reasons you better be bright-eyed and bushy-tailed when dealing with them.

b) Being **physically well rested, you will also be able to be MENTALLY STRONG.** You are going to be in for a battle of wits and somebody is going to make a sale tonight: either you will sell the owners on the idea of listing with you or else they will sell you on the idea of going home empty handed.

c) During your listing presentation you will, in effect, ask the Sellers to entrust you with the handling of many thousands of Dollars in real estate. In order to **GAIN THE OWNERS' CONFIDENCE** you must **LOOK THE PART OF A BUSINESS-PERSON: you must make a reasonably GOOD IMPRESSION... from HEAD-to-TOE:**

MEN: hair combed, suit pressed, shoes polished, clean shirt and no loud neckties. No outlandish body-piercing in ears, nose, lips or tongue.

LADIES: subdued, natural-looking make-up; whatever you are wearing it shouldn't be too short or too tight or too low-cut or too see-through to attract Mr. Seller's undue attention. His surreptitious ogling will be noticed and resented by "Mrs." Seller who also has to sign the listing.

Mile-long fingernails will resemble claws and massive or multiple rings on every finger will make it tough to write.

d) In order to **leave yourself sufficient time** to have a fair chance of getting the listing, do not make any other appointments for that evening or time period. If you have to rush off to be somewhere else (e.g. to present an offer), the customer will not see you as super-busy high-octane Realtor, but as somebody who puts HIS business interests ahead of THEIR welfare.

e) **VISUALIZE in your mind** the events which will take place during your forthcoming appointment and **REHEARSE what you are going to say.** With accumulating experience you will need less and less rehearsal time.

4) **SUPPLIES you will need for a listing appointment.**
   a) Several copies of Listing Contracts (in case you spoil one)
   b) A calculator and amortization book.
   c) Several ballpoint pens (it is embarrassing to have your only ballpoint pen run out of ink at the crucial moment).
   If you have ballpoints with your name and Company logo, give one to each of the Sellers as "lucky pens" when they sign the listing contract.
   d) Scratch pads to take notes or to give out as closing gifts.
   e) A good supply of your business cards because you will leave several with the Sellers to be given out
      - to their friends and relatives (bird dogging) or
      - to give to potential Buyers who may be unable to resist the temptation of knocking on their door without an appointment. (You should prepare your Sellers to say to these people: "Would you please call my Realtor to view the house. Here is his card.")
   f) A measuring tape (to measure the room sizes).
   g) A properly completed CMA.
   h) Many companies have a special form to calculate the Seller's "Estimated Net Equity" (net sales proceeds).
   i) A brochure with handy tips to make the house more saleable and showable.
   j) Referral or Relocation forms (in case the Sellers move out of town).
   k) A brochure explaining "How long does it take to sell a house?"
   l) A small powerful flashlight. Some owners do not leave the front porch light on when you arrive. Rather than stumbling around in the dark and stepping into sundry puddles or potholes, use a small flashlight to light your way safely from your car to the house. When you arrive at the front door you can slip it into your pocket.

5) **WHEN YOU ARE FINALLY GOING FOR THE APPOINTMENT:**
a) Taking traffic conditions into account, leave in plenty of time, in order to **arrive on time.** If you are 15 minutes early, park your car around the corner and quickly

rehearse in your mind what will shortly take place.

b) If you are nervous, please do NOT smoke in the car; your clothes will simply soak up the smoke and you will arrive in a cloud of tobacco stench.
Alternatively do not fortify yourself with alcohol. A quick pull from a bottle of cheap plonk will not put fire into your belly, but merely alcohol smell on your breath.

c) About 5 minutes before the appointed time, drive up to the house.

d) As you walk towards the house, clear your mind of all of your personal problems and concentrate exclusively on the task at hand. For the next hour or so nothing else in this world should matter other than these Sellers and you.

e) Take 2 deep breaths before ringing the doorbell or before knocking. The extra oxygen in your lungs will help to calm your nerves.

f) **A WORD OF CAUTION:**
Front doors open inwards; screen doors open outwards.
Therefore, don't stand flush against the screen door; if you do, then the owner will not be able to open the screen door to let you in. After an awkward moment you will have to take a step sideways or backwards. What an embarrassment: your opening salvo is a retreat!
If you are tall you should stand one step down in order to be eye-level with the Seller when he opens the door. If you don't do this, then the Seller's gaze will be on your chest instead of on your face. His first impression of you will be your overpowering and looming physical presence.

g) Put a sincere smile on your face, **because your LISTING PRESENTATION STARTS THE MOMENT THE OWNER OPENS HIS FRONT DOOR.**

The Listing Appointment - Part I

(I) **"SEEK AND YE SHALL FIND" are the basic elements** for a successful listing presentation.

1) **YOUR OBJECTIVE is** to leave with **a good and realistically priced listing.** Always remember that the RIGHT PRICE will remedy all defects and shortcomings of the property.

2) The Listing Salesperson is selling an **INTANGIBLE**, namely HIS and his COMPANY'S **SERVICES**. To **ACHIEVE** that objective the Realtor must convince the Seller of the **VALUE OF THOSE SERVICES**. This can be done by presenting to the Customers in a convincing way how your **SERVICES, RESOURCES, TRAINING and EXPERIENCE**
    - will relate to the Sellers' **objectives** and solve **THEIR problems.**
    - You will gain their goodwill and confidence by explaining
    - how they will **benefit** from dealing with you
    - and how you propose to **fulfil their needs.**
    - You also have to know how to **put your customers at ease**
    - to eventually **GAIN THEIR GOODWILL and CONFIDENCE.**

3) **YOUR LISTING PRESENTATION starts the moment the owner opens his front door.** Therefore, it is important for you to appear to be pleasant, confident and competent.
   In order for YOU to be confident and appear as competent,
    - your listing presentation **must be well PLANNED and carefully REHEARSED.**
    - **Choose your words carefully.** E.g. if you say: "Let me be honest with you for a minute" … does that mean to an unprejudiced listener that you have been lying up to now?
    - **EVERYTHING you say and do should impress the customer that YOU and only you are the right person to sell his house.**
    - For that purpose you must learn to use only
    - **powerfully descriptive and winning words** and
    - **soothing, reassuring phrases.**

4) To improve his chances of succeeding, the Realtor has to "set the stage." A listing presentation has the components or basic elements, if you will, of a classical drama:

CLASSICAL DRAMA:
(a) Start of action
(b) Escalating events leading up to the

LISTING PRESENTATION:
(a) First impression
(b) House tour and establishing rapport

(c) Climax
(d) End of play

(c) Closing for the listing
(d) Departure

5) Similar to any stage performance it is essential that what takes place during your listing presentation should be
   - **flowing smoothly**
   - **in a well organized manner** from the beginning right up to the time when you leave.
   - **Appearing to be "spontaneous"** (no painfully obvious artificial sales techniques). This "spontaneous" appearance is very difficult to achieve:
   - it requires a lot of practice and
   - whatever you do and say should be consistent with YOUR personality (do not copy somebody else!).

II) "KNOCK AND THE DOOR WILL BE OPENED FOR YOU."

As the Realtor is essentially selling **INTANGIBLES**, namely HIMSELF (his experience, his willingness to work hard and his Company's SERVICES), it is very important that he makes a **GOOD FIRST IMPRESSION.**

(a) Regrettably there is NO SECOND CHANCE to make a good "FIRST" impression.

(b) Without the VISUAL LINK of a good first impression the Realtor may not get a chance to go on to show off his business acumen and abilities.

(c) Therefore, before you leave your home, look into the mirror and ask yourself:

"Do I look like I am ready to be employed?"
"Would I hire this person to sell my house?"

First ... WHAT MAKES A "BAD FIRST IMPRESSION?":

1) Some Realtors are nervous because of lack of experience or lack of confidence. Experience is gained by making mistakes
   - in the field where it costs you money. The secret is to **learn from your mistakes, so you will not repeat them. With accumulated experience your confidence will increase.**

2) A Realtor's nervousness could be aggravated by the mistaken worry that the Sellers will be on the lookout for his weak points and flaws. This is absolutely not true. In reality the customer is just as nervous as the Realtor may be. **All the Customer wants is**
   - to find a competent and compatible Realtor
   - with whom he can work with comfortably and
   - with whom he can enjoy a good level of communication.

3) As a result of being apprehensive the Realtor's **mind may go blank or his throat**

will go dry and his hands will tremble.

If his mind goes blank, he will stammer "ah's" and "oh's." Because of his dry throat, he will be either unable to speak or if he manages to say something then his words will come out in a hoarse or squeaky voice. Trembling hands make a pitiful impression.

Here is an ANTIDOTE:

The best way to reduce the painful pounding of your heart is the QUIETING OF YOUR MIND by simply focusing on the task at hand.

4) For some unfathomable reason, a Realtor may also think that he is "intruding" and consequently will act apologetically. This is sheer nonsense because he is there by appointment.

5) It is impossible to radiate self-confidence if you stand in front of the customer in soiled, ill-fitting, wrinkled clothing and are poorly groomed (e.g. unshaven). Right or wrong, **people will often judge you by your appearance.** If you make a bad impression during the first few seconds of your meeting then unfortunately the odds are that the customer will assume that your poor appearance is indicative of your attitude and the quality of your work.

Any uneasy feelings are conveyed to the customer as a NEGATIVE FIRST IMPRESSION which subsequently is hard to overcome.

Well then ... WHAT COUNTS IN MAKING A "GOOD FIRST IMPRESSION?"

1) An important part of any first impression is the VISUAL IMAGE. The Realtor's overall general APPEARANCE must be pleasing to the Seller's eye. This means:
   - clean, well pressed and good fitting clothes
   - clean body (well groomed and no offensive odours)
   - clean breath
   - **IMMEDIATE eye contact** (which requires that you stand at eye level with the customer). To look the other person in the eye establishes not only CONTACT, but also simultaneously gives the impression that you are interested in him.

   A pleasing general overall appearance does NOT mean:
   - That you have to be a "beauty queen" or a "gorgeous hunk"; people come in all shapes and sizes.
   - That you have to be "young." Time marches on and has the habit of catching up with all of us.
   - That you have to be dressed in the latest fashion or in expensive clothes.
   - That you have to sport flashy jewellery (to impress the customer that you are "successful").

2) **A pleasant smile on your face** will help the customer to relax. It will also be the FIRST STEP in convincing him that you are:
   - non-threatening (no high-pressure tactics)
   - trustworthy
   - and, if given a chance, will be helpful and sympathetic (in solving their problems).

3) You must be physically, mentally and emotionally fully prepared and ready in order to **MOVE WITH PURPOSE** to get the job done.
   By subtly taking charge of the situation, you will get the customer's attention and simultaneously start creating the impression that you are EFFICIENT and COMPETENT.

   (a) Have an **OPENING REMARK** ready to start the conversation: "Good evening, Mr. Seller, I am .... of ... Realty."
   Hand him your business card.
   It might be a good idea to practice your opening words in front of a mirror to avoid artificial grins and other forced facial grimaces.
   - Like any good actor you want to achieve a "natural," spontaneous and unrehearsed appearance.
   - People like to be addressed by their own names, therefore, do so.
   - Be sure that you pronounce their names correctly. If in doubt, ask for the correct pronunciation.
   - If the customers are older than you it might be a good idea to address them (at least in the beginning) as Mr. or Mrs. and use their last names. People of an older generation (who are strangers to you) often do not take kindly to being addressed right off the bat by their first names. Somebody who is old enough to be your father may consider it as disrespectful if you call him "Mack" or whatever in the first few minutes.
   - If you end up shaking hands, make it a firm handshake. But not so firm that it feels like you are trying to crush his fingers; on the other hand don't make it a limp-noodle type of handshake either.
   - If you have never seen the Sellers before, don't greet them like long-lost relatives. Just be friendly and sincere, anything else will come across as phony.

   (b) The events which are going to happen during the next hour depend to a good extent on YOU. **YOU are the star and the director of the forthcoming action, therefore it is only logical that YOU TAKE CHARGE (CONTROL).**
   As it is difficult to conduct business through the screen door say:
   - "May I come in, please?"
   - "Where may I hang my coat, please?"
   - "Would you like me to take off my shoes?" (Alternatively some Realtors carry little plastic booties with them which they can slip over their shoes).

- "Before we sit down to talk, can you show me around the house first, please?"

YOUR "TALK" (listing presentation) MUST TAKE PLACE IN AN UNDISTURBED PLACE. Therefore, at the beginning of the guided tour of the house, **leave your briefcase in the kitchen,** because eventually you will want to sit down with the Sellers around the kitchen table. The close physical proximity will ensure that you can show them things; also you will be able to write on the kitchen table. For these reasons, the living room is "out."

III) **THE HOUSE INSPECTION.**

(a) During the inspection of the house take extensive notes on a clip-board; this will impress the Sellers because other Realtors often rush through the house. By inspecting the house in a whirlwind fashion, they inadvertently create the impression that they either haven't seen it all or that they are not too interested. Your notes will also refresh your memory later on when you will be writing a newspaper ad or prepare a Handout-Sheet.

(b) Everybody likes compliments; so during "The Tour" be COMPLIMENTARY, but only if it is truly warranted. Note and praise improvements and "extras" but do not exaggerate. Any compliments should be sincere and honest and stated in simple words. A gushing rhapsody about a standard paint job will come across as phony.

(c) Make sure that **the tour of the house ends in the kitchen**, where you have left your briefcase. If the owners suggest sitting in the living room, then say: "At home we usually sit around the kitchen table when we talk about important things. It's more comfortable."

(d) Arrange for **STRATEGIC SITTING around the kitchen table**, so that you don't end up playing "ping-pong": if husband and wife sit at opposite ends of the table and you sit in the middle, then you will have to constantly look from left to right and vice-versa. Therefore, it is important that YOU sit at one end of the table so that you can face both Sellers simultaneously.

IV) **"BREAKING THE ICE"** will control the Sellers' ANXIETY LEVEL

While everybody is getting settled around the kitchen table, engage in a little small talk to **establish PERSONAL RAPPORT.**

In order to overcome the owners' suspicion, apprehension and any disappointment (from a previous unsatisfactory dealing with a Realtor), **you must try to establish A PERSONAL BOND.** E.g. common experiences like children, school, hobbies etc.

(a) **At all costs avoid talking about religion or politics.**

(b) **If YOU are doing all the talking,** then chances are that sooner or later you will make a mistake: you will say something which you shouldn't have and which you will come to regret later on.

(c) **It is preferable that you let the Owners talk** about themselves because YOU WILL LEARN MORE ABOUT THEM if they do the talking. **A good listener** will SORT and SIEVE this information.

This "ice breaking period" should be no more than 5 or 10 minutes because **too much small talk can and will kill the "sale"** (getting the listing).

(a) Regrettably many Realtors get themselves involved in a lengthy discussion about something or another and forget the original purpose why they are there in the first place.
(b) Or else, they don't know how to stop the pleasantries and get down to business.
(c) Don't ever rely on the Owners because they certainly don't know how to switch the conversation back to business - THEY are the lay people and after all YOU are the expert! The only day when the owners will suggest to you to take out your Listing pad and start writing is on a frosty morning in August, when the temperature is 50 degrees below zero and when a red-horned gentleman comes up for air and announces to the world that his living quarters are frozen over.
(d) Therefore YOU must take charge again:
"Mr. and Mrs. Seller! I would love to continue talking to you about children and school. We will talk more about it in the future. In the meantime you have invited me to come over here tonight, to talk to you about the marketing of your beautiful house."

AT THIS STAGE good transitional questions to ask the owners are:
(a) "How long have you lived here?"
(b) "What prompted you to buy the house in the first place?" (This could be an important clue, because it may also motivate the NEXT Buyer).
(c) "What do you presently owe on your property?"
(d) **Ask to see the mortgage documents, Survey Certificate (Certificate of Non-encroachment), the Deed and any other documents they have for the house.**

The following questions will enable you to judge and determine the DEGREE OF MOTIVATION which the Sellers have:

(a) "Why are you selling?"
(b) "When do you have to move?" OR "When do you want to move?"
(c) "What are your future plans?" (e.g. to buy another house locally or to move out of town).
(d) "If you are transferred and have to leave immediately, will you leave your family behind until the house is sold?"
(e) "If the house is not sold by the time all of you are leaving, then for how long are you in a position to keep up the mortgage payments and house maintenance costs?"

THE ABOVE QUESTIONS ...
- will continue building your rapport with the Sellers and

- simultaneously they will give you valuable information and insights into their needs and wants which you can use later.

CAUTION:

At this stage, the Sellers' pressing need is to hear what his house is worth.

If you tell him, then you will never get a chance to inform him about your services. He will be too pre-occupied trying to figure out in his head what his "net equity" is.

You will just have to grab the bull by the horns again and say:

"Mr. and Mrs. Seller! I know that you have many questions and that you want to hear about the Market Value of your house. **But before we discuss price,** please allow me
- to review with you some of the highlights of my services.
- Also I want to tell you a little about myself and my Company
- and **how I propose to go about marketing your house in order to obtain top price for you.**
- Please feel free to interrupt me anytime and I will answer all of your questions to the best of my ability."

TO RELIEVE the time pressure on the (impatient) Sellers that it will NOT be an all night affair ... take your watch off your wrist and place it in front of you as a reminder.

This simple but powerful gesture should relieve any time concerns which the Sellers may have.

Communication should be both audio AND visual.

Talk is cheap and therefore your listing presentation should contain something (proof, statistics, sales awards etc.) which the Sellers can see.

"Mr. and Mrs. Seller! It will help me to express myself a little better if I have some visual aids."

If on the other hand you keep on talking too much (e.g. how great YOU are) then your words are liable to go into one ear of the Seller and out the other.

LISTING WORK SHEET

OWNERS: _____ Phone # _____

PROPERTY ADDRESS: _____

Legal description: _____

Tax Roll # _____

Current gross taxes: $ _____ Paid _____

                                             Outstanding _____

Water, sewer, garbage $ _____ (included: yes/no)

Assessment: Land $ _____

                Building $ _____

Zoning: _____ Age of house: _____

LOT size: North side _____ West side _____

                South side _____ East side _____

LOT grade: _____ or sloping: _____

LANDSCAPED: fenced _____ grass _____ trees _____ shrubs _____

LANDSCAPING (circle one): well-kept   fair   poor

Driveway: paved _____ or "dirt & gravel" _____

              private _____ Is there a backlane? _____

Garage: single/double/multiple car: size _____

Carport: single/double/multiple: size _____

ROAD: paved _____ or "dirt & gravel" _____

Sidewalks: _____ Curbs: _____ Street lights: _____

Distance to Hydrant: _____ On municipal water: yes/no

Shopping: _____ Elem. school: _____

Transportation: _____ High school: _____

Park: _____ Churches: _____

Sanitary sewer (connected to the house): yes/no

Septic tank (if any): _____

Date last serviced (pumped out): _____

The Listing Appointment - Part I

WELL water: (well certificate) type of well _____

produces _____ gallons per minute

Certificate for quality of water _____

Capacity of the water storage tank: _____

EXTERIOR of house: _____ Roof: _____

Eavestroughs: wood/aluminum … good…fair…poor

Downpipes: good…fair…poor

INTERIOR walls: drywall/plaster/panelled/wallpaper

Need painting: yes/no

Windows: single glazed/double glazed _____

Furnace: forced air _____

Fuel: gas _____ oil _____ If "oil": location and condition of oil tank _____

                                            Capacity (size) of oil tank _____

Radiant heat: electric _____

Gas/oil fired radiant heat: number of zones:_____

Number of fireplaces: _____ wood/gas/elec.

Hot water tank: gas/elec.   age: _____ capacity:_____ gallons

Plumbing: _____ Wiring: _____

Living room size: _____ floors _____

Dining room size: _____ floors _____

Family room size: _____ floors _____

Kitchen size: _____ floors _____

Eating area: _____ floors _____

Master bedroom: _____ floors _____

Ensuite bathroom: toilet/sink/shower/tub

Bedroom: _____ floors _____

Bedroom: _____ floors _____

Bathroom: toilet/sink/shower/tub

Bathroom: toilet/sink/shower/tub

Other rooms: _____ floors _____

BASEMENT: yes/no

Recreation room: _____ floors _____

Bedroom: _____ floors _____

Bedroom: _____ floors _____

Bathroom: toilet/sink/shower/tub

Laundry: _____ Workshop: _____

Storage: _____ Other: _____

Foundation: _____ (continuous cement/cement blocks/ other _____)

Crawl space: (Access)_____

Height of crawl space: _____

Is there a continuous cement floor in crawl space under the house _____ or is there a dirt/gravel floor _____.

Is there an insulating tarp or poly sheet spread over the dirt floor? _____

Are there any signs of dry rot in the crawl space?_____

Dimensions of building: _____   Location on street:_____

The Listing Appointment - Part II

V) **The actual LISTING PRESENTATION.**

The basic idea is to capture and retain the Sellers' attention to what you have to say. As the Seller can listen at a higher rate of speed than you can talk, there is the danger that his mind will wander, while you are trying to get your message across.
If you drone on about
- how great you are or
- if you just talk about what is not important to the owners,
- or you talk too much because you forgot that talk is cheap, **then chances are that you will lose your conversation partners.**

Therefore, it is best to interrupt your stream of words by showing the customers something. In other words, your communication should be both audio and visual. (Pictures can have subliminal messages).

An organized, planned **VISUAL listing presentation** is best done with the help of a flip chart. This is simply a 3-ring binder into which you can clip some of the following material:

1) Licenses, diplomas and awards (in order to gain the Customer's confidence that you are COMPETENT and TRUSTWORTHY).
   (a) A photocopy of your real estate license.
       This may be a good time to tell the Customers how long you have been selling real estate:
       - if you are a seasoned veteran, then you have "experience, knowledge, mortgage connections etc.."
       - If you are new in the business, then you are "enthusiastic, a tireless, hard worker and you are being guided by your Manager or a seasoned Realtor.
   (b) A photocopy of a real estate designation or degree which you have achieved.
   (c) A photocopy of educational certificates (from seminars which you have attended) or diplomas of advanced studies.
   (d) A picture of you receiving a Sales Award (either in your Company or from the local Real Estate Board).

2) A picture of you sitting at your desk speaking into the phone. (In order to suggest that you are ORGANIZED, the desk should NOT be cluttered with piles of paper).
   This might be a good time to tell the prospects that:
   (a) you are familiar with the market in this area.
   (b) If they were to list their home with you, you could start with your marketing efforts IMMEDIATELY.
   (c) That you are constantly in touch with other local Realtors and will promote their house to them.

3) A picture of all salespersons including the Manager in front of your office. (This may depict happy team work).

4) In various locations throughout this presentation folder there should be interspersed:
   (a) pictures of homes which you have sold: these should have little "sold" stickers affixed across a corner.
   (b) Pictures of YOU (and possibly the Sellers' children) putting up a "SOLD" sticker on your "For Sale" sign in front of a house which you have just sold.
   (c) Pictures of you shaking hands with smiling Sellers (satisfied Clients) and their children, dog etc. in front of your "SOLD" sign.

CAUTION: **don't get too carried away tooting your own horn.**
If you are on an extensive ego trip bragging about the Multi-Million Dollar Sales Volume of houses you claim to have sold, then don't be surprised if the the customers will silently start adding up in their heads the amount of commissions which you will have earned. As a consequence they may decide not to contribute further to your growing wealth.

5) An **"ACTION WARRANTY"** to allay the Sellers' fear that you might vanish without a trace never to be heard of again once they have signed the listing contract.

6) A handout brochure detailing what your **Marketing Strategy** for the Sellers' property will be. A copy thereof should be given to the Sellers.
   The following are some of the items which could be included:

"MY MARKETING PLAN FOR YOUR PROPERTY"

(a) I will submit **complete details** of your property to the local Real Estate Board for publication on the Multiple Listing Service, the Board computer, the Internet and the printed MLS catalogue.
(b) A distinctive (nationally recognized) **"FOR SALE" sign** will be placed on a **strategically visible spot** on your property.
(c) For various promotional purposes (e.g. internet, display case in our office) I will arrange to have pictures taken of the outside and inside of your house.
(d) For potential Buyers and the use of other Realtors I will prepare a **FEATURE or HIGHLIGHT sheet** detailing all attractive features and benefits of your house.
(e) All showings of your property will be **"by appointment only."**
(f) All appointments to show your house will only be made through me. I have a pager and cellular phone.
There will be no need for you to stay home waiting for the phone to ring.

(g) I will provide you with a **list of suggestions** to make your house more attractive/saleable to a prospective buyer.

(h) When convenient,
- I will arrange to have the salespersons in my office view your house **(Office Tour).**
- I will arrange to have Co-Operating Realtors from other companies tour your house **(MLS Tour)**.
- You will be informed of the Tour Average Appraisal.
  (Each attending Realtor will give an estimate of what could be the anticipated Selling Price).

(i) Whenever possible, I will **pre-qualify all prospective buyers** (to ensure that they are interested in your type of house and that they can afford it).

(j) **I will follow up** on all salespersons who have shown your house and solicit from them their buyers' reaction and comments about your house. I will communicate this information to you.

(k) I will set up an **ADVERTISING RECORD** for your house and **you will receive a copy of every newspaper ad** which I am running together with comments of persons who have called me on my ads and sign.

(l) If it is agreeable with you I will hold an **"OPEN HOUSE"** whenever possible.

(m) **I will keep in touch with you** and will communicate to you regularly the results of all other marketing activities.

(n) I will constantly update you as to any changes in the market, both in prices and interest rates and **their effects on the saleability of your property.**

PRESENTATION OF OFFERS.

(o) I will represent you during the presentation of all offers;
I will scrutinize and discuss all offers with you.
I will do my utmost to negotiate the best possible price and terms for you.

AFTER-the-sale-SERVICE.

(p) I will give you my attentive "after-the-sale-service" which includes:
- I will handle all follow-up instructions and paperwork to lawyers and/or notaries public.
- I will keep you informed of all appraisal, mortgage, title and other closing procedures.
- If you so wish, I will be happy to attend with you when you sign the final documents in the lawyer's office.
- I will phone your Insurance Agent and ask him to contact you to discuss with you all insurance matters both on the house you have just sold and/or the next house you are buying.
- I will give you a **"LIST OF THINGS TO DO and people to notify when moving."**

- I will arrange for the transfer of the house keys.

I will take care of everything and leave no loose ends.

==

Hopefully by this time you will have won the Sellers' **CONFIDENCE** and established with them your **CREDIBILITY**.

IT IS NOW FINALLY TIME TO DISCUSS "THE PRICE."
(1) Take out your **neatly typed MARKET ANALYSIS** with **pictures** (pictures say a thousand words) of
   (a) **comparable, recently SOLD houses** (indication of value)
   (b) **comparable, currently LISTED houses** (the competition)
   (c) **comparable, recently EXPIRED listings** (indication of over pricing)
(2) Discuss the suggested Listing Price and give them a "guesstimate" of the **anticipated** Selling Price or **Price Range.**
(3) Discuss the **DANGERS of OVERPRICING.**
(4) Prepare a **Seller's "NET EQUITY" sheet:** they want to know roughly how much they get out of the sale after the dust settles.

VI) **NOW COMES "THE (real) CLOSE."**

EVERYTHING that you have done up to now should have been **leading up to and been part of "THE CLOSE."**
The CLOSE, which so many Realtors fear, is nothing more than asking for the order (see Trial Closes below) by giving
(a) a brief summary of what you have just said emphasising **FACTS, EVIDENCE, BENEFITS and ADVANTAGES.**
(b) **NEVER FORGET TO ASK FOR THE ORDER** with a simple question. Don't beat around the bush. It's decision time!

The 1st TRIAL CLOSE:
"As you have just heard, you will get the maximum in service and the maximum in results if I handle the sale of your house. **Can we go ahead and put it on the market, please?"**

At this stage it will be necessary for you to hold your tongue and bite your lips, not to move and to keep quiet while giving the husband and wife a chance to "exchange glances" (e.g. silent approval to go ahead).

- If YOU are the first party to break the silence then chances are that you will shatter the magic moment and lose out.
- If their answer is "yes" then quickly take out your pad of Listing Contracts and

start writing. While you are doing that don't forget to keep them involved by asking questions; e.g.: "What are your full names, please?" (You will need this information at a future date, when the house is sold and you are filling out the Sales Record Sheet/conveyancing instructions to the lawyer).
- As a gesture of courtesy, reconfirm the Asking Price with the Sellers, before inserting it in the Listing Contract.
- When the chips are down, it happens occasionally that the Sellers will decide in the last minute on a more realistic price. Of course, the opposite can happen also.
- Without saying anything further, shove the completed Listing Contract together with your ballpoint pen towards the Sellers for their signatures.
- **ALL registered owners must sign the listing contract and**
- **each one of them must be given a copy thereof.**
- **If the Sellers have any hesitations, then offer again to answer completely all questions, concerns and objections.**

The 2nd TRIAL CLOSE.
"I have 4 objectives for you, Mr. and Mrs. Seller:
- To get as many QUALIFIED Buyers as possible to see your house.
- **I will not quit UNTIL your house is SOLD.**
- My goal is to assist you in getting
- **the highest possible Dollar value** for your property,
- in the **shortest possible time** and
- with the **least amount of inconvenience and problems to you**.
- By doing all of this, I hope to give you **PEACE OF MIND** that you as a consumer are **getting GOOD VALUE** for your commission Dollar. **I am ready to start immediately: can we go ahead and put your house on the market now, please?**"

The 3rd TRIAL CLOSE.

"Mr. and Mrs. Seller! Everything that reasonably can be done to sell your house WILL be done. I promise you my honest hard work - and I will keep my promise. That is all that anybody can reasonably ask for.
Can we go ahead with the paperwork to market your house?"

NOTE:
(a) Avoid the words "sign" and "listing" - use euphemisms instead.
(b) Consult the Chapters on "Overcoming Objections" and "27 Obstacles in the way of getting a listing signed."

VII) For a Realtor who wants to succeed under difficult circumstances it is important to understand some of the **REASONS WHY** customers sometimes **DON'T BELIEVE or TRUST REALTORS.**

(a) **A bad past experience.**
   The Sellers may have been misled by exaggerated claims or disappointed by unkept promises of other salespersons.
(b) They may have heard **bad stories** from friends and relatives or they may have read in the media about an unfortunate real estate incident.
(c) Some people are **sceptical by nature.**
(d) **A poor listing presentation:**
   - Because of another appointment, the Realtor was in a hurry and didn't give the "whole story."
   - The Realtor **didn't listen** (to the Sellers' concerns) **with his ears, eyes and heart.**
   - The Realtor only talked about things which HE thought were important and didn't deal with items which were of interest to the Sellers.
   - The Realtor did not listen when the customer told him what he wanted or needed. Instead, he tried to change the Owner's mind by addressing something else in the hope that the customer will change his mind.
   - When the Realtor didn't have an answer for something, he decided to "wing" his reply and bluff his way out … and the customer recognized it.
   - The Realtor only spoke about "benefits" which meant absolutely NOTHING to the Sellers. E.g.: "Our company is financially strong and trading on the …stock market because we are associated with/a subsidiary of So-and-so who is a Land Developer/Builder/Mortgage Company."
   - The Realtor totally missed the things which were really important to the Sellers. E.g.: "How much advertising are you willing to do to get our house sold?" ANSWER: **"As much as it takes to get it sold."**
(e) The Realtor made **exaggerated claims**. All claims or statements should be backed up by **FACTS, EXHIBITS, STATISTICS and TESTIMONIALS.**
(f) Poor manners (e.g. unthinkingly lights up a cigarette), unprofessional conduct (e.g. runs down his competition), unfavourable personal appearance (e.g. lack of hygiene).

VIII) **THE DEPARTURE.**

ONCE THE LISTING IS SIGNED **you will have to do 3 more things:**

(1) Courtesy costs you nothing, but will go a long way with your new Clients: don't forget the value of a **sincere "THANK YOU for listing with me."** (See sample letter).
(2) If you feel the need that you have to promise something, then simply say: **"I promise you only what I can control and deliver: I promise to work hard for you and will try my best to sell your house."**
(3) If the hour is late, then make an appointment for the next day to measure the house inside and out. At that time also take pictures of the front and/or back of the house for your newspaper ads.

(4) AFTER THIS ... **you must LEAVE!**
This was a business appointment and not a social call. If you stay for coffee or tea or something stronger, you will invariably end up
   (a) "blabbing" about how desperately grateful you are to have obtained their listing. **Some Sellers may interpret this as a sign of weakness** and could reward you in due course by asking you to cut your commission when you bring them an offer.
   (b) You are also liable to make foolish promises which you will not be able to keep. E.g.
      - "I will work my fingers to the bone for you."
      - "I will work 24 hours a day 7 days a week for you."

      These exaggerations are unbelievable.
      - "I have sold everything and can, therefore, advertise your house every week."

      You may regret this foolish promise later on when you pick up a few more listings before this one sells.

Therefore, AFTER YOU HAVE FINISHED YOUR BUSINESS ... PACK YOUR BAGS, **say "Good night" and actually L-E-A-V-E!**

IX) FOR YOUR FUTURE EXPECTATION OF SUCCESS.

What happens if you don't get the listing? Many salespersons **fail because of an IMPROPER EXIT,** which conceivably could damage or adversely affect any future chances or expectations of success with this particular Seller. (See sample letter).

(1) If the Seller's answer is **"NO" and you don't get the listing,** then be a gentleman and **LEAVE GRACEFULLY.**
(2) Don't look at the customer as a mere body who didn't give you a listing. When you are turned down, **do NOT show any displeasure whatsoever.** This is very hard to do and requires a lot of self control.
(3) Instead, **leave the prospect with such good grace that he REGRETS that he didn't list with you.** Who knows, after he has tried somebody else and failed, he will remember YOU and your sincere attitude at some future date, at which time he WILL do business with you.
(4) You know the house, you have an idea what the Seller will take; isn't this a wonderful set-up when you in your travels come across a good buyer for it?
(5) There is another and just as important reason why a Realtor should not become unhappy and emotionally down: it will give the salesperson a **NEGATIVE MENTAL ATTITUDE.**
(6) If a salesperson with a Negative Mental Attitude approaches his NEXT Listing PROSPECT, chances are that because of his poor attitude **he will repeat his failure** because:
The Realtor's **NEXT PROSPECT**
   - not only doesn't know what had gone on BEFORE him,

- but he also doesn't care.
- For HIM it is a brand new ball game.
- What is important for HIM is
- the PRESENT
- his GOALS and NEEDS
- and his CONCERNS.

For these reasons, it should also be a brand new effort (performance, ball game etc.) for the REALTOR who must call on his NEXT PROSPECTS **with ENTHUSIASM and the EXPECTATION OF SUCCESS.**

X) SUMMARY.

It should be evident that only an enthusiastic, hardworking and persistent Realtor with a GOAL and PLAN will consistently get listings. The pillars of staying on the right track **to ensure a continuous flow of new listings are:**

(1) A lot of hard work and long hours must be devoted to **prospecting. You must resolve that you will NEVER quit prospecting.**

If you (on any particular day) suddenly find yourself not knowing what to do next, then **do some prospecting.**

Here is some good news for those who are worried about over working themselves:

Armpit sweat is not life-threatening and by the latest report nobody has ever died from it.

(2) **The better your listing presentation is,** the better are your chances of getting a listing. Therefore it is desirable that you **constantly update, review and rehearse** your listing presentation **until it becomes second nature to you.**

(3) **The more experience and accumulated business knowledge you have,** the better are your chances of getting the listing.

(4) **The more SERVICE, BENEFITS and ADVANTAGES** you can offer to the Seller, the better are your chances of getting the listing.

(5) Sellers have an inexhaustible arsenal of questions and objections. This will never change.
The SMART thing is to be prepared for them.

(6) In spite of the best laid plans of mice and men, the Sellers are liable to come up with some last minute objection why they don't want to sign the listing contract.
HOLD YOUR TEMPER and DON'T PANIC.
   (a) **An astute Realtor will first determine if these refusals are:**
   - based on valid concerns which he must address and diffuse immediately
   - if the Seller is stalling for time because he has some undisclosed and/or unspoken problems.
   - If they are merely "gripes" which can be politely set aside.
   (b) Due to lack of experience and/or confidence a lot of Realtors give up too easily when the owner refuses or makes some sort of objection.

(c) **Refusals and objections are part of the Selling Game**. That is why we are called "SALESpersons" and not "Order Takers."
(d) A Realtor must be organized and able to overcome ALL objections. Admittedly that requires **a lot of practice** which preferably should be out in the field "nose-to-nose" and "toes-to-toes" with customers. Play acting at the office takes place under controlled circumstances and if you make a mistake then nothing drastic will happen. However, if you strike out in real life it will cost you some real money. That is why such lessons are learned in the school of hard knocks.

Hopefully you will learn from your mistakes and remember the lessons they taught you so you will not repeat them the next time you are dealing with a customer under similar circumstances.

Suggested "THANK YOU" letter on your Company's Letterhead

Dear Mr. and Mrs. ....

I would like to thank you for the confidence you have shown to me by accepting my services for the marketing of your property at ....

In order to sell your house for the best possible price and with a minimum of inconvenience to you, I will make an extensive effort to expose the desirable features of your property to the buying public, as well as my colleagues in the business. I will also keep you informed of all developments favourable and otherwise that may arise out of my marketing efforts. For your perusal I am enclosing herewith an informative pamphlet dealing with the question "HOW LONG DOES IT TAKE TO SELL A PROPERTY?"

Should you at any time have any questions or problems, please feel free to call me right away. Looking forward to a happy cooperation, I am,

Sincerely Yours,

Suggested courtesy letter on your Company's Letterhead in case you didn't get the listing right away.

Dear Mr. and Mrs.......

I would like to thank you for giving me the opportunity of meeting with you and listening to my Listing Presentation. I hope that I was able to answer many of the questions which you may have had.

Based on the Market Data available, a Realtor will suggest a realistic price range for the Asking Price. However, the actual final Selling Price will be determined by supply and demand and is achieved by a meeting of the minds of the Sellers and their prospective Buyers (Fair Market Value).

I take great pride in competing for your valued business on the basis of
- my GOOD SERVICE and intensive MARKETING PLAN for your property. (A summary copy of which I have already given to you).
- My ... years of experience in the business.
- My integrity and hard work (I am a tireless worker)
- and my good reputation with my fellow Realtors, which I have earned over many years of fair dealings.

I look forward to hearing from you soon and remain,

Sincerely Yours,

The Listing Appointment - Part II

HOW LONG WILL IT TAKE TO SELL YOUR HOUSE?

There are 6 factors which will determine how long it will take to sell your house:

(1) **THE PRODUCT.**
   The CONDITION of the property.
   a) If the house shows poorly because of
   - neglect (dirt or lack of maintenance) or
   - other defects which haven't been corrected, then a sale may not take place for a long time; or at least until such time when a handyman buyer is prepared to take on the burden of the deficiencies.
   Such a Buyer will do that only PROVIDED that the Selling Price is adjusted accordingly to compensate him for his work, time, costs and risks.
   b) **Another factor is the LOCATION.** If the property is on a busy through street, next to a noisy business, garage, factory, railway tracks etc. then many Buyers may shy away from buying your property.
   c) However, there is an old saying in real estate:
   "The (right) PRICE will REMEDY ALL DEFECTS." In other words, if the right Buyer feels that the Asking Price warrants his attention, then he will make an offer.

(2) **THE PRICE.**
The (wrong) Price may delay or prevent a sale. Serious and qualified buyers look for a house in THEIR PRICE RANGE or perhaps slightly above it. If you OVERPRICE your house then you will put it into a price bracket where they won't look.
On the other hand buyers who can afford the price range in which you have listed, may want a better and bigger house.
The wrong price will attract the wrong buyers.

(3) **THE COMMISSION.**
   a) Realtors earn a commission only if they sell something. It is entirely possible, that a Realtor may do a lot of work and incur considerable expenses in the promotion of a property; if the property isn't sold, then in the end he will not even be reimbursed for his cash-outlay (expenses).
   b) The Competition Act allows the "floating" of real estate commissions. There is no such thing as a "regular" commission and no Realtor may charge a commission "like everybody else."
   c) The Listing Broker splits the real estate commission with the Selling Broker. It is the Selling Broker's privilege to select houses for showing to his Buyers.
   d) If the commission which you are prepared to pay is non-competitive (namely drastically below the level which is offered by other Sellers for similar, competing houses in your area) then the successful cooperation with other Buyer's Agents may be influenced.

(4) **THE REAL ESTATE MARKET.**
No Realtor can change the real estate market. It is a matter of supply and demand.
  a) In a SELLER's MARKET many Buyers compete against each other for the few houses which are for sale. Prices tend to rise; multiple-offer situations happen.
  b) In a BUYER's MARKET there are many houses for sale. They all compete against each other for the attention of the few Buyers which are around. Prices tend to drop.

(5) **YOUR COMPETITION.**
The real estate market has a tendency to change constantly. The number of houses coming on the market may change weekly or monthly. Your CURRENT COMPETITION of similar houses to yours in the area will determine a **Buyer's DECISION to buy and at what price.** In other words, a Buyer makes his decision to buy and the price he is willing to offer **BY WHAT HIS OTHER CHOICES ARE.**

(6) **THE PROMOTION.**
  a) My company and I will make every effort to promote the sale of your house.
  b) We will report to you periodically about the comments made by prospective Buyers who have viewed your house.
  c) We will also keep you up-to-date about interest rates and about the state of the real estate market.
  d) However, the best **PROMOTION cannot overcome the first 5 factors:** if they are out of balance your house will most likely not sell.

The Listing Appointment - Part III

ANALYZING the difference between a SELLING Salesperson and a LISTING Salesperson.

The **"SELLING" Salesperson** is selling something **tangible**, namely a property. In essence, after analyzing what the prospective Buyer wants and needs, he selects several appropriate type of houses and shows them to the Buyer. The popular myth is that the house usually sells itself and that the Selling Agent ends up more or less just taking the order. This is not so. "Selling" is by no means that easy.

(a) A Selling Agent must be familiar and keep constantly up-to-date with the current inventory of houses which are for sale.
(b) He must tactfully prequalify (financially) the Buyers.
(c) He must be skilled to make the right value judgment when selecting houses which he is going to show to his Buyers.
(d) Then he has to do a lot of exhausting running around with the Buyers showing them various selected properties.
(e) There will be nerve wrecking times when thoughtless and/or disloyal Buyers will be out of sight of the Selling Agent during which time they could buy from somebody else.
(f) Finally getting everything down on paper and walking the fine line between obliging his Buyers' wishes to offer low and simultaneously making tactfully sure that such offer is not so low-ball that it will antagonize the Sellers.
(g) Then comes the potentially difficult task of negotiating with (potential) strangers who are:
  - the apprehensive Sellers and
  - the Listing Salesperson who - aware of his Agency Duties vis-a-vis his client, the Seller - acts occasionally more like a confrontational advocate instead of trying to be helpful in bringing the parties together.

The **"LISTING" Salesperson is selling**
- **an INtangible, namely HIS and his Company's SERVICE.**
- **In effect he must convince the owner of the VALUE OF THAT SERVICE.**
  It should be evident that only an enthusiastic, hardworking and persistent Realtor with a GOAL and PLAN will consistently get listings. The pillars of staying on the right track **to ensure a continuous flow of new listings are:**

(1)
(a) **A lot of hard work and long hours devoted to PROSPECTING.**
(b) **You must resolve that you will NEVER quit prospecting.**
  If you ever on any particular day suddenly find yourself not knowing what to do next, **then do some prospecting.**
  Here is some good news for those who are worried about overworking themselves:

Armpit sweat is not life-threatening and by the latest reports nobody has ever died from it.

(2) **The better your listing presentation is,** the better are your chances of getting a listing. Therefore it is desirable that you constantly update, review and rehearse your listing presentation until it becomes second nature to you.

(3) **The more experience and business knowledge you have,** the better are your chances of getting the listing.

(4) **The more service, benefits and advantages you can offer** to the Seller, the better are your chances of getting the listing.

(5) Sellers have an inexhaustible arsenal of questions and objections. This will never change.
The smart thing is to be prepared for them.

(6) In spite of the best laid plans of mice and men, the Sellers will come up with some last minute objection, why they don't want to sign the listing contract.
Hold your temper and don't panic.
  (a) **An astute Realtor must first determine** if these refusals are:
- based on valid concerns which must be addressed and diffused immediately or
- if they are merely gripes which can be politely set aside or
- if the Seller is stalling for time because he has an undisclosed and/or unspoken problem.

  (b) Due to lack of confidence and/or experience a lot of Realtors give up too easily when the owner refuses or makes some sort of objection. **Refusals and objections are part of the Selling Game.** That is why we are called **"SALESpersons"** and NOT "Order Takers."

  (c) A Realtor must be organized and able to overcome ALL objections. Admittedly that requires **a lot of practice which preferably should be out in the field** (meaning "in the trenches" and "nose-to-nose and toes-to-toes" with the Customers).

Play acting at the office takes place under controlled circumstances and if you make a mistake it costs you nothing. However if you strike out in real life it will cost you real money. That is why such lessons are best taught in the proverbial "School of Hard Knocks." Hopefully you will learn from your mistakes and remember the lessons they taught you so you don't repeat them the next time you are facing a Customer under similar circumstances.

Disclosure Of Agency Representation

Since January 1, 1995 Article 3 of CREA's (Canadian Real Estate Association) Code of Ethics requires written and receipted agency disclosure during
- the first substantial and meaningful contact or
- at the first available reasonable and appropriate opportunity with the Client(s)-to-be.

The brochure "Working with a Realtor" describes
(a) the various types of working relationships between a Realtor and the Client(s): Single Agency, "No Agency"/ Transaction Broker and Limited Dual Agency.
(b) The Realtor's **FIDUCIARY DUTIES which are:**
   - To act in a competent manner and to exercise reasonable **CARE and SKILL**.
   - **LOYALTY**: to act at all times
     - only in the interests of his Client(s) and
     - even to put the Client's interests above his own.
   - **DISCLOSURE** of all pertinent facts which may affect the Client's decisions.
   - **OBEDIENCE**: to obey promptly all lawful instructions given by the Client.
   - **CONFIDENTIALITY**: not to reveal any confidential information given by the Client(s).
   - **ACCOUNTABILITY**: of all monies entrusted to him.

With the exception of one duty (see below) **the Listing Broker's agency obligations END ONLY when the sale is completed.** E.g. this means that the Realtor has an obligation to present back-up offers even in the case of a firm and subjects-free sale; the decision if back-up offers should be considered is made by the SELLER and NOT by the Realtor.

As mentioned above **THERE IS ONE EXCEPTION: the agency obligation of "CONFIDENTIALITY" NEVER ends.** It does NOT end
   - when the sale is completed or
   - when the listing (of the unsold property) expires.
(c) The services which a Customer will receive when there is "No Agency" relationship.
(d) Certain limitations which will be imposed in **a mutually consented Limited Dual Agency situation.**

In **"LEE v. ROYAL PACIFIC REALTY CORP."** B.C. Supreme Court, Date 2003-06-12, Docket No. C995919 the Honourable Madam Justice D. A. Satanove outlined at [26] **the STATUTORY DUTY of a Realtor** by referring to Section 36 of the Real Estate Act, R.S.B.C. 1996, C.397 which says:
36 (1) Before assisting or representing any person in a real estate transaction, a licensee must disclose to that person

(a) the nature of the assistance or representation that the licensee will provide to the person.
(b) whether the licensee is, or will be, acting in the real estate transaction on behalf of any other person, in any capacity,
(c) whether the licensee is or will be, receiving remuneration relating to the real estate transaction from any other person,
(d) the nature of the licensee's relationship with any other person from whom the licensee is, or will be, receiving remuneration relating to the real estate transaction,
(2) If, during the course of a real estate transaction in which a licensee is assisting any person, there is any material change in the facts that the licensee has disclosed under subsection (1) to that person, the licensee must disclose the change to that person immediately.

Some readers may question if the above requirements are sufficient to enable the Clients (Sellers and Buyers) to give their **"INFORMED CONSENT" to the CHOICE of Agency Relationship which is to be established.** In this connection the following 2 law cases may be considered:

(A) "**HODGKINSON v. SIMMS**" B.C. Court of Appeal CA 011048 and Supreme Court of Canada [1994] 3 SCR 377 which deals with the duty of proper disclosure during pre-contractual negotiations of material facts which were **ADVERSE to the Plaintiff.** Had the Plaintiff been aware of the full nature and extent of these facts, his decisions and actions may have been different.

The following salient point may be considered:

(1) **BEFORE** the Client chooses **"PERSONAL representation" and becomes the PRINCIPAL in an Agency Relationship** should he not be told that **a PRINCIPAL becomes VICARIOUSLY LIABLE for the actions of his SERVANT** (the Agent/Realtor)? E.g. any MISCONDUCT and NEGLECTS committed in the course of the Principal's business even though only committed for the Agent's benefit (e.g. the earning of a commission).
See the following law cases:
(a) "ORRIS v. COLLINGS" (1929) 36 O.W.N. 172; varied 37 O.W.N. 233 (C.A.)
(b) "SCHOLL et al v. ROYAL TRUST CORP. OF CANADA" (1986) 40 C.C.L.T. 113 (Ont. H.C.)
(c) "PAVENHAM v. SLADEN & SUTTON GROUP RESOURCE REALTY" BCSC, Docket No. S5182, Date Sept. 11, 1997
(d) "TAN v. ENG" B.C. Supreme Court, Docket C872273, Date 1990-12-20

(2) As an Agency Relationship should be built
- on **mutual trust** which requires **full and candid disclosure of everything**
- shouldn't the Realtor have at least a **MORAL OBLIGATION** of

CANDOUR to disclose the future Principal's vicarious responsibility?
- Natural justice requires a **duty of common honesty between negotiating parties** (the future Client and the Realtor are negotiating the terms of the Agency Relationship).

(B) This very subject was addressed in **"QUEEN v. COGNOS INC."** (1993), 99 D.L.R. (4th) 626 at 643. The Court found that QUOTE "the respondent and its representative" (in our case this would be the Real Estate Company and its salesperson) "owed a DUTY OF CARE to the appellant" (in our case the Seller/Buyer) "during the course of the hiring interview" (in our case the Agency Disclosure prior to entering into a listing contract or a Buyer's Agreement) "to exercise such reasonable care as the circumstances required to ensure that the representations made were accurate and not misleading. This duty of care is distinct from and additional to the duty of common honesty existing between negotiating parties ... while a subsequent contract" (in our case the Listing Contract or Buyer's Agreement) "may, in appropriate cases, affect a Hedley Byrne claim relying on pre-contractual representations ..." UNQUOTE.

TORT LIABILITY on the basis of **"HEDLEY BYRNE & Co. v. HELLER & PARTNERS LTD."** (1964) A.C. 465 (H.L.) is discussed in "SLEIGHTHOLM v. EAST KOOTENAY REALTY LTD." (1999-02-18), B.C.S.C. 8929

(C) The test for negligent misrepresentation in the context of pre-contractual representations is found in **"KINGU v. WALMAR VENTURES LTD."** (1986) 10 B.C.L.R. (2nd) 15.

(3) As the "Agency Relationship" is with the REAL ESTATE COMPANY and NOT with the individual Agent, the Principal (Seller/Buyer) also becomes vicariously liable for the misconduct of all other licensees working for that Company, albeit of course, only for wrongs committed in the course of that particular Principal's business.

(4) Whereas some may consider this point to be far fetched and/or unimportant, **for the sake of completeness,** common honesty would require that this also should be disclosed **in order to truly achieve "INFORMED CONSENT."**

(5) Whereas Agency Disclosure complaints by themselves may be rare, they are usually attached to other complaints: e.g. breach of fiduciary duties, misrepresentation, negligence etc.

(6) TO SUMMARIZE:
An agency relationship which exists between the Clients and the Realtor

- **must be clearly understood and consented to**
- must be **in writing**
- if there is **any material change** in the agency relationship during the course of a transaction then the Realtor must disclose it IN WRITING.

In the SELECTION of a Realtor the future Clients' concerns are:
- to find a professional who will assist them in achieving their real estate goals.
- who is compatible and with whom they can communicate easily and properly.
- Who is experienced and knowledgeable enough to keep them out of any legal and other troubles.
- Who is familiar with the local Real Estate Market.
- Who is willing to work hard enough
  - to sell their house and/or
  - to find them the right house and
  - who is a skilful negotiator so that they will get the most value for their (hard earned) money.

Many Clients are not particularly interested in a dry, lengthy and convoluted legal lecture about "Agency."

AGENCY RELATIONSHIP WITH THE SELLER.

(I) The Listing Broker will work for the Seller.

(II) DISCLOSURE of the Listing Broker's SERVICES.

(1) This is best achieved by "packaging" them in an easy to understand list of benefits:
- **what the Realtor will do for the Sellers,**
- **how he proposes to go about it and**
- **how he will protect them from problems.**

(2) **The Listing Broker's OBJECTIVE** is to obtain for the Owner/Seller
- the HIGHEST amount of money
- in the SHORTEST possible time and
- with the LEAST amount of inconvenience.

The following points can be summarized in the form of a printed brochure or hand-out presentation kit:

(3) **PRELIMINARY SERVICES OFFERED.**
- The Listing Salesperson will prepare a Comparative MARKET ANALYSIS to
  - arrive at a realistic Market Value
  - and to be able to assist the Sellers in determining an attractive Asking

Price.
- He will discuss with the Sellers all favourable and other items about the property which may have a bearing on the Market Value and saleability of the property.
- He will give to the Sellers a list of "Things to do to improve the marketability of the property."
- He will discuss with the Sellers **the procedure how the property will be shown:**
  - all showings will be "by appointment only."
  - Efforts will be made that all showings should be at the convenience of the Sellers.
  - When making the appointment to show the house, the Sellers will be given sufficient time to prepare the property for the showing.
  - The Sellers will be asked to save all business cards from Realtors who have shown the house so that the Listing Salesperson can follow-up and obtain the prospective Buyers' reactions.
- The Listing Salesperson will discuss the use of a Lock Box on the house.
- Before the Sellers sign the Listing Contract, the Realtor should/will
  - go over all major points in the document,
  - answer readily and completely all questions the Sellers may have and
  - address all other concerns which may come up.

(4) **RESEARCH.**
   (a) The Listing Salesperson will measure all rooms and calculate the floor area of the house.
   (b) He will photograph the house (front and back).
   (c) He will take extensive notes during a thorough inspection of the property.
   (d) The Sellers will be asked to execute a "Property Condition Disclosure Statement." (This is not a warranty but merely states what the Sellers know about the property).
   (e) He will discuss with the Sellers all **observable (patent) defects** of the house.
   (f) He will discuss with the Sellers all **latent (hidden and not readily observable) defects** which must be disclosed to a prospective Buyer.
   (g) He will verify
   - the lot size.
   - Any easements and Right-of-Ways.
   - The zoning (e.g. a prospective Buyer will have to be advised if the building is "non-conforming").
   - The age of the house.
   - The existence and locations of the sanitary and storm sewers.
   - If the sanitary sewer is hooked up to the house.
   - If there is a septic tank then to ensure that it is functioning properly and that it has been maintained regularly.
   - If the property is on a well then details about the adequacy of the water

produced, the depth of the well, a "well certificate," the quality of the water etc.
- If the Sellers have obtained the necessary municipal permits and inspections for all major renovations.
- The current property taxes
- and any outstanding unpaid tax balances (this is necessary in order to calculate correctly the Net Sales Proceeds for the Seller when an offer is received).
- The current Property Assessment figures.
  - Obtain **in writing** details of **all financial encumbrances:**
    - outstanding mortgage balances,
    - monthly mortgage payments,
    - interest rates,
    - mortgage renewal dates,
    - prepayment privileges,
    - if the mortgage is assumable or not (with or without qualifying)
    - amount of any pay-out penalty,
    - administrative charges by the Lending Institution for preparing the pay-out.
  - **As soon as the Lending Institution's reply is received a photocopy thereof should be given to the Sellers.**

(h) The Listing Salesperson will enquire about
- the distance to transportation,
- the distance to elementary and high schools,
- the distance to shopping,
- the distance to various churches etc.,
- the monthly cost of heat and light.

(5) **MARKETING**.
   (a) A "For Sale" sign will be placed in the most visible spot in front of the house.
   (b) "House for Sale" arrows will be placed at strategic intersections in the neighbourhood.
   (c) The Listing will be submitted promptly to the Real Estate Board for publication and circulation.
   (d) The listing will also be published on the Internet.
   (e) With the Sellers' agreement the house will be scheduled
      - for the Office Tour and
      - for the Multiple Listing Tour. **The "Tour Average Estimated Selling Price" will NOT be disclosed to the other Realtors attending the Tours because**
         - they are potential Buyer's Agents
         - of the fiduciary obligation of "confidentiality."
   (f) The Listing Salesperson will discuss with the SELLERS the "Tour Average Estimated Selling Price" and possibly suggest a price adjustment.

(g) The Listing Salesperson will promote the house
- to other sales associates and
- mail out "Just Listed" cards in the immediate neighbourhood (because somebody might have a friend or relative who may want to live nearby).

(h) The property will be advertised in the local newspaper(s).
- The wording of the ads and the pictures of the house will be changed periodically.
- If the house contains unauthorized accommodation (e.g. an illegal basement suite) then the Realtor has to obtain the Sellers' permission **in writing** before he can mention it in the ad (e.g. "mortgage helper").

(i) **The Sellers will receive a copy of each ad placed.**

(j) After each showing the Listing Salesperson will follow up and will report to the Sellers the results and comments (favourable and otherwise) made by all prospective Buyers who have seen the house.

(k) To facilitate a sale, information about possible new financing will be obtained.

(l) The Listing Salesperson will keep the Sellers up-to-date of
- any fluctuations in the Real Estate Market,
- changes in interest rates and
- anything else which may have a bearing on the Market Value of the house.

(m) By mutual agreement the Listing Salesperson will hold an "Open House" and report the results to the Sellers.

(n) The Listing Salesperson will review periodically with the Sellers the saleability of the house.

(6) **OFFERS.**
The Listing Salesperson may NOT discuss with or disclose to other Realtors or prospective Buyers (or anybody else)
- **details of previously received UNACCEPTABLE offers**
- **or details of any collapsed sales** on the property.

(a) The Listing Salesperson will carefully review all offers received:
- to ensure that it is an enforceable contract,
- to ensure that there are no ambiguous terms (to avoid possible misunderstandings),
- to ensure that the Sellers understand all terms and risks (if any) in the contract.
- To ensure that latent defects (if there are any) are disclosed to the Buyer(s) in writing (by way of "acknowledgment" clauses: "The Buyers hereby acknowledge that they have been informed of …..").

(b) He will discuss the offer with the Sellers and assist them in coming to a decision.

(c) The Realtor must suggest to the Sellers to **obtain legal advice** in case there are areas in the contract which are beyond the Realtor's expertise and/or competence.

(d) He will deal with and help draft counter offers.
(e) In case the Listing Salesperson obtains an offer from
- a Buyer of his own or
- if another Realtor from his office brings an offer

then the Realtor(s) will
- discuss with the Sellers and Buyers all aspects of the (disclosed) **"Limited DUAL AGENCY"** and
    - **obtain their written consent to it PRIOR to**
    - **the presentation of the offer and**
    - **any ensuing negotiations:**
- **Unless authorized in writing to do so** the Realtor(s) will not disclose any personal information of either the Buyer or the Seller.
- The Realtor(s) will deal with the Buyers and Sellers **IMPARTIALLY**.
- **The Realtor(s) will not disclose**
    - the Buyers' motivation to buy or
    - the Sellers' reasons for selling.
    - That the Buyers may be willing to pay a higher price than what is shown in their offer.
    - That the Sellers are or may be willing to accept a price lower than what is shown in the Listing Contract.

(f) In case of receiving several offers simultaneously from several different Realtors the Listing Salesperson will adhere to the practice of **how to present MULTIPLE OFFERS as it is recommended by the local Real Estate Board.**

(7) AFTER SALE SERVICE.
(a) The Listing Salesperson will cooperate to make the house available for
- the Buyers' Certified Home Inspector
- the Buyer's Surveyor (if a survey is required) and
- the Lending Institute's Appraiser.

(b) The Listing Salesperson will **keep track of deadlines and subject removals.**

(c) If the offer says that the Buyers' deposit will be tendered "within 24/48 hours of acceptance," then the Listing Salesperson's duty is to **verify with the Selling Salesperson that this has indeed taken place.**

(d) The Selling Salesperson (Buyer's Agent) has an obligation to notify the Listing Salesperson and the Sellers if the Buyer's deposit cheque was returned as "NSF" (insufficient funds).

(e) In such a case, the Listing Salesperson will discuss with his Clients (the Sellers) what their options are:
- either grant the Buyers a short period of time to rectify the situation or alternatively
- the Contract of Purchase and Sale may be treated as being at an end.

(f) When the Listing Salesperson receives any "notice" on behalf of his Clients

(e.g. subject removal or a 72-hour clause notice) he will communicate this information immediately to his Clients.
(g) When all subject-to clauses have been removed (the sale has become "firm") then the Listing Salesperson will
- place a "Sold" sign on the property and
- immediately report the sale to the Real Estate Board.
- If required, he will assist the Clients in selecting (from a list of several lawyers) a suitable lawyer who will act on their behalf to take care of the required formal documentation.
- Will prepare and send the necessary information and instructions to the Conveyancing Solicitor.

(h) The Listing Salesperson will give to the Sellers a list of "What to do and People To Notify when moving."
(i) If the house will be vacant for a period of time before Possession Date, then the L.S. should remind the Sellers to arrange for a special insurance coverage.
(j) If required, the Listing Salesperson should be willing to attend with his Clients when they are signing the final transfer documents in their lawyer's office.
(k) The Listing Salesperson will arrange for the transfer of the house keys to the Buyers or their Agent.
(l) If keys are to be released before the Possession Date then the Sellers must **obtain legal advice (because of legal and insurance ramifications).** The keys can only be released when **so authorized in writing by the Sellers.**

AGENCY RELATIONSHIP WITH THE BUYER.

After having made the required agency disclosures, a prudent Buyer's Agent will endeavour to obtain from the Buyer a written Agency Contract (employment and fee agreement) which is the equivalent of and/or similar to what a Listing Contract is with a Seller.

A Realtor can work with a Buyer without such a contract, as long as he realizes that
- he is not protected because the Buyer might be working with several other Realtors at the same time and
- the situation is the same as if he was showing an unlisted property.
- He might attract fiduciary duties without having anything in writing confirming his employment.

In case there is no signed "Buyer's Contract" then the acknowledgement of the agency relationship will be shown only on the Contract of Purchase and Sale.

About the Principal's Vulnerability - Part I

Are you "Disclosing" or "explaining" Agency?
The Principal's VICARIOUS LIABILITY.

The Defendant in the expensive litigation of **"HODGKINSON v. SIMMS"** (B.C. Court of Appeal, Date 1992-03-16, Docket CA 011048 (65 B.C.L.R. [2d] 264) and Supreme Court of Canada [Date 1994-09-30], Docket 23033 (3 SCR 377) **owed a duty of PROPER DISCLOSURE of MATERIAL FACTS which were adverse to the Plaintiff.** Had the Plaintiff been aware of the full nature and extent of these facts, his decisions and actions may have been different.
This law case should be of interest to all Realtors who are disclosing Agency to the public.

In 1990 Canadian Real Estate Boards through CREA decided to attempt voluntary "soft" (verbal) agency disclosure. The experiment failed because the large majority of Realtors did not participate. Since January 1, 1995 Article 3 of CREA's Code of Ethics requires written and receipted agency disclosure. This is done during the first substantial or meaningful contact with the Client-to-be.

In spite of the fact that Realtors have taken courses about "Agency Disclosure" and "Agency Duties" it is an open secret that many still have problems understanding and dealing with the intricacies of "Agency." The reasons for these problems are many. Little thought, if any, may have been given to the following practical problems:

(I) There is a difference between **"disclosing"** agency and **"explaining"** agency.
   (a) While the Realtor is **"disclosing" agency he is merely reciting the nature of his services and duties**.
   (b) On the other hand the average member of the public (and possibly also many a Realtor) may often be under the understandable but erroneous impression that the Realtor is **"explaining EVERY aspect" of Agency**. This incorrect impression may be created by talk about legal matters like fiduciary duties.
   (c) Seeing that the future Client makes decisions on his legal and practical interests by relying to a certain degree on what he hears from the Future Fiduciary (namely the Realtor) **the Customer should be entitled to have a reasonable expectation of being told EVERYTHING HE needs to know about "Agency."**
   (d) If inadvertent misunderstandings and non-disclosure of material facts take place during the disclosure process, then it is doubtful that the future Client is giving his "INFORMED CONSENT" before entering into the agency relationship.

(II) Specifically what MATERIAL facts are often NOT mentioned during the disclosure process? Please consider the following:
   (a) Does the average member of the public or for that matter does the average

rank-and-file Realtor realize that their Agency relationship is a TWO-WAY street?

(b) How many Realtors - when they talk about Agency - do inform their future "Principals/Masters" that they - even if innocent - will become VICARIOUSLY LIABLE for the Realtor's (Agent - Servant) misconduct (e.g. fraud) and neglects committed in the course of the Principal's business, even though only committed for the AGENT's benefit (e.g. the earning of a commission).

(1) See **"Orris v. Collings"** (1929), 36 O.W.N. 172; varied 37 O.W.N. 233 (C.A.);

(2) See **"Evetts v. Taylor"** (1925), 28 O.W.N. 57: if the Principal's behaviour is blameless, then he in turn may be entitled to be indemnified by the Agent.

(3) See **"Scholl et al v. Royal Trust Corp. of Canada"** 1986, 40 C.C.L.T. 113 (Ont. H.C.). The Seller's Agent misrepresented the presence of UFFI foam insulation to the Buyer, who then successfully sued everybody for damages; the Sellers were entitled to be indemnified by the fraudulent Agent.

(4) See **"Pavenham v. Sladen & Sutton Group Resource Realty,"** BCSC, Docket # S5182, Sept. 11, 1997 where a house was sold which was not habitable.

(5) See **"Tan v. Eng"** (1990-12-20) BCSC. C872273 Here the Court found that the Defendant Sellers vicariously through their Realtor had a duty to disclose certain items to the inexperienced Plaintiff-Buyers (e.g. Non-conforming zoning, the Municipality's long-term intent of acquiring the property for public purpose; all of which affected the market value of the property).

(c) Seeing that the Agency Relationship is with the Real Estate COMPANY (and not the individual Salesperson), **the Principal would also become vicariously responsible for the misconduct of all other salespersons who are working for that firm (all of whom may be total strangers to him)** albeit of course, only for wrongs committed in the course of that particular Principal's business.

(d) The point is this:
An Agency Relationship should be built on mutual trust which surely requires full and candid disclosure of everything, warts and all. Although the subject of Agency is brought up BEFORE an agency relationship is established **shouldn't the Realtor have at least a moral obligation of candour** to disclose to the Beneficiary (the Customer who will be the future "Principal") his vulnerability, namely his vicarious liability/responsibility for the actions of the Fiduciary (the Realtor who will be the future "Servant")?

(e) This very subject was addressed in **"QUEEN v. COGNOS INC."** Supreme Court of Canada, 1 SCR 87, Date 1993-01-21, Docket 22004. The Court found that
- "the respondent and its representative" (in our case this would be the Real Estate Company and its salesperson)
- **"owed a DUTY OF CARE to the appellant"** (in our case the Seller/Buyer)

- "during the course of the hiring interview" (in our case the Agency Disclosure prior to entering into a Listing Contract or a Buyer's Agreement)
- "to exercise such reasonable care as the circumstances required to ensure that the representations made were accurate and not misleading.
- This duty of care is distinct from and additional to the duty of common honesty existing between negotiating parties ... while a subsequent contract" (in our case the Listing Contract or Buyer's Agreement) "may, in appropriate cases, affect a Hedley Byrne claim relying on pre-contractual representations ...."

Tort liability on the basis of **"Hedley Byrne & Co. v. Heller & Partners Ltd."** (1964) A.C. 465 (H.L.) is briefly discussed in **"Sleightholm v. East Kootenay Realty Ltd."** B.C. Supreme Court, Date 1999-02-18, Docket 8929.

(III) Thus the crux of the problem is this:
When Realtors are disclosing, discussing and/or explaining Agency are they making unwittingly, inadvertently or unintentionally - during that talk (the interview prior to being hired) - certain representations to their future Principals which are incomplete, inaccurate or misleading in a negligent manner?

(a) The test for negligent misrepresentation in the context of pre-contractual representations is found in **"KINGU v. WALMAR VENTURES LTD."** B.C.C.A., (1986), 10 B.C.L.R. (2nd) 15.

(b) Whereas Agency Disclosure complaints by themselves are rare, they are usually attached to other complaints: e.g. breach of fiduciary duties, misrepresentation, negligence, etc.

About the Principals's Vulnerability - Part II
The SELLERS' DUTIES and obligations.

In Part I we have touched on some practical problems in connection with "disclosing" Agency relationships.

Here are a few more:
(1) Due to
- different levels of experience,
- lack of adequate training,
- business and time pressure,
- some Realtors' frustration and resentment of Agency in general or
- just plain because of a lack of interest **the average Realtor may not be the ideal lecturer to expound on a complicated legal subject in a concise way.**

(2) Whereas the average consumer may politely endure for a while the Realtor's torrent of words about "disclosure," eventually their minds will impatiently wander ahead to their overriding priorities, which is the listing, selling or buying of a property.

What consumers do want to hear is
- an assurance that their Realtor is trustworthy and
- experienced enough to protect them from all problems;
- that with the Realtor's help they will achieve their real estate goals and
- in the process they will receive good value for their money.

(3) Let's be frank: if a discussion of Agency would include a full explanation of the Principal's obligations, then would the average member of the public really be inclined or willing to become a Realtor's PRINCIPAL? If the Client would know before-hand what he could learn later on during a law suit, would he insist on a "PRINCIPAL/AGENT ["personal representation"] Agency relationship?

A partial quote from Part I's **"Hodgkinson v. Simms"** law case may shed some light on this problem: Partial QUOTE: "The language used by the Judges in **"International Corona Resources Ltd. v. Lac Minerals Ltd."** Date 1989-08-11 Docket 20571 Supreme Court of Canada 2 SCR 574 suggest that a fiduciary duty will not be imposed unless the victim is in the hands of the alleged fiduciary and, if not at his mercy, is seriously disadvantaged and unable to protect himself."

(4) On the other hand would a Realtor (working on a commission basis) be willing to take the chance of loosing business by frightening and/or possibly antagonizing the average (often anyway already apprehensive) Sellers with such blunt, full and candid disclosure?

In this respect the Reader may have heard about an Alaskan Realtor who unwisely had the courage of saying during a Court hearing that "following statutes regarding agency disclosure was impractical." Of course, the judge promptly ruled against her. ("Columbus v. Mehner")

(5) Sometimes Agency has not been fully explained to the public because the information being circulated to the public is INCOMPLETE.
For example:
the commonly used hand-out pamphlet entitled "Working with a Realtor" does not mention the Principal's vicarious liability and his other obligations.

(6) Furthermore sometimes Agency has not been fully explained to a consumer because of the average Realtor's unfortunate IGNORANCE about various other aspects of Agency. For one it would appear that the Rank-and-File Realtors' training occasionally has been incomplete about
- **the various types of agency** (e.g. Single Agency, No Agency, Transaction Broker/Facilitator) and
- next to nothing about the Principal's obligations and involvement.

(7) In this connection here are **a few more obligations of the Seller/Principal** which are noteworthy:

The duty of performing the terms of the Listing Contract with his Agent/Servant which includes:

Referring any potential Buyers to his Realtor.

(a) See **"BLOCK BROS. REALTY LTD. v. BALWINDER SINGH RAI"** B.C. Supreme Court, Date 1990-02-12, Docket F884203 where the Defendant Seller entered into a sham rental agreement with a Buyer in order to avoid having to pay a commission. The Realtor got his commission.

(b) See **"MOLLOY PEMBERTON AGENCIES LTD. v. MERRICK,"** B.C. Supreme Court, Date 1990-04-18, Docket # 88023 Powell River Registry.
Where the owner - 5 days before expiry of the listing refused to give a potential Buyer's name and phone number to his Realtor and sold the property to this Buyer on the day after the listing had expired. The Judge ruled that the owner's obligation was not only to tell the licensee of an enquiry, but to provide sufficient information to enable the licensee to meet with the prospective Buyer. The failure by the owner to do this was a breach of the Listing Contract. The Realtor's right to recover damages depended on the Judge being satisfied that on a balance of probabilities, the licensee would have been able to bring into being a binding contract, if he had been given the name and telephone number of the Buyer. The Realtor was entitled to damages in the amount of the commission.

(c) See **"WOLSTENCROFT REALTY CORP. v. ASHCROFT HOLDINGS LTD."** (1984), 33 R.P.R. 206, BCSC
The Realtor was entitled to damages for the Defendant's failure (breach of the Listing Contract) to refer all enquiries and offers to the Agent.

(d) See **"SMALLEY AGENCIES LTD. v. HILL-EVEREST HOLDINGS LTD."** Manitoba Court of Queens Bench (1992), 80 Man. R (2d) 56, (1992) M.J. No. 217, (Q.I.) (Q.B.) affd. (1993) M. J. No. 74 (Q.L.)(C.A.) 4 W.W.R. 233
The Listing Contract required the Seller to forward to the Agent all inquiries and offers; meaning that only the agent had the right to effect a sale during the listing period, even to the exclusion of the owner.

(2) **To pay a commission once a firm and subject-free contract has been entered into between himself and a Buyer who is ready, willing and able to complete.**

(a) See **"KELLNER v. STICKLAND,"** BC Court of Appeal, Date Sept. 25, 1998, Docket CA 023249
The prospective Client should be informed as to his potential obligation to pay a commission given the form of the wording contained in the Listing Contract **in the event of default, whether by the Buyer or by the Seller.**

(b) See **"DAVIDSON v. MILLER,"** BCSC, Nanaimo Registry, Docket 35207, January 8, 2003. It deals with a valid commission claim in a case where the Client had died before the completion date (and the executor of the estate refused to complete).

(3) (a) **A Principal cannot avoid paying a commission by holding off closing of a sale until the listing has expired;**
 (b) **The Seller cannot act in complicity with a Buyer to deprive the Realtor of his commission; e.g.**
- to ask his Realtor for an cancellation of the Listing Contract in order to be able to sell the property privately and without paying a commission. Taking the property off the market is an INDULGENCE by the agent to forego the active pursuit of a sale in keeping with the Seller's wishes, but it does not necessarily amount to a termination of the agreement.
- **To collusively conspire with the Buyer to outwait the Listing Contract.**

(4) When the Realtor's EFFORTS were the "effective cause of sale." (also the For Sale SIGN, Advertising, TV etc.).
 (a) See **"Re/Max CENTRE CITY REALTY v. John and Helena FRIESEN"** Provincial Court of B.C., Date 2002-06-19, Docket SM 14266
 (b) See **"HOMELIFE OKANAGAN REALTY INC. v. GALVAGNO,"** BCSC, Date 1994-11-07, Docket 9242

On the other hand the training of Realtors has focused to a large extent on their fiduciary duties. No doubt the future Client should know what the Realtor's fiduciary duties are.

However, such disclosure of fiduciary duties can also be a surprisingly detailed road map of how Realtors could be sued in case they misstep (fail in their obligations).

Regrettably sundry dissatisfied Clients-from-hell will find this information eminently useful when lodging a frivolous, but free-for-the asking complaint with the local Real Estate Board.

As the fiduciary duties also include full disclosure of all pertinent facts a future Client should be entitled to learn that there are other forms of working with a Realtor which may be more attractive and less worrisome to him.

E.g. "no agency" instead of Single Agency. Being a "Non-Agent" (or Transaction Broker) does not mean watered down services, it means less liability all around. By eliminating an Agency relationship there is less liability for Realtors and none for the consumer (if he is not the Principal, then it follows that there can be no vicarious liability).

About the Principal's Vulnerability - Part III
INFORMATION ABOUT A TRANSACTION BROKER.

Agency in the form of "individual (personal) representation" to Buyers and Sellers provides **advocacy services**. In their efforts to justify their existence (and to earn their keep in the eyes of their respective Clients), a few Realtors have unfortunately taken to imitating opposing lawyers in Court.

Many a times harmonious and friendly cooperation between Realtors has been replaced by more or less open and confrontational advocacy.

When offers are presented in an atmosphere of suspicion, then
- artificial difficulties and
- legalistic stumbling blocks can be placed in the way of a sale.

Sadly, these type of Realtors don't even realize that their poor attitude and lack of cooperation with fellow Realtors are
- NOT doing their own Clients any favours,
- but may in fact be a breach of their fiduciary duties vis-a-vis their Principals.

With the advent of multiple offers in a super heated real estate market "advocacy" is often misused
- for the benefit of the Listing Salesperson and
- to the detriment of the Client (the Sellers) and
- to the detriment of other Co-Operating Brokers and their respective Clients.

On the other hand Transaction Brokers (No Agency) are the IMPARTIAL and NEUTRAL salespersons in the transaction (in some ways similar to a Consented Limited Dual Agency situation). They act more like a "Broker," a "go-between," a Facilitator and NOT as an "Agent" (in the true sense of the word).

Regardless of how fair and impartial a Realtor is endeavouring to be in a "Limited Dual Agency" situation, the fact remains that he is the ONLY person who knows ALL details about the Sellers and Buyers. He is the only person who knows all of the strengths and weaknesses of and all secret details about the contracting parties. As the Realtor gets paid his commission only upon effecting a sale and as he has a family to support, it is only natural and almost inadvertent that the Realtor will use (most likely subconsciously) all of the information he is privy to in order to nudge one or the other of the parties (or both) towards a compromise resulting in a sale. But achieving a meeting of the minds is part of his job as a "broker of deals" and this "nudging" may be alright
- as long as the Realtor doesn't high-pressure one of the parties into financial difficulties or some sort of other predicament.
- As long as he is doing his job fairly and impartially as a "mediator" between the parties

in order to facilitate a successful compromise leading to a mutually satisfactory sale.

There are other alternatives to a Limited Dual Agency:

(a) The Listing Salesperson remains the Seller's Agent and will treat the Buyer as a "Customer" (he gives "No-Agency" to the Buyer).
(b) The Realtor will act as a neutral Transaction Broker ("no agency" is given to the Seller at the time when the listing is taken AND "no agency" is given to the Buyer during the transaction).

INFORMATION about a TRANSACTION BROKER (Facilitator)

- A Transaction Broker is a licensed real estate salesperson who is NOT giving "individual, personalized representation" to the party he is dealing with.
- Contrary to "Single Agency"
  - there is NO Master/Servant relationship.
  - There are NO fiduciary duties.
  - The Customer is NOT the Principal and therefore he has no vicarious liability.
  - **A Transaction Broker (a Realtor giving "NO agency") works "WITH" the Customer instead of "FOR" the Client.**
  - The public is fully protected by the Realtors' Code of Ethics and by the LAW.
  - A Transaction Broker can give out public information about comparable listed and sold properties (just like any other Realtor).
  - A Transaction Broker can select and show properties (just like any other Realtor).
  - A Transaction Broker can prepare and has an ethical obligation to promptly present offers and counter-offers. (Just like any other Realtor).

Here are some popular MISCONCEPTIONS about "No-Agency" and the Transaction Broker:

(1) A Transaction Broker is illegal or unethical.
   NOT true:
   - he has a valid real estate license same as all other Realtors.
   - He must adhere to the Realtors' Code of Ethics (same as all other members of the Real Estate Boards).
   - He cannot break the law.

(2) A Transaction Broker works only for a minimum commission. Realtors must have fiduciary duties in order to be entitled to a (full) commission.
   Both statements are NOT true.
   - Acting as a Transaction Broker does NOT mean rendering watered down services.
   - The amount of the commission is NOT based on the type of Agency

(representation).
- The commission is negotiated between a Realtor and the Consumer and
- its amount should be based on the Realtor's experience, skills, resources, quality of service, hard work etc.
- What could fiduciary duties possibly have to do with the amount of the commission?
- Fiduciary duties are legal obligations and liabilities, similar to the Principal's vicarious liability.

(3) The Client doesn't get his money's worth unless the Realtor "represents" him and "extends to him fiduciary duties."
NOT true.
- What have "representation" and fiduciary duties got to do with a Realtor's quality and quantity of service?
- The Consumer gets his money's worth after the Realtor has spent money, time and effort to successfully conclude a sale.
- If there is no sale then the Seller will pay to the Realtor NOTHING regardless of fiduciary duties and what kind of "representation" there was.
What a bargain for the public!

(4) A Transaction Broker cannot advise about Market Value.
NOT true.
- Market Value is determined by Buyers and Sellers and not by Realtors.
- A Transaction Broker (same as all Realtors) has a legal and ethical duty to provide accurate and honest answers about the Seller's property. The same applies in the case of a Buyer.

SUMMARY:
(a) Who can become a Transaction Broker? Everyone of you, because it is YOUR decision in what sort of capacity (liability) you want to conduct your business.
(b) With the possible exception of your employer (the Real Estate Company which you are working for) you don't have to ask for anybody's permission to act as a Transaction Broker.
(c) Is Transaction Brokerage an alternative to Single Agency? YES.
(d) Is Transaction Brokerage for everyone? No. There is nothing to stop anybody from continuing to work as a Buyer's Agent or a Seller's Agent.
(e) It is only a question of pre-contractual honesty:
- informing (disclosing to) the future Principal of his vicarious liability and other (Listing) contractual obligations.
- If the Consumer is not a "Principal" then it follows that there can be no vicarious liability on his part.
- In the case of "No Agency" the Realtor becomes a Transaction Broker and there is less liability for him.

The Property Condition Disclosure Statement - Part I

The Realtors' Code of Ethics requires that:
- Realtors must **discover all facts** about any property which they are handling in the course of their business.
- They have to **independently verify** all data and information in order to avoid possible errors, misrepresentations of various kinds and possible concealment of pertinent facts.
- **The level of care** which they have to exercise is that which a reasonably prudent and competent Realtor would employ.

They are required to do this in order
- to protect their Clients' interests.
- Simultaneously, Realtors also protect themselves from expensive legal actions.

One of the ways of fulfilling the above obligations is for the LISTING BROKER to ask his Seller to complete a preprinted form which will disclose the current condition his property is in. Such a representation (often in the form of a questionnaire) which the SELLER COMPLETES, is called the Seller's "PROPERTY CONDITION DISCLOSURE STATEMENT."

In areas where there is no such a report available individual Realtors may wish to prepare one. Alternatively they could approach their local realty association to issue one.

Reasons for the use of a Seller's Information Questionnaire:

(a) as time goes by, people sometimes forget what they have said. A PCDS will eliminate any contentious "I said-he said" controversies later on.
(b) In case of a disagreement later on, a prior executed written statement - signed by ALL contracting PARTIES - will eliminate a lot of unnecessary excitement, stress, frustration, waste of time and costly legal fees.
(c) Realtors may elect to incorporate the PCDS as an addendum into the Contract for Purchase and Sale.
(d) **Additional benefits for the Realtor are:**
- the more a Realtor knows about a property, the better is he equipped to talk about it intelligently and with authority and
- the better is he able to overcome objections as they may arise and the better to deal with the Client's concerns in a timely manner.

As a PRECAUTION please note the following:

(1) The PCDS should be completed by the Seller in his own handwriting. Instead of a "check mark" he should write his initials into the appropriate box. ("yes," "no,"

"don't know," "doesn't apply").
(2) All questions should be answered by the Seller himself.
(3) Any person (e.g the Listing Salesperson) who assists the Sellers in the completion of this form in any way should take great care that the owners understand ALL questions and that they answer them COMPLETELY and TRUTHFULLY.
(4) If "language" (English or French) is a problem, then the services of a competent Certified Translator should be engaged. The reason for this is as follows:
(5) Any well meaning Realtor who happens to be able to speak the Seller's primary language should realize that his "helpful translation assistance" can and will expose him (the Realtor) to a certain amount of legal responsibility.
(6) The Seller is legally responsible for **the ACCURACY of the information** in the PCDS. The reason for this is because the Buyer may be relying on this information which in turn may motivate him to buy the property.
(7) The Seller must answer **all questions not only ACCURATELY but also COMPLETELY;** and this information is to be given FREELY.
(8) For that reason a Seller cannot
   (a) hold back some of the information by answering a question with "I do not know";
   (b) or avoiding (for him) potential problems by
      • giving only a partial or evasive answer
      • or by saying "This doesn't apply"
      • **if in reality he DOES know the answer.**

The Sellers are obliged to disclose to a Buyer ALL KNOWN FACTS which may materially or adversely affect the SALEABILITY and VALUE of the property - especially the ones WHICH ARE NOT READILY OBSERVABLE. This includes recent repairs of a serious defect; even if the situation has been fully remedied it is best to come clean and make full disclosure. See **"Curtin v. Blewett,"** 28 R.P.R. (3d) 115, November 14, 1999, BCSC, Kamloops" which dealt with the recurrence of termites infestation, after it had been remedied before.

(9) The information provided by the Sellers must be upon their BEST INFORMATION and BELIEF and KNOWLEDGE.
(10) **To avoid future problems or misunderstandings** any Buyer should be made aware of the following:
   (a) The PCDS is NOT a guarantee or warranty of any kind.
   (b) Nor is the PCDS a substitute for a building inspection
   (c) The PCDS merely sets out answers to motivate the Buyer to make further enquiries about potential concerns which he may have. In **"Arsenault v. Pederson"** (1996) BCJ No. 1029 (SC)" the Judge ruled that the Sellers merely said what they knew about the property.
   (d) **The Buyers should keep in mind that the Sellers are not experts in building construction and that their knowledge of some defects or facts may be incomplete.**
   (e) If the Buyers are not satisfied with or do not wish to rely on the Seller's written

declaration, then the Realtor should advise them to avail themselves of the services of **an Independent Professional or an Accredited Home Inspection Service.**

(f) If the Buyer wishes to rely on the opinion of somebody else (e.g. a relative or friend), then he will do so on his own peril.

(11) Some Sellers who may rightfully refuse to complete and sign a PCDS are EXECUTORS in an Estate Sale: most likely none of them has ever lived in the house and therefore, they would be reluctant to sign such a statement.

(12) ABSENTEE LANDLORDS of rented properties may also have never lived in the property; but if they are conscientious Landlords or if they have a Property Manager handling the rental, then they should be aware of any defects or outstanding repairs. For that reason they should consider completing a declaration about the state of the property.

THE FOLLOWING ARE POINTS OF CONCERN dealing with HEALTH, SAFETY, ENVIRONMENTAL AND LEGAL MATTERS which should be addressed in a Seller's Report:

(1) **THE LAND:**
Is the land or any immediate neighbouring property
  (a) subject to flooding?
  (b) Are there any drainage problems?
  (c) Is there a Municipal storm drain system in place?
  (d) If there is none, then are there ditches and who will maintain them?
  (e) What is the quality of the soil?
  (f) Are there any soil STABILITY problems due to fill, settling, movement or the lay of the land (e.g. a steep hillside)?

(2) **THE SEWER SYSTEM:**
  (a) Is the house connected to a Municipal sanitary sewer system?
  (b) If the sanitary sewer is not connected to the house, then is it available on the street or in the area?
  (c) If yes, then what will it cost to bring the sewer to the property line?
  (d) What will it cost to bring the sewer from the property line to the house and to hook it up to the house?

(3) **If there is a SEPTIC SYSTEM,** then
  (a) was it properly installed?
  (b) When was the septic tank last serviced and/or pumped out?
  (c) Is the septic tank leaking? Are there any backup or other problems?
  (d) Is the topography of the septic field suitable?
  (e) Is the septic field contaminating nearby wells?
  (f) Are there any other health or environmental concerns with the septic tank or the septic drainage field?

The Property Condition Disclosure Statement - Part I

(4) **DOMESTIC WATER SUPPLY.**
   (a) Is the house connected to a public (Municipal) water supply?
   (b) If the source of the domestic water supply is a WELL, then:
   - What type of well is it? Surface (Artesian) or a "drilled" well? If the well is drilled, then how deep is it? Does it have a SUBMERSIBLE PUMP?
   - **Is a recent (current) WELL CERTIFICATE available?**
   - When was the well last checked for safety and what was the test result?
   - What is the purity (quality) of the drinking water?

NOTE: properties out in the country (e.g. farms, recreational properties etc.) may have a water system which does not have **an adequate filtration system** which is the most effective protection against a hardy water-borne parasite called **cryptosporidium** (which is resistant to the common chlorine treatment). This parasite is usually spreads through the feces of (infected) wild animals or possibly through animal husbandry. In healthy people this parasite can cause stomach cramps and diarrhea. It can be fatal for people whose immune system is compromised by HIV or AIDS, or people who are taking immune suppressing medication for organ transplants; or for persons undergoing cancer treatments.

- What is the potability of the water?
- Are there any health concerns emanating from a nearby septic field?
- What is the QUANTITY of water produced? How many gallons per minute does the well produce?
- During dry spells and in the summer months will the domestic well water supply be adequate for cooking, laundry, bathing and showering? E.g. The water supply may be "adequate" for a retired couple, but would not be adequate for a family with children.
- Is the water storage tank of adequate size?

(5) **THE BUILDING:**
   (a) What is the age and general condition of the house? Is there a lot of "deferred maintenance" (neglect)? Are there any problems with the plumbing, wiring or heating system?
   (b) Are there any guarantees or warranties (e.g. new construction).
   (c) Are there any termites or pests (e.g. mice) of any kind?
   (d) Is there any dryrot, mould and/or fungus in evidence?
   (e) **STRUCTURAL INFORMATION:**
   - Are there any structural problems?
   - Is the owner aware of any past or present **cracks, flaws, shifting, deterioration or movement in any of the walls or the foundation?**
   - Have there been **any structural changes or renovations** made during the current ownership?
   - Did any former owner make any structural changes, additions or alterations of any kind?

(f) If yes, then have the required Municipal permits been taken out and were Municipal inspections made? Have final Municipal approvals been received?

(g) Have there been any CORRECTIVE MEASURES TAKEN **for problems of a more serious nature?** (e.g. engineered footings to counteract excessive settlement due to unstable soil conditions; water leakage; damage caused to foundations and drains by encroaching tree roots). **Buyers' Agents should specifically ask the Sellers and the Listing Broker if there have been any recent major repairs which are not declared or shown in the PCDS.** See "**Dirksen v. Au**" (1996) BCJ No. 2738 (Prov. Ct.)" and "**Chamberlain v. Jenner**" (1997) BCJ No. 32164 (SC)."

(h) Has a **FINAL BUILDING INSPECTION** been done and has a **FINAL OCCUPANCY PERMIT** been issued?

(i) **INSULATION:**
   - What kind of insulation is in the walls and the ceiling? What is the "R" factor?
   - Does the building contain or has it ever contained urea formaldehyde foam insulation?
   - If yes, then when and by whom has the UFFI been removed? (NOTE: UFFI was used as insulation in some older type homes for a short period of time: approximately in the late 1970's to the early 1980's).
   - Has there ever been **asbestos insulation?**

(j) **BASEMENTS and CRAWL SPACE:**
   - Does the basement leak?
   - Has there ever been any dampness or accumulation of water or water leakage of any kind in the basement?
   - Is there any moisture, dampness or water accumulation in the crawl space?
   - Is there any dryrot in the crawl space?
   - Does the crawl space have a vapour barrier (heavy plastic sheet and gravel)?
   - Is the floor of the crawl space cemented?
   - Does the crawl space have sufficient ventilation?

(k) **What is the age and condition of the roof?** Does the roof leak? Are there any transferable guarantees in existence?
NOTE: See "**Ross v. Hobbis**" 27 R.P.R.(2nd) where the Sellers knew that their 4 year old roof was leaking, but lied to the Realtor and the Buyer. After having been successfully sued by the Buyer for the cost of roof repairs, the Sellers in turn tried (unsuccessfully) to collect damages from the Realtor (damages which originally had arisen out of their own fraudulent misrepresentation).

(l) What type of **PLUMBING** (pipes) is there? Are there any problems?
NOTE:
Before the 1950's "galvanized lines" were used for the water/heating distribution

lines. They were eventually replaced with copper or plastic.

For plumbing WASTE pipes (toilet, kitchen) usually cast iron was used until the mid-1950's when it was changed to copper. This in turn has been replaced in the late 1960's to plastic.

The age of toilets can sometimes be determined by looking into the inside of the water tank where the manufacturer may have stamped the date of issue.

- What is the age and condition of the **domestic hot water tank?**
- How is the water being heated? Gas or electric?
- What is the tank's size? How many gallons of water does it hold?
- Has the hot water tank been properly maintained? (e.g. periodic draining of the water)

(m) What type of **WIRING** is there?

NOTE:

Aluminum wiring was used from about the mid-1960's to roughly the late 1970's. Allegedly many homeowners were dissatisfied with it. The wiring had to be upgraded to accommodate today's standard of 100 amps service. The old "fuse box" was replaced by multibreaker circuits.

(n) What are the **inside walls and ceiling?**

NOTE: Plaster was used before the 1960's; it was replaced by drywall.

(6) **FIRE HAZARDS** from:

(a) **a free-standing wood burning stove OR fireplace:**

The Sellers should be advised that - if they have a wood burning stove or free-standing fireplace - which does not comply with the current applicable codes they should carry out the necessary repairs and/or renovations so that they do comply; OR, alternatively, they should remove the wood burning stove or free-standing fireplace PRIOR to the sale of the property. If these are a fire hazard, then the insurance company may refuse to insure the house.

(b) When was the last time that the flues have been cleaned out on any wood burning masonry fireplaces?

(7) **CURRENT ZONING REGULATIONS:**

(a) A building could be **"NON-CONFORMING"** in which case it will not be possible to rebuild it in its present form should the structure be destroyed by fire etc.

(b) Has the current owner ever been served with any kind of notice from the Municipality or some other public entity for bylaw infractions or outstanding fire and safety orders? (e.g. sprinkler system, smoke detectors, fire hazard from flammable material stored on the property).

(c) Some properties contain **secondary suites** which are contrary to current local zoning regulations. In some municipalities such illegal suites are not allowed. Has one of the neighbours in the immediate vicinity complained? Has the current owner been served with a notice from the Municipality to discontinue the illegal suite?

The sale of properties with **unauthorized accommodation** can create serious problems for the Seller, the Buyer AND the Realtor.

THE SELLER's PROBLEM:
If a Realtor **advertises** the existence of illegal accommodation then it is possible that Municipal Officials will read the ad and will take action requiring the current owner to remove the illegal suite. A cautious Realtor will **obtain in advance the Seller's CONSENT IN WRITING BEFORE** he publishes the first ad for such a property.

THE BUYER's PROBLEM:
Buyers of property with illegal accommodation may intend to depend on the revenue from the illegal suite to subsidize their monthly mortgage payments.
The Realtor must explain to all parties involved that such a **"MORTGAGE HELPER"** situation is fraught with financial risk. The Realtor should play it safe: his explanation should be **backed up by the insertion of an appropriate clause** into the Contract of Purchase and Sale stating that the **BUYERS HAVE BEEN MADE AWARE OF THE FACT** that the existence of such **UNAUTHORIZED ACCOMMODATION is subject to Municipal disapproval and consequently - at some future time - the INCOME from the suite could be DISCONTINUED.**
For that very reason some lending institutions in the past have refused to include such dubious rental income into their mortgage qualification calculations.

THE REALTOR's PROBLEM:
Realtors are required to deal fairly and honestly with ALL parties in a transaction. Failure to give the appropriate warning to his Sellers or Buyers will often result in disciplinary action or worse.

(8) Disclosure of **existing TENANCIES.**
   Is the entire building or any portion thereof presently rented out or leased? If yes, then what type of rental is it? (e.g. month-to-month rental or long-term lease). Is there a written rental contract and who pays for what? When does the lease expire?
(9) Do any of the appliances (fridge, stove, washer, dryer) belong to the tenants?
(10) Is any of the equipment in the house rented or leased?
   E.g. the alarm system.
(11) Is there an underground old oil storage tank buried on the property? Even if it was pumped out once upon a time, there could still have been a residue amount left at the bottom of the tank. The tank could be rusting and the residue oil may be leaking into the ground contaminating the soil.
(12) **LEGAL MATTERS:**
   (a) Is the Seller aware of any pending or proposed change in the neighbourhood which could adversely affect the desirability and/or the value of the subject property e.g. zoning changes, street alignments, road changes etc.

(b) Are there any current or threatened legal actions concerning the property: e.g. expropriation.
(c) Are there any encroachments, easements and/or Right-of-Ways?
(d) Are there any "covenants?"
(e) Are there any zoning violations, setback and sideyard violations?
(f) Are there any boundary line disputes? Fence disputes?
(g) Are there any Municipal Bylaws which forbid the deposit of fill of any kind on a vacant lot?

(13) **On STRATA PROPERTIES:**
(a) Does the information contained in the PCDS solely apply to the individual unit which is being sold OR is the information applicable to the entire complex?
(b) What is the monthly maintenance fee?
What is included in the maintenance fee?
Have all maintenance fees been paid in full and are they up to date?
Will there be a possible increase in the maintenance fees in the near future?
(c) What is the number of and location of PARKING STALLS for the unit?
Is additional parking available?
At what cost?
Is the underground parking "secured?"
(d) Is there a STORAGE LOCKER and where is it?
Is there additional storage available?
(e) Is there any pending litigation or claim against
- the unit being purchased OR
- the entire complex?
(f) Are there any problems with the swimming pool, hot tub, any of the exercise equipment, playground equipment etc.
(g) What restrictions are there? Rentals, pets, minimum age?
(h) (Because of the "leaky condo problem" in B.C.) the Sellers should SPECIFICALLY WARRANT that they are NOT aware of:
- any rotting or mould or fungi of any kind
- any water penetration problems or
- building envelope failures.
(i) There should be various **documents available:**
- **Current Bylaws;** are there any contemplated or pending bylaw amendments or resolutions which could materially influence or change the use of the unit(s) which the Buyer is considering to buy?
- Current House Rules (if any)
- The name, address and phone number of the **Strata Management Company** (including the name of the individual Manager and Caretaker)
- The names and phone numbers of the **Strata Council Members.**
- **Financial Statements** for at least the past 3 years
- **The Current Operating Budget.**

- Are there any current or contemplated special assessments?
- For the last 12 months …
  - **all Council Minutes of Meetings**
  - **all resolutions, extraordinary and otherwise**
  - **Annual General Meeting Minutes.**

NOTE:
(a) Realtors should give ALL pertinent documentation to the Buyers. This means that Realtors should NOT make arbitrary decisions by themselves about what the Buyer should see and what he shouldn't see.
(b) A LIST of these documents should appear on an ADDENDUM attached to and forming part of the Contract of Purchase and Sale together with the Buyers' ACKNOWLEDGEMENT that they have received the documents.
(c) It is not wise for a Realtor to review any financial statements with the Buyers; an accountant is more qualified to do that.
(d) In order to shift responsibility to the appropriate expert it is preferable that other documents should be reviewed by and with the Buyers' LAWYER.
(e) In a further ADDENDUM to the Contract of Purchase and Sale the Buyers should state that they have reviewed all documents and that they are satisfied with them.

Those who think that the completion of a thorough Seller's declaration about the property to be marketed is too much trouble and who wish to take short cuts instead, they should consider the following saying:

(1) "An ounce of prevention is worth a pound of cure." INITIALLY you may save some time and effort; but there is always the possibility that you will have to repent at leisure in Court later on; even if you are innocent you may still have to incur a huge bill for legal fees defending yourself.
(2) It will also be beneficial to keep the following in mind: "In order to conduct business seamlessly and to succeed, it is best to first line up all of your ducks in a row."

This simply means:
If you do your groundwork then you will be:
- prepared for all eventualities (objections).
- Able to talk with authority and conviction about the property you are selling.
- Able to write up an offer on the spot without having to take the risk that the Buyer might cool off while you are searching for an answer to one of his concerns.

The Property Condition Disclosure Statement - Part II

Generally speaking some of the BASIC PURPOSES of the PCDS are
- to raise possible questions and concerns in the mind of a Buyer
- Both the Seller and his Realtor (the Listing Broker) want to prevent **potential problems** resulting in **legal liability.**
- To document what was actually said (to avoid the retroactive situation of "he said - she said")

How does the existence of the PCDS effect the various parties?

(1) **The SELLER.**
   By completing the PCDS
   - the Seller is making a full and truthful written disclosure in plain language of what is known to him.
   - The Seller does **NOT give a warranty,**
   - nor is he required to warrant a certain condition or state of affairs: he merely says if he is or is not aware of any problems. See **"ARSENAULT v. PEDERSEN"** (April 26, 1996) B.C.J. No. 1026 (QL), BCSC New Westminster S021575.

Also see **"LIND v. MacLEOD"** BCSC (1997-10-20) Docket # 8389, BCJ No. 3134: The Seller Mrs. MacLeod stated in the PCDS that to the best of her knowledge the quantity and quality of the well water was adequate for her and her husband's needs (They were also away for a part of the year): "provides adequate water for small family, but not abundant." Because she did not represent that there was enough water for a larger family, the Plaintiffs' (Buyers') claim was dismissed with costs.

In **"CHAMBERLAIN v. JENNER"** BCSC (1997-01-23), Docket 32164 the Seller said in the PCDS that she was not aware of any moisture or water problems in the basement. A year prior to that some water had seeped onto the basement floor after a sprinkler system had been installed. She had the problem repaired and didn't experience any more difficulties. After the Buyer had moved in he discovered a puddle of water on the basement floor in May 1996 which may have been caused by the improper placement of concrete footings at one end of the house. At trial the Judge found that the Plaintiff had failed to show on a balance of probabilities that the Defendant had made a misrepresentation or that the Plaintiff had relied upon it (allegedly the Buyer had made his first offer before he saw the PCDS). The Judge further found that the Defendant was not aware of either the seepage (there had been no water problem for a year) nor was she aware of any structural problems. There was neither misrepresentation nor wrongful failure to disclose. The Plaintiff/Buyer had failed to make a reasonably careful inspection of the premises nor had the Buyer made any reasonably careful inquiries (see **"ROBERTS v. CORRIGAL"** (1993) 84 BCLR (2d) 155 p. 158).

In **"ANDERSON v. KIBZEY"** (1996-10-08) BCSC Kamloops Registry Docket No. 22662 the Sellers of a double wide mobile home on acreage indicated in the PCDS that they were aware of unrepaired damage due to a leaking roof ("Ceiling to be repaired"). The Plaintiff's claim was dismissed.

Although PCDS are widely used, there is no actual law which requires that a Seller must complete one. Those Sellers who do not wish to complete one (e.g. the Executor of an estate who has never lived in the house) should be reminded by their Realtor that they nevertheless have **a legal obligation to disclose to a Buyer any known LATENT defects in the property EVEN IF the Buyer never even asks or enquires about the matter.**

In **"MALENFANT v. JANZEN"** (October 19, 1994) BCJ No. 2372, Vancouver and New Westminster Registry No. S0-9962 the Sellers told the Buyers during an inspection of an old converted barn that the septic tank and field were fine and in the PCDS they stated that they were not aware of any problems with the septic tank and plumbing system. The Plaintiffs failed to have the property and septic system inspected by a Property Inspector. A week after the Buyers took possession, the downstairs toilet backed up and overflowed. The Plaintiff-Buyer's action was dismissed because the Defendant-Sellers merely said in the PCDS what they thought to be true.

(2) The LISTING BROKER.

He is the Seller's Agent and is legally and ethically obliged to investigate, discover, verify and disclose all material facts which can and are effecting the value of the listed property.

The Listing Broker has an obligation to **disclose to a BUYER and/or his Agent any known LATENT defects even if the Buyer or his Agent never even bring up the subject matter.**

(3) The BUYER.

(a) The Buyer has the satisfaction, reassurance and advantage of detailed information about the property being disclosed to him.
(b) If he has any concerns as a result of reading the PCDS he can make further enquiries.
(c) As a result he will have increased confidence in his decision making process.
(d) If for some reason the Seller chooses NOT to complete a PCDS, this should alert the Buyer to conduct his own thorough investigation and/or to seek professional help by **hiring an appropriate expert** (e.g. a Licensed Property Inspector) to do so on his behalf.

See **"ZAENKER v. KIRK"** (1999-12-20), 30 R.P.R. (3d) 9 (BCSC) Kamloops Registry, Docket No. 24348 A PCDS can be part of a Contract of Purchase and Sale, but that isn't necessarily a warranty if the items which the Plaintiff/Buyer complains about require continuous attention and maintenance.

The Property Condition Disclosure Statement - Part II

(4) **The SELLING BROKER (Buyer's Agent).**
This Realtor acts for the Buyer and therefore he must ensure that his Client has
- a full understanding of the condition the property is in,
- what outstanding repairs may be necessary
- and **the Buyer's Agent should always suggest to his Client to have an independent inspection made of the property.**
- **Should the Buyer decide NOT to have an inspection done, then a wise Realtor will DOCUMENT that fact**
   - in his work diary or the Deal File
   - or possibly even by inserting into the Contract of Purchase and Sale an appropriate "acknowledgement" clause.

(E.g. The Buyer hereby acknowledges that he has been advised to obtain the services of a Certified Property Inspector before entering into an unconditional contract).

If the Seller and Buyer agree in writing that the Seller's answers to the questions in the PCDS and **the PCDS document itself forms a part of the Contract of Purchase and Sale,** then it can be **a breach of contract** if the answers provided by the Seller **are untrue based upon his current ACTUAL knowledge.**

Due to the recent increase of illegal drug manufacturing and wide-spread marijuana grow operations in residential properties, the following items should be addressed by a careful Real Estate Agent:
Illegal activities can result in major defects to the property
- fire hazards of improperly installed electrical wiring,
- the installation of many heavy duty fans which may overload the electrical system,
- movement of load bearing walls or other damage to walls,
- the health hazard of mould stemming from an unusual amount of humidity or moisture etc.

The problem of "leaky condos" (condominiums suffering from sundry construction defects resulting in moisture and mould problems) also needs to be addressed by a cautious Realtor. Leaky condos are not only a health hazard, but in due course they will often result in an extraordinary "special assessment fee" (possibly in the tens of thousands of Dollars) to repair the problem. Such high one-time assessment fees have unfortunately resulted in many a personal bankruptcy.

WARNING: **REALTORS SHOULD BEWARE of UNTRUTHFUL PCDS** completed by a Seller.

See **"BAYNHAM and BAYNHAM v. TERRY and BLACK"** (2003-03-19) BCSC Chilliwack Registry, Docket S0010315. The Plaintiffs claimed damages for certain deficiencies (leaky roof, structural and septic tank problems) on the basis of negligent or fraudulent misrepresentation. The Dept. of Health had even required a written assurance from the Seller that any future Buyer would be told that the holding tank operated under a special permit and that any subsequent Buyer would have to make a personal application to the Health Department.

In **"PAVENHAM DEVELOPMENT CORP. and KAAM CONSULTANTS LTD. v. SLADEN et al."** (1997-09-11) BCSC Duncan Registry, Docket S5182 the Seller sold a house which was uninhabitable. Instead of making a full and frank disclosure, the Judge found that the Seller employed "circumlocution" in the PCDS. The Seller not only did not tell his Realtor of the public health order, but due to his comments in the PCDS he represented that the house could be rented out. Regrettably the Realtor accepted the Seller's explanatory entries in the PCDS at face value without any further questioning or verification. As the Seller had a positive duty to inform the Buyers that the house was not habitable, he was liable to the Plaintiffs in damages for fraudulent misrepresentation.

In this connection PLEASE NOTE THE FOLLOWING:
   (a) The Listing Salesman should have asked the Seller what some of his confusing answers to the questions in the PCDS meant.
   (b) The Listing Salesman made no enquiries of his own.
   (c) The Listing Salesman forgot to give the PCDS to the Selling Salesman and the Buyer thus depriving the Buyer of an opportunity of discovering the hidden defect.
   (d) **The Listing Salesman was found liable to the Plaintiff Buyer in negligence.**
   (e) The Real Estate Company which employed the Listing Salesman was vicariously responsible for its Salesman's acts of negligence.
   (f) The Seller was vicariously liable for the acts of his Realtors.

In **"ROSS v. HOBBIS"** (1992-07-06) BCSC Docket 891157 the Defendant Sellers tried to collect from a Third Party (namely the Realtors involved) indemnification for damages arising out of their own fraudulent misrepresentations.

The case of **"DAVIS v. STINKA"** (1995-05-15), BCSC Campbell River Registry, Docket S 1135 dealt with a semi-rural three-quarter acre parcel of land, with a one year old house, some outbuildings, a wood shed and barn. The property was adjacent to a creek with an environmental restrictive covenant over a portion of the land. The property was bought during a relatively dry summer. When the Buyers moved onto the property in fall, the rains started.
Some of the problems encountered were: a leaky roof, the upstairs toilet was not flushing properly (it bubbled and splashed the cedar wall behind it), water dripping inside of the wall down past the window onto the sill; dry rot in the deck; problems with the septic system (the field was low and was under water some or all of the time), dampness in the crawl space, some of the buildings were not set back from the property lines.
The deck was obviously in poor condition, so it was a patent defect.
The Plaintiff Buyers succeeded on most of their other claims.

Defects

There are 2 kinds of defects: patent and latent.

(1) **PATENT DEFECTS.**
Patent defects are those which an ordinarily vigilant and alert Buyer can readily discover during his inspection of the property. In this respect the general rule of the law is **"CAVEAT EMPTOR" (Buyer BEWARE).**

NOTE:
  (a) **The Seller has NO DUTY to disclose PATENT defects to a Buyer.**
  (b) But at the same time the Seller cannot and must not act in such a way as to **mislead** the Buyer or to **allay** the Buyer's suspicions.

It is the Buyer's responsibility to ascertain patent defects by
- conducting his own reasonably thorough inspection of the property (building[s] and land)
- in case he has a concern of any kind (e.g. leaky basement, roof problems or the importance of the quality of material used and/or the workmanship employed), then he should make further reasonable enquiries
- he should hire an expert (e.g. an Accredited Building Inspector) to do an inspection.

CASE LAW:

In **"ANDERSON v. KIBZEY"** (1996-10-08) BCSC Docket 2262 the Defendant Seller had disclosed to the Plaintiff Buyer that there was a problem due to the mobile home's leaky roof. This law case also referred to 2 other important cases involving defects, namely

"ROSS v. HOBBIS" (1992-07-06) BCSC Docket 891157
The Seller's false representations about
(a) the leaky roof and
(b) the 50 year warranty is without value because the roofing company was out of business.
(c) The third party claim against the Realtor was dismissed.

and **"DAVIS v. STINKA"** (1995-05-15) BCSC S 1135 deals with a leaky roof, dry rot, septic system, some of the outbuildings encroach on the neighbour's property. The Plaintiff-Buyers succeeded because "there was an element of carelessness in the answers given … in the Disclosure Statement."

Defects and the Property Inspector.

See **"ISSLER v. WALL"** (2002-11-08) Provincial Court of B.C., Docket # 27070. Over a period of time, sundry repairs and improvements had been made on an old mobile home. The Buyer had inspected the mobile home 3 times and at no time was the viewing impeded by any of the Sellers. The Buyer had hired an experienced inspector whose report said exactly what the mobile home was (namely an old mobile home). It was found that condensation in the windows, mould, water staining, roof and deck repairs were all patent defects. As there was no fraudulent or negligent intent to conceal any defects, "caveat emptor" applied and all claims against the Defendant Sellers and the Property Inspector were dismissed.

In the following case **the claim against the Seller was dismissed, but not against the Property Inspector:**

"KHAIRA v. NELSON and LIDDER" (2002-07-11) BCSC Docket 9553 There was a 12 inch slope over the entire house from the West wall to the East wall, a distance of approx. 48 feet (resulting in a 2 degree incline). Apparently the house had been built with the slope. The slope was discovered by the Buyers only when they moved into the house and were placing their furniture. Prior to their purchase they had hired an inspector who inspected the property on June 12, 1997. Regrettably the inspector did not use a level on the day when he conducted his inspection. As the inspector owed a duty to the Plaintiff Buyer to detect the slope, he had breached that duty by not detecting it. (An "exemption clause" in the Inspector's contract cannot be construed to excuse liability for a "fundamental breach" of fundamental terms of the contract). The third party notice against the Seller was dismissed. The inspector had to pay for general damages suffered by the Plaintiff (diminution in value of the property and diminution in the enjoyment of the property).

Similar cases where **the "exclusion clause" was unenforceable** to limit the Home Inspector's liability are **"BROWNJOHN v. PILLAR TO POST,"** (2003-11-09) Provincial Court of B.C., Kelowna Registry, file No. 52779 and **"SIMARD v. TAYLOR"** (2000-01-10), Provincial Court of B.C., New Westminster Registry, file No. C 9137

If certain misrepresentations were made to a Buyer and that Buyer **fails to make reasonable enquiries,** then it may result in **"CONTRIBUTORY NEGLIGENCE"** (see **"UNITED SERVICES FUNDS** (Trustees of) **v. RICHARDSON/ GREENSHIELDS OF CAN. LTD."** (1988), 22 B.C.L.R. (2d) 322 (S.C.). Once the Plaintiff/Buyer is aware of or knows of a fraud, **he must mitigate his loss.**

(2) **LATENT DEFECTS.**
   Latent defects MUST be disclosed by the Seller as well as his Realtor (the Listing Broker).

Latent defects are those which
(a) are not readily apparent to a Buyer during an ordinary inspection of the property
(b) Often latent defects have to do with
- **structural problems** (e.g. foundation problems, termite infestation (see "**JUNG et al v. IP et al,**" Ontario District Court (York), January 15, 1988),
- land subject to flooding or landslides

In "**THOMAS v. BLACKWELL**" (1999) S.J. No. 769 the Seller failed to disclose significant foundation problems which could only be discovered by the removal of wood panelling from interior basement walls.

See "**PATON v. LITTLE**" (2003-01-28) Saskatchewan Court of Queen's Bench, Docket QB03040; QB182/01JCMJ. The Seller had built his own house; instead of the originally contemplated concrete foundation he installed a preserved wood foundation without submitting to the Municipality the required plans or engineering certification (as he was required to do). There were a number of design and construction deficiencies and consequently various problems were not disclosed to the Buyer.

In "**PROZNICK v. KJARGAAD**" (2000) S.J. No. 758 other problems were dealt with: a settled driveway, water softener problems etc. The Judge in that case referred to the well-known law suit of "**McGRATH v. MacLEAN**" (1979) 22 o.r. (2D) 784: The Buyer alleged a loss arising not as a result of negligent misrepresentation, but rather as a result of the Defendant Seller's failure to disclose a latent defect.

To succeed a Buyer must be able to prove and satisfy the following 3 items:

(1) that the defect was latent (which means that it could NOT have been identified by or during a reasonable inspection).
(2) The Seller KNEW of the defect and/or was guilty of CONCEALMENT.
(3) As a result of these defects, the premises are not fit to be lived in; or rather the defects may have caused a certain amount of **loss of use:**
- loss of enjoyment of many meaningful or material portions of the premises
- AND as a result of which perhaps the loss of enjoyment of the premises as a whole. See "**MOORE v. PAGE**" (2002) O.J. No. 2256

"**ROWLEY v. ISLEY et al**" [1951] 3 D.L.R., 766 at p. 767, 3 W.W.R. (N.S.) 173. The failure to disclose to the Buyer **the true condition of the property** (regarding the previously excessive cockroach infestation and the subsequently necessary fumigation) was **a fraudulent misrepresentation arising from the SUPPRESSION of the truth.** This condition was also the Agent's duty to disclose.

See the Manitoba Court of Queen's Bench case of **"GRONAU v. SCHLAMP INVESTMENTS LTD."** (1974), 52 D.L.R. (3rd) 631 (Man. Q.B.) where the Seller of a 9-suite apartment block concealed a crack in the wall of the building by patching it with bricks which matched the surrounding area. Although the Defendant Seller claimed that he had no intention to conceal the damage or the repairs, the Judge found that **the Seller's knowledge and his failure to disclose** the (repaired) defect was enough to attract **LIABILITY**.

Therefore in the case of a latent defect which is not readily apparent during the Buyer's ordinary inspection of the property, because it is **ACTIVELY CONCEALED by the Seller,** the rule of "caveat emptor" does not apply. The deceived Buyer can ask either for a rescission of the contract and/or compensation for damages.

In **"PADDA v. ROYAL LePAGE RELOCATION SERVICES LIMITED & Guerriero"** (2002-02-22), Surrey Small Claims Court No. 47500 it was found that withholding information about a leaky basement was fraudulent. **Nor could the Defendant hide behind the Disclosure Statement of the PREVIOUS owner, nor behind the "AS IS" disclaimer printed in the Contract.**

In **"FROST v. STEWART"** (1998) 19 R.P.R. (3d) 281 (Ont. C.J. - Gen Div.) the trial judge commented that QUOTE "the suppressing of the truth and the telling of a falsehood are first cousins" UNQUOTE.

THE REALTOR'S RESPONSIBILITIES IN CONNECTION WITH DEFECTS.

Most likely incorporated in the Articles and/or Code of Ethics of Real Estate Boards is an admonition that their Realtor members have the duty to:

(a) discover **all FACTS** (both important and/or deemed otherwise) about each and every property which the Realtors are handling in the normal course of their business.

(b) It cannot be emphasized enough that wise and cautious **Realtors should independently VERIFY all information and data**. From a practical point of view this specifically means that a Realtor should not merely accept the Seller's word for something REGARDLESS of
   - how sophisticated or sincere the Client appears to be
   - or if in the mind of the Realtor the matter is "a mere trifle" or "unimportant." Many a "trifle" like e.g. the age of the house, the house floor area or the exact square footage of the lot have come to haunt a Realtor later on.

(c) And the Realtor has to do a conscientious and good job, because **the level of care** is set at that which a reasonably prudent and COMPETENT Realtor has to exercise.

(d) The purpose for the existence of these requirements should be obvious: **to protect the Client** from expensive law suits which may arise as a result of
- sloppy work habits resulting in avoidable errors,
- the various types of misrepresentations,
- uncalled for exaggerations and
- possible concealment of pertinent facts or defects.

What BENEFITS will REALTORS receive for acting prudently and thoroughly?

(a) First of all they will protect themselves from law suits which are usually very time consuming, frustratingly unproductive and cost a lot of money.
(b) As a result of their research, Realtors will also have **as an added bonus:**
- FIRST HAND KNOWLEDGE of all facts about the property
- as a direct consequence of this he will be able to talk with **more confidence and authority** about the property and
- in turn he will appear to be **more sincere and convincing** in his sales efforts (he is instantly able to address the Buyer's concerns with answers based on facts instead of guessing, waffling or "finding out later").
- Because of all of the above, the Realtor will be **more successful in his sales efforts**. In plain English, he will make more commission money with less of a chance of being involved in unproductive, expensive and protracted law suits, disciplinary hearings, sleepless nights, shot nerves etc.

(1) **The LISTING Agent's DUTIES are**

(a) to ascertain and verify all pertinent facts about the property BEFORE he is putting it on the market. See **"FLANDRO v. MITHA"** (1992-06-05) BCSC C892488, 93 DLR (4th) 222. One section deals with the **LIABILITY OF REALTORS.**

Occasionally the verification and gathering of information may be somewhat difficult to do in a short period of time, because
- in a hot market Buyers will jump on a new listing as soon as the "For Sale" sign goes up or
- it may take longer than the time limit normally allocated by the Boards (for the submission to them of the Listing Contract). When a listing is submitted late to the Board, it may be a nice gesture of courtesy to attach a little explanatory note.

(b) As mentioned before: whenever possible, the Listing Salesperson **must independently check and confirm** the accuracy of all information provided to him by the Seller. E.g.
- on an existing mortgage the interest rate, outstanding unpaid balance,

- is the mortgage assumable or not, with or without qualification;
- is the sanitary sewer connected to the house?
- Does the well produce an adequate amount of water? (see **"WARD et al v. SMITH et al"** (2001-10-24) BCSC Golden, Docket No. 2303 (Damages due to negligent misrepresentation of the quantity and quality of the water supply). Also see **"SEDGEMORE et al v. BLOCK BROS. REALTY LTD."** BCSC, December 12, 1985 (Agent under duty to Buyer to verify Seller's representations; Seller liable for fraudulent misrepresentation, Realtor liable for negligent misrepresentation).

(c) Another reason why the Listing Salesperson must obtain all information which is relevant and necessary is:
- **to enable a prospective Buyer to make an INFORMED decision and value judgment whether to buy the property or not.**
- If the Listing Salesperson fails to exercise a degree of care and skill in the discharge of his duties, then he may possibly deprive his Client (the Seller) of an opportunity to sell (lost opportunity).

(d) The Listing Salesperson must disclose to a Buyer
- not only reasonably discoverable defects (no "belittling" or covering up)
- but also **all LATENT DEFECTS which are known to him.**

(e) All of the above-mentioned information is
- to be GIVEN FREELY and
- is to be COMPLETE.

(2) **The SELLING Agent's responsibilities** are somewhat narrower. See **"BOLTON v. SALAGA et al"** (August 17, 1989), Victoria SCBC, 85/0287. In this case the Selling Broker was not required to verify the legality of a utility line. The Selling Broker was deemed to be merely an unwitting bystander to the wilfully reckless disregard by the Sellers for the Buyers.

From a practical point of view (but only to a certain degree) it is not entirely unreasonable for a Selling Agent to rely on the Listing Broker to disclose all material information. However, BEFORE giving any information to his Client (the Buyer), **the Selling Agent must check:**

(a) the completeness and accuracy of all information which is usual or customary for brokers to verify: especially if the item involved **is of paramount and/or essential IMPORTANCE for the Buyer.** (E.g. that the well produces an adequate amount of water for the Buyer's family; or that the interest renewal date on an assumed mortgage meets the Buyer's hopes and specifications).

(b) the completeness and accuracy of any and all other information of which he (the Realtor or his Client) is or might be in doubt.

(3) **For the BUYER, the presumption is**

(a) **"CAVEAT EMPTOR" (Buyer beware)** for any defects which they can SEE or otherwise NOTICE during a reasonably alert inspection.

(b) The Property Condition Disclosure Statement completed by the Seller should encourage the Buyer to SEEK FURTHER EXPLANATIONS about any possible inconsistencies in the information provided therein.

(c) Moreover, the Buyer can protect himself by
- hiring an expert for an independent inspection or examination of the property OR
- by seeking (from the SELLER) an EXPRESS WARRANTY.

If the Buyer fails to do either, then he may find himself without remedy in the absence of fraud or a fundamental difference between that which he had bargained for and that which he eventually obtained.

The distinction between what is a **REPRESENTATION** and what is a **WARRANTY** can often be tenuous for the Realtor and even more so for the contracting parties (if they are lay persons).

(a) Generally speaking a **REPRESENTATION is that which PRECEDES and INDUCES a Contract of Purchase and Sale.**
(b) A **WARRANTY** is a term embodied in a contract which
- does not go to the root of the agreement between the contracting parties
- but simply expresses some lesser obligation, the failure to perform which can give rise to an action for damages.

ANY WARRANTY WRITTEN into the Contract of Purchase and Sale **must EXPRESSLY PROVIDE that the contracting parties INTENDED the warranty to SURVIVE the closing.**
If such "express terms" are not used, then an unwary Buyer may find himself in a trap, because the responsibility of the Defendant/Seller could be extinguished by the conveyance.
E.g. who in his right mind would enter into a contract containing an express warranty that the house he is buying complied with all applicable building by-laws and regulations and, at the same time, intended that the warranty will be extinguished when he takes possession of the house. Furthermore, this is especially relevant in the case of defects which are NOT REASONABLY DISCOVERABLE at or PRIOR to the time of "closing."

EXAMPLES of warranties:

See **"FRASER-REID et al v. DROUMSEKAS"** (1980) 1 S.C.R. 720. In the sale of an uncompleted house, there exists an implied warranty that upon completion, the home will be fit for human habitation. The missing foundation drain tiles were latent defects. Implied and express warranties should survive the completion date.

In **"WINNIPEG CONDOMINIUM CORP. #36 v. BIRD CONSTRUCTION"** Supreme Court of Canada (October 12, 1995), 1 S.C.R. 85. In 1972 a general contractor built a 15-storey apartment block which was converted into condos in 1978. On May 8, 1989 a one-storey-high section of the exterior cladding fell from the 9th storey of the building to the ground below. The cost of removing and replacing the entire cladding was estimated at $ 1.5 Million. The Supreme Court of Canada ruled that a subsequent Buyer is entitled to recover the cost of repairing the defect, if the work was originally done so negligently that the defect posed a serious danger to the **subsequent (current)** occupants of the building.

See **"SWEENEY v. BREEDVELD"** (2003-04-14) Abbotsford Provincial Court of B.C., File # S13153. The house was built by the Defendant Seller about 6 years before he sold to the Plaintiff Buyer. He subcontracted and/or did some of the work himself. The Sellers had been living in the house at all times. The house was situated at the lowest end in a cul-de-sac and water was flowing towards the house. The Seller did make some attempts to solve the water problem. There was a PCDS; based on the assurances given to them prior to purchase the Buyers failed to hire a property inspector. The Judge found that the water leakage problems were caused by latent defects in the structure. Also construction had been negligently supervised and completed. The Defendant Sellers were liable to the Claimant Buyers for damages.

A Few Thoughts About Fixtures And Chattels

At one time or another every Realtor has encountered the problem of "WHAT" stays with the house and what doesn't. In the "Good Old Days" of the 1950's and early 1960's some Sellers used to literally strip the house on the way out the door. Horror stories were told about light fixtures and even the light bulbs having been removed, as well as the kitchen floor linoleum (if it wasn't glued down).

Generally speaking, anything that is a FIXTURE must stay with the house.

What determines what a FIXTURE is?
(a) **the degree of annexation**: the item is a fixture if the removal of the item in question will cause damage or some sort of an alteration to the property; e.g.
- the removal of nails, screws, bolts and glue,
- the cutting into walls (e.g. if the item is so large that it cannot be taken out through a door or window)
- the necessity of cutting wires and/or pipes to be able to remove the item.

(b) **the object of annexation which means the PURPOSE to which the article is being put.**
It goes without saying that certain items necessary for the operation of the house must stay:
- the furnace and the hot water tank,
- the built-in air conditioning unit,
- plumbing and bathroom fixtures,
- an inground pool
- wiring, light fixtures, door chimes, switch plates, intercom and alarm system, smoke detectors, ceiling fans, a built-in dishwasher, garborator, compactor.
- Fixed wall-to-wall carpeting, venetian blinds, drape tracks, a built-in bookcase, storage shelves attached to the walls by screws (because the removal of the screws will damage the wall).
- A built-in vacuum system (the canister could sometimes be an exception because the canister can be unplugged and lifted out of the brackets without damaging the wall. Of course, the brackets must stay).
- Gutters, garage door openers, thermo windows, window screens and screen doors to name a few.

THE OWNERS SHOULD VOUCH THAT
(a) **ALL OF THESE FIXTURES ARE HIS PROPERTY** (they are not rented or leased or belong to a tenant or somebody else).
Obviously the Seller/Landlord cannot give away something that belongs to somebody else. E.g. a Tenant may remove a fixture which belongs to him during the lifetime of his tenancy provided he doesn't cause any irreparable damage and leaves the premises in exactly the same condition as it was when he rented it and first moved in.

AND

(b) that these fixtures WILL BE IN GOOD WORKING CONDITION ON POSSESSION DAY. But no future guarantees or warranties beyond that date will be given. This simply means that if the hot water tank suddenly quits working a week after the Buyer has taken possession, then it is the Buyer's problem.

CHATTELS are generally items which are NOT attached to the land or building (by nails, screws, glue etc.) and can be removed without creating damage or having to make some sort of alterations. Therefore, anything that is merely plugged in or hanging on something and can be removed without causing any damage is a CHATTEL.
E.g. PICTURES hanging on a hook or nail on the wall, hang there by their own weight (gravity), but can be removed without damage, therefore they are chattels. But the hook or nail must stay.
Similarly it is with a MIRROR held to the wall by brackets. The mirror retains its use and essential character even if it is removed. It can be lifted out of the brackets without causing any damage and is therefore a chattel. But the brackets must stay.
A SWAG LAMP is a chattel because it can be unplugged (from the electrical socket) and removed without causing any damage. The hook in the ceiling must stay.

One of the more unusual problems are GARDEN ORNAMENTS like a bird bath, gnomes or a little stone pagoda. It can be argued that each item is not attached to the land (except by its own weight) and can be removed without damage. However, if these items are an integral part of an elaborate ornamental garden which was prominent in the Buyer's purchase decision, then they may have to stay (same as all flowers, plants, shrubs etc.). (See **"Freeman v. Champagne,"** B.C. Supreme Court Docket # 871193, Date May 11, 1989).

Other items which may be borderline and have the POTENTIAL of becoming a possible problem later on are for example:
- Ornamental curtain rods and special track lights.
- Hanging flower baskets, a greenhouse and storage shed.
- Novelty items like e.g. a fancy acrylic toilet seat (showing coins or flowers).
- Children's play equipment: a swing, a tree house.
- Fireplace screens which are not attached.
- A "built-in" breakfast nook which is not actually fastened to the wall and floor (in case of doubt, ask the Seller if it is fastened onto anything in any way).
- Possibly the canister and accessories of a built-in vacuum system: the canister can be unplugged and lifted out of the brackets which are holding it to the wall. The various vacuum attachments are portable. But the pipes in the walls must stay.
- An above-ground pool; pool equipment and pool chemicals.
- A recreation room bar (which is not fastened to the floor)
- A freestanding fireplace or wood stove.

IN CASE OF DOUBT it is best to play it safe in a sale: as a wise precaution the Realtor should prepare an ADDENDUM which
- will form part of the Contract of Purchase and Sale and
- which will have to be signed by all contracting parties,
- **DETAILING exactly what will stay and what will not.**

When a Realtor is in the process of taking a LISTING, it should be STANDARD PROCEDURE to determine IN ADVANCE with the Sellers
- what CAN stay (to be used later on as a bargaining chip) and
- what WILL definitely NOT stay. E.g. a refrigerator may have been a wedding present. A rose bush COULD have some sentimental value for the owner.

Former occupants of a house (e.g. tenants or a disappointed/ frustrated former owner who has lost the house through foreclosure) **are not allowed**
- **to trash the house on the way out the door or**
- **to remove fixtures.**

It is an offence under the Criminal Code of Canada (because this act would be prejudicial to the foreclosing bank and/or the next owner).

If the contracting parties agree in the Contract of Purchase and Sale that certain chattels stay (like a fridge, stove, washer, dryer and drapes) **then they must be the ones "as viewed by the Buyer" on the date of inspection. The Seller cannot substitute or exchange any of the items mentioned in the Contract.** See **"Laski v. Chan"** Ontario Superior Court of Justice (July 24, 2003) O.J. No. 3033, Court file No. 01-CV-205974 CM, where the Sellers were fined for switching sundry items (the fridge was exchanged for a non-working fridge etc).

The following are some law cases which deal with fixtures and chattels:

- "Stack v. Eaton" (1902), 4 OLR 335, at 338
- **"La Salle Recreations Ltd. v. Canadian Camdex Investments Ltd."** (1969), 68 WWR 339 (BCCA)
- **"Homestar Holdings Ltd. v. Old Country Inn Ltd."** (1986) 8 BCLR (2d) 211 (SC)
- **"Pemberton Holmes Ltd. v. Ulaszonek"** (1996-01-31) BCSC Victoria Registry No. 95 1452 deals with
- a display shelf in the kitchen (fixture)
- the Jennaire cooktop (fixture)
- frigidaire convection oven (not a fixture)
- the blinds (a fixture)
- the canister portion of the built-in vacuum system (not a fixture),
- the electrical unit of the garage door opener (a fixture)
- **"Royal Bank of Canada v. Maple Ridge Farmers Market Ltd."** (July 28, 1995,

B.C. Supreme Court, Vancouver Registry No. A 950858
- **"Boxrud v. Canada"** (1996-12-04) Federal Court of Canada, Docket T-1162-93 (improvements in the sale of a resort business)
- **"Playmakers' Adventures Inc. v. Cariboo Mountains Fishing and Outdoor Adventures Ltd."** (2002-09-10) B.C. Supreme Court, Docket # 113878 (fixtures, chattels and rights and other assets relating to or connected with the sale of a Wilderness Resort. E.g. Angling Guide Licenses and Park Use Permit for guided and non-guided angling opportunities).

_____, 200____ Page # _____ of _____

ADDENDUM to and FORMING PART of Contract of Purchase and Sale dated _____ 200_____ for _____

The following items are **INCLUDED IN THE SALE** (at no extra charge) **"as viewed on"** _____, 200_____

Refrigerator: Make _____ Colour _____ Serial # _____

Range/stove: Make _____ Colour _____ Serial # _____

Washer: Make _____ Colour _____ Serial # _____

Dryer: Make _____ Colour _____ Serial # _____

Dishwasher: Make _____ Colour _____ Serial # _____

Compactor: Make _____ Serial # _____

Garborator: Make _____ Serial # _____

Venetian blinds _____

Drapes & Sheers _____

All window coverings except _____

Humidifier _____

Built-in vacuum: Make _____ Canister _____ Attachments _____

Intercom: Make: _____

Alarm system: Make: _____ Monitored: _____

Ceiling Fan _____

Attached mirrors _____

Automatic garage door openers: Make: _____

Bar in recreation room: _____

Kitchen nook: _____ Built-in _____ NOT built-in _____

Fireplace insert _____ Is installed according to applicable code _____

Freestanding fireplace _____ wood burning stove ____ Is installed according to applicable code _____

Swimming pool and all accessories _____

Hot Tub and all accessories _____

Storage shed _____ OTHER: _____

Greenhouse _____ _____

Gazebo _____ _____

The Sellers WARRANT that all items which stay will be in GOOD WORKING ORDER on the Possession Date. However, no future warranties or guarantees are given.

_____ _____
Seller's signature   Witness

_____ _____
Seller's signature   Witness

_____ _____
Buyer's signature   Witness

_____ _____
Buyer's signature   Witness

About Existing And New Financing

It has been said, that **"financing" is the key** to selling real estate. Never were truer words spoken, unless, of course, the Buyer is able to pay "all cash"; and even in that situation, the question of "financing" comes into play, because the Seller has to deliver "Clear Title" (title free and clear of all financial encumbrances). If the Seller has to pay off an existing mortgage on which there is a huge prepayment penalty then the "all cash for clear title" stipulation will profoundly influence **his bottom line - his "NET EQUITY."**

From the above example it can be seen that a Realtor will have to consider the 2 aspects of the financing problem:

(A) **the EXISTING financing presently registered against the property:**
  (a) **If it is assumable or not.**
  (1) Some existing mortgages can be assumed, either with
   - **the Buyer qualifying** with the lending institution for the assumption, in which case **the previous owner/mortgagor can ask to be released from his "personal covenant."** The "personal covenant" is a clause in the fine print of the mortgage which says "I promise to pay" or words to that effect. If that clause is not deleted and the Mortgagor is not released from it, then the Lending Institution can (in case of foreclosure at some future date) go back to all previous Mortgagors who were ever on the mortgage and sue them on their "personal covenants." Of course, they will most likely go after the most credit worthy ones. The average consumer is not aware of this. For that reason a conscientious Realtor should make the appropriate arrangements (through the Seller's lawyer).
   - **or without qualifying** (which means that it is not necessary to obtain the Lender's prior approval of the assumption). In that case it is also not possible to obtain a "release" from the lender of the original personal covenant.
  (2) There are certain **ADVANTAGES for a Buyer to assume an existing mortgage,** e.g.
   - the mortgage may carry a **LOWER interest rate** than what the currently going rate is
   - there may be **a distant (long) mortgage renewal (due) date**
   - by assuming the existing mortgage the Buyer may be able to save some money for
     - a new appraisal
     - a new Survey Certificate
     - the legal fees of drafting a new mortgage
     - the Land Title Office costs of registering a new mortgage
     - the Buyer may get the house at a lower Selling Price, if the Seller does

not have to pay a prepayment penalty (to pay off the old mortgage) in order to clear the title.

(3) **Some existing mortgages CANNOT be assumed and must be paid off upon a sale.** This is often the case with privately held mortgages where e.g. a Seller provides financing for a particular buyer, but doesn't wish to do business with anybody else.

(4) Occasionally there may be a (privately held) mortgage which MUST be assumed and cannot be paid off before a certain date.

(b) **The Seller's COST of discharging an existing mortgage**

(1) There may be a PREPAYMENT PENALTY which is required to clear off an existing mortgage. The amount of this penalty will obviously have an effect the Seller's Net Equity.

The prepayment penalty could be negotiable (and reduced or even totally eliminated) if the Buyer agrees to take out his new financing through the **current** mortgagee (for a higher loan amount and if the current interest rate is higher than what the old [former] mortgage rate is).

(2) In addition, there may be ADMINISTRATION FEES charged by the Lending Institution to process the discharge paperwork and, of course,

(3) there will be LEGAL FEES to discharge the mortgage. Please note that the legal fees consist of the following 2 components:
- what the Lawyer or Notary Public charges for his work.
- Scheduled fees charged by the Land Title Office for the registration of the discharge document.

FOR HIS CLIENT'S (and his own) PROTECTION ... a Realtor should at the **BEGINNING of his marketing efforts, verify IN WRITING and from INDEPENDENT SOURCES** (other than from the Seller) **complete details of all existing mortgages and other financial charges** registered against the property. (See sample of Mortgage Information Request form at the end of this Chapter).

WHY should and would a prudent Realtor do this?

(1) **The Sellers may not be sure what the exact current BALANCES of their existing mortgage(s) is/are.** The total amount of indebtedness could be MORE than what the Seller thinks it is.

This means that he has LESS equity and consequently will have LESS downpayment for the purchase of his next house. In the worst case scenario the shortfall may come to light only late in the day, e.g. in the lawyer's office when the Seller is signing the Statements of Adjustment. At that time any discrepancies or shortfalls have little chance of being resolved satisfactorily in the short time period available before the registration of documents will have to take place. Tempers will flare, moving vans will sit idle and several families may find themselves in an expensive predicament. Sometimes deals collapse resulting in expensive law suits.

(2) Alternatively, if the outstanding mortgage balances are obtained right at the beginning (shortly after listing the property) and the Seller for some reason doesn't agree with them, **then he has an opportunity to contact his lending institution** and make the necessary enquiries - at his leisure and under no "last minute" time pressure.

(3) The Seller may not be sure what the existing INTEREST RATE and DUE (Renewal) DATE on his mortgage is. If the Buyer assumes the existing financing and the interest rate and/or renewal date turn out to be different from what he was led to believe and from what was contracted for, then the bad surprise could lead to the last minute collapse of the sale and again to some expensive legal action. See **"AVERY et al v. SALIE et al"** Saskatchewan Queen's Bench, (March 10, 1972) Dominion Law Reports 25 D.L.R.(3d)

(4) If the Realtor makes his **mortgage verification enquiries by phone,** then he is running the risk of a clerical error or a misunderstanding. The person who has given him the information verbally may later on either not recall having done so or alternatively, may for a number of reasons, not be readily available. (E.g. he may have left the company, he may have been transferred to another location or he may simply be on holidays). Therefore, **it is of paramount importance to get everything in writing.**

(B) **NEW FINANCING arranged to finance the purchase.**
    (a) CONVENTIONAL mortgages are loans up to 75% of the Selling Price or Appraised Value, whichever is lower.
    (b) HIGH RATIO mortgages are loans in excess of 75% and require an insurance premium (which is often added to the loan amount). The insurance is in favour of the Lending Institution as protection in case the mortgagor defaults. This type of insurance is available through the Federal Government (CMHC) and a limited number of private insurance companies. In case of default, the mortgagee doesn't have to foreclose, but merely collects the outstanding balance from the Insurer. In turn the Insurer will do the foreclosing and sell the house in due course (sometimes at a loss).
    (c) **The RISK factor determines the INTEREST RATE.** Obviously a First Mortgage is better secured than a Third Mortgage.
    (d) **Seller financing.**
        If the Seller provides a part of the financing, (e.g. a 2nd mortgage), **then GREAT CARE must be taken to ensure that his equity is PROTECTED.**
        • the Buyer's downpayment must be his own money (and not borrowed),

- the Buyer's credit rating must be checked,
- his current employment and income verified
- the Buyer should NOT achieve 100% financing, because in that case the Seller (if he carries a balance himself) would NOT be protected. The Buyer has no equity and if there is a severe fluctuation in market value, the Buyer is liable to just walk away and leave the Seller (2nd mortgagee) holding the bag. The 1st mortgagee is foreclosing against the defaulting current owner and the 2nd mortgagee (as well as against any other subsequent financial charges). In that case, to protect his equity (and investment) the Seller (or 2nd mortgagee) would have to continue servicing the existing 1st mortgage (by making the monthly mortgage payments). Otherwise the 2nd mortgagee will run the risk of losing it all.

(e) Alternatively, **a NEW "BLENDED" 1st mortgage** could be secured where the INTEREST RATE IS BLENDED between the old (lower) rate of the former existing mortgage and the new (higher) current interest rate.

(C) IF THE REALTOR IS CUTTING HIS COMMISSION.

Supposing that negotiations have bogged down: the Seller is unwilling to settle for any LESS NET EQUITY. On the other hand the Buyer is unable to come up with anymore downpayment and/or he cannot qualify for a higher mortgage loan amount. Rather than losing the whole thing, the Realtor decides to cut his commission.

By doing so, he is **GIVING A BENEFIT to the Buyer** and indirectly to the Seller. **The Buyer's downpayment**
- is boosted (increased) by the amount of the commission cut, OR alternatively
- one may consider that **the Selling Price is reduced** by the amount of the commission cut subsidy.

THEREFORE, it should be fairly obvious that

(1) **the lending institution** who is granting the new financing MUST BE INFORMED of this development.
Armed with that information, they in turn may
- either reduce the new loan amount (in which case the Buyer has again a cash flow problem) or else
- they may decide to do nothing and leave the loan amount the same as before.

(2) **Also the SELLER must be informed** that the Realtor is cutting his commission and (indirectly) giving that amount to the Buyer.
The reason why the Seller must know about the commission cutting is that he must be able to make a decision to
- either approve the kick-back arrangement with the Buyer

- or the Seller could reduce the Selling Price and pay a lower commission
- or alternatively he could chose not to proceed with the sale.

See **"Ocean City Realty Ltd. v. A & M Holdings Ltd. et al"** (March 6, 1987), B.C. Court of Appeal, 36 DLR (4th) 94 During negotiations the Buyer told the Realtor that he would not continue with negotiations, unless he receives a portion of the real estate commission. She agreed, but failed to inform the Seller. During the conveyancing, the Seller's lawyer discovered the commission kick-back to the Buyer and the Seller refused to pay commission. When the real estate company sued, the Judge found that the Realtor had a fiduciary duty to disclose to the Seller everything known to her regarding the subject matter of the contract. The Realtor testified in Court that she hadn't disclosed to the Seller the proposed kickback to the Buyer, because she was concerned that as a result of that information, the Seller in turn would back out of the negotiations and then she would not even receive the reduced commission. Nevertheless the Judge found that she should have advised the Seller of her concern that there might be no sale unless she agreed to reduce her commission. The Judge further found that the Realtor was not entitled to any commission at all, because of the breach of her fiduciary duty to the Seller.

(D) **BEWARE OF FRAUD.**

Supposing that you have a desperate Seller who is on the verge of losing his house through foreclosure. The Realtor has tried everything to unload the house and for some reason has been unable to do so.

Then one day an "Investor" shows up who has seen too many Infomercials on TV about getting rich quick by buying houses with NO DOWNPAYMENT and 100% financing. He proposes the following scheme:

(1) In order to achieve 100% financing, the Selling Price is to be increased by a certain (fictitious) amount. The amount of increase is merely "puff" or an "overallowance"; in due course, that non-existent amount will be "credited" back to the Buyer as an "allowance for repairs" or "for the purchase (from the Seller) of items of furniture."

(2) The Contract of Purchase and Sale will show that the Buyer's ENTIRE DOWNPAYMENT (not the deposit, but the amount of the fictitious "puff") is or has been paid directly to the Seller. (The Realtor holds nothing "in trust").

(3) A new 1st mortgage is applied for. The loan amount of that new 1st mortgage is in reality the amount of what the Seller's original (lower) Selling Price used to be.

(4) If the mortgage is granted, then the Buyer has obtained 100% financing by fraudulent means. The Seller, the Buyer and the Realtor are co-conspirators in the scheme to defraud the Lending Institution.

(5) A variation of this scam is that the Seller purports to "carry" a new 2nd mortgage (in the amount of the "puff/over allowance").

(6) **SAFEGUARDS:**
   (a) An experienced and alert Appraiser has an opportunity to question the inflated Selling Price.
   (b) The Lending Institution can request proof of the downpayment: e.g. verification of the bank account where the funds (downpayment) were allegedly deposited;
   (c) Alternatively the Lending Institution can ask to see "a gift letter" (if the Buyer's downpayment comes from somebody else other than the Seller).

MORTGAGE INFORMATION REQUEST SHEET

_____,20_____

TO:
_____ **(Mortgagee)**
_____ **(Address)**

FAX #_____ **Telephone #**_____

DEAR SIRS:
Re:
_____ **(Mortgagors)**
_____ **(Property Address)**
Mortgage Loan Number_____

We have listed our property with ... Realty and wish to confirm the status of our mortgage, in order to be able to make an informed decision when we receive an offer to sell.

Please complete the details below and return the completed form to our Realtor:
Mr./Mrs./Ms. ....
... Realty Ltd.
Address ... FAX #

Thank you for your co-operation.
Yours very truly,

_____   _____
Signature of Seller   Signature of Seller

MORTGAGEE'S REPLY:
1) The outstanding **PRINCIPAL BALANCE** of this mortgage as of _____ was $_____
2) **Arrears** (principal and/or interest) as of the same date were $_____
3) The **DUE DATE (Renewal Date)** of the mortgage is: _____
                                    Day/Month/Year
4) The current **INTEREST RATE** of this mortgage is: _____%
5) The **Monthly Payment of PRINCIPAL & INTEREST** is: $ _____
6) If the monthly payments are "P.I.T." (principal, interest AND taxes) then how much is the **ACCUMULATED TAX RESERVE FUND?**
   $_____ as of _____ 20 _____
7) (Please circle one) This mortgage **CAN/CANNOT** be assumed.
8) (Please circle one) This mortgage can be assumed **WITH/WITHOUT** qualification.
9) **The Administration fee for an assumption** is $ _____

About Existing And New Financing

10) The **DISCHARGE FEE** in case of a pay-out is $ _____
11) The **PRE-PAYMENT PENALTY is** _____ **months' interest OR a total of $** _____ **if this mortgage is prepaid before** _____ **(date).**
12) Will you eliminate or reduce the pre-payment penalty if the NEW buyer of this property takes out a NEW mortgage with you for a higher loan amount and at the current interest rate? **YES/NO** _____
13) If the Buyer assumes the current mortgage WITH qualification, then will you automatically release the Sellers from their PERSONAL COVENANTS ("I promise to pay") or will the Sellers/Mortgagors have to make a separate application for that with you? **YES/NO** _____
14) Are there any other ...
    a) Administrative Charges ... $ _____
    b) Bonus payments ... $ _____
    c) Miscellaneous Charges ... $ _____
15) **Name and job title** of the person providing this information:

_____(Please print NAME)

_____(Please print JOB TITLE)

_____ (Signature)

Market Value And Saleability

(I) **FAIR MARKET VALUE** has been defined as
- the highest price a ready, willing and able BUYER will pay
- and the lowest price a SELLER not under duress will accept
- and both parties are acting "at arm's length"
- and the property has been exposed on the market for an adequate (or reasonable) period of time.

Fair Market Value is an appraisal term which denotes the value of the subject property after comparing it to similar properties in the same area which sold recently. **("Comparative Method" of appraisal).**

Another method of appraisal is the **"Cost or Reproduction Method"**: cost of land plus cost of the building, less the various types of depreciation: physical, functional (obsolescence), remedial, non-remedial etc. This method works best with new construction where there is no depreciation. On an older house, this method becomes very complicated and somewhat inexact because **the amount of depreciation to be calculated is a Value Judgement based on the extent of the individual appraiser's experience.**

FOR PRACTICAL PURPOSES REALTORS USE THE aforementioned **"COMPARATIVE METHOD"** which is the best and most reliable way in which to **DISCUSS** with the Seller intelligently the **"ACTUAL VALUE"** of his property. The Realtor is not talking to the Seller as an **APPRAISER or an ADVISOR.** The Realtor is merely **INFORMING the Seller** of the results of his research, based on his experience and skill.

The **"ACTUAL VALUE"** is an amalgam of 3 different perspectives:

(1) First there is the **"COMPONENT VALUE"** which is made up of
   - the land value
   - the value of the lumber, nails, brick, shingles etc. and
   - the general utility (condition and location) of the property.
(2) Then there is the somewhat nebulous **"SENTIMENTAL VALUE"** which is difficult to define and partly consists of the Seller's
   - **pride of ownership**
   - **sentimental memories** of joy and good times in the house
   - **the value of friendly neighbours and the peaceful relationship and coexistence with them.**
   - **The value of improvements,** may they be self-made or other.
   - **The value of regular maintenance and upkeep**
   - and last but not least a certain measure of greed.

It is part of the Realtor's job to TACTFULLY
- help bring the Sellers' thinking into line with the reality of the current Market Value and
- to dispel any misguided illusions which the owners may have about the value of their property.
- The Seller must come to realize that his cherished "HOME" to a prospective Buyer is nothing more than another "HOUSE" - one of many that the Buyer is looking at.

(3) Finally there is a third party, namely the **Buyer, who will contribute HIS opinion to the concept of MARKET VALUE in the form of "HIS EMOTIONAL VALUE":**
- What sort of (strong) emotions will **MOTIVATE the Buyer** in the first place to make an offer to buy?
- What is it that will trigger his decision to make an offer?
- What motivates him to change his perspective that this particular "HOUSE" should become his "HOME?"

At the time of preparing the listing contract the Realtor will have his opinion of the value of the house, but so will, of course, also have the Seller. The Realtor should at all costs **avoid arguments**. The basic idea is to make your point pleasantly and convincingly without insulting, upsetting or aggravating the Seller.

In this regard the Realtor must walk a fine line:
- he will not make a good impression if he is unable to support his statements of value with facts or
- alternatively have no firm opinion at all.
- Sometimes it can happen that a stubborn Seller's opinion will determine the Listing Price.

What happens if a Realtor is unable to convince a Seller that the price he has in mind is unrealistically high?

(a) By accepting such a listing price the Realtor **by inference unwittingly confirms in the Seller's MIND the Seller's PRICE.**
(b) By apparently succeeding in bending the Realtor to his will, the Seller will form the impression that HIS price might be alright after all. Why else would the Realtor agree to list his house at that (allegedly high) price?
(c) Subsequently the owner will not be easily persuaded to reduce his asking price at a future date.

DAMAGE CONTROL.
If a Realtor lists at the Seller's Price
- he has an obligation to warn the Seller of the **CONSEQUENCES OF**

OVERPRICING.
- By giving good service (ads, Opens, showings) resulting in little or no success (no showings by other Realtors, no offers) he will indirectly supply evidence that the Market will not support the Seller's price. This **LACK of RESULTS should be discussed with the Sellers periodically.**
- A few Realtors also insert into the "remarks" column of the listing "listed at Seller's price" or words to that effect.

No doubt, this is a face saving device vis-a-vis their peers; however, as the listing (or portions thereof) are available to the public (e.g. through the Internet, computer printouts of listings given to the Buyer, Clients' perusal of listings in the catalogue), such remarks will turn out to be counter productive to the saleability of the house.

(II) WHAT FACTORS WILL DETERMINE THE SALE PRICE?

When comparing the subject property to other similar homes which recently sold, the Realtor will find that there are **many variables**. This will make it a lot more difficult to accurately determine the Fair Market Value of the subject property.

A) In no particular order, **the following will influence what the Sale Price will be:**

1) **Cleanliness**. Buying a home is an emotional process. Most Buyers are looking for homes that are clean, bright and well cared for. Unless the price is very cheap, they will be reluctant to clean up somebody else's mess and dirt.

2) **Condition** of the building.
   "In good repair" is ideal. E.g. newly painted, fairly new roof, upgraded plumbing, safe wiring;
   "neglect (rundown)" is politely referred to in the business as **"deferred maintenance."**

3) **Utility** of the property: floor area and floor plan, the number of bedrooms and bathrooms, finished basement, big and bright rooms etc.

4) **Location.**
   In a good neighbourhood real estate values are likely to hold firm and be stable.

What contributes to "a good neighbourhood?"
(a) To start with the City or Municipality must have **good planning, sensible zoning and conformity of land use** (e.g. a homogeneous population occupying all single family dwellings which are not interspersed with commercial or multi-family rental properties).
(b) **Adequate utilities:** municipal water, gas, electricity, sewers, no ditches, police and

fire protection.
(c) **Near** schools, good access to public transportation and highways, shopping, churches, etc.
(d) **Visual appeal** or prestige of the entire neighbourhood.

What contributes to depreciating values in a neighbourhood?
(a) **Lack of municipal zoning protection** allowing the creeping encroachment of commercial and industrial uses into a basically residential area, resulting in increased traffic, noise, smoke, obnoxious fumes and smells.
(b) **Lack of adequate municipal planning** allowing a mixture of architectural styles (e.g. revenue properties like duplexes and fourplexes amongst single family residences, resulting in traffic congestion on the street because of inadequate parking for the tenants.)
(c) **Lack of upkeep** of such interspersed rental properties by absentee landlords
(d) which in turn will result in **lack of community pride.**
(e) A reduction in the cohesion of a community and its subsequent loss of community pride can unfortunately also happen by the influx of a large number of mobile tenants of different economic, social and cultural backgrounds.

5) **Scarcity.** Demand and supply will dictate the price.

6) **Competition.** Number of other similar properties for sale.

7) **"Extras,"** unusual features, quality of construction, amount of finishing; e.g.
   - Finished basement (recreation room, extra bedroom, extra bathroom, in-law suite; lay-out of the basement).
   - Renovated kitchen.
   - Family room off the kitchen.
   - Updated bathrooms.
   - Ensuite bathroom to master bedroom (with or without shower).
   - Upgraded flooring (new carpets, hardwood floors).
   - Fenced backyard.
   - Upgraded insulation.
   - Double-glazed windows.
   - Wood-burning fireplace(s).
   - Air conditioning.
   - Resurfaced driveway (all potholes should be filled in and any cracks should be repaired).

8) **Lot size and landscaping.**
   In summer the Seller should keep the lawn trimmed and edged; rake all leaves, remove weeds, clear away any refuse, grass cuttings and sundry debris.
   In winter he should remove the snow and ice from the walkway, driveway, front

door steps and porch.

9) **Curb appeal.**
A good first impression (high emotional appeal) starts with the outside frontal appearance of the house; ideally it should emanate a feeling of the "welcome mat" being put out for the buying public.

10) **Surrounding area.**
Preferred are a quiet area of well-kept homes near a peaceful park.
The nuisance from heavy traffic, congestion, noise, fumes etc. is encountered by properties on a busy street; across from or next to a high-volume gas station; near a factory.

11) **Financing**.
A "plus" is a big assumable mortgage with a low interest rate and a long interest rate renewal date.
A "minus" (not attractive to a Buyer) is:
- A small existing mortgage requiring a big downpayment.
- An existing mortgage with a high interest rate; (higher than the current rate available).
- A property which can only be refinanced if the Seller pays a (huge) prepayment penalty. By being tougher on the Selling Price the owner will try to pass on a portion of the cost of the mortgage pay-out penalty onto the Buyer. The Buyer will be inclined to refuse this.

12) **Floor plan.**
"Plus": Good traffic flow; bedrooms away from the living area.
"Minus": Cut up basement development.

13) **Parking.**
Desirable features are double or multiple garages, a backlane or access for RV parking. "Minus features" are: no covered parking, no parking adjacent to the dwelling (a long way to carry the groceries), single carport only (where are the owners going to park the 2nd car?).

14) **Ample storage space.**

B) **Factors which have an uncertain influence on the Market Value:** (these type of properties will appeal only to a certain type of and limited number of Buyers).
1) An in-ground pool or a sauna could be a plus or minus.
2) Sentimental home improvements: a jerry-built recreation room with a distinct "flavour" (e.g. a pub-style); an amateurish paint job with unusual colours, a poorly tiled basement shower.

3) A huge garage with heavy duty power, a grease pit and motor winch will appeal only to car specialists.
4) A greenhouse.
5) An overwhelmingly extensive and intricate garden with wall-to-wall flowers, shrubs etc. requiring a lot of upkeep (not everybody is a green thumb hobby gardener).

C) Fair Market Value is NOT calculated by
- adding up the cost of the various improvements and the
- commercial value of the many hours the owner spent on "upkeep."

A more realistic approach is to consider **if the home improvements will be essential for or of any importance to or even appeal to a prospective buyer.**
- With painting and wallpapering the question is if the current owner's taste and colour scheme will suit and be agreeable to the future Buyer.
- Any unusual overimprovements (in comparison with the surrounding houses) will not necessarily return to the Seller the full cost of its installation (e.g. an inground concrete pool). A Buyer (when considering to make an offer) will most likely only give it a fraction of the original cost. **Overimprovements will not make the current owner any money (or profit).** They should be viewed as merely suiting his lifestyle and in order to get his money back, the owner will have to "live it out" (stay there for some time during which he will enjoy its use).

(III) WHAT INFLUENCES THE SALEABILITY OF A HOUSE?

1) **The PRICE.**
Regardless of how beautiful, clean and well maintained a house is, if it is greatly overpriced, then it will not sell.
Regardless of how rundown and dirty a house is, even in a poor location ... if it is cheap enough, then somebody will buy it.
"THE RIGHT PRICE WILL REMEDY ALL DEFECTS" (shortcomings, poor location etc.)

2) **The SELLER.**
Depending on the **URGENCY and REASON FOR SELLING,** there are basically 3 types of Sellers:

a) **Sellers who MUST sell:** persons who are transferred, have bought another home (firm, no-subject purchase), separations, death (to settle an estate), foreclosure etc.

b) **Sellers who WANT to sell** because they have a good reason: they need a bigger house with more bedrooms; they want to downsize to a smaller house or a condominium because the children are grown up and have moved out; anything that will prompt an owner to move soon.

c) **Sellers who WILL sell (only) IF THE PRICE IS RIGHT.**
The "Profit Motive" is a poor reason for selling. Such owners are merely testing the market and generally are playing games: they don't care what the Market Value of their home is. All they are interested in is making a whopping profit in a relatively short time with no work or cost to them. Smart Realtors will avoid these type of Sellers because they are only heart-breakers, emotional roller coasters and time wasters.

It is important that a Realtor learns to
- categorize the various types of Sellers by recognizing their degree of motivation;
- and then make a judgement on HOW MUCH TIME he should spend on them
- and what his chances are of earning a commission.

3) **ACCESSABILITY.**
   (a) Tenants who don't want to move will make it difficult to show a rented property. Usually a stipulated amount of advance notice (e.g. 24 hours) must be given before the property can be shown. If the Realtor and his Clients are not there right on the button, uncooperative tenants will refuse access. They do this in order to discourage the Buyers, frustrate the Realtors and spoil a prospective sale. Tenants may also deliberately mess up the inside of the house so that it will make a bad impression: dark and untidy rooms with drawn curtains, cooking smells, tobacco smoke, filthy bathroom, dirty dishes in the kitchen sink etc.

   (b) Another example of an obstacle in the way of accessibility is a (vacant) house where the Listing Broker doesn't place a "Lock Box" on the house. Realtors wanting to show the house have to pick up the key from the Listing Broker's office which could be miles away. (Of course, the key will have to be returned to the L.B.'s office right after the showing). Unless the Listing Broker is prepared to meet the Selling Broker and his Clients at the house in order to open it up for them, he may find that the house will not be shown very often by other Realtors.

4) **SHOWABILITY.**
   Actions speak louder than words. If a Seller really wants to sell, he will be open to suggestions (price, fixing up the house etc.) and consistently do everything to **help bring about a sale.**

There are many things which an owner can do, without having to spend a fortune. Investing some effort and work can earn him Big Tax Free Bucks in the end ("tax free" if it is his principal residence).

FIRST IMPRESSIONS ARE LASTING IMPRESSIONS.

(1) **Clear out and dispose of all junk**; this can be an arduous and psychologically

painful undertaking, because a lot of things may have sentimental value or their possession may give the owner emotional comfort. If you have to - then keep them. But for the rest the Seller should ask himself the following questions:
(a) have I used this item in the last 2 years?
(b) What is its commercial value?
(c) Will I have any use for it in the near future?
If the answer is "no-nil-no," then get rid of it.

SOME EXAMPLES OF JUNK:
- stacks of old newspapers and magazines.
- A basement or garage full of discarded never-to-be-used-again tools; broken old lawnmower, old tires, broken lawn ornaments and damaged lawn furniture, not working washing machine and all sorts of useless and unused appliances.
- Buckets of unsorted rusty nails and screws; pieces of pipe; odd pieces of lumber; luggage in damaged condition; empty boxes, plastic and paper bags, jars, tins, bottles etc.
- Rusting disabled cars (used for spare parts).

(2) **Avoid cluttered appearances:**
(a) clear halls, stairways, driveways etc. of toys and various objects. (These could also be hazardous for a visitor to trip over).
(b) Rooms crammed with a lot of bulky (excess) furniture, many house plants, ashtrays, knickknacks, figurines and **anything that will make the room look SMALL.**
(c) **Cluttered closets:** suits and dresses properly hung, shoes and other items neatly placed will make closets appear as "adequately spacious" to the Buyer.
(d) **Cluttered storage space:** if the attic and the basement are full of junk, then they will
  - create the impression that there is insufficient storage space;
  - also that it will take an eternity for the Seller to clear all of the junk out (the Buyer will silently wonder how long the Seller will need before he can move out).
(e) **Cluttered kitchen counters** and kitchen sinks full of dirty, unwashed dishes. All work space in the kitchen should be clear, the refrigerator, sink and range should be spotlessly clean.
(f) **Cluttered bathrooms:** empty old toothpaste tubes, rusty razor blades, empty perfume bottles; bits of soap around the sink. Bathrooms should be clear and neat and the air in them should be fresh.

(3) **Make minor repairs** (it is the little things that count):
  - Put new washers into dripping faucets.
  - Repair leaky toilets.
  - Repair loose door knobs, sticking drawers and warped cabinet doors.
  - Make sure that the doorbell is working.
  - "Unmarred walls": wipe off finger marks and children's crayon drawings from the walls; repair any holes in doors or walls; repair cracked plaster, touch up

paint, glue back loose and dangling wallpaper.
- Oil squeaky door hinges.
- Replace broken or cracked window panes.
- Clean all windows inside and out.
- Replace a faulty light switch.
- Get all dead flies and bugs out of ceiling light fixtures (because their shadowy outlines are visible when you turn the lights on).
- Replace burned out light bulbs, especially in high traffic areas.
- Put an adequately strong light bulb into all light fixtures which are in a windowless area (e.g. hallways, staircases).
- Shampoo carpets, if needed.
- Clean out last winter's ashes from the fireplace.
- Nail down loose roof shingles.
- Attach all downspouts to the gutters.

(4) **Have the house properly aired out.**
- Eliminate spicy and strong cooking smells, tobacco smoke and offensive pet odours, all bathroom odours.
- Deodorize the chesterfield or blanket on which your old hound is accustomed to on lounging.

(5) **Keep pets under control** (preferably out of the house):
Some people may be afraid of, allergic to or simply dislike animals. A friendly dog who greets visitors enthusiastically by jumping up at them, may tear (with his claws) nylon stockings or knock over a small child. The frightened child will cry. The parents (Buyers) will be upset and distracted from looking at the house.

(6) **SET THE STAGE FOR THE SHOWING AND CREATE A "BUYING MOOD."**
   (a) All drapes should be opened, shades pulled up and lights turned on where needed.
   (b) The house should be aired out with possibly some subtle air freshener sprayed in the kitchen and bathrooms.
   (c) Blaring radios, stereos and TVs should be turned off because they are distractions.
   (d) **The Buyers must feel at ease** while they are looking through the house; under no circumstances should they feel like an intruder. If they are disturbed by anything, they will hurry through the house and not buy it.
   (e) For that reason the owners, their children and pets should preferably be out of the house during a showing. Be sure to explain to them the reasons why.
   (f) **If the owners are home during a showing then**
   - they should not follow around or anxiously tag along with the Realtor and his Clients; inadvertently the owners will interfere - if not with words, then by

their presence. Let the Realtor do his job.
- The Sellers should never apologize for the appearance of the house. If they feel that something is amiss, then they should attend to it before the next showing.
- If asked a question, the owners should give a courteous, but brief reply.
- Talk is silver, silence is golden. The owners should not enter into an extensive conversation with the prospective Buyers and **thereby distract them from their original purpose**, which is "inspecting the house" (and NOT socializing with the Sellers).
- Socializing between the Buyers and the Sellers will invariably end up with a **discussion of "what stays with the house"** (e.g. appliances). Possibly even worse are conversations about price, terms and possession dates. If that subject ever comes up then the Sellers' standard reply should be: **"Please discuss this with my Agent."**
- If pressed further by anybody (the Buyer or his Agent) **the Seller should shift the responsibility from himself onto the absent Listing Broker by saying that:**
  (a) he has placed the marketing of his house into the hands of his Agent (the absent Listing Broker).
  (b) That he is paying good money for that service
  (c) and would they please discuss this matter with him.

What happens if the Sellers discuss price and terms?

THE SELLERS may think that they are helpful in enticing the Buyers to make an offer by disclosing prematurely what price and terms they will take.

In fact what will happen is that THE BUYERS will disregard the Listing Price and take the Seller's disclosed "bottom price" **as their starting point.** In other words, whenever they get around to making an offer, it will be for less than what was discussed previously.

The owner may say: **"If the price is right, then the fridge and stove can stay."**

With these words the Seller has given away "for free" his appliances without getting anything (any concessions) in return.

Speaking of appliances and sundry chattels:

In order to justify a high asking price, Realtors (on behalf of their Sellers) often advertise a home with "all appliances and drapes included at no extra charge."

Chances of this really working are remote, because the commercial resale values of used appliances (regardless of how "new" and "good" they are) are generally low. Just read any newspaper. It is more a matter of convenience
- for the Seller not having to move the appliances out (his wife will get new ones for the next house) and
- the Buyer not having to install them.

Both parties know this. The problem with the high price will still have to be resolved through negotiation.

Reasons For Overpricing A Property

Most likely all of you have seen at some time or another in the MLS catalogue or on the computer a listing which was so badly overpriced that the Listing Broker was embarrassed by the asking price. To justify himself to his peers he felt it necessary to point out that the listing price was the "Seller's Price" and that it wasn't his idea.

Of course, and rightfully so, all Sellers want to obtain the highest possible sale price for their property. The following should be kept in mind when dealing with Sellers:

(a) **the Seller**
- is a lay person
- is unfamiliar with "current market conditions" and "values" in general
- although he may have a ball-park idea of what his property is worth, his value judgment may nevertheless be inaccurate. Chances are that it is often too high because he is emotionally involved. E.g.
    - good family memories (Christmas, weddings etc.),
    - expensive over-improvements made for the convenience of him and members of his family,
- all of which mean something to him but not necessarily to somebody else.
- As a result of the above-mentioned points he is not really sure what the **"realistic market value" of his property is.**

(b) **It is up to the Realtor**
- with his thorough knowledge of market conditions and
- with his appraisal experience and
- with his detached professional judgement

to **CONVINCE the Seller that only the "RIGHT" price will produce the BEST RESULTS AND the BEST RETURN for him.**

There are many REASONS for the existence of overpriced listings.

(1) The average person deals in real estate only a few times during his life. When he decides to sell, he first embarks on a **QUEST FOR INFORMATION.** This may include some or all of the following:
   (a) GOSSIP in the form of second or third hand rumours about the fantastic price which the neighbour down the street (allegedly) sold his house for last year; and of course, that neighbour's house was FAR inferior to his own. Therefore, logic says that he should get more for HIS house than what the other fellow got. In the parlance of the business this is called **Unsubstantiated Selling Price.**
   (b) Then there are the opinions of well-meaning friends and relatives who are only too willing to be helpful with good advice. Inevitably one of them is Uncle Joe who 30 years ago had built a garage or a dog house on the Prairies. Ever since that time he

has been the self-styled construction and real estate expert in the family.
(c) Another source of information for the public are the MEDIA:
- Special Reports and interviews during the TV News Hour which report exciting news about local real estate.
- Newspapers who carry carefully worded monthly statistics and sundry releases by the local Real Estate Board or some government agency. Such releases are eagerly read and promptly misunderstood by the public. E.g.: "Sales have risen by 30% over last month." This sort of triumphant blather will invariably make some Sellers think that the market is booming. What the short memory of the public doesn't recall and what the statistics often don't say is that "last month" the market was stone-cold dead and the 30% increase amounts to nothing more than the first weak signs of life. Furthermore for some unfathomable reason, many an Owner will somehow be under mistaken impression that real estate PRICES and VALUES also have risen by 30%. Another example is "Listings have risen by 40% over last year and Buyers have a large selection of homes to chose from." These innocent words may give the unintended impression of exhilaratingly increased real estate activity. What people don't understand is that this could be the signal that the market has changed from a Seller's Market to a Buyer's Market. Because of the increased (by 40%) competition between more Sellers for the attention of the same amount of Buyers anybody who is serious about selling would be well advised to reduce his asking price before all the other Sellers do.

(2) Regrettably, many a Seller will also be MISGUIDED by us Realtors. E.g.: An owner may call upon several Realtors to obtain their expert evaluation of his house. Instead of giving the Seller
- an honest opinion and
- trying to impress him with our integrity and
- compete on the basis of
  - our experience
  - the splendid service which we are prepared to give
  - and our negotiating skills

we instead CONDUCT AN AUCTION to get the listing. Cleverly we find out what the previous salesperson BEFORE us has quoted.

Then we state a price a few thousand Dollars higher in order just to humour/impress the Seller enough to get him to sign on the dotted line. After 3 or 4 salespersons playing this unfortunate game, the eventual highest bidder will get stuck with a hopelessly overpriced listing which will instantly become a millstone around the successful bidder's neck:
- Not only will he encounter stiff buyers' resistance,
- but the overpriced listing will be shunned by his fellow Realtors.

- Should he be lucky enough to get an offer somewhere along the line, the Realtor will find to his dismay that the owner will not be inclined to accept it.
- After all he (the lay person-Seller) had been assured by a number of "experts" (including the current Listing Broker) that his house is worth a lot more than the paltry offer which is before him on the table.

(3) A repeat of the over-pricing situation may arise when Realtors relist an expired Multiple Listing.
If a property listed on MLS is not sold within 90 days and the market hasn't changed, is there any point in relisting it for the same price or for a (much) higher price, just to get a listing? It doesn't make sense and yet, it is being done all the time. Why?

Here are several reasons why this takes place:
(a) Some Realtors subscribe to the philosophy that the product can be sold the second time around if it is repackaged with a different label: for sale by another Company which is "better known"/bigger/smaller/"active" etc. If the salesperson says that he is better/more aggressive/more experienced/harder working than his predecessor was, then he is running his competitor down (and that is a violation of the Real Estate Board's Code of Ethics).

(b) Others will feel that out of sheer self-protection they have no choice but to take this overpriced listing. They justify doing so as follows:
- "If I don't take this listing at this price, then somebody else will. Should it sell after all, then that somebody else will make the money instead of me."
- "Maybe I will be able to get the price down to a saleable level after it has been on the market for a while. Maybe the owner will get fed up clinging to his high price and with time he just might relent."
- "If I put it on MLS, maybe some sucker from out-of-town might buy it or a Realtor from another area (who is unfamiliar with our local prices) will sell it to one of his buyers."

(4) Then there are the Realtors who **do not have enough TIME to explain to the owner what a realistic asking price is**, because
- the appointment has dragged on for too long and
- it is close to lunch time or
- the Realtor has another appointment to go to or
- the Seller has to go to work or
- it is past midnight, everybody is tired and it is time to go home.

(5) **What are some OTHER REASONS why overpricing occurs?**
  (a) Unfortunately one of the most fundamental reasons is
   - **that the Owner DOESN't believe you**
   - **because you did not back up your pricing presentation with**

CONVINCING FACTS: in plain English, you didn't prepare a thorough CMA, together with the necessary supporting documentation:
- COLOUR pictures and
- complete DETAILS about each similar house which has recently been SOLD in the area.

(b) As a consequence the Seller may have **a problem with TRUSTING you because:**
- you are a potential stranger to him
- you have presented to him a somewhat less than enlightening CMA as a result of which he will be under the impression that you are
  - not very good
  - not experienced enough
  - not thorough enough etc.
- unfortunately he may also think that
  - most likely you want to make a quick commission
  - and therefore, you have a vested interest in selling his house at a low price.

(6) Another reason why overpricing can occur is that **the Realtor may fear to confront the Seller too assertively,** lest he runs the risk of not getting the listing at all.

E.g.: The owner may say: "Mr. Optimist from X Realty GAVE me $ 10,000 more than you do." At first blush the temptation is great to lecture the Seller that the other Realtor has not "GIVEN" him anything. The other Realtor is NOT buying the house, he merely quoted a higher suggested listing price in order to get the listing. **Lecturing the owner on his poor choice of words may backfire on you:** you could win the argument, but lose the listing.

A better strategy may be to inform the Owner diplomatically that **a Realtor has NO CONTROL over the market.**

Realtors can control ONLY the MARKETING of the property, in other words:
- how hard the Realtor is **willing to work** (" Mr. Seller I'll work my fingers to the bone for you")
- how much **experience and negotiating skills** the Realtor has ("I am a good negotiator and will try my best to get you top price for your house").
- **how competent** the Realtor is in solving problems which may arise ("I will make sure that there are no loose ends")
- and how the Realtor will **protect the Seller** from pitfalls, legal or otherwise.

For the above reasons, **the Seller's concern should be to select a Realtor**
- who will be able to do the best job for him
- and with whom he is comfortable with.

The Seller should **never select** a salesperson based on

- the highest quoted price or
- who is the most agreeable to his (the Seller's) price.

(7) **Frequently, the Seller bases his asking price on his FINANCIAL NEEDS. In a misguided frame of mind, the old (present) house has to atone for a multitude of sins and to finance all sorts of unreasonable expectations:**
   (a) First of all the sales proceeds from the old house have to get him into the "next house"
   - preferably "Clear Title" because he no longer wants to make mortgage payments.
   - Of course, the next house must be "newer" (no more repairs) and "bigger" (he is "upgrading" otherwise what's the use of moving).
   - An interesting variation of this theme is that his (newer/bigger) next house should be in a better area (read: HIGHER PRICED area). In this respect you can tactfully mention that everybody knows that **real estate values ARE location specific.**
   - The Seller had promised his "Mrs." that in the next house she will get new drapes and appliances.
   - To qualify for new financing, he needs to bring his financial house in order. Specifically, all outstanding credit card debts (with their high interest rates) must be paid off.
   - He had promised the kids a holiday in Disneyland.

The long-suffering Realtor's task is to explain to this kind of Seller that his financial NEEDS (however pressing or worthwhile they may be) **will neither DETERMINE VALUE nor will they INCREASE the Market Value** of his present property. In fact his "needs" have absolutely nothing to do with the Market Value of his present house.

(8) **The Seller may have a POOR REASON for selling.**
Unless he is able to obtain a certain predetermined price which he has in mind, the owner is not willing to sell. **The benefits of moving are not important enough for him UNLESS he gets "HIS PRICE."**

(9) Another difficult aspect may be **the owner's original PURCHASE PRICE** because it may influence his current asking price.

If he has bought when the market was high, he may be reluctant to sell for less than what he paid for way back when. Try to explain to him that
   (a) the real estate market has a tendency to go up and down
   (b) when he bought a few years ago he had most likely paid the **"THEN-Market-Value."**
   (c) only when you compare his original purchase price to **TODAY's Market**

Value that it looks as if he had paid too much.

(d) if he sells "low" at the present time, then he will also buy "low" locally: it is the DIFFERENCE between the 2 (local) houses which counts. This situation may not apply if he moves to another town or province where there is an entirely different real estate market.

(10) Alternatively, if he has arranged for high ratio financing when he bought and the market has dropped since, then he may endeavour to at least walk away debt free by hoping that somebody will just assume his existing financing. (The owner is willing to lose his original downpayment as long as somebody takes over his house debts). **Tragically, he may OWE MORE on the property than what its Current Market Value is.** This situation is a real heart-breaker because the owner may elect to just walk away from the property. After foreclosure proceedings he will still be liable for the difference between the outstanding unpaid mortgage balance and the sale price achieved in the foreclosure sale. This liability is based on his personal covenant (a fine-print clause) in the mortgage contract. To avoid having to pay for this shortfall he will have little or no choice but to declare personal bankruptcy.

(11) **There are also the problems of OVER-IMPROVEMENTS.**
These may come in 2 forms:
(a) **The entire house may be over-improved** (too big, too fancy) **for its surrounding area.** E.g. somebody got a cheap lot in an area where there are 30 year old 1,100 sq.ft. no basement homes. If he builds a new 5,000 sq.ft. deluxe basement home, then he will have trouble recouping his investment (the actual construction costs). The Market Value of the fancy and over-improved new house will be dragged down by the lower values of the surrounding more modestly valued homes.
- Buyers who are looking for and can afford the calibre of such a new home, will not want to live in the area.
- Buyers who wouldn't mind living in the area couldn't afford the Seller's asking price (replacement value).
- What eventually will happen is that the owner will have to live in the house for a period of time and thus "live-out" the cost of over improvements
- or else the house will be snapped up by somebody at a bargain basement price.

(b) If an owner goes **overboard with remodelling** and/or makes expensive improvements (an English-Pub style recreation room, an inground concrete pool etc.) then he should understand that these improvements were made for his personal enjoyment while he is living in the house. It is unrealistic for him to expect that a Buyer will refund the **ORIGINAL improvement costs** (because the improvements may now be several years old).

(c) While some improvements may make a property more saleable (new kitchen cabinets, remodelled bathrooms, exterior painting), it is often uncertain what their **RESIDUAL VALUE MIGHT BE.** By this is meant:

- what amount of Dollars and Cents can be safely added to the asking price?
- **BY HOW MUCH will the Market Value be INCREASED** (because of these improvements) **and still be REALISTIC?**

Consequences Of Overpricing A Property

The Professional Realtor has an obligation to make the Seller understand that the **CONSEQUENCES** of overpricing can be very high for him. The pricing process, based on **a Market Analysis of PRICES paid in recent SALES for SIMILAR properties in the area**, is coldly scientific and starkly analytic.
- **To diplomatically** break the (potentially disappointing) facts of life **(REALITY)** to the Seller (who may not like to hear what he is hearing) and
- **to psychologically know how to go about tactfully CONVINCING the Seller** to list his property at the **RIGHT PRICE … IS AN ART FORM** which can be mastered only **after many years of diligent practice.**

Overpricing may cause the property to miss its market.

(1) When Realtors use computers to find homes, they search by **the price range which their Buyers can afford.** MLS catalogues are arranged in ascending price, but the general idea is the same.
(2) The computer cannot tell what is overpriced and what is not. If the house is overpriced and above the value range of the Buyer, it will not appear on the Realtor's print-out and as a consequence the right Buyer will not see the house.
(3) Those buyers for whom this particular house would be perfect, will not even look at it because they will think that it is out of their price range.
(4) On the other hand Buyers who can afford the (higher) price range will reject this property, because in their opinion it is not good value for that price. (For that SAME amount of money bigger and better quality houses are available).
(5) The public is a lot more sophisticated than it was a few years ago. Buyers are shopping by comparison and are not gullible fools.
(6) Looking at the overpriced home will only convince them to buy a different property. Thus overpricing will turn out to be counter-productive.
(7) Other Realtors will be reluctant to show an overpriced house, because as Agents for the Buyer they have an obligation to their clients to show them homes which are fairly priced and good value. Buyers' Agents know that and take great care not to antagonize their buyer-clients and lose their goodwill.
(8) Occasionally an overpriced property will be shown by a Realtor but only for the simple reason to make another competing property look good in comparison with the overpriced one.

TIME is of the essence.
Many Sellers make the mistake of wanting to **"test the market."** They feel that there is no harm in initially starting high. They may say: "We are in no rush to sell. We want to try it at our price for a while." They reason that:
- if necessary, they can always **"come down later on"**
- or **they can "come down" when somebody makes an offer.**

Regrettably, it doesn't work that way.

(1) There is a certain amount of "excitement" when a property first comes on the market. During the first two to four weeks or so, a property receives the attention of the best potential buyers around, namely those who are at that point in time actively searching the market for a suitable home. **These active buyers**
 - either diligently peruse the newspapers for new ads or
 - they are updated by their Realtors of any new listings coming on the market.

If these good prospects refuse to see the property because it doesn't appear as good value to them (the price being too high) **then the price alone will have killed a potential sale.**

(2) Even if after some time the Seller reduces his market-testing "exploratory price" to a more realistic level, chances are that he will have missed the boat. It is doubtful that any of these original buyers will be still around; most likely they will have bought by then.

(3) A property left on the market for an extended period of time becomes "stale" or "shopworn." Buyers will be reluctant to come back to it, because they may fear that there is something wrong with it. ("Is it still for sale? What is wrong with it?")

(4) Alternatively, **some Buyers may be willing to play the WAITING GAME:** they assume that they will be able to buy it for even less if they wait long enough ("We are in no rush to buy and want to wait to see if there is another price reduction coming along").

(5) As a consequence of persistent Buyers' resistance the unlucky owner of the initially overpriced house may have to keep on reducing his asking price until it becomes an irresistible bargain for somebody. Thus chances are that in the end the owner will ultimately achieve a lower selling price than he might have realized if he had put on a more realistic price tag to start off with.

The fallacy of "Room for Bargaining."
Many Sellers reason (and are encouraged by well-meaning friends and relatives) that Buyers will offer less regardless of what the asking price is.
Therefore they feel that unless they have an adequate (safety) allowance providing for a generous negotiating margin, there will be no room left to dicker when an offer comes in.
Whereas it is true that Buyers will almost always offer less than the asking price, it should be pointed out that it is easier and more realistic to **NEGOTIATE UP TO FAIR MARKET VALUE** than to negotiate up to an inflated and fictitious price.

When things go wrong.
(1) Even should the Buyer for some reason be willing to pay the too-high-price, there is a good chance that the sale will eventually collapse:
- a friend or relative will clue him in
- he may have "Buyer's Remorse" or
- if the Buyer has to arrange for outside financing the following scenario will take place:
    (a) **Lending institutions require an appraisal;**
    (b) the appraiser has an obligation to his principal (the Lender) to come up with a realistic value (he will not merely rubber-stamp the Selling Price).
    (c) The Buyer's new 1st mortgage will be based on the Selling Price or the Appraised Value, **whichever is lower.**
    (d) If the mortgage is based on the lower Appraised Value, then it could be that the Buyer will not have the extra cash needed to make up the difference in the down-payment required.
    (e) In addition, the Bank Manager will most likely inform the Buyer of the discrepancy between Appraised Value and Selling Price.

For these reasons the whole enterprise will turn out to be an exercise in futility.

A REALTOR's INITIALLY HARMONIOUS WORKING RELATIONSHIP WITH HIS CLIENT MAY BECOME STRAINED.

(1) After ramming his head against the wall for a period of time, and having no luck in selling the overpriced listing
- **the Realtor will get frustrated** and might give up;
- or (for financial reasons) he will have to turn his attention to endeavours which have a more realistic chance of earning him a living.

(2) Simultaneously the Seller may come to believe in his (what was originally only intended to be an "exploratory") price and will blame the Listing Salesperson for any lack of action. At this point the relationship between the Agent and the Owner will start to deteriorate.

(3) The next step is that the Seller will be unwilling to reduce his asking price because he hasn't seen any "action" (no prospective buyers viewing his house and no offers). This situation is the result of what the Seller perceives to be an inadequate market exposure of his property. He complains: "You only advertised my house twice in 6 weeks and you have held no Open Houses. Nobody has shown my house."

(4) OR EVEN WORSE, because of his ignorance of the market place, the Seller may turn down a good and realistic offer.

(5) The house stays on the market and the listing will eventually expire.
- The Seller is disappointed and
- somewhat resentful,
- the Realtor is frustrated (he wasted his time and money).

An unhappy situation all around for everybody involved.

(6) Such a Seller could go through several Listing Brokers before the property finally sells (after many a hard-fought-for price reduction).

(7) And then there are the perennial Sellers whose asking prices are always one steps ahead of Market Value. Their houses may never sell.
Actually even these houses will sell some day but only after the occurrence of a catastrophic event (e.g. the incapacity or death of the dominant-hold-out owner. At that stage the surviving partner or any heirs will unload the property without much ado).

Price "REDUCTION" is a misnomer.

(1) When a Realtor asks his Seller for a price reduction, he should try to avoid using the word **"reduction."**
(2) The correct terminology is a **"price ADJUSTMENT."**
(3) When a Realtor talks about "reducing the price," the Seller will automatically be reluctant **"to come down,"** because it means that he will be **losing EQUITY DOLLARS.** In his mind this **translates into actual CASH MONEY.**
(4) It is incumbent on the Realtor to explain to his client tactfully that **the objective of the exercise is to put the price THERE where it should have been to start off with.**
(5) **In REALITY the HIGHER VALUE NEVER EXISTED.** One cannot lose that which never existed.

PRESCRIPTION for an easy way to obtain price "adjustments."
If the Realtor has
- done his job properly and
- rendered the right kind of service,

then it should be relatively easy to obtain a price adjustment from a serious Seller who has a good reason for selling.

Some of these above referred to services are:

(a) **The Realtor should keep in touch with his client on a regular basis**
- After the MLS Tour he should discuss with him the "Tour Average Appraisal" (which is a cross section of opinions obtained from various salespersons of different companies of what the anticipated Selling prices might be).

- The Realtor should report to the Seller all Buyers' reactions and comments whenever his house was shown (that also includes buyers brought by other Realtors).

Put yourself into the Sellers' shoes: people come day in and day out to look at his house and nobody makes an offer. Isn't the owner entitled to some sort of explanation or update?

(b) Make a reasonable effort in exposing the house on the market through
- advertising in various newspapers
- be sure to deliver a copy of each ad and its results (responses) to the Seller (so that he knows what is going on),
- Open Houses (held by mutual agreement)
- displaying the property on the Realtor's website,

(c) Another piece of ammunition in a Realtor's arsenal is to point out to the Seller that an unsold house is a non-productive asset: it prevents him from getting on with his life: e.g. buying another house, moving to another area.

(d) It is stressful and unpleasant to confront the Sellers and ask them to make a price adjustment. Unfortunately many a Realtor is reluctant to undertake this service. It should be remembered that it is the Realtor's fiduciary duty to serve his Client/Principal well and this includes some unpleasant jobs.

(e) Great care should be taken that **the price adjustment is adequate. Especially in a falling market, there is a danger of chasing the price downhill by always being one step behind the market.** (Too little ... too late).

TO TAKE an overpriced listing or NOT ...
THAT is the question!

Over a period of time, real estate markets and prices will rise or fall. In a rising market, prices may actually catch up to what originally was a too high listing price. That is provided the misguided owner doesn't keep on adjusting his asking price upwards.
But in a flat or declining market, overpricing is a killer.
Realtors whose listing inventory continuously consists of overpriced product will not last for very long in the business. The reasons for this are:

(a) **Psychologically** the Realtor will be caught between a rock and a hard place:
- **the Seller will press for service:**
  - expensive advertising,
  - holding "Open Houses" (which is an investment of the Realtor's precious time)
- **the Seller wants "action":** he wants to see offers.
- Due to lack of action, the Seller will become unhappy and confrontational
- very quickly the Realtor will learn that in REALITY

- other Realtors refuse to waste their time in showing an overpriced listing to their Buyers
- Buyers who phone him on his costly ads are no fools and will decline to view the property.

Although listings are the "life blood of a Realtor" and the "backbone of the industry," it may be better for some Realtors to have no listings at all rather than a bunch of hopelessly overpriced ones.

Having low-quality listings might give the Realtor a false sense of security: the Realtor runs the risk of deluding himself that one of them might sell after all and bring in some money. On the other hand, with no listings of his own, he knows that there is no chance for an income from listings. Hopefully this will motivate him to go out and do something constructive.

(b) **Financially**, the Realtor who markets an overpriced listing is faced with the following problems:
- he must spend some of his hard earned after-tax-Dollars on promotion which has little or no chance of giving him something in return or at least to recoup his expenses.
- Instead of doing something constructive he must squander his valuable time on a hopeless enterprise.
- If the above is not enough, he will have the continuous frustration of Buyers and other Realtors enquiring why the asking price is so unrealistic.

And that brings us to the next item which is of importance:

(c) There could be a possible **legal problem:**
- The Realtor owes certain **fiduciary duties** to his Client, the Seller.
- The Realtor must also adhere to his Code of Ethics which require **honest and fair dealings.**

Does the Realtor breach any of these requirements, if he tells **(without his Client's knowledge and consent)** to other Realtors and/or enquiring prospective Buyers that his Client's property is overpriced?

What do you think how this Seller will feel when he finds out what his Realtor has been saying behind his back? (Namely badmouthing the asking price).

How can a Realtor protect himself and his Company?

(1) When he makes his Listing Presentation, the Realtor should have 2 copies of his Competitive Market Analysis. One for himself and the 2nd one for the Seller (as a gesture of courtesy, so that the Seller can follow all of the proffered information on his own during the meeting).

(2) If a listing contract is entered into, then the Realtor should:
- leave the 2nd copy with his Client (the Seller)
- **and ask the Seller to acknowledge receipt thereof in writing; the simplest way is to get the Seller to sign the Realtor's copy of the CMA.**

(3) If no listing contract results, then the Realtor should NOT leave his CMA behind with the Seller because the Comparative Market Analysis is
- the product of the Realtor's work,
- it is his intellectual property,
- it contains confidential information (about other sold or expired properties) and therefore
- it should not be seen by or available to anybody else.

(4) If the property is overpriced, then it should be explained to the Seller that Realtors and Buyers are entitled to some explanation for the price; e.g. "The Seller has made many expensive improvements and hopes to find a Buyer who will appreciate the quality and is willing to pay a premium price for it." Or whatever other reason the Seller is willing to advance. **Again for the Realtor's protection** it may be worth considering that this discussion should be formalized **in a brief written and signed statement (to be kept in the Realtor's file).**

(5) The Realtor may suggest that the Seller - for his own protection - should obtain an independent opinion from a Certified Appraiser. A certified appraisal could be tendered to a serious Buyer when he makes an offer or alternatively, the Buyer may be persuaded to make a better offer if he can use (at no extra charge) that appraisal for mortgage purposes (his Lending Institution will require an appraisal before approving new financing).

(6) After marketing the property for an adequate period of time, the Realtor should be willing to approach his Seller with
- a report of his activities and
- ask for a revision of the Asking Price to a more realistic level (as outlined before).
- **If the Sellers are persistently difficult and decline to make a price adjustment, then the Realtor should keep a separate Activity Log for this specific property** in order to
  - be able to supply proof of his marketing efforts
  - and to record that he has made periodic efforts to obtain reductions of the Asking Price (which could have resulted in an increased flow of activity).
  - In a dropping market a stubborn Seller may lose out on sales because of his unrealistic asking price.

To PROTECT himself from allegations of incompetence, negligence and breach of fiduciary duties by a litigation happy Client, **a cautious Realtor will keep faithfully**

the above-mentioned extensive and detailed ACTIVITY LOG.

(7) Another alternative to achieve eventually a realistic Listing Price is to make an agreement with the Sellers right at the beginning that (if the property is not sold within a certain period of time)
- they commit themselves to reducing the price to a certain predetermined and agreed-to level.
- price reductions could be made in several stages.
- Some Realtors even manage to get the Sellers to sign post-dated price reduction agreements (thus eliminating the necessity of periodic unpleasant haggling or unforeseen back sliding by the Sellers).

OVERPRICED LISTINGS where the Realtor surrenders to the Seller's whims are naturally easier to get; however they have an unfortunate habit of not selling …

On the other hand, as soon as the Seller signs the Listing Contract for **a realistically priced listing, the property is (as good as) "SOLD" …SUBJECT TO FINDING A BUYER**. These type of listings are hard(er) to get, even at the best of times.

So which one is it going to be?
- **List at or near market value and PROSPER or**
- **list at any price and STARVE?**

Suggested Guidelines To Determine The Value Of Raw Acreage Before It Is Subdivided Into Residential Lots

The PURPOSE of this Chapter is to offer some guidelines:
(a) to ensure that the Realtor is CAREFUL in determining (for his Client) a realistic estimate of value of the raw, unsubdivided acreage.
(b) It is recommended that the Realtor keep detailed records and other proof of his investigative efforts in order to AVOID (at a future date) a possible accusation of negligence, breach of fiduciary duty etc.

CHECK LIST.

1) The Realtor may obtain **from the Office Computer:**
   - the legal description
   - the civic address
   - the names of ALL registered owners
   - when the property was last bought and the PURCHASE PRICE which the current owners have paid
   - the amount of gross taxes
   - the municipal assessment (Land and Buildings)
   - The Realtor should **search for previous OLD listings on this property.**

2) The Realtor should also obtain **a TITLE search** from the Land Titles Office showing
   - the names of all registered owners,
   - registered financial encumbrances: e.g. mortgages, liens etc.
   - registered non-financial encumbrances: e.g. easements, Right-of-Ways, Covenants etc.

3) **From the Municipal Hall:**
   (a) Consult municipal **maps** to determine:
   - the **dimensions** of the property (maps will often also show the total amount of acreage)
   - the **zoning**: obtain a copy of the zoning to determine
     - its present (permitted) USE
     - rezoning potentials for possible future use
     - and any subdivision potentials.
   - size and location of the existing SANITARY SEWER, STORM SEWER and municipal drinking WATER LINES in relation to the property

   (b) **Check with the appropriate Dept.** (e.g. the PLANNING Dept.) **if there is a proposed**
   - **SUBDIVISION LAYOUT for the property OR if there is any record**

of a previous attempt to subdivide.
- **OBTAIN AN ESTIMATE OF SUBDIVISION COSTS** (to bring the required services (sewers, water etc.) to the property line.
- The ENGINEERING Department could give **the location, depth and size of sewers and water lines)**
- The TRAFFIC Department:
  - what type of ACCESS is there?
  - What are the **dimensions of existing (paved) roads** and will they have to be **upgraded?**
  - What are the costs of new ones to be built?
- The TAX Department:
  - the names of ALL REGISTERED OWNERS.
  - Are there any taxes unpaid or outstanding? If yes, what are the penalties and accumulated interest for late payment?

4) **PHYSICAL INSPECTION of the property.**
   - Look at the soil condition IN A GENERAL WAY (the Realtor is NOT a soil expert): are there shrubs or trees or an unusual amount of garbage to be removed?
   - Most likely it will be too difficult to try to find the CORNER PINS (the Realtor is not a Surveyor).

5) **Investigate with the proper authorities and specialists:**
   - Is there any contamination of the soil?
   - Waste Management
   - Are there any archeological considerations? (Indian artifacts, heritage designation etc.)

6) **GET AN IDEA OF WHAT CAN BE DONE WITH THE LAND:**
   - what types of properties are surrounding it?
   - Tour the area to see if there are any SOLD or FOR SALE signs (and find out prices and sales data)

7) **FEASIBILITY STUDY:**
This involves
- **A rough ESTIMATE of what a potential buyer could afford to pay for the property given:**
- the Costs to subdivide
- the Costs to service the lots
- Development costs:
  - municipal fees (application, processing fees etc.)
  - amount of park land which may have to be donated to the Municipality
  - all off-site costs

Suggested Guidelines To Determine
The Value Of Raw Acerage Before It Is Subdivided Into Residential Lots

- - architects' fees, engineering costs, sidewalks, street lighting, hydro and telephone
  - LEGAL fees required:
    (a) to TRANSFER title into the Buyer's name
    (b) to create new titles for the subdivided lots.
- **Interest and holding costs**
- The Developer should be able to make a reasonable profit (for his risk in undertaking the venture and for the work involved).

8) Prepare a COMPARATIVE MARKET ANALYSIS based on:
   (a) recent sales of similar parcels of raw, unsubdivided acreage in the area
   (b) recent sales of serviced, subdivided lots in the area

9) This will give you an idea of
   - the total YIELD of number of finished lots per acre (provided the Municipal requirements haven't changed)
   - Establish the retail sale price of a lot in the area (watch out for Market Conditions! E.g. active or slow, rising or falling prices). As it usually takes a long time to subdivide, particular attention should be paid to TRENDS (future market conditions).
   - Calculate how many lots you will have once the acreage is subdivided.
   - Multiply the number of newly created lots (of the acreage) with the AVERAGE Selling Price of similar lots in the area.
   - From this figure (grand total) DEDUCT all development costs, legal fees etc.
   - and the END PRODUCT should give you a rough idea of what the unsubdivided piece of acreage could be sold for.
   - Developers are RISK TAKERS and therefore, their offers will vary.

Activity Check List
___

To be kept in the Listing file.
ACTIVITY CHECK LIST
for the marketing of the property at
___

MLS # _____   **SIGN: Yes/No**   **Lock Box: Yes/No**
Directional arrows: Yes/No

(1) RESEARCH:
Full names of all registered owners _____
_____

LAND:
    Fee simple or
    Leased land: terms of lease _____
    Lot size _____
    Easements, Right-of-Ways, Covenants _____
    Zoning: _____

For a house on ACREAGE:
    Type of well: _____
    Well Certificate .... Yes/No
    Quality and quantity of domestic water supply _____
    Condition of septic tank/field _____

LOCATION:
    Quietness of neighbourhood _____
    Distance to transportation _____
    Frequency of bus service _____
    Distance to schools: elementary _____
                       high _____
    Distance to shopping _____
    Parks and playgrounds _____
    Churches _____

THE HOUSE:
    Age: Date of building permit _____
        Final occupancy permit _____
        Date of water connection _____
        Date of sanitary sewer connection to the house _____
    Current gross taxes $_____
    Tax arrears and penalties $_____
    Current Assessments: Land _____
                    Building _____

(2) PROPERTY INSPECTION at the time of taking the listing
    (see separate Work Sheet):
    (a)   Was one of the owners present? Yes/No

(b) Were any recent upgrades and improvements discussed?_____
(c) Floors _____ Cabinets _____ Clothes closets _____
Condition of bathrooms _____ Plumbing fixtures Old/New
Furnace _____ Hot Water Tank _____ Wiring _____
Oil Storage Tank _____ Roof _____ Insulation _____
Is the basement leaking? Yes/No_____
Foundation _____
Crawl space (access & ventilation) _____
Interior paint _____ Wallpaper _____ Doors _____
Exterior paint (trim, colour scheme) _____

(3) MEASURE all rooms and the EXTERIOR _____
Calculate the floor areas (finished & unfinished)
Basement _____ Main Floor _____ Upstairs _____

(4) The PROPERTY CONDITION DISCLOSURE STATEMENT
(a) Patent defects _____
(b) LATENT defects _____
(c) Defects which have been repaired _____
How long ago? _____
Has there been any recurrence of the problem?_____
(d) Unauthorized accommodation _____
Ramifications of advertising U.A. _____
Owners' written permission to advertise U.A. _____

(5) PHOTOCOPIES MADE of
Existing mortgage documents _____
Survey Certificate (Certificate of Non-Encroachment) _____

(6) The SELLERS
(a) Have all registered owners signed
- The Listing Contract? _____
- The Mortgage Verification Letter? _____
- The Property Condition Disclosure Statement? _____
- Your copy of the Competitive Market Analysis? _____
- **Did each owner receive a copy of the Listing Contract?** _____
(b) Discuss with the Sellers:
- the showing of the house (including "Open House") _____
(hide valuables; bright airy rooms, etc.)
- save other Realtors' business cards for "follow-up"
- **caution the owners**
  - not to follow other Realtors/Buyers around
  - not to discuss price, "what stays" etc.

Activity Check List

- do not let in people who come to the door without an appointment
- **leave a number of your business cards** (to be given out to people without appointments ____
- Discuss with the Sellers **how to prepare the house for showings** ____
- Pamphlet **"Helpful Suggestions to show your house to its best advantage"** _____

(7) **PRELIMINARY ACTIVITY AFTER the Listing Appointment**
  (a) Submit the Listing Contract and the completed Computer Data Sheet to the office _____
  (b) FAX the Mortgage Verification Letter to the Lender
    Done on _____
  (c) Place a "For Sale" sign and "Directional Arrows"
    Date: _____
  (d) Take pictures of the house (front, back, interior)
    Done on _____
  (e) **PREPARE A LIST of all good points of the property** _____
    - prepare a FEATURE [or HIGHLIGHT] SHEET _____
  (f) **PREPARE A LIST of all BAD points of the property and prepare ADEQUATE REBUTTALS** (to overcome objections made by future, potential Buyers). _____
  (g) FOR FUTURE REFERENCE glue the "Good/Bad Sheet" onto the inside of your Listing file.
  (h) Check the **published** MLS listing for **accuracy** _____

(8) **First MARKETING EFFORTS:**
  (a) Hand deliver to the Sellers the **"Thank you for listing with me" letter.**
  (b) **Give to the Sellers a copy of the Lender's reply to the Mortgage Verification letter.** Keep a copy thereof for your records _____
  (c) If necessary, correct the published MLS listing (loan amount, interest rate, renewal date etc.) _____
  (d) Schedule the OFFICE TOUR _____
    Schedule the MLS TOUR _____
    Report and discuss with the Sellers the "Tour Average Anticipated Selling Price" _____
    Written "Tour Average Report" _____
  (e) Give to the Sellers several copies of the FEATURE/HIGHLIGHT sheet, to be available for other Realtors and their Buyers _____
  (f) Run the first ad _____
  (g) **PROMOTE** enthusiastically your new listing to your fellow Realtors
    - in the office _____
      in other Companies _____
  (h) Prepare the ADVERTISING RECORD _____

ACTIVITY CHECK LIST

       Keep the ACTIVITY RECORD up to date _____
- (i) Canvass in a 2 block radius and deliver the **"Just Listed"** cards _____
- (j) Publish your new listing on your website _____
- (k) ADVERTISING:
    - Write several ads _____
    - ADVERTISING RECORD: Periodically mail to the Sellers a copy of each ad together with results _____
    - Discuss with the Sellers and schedule an "OPEN HOUSE" _____
    - Advise neighbours of your "OPEN HOUSE" _____
    - Obtain permission to place **"OPEN HOUSE" arrows on private property** _____
- (l) Hold an "OPEN HOUSE" _____
    - Arrive a little ahead of time.
    - "Open House" GUEST BOOK _____
    - If necessary open drapes, windows, turn on lights _____
    - When leaving make sure that **the house is SECURE** _____
    - **REPORT to the Sellers the RESULTS of the "Open House" and DISCUSS potential Buyers' REACTIONS** _____
- (m) **Price Reduction** _____

(9) 2nd MARKETING EFFORTS.
- (a) Pick up business cards from other Realtors who have shown the property _
- (b) Obtain their Clients' REACTION _____
- (c) **UPDATE the ACTIVITY RECORD** and report prospective Buyers' Reactions to the Sellers _____
- (d) **Constantly update** the Sellers of local Market Conditions, mortgage interest rates etc. and discuss their effect on the saleability of their house _
- (e) Write a new ad _____
- (f) Deliver the updated ADVERTISING RECORD to the Sellers _____
- (g) Hold another "OPEN HOUSE" _____
   Same procedure as before _____
- (h) **If warranted update the "Competitive Market Analysis" and discuss it with the Sellers** _____
- (i) Discuss **new MARKETING STRATEGY** with the Sellers _____
- (j) **Discuss PRICE ADJUSTMENT and LISTING EXTENSION** _____
- (k) Recommend changes _____
- (l) **Privately (and for your own benefit) review how MOTIVATED and REALISTIC your Sellers are based on**
    - their cooperation to date _____
    - previous offers received (if any) _____
    - the Sellers' counter offers (if any) _____
    - Sellers' additional reasons for selling _____

Activity Check List

(10) FURTHER MARKETING EFFORTS:
  (a) REPEAT the above until the house is SOLD _____
  (b) NEVER QUIT.

(11) WHEN THE HOUSE IS SOLD:
  (a) Are all "subject-to" clauses removed? _____
  (b) Place "SOLD" sign, remove the lock box _____
  (c) Canvass the vicinity with "JUST SOLD" cards _____
  (d) Follow procedure for **"After Sale Service."**

MEMO FROM THE DESK OF

Affix your business card here

HELPFUL SUGGESTIONS to show your property to its best advantage.

EXTERIOR:
An attractive, well-kept exterior invites inspection of the interior.
- The lawn should be kept edged and cut.
- Flower beds should be cultivated.
- Shrubs should be trimmed.
- The front and backyards should be clear of junk and refuse.
- In winter time, snow should be removed from the driveway, walkways and porches.
- Peeling exterior paint should be touched up.

INTERIOR:
The objective is to create the impression of a neat and clean home which is comfortable to live in.
- All rooms, especially the bathrooms, the kitchen and all windows should be sparkling clean.
- Keep all drapes open to allow plenty of light to enter. It will make the rooms look bigger and more cheerful.
- If the house is shown after dark, turn on all lights.
- On hot summer days, open windows for fresh air to enter.
- In cold, damp weather, turn on the heat, which will give a feeling of cosiness.
- Clean out all junk from the basement, garage and various closets. That way you will make sure to attractively display all of your storage and utility spaces.
- Keep all bedroom and hall closets neat inside.
- Make sure that all stairways and halls are clear of junk and toys. (Somebody may trip and fall).
- Shut off the TV and/or tune down the radio.
- Keep children and pets under control.

Make low-cost minor repairs:
Fix
- dripping faucets and leaky plumbing
- loose door knobs and broken light switches,
- broken hinges in a gate
- sticking drawers
- warped cabinet doors in the kitchen and bathroom.
- Replace cracked or broken windows.
- Ripped wallpaper.
- Touch up paint or repaint a room as needed.

Helpful Suggestions To Show Your Property To Its Best Advantage

A few "DONT'S" while your house is being shown:

(a) Do NOT accompany the Buyers and their Realtor during the inspection. You will only make them nervous and they will hurry through the house and leave (and not buy).
(b) Answer honestly and pleasantly all questions about the house and neighbourhood and neighbours.
(c) Be courteous but do not engage in a lengthy conversation with the Buyers or their Realtor; this is not a social call - they are there on business.
(d) Don't discuss **PRICE, terms and possession**. If you tell the Buyers what your rock bottom price is, then they will often treat it as their "starting" point.
(e) Don't discuss **"what stays and what doesn't."** Your fridge and stove etc. could be future bargaining chips.
(f) For all of the above refer them to YOUR Realtor.

IF YOU WILL HOLD A GARAGE SALE then you could turn some of your accumulated, disposable junk into cash!

- Advertise the "Garage Sale" in your local newspapers.
- Post notices on corners and the bulletin board of your local Supermarket.
- Place directional signs: they should be "readable," which means that if you cannot read them, then nobody else can't either.
- Make a trial run to ensure that the directional signs can be SEEN and that people can follow them to your house.
- Talk to your neighbours and ask them if they would be interested in holding a "Multi-Family Garage Sale" which is sure to attract more Buyers.
- Put **realistic prices** on everything.
- The price tag should be on top of each item (easy to see) and not underneath at the bottom.
- To avoid future complaints, all items to be sold must be clean and in good working condition.
- Display everything in your driveway; **do NOT let people wander through your house.**
- To attract people and in order to entice them to stop the car (instead of keeping on driving) **display the more interesting items closest to the road.**

Activity Record

MEMO FROM THE DESK OF

=====================
Attach your business card here
=====================

ACTIVITY RECORD

for the property at _____
Date of Inspection _____
Date of Market Analysis _____
Date of Listing _____ Marketing Price $ _____
Date when the "For Sale" sign was placed _____ ("By Appointment Only" sticker)
The Listing was processed to the Real Estate Board on _____
Date of checking details of the published listing _____
Date when the pictures were taken _____
Internet _____ Display Board for the Mall Kiosk _____
The "Feature" or "Highlight Sheet" was prepared on _____
A Lock Box was placed/house key obtained on _____
Date of the Office Tour _____
Number of Salespersons who attended _____
Tour Average Anticipated Selling Price $ _____
The Tour results were discussed with the Sellers on _____
Date of the Multiple Listing Tour (or Agents' Open House)_____
Number of Salespersons who attended _____
Tour Average Anticipated Selling Price $ _____
The Tour results were discussed with the Sellers on _____
Price Adjustment as a result of the Tours $ _____

FINANCING:

The Mortgage Information Request Form was mailed on _____
A photocopy of the Lender's reply was given to the Sellers on _____
New financing was lined up on _____
Details of the new financing _____
CANVASS THE NEIGHBOURHOOD ("Just Listed" cards) _____
"OPEN HOUSE" _____ Number of people who attended _____
Results of "Open" _____ Discussed with the Sellers _____
"OPEN HOUSE" _____ Number of people who attended _____
Results of "Open" _____ Discussed with the Sellers _____
KEEP IN TOUCH WITH THE SELLERS!
Dates of periodic Reports to Sellers _____, _____, _____
_____, _____, _____, _____, _____
Date of Price Adjustment _____ to $ _____
Date of Price Adjustment _____ to $ _____

Activity Record

Date of Listing Extension _____ to _____
Date on which an offer was presented _____ $ _____
Result _____
Date on which an offer was presented _____ $ _____
Result _____
Dates of "subject" removals _____
Date and details of Sale _____ $ _____
Date when the Sales Record Sheet was completed _____
Conveyancing instructions were sent on _____ to _____
The "SOLD" sign was placed on _____
Courtesy closing letter to the Sellers _____
(Pamphlet "What to do and people to notify when moving").
"Just Sold" cards delivered in the neighbourhood on _____
The "Sold" sign was taken down on _____
Date of the transfer of the house keys _____

Suggested letter on your Company's Letterhead reporting the monthly statistical **MARKET ACTIVITIES.**

MEMO FROM THE DESK OF _____ **Date** _____

Dear Mr. and Mrs...

    In accordance with my Agency Obligations it is my pleasure to keep you up to date of real estate developments and the current real estate market in our area. The following information was taken from the latest Multiple Listing STATISTICS of the … Real Estate Board. If you wish, I will be happy to discuss with you the meaning of these statistics and as they reflect on the CURRENT SALEABILITY of your property at

_____

MLS STATISTICS for the month of _____, 2_____

(1)   **Number of SALES in THIS month LAST YEAR** _____
        Number of SALES in THIS month CURRENT YEAR _____

(2)   **ACCUMULATED number of SALES "year to date LAST YEAR"** _____
        ACCUMULATED number of SALES "year to date CURRENT YEAR" _____

(3)   **Number of NEW LISTINGS received in THIS month CURRENT YEAR** _____

(4)   **TOTAL NUMBER of CURRENT Listings "year to date CURRENT YEAR"** _____

(5)   **RATIO of CURRENT SALES to CURRENTLY ACTIVE LISTINGS:**
        "Year to date - LAST YEAR" _____%
        "Year to date - CURRENT YEAR" _____%

Advertising Record

With the compliments of

Affix your business card here

The following is the
ADVERTISING RECORD
for the property at

_____

Valued Clients: _____
===
This property was advertised as follows:
=============================

Name of the newspaper: _____	Affix a copy
Date of the ad : _____	of the ad
Number of calls received: _____	here
Comments (if any): _____	

===

Name of the newspaper: _____	Affix a copy
Date of the ad: _____	of the ad
Number of calls received: _____	here
Comments (if any): _____	

===

Name of the newspaper: _____	Affix a copy
Date of the ad: _____	of the ad
Number of calls received: _____	here
Comments (if any): _____	

===

Name of the newspaper: _____	Affix a copy
Date of the ad: _____	of the ad
Number of calls received: _____	here
Comments (if any): _____	

MEMO FROM THE DESK OF

====================

Attach your business card here

====================

RECORD OF SHOWINGS

for the property at _____

DATE SHOWN	Name of Buyer	Name of Realtor	Phone Number	Comments

OPEN HOUSE

DATE	Name of Buyer	Name of Realtor	Phone Number	Comments

Servicing A Listing - Part I

WHAT IS A "LISTING?"

A "Listing Contract" is a **CONTRACT** between
- the Seller(s) of a property and
- a Real Estate Company (represented by an individual Realtor)
- to **MARKET** the Sellers' property to find a suitable Buyer
- for a specific, limited time period
- and for a certain asking price, terms and conditions.

For the Realtor a Listing Contract is
- an **ASSET** because it offers him the possibility of earning a commission should the property sell.
- Simultaneously it is an **OBLIGATION** because - during the time period before it is sold - it requires from him
  - **WORK** (showings, Open Houses etc.) and
  - the expenditure of **MONEY** (for signs, advertising etc.)
  - without the Realtor having any sort of guaranty that he will be able to recoup his investment of time, work and money.
- Because of the Realtor's **FIDUCIARY DUTIES**, it also creates a certain amount of legal LIABILITY.
  In **"CHAND et al v. SABO BROS. REALTY LTD. et al"** [1979] 2 W.W.R. 248 at 258 (Alta. C.A.)
  the Court held that the test for determining a Realtor's liability was:
  - Does or did the Realtor possess **a special skill?** (e.g. to be an expert in acreages, to prepare an enforceable Contract of Purchase and Sale etc.)
  - Did the Realtor (regardless of a contract) undertake to apply that skill for the benefit and assistance of the Client?
  - Did the Client rely upon such skill?
  - Did the Realtor negligently fail to apply such skill?
  - Did the Client suffer damage as a result of such failure?

A two-way **AGENCY RELATIONSHIP is established between**
- the Realtor (the "Agent"/Servant) and
- his Client (the "Principal"/Master);

This business relationship is based on MUTUAL TRUST.

(a) **OBLIGATIONS OF THE SELLER.**
The Seller (PRINCIPAL/Master) - even if innocent - **becomes VICARIOUSLY liable for the Realtor's** (AGENT/Servant) **misconduct** (e.g. fraud) **and neglects committed in the course of the Principal's business, even though only committed for the AGENT's benefit** (e.g. the earning of a commission).

SEE **"Orris v. Collings"** (1929), 36 O.W.N. 172; varied 37 O.W.N. 233 (C.A.);
SEE **"Evetts v. Taylor"** (1925), 28 O.W.N. 57 If the Principal's behaviour is blameless, then he in turn may be entitled to be indemnified by the Agent.
SEE **"Scholl et al v. Royal Trust Corp. of Canada"** (1986), 40 C.C.L.T. 113 (Ont. H.C.)
The Seller's Agent misrepresented the presence of UFFI foam insulation to the Buyer, who then successfully sued everybody for damages; the Sellers were entitled to be indemnified by the fraudulent Agent).

(b) **Other OBLIGATIONS of the PRINCIPAL include the following:**
- The duty of performing the terms of the Listing Contract with his Agent: e.g.
    - referring all potential Buyers to his Realtor.
    - To pay a commission once a firm and subject-free contract has been entered into between himself and a Buyer who is ready, willing and able to complete.
- **A Principal cannot avoid paying a commission by**
    - holding off closing a sale until the listing has expired; or
    - by acting in complicity with a Buyer to deprive the Agent of his commission. E.g.
    - to ask his Realtor for an unconditional cancellation and then selling the property privately without a commission or
    - to collusively conspire with the Buyer to outwait the Listing Contract.
    - Or to accept an offer and then by his own default preventing the carrying out of the contract.

(c) **OBLIGATIONS of the REALTOR.**
The Realtor's ("Agent"/Servant) duties towards his Principal(s) are enshrined in his **"FIDUCIARY DUTIES."** These are:
- Undivided **Loyalty**
- To keep the Seller's personal information **confidential**
- To use reasonable **care and skill**
- **Full disclosure** of all pertinent and material facts which may influence the Seller's decisions. (Please note: For the SELLER'S PROTECTION "Latent Defects" must be disclosed to the Buyer).
- To **obey** the Principal's LAWFUL instructions.
- To **account** for all monies handled.

Numerous courses have been given and articles have been written about "Agency Disclosure," "Agency Duties" etc. but in the end, it all boils down to a few very simple rules:

1) **THE GOLDEN RULE:**
Ask yourself the following question: **"If I would be the Principal, what would I expect from my Agent under these circumstances?"**

2) Article 4 of the Canadian Real Estate Association's CODE OF ETHICS and STANDARDS of BUSINESS PRACTICE requires of a Realtor to **discover all facts** pertaining to every listing of properties which the licensee handles.

The degree of care must be that which a reasonably prudent salesperson would employ to protect his principal and the public from errors, misrepresentation or concealment of pertinent facts.

The "DISCOVERY of facts" entails "BEING ACCURATE":
- Never take short cuts. In case of doubt, always choose the high road.
- **Obtain and verify all information from an independent source**. This means that the Realtor cannot just take the Seller's word; he must verify the information with the Municipality, the Bank etc.).
- **Double-check EVERYTHING.**
- Do NOT copy any information from a previous listing, because you might be copying your predecessor's mistakes.
- **Disclose EVERYTHING** (that you can legally do); clear guidelines have been set down dealing with questions of "confidentiality."
- **Qualify** what you say and **quote your sources.**
- **Distinguish** between **relaying INFORMATION** and **giving ADVICE.**
- Your job is to be a CONDUIT of information and not an ADVISOR.

3) **WORK with SKILL and DILIGENCE or else LEARN HOW to do it.**

   (a) The Courts are expecting Realtors to write ENFORCEABLE CONTRACTS. See **"SHULIST v. HUNT"** [1987] 51 Alta. LR (2d) 69 (Q.B.) Realtors owe Buyers and Sellers a standard of care.

   To protect the Client:
   - A Realtor must avoid inconsistencies and ambiguous "subject-to" clauses which might render the Contract of Purchase and Sale void for uncertainty.
   - A Realtor must not fail to include appropriate "subject-to" clauses in the Contract of Purchase and Sale.
   - A Realtor must describe easements, Right-of-Ways and other non-financial encumbrances and **make the Buyer aware of their effects on the use of the property.**
   - "Time is of the Essence" … always!
   - Know what the difference is between an "unidentified" Buyer and an "undisclosed" Buyer.

   (b) The Realtor should also **protect HIMSELF** because the "Client From Hell" can and often will sue. Whereas it is probably difficult for the average Realtor to make himself completely legally bullet proof, the following are a few suggestions which may be of some assistance in reducing his exposure.

- Consider the risks of dealing with and accepting a listing from a "Grinding-you-down-Seller." Such a person is not only difficult to deal with, but he will expect and demand "Gold-Plated Service" while paying a marginal Commission. It is the Seller's right to negotiate how much of a commission he will be paying; but at the same time it is also the Realtor's right to choose not to do business with such a person.
- Evaluate the Seller's property CAREFULLY.
- Give him a copy of the CMA and get him to initial YOUR copy of the CMA (which you should keep on file). This will be your proof that you have fulfilled your agency duty of quoting him a realistic asking price.
- Warn him of the risks of overpricing.
- Market his property to the best of your ability in order to get him the best possible price.
- **Take notes and keep a "working diary"** (Advertising Record and Activity Sheet to back you up in case you ever end up in Court).
  By the way: your regular appointment diary should include a **daily work-mileage record**, which will be of invaluable help should you ever be **audited for income tax purposes (car expenses).**
- Keep the Seller informed about
  - changes in the real estate market (rising or dropping sales activity) and
  - interest rates and
  - how they will effect the saleability of his house.
- Protect your Clients AND yourself by **shifting various risks onto EXPERTS.** E.g.
  - legal advice should be obtained from a lawyer.
  - Income tax ramifications should be discussed with an income tax accountant.
  - A building's condition should be evaluated by a Certified Building Inspector.
  - Protect yourself by giving your Clients the names of MORE than just ONE expert (e.g. building inspector). You could be sued for recommending an incompetent person.

- In the form of an ADDENDUM to the Contract of Purchase and Sale, attach a **"Disclaimer Form"** with an **ACKNOWLEDGEMENT CLAUSE.** E.g.: "The Buyers have refused to have the property inspected by an Independent Professional or Accredited Home Inspection Service; it is hereby expressly agreed that notwithstanding of the "Sellers' Property Condition Disclosure Statement," the Buyers are buying this property and any included items and fixtures on an 'As Is - Where Is' basis." From a legal point of view this may not be 100% foolproof, but it should go a long way to

convince a Judge some day that you have tried to be careful and fair.
- Stay away from **"secret commissions"** and **"under-the-table" arrangements.** (E.g. a "list-back" from a Buyer [in order to "make the deal fly"] must be disclosed to the original Seller).
- Resist getting involved in "flipping" properties for a quick profit: this is buying real estate for the sole purpose of immediate resale - especially a resale to a ready-made buyer. These situations are law suit magnets.

(c) A Multiple Listing of a property is **a form of advertising** designed to stimulate the interest of other Realtors to show this house. For that reason it is important that the Data Input Form be filled out by the Listing Salesperson correctly and completely in every respect. If it is poorly or sloppily written it will reflect badly on the Listing Salesperson because it will create the impression that he doesn't care. **Consequently it can also adversely affect the MARKETING and PROMOTION of the Client's house.**

MAKE SURE that you OBTAIN the FOLLOWING INFORMATION:

(a) **A Title Search** will give you
  - the names of **all registered owners.**
  - The correct and **complete legal description.**
  - It will also show all
    - financial charges (mortgages), liens and
    - non-financial charges (easements etc.)

(b) Is the land leased or is it freehold (fee simple) property?

(c) Is the building a Co-operative?

(d) Is any part of the property currently rented out or leased to somebody? (e.g. the rental of a secondary suite).

(e) What are the current **gross taxes?**
  - Do they include charges for sewer, water and garbage collection?
  - Are the taxes paid in full? If not then what are
    - the tax arrears,
    - the penalties and
    - the accumulated amount of outstanding interest?

(f) What is the current **zoning?**

(g) Is the building "legally non-conforming?"

(h) **The lot size** (convert meters to feet for Clients who are not up to speed with "metric"); dimensions and area.

(i) Details of any "Covenants" and non-financial encumbrances.

(j) Also outline the location, purpose and dimensions of any easements, Right-of-Ways etc. (e.g. a shared driveway)

(k) Is **the sanitary sewer** connected to the house?

(l) If there is a septic tank and septic field, are they in good operating condition? When was the last time that the septic tank has been serviced (pumped out)?

(m) What is the source of the domestic water supply? Is it supplied
   - by the Municipality or
   - by a private well? Is the well water supply adequate for the prospective Buyers?
     BEWARE OF THE WORD "ADEQUATE": If the Sellers are a retired couple, then the well water supply may be adequate for them; but if the Buyers are a family with several children then the water supply may be insufficient for them.
(n) The age and condition of the house; are there any guaranties or warranties? (e.g. new construction, new roof). Are the Contractor and/or Roofing Company still in business? (If not, then the "guaranty" is worthless).
(o) What is the type of construction? Wood frame, reinforced concrete, brick, wooden logs?
(p) What is the exterior finish? Wooden siding, stucco, brick, vinyl siding, aluminum siding etc.
(q) What kind of insulation is in the walls and the ceiling? What is the "R" factor?
(r) Are the windows single-glazed or thermopane?
(s) What type of roof is there? (Asphalt shingle, wooden shakes, tar and gravel, aluminum tile)
(t) What type of heating is there? Forced air (natural gas, oil, propane gas) or radiant heat (electric or hot water heat); how many heating "zones" are there?
(u) **The age of the Furnace.** Furnaces often have a DATE CODE incorporated in the serial number or the model number.
(v) What type of hot water tank is there? (gas or electric). Occasionally hot water tanks also have a DATE CODE included in their serial number. How many gallons does the hot water tank hold?
(w) What type of flooring is there? Wall-to-wall carpets, hardwood floors, vinyl, linoleum, tile.
(x) **MEASURE carefully all room sizes and accurately calculate the floor area of the house.**
   - What are the **finished and unfinished floor areas** in the basement, on the main floor and upstairs?
(y) Are there any additions or alterations? Have the necessary permits been taken out and inspections made?
(z) Is there a full basement, a part basement, a low basement, a crawl space? On older ranchers: is the crawl space vented? Is there a concrete floor or at least a poly ground sheet in the crawl space?
(aa) Is the foundation made of continuous concrete? Or is a part of the foundation made of concrete blocks?
(bb) What are the site influences? Cul-de-sac, private setting, view, waterfront; level or sloping land.
(cc) What are the amenities?
   - Distance to shopping, transportation, schools, churches and recreation

centre.
- Indoor/outdoor pool, sauna, sundeck, patio, balcony.
- What type of parking is available?
- Carport: single, multiple, detached, attached
- Garage: single, multiple, detached, attached. What is its size?
  - Is RV parking available?
  - What is the access for parking? Front, rear (backlane).
- Fireplaces: masonry or freestanding cast iron
  - wood burning
  - gas or electric

(dd) **Existing financing:**
Contact the lending institutions who are holding the existing mortgage(s) and **obtain complete details IN WRITING.**

STRATA PROPERTIES.
- The "Unit Entitlement" can be found in the original Prospectus.
- Secure from the Strata Management Company the **current Bylaws and Financial Statements.** Also a **current Operating Budget.**
- Is Council approval required for a new owner?
- Is there a minimum age limit? (e.g. is the complex "adult oriented," say over 40 years of age?)
- Are pets allowed? If yes, are there any restrictions?
- Are rentals allowed? If yes, are there any restrictions?
- How much are **the monthly maintenance fees** and **what do they include?** (e.g. management, caretaker, recreational facilities, maintenance of common areas, exterior insurance)
- Are there any pending **"special assessments?"**
- During the past few years sundry Strata Title properties have been known to suffer from water penetration in the building envelope and/or to have condensation problems (the so-called "Leaky Condos") and mildew problems. **It is therefore very important to peruse for clues all communications from the Strata Council and/or the Management Company for the last 3 years. (Longer if available).**

Apartments may have "in suite laundry" or "shared laundry" in the basement; visitor parking, secured underground parking,, wheel chair access, workshop, playground, daycare centre, a club house or recreation area, exercise area, storage lockers etc.

Mobile Homes in a mobile home park.
- Does the prospective Buyer of the mobile home have to be approved by the park management? Will he have to sign a rental agreement (for the pad)?
- How much is the monthly pad rent? When was the last rent increase?
- Are there any other charges (monthly or otherwise)?
- Are pets allowed? If yes, are there any restrictions?

- Is there a minimum age limit in this park? Are children allowed?
- What are the park's amenities? (Club house, pool etc.)

LAST BUT NOT LEAST:

(1) Each registered owner of the property MUST sign individually the Listing Contract.
(2) The Realtor cannot sign the Listing Contract on anybody's behalf even with verbal instructions or a letter. To do so legally the Realtor must have a Notarized Power-of-Attorney.
(3) **All changes and/or alterations** (in the Listing Contract, e.g. expiry date, asking price etc.) **must be initialled by all registered owners.**
(4) **Each registered owner must receive a separate copy of the completed and signed Listing Contract.**

Servicing A Listing - Part II

GOOD SERVICE is one of the controlling factors of any listing.
GOOD SERVICE will create Client Satisfaction.
GOOD SERVICE will generate referrals and repeat business.
GOOD SERVICE will result in sales and money in your pocket.

Having sent a copy of the Listing Contract and the carefully completed Data Input Form to your local Real Estate Board for processing and circulation, the next things on the agenda of "service" are:

(1) **YOU should check the PUBLISHED listing** (in the catalogue and on the computer) for CLERICAL ERRORS and TYPOGRAPHICAL MISTAKES. The Clerks at the Real Estate Board are processing literally hundreds of listings. Whereas, no doubt they are as careful as possible, mistakes do and can happen.
In the final analysis, **it is the Listing Salesperson's responsibility to ensure the accuracy of the published and circulated listing.** People who may not agree with this view
- should remember their fiduciary duty of CARE, like in CAREful and good quality work.
- Finally those who still feel that they do not need to double check their published listings, they should consider **what their LIABILITY is** if another Realtor relies on the accuracy of the published listing and there is something wrong with the lot size or the floor area of the house.

(2) **Talk to the owners:**
  (a) Obtain their permission to place a "For Sale" sign on the property in a strategically visible place.
  (b) Discuss with the Owners the procedure for **the showing of the property.**
   - They should NOT follow other Realtors and their Buyers around.
   - They should NOT discuss with other Realtors or their Buyers PRICE, terms, possession dates or "what stays with the house" (e.g. washer & dryer); their standard answer to all of these questions should be: **"Please discuss this matter with my Realtor."**
   - Leave a number of your business cards with your owners in case somebody should knock on their door without an appointment wanting to see or show the house. In that case they should refuse admittance and give to the unannounced strangers pleasantly one of your business cards and ask them to contact you for a showing. If they are serious Buyers, then they will do so. Those who don't were most likely only lookeeloos anyway.
   - If other Realtors make appointments directly with your owners, then they should leave their business cards so that your Client can give to you their names and phone numbers.

You in turn will "follow up" and obtain the Buyers' reactions and comments which you will pass on to the owners. **It will pay great dividends to keep the Sellers INFORMED.**
- Discuss with the owners how they can prepare their home for showings. First impressions count a lot with prospective buyers:
  (1) Curb appeal
  (2) Cleanliness and good maintenance
  (3) Create an inviting "welcome home" feeling.
  (4) Discuss recommended changes and improvements.
- Discuss the Office and MLS Tours and the holding of "Open Houses."
- Discuss the installation of a Lock Box and common sense precautions: no cash, jewellery or other valuables are supposed to be laying around in plain sight on top of dressers etc.
- Alternatively, make arrangements to obtain a key, so that the house can be shown when the owners are out. Enquire if you can hand out the house keys to other Realtors for showings or if YOU are supposed to be there to keep an eye on things.

(c) **In order for you to be able to write an effective ad**, ask the owners
- **what were THEIR reasons for buying this house in the first place?** (Chances are that these may also attract another/the next buyer).
- **What did the current owners enjoy most while they were living in this house?**

(3) **Compile a list of outstanding features of the property.**
- **Write several ads** emphasizing the BEST features. By using powerfully descriptive words you will add colour to your ads.
- **Prepare a Highlight or Feature Sheet.**

(4) **Forewarned is forearmed.**
Compile a list of all the BAD features and any draw backs which the property might have. Then prepare in advance the appropriate rebuttals and answers for them, so that you can **MINIMIZE ANY BAD IMPRESSIONS.** In modern parlance this is called "DAMAGE CONTROL" and/or "OVERCOMING OBJECTIONS."

(5) **Take PICTURES of the house - front and back.** Some Realtors will also take pictures of the inside of the house for publication on the Internet or for exhibition at a kiosk in a shopping mall. For inside pictures it would be best to obtain first the owners' WRITTEN permission, because INSIDE pictures show the location of the TV, VCR, computer etc. and could serve as a road map for criminal elements.

(6) Mail or FAX the Mortgage Information Request form.

(7) As soon as you receive **the completed Mortgage Information Request form**, give a PHOTOCOPY thereof to the Sellers for their perusal.

(8) If the financial information which you received from the Lending Institution is different from what it is on the published listing, then don't forget to phone the MLS Department of your Real Estate Board to make the necessary corrections.

(9) It is NOT professional to wait with finding (new) financing until you have a Buyer.
- Discuss methods of new financing with your Mortgage Broker:
    - a new conventional mortgage,
    - a new high ratio mortgage,
    - assume the existing mortgage plus a new 2nd mortgage.
- If the existing 1st mortgage has a low balance, but has an attractive low interest rate and there are at least 1 or 2 years to go before the mortgage is up for renewal then contact the existing mortgagee and enquire if they are interested in **rewriting the mortgage by granting a higher loan amount** (for a qualified buyer) **AT A "BLENDED INTEREST RATE."**
NOTE: This may also save the Seller some or all of the prepayment penalty.
- Occasionally there is also the possibility of the Seller carrying either a 1st mortgage or a well-secured 2nd mortgage. The risks of a "Seller-take-back" mortgage should be explained to the Client and obviously, the Buyer would have to qualify in the same way as if the mortgage would be granted by a Lending Institution (e.g. credit report, work and income verification etc.). **Great care must be taken**
    - NOT to provide 100% financing and
    - NOT to provide any type of Seller financing (e.g. a 2nd mortgage) for a marginal buyer with a poor credit history.

(10) **PROMOTE your new listing by CREATING EXCITEMENT:**
Discuss your listing with
- your fellow Realtors in the office;
- Realtors from other Companies;
- old clients and anybody who might be in the market to buy a house.

(11) Your new listing should become a **CENTRE OF INFLUENCE for you:**
- Deliver **"JUST LISTED"** cards in the neighbourhood and canvass all houses in a 2 or 3 block radius. If somebody is not home, phone them in the evening.
- If you haven't already done so, inspect all other homes which are currently for sale in the neighbourhood (this is your competition. You also may be able to switch a Buyer who doesn't like your listing to buy one of the other houses which are for sale.)
- Take courage and speak to all FSBO's.

Servicing A Listing - Part II

(12) Schedule your new listing for the **OFFICE and MLS TOURS**. After the tours **DISCUSS** with the owners the **TOUR AVERAGE APPRAISAL** and any comments made by other Realtors.

(13) Hold an "Open House" and afterwards report to the owners the results of the "Open" and the prospective Buyers' reactions and comments (but be diplomatic when relaying remarks of harsh criticism).

(14) Set up an **ACTIVITY RECORD** on which you **keep track of your service and systematic marketing activities.** This should also include a **SHOWINGS RECORD** which will detail the dates of all showings, including showings by other Realtors and the comments from all Buyers who have seen the house. **All of this will come in handy at the time when**
- you present an offer or
- ask for a price reduction or
- endeavour to obtain a listing extension.

(15) **Set up an ADVERTISING RECORD** onto which you will glue a copy of each ad you are running on this house. This also will be of help at the time when you present an offer or ask for a price reduction or listing extension.

(16) **Deliver to the owner a copy of ALL ADS** which you are publishing for his house, together with the number of calls received and Buyers' comments.

(17) **Keep in touch with the owners and report to them regularly by phone AND by sending them a photocopy of the constantly updated SHOWINGS RECORD.**

(18) Discuss periodically with the owners
- the general real estate market,
- the level of sales activities,
- interest rates and
- anything else which may influence the saleability of their house.

(19) **IF AFTER 30 DAYS** the house is still not sold
- review and if necessary update your CMA
- discuss with the owners a possible **price adjustment** (reduction) **at which time you will refer to your ADVERTISING AND SHOWINGS RECORDS.**
- This "interview" may be uncomfortable, but it will have to be done for their sake and your sake:
  - **it will be a test of their motivation and urgency to sell! ON HAND OF THIS you will be able to "qualify" your Sellers!**
  - What are your chances of making a sale and earning a commission?

- Are they intransigent, unreasonable and obstinate?
- **Are you just wasting your time?** This may mean having to part company with them, so that you can devote yourself to more productive efforts with somebody else.

In this connection **PLEASE NOTE and remember the following 3 RULES:**

(a) **Often people don't mean everything what they say,** so don't be intimidated, overwhelmed or offended.

(b) **Often people don't say everything they mean,** so learn to read "between the lines."

(c) What **a Client DOESN'T say may be MORE important** than what he does say.

(20) AFTER a successful price reduction INTERVIEW
- submit without delay the price reduction (amendment) form to the Real Estate Board for processing.
- Amend your marketing plan.
- Advise other sales associates in the office and Realtors from other companies of the new price.
- Write a new ad!
- Place a "reduced" sticker on your sign.

(21) **Don't quit or give up until the property is SOLD:**
Repeat the items mentioned above:
- Hold another "Open House."
- **Review with the owners the comments and results of all showings.**
- **Change the picture in your ads.**
- **Write a new ad with a better/different heading.**
- Deliver a copy of all ads to the owners.
- **KEEP IN TOUCH WITH THE SELLERS.**
- Initiate ANOTHER price review and obtain
- possibly ANOTHER price reduction.
- **Don't wait till the last minute for a listing extension.**
- **Get the extension at the time of the price reduction.** ("Mr. Seller, I am going to spend more money on advertising your property and I need the assurance of being able to recoup my advertising expenses and the cost of my hard work, before the listing runs out").
- **DON'T GET DISCOURAGED.**
- Keep up the good work until the property is "S O L D"!

Advertising

The most "READABLE" AD will be the ad which WILL BE READ THE MOST.

The purpose of any kind of advertising is to make the Realtor's phone ring with NEW business:
- new prospects wishing to either buy or sell or
- who may enquire about property management, rentals etc.

In addition to the investment of **TIME and EFFORT** advertising can become a large **EXPENSE** item. Considering that all promotion is paid for with hard-earned after-tax Dollars, it stands to reason that a Realtor, just like any other smart business person, has to be careful how he is spending his cool cash.

Many surveys have been made to gauge the effectiveness of all types of advertising and many learned books have been written about these surveys. But in the end most of them have to admit, that **there is no 100% foolproof and accurate way of measuring the results of promotional efforts**. The reasons for that are actually quite simple:
(a) the ever-changing ups and downs of the economy.
(b) A constantly changing population mix of different tastes, spendable income etc.
(c) A further unknown factor is the uncertainty and fluctuation - at any given time - of the number of genuine "prospects" in the market place.

There are various types of advertising.

(I) **INSTITUTIONAL ADVERTISING.**
The justification and reason for Institutional Advertising are
- **to get NEW business NOW.**
- To **build a strong and positive public image** by keeping the real estate company's name in front of the public on a regular basis (monthly, weekly or perhaps even daily).
- To **get new business IN THE FUTURE**: many people have no intention of moving and yet they read real estate ads. The expectation is that some day they will be moving and if they have heard of you and are familiar with your Company's name, then chances are that they will remember you and call.
- **To build staff morale:** Salespersons will be proud of the Company's public image and they will feel secure in the knowledge that they are working for a good company.
- The Company's **instant name recognition** will hopefully assist salespersons in their conduct of business: in a tight competition it may help them to clinch that listing.
- Because of the increased name recognition and accompanying increased

staff morale, **management will find it easier to recruit new and seasoned salespersons.**

Institutional advertising is a long-term effort and investment. The results will not come overnight. However over a period of time both management and staff should imperceptively sense a gradually and ever increasing sense of general financial well being: perhaps the telephone is beginning to ring more regularly and salespersons from other companies may sense the excitement and come to join up.

Some suggestions for Institutional Advertising:

(a) Think up a **GOOD SLOGAN** and use it in ALL promotions.
(b) Have a **professionally designed GOOD and CATCHY LOGO** and use it everywhere. E.g. on handouts like ballpoint pens, scratch pads, oven mitts, fridge magnets, key rings etc. Use it also on office stationery and business cards.
(c) **Periodically publish in a local newspaper** a picture of the office. Alternate it with a picture of the entire sales staff.
(d) "Word of mouth" advertising will result from being a good corporate citizen. E.g. by sponsoring a team of the Little League or a float in the annual local parade (e.g. Family Day parade).
(e) Yellow pages.
(f) Radio and TV (expensive).
(g) The Sales Staff will appreciate and the public will notice **attractive Business Cards.**
(h) Billboards and benches: By necessity the ad message must be short and to the point. A reader's attention is literally limited to a few seconds of reading time while he is driving by in his car or on the bus.

(II) **ADVERTISING to promote a specific property.**
- What is uppermost on the Seller's mind as soon as he signs the listing?
- And what is the most obvious question which he is going to ask his Realtor?
ANSWER: "When are you going to advertise my house?"

It may be good to advise him that besides newspaper ads there are OTHER EFFECTIVE METHODS TO ADVERTISE a property:

(1) The local Real Estate Board's **MULTIPLE LISTING SERVICE.**
Is there a better way to advertise that a property is on the market, than to promote it to men and women who are earning their living from selling real estate?

(2) **SIGNS OF ANY TYPE.**
"House For Sale" signs should be placed in a strategically prominent and highly visible place.

"House for Sale" **DIRECTIONAL ARROWS**.
"OPEN HOUSE" arrows.

(4) **"JUST LISTED" CARDS:** to be delivered in the neighbourhood.

(5) **"JUST SOLD" CARDS:** to be delivered in the neighbourhood.

(6) OFFICE and Multiple Listing **TOURS**.

(7) A **"FEATURE SHEET": This should preferably include:**
- A colour picture of the house.
- A summary of various good features and amenities.
- All room sizes (in order that the prospective customer may be able to determine if his furniture will fit into a particular room).
- The number of bathrooms and their individual number of fixtures (e.g. 2-piece, 3-piece, full).
- A sketch of the lot, especially if it is irregular.
- The gross taxes.
- Any existing assumable financing (provided the Seller approves its publication) which would be advantageous for a Buyer to assume.

(8) An **"OPEN HOUSE."**

(9) Periodic mailings of a **"Newsletter"** in a farm area.

(10) **"WORD OF MOUTH" PROMOTION** to:
- Other Realtors in the office and
- other Realtors working for other companies.
- Former Clients, friends etc. in fact anybody who might know of somebody who is looking for a house.

(11) **NEWSPAPER ADVERTISING.**
   DAILY newspapers have an anticipated shelf life of 1 day.
   Then they are superseded by the next day's edition.
   WEEKLY newspapers last a little longer.

7 REASONS why Realtors advertise a house in the newspaper.

(a) To pacify the impatient Seller.
(b) You might actually sell the house.
(c) You might get a **PROSPECTIVE BUYER** (who is ready, willing and able to buy **NOW**) but doesn't find the advertised house as suitable and you manage to sell him something else.

(d) You might get a **LISTING** (from a prospective Buyer who has to sell his house first before he is able to buy).

(e) You might get a **SUSPECT**. He is an undecided Buyer who for some reason is not yet quite ready, willing or able to buy NOW. If he is genuine and has good intentions then he might have the potential of becoming a "PROSPECTIVE BUYER."

(f) And finally you might also get a **"PERPETUALLY SEARCHING SUSPECT."** That is a person who is uncertain what he wants. **In his seemingly endless search he is difficult to satisfy:** " When I see the RIGHT house I will buy it."
Upon investigation (you should routinely "qualify" your Buyers) it turns out that he is not only NOT yet ready and willing to buy, but often he is also UNABLE to buy NOW or in the near and foreseeable future. **THIS type of CUSTOMER IS CALLED A "TIME WASTER." He is not only demanding, but will also unscrupulously waste your precious resources (time, work, health etc.)**

(g) Individual name recognition, public image, prestige etc.

PROBLEMS and DIFFICULTIES which can be encountered when advertising in a newspaper.

(1) Many houses are quite similar to each other; if you recite their "virtues" and "good points" then the end result may turn out to be quite similar to ads from your competition. It will remind a reader of "deja vu."

(2) What works for one Realtor may not work for another.

(3) One of the reasons why Realtors advertise is to get a Buyer. Frustratingly some of these callers can engage in some irrational behaviour.
NEW SALESPERSONS PLEASE NOTE and learn:
A Buyer may claim to be looking for a 4 bedrooms basement home out in the country for privacy and then he ends up buying a 2 bedroom townhouse in the middle of the city. Why would he do that?
- Because he fell in love with something that the townhouse offered.
- He then made an EMOTIONAL DECISION and
- his mind immediately supplied LOGICAL REASONS to JUSTIFY what his heart had foolishly decided.

Although a Realtor must basically adhere to the **FACTS** as he hears them, he must be simultaneously on the lookout for **the Client's tell-tale EMOTIONAL REACTIONS.**

(4) For many people buying a house is the biggest single investment of their lives. Many are sure of only 2 things:
 (a) what they do NOT WANT and
 (b) what they CANNOT AFFORD.

Other than that they have a more or less admittedly nebulous idea of finding the "MOST house" which offers them the "most amenities" for what their money can buy.

(5) **BUYERS ARE BASICALLY INTERESTED IN 3 THINGS:**
  (a) The **AREA**: meaning
   - a quiet street of well-kept similar residences.
   - The proximity to public transportation, schools, shopping, recreational facilities and churches.
   - Good freeway access for an easy commute to work.
  (b) **DETAILS:**
   - Number of bedrooms and bathrooms.
   - Age and condition of the house.
   - The lot size and floor area of the house.
  (c) **THE COST:**
   (a) Notes about the total **ASKING PRICE:**
    - **IF THE PRICE IS NOT MENTIONED** in the ad then some people will not phone because they jump to one of 2 conclusions:
    - Some people think of the motto: "If you have to ask then you can't afford it." They rather will not phone you because they want to avoid the embarrassment of having to admit it that they cannot afford the house.
    - Alternatively, people may not phone because they assume that the house is so badly overpriced that the Realtor is too embarrassed to mention the asking price in the ad.
   (b) **The downpayment and the monthly mortgage payments.**
    Talking about "easy terms" is meaningless, unless the prospect can raise the downpayment and is able to handle the monthly payments.

VARIOUS "DON'Ts"

(1) Don't write an ad when you are in a rush, worried or tired. If you do it then you will most likely throw away good cash. It is somewhat akin to lighting a cheap cigar with a $ 100 bill.
(2) Don't write an ad for a house which you haven't seen.
(3) Don't advertise a house that is sold or which the owner has taken off the market, in the hope that you will "catch a Buyer" whom you could switch to something else. This is called **MISLEADING ADVERTISING**.
(4) **AVOID USING TOO MANY ABBREVIATIONS.** It might save you ad space, but the reader may not be able to understand what you are trying to say. In frustration he will give up and move on to read another ad.
(5) **AVOID THE USE OF REAL ESTATE JARGON and/or difficult technical terms.** Unless you are mechanically inclined you will not understand and appreciate the technical intricacies of a car motor. The same applies to real estate and a lay person.

(6) Try to **AVOID "BREATHLESS" and NEBULOUS LANGUAGE.**
Expressions like "features galore," "loaded with extras," "stunning executive home," "too many extras to mention," "charming dream home" sound nice, but are **OVERused and UNDEReffective. Home Buyers want FACTS.**

(7) **AVOID FALSE CLAIMS and INACCURACIES:**
Sometimes an owner gives to a Realtor information which he truly believes to be correct. In reality this information may subsequently turn out to be either misleading or even worse, incorrect. A Realtor as a "Professional" has an obligation (for his Client's and his own PROTECTION) to independently investigate and verify all representations and information supplied by the Sellers. Of course, this should be done discreetly in order not to embarrass or antagonize the Sellers.

(a) **Be certain to comply with all relevant provisions of the law and existing legislation.** Canadian Realtors should familiarize themselves with the COMPETITION ACT.

(b) Minimizing any flaws or defects could be viewed in Court as **artful or creative CONCEALMENT.** It is better to stick to the facts.

(c) Why start a Realtor-Client relationship on the basis of a DECEPTION? Avoid "puffing" (exaggeration) and don't stretch the truth. If the Buyer's dream of a lifetime is to have an "ocean view" he will be disappointed and frustrated when he sees the real thing and realizes that he has to stand on top of a 10 ft. step ladder in the North-East corner of the sundeck to get a glimpse of the water. The same goes for the **"winter view"**: you can see the water only in late fall and winter after all the leaves have fallen from the trees (which block the view during spring, summer and early fall).

(8) **SOME ETHICAL CONSIDERATIONS which should be pondered.**

(a) Is there anything wrong with advertising a **"ROCK BOTTOM BARGAIN?"** Of course NOT! As long as it truly is a bargain in comparison with other similar houses which are currently for sale. Anyway people have become rather sophisticated and won't be fooled.
Same as there is no such thing as a "free lunch" everybody knows that nothing of value will be given away for "free." So if it is too good to be true, then it usually is. On the other hand **BARGAIN HUNTERS are not necessarily qualified Buyers.**

(b) Legitimately, however, a **"HANDYMAN's SPECIAL"** may appeal to somebody who has initially little money, but wants to build up some **"SWEAT EQUITY."**

(c) The word **"NEW."**
"New" means exactly that, namely brand new:
- construction was recently completed and
- nobody has ever lived in the house.
- A one year old roof is not "new."

Appliances like a fridge and stove are "new" only
- if they have recently been delivered from the store and

- have never been used by anybody.

(d) **"DISTRESS SALE," "FORECLOSURE" and "DIVORCE."**
 These headings could cause embarrassment to the Seller and could generate fear or suspicion in a prospective Buyer. Some people may get turned off and may not want to take advantage of the financial woes or personal misfortune of others. The same goes for the **"SACRIFICE SALE."** Before using these type of headings, the Realtor may wish to consult first with the Sellers and obtain their permission to do so.

(e) Another favourite headline is the **"REDUCED FOR QUICK SALE."** To some Buyers this means that the price was too high before and now the Seller must bite the bullet because he is running out of time. A savvy Buyer then might ask himself the following question: "How desperate to sell is the Seller really... NOW?" Perhaps it may be to the Buyer's advantage to wait a little longer to see if there will be any further price reductions.

(f) A similar thought process might be elucidated from advertising an **"ESTATE SALE"** or **"TO SETTLE AN ESTATE."**
 The implication is that this is not a regular arms-length sale, but that the Buyer can get it CHEAPER because the Executor of the Estate wants to wrap up things quickly and the heirs are anxious to get their share of the inheritance. Any thinking Realtor must realize that an Executor has an obligation to sell the property at fair market value and not to give it away. In a similar vein is the **"COURT ORDERED SALE"**: the lawyer for the party who is foreclosing has an obligation to try to obtain the maximum available sale price. It is also very doubtful that a Judge will endorse a give-away price.

(g) References of **"CLOSE TO"** or **"NEAR"** or **"WALKING DISTANCE"** are open to interpretation. If the nearest bus stop is 1 km away from the house, a marathon walker in good shape will find it to be a brisk little walk. On the other hand a person with painfully arthritic knees will find the same distance rather too far. It may be better to say "2 blocks" etc. The same thoughts apply to the expression **"CONVENIENTLY LOCATED TO ..."** What may be "convenient" for one person could be inconvenient for another.

What makes an ad an EFFECTIVE AD WHICH DRAWS CALLS v. just another routine ad which doesn't?

(1) **PREPARATION.**
 (a) It is difficult to compose a good message just off the cuff. To assist your memory when it is time to write the ad, you may wish to **use a tape recorder or a little note book to record ALL THE GOOD FEATURES about the house.** Do this **while you are inspecting and/or measuring the house**. Later on write your observations down into your LISTING FILE for future reference.
 (b) Ask the current owners:
   - Why did they buy this property in the first place?

- What was it which they enjoyed most while living there?

Write that information also into your listing file so that you will be able to incorporate it in your future ads. Chances are that what worked for the current owners will also attract and work for any future owners.

(2) **DEVELOP A KNACK FOR WRITING GOOD ADS.**
This requires from a Realtor a big investment:
 (a) **Time-consuming research.**
  Carry a little note book around with you. Whenever you see a good heading or some attractive wording write it down into your booklet. This works especially well when you are on holidays and read a newspaper from another town. Chances are that you will glance at the real estate ads and what catches your sophisticated eye will surely work on a lay person back home.
 (b) **Increase your word power.**
  Accumulate a treasure horde of powerfully descriptive words. This also requires a lot of patience and hard work.
 (c) **Set aside a regular time** or day for ad writing. Of course, it should be a time when interruptions are at a minimum and least likely to occur.
 (d) **CONCENTRATE on what you want to say.**
  - Carefully select the attractive features and strong points of the house.
  - Stick only to the facts.
  - Try to be brief and selective.
 (e) All Realtors' ads are competing with each other for the Reader's attention. Therefore, it is important to compose a message which is
  - designed to attract the Reader's attention,
  - appeal to him as a "Buyer" and
  - stimulate him to action (namely to pick up the phone and call you).

KEEP IN MIND THE FOLLOWING 2 ACRONYMS:

(I) **"AIDA":**
 "A" stands for "ATTENTION"
 As the ad reader's eye glances over the newspaper page, your precious and expensive ad probably only has 1 or 2 seconds of time to catch his **ATTENTION**.

 "I" stands for "Interest"
 Ask yourself what will be of INTEREST to the reader.
 What will change his mind from hurried and bored indifference to a feeling of anticipation that he may read something - to him - fundamentally IMPORTANT?

"D" stands for "Desire"
What will transport the Reader's mind to a state of eager URGENCY that it is beneficial for him to make further enquiries?

"A" stands for "Action"
What will EXCITE the Reader and MOTIVATE him to pick up the phone and call you?

(II) **"NIHAM":**

"N" stands for "Noticed."
For **the ad to be NOTICED** it must have
- **a smart HEADING** because it is the ATTENTION GETTER.
- The Reader must be INTRIGUED by the heading, which should be either unique, imaginative or humorous.
- Try to leave some WHITE EMPTY SPACE around the ad.
- Possibly an attractive or interesting BORDER.
- The use of different sizes of TYPE SETTING; e.g. all caps, italics, bigger and bolder letter types.

"I" stands for "Interesting."
What makes an ad appealing and interesting? **BENEFITS.**
Only BENEFITS make it worthwhile for a prospective Buyer to read the ad. **Dramatize the emotional aspects** of the desirable features: comfort, closeness to amenities, seclusion, the value of the "extras," prestige, quality, good and safe investment etc.

"H" stands for "Honest."
- Stick to the facts.
- Eliminate the meaningless and unessential.
- Let the property speak for itself.
- Arrange the facts in their most effective order.

"A" stands for "Appealing."
- **The BODY OF THE AD should create and stimulate desire and arouse curiosity.**
- The ad should be **EASY and INTERESTING to read.** Therefore USE **PLAIN TALK.** Write in enthusiastic, but in simple, EVERYDAY LANGUAGE as if you were talking normally.
- Use **SHORT SENTENCES** because they **will improve READABILITY. The MOST READABLE AD will be the ad which will be read the most.** The average Reader's ATTENTION SPAN (patience) is SHORT; therefore, don't write a book. It is not true that the more you tell, the more you sell. You will have an opportunity to do that in person at a later stage.

- Streamline the information.
- Break the ad into NATURAL TOPICS.

"M" stands for "Motivating"
The ACTION LINE at the end of the ad should stimulate and motivate the reader to pick up the phone and call you ... NOW!

(f) FIT THE RIGHT BUYER TO THE ADVERTISED HOUSE.
- VISUALIZE IN YOUR MIND what type of Buyer will most likely buy this house. (A retired couple, a young couple, a family with children etc.)
- Ask yourself what is it that will most likely
    - APPEAL to him and
    - what will ATTRACT him?
    - Exactly WHAT is it that
        - will EXCITE this Buyer to call and
        - MOTIVATE him to buy?

It can be summarized in one word: "BENEFITS."

"BENEFITS" are:

I) **MONEY** matters:
   (a) **Affordability:** try to guess what (most likely)
   - would be the income of a typical Buyer for this property?
   - This will determine the amount of new financing (mortgage) which he can qualify for.
   - The downpayment is a "variable" and an "unknown factor" (because the Buyer may get some outside help from a relative).
   - Having reconstructed the above "guesstimates" you should address you advertising to such a Buyer.

   (b) **Profit:**
   - yes, everybody likes a bargain.
   - **Avoidance of loss** (don't procrastinate and loose out) "you snooze - you loose."

   (c) **APPEAL TO BASIC HUMAN NEEDS:** convenience, comfort, love of family, happiness, security, health, contentment, satisfaction.

II) The prospective Buyer's **"EGO"**
   - status and prestige
   - INDIVIDUAL TASTE or PREFERENCE.

III) **LEARN FROM THE PROFESSIONALS** when talking about **"BENEFITS."**
Ads for cars, toothpaste, mouthwash, deodorants etc. on TV and in magazines are written by professional ad agencies. These ads don't describe the components

of cars or the ingredients of the mouthwash. Instead they talk about BENEFITS and stimulate the imagination of the viewer or reader and flatter his ego. So **why are real estate ads so dreadfully descriptive and simultaneously so similar to each other?**

(3) **You should not only PLAN, but also EDIT and POLISH your ads.**
   (a) Eliminate weak, meaningless words and shop worn phrases.
   (b) Don't change a good ad that works for you. Only change a poor ad.
   (c) Vary your ad; try out different newspapers; experiment around by varying the days on which you are running ads.
   (d) **A picture is worth a thousand words.**
   A good picture will show the property to its best advantage. Therefore, it should be:
   - properly focused.
   - Adequately exposed (well lit, not too dark, not too light).
   - Experiment around and take a shot from different angles. Only a shot from the most advantageous angle will show off the property from its best side.

(4) **FIVE FINAL THOUGHTS.**
   (a) COMMUNICATION IS IMPORTANT.
   - Mail a copy of each ad to the Sellers so that they know what you are doing.
   - Let them know how many responses you have received on each ad and what the callers have said.
   - In due course this will help you greatly when you present an offer. The Seller will not be able to say: "You never advertised my house. I never saw an ad." Alternatively he cannot say: "Nobody ever looked at my house" if you mailed him the ads and relayed the information that prospective Buyers declined to make an offer on the house because they felt that the price was too high.
   (b) **Various advertising programs should be discussed periodically at sales meetings.**
   (c) BRAINSTORMING will pay huge dividends.
   (d) Don't be discouraged: the law of average works for you. **The watchword is "PERSISTENCE."**
   (e) **A Salesperson MUST be accessible and available to return all incoming ad calls promptly.** If you are going to be out of town on the weekend, then there is no point in advertising. If you attend a concert, theatre, movie or some live performance, then turn your pager to "silent"; but check it during the intermission and use your cell phone to return calls. Both of these gadgets have become very affordable. If you use them judiciously then they will pay for themselves.

A Few More Thoughts About Advertising

As soon as the Sellers have signed the listing contract, their first question will most likely be: "When are you going to advertise my house?"

For the Realtor, this is a LARGE EXPENSE ITEM (involving cool cash, effort and time).

Negative reasons for advertising:

1) To pacify an impatient Sellers is a poor reason to advertise.
2) The Realtor may get a phone call from an **"EXPECTIVE SUSPECT."** An "ES" is
   - uncertain what he exactly wants. Therefore, he is not yet ready and willing to buy.
   - For that reason he has been "looking" for a long time.
   - Upon investigation (qualifying) it turns out that he is also UNABLE to buy NOW or in the near future.
   HE IS A TIME WASTER - avoid him like the plague!

Positive reasons for advertising:

3) A **"SUSPECT"** may call the Realtor. A "SUSPECT" is a Buyer who is not yet quite ready, willing and able to buy NOW. **Put him on the back burner:** if he has good intentions then he may have the potential of becoming some day a PROSPECTIVE BUYER.
4) The Realtor might get a phone call from a **"PROSPECTIVE BUYER"** (who is ready, willing and able to buy NOW) and
   - who will actually end up buying the advertised house or
   - the Realtor is able to sell him something else.
5) The Realtor might get a LISTING from a prospective Buyer who has to sell his house first before he is able to buy.
6) **Public image, prestige, becoming "known" in the local market place:** many people who have no intention of moving read real estate ads. But some day when they will be moving, then they will call you, because they are familiar with your name.

As many houses are quite similar to each other … reciting their virtues and good points may end up as "deja vu."
So what makes an ad
"a good ad which draws calls v. "just another routine ad?"

(1) The answer is simple: the Realtor must **develop a knack for writing effective ads.** Not every salesperson is able to compose a brief, simple message just off the cuff.

- To assist your memory **take NOTES while you are inspecting the property** (when you are listing it).
- Set aside a regular day or time for ad writing. Preferably a time when the phone rings the least.
- **Concentrate** on what you want to say.
  - Carefully select the facts and strong points of the house.
  - **Be BRIEF and descriptive** (increase your word power)
  - Don't write a book; it is not true that the more you tell the more you sell.
  - Readers have a short attention span.
  - Short sentences will improve readability.
  - PLAN, EDIT and POLISH YOUR ADS, eliminate weak words, shopworn phrases (e.g. "Executive Home," "Easy Terms" (are meaningless), "This is good!" and "This won't last" mean that you cannot think of anything else to say).
  - Therefore, eliminate the meaningless and unessential.
  - **OVERused words are often UNDEReffective:** "nice, charming and gracious" mean different things to different people.
  - The ad will be easy and interesting to read if it is written in YOUR everyday language, in **plain talk but simple and enthusiastic**.
  - Let the property speak for itself (spacious, loaded with extras)
  - The MOST readable ad will be the ad which will be READ THE MOST.

(2) Generally, the AD MUST BE NOTICED by being
- APPEALING (white space, border, different sizes of type setting: all caps, italics, bigger or bolder type etc.
- and **INTERESTING:**
  The **HEADING** should attract attention in a unique, imaginative or humorous way.
  The **BODY** of the ad should
  - create and stimulate desire and arouse curiosity.
  - Try to break the ad into natural topics.
  - Arrange facts in their most effective order.
- As the ad reader's eye glances over the page, your ad will literally only have one or 2 seconds of time to catch his attention and create a feeling of URGENCY in him that he will read something fundamentally IMPORTANT.
- Put yourself into the ad reader's shoes:
  - what will be of interest to him?
    - **Area:** meaning the proximity to amenities (public transportation, schools, shopping etc.)
    - **Utility:** number of bedrooms and bathrooms, basement or no basement.
    - **Cost:** asking price and terms.

- What will excite/attract/motivate him to read the ad?
- What will transport him from a state of bored indifference to a state of eager anticipation?
- What will change his mind from "hm, sounds interesting,"
- to "maybe I should check this out"
- to "I am going to call this Realtor right away?"

(3) The relative **PULLING POWER** of the ad.
There have been many surveys made and books written about effective advertising, but there seem to be no clear answers.
- What works for one person may not work for others.
- There seem to be no or few set formulas or rules.
- However, the law of average works for you.
- Don't change a good ad that works.
- Only change a poor ad.
- Many prospective Buyers are sure of only 2 things:
    - What they do not want and
    - what they cannot afford.
    - Other than that they have only a nebulous idea of finding the MOST house, offering the MOST amenities which their money can buy.

(4) **FIT the RIGHT BUYER TO the ADVERTISED HOUSE.**
- Visualize the type of prospective buyer who is most likely to buy this house and TRY TO ATTRACT HIM!
- What could be the composition of the family? E.g. a retired couple or a growing family, perhaps with pets.
- Ask yourself what will most likely appeal to that type of buyer?
- What could be his average income (which will determine how much of a mortgage he can qualify for).
- What will **MOTIVATE** this Buyer to buy?
  BENEFITS:
    - money (affordability or profit),
    - love of family, convenience, security
    - ego (status & prestige),
    - individual taste and preferences.
    - A picture is worth a thousand words.
    - **Ask the present owners**
        - what made them buy this house in the first place and
        - what they enjoyed most about living in it.
  This will most likely appeal to the next buyers, also.

(5) **Vary the ad,**
- vary the days on which you are running ads,
- try out different newspapers.

(6) DOUBTFUL EMPHASIS:
- DON't write an ad when you are in a rush, worried or tired. If you do this, you will be throwing away good hard cash.
- Don't write an ad for a house you haven't seen.
- **Avoid "puffing" (exaggerating).** Why start a Realtor-Client relationship (with a prospective Buyer) on the basis of a deception?
- Minimizing any "flaws or defects" could some day be viewed in Court as **artful or creative CONCEALMENT.**
- Stick to the facts.
- Avoid false claims and inaccuracies: an "ocean view" is not an ocean view if you have to stand on top of a 10 ft. ladder in the NE corner of the sundeck in order to glimpse a bit of water.

OTHER WAYS OF ADVERTISING:

- Billboards and benches:
  By necessity the messages must be short. They literally must be limited to seconds of reading time while the prospect is driving by.
- Business cards (consider "splurging" and have them professionally designed).
- Pens, scratch pads, oven mitts, key rings, coffee mugs etc.
- Radio and TV advertising (is often expensive)
- **Periodic mailings of "newsletters," annual greeting cards etc.**
- Former Clients "Appreciation Night."
- Teaching at night school.
- **The BEST ADVERTISING is by word-of-mouth: "REFERRALS"**
- Same as "REFERRALS" … "REPEAT BUSINESS" is earned by GOOD SERVICE.

Advertising Lead Lines

TO ADVERTISE THE REALTOR's SERVICES.

(1) List your house with me and I'll spoil you rotten with good service
(2) List today - sell tomorrow
(3) I want to sell your property as much as YOU do
(4) The properties I list are selling like HOTCAKES. To find out how much I can get for yours, please call me at…
(5) The sale or purchase of a home deserves organized and complete attention … from an expert!
(6) I will find the right buyer for your property … wherever he may be.
(7) Do you have to sell before buying? I will solve your dilemma.
(8) My work: Professional - productive - efficient - courteous
(9) The "Action" Agent: Working harder than many …
(10) When you let me go to work for you, this is what I am going to do for you!
(11) To work hard and long hours each day
   Is ALBERT's tireless way.
   To sell your house is what I need,
   Because I sell houses at breakneck speed.
(12) Do you have a house you want sold? Call …
(13) I work hard and get results
(14) To hire me to sell your house is INCREDIBLY SIMPLE.
   The good service I will give you is SIMPLY INCREDIBLE.

VALUE

Accent-on-Charm
Accent-on-Value
Read my lips - MOM's delight
The answer to your dreams is within your means
The Power of Your Dollar
Lasting Value
Prudent Buyer - Super Value
Ca$h Cow
$mart Buyers
Home with many extras
All spruced up & ready to sell
NOT your average "box"
Gorgeous big rancher
$prawling rancher
Honest to goodness Value at $…
A LOT for a little

L(.)(.)K
Wine Cellar or Bomb Shelter
It's close to everything but nothing comes close to it
Buy a home a builder would buy
Large lot lovers
Crackling fire - sizzling price
Your hectic days of house shopping may be over
This home feels so good
Sensible & special
Don't wait for the "Sold" sign - see today …
A gem for a wise buyer
A Memory Maker
Step-saving floor plan
Innovative features
You sometimes know you're going to love a house before you walk inside.
Better "see" than be "sorry"
Value with variety
Your family's delight
Many happy hours will be yours in …
Soft carpeting & tastefully chosen draperies
In flawless taste & condition
Outside average - inside AAAHHH
The "N" word: NICE
Come see - come sigh
Custom-built with meticulous attention to all details
Ideal for lazy gardeners
Picture perfect
Charm personified
Morning coffee on the patio
Plop - plop … Fizz-fizz
All the right stuff
Spiffy
Wall-to-wall Value

KITCHEN

Wanted! Good cook to go with this charming oak kitchen
Step-saving kitchen
Practical "wife-saver" kitchen
Woman's delight kitchen
A kitchen made for holiday cooking

LUXURY

Sumptuous & pampered
Quality & class
Elegant good taste
Practical luxury
High end living
Languish in luxury
Sophisticated - elegant charm
Stunning & prestigious
Elegant gracious living
In flawless taste & condition
Elegance blended with livable informality
Understated elegance
Classic elegance
Symbol of success
Tradition
Gracious and spacious

BARGAIN and ECONOMY

A lot for a little
Economy & convenience
Dollars at a discount
Hard to beat at this price
Budget Pleaser
Budget Priced
Nifty for the Thrifty
Sizzling Price
So much for so little
$pecial
For low-calorie budgets
Squeezing pennies
The price is wrong - it's much too low
Priced to sell by transferred owner
A little tear falls from my eyes when I think of you paying rent when you could be investing your money in this …
New York Steak Value - but this home is "hamburger" priced
AAhh-choo - are you allergic to high prices?
Rent slips are like quicksand
Famous last words: "We should have looked at that home"
Wallet watcher
You'll know where your money went - if you buy this home instead of rent.

Long on value - short on price
Always sought - seldom found
Hagglers invited
Pinch-yourself price
Be QUICK & start SMART
$top! Circle Ad! Call me!
Worth every penny
Low calory income?
You snooze - you loose
Next to everything for next to nothing
Buy today - reap tomorrow
Even your parents would approve
Hard to find - easy to own
Your instinct for a good buy will tell you …
Wallet Watcher
The 3 "R's": roomy, ready, reasonable
Prehistoric interest rate
Prehistoric asking price
Asking $ … and worth a lot more
Steal it legally
Lucky Nine! Asking $ 99,999
Cannibal Casserole … price chewed to the bone
Pick of the crop
Top area - bottom price
Too good to resist
Affordable elegance
Be the early bird
Don't pass this "buy"
Bushels of benefits
Luxury family living at an affordable price
Starting out or slowing down
Bonanza for Bargain Hunters
Pocketbook appeal
Beginner's bargain
Realistically priced
When $ is the object and value a must, this … heads the list
PURSE-anality
This is the age of ACQUIRE-us
An EYE teaser - a PURSE pleaser
It's got high price written everywhere except the price tag
Well trimmed price
PSST … the price is so low that I don't dare to print it
Best value for your Dollar

Squeezing Pennies?
Beginner's Bargain
A gem for the 1st time buyer
Don't you wish you'd bought in 1970?
"Champagne-class" home for MINI-BUDGET pocketbook
Skimpy heating bills
Take the landlord off your payroll
Are you tired of paying rent?
Buy low - live high
He who hesitates lives in an apartment
Won't last long - these never do
Mini price - maxi value
Newlyweds and retired
Bull's eye bargain
"B" fast - "B" FIRST
This price is not a misprint
The MOST for your money

RETIREMENT

When the kids are all gone, this is such a special home for those that want to be alone.
Precious rancher for those not needing a large home.
Easy carefree living
Retirement rancher
Dream rancher
No-steps rancher
The proverbial "Doll House"
Carefree - stair free
Empty nesters trading for elegant living
Cosy comfort
The yard is small, but there is less grass to cut & there is still room to grow things (flowers, vegetable garden)

VIEW

A view to unwind with
View the city
Fabulous sunsets
Soak in the view
City lights
VIEW-tiful
Sweeping unobstructed view
Stunning view

High on the hill
Accent on view
Facing the sunrise
On a clear day you can see forever

SECLUSION

Close in but totally secluded
Secluded setting
The loudest noise you hear is the breeze in the trees
Towering trees provide cool shade in the fenced back yard
Privacy yes! Isolation no!
Wooded privacy
Enchanted retreat
Bubbling brook
Artist's retreat
Tall towering timbers
Your dream refuge
Quiet location
Sounds of Silence
Nestled behind trees
So quiet even the squirrels tiptoe.
Treed lot
Murmuring Creek & tall trees
Huge treed lot
City close - country quiet
Country splendour
You need a map to find this
Pastoral tranquillity
Sleep to the music of crickets
A Million Miles away & yet close to bus & shops
Secluded cul-de-sac lot
Do you enjoy tranquillity?
The hush of country seclusion on this lush 1/2 acre
FAR from the maddening crowd, but only minutes driving time to
Seclusion anyone?
Privacy abounds
Country? Yes! … Bumpkin? No!
A part of the city and yet apart from the city
Wooded privacy
Secluded setting
TREE-menduous
Wooded wonderland

After a busy day come home to a haven of comfort
Picturesque park-like setting
Fresh air with some flair
A very private place
Natural beauty - sought after location

HANDYMAN's SPECIAL

Handyman's dream: Not just another pretty place!
This custom-rundown … is sure to please any discriminating bulldozer.
The yard is ablaze with knee-high grass, melancholy junk and several derelict cars.
This will appeal only to the stout-hearted with good working hands.

A legend becomes reality: Classic custom-neglected 2 bedrms. stucco rancher on treed 1/2 acre lot (Be a land baron!). Imagine yourself perspiring while you are slaving to clean up the nightmarishly messy yard. But it has one redeeming feature: It can be bought CHEAP! (no extra charge for the dirt and termites)

El Fixo - Zorro never slept in this neglected gem
Solid home but needs some work
Earn sweat equity
Handyman's dream
Bring your working hands
Decidedly damaged
El Dumpo
Paint & $ave
Neglected jewel
Not for the faint of heart!

REMODELLED

Lovingly remodelled and updated kitchen
Just open the door and you'll search no more
Mr. Handyman is selling his house
Masterfully renovated

LOCATION

Closer to work
Near … Mall
Quiet street
Convenient to everything
Home for lunch

Child in school?
Close in
Tucked away on a dead-end street

COUNTRY

Country atmosphere
Quiet country living
Fresh air
Mother Nature
Good old country feeling
Country Gentleman
Here is the rare chance to buy the country place you've been wanting for your family
An adventure in living
Family with Horse Sense?
Rustic charm
Park your horse
A perfect place for horses, dogs and their friends

FARM

Features to be included: ...
Size of acreage
Pastures, wooded land,
Type of fencing
Crops & livestock
Equipment & machinery
Description of the main house
Any other buildings

CLEAN

A speck of dust would die of loneliness in this lovely ...
Mrs. Clean is selling her house
Mrs. Clean and Mr. Fussy are selling their home
Clean & Ready
Neat as a pin
Meticulously clean
You can eat off the floor
Apple pie order
Dutch clean

LARGE HOUSE

Perfect for the large family
A warm, wonderful home for the large family
Large home - great price
The best room is elbow room
Ballroom-sized bedrooms
Home with lots of room
Ease the squeeze
Help stamp out small rooms

How To Hold A Productive "Open House"

There are 3 reasons for holding an "OPEN HOUSE":
(a) To get the house **sold**.
(b) To test its **saleability**
- selling a house is a joint effort between the Realtor and the Sellers.
- Constructive comments from genuine Buyers about price, physical condition of the house, cleanliness etc. are - if heeded - important pieces of information leading to a sale. Everything should be relayed to and discussed **diplomatically** with the Sellers.
- At the same time, **this discussion is a test** of how seriously motivated to sell the owners really are.
    - If they are open to suggestions and cooperate within reason, then you have a good listing.
    - If they put up resistance (especially against a price reduction after numerous Buyers have complained about the price), then you have a poor listing.

(c) **To generate other business** for the Realtor:
- prospective buyers who may be interested in seeing other properties,
- local sellers who need to sell their present home before they are able to buy (prospective listing).
- persons visiting from out of town and here on a fact finding trip could result in a REFERRAL being sent to a Realtor in their home town (if their house is not yet listed there).

(I) To hold a successful "Open House" there must first be **ADEQUATE PREPARATION.**
1) **DISCUSS with the Sellers the holding of an "OPEN HOUSE"** at least one week in advance before the proposed day.
    - Don't take the Sellers' consent for granted.
    - You should also have adequate lead time to advertise the "Open House" in local newspapers.
(a) A date and time suitable for all parties must be agreed upon. This should be reconfirmed with the Sellers 2 or 3 days before the "Open."
(b) If the owners will be away during the Open House, then -for obvious security reasons - they should not leave valuables (cash in the form of loose change or jewellery of any kind) laying around in the open, e.g. on top of a dresser. Explain that occasionally several parties may be in the house simultaneously and you cannot be everywhere at the same time to stand guard.
(c) Ensure diplomatically and tactfully that the house will be **in a tidy condition:**

Curb appeal:
- the yard should be neat, the lawn should be mowed and watered. There should be no knee-high weeds.

- If necessary, the exterior painting should be touched up.

House appeal:
- no laundry on the floor;
- no dirty dishes in the sink;
- all garbage and old newspapers must be disposed of,
- all toys should be put away so that the rooms look neat
- all staircases and steps should be free of toys and sundry debris, so that nobody should stumble and fall.
- The beds should be made,
- all closets should be rearranged, so that nothing falls onto an unsuspecting visitor's head when he opens the door
- All cupboards should be in a neat condition.
- The fridge and oven must be clean,
- the garage should be tidy.
- the house must be aired out
- all interior rooms should be bright. "Bright" rooms look bigger. In **summer** open the drapes, in **winter** put on the lights.

Minor repairs:
- fix leaky faucets,
- replace or repair torn wallpaper,
- replace broken windows,
- replace burnt out light bulbs.

No distractions:
- Family pets (cat or dog) should be out of the house.
- Pets may be harmless but some people are afraid of dogs. Some people may be allergic to fur.
- Dogs may be friendly but in their enthusiasm they could knock over or frighten a small child.

2) If you haven't done so already, prepare a **FEATURE SHEET or HIGHLIGHT SHEET** giving
- **ALL room sizes,**
- the **AGE** of the house (usually the date of the final occupancy permit or the water connection. The date of the sewer connection is not reliable, because the house could first have been connected to a septic tank for some time).
- a sketch of the lot (if the dimensions are irregular),
- gross taxes,
- (if permitted by the Seller) the assessment figures for land and building
- proximity to schools, transportation, shopping etc.
- a colour picture of the house.
- (if permitted by the Sellers) details of existing financing (provided it has some

outstanding feature which could be of interest to a Buyer, e.g. a low interest rate which is good for a number of years).

Buyers will look at several houses on any given day. **The Feature Sheet will refresh their memories** when they are back home (e.g. the room sizes will tell them if their chesterfield will fit into the living room and if the king-size bed and their dressers will fit into the master bedroom).

3) As with ALL of your listings **you should be thoroughly familiar with ALL features of the home,** like e.g.
   - the age of the roof,
   - the age and capacity of the hot water tank,
   - the average cost of utilities (heat and light),
   - gross taxes and other assessments (e.g. water, sewer and garbage collection if they are not included in the tax bill),
   - what kind of neighbours there are: children, a retired couple, noisy neighbours etc.

Forewarned is forearmed:
(a) Be acquainted with **the home's best features**, so that you can eloquently demonstrate its highlights.
(b) At the same time you should also be well prepared to be able to minimize or overcome all objections to **any drawbacks the home may have.**

4) Discuss with your Mortgage Broker various financing options for the house; most likely, he will be happy to give you handout material covering interest rates, suggested financing packages etc.

5) **Familiarize yourself with other houses which are CURRENTLY FOR SALE** in the neighbourhood. Make an appointment and actually inspect them. This will give you the following benefits and advantages:
   (a) you will know what your competition is and you can report about them to your Sellers.
   (b) You will be able to switch a Buyer (who doesn't like your listing) to one of these other currently-for-sale houses and make a sale.
   (c) The listing on one of those houses could be expiring soon and a disappointed Seller might list with you at some future date.
   WARNING: Please refer to your Real Estate Board's guidelines regarding presoliciting a listing before its expiry.

6) From the market analysis (of your "Open House" listing) you should know **which houses had SOLD recently in the area.** If you haven't done so already, drive by them and look at them from the outside, so that you can talk about recent sales intelligently, if the need arises. Nowadays clients are both inquisitive and rather sophisticated.

7) Familiarize yourself with **houses in the neighbourhood on which the listing has recently EXPIRED.** Your upcoming "Open House" could be **a marvellous**

door opener to a potential future listing; even if you don't get a listing right away, there is the possibility of a double-ender by switching one of your leftover Buyers to one of these properties (where the seller won't list right away, but is willing to accept an offer).

Sometimes a listing expired a long time ago: you might be able to rekindle the owner's interest in selling again, by telling him that the market is active, interest rates are attractive, prices have risen and he might now be able to get his price (which he couldn't obtain last year). Familiarize yourself with all **"For-Sale-by-Owner" houses in the neighbourhood.**

(II) **Don't overlook the importance of PROMOTION.**
8) (a) Distribute "I am going to have an OPEN HOUSE" flyers in the neighbourhood; these are similar to the "Just Listed" cards.
   (b) A good ad is vital for the success of your Open House.
   - **Write an effective ad** for the newspaper (preferably with a picture).
   - Then polish the ad for "flow" and "clarity."
   - Give enough information to interest people and to motivate them to come.
   - Try to communicate the "flavour" or any special advantages of the house.
   - Include the asking price (unless the house is unrealistically priced)
   - and **don't forget to mention the address**. (I bet that you have seen Open House ads without an address).

   (c) **Promote your Open House in the office** and to Realtors working for other companies (e.g. your Real Estate Board's computer may have a category or site where you can advertise upcoming Open Houses).
   (d) **Coordinate your Open House with other Realtors who will hold "Opens" in the area on that weekend.**
   (e) A few days before the Open House, **place your sign-rider** (strip-sign reading "Open Sunday 2 - 4" fastened to your regular For-Sale-sign).

9) **Scout the best route where to place your DIRECTIONAL Open House ARROWS** and count how many you will need. (If you don't have enough, make arrangements in advance to borrow some from somebody at your office).
   (a) Drive the route yourself to make sure that all arrows will be visible and not hidden by trees, shrubs or telephone poles.
   (b) Make sure that **the arrows go all the way out to a main traffic artery.**
   (c) Consider having signs leading to the house from 2 different directions.
   (d) **Don't confuse** prospective buyers by placing your directional signs too close to your competitors' arrows.
   (e) **All of your directional signs should be clean and in good condition.**
(10) **Talk to the "owner on the corner"** where you will stick your "Open" arrow and obtain his permission to do so. This is not only the polite thing to do, but it is

another door opener to talk to somebody about a possible future listing or sale:
- "Have you thought about moving to a larger/or smaller house?";
- Or that person may know of a neighbour who is thinking about selling.
- Alternatively he may have a friend or relative who wants to live nearby and buy in the area.

Ask "the owner on the corner" if he would consider keeping an eye on your sign; because kids sometimes mischievously turn the arrows into another direction.

(III) ON THE DAY OF THE "OPEN HOUSE."
11) **Allow yourself plenty of time** for placing your directional arrows.
12) **Arrive ahead of time** at the house to:
    (a) be there for any early-bird customers.
    (b) place your car roof-top arrow, balloons, flags etc.
    (c) have the house thoroughly vented:
    - fresh air,
    - non-perfumed room deodorizer;
    - a sprinkling of cinnamon in a pot of warm water will smell like freshly baked bread creating that "home" feeling.

    (d) if you want music then make it soft and non-intrusive.
    (e) Turn the TV off (it could be a source of distraction).
    (f) Open all drapes and make sure that all rooms look airy and bright. Turn on lights where needed (e.g. in a dark hallway).
    (g) Make sure that all valuables are safely hidden away
    (h) Position yourself in a place from where you can observe the street (and see customers coming).
    (i) Garage doors facing the street should be closed.

13) Place an **OPEN HOUSE GUEST BOOK** near the entrance and ask all visitors to sign in.
    Have **a monthly draw for a complimentary hamper** (which should be displayed next to the guest book); this will encourage people to sign the book and simultaneously discourage them from giving you a phony name and phone number.

14) Be equipped and prepared for all eventualities.
    Bring
    - a current MLS catalogue,
    - an adequate supply of your business cards,
    - complimentary ballpoints and scratch pads with your name and phone number on them and
    - any other promotional material you may have.
    - There is always a possibility that you will have to see a prospective client immediately after the Open House. Therefore you should have with you a pad

of blank MLS Listing forms, Contracts of Purchase and Sale etc.
- Your cell phone should be fully charged.
- The gas tank in your car should be reasonably full.

15) **DURING THE "OPEN HOUSE":**
   - **Control the showing,**
   - be attentive to everybody and
   - **watch out for "buying signals."**
   - **Ask "qualifying questions":** "This home has 3 bedrooms. Is that what you need?" OR "The asking price is $ 200,000. Is this within the price range you are looking for?"
   - **Qualify for a potential SALE:** "Have you been looking for a suitable home for long?"
   - **Qualify for a potential LISTING:** "Are you renting now or do you own your own home?"
   - **Allow prospects time to leisurely inspect the house and absorb its features.**
   - Do NOT point out obvious things (e.g. by saying "this is the kitchen").
   - Instead you should emphasize facts and good features which viewers may not be aware of.
   - Answer all questions fully and freely;
   - if you are unable to give a satisfactory answer, say that you will find out and call them later.
   - **LISTEN to what people tell you about their needs and wants,**
   - **determine their priorities** and
   - obtain **their reaction to this house.**

16) In the absence of the owners, you are responsible for the house and its contents. **Never leave the (Open) House unattended** — for any reason. Not even for a few minutes.

17) **Stay a little "overtime,"** because there might be some stragglers. (If you are not there, they will call you at supper time and you will have to go back that evening or some other time and open up the house for them. Thus staying late may save yourself an extra trip; it will also impress the Seller.

(IV) SECURITY

If you don't carry a pager or cellular phone, then leave the phone number of your Open House location with the office, your husband or wife or a friend.
This will serve 2 purposes:
(a) messages can be relayed to you.
(b) more importantly, caution suggests the wisdom of a periodic security check-up (phone call) during your Open House ("Hello! How are things?") After all, isn't it a fact that you are inviting total strangers to come into the

house, where you are alone…?

(V) AFTER THE OPEN HOUSE

18) **Leave the property in the same condition as you found it:**
    (a) turn off lights (except for those which the owner had left on),
    (b) Close all windows and lock all doors.
    (c) Don't forget to check the (furnace) thermostat and the elements on the kitchen stove (people sometimes fiddle with them). Make sure that the fridge door is closed.
    (d) Make sure that all faucets are turned off.
    (e) Pick up all of your arrows and "Open" signs.
    (f) Put yourself into the owners' shoes: they are curious and want to know what went on during the Open House. Therefore, as soon as possible you should call the Seller with the results of the Open House (how many people came, were there any interested parties; you may have to use your discretion when relaying overly critical comments made by some of the visitors).

(VI) ON THE NEXT DAY (following the Open House)

19) (a) **Immediately follow up all leads**, especially those who may be thinking of buying or listing in the near future.
    (b) Call all Realtors who have brought prospects through the Open House and obtain their clients' reactions.
    (c) Send "THANK YOU" notes to the "owners on the corners" (arrow locations). This is not only good manners, but also good public relations. At some future date it could result in a listing or sale.
    (d) Touch base with other Realtors who have held "Opens" in the area on the same weekend and compare notes.
    (e) Start planning for your next Open House.

Conducting a successful and productive Open House is a test of your professionalism, ingenuity, willingness to work (careful preparation and execution) and above all the exercise of your communication and selling skills.

WELCOME TO OUR OPEN HOUSE

_____ 2 _____

_____

The owners will appreciate it if you would kindly sign this

GUEST REGISTER

PLEASE PRINT YOUR NAME	TELEPHONE NUMBER

THANK YOU!

Staple your business card here

Showing Properties Is An Art

When a salesperson selects a property to show, then he does so based on
(a) His **knowledge and accumulated experience** of
- the real estate business and
- human nature

(b) His **familiarity** with what is currently for sale
(c) His **personal judgment** (decision) if the property he selects to show will meet the Buyers' needs, wants and financial criteria.
(d) the salesperson's **skill** in combining
- a thorough knowledge of the selected property and
- the requirements and specifications of his Buyers.

The "showing of houses" to a prospective Buyer is an **EDUCATIONAL process:**
(a) A lot depends on
- the sophistication of the Buyers and
- how long they have been "looking" and
- to what extent they are familiar with "values."

(b) **The Buyers** find out what is available in their price range; they may have to realize that within their budget they cannot get everything they want.
(c) **The Realtor** has to be alert and observant to interpret (and learn) from the **verbal and non-verbal (body language) reactions** of the Buyers what is important for them (and what isn't).
(d) Ideally a salesperson should make the selection of
- a suitable house and
- the Buyer's decision to buy

    a **comfortable, natural and easy experience** (and not a high pressure nightmare).

(e) When showing properties, the Realtor **also "shows" himself**.
    Therefore, it goes without saying that the Realtor should show himself in the best light possible:
- neat appearance
- well spoken
- **he SHOULD NOT**
    - stifle free communication
    - alienate the Client by being a sarcastic "know-it-all" or by discussing politics or religion or
    - make foolish promises which he cannot keep.
- **INSTEAD the Realtor SHOULD be**
    - **knowledgeable:** he should know as much as possible about the properties he will be showing. He will loose credibility, if he tries to fake an answer. If he doesn't know the answer, then he should admit it and offer to find out the required information as soon as possible.

- **enthusiastic** (enthusiasm is infectious).
- Punctual and keep his word.

Obviously there is no set formula of how properties are shown. Each salesperson must develop his own **personalized method.** However, there are some **basic guidelines** which should be adhered to:

TO START the process:

(a) A Realtor **must know what is available on the market (=Inventory).** He will keep himself up-to-date by
- frequently attending Office and Multiple Listing Tours.
- Inspecting properties on his own (e.g. look at the most realistically priced listing of the day. This should be done every day).
- By taking extensive notes while inspecting a house (in order to be able to refresh his memory when needed later on).

(b) Before the first outing the Realtor should try to **establish a rapport** with the prospective Buyers. This rapport should be continuously reinforced during the subsequent house showings by offering friendly, sincere and helpful service (e.g. by pointing out not only the good features of a property, but also some of its drawbacks). That way the Realtor will **gain the Buyer's CONFIDENCE and LOYALTY.**

(c) The Realtor should interview the Buyer as to his
- **needs and wants** and
    - qualify what his **financial abilities are:**
    - **amount of downpayment** available (his own money)
    - the **Debt Service Ratio:** how much they can afford to pay in monthly mortgage payments plus 1/12 of the taxes.
    - the **Total Gross Debt Service Ratio**: the PIT (principal interest and 1/12 taxes) PLUS monthly payments on **all other debts.**
    - job security and prospects.

A lot of Buyers prefer to **get prequalified** for a mortgage by a bank or lending institution. This will be very helpful because
- the Buyers will look only at houses which they can afford (the Buyer's downpayment plus his maximum available mortgage = realistic price range of houses suitable for viewing).
- When the Buyer makes an offer the Seller can be assured that the Buyer is serious because he has already qualified for the new financing.
- If the Buyer is renting then the Realtor should make sure that he knows how and when to give the proper notice to his landlord.

- The Realtor should also find out which houses the Buyers have already seen from the outside and didn't like for one reason or another. This way a last minute cancellation can be avoided.
- Worse still is a situation where the Realtor drives up to the house and the Buyers inform him that it didn't appeal to them BEFORE (when they have seen it with another Realtor); in that case the proper thing for the Realtor to do is to walk up to the door and advise the Seller that the Buyers do not want to see his house.

  It is very impolite to just drive off without telling the Seller that he does not need to wait for you. If you don't tell the Seller, then he may sit there inside the house for hours in silent frustration wondering when you are finally going to show up.

(d) Never leave your office, unless you are **fully prepared**. This means having with you
  - street maps
  - any information (and make sure that it is correct) you may need about the properties to be shown (e.g. distance to schools, shopping and transportation; complete details of attractive assumable existing financing which could be of interest to the Buyer).
  - A full pad of Contracts of Purchase and Sale forms (the Buyer may want to make an offer on the spot).
  - A pad of Listing Contracts (in case the Buyer has to sell first and his offer is subject to the sale of his house).
  - A full tank of gas in your car.

(e) The Realtor should make sure that the Seller has adequate time (before the showing) to ensure that the property is in a presentable condition. Also the showing should fit into the Seller's time schedule on that day.

(f) Some Realtors prefer that the owners should not be present during a showing, in order to enable the Buyers to look around at their leisure and without being embarrassed or self-conscious.

THE ACTUAL "TOUR OF HOMES"

(a) The Realtor should line up the houses he wants to show
  - in geographical sequence. No driving back and forth all over the map.
  - When making the appointments with the various owners make sure
    - to allot sufficient time to show the house and
    - enough time to get from one house to the next.

(b) **As a safety precaution** before you depart
  - leave an **itinerary** of the homes you will be showing and
  - **a time schedule** with somebody (the office receptionist, your significant other,

a friend, another Realtor in your office).
- Fix a time when you will report back to that person. If that person doesn't hear from you within a certain time frame then they will know that you could have encountered some kind of difficulty.

(c) If you show vacant houses in a remote or isolated location then it may be preferable to **bring another Realtor along** "to assist" you. An ounce of prevention is worth a pound of cure.

(d) If for some reason you end up showing a vacant house in an isolated location **alone by yourself,** then
- always let the Buyer walk **in front of you** while making your way through the house. That way you cannot be surprised and attacked from behind, should he have bad intentions.
- Carry your cellular telephone in your hand.
- Never walk into an isolated room (e.g. a bedroom or bathroom) with the Buyer because
    - the room might look smaller with both of you being in there
    - if he blocks the door (in order to attack you) then you may find yourself trapped in the room without a chance for escape. It is better if you stay in the hallway.

(e) **If the owners are not going to be home** then find out if there are any special conditions you should watch out for:
- learn how to turn off and reset the burglar alarm
- alternatively make arrangements that somebody should be there who can do it for you.
- If there are any pets in the house and what their names are. **Cats** may either hide somewhere or else they are liable to bolt out of the front door as soon as you open it. **A small dog** may bark: bring along some dog cookies to pacify it. If there is a **big dog** running loose in the backyard then the smart thing is not to open the back door because he is liable to run to you. Instead view the backyard only through the windows. Should the Buyer be interested in the house, he will want to see it for a 2nd time anyway. Make sure that the owners are home on that occasion in order to keep the dog under control while you and your Clients are walking in the backyard.

THINGS TO DO WHEN YOU ARE ACTUALLY SHOWING HOUSES:

(a) When taking the Buyers to a property, choose the most attractive route to get there and point out interesting things on the way.
(b) Try to park your car across the street from the house, in order to afford the Clients the best overall view.
(c) While walking towards the house, point out good features of the house and the

immediate neighbourhood.

(d) If you and the Buyers go in separate cars, be sure to be on time when you meet them at the first house to be shown.

(e) When the owner opens the front door, introduce yourself and your clients. **Give him your business card.**

(f) If the owners are not home or the house is vacant, leave your business card in a conspicuous place; e.g. the kitchen counter. The reason for this is so that the Listing Broker and the owner know who has shown the house.

(g) When showing the inside of the house, make sure that the Seller is not following you around: he may interfere with well-meant, but unwelcome remarks. His continued presence and persistent chatter may disturb the Buyers.

If the Seller does that then a polite and diplomatic "word in confidence" (away from the Buyers) might be in order. (E.g.: "Mr. Seller, I am perfectly capable of showing your house to its best advantage").

(h) Never let the Buyers and Sellers enter into verbal negotiations. E.g. Buyer to Seller: "Are the appliances going to stay?" or "Are you open to offers?." This kind of question will put the Seller on the spot. Being anxious to sell, he doesn't want to discourage the Buyers from making an offer. He may say something which he will regret later on.

(i) Do not insult the Buyers' intelligence by announcing: "This here is the kitchen." Instead talk about benefits: spacious, sunny kitchen; step-saving kitchen; attractive lay-out of kitchen counters and cabinets.

(j) Before leaving the house, **get a summary reaction from the Buyers**: "Before we leave, is there any particular portion of the house which you want to see once more?"

(k) After showing a house, the Realtor should **give to the Buyers an Information Sheet** containing all details about the property. This Information Sheet will be very helpful to refresh the Buyers' memory when they discuss later on what they have seen. All room sizes should be shown so that the Buyers can determine if their furniture will fit or not (e.g. the king-sized bed in the master bedroom or the chesterfield in the living room). Especially if the lot is irregular, a sketch of the lot together with its dimensions would be good. The lot sketch should also show any easements and Right-of-Ways.

(l) If it is painfully obvious that the Buyers are not at all interested after having seen only a portion of the house, then do not insist that they see the rest. If the Seller is home - excuse yourselves diplomatically and say that he will receive a call later on with an explanation. Then as quickly as possible you should phone the Listing Salesperson and tell him the reason why the showing was cut short. It is the Listing Broker's obligation to inform his Client accordingly.

(m) If the house is vacant or the owners were not at home, **it is very important that you leave the house in a secure state:**
- make sure that all doors are locked and windows closed.

Your Buyers may have opened something and forgotten to shut it.
- Turn off all lights except for those which the owners have left on.
- Check that
  - all water faucets are turned off,
  - the burners on the stove are turned off
  - the furnace thermostat is set to a proper level. Sometimes Buyers or their children may "test" these items and then forget to turn them off or to reset them.
  - Replace the house key in the lock box (instead of walking off with it in your pocket).

METHODS OF SHOWING HOUSES:

Buyers will find the right house by a process of ELIMINATION.

(a) Some Realtors sell houses "by exhaustion." They show the Buyers numerous houses during several sessions and hope that somewhere along the line they will find a house which will appeal to them. Alternatively, the Buyers eventually will be so fed up looking that they will buy something… anything (!) (which might not necessarily be the right house for them).

(b) Some other Realtors carefully prequalify the needs, wants and financial abilities of their Buyers. Being thoroughly familiar with what is available on the market, they often only have to show less than 6 houses, before the Buyers find the "right one."

There are 2 schools of thought or methods of showing a limited amount of carefully selected homes:

- Showing houses **in ascending suitability order:** the Realtor shows first the house which he judges will fill the least amount of the Buyer's needs and wants. Subsequently the Realtor will build excitement and anticipation by proceeding to show in sequence houses which gradually will be more and more satisfactory to the Buyers. Finally and as LAST one he will show the "best and most perfect" of all selected houses. At that stage it is time to make a trial close to obtain an offer.
- Some other Realtors surprise and try to sweep the Buyers off their feet by **showing them the "perfect" house right off the bat.** The drawback with this is that the Buyers might want to see "more" houses and then they will be disappointed by the subsequent selections.

Representations

For a detailed analysis of the law regarding "representations" please read **"PACIFIC PLAYGROUND HOLDINGS LTD. v. ENDEAVOUR DEVELOPMENTS LTD. et al"** (2002-01-31) BCSC, Docket S 2791, Campbell River Registry.

During precontractual negotiations (which - from a practical point of view - may include many things **which take place before the Client signs on the dotted line**) Realtors can and often will make various types of representations. Such **representations can be conveyed either by words or by conduct and may involve (past or present) material facts with the intent of inducing** the other party to act. In this sense the word **"material"** means that whatever was "represented" will have a **TENDENCY TO INDUCE** the other party to act upon it. An English dictionary usually defines the verb **"to induce"** as **"to lead a person by persuasion or some other influence to some action."** And it is a fact of life (as well as a part of selling) that a Realtor obviously wants (or at least expects) that his words are relied and acted upon.

The various types of representations are as follows:

(1) Puffing (or "puffery," "dealer's talk")
(2) Innocent misrepresentation
(3) Negligent misrepresentation
(4) Fraudulent misrepresentation

(1) **PUFFING**.

In order to attract somebody to buy something, the offered item and/or its advantages are generally praised. When the "praise" is almost too good to be true and obviously an exaggerated statement, such practice is called **PUFFING**. Because this is a somewhat grey area with a hazy borderline a certain amount of latitude is often granted in a case of "mere puffery." A reasonably alert person is therefore not justified in placing reliance on a mere statement of opinion, judgment, expectation or a conjecture.
In **"ARSENAULT v. PEDERSEN"** (1996-04-26) BCSC, Docket S021575 the Plaintiff Buyer claimed (amongst other things) that he relied on a written advertisement containing the phrase "Nothing to do but move in." The Judge found that this sentence was so vague as to be meaningless absent of deceit.

Nevertheless, a Realtor should be cautious when engaging in an **INDISCRIMINATE PRAISE** of a property by **detailing SPECIFIC facts.** Such "praise" could be (mis)interpreted by Clients as a "statement of fact." E.g. Realtors are deemed to have expert knowledge of property values. Therefore, a grossly exaggerated expression of value cannot be honest, if the Realtor is trying to induce a Buyer to contract.

THE VARIOUS TYPES OF MISREPRESENTATION ARE:

Claims of misrepresentation are often brought by Buyers. Because there are usually only 2 parties involved (namely the Plaintiff and the Defendant), it is difficult to defend (Sellers and) Realtors against whom misrepresentation is alleged. It is the old story of "he said - she said."

The Judge has the difficult task of **deciding "on the balance of probabilities" who is to be believed.** So what exactly is the Judge looking for "on the balance of probabilities" and on what does he base his decision?

Basically how a witness, plaintiff or defendant **acts and talks when giving evidence (his demeanour):**
(a) A confident witness, who is composed and knows his facts.
(b) Is it generally reasonable (believable, fits the facts) in what he is saying?
(c) What (important to him) reasons may the party who is testifying have had for remembering (or forgetting) something crucial?
(d) Are there any mistaken recollections?
(e) Is he "guessing" because maybe he forgot or because he can no longer remember accurately?
(f) Is the party confused, evasive or is he deliberately lying?
(g) Is the person on the stand a shrewd person adept in the half-lie? Is he one of those who can skilfully combine exaggeration with a partial suppression of the truth?

To succeed in Court with a claim for misrepresentation the Plaintiff/Buyer cannot simply say that he has spent money on repairs and request compensation from the Defendants (the Seller and/or Realtor).

(a) The burden of proof is on the Plaintiff to establish his claim "on the balance of probabilities" as required by law. See **"MILLER v. MINISTER OF PENSIONS"** (1947) 2 All E.R. 372 at 374

(b) **DAMAGES must be proven.** The Plaintiff must come up with **EXPERT REPORTS from INDEPENDENT SPECIALISTS** confirming that they have indeed suffered damages; such reports **cannot** be obtained from "Contractors with a commercial interest." (E.g. somebody who may have submitted an "estimate" of how much he will charge if he is given the job to repair the defects or problems).

(2) **INNOCENT MISREPRESENTATION.**
In law, the word "innocent" means to say **"not knowingly."** An innocent misrepresentation takes place when the person (who makes the untrue statement of

fact or gives an erroneous opinion honestly held) is actually and honestly convinced that the statement he is making is true.

CAUTION: However, the representor (the person who is making a statement of fact) can still have a legal problem in spite of the fact that he doesn't actually know that THAT which he is saying ("representing") is untrue:

(a) if he is **INDIFFERENT as to the truth or falsity** of his statements. Indifference can be deduced from a **lack of inquiry** (or lack of effort) to **INVESTIGATE (verify)** if his statements are true or false.
(b) This may lead to the conclusion that the maker of the statement is or was **reckless** and
(c) **that he INTENDED his words to be believed and ACTED upon** even if there was no basis whatsoever in truth.

(3) **NEGLIGENT MISREPRESENTATION.**

A negligent misrepresentation is making statements **carelessly when there are NO reasonable grounds for believing them to be true.**

In **"QUEEN v. COGNOS INC."** (1993) 1 S.C.R. 87, 99 D.L.R. (4th) 626 (S.C.C.) at 643 the Supreme Court of Canada cited general requirements for establishing liability based on a negligent misrepresentation. These are as follows:

(a) There must be a **DUTY OF CARE** based on a **SPECIAL RELATIONSHIP** between the representor and the representee. This type of duty arises from 3 things: See **"EDGEWORTH CONSTRUCTION LTD. v. N. D. LEA & ASSOC."** (1991), 53 B.C.L.R. (2d) 180 (C.A.)
  - foreseeability
  - reliance and
  - proximity (it should be obvious that the "proximity" of a Realtor or even a Seller who is a builder may carry the heaviest burden in the Buyer's decision-making process).
(b) The representation must be **untrue, inaccurate or misleading.**
(c) The representor must have **acted negligently** in making the misrepresentation.
(d) The representee must have **relied** (in a **reasonable manner**) **on the negligent misrepresentation**.
   For what **"reasonable reliance"** is see **"HERCULES MANAGEMENT LTD. v. ERNST and YOUNG"** (1997) 2 SCR 165, 146 DLR (4th)577 The Court ruled that the following are **indications of "reasonable reliance":**
  - The Defendant has either a direct or indirect **financial interest** in the transaction.
  - The Defendant is either a professional or somebody who possesses a special skill, judgment or knowledge

- The representation (information or advice) was given **deliberately**:
  - in response to a specific inquiry or request
  - during the course of the Defendant's business dealings (and not on a social occasion).

(e) The **reliance must have been DETRIMENTAL** to the representee who (as a consequence thereof) **has suffered damages.**

The test for negligent misrepresentation in the context of precontractual representations can be found in **"BANGO v. HOLT et al"** (1971) 5 WWR 522 at 528.

Also see the case of **"HEDLEY BURNE & CO. v. HELLER & PARTNERS LTD."** (1964) A.C. 465, [1963] 2 All E.R. 575 (H.L.)

In **"KINGU v. WALMAR VENTURES LTD."** (1986), 10 B.C.L.R. (2d) 15 (C.A.) the Judge said that the "duty of care" does NOT arise UNLESS:
- the person who is making the statement has a special skill or **knowledge about the matter in question**
- that a reasonable person in his position would realize and know that the recipient of the statement is relying on his skills, knowledge and judgment.

EXAMPLES:

In **"SEDGEMORE et al v. BLOCK BROS. REALTY"** (Dec. 12, 1985) BCSC (inadequate water supply from a 300 ft. well) dealt with the Seller's precontractual fraudulent misrepresentation and **the Realtor's liability for NEGLIGENT misrepresentation** for his failure to verify the Seller's information.

Cases about a Buyer complaining about **floor area (square footage)** are: **"SLEIGHTHOLM v. EAST KOOTENAY REALTY LTD."** (1999-02-18) BCSC 8929 and **"DAVIE v. HUCKSCHLAG et al"** (July 5, 1993) BCSC Vancouver Registry No.1 C910767.

(4) **FRAUDULENT MISREPRESENTATION.**

In order to succeed in Court on a claim of civil fraud, the Plaintiff Buyer must prove that he was **induced** to enter into the Contract of Purchase and Sale by a fraudulent misrepresentation made by the Defendant (Seller or Realtor). Two leading cases are **"DERRY v. PEEK"** (1889), 14 App. Cas. 337 and **"REDICAN v. NESBITT"** (1924) SCR 135 at 154 (Ont.).

To prove that a fraudulent misrepresentation (fraud, deceit) was made, the following requirements must be met: That the **false representation** was made:
(a) **knowingly** either by words or conduct.

(b) **Without any belief in its truth** (knowledge of the falsity or the absence of any genuine belief in the truth of the statement).
(c) **Recklessly** and/or **CARELESSLY (with a wicked INDIFFERENCE)** whether such representations were true or false. (Moral turpitude).
(d) With the **wilful intent (MOTIVE) to deceive or mislead** a party in a material way.
(e) And with the intention of inducing the other party **to act to his detriment** (to do something, e.g. make an offer).
(f) There must be **damage caused** to the Plaintiff **as a consequence OF RELYING (or acting) upon the false statement.**

Fraud can also be established when the Plaintiff Buyer can prove that the Seller has
(a) actively, deliberately and dishonestly deceived him by **concealing a DEFECT or concealed (withheld) a PERTINENT FACT.**
(b) Or "with a wicked mind" deliberately and fraudulently **suppressed information about the defect.**

For example in connection with a **latent defect** the Buyer must prove that
- the latent defect was known to the Seller or
- that the circumstances were such that the Seller may be guilty of concealment or
- a reckless disregard of the truth or falsity of any representations made by him.

EXAMPLES:

"SORENSEN and SORENSEN v. KAYE HOLDINGS LTD." (1979) 6 W.W.R. 193 (BCCA)
A person is wrong in law and also morally wrong by:
- saying only "half of the truth."
- Studiously avoiding the complete truth.
- Selecting to talk only about facts which are in his favour and/or to his advantage
- while keeping silent about the rest (the disclosure of which may be to his disadvantage).

"BRAR v. MUTTI" (October 14, 1994), BCSC New Westminster, Docket C914347: the Defendant knew of and failed to mention restrictive covenants which affected the Buyer's planned use of the property.

"McGRATH v. MacLEAN" [1979} 22 O.R. (2d) 784. The Buyer alleged a loss arising not as a result of negligent misrepresentation, but rather as a consequence of the Defendant Seller's failure to disclose a latent defect.

"PEEK v. GURNEY" (1873), L.R. 6 (H.L.) 377
"LEESON v. DARLOW" (1926) 4 D.L.R. 415 (Ont. C.A.)

REMEDIES.

In the case of a fraudulent misrepresentation, the Plaintiff Buyer at his option can ask for

(a) **rescission** of the Contract (the contract is voidable by the Buyer). On the date of the Contract of Purchase and Sale the Buyers bind themselves to buy the property. **If the Buyers were deceived BEFORE that date, then it becomes also relevant to consider whether the deceit was COMPOUNDED, REINFORCED or CONCEALED by the SELLERS in the period BETWEEN the making of the Contract and the time of closing.** It is in that period of time that RESCISSION would be a relatively simple matter. However, if there is an undue delay by the Plaintiff in commencing an action (perhaps several years after he had discovered the misrepresentation), then rescission may be rejected. See **"BETKER v. WILLIAMS"** (1991-12-18) BCCA Vancouver Registry, CA 010502

(b) The Buyer can ask for **DAMAGES**. The proper measure of damages is the difference between the price paid for the property and its actual value.

Should Your Client "BUY First" Or "SELL First?"

Similarly to the old question of "What comes first? The chicken or the egg?" there is no generally correct answer to this classic real estate problem. The move from rented premises to a house is relatively simple in comparison with the move from one house to another.

The latter involves
- the financial risk of possibly having to carry 2 houses simultaneously for a period of time or
- alternatively to maybe ending up on the street, having to rent for a while and having to move twice.

Let us investigate both alternatives in order to determine which one has the lesser disadvantages.

If the Client BUYS first:
(1) then he may have the satisfaction and security of knowing where he is moving to... but only perhaps!
(2) The smart thing to do is to include in the offer-to-purchase a clause stipulating that the purchase is "subject to the sale of the Buyer's house by a certain date (say, 60 days hence).
(3) If the buyer needs new financing, there would also have to be an appropriate clause to that effect.
(4) Because of these 2 precautionary "subject-to" clauses the Seller will not be as impressed as he would be with a "subject-free all cash" offer. After all there is the uncertainty if the Buyer's house will sell (or not) during the stipulated limited time period. **The BUYER WILL HAVE REDUCED BARGAINING POWER, because**
    - the possibility exists that for some reason his old house may not sell before the time limit stipulated
    - in which case the Seller (having taken his house off the market)
        - would have wasted his time or worse still, would have
        - missed out on the possibility of selling to somebody else who had the cash and may even have paid more.
(5) In order NOT to tie up his Principal's house needlessly the Listing Broker will insist on inserting an "escape" clause: "The Seller's acceptance of this offer is subject to him being able to continue to market his house during the next 60 days. If another acceptable offer should materialize during those 60 days then the Seller will give to the Buyer 24 hours notice to remove ALL subject clauses and to make this a firm and binding contract. Failure to do so (within the 24 hours) will render this contract null and void and the Seller will be free to accept the next (other) offer."
From a practical point of view thus the Buyer's so-called "purchase" is little more than some sort of vague option or a "right-of-first-refusal."

(6) Next the Lending Institution will not give a firm mortgage commitment until such time when the Buyer's house is sold and it is firmly established
   - how much of a downpayment he will have (from the sale proceeds of his old house) and exactly
   - how much of a new mortgage he will actually need to buy the next house.

Another concern which the Lender may have is the Buyer's ability to carry 2 houses simultaneously. This situation will arise when the prospective Buyer is served by the Seller with the afore-mentioned "escape clause" BEFORE the Buyer's old house is sold. The Buyer may decide to gamble that his old house will sell in time before the set Completion Date; if it does not then the Buyer is willing (and able) to carry 2 houses at the same time by arranging for "bridge financing." (Borrow money to complete his purchase and carry 2 houses at the same time which may represent a serious financial burden).

(7) Even BEFORE the Buyer is served by the Seller with the "escape clause" he will find himself under some pressure to sell (quickly) because he has only a limited time frame (e.g. 60 days) to sell his house.
   Precious time will be wasted on getting the show on the road:
   - processing, publishing and circulating the listing.
   - It may be on the computer quickly, but possibly initially without a picture.
   - The deadline for the next MLS catalogue might be missed.
   - The MLS Tour could be fully booked for the next few weeks.

(8) Selling in a "Buyer's Market" often compounds additional problems. **Over optimistic and/or unrealistic Sellers tend**
   - **to OVER-estimate their house's Market Value** (there is no time for wishful thinking) and
   - **UNDER-estimate the length of time which is required to sell their house AND to complete documentation on time.**

(9) The Buyer will not have the luxury of being able to hold out for a good price on his old house; in fact, he may be forced to progressively reduce the asking price on his old house in order to attract an offer. Everybody has seen the ads "Owner has bought and must sell." Some ruthless Bargain Hunters may decide to see how low the unfortunate owner is willing or able or forced to go. Stress levels will be high.

(10) To add insult to injury, the Buyer may be served (during the 60 days time period) with the (24 hour) "escape clause" before his old house is sold. As for most people it is too risky to borrow bridge financing and to carry 2 houses, they will have no choice but to step aside and loose out on the home of their choice.

Therefore **if somebody buys first**, then chances are that
- he will buy high (little bargaining power) and
- sell low (due to time pressure)
- and/or he may loose out anyway on the chosen house.

If the Client LISTS and SELLS first:
(1) The preliminaries of putting the house on the market can be taken care of without wasting precious time.
(2) While their house is for sale, there is nothing to stop them to familiarize themselves with what is on the market; should they find a suitable home before they have a firm offer on the old house, then there is always the "subject-to-sale method # 1" available.
(3) If they receive an offer on their "old" house before they have found something suitable, then they have the luxury of being able to drive a hard bargain (namely to make only small concessions on the asking price etc).
(4) If the Buyers (of the Buyer's house) are renting, then a long possession date should be no problem. A long possession date on the "old" house
   - would give the Sellers ample of time to find another suitable house (especially if they already are familiar with what is on the market) and
   - it could be a bargaining factor when they make an offer on something. (The Seller of their "next" house may appreciate the fact that he doesn't have to move quickly).
(5) After the Buyers have received a firm offer with a substantial deposit (for their peace of mind) on their "old" house, then they can
   - get their new mortgage approved and
   - drive a hard bargain on their next purchase.
     The owner of the house they want to buy will view them as "Cash Buyers" and most likely will be more disposed to making concessions on the price and terms.

Thus **if the Client LISTS and sells first and buys later**, he has the luxury of
   - marketing his old house at leisure to achieve the maximum Selling Price.
   - He can familiarize himself with the Market and
   - he can still search for the next house (before his current house is sold).
   - Should he find a property which he likes, then he still has the option of making an offer "subject-to-the-sale" of his old house.
   - If he receives an offer on his "old" house BEFORE he has bought something else, then he will be able to drive a hard(er) bargain on HIS sale.
   - If he has sold his "old" house then he will be able to drive a hard(er) bargain on his next purchase.
   - **If the Client plays his cards right he will SELL HIGH and BUY LOW.**

Regrettably there is no universally perfect solution to this dilemma. Each individual Client will have to weigh the risks of having to move before the next place is available. If they bunk with friends or relatives or rent temporary quarters, then there is the inconvenience and expense of
   - having to move twice,
   - storing the furniture somewhere and
   - possibly having to put a pet into a kennel.

- Worse still, where will the children go to school?

For whatever it is worth, all of these problems are surmountable and merely inconveniences in comparison with the financial burden and fiasco of having to carry 2 houses for an indeterminate period of time.

An example of what I have said above is illustrated in the law case of **"Re/Max Central Realty v. Holmes"** B.C. Supreme Court Docket S020693, March 24, 2003.

A couple bought a new home under construction in Vernon before they listed their West Vancouver house on May 15, 2001 on MLS with an experienced and very meticulous Realtor (a retired teacher). Contrary to their Realtor's advice, they insisted on an Asking Price of $ 748,000.00, because a neighbour's house had allegedly sold for $ 719,000 and theirs (allegedly) had a better view. To his credit the Listing Salesman kept copious notes of his involvement and marketing efforts. In addition to his general appointment book in which he diarized telephone calls and meetings, he maintained a comprehensive "Record of Action" document which contained detailed notes on this particular property. The Realtor also contacted the Sellers weekly to keep them informed of all developments and feedbacks from various showings. Between May 15 and August 18 the price was progressively reduced (although always too little and not quickly enough) to the still unrealistic Asking Price of $ 629,000.00.

On August 31, 2001 the Sellers had to complete their Vernon purchase. On September 6, 2001 the listing price was reduced to $ 519,000 and on September 7 the property was sold for $ 480,000. The transaction completed on October 1. The Realtor had to sue for his commission and the Sellers counterclaimed for negligence or breach of fiduciary duty. While the Court had sympathy for the Sellers' plight, it did recognize that the Sellers had been constantly (and stubbornly) controlling the listing price contrary to their Realtor's advice. This resulted in a complete dearth of offers and as a consequence they found themselves in desperate financial circumstances. The Realtor was absolved of all allegations of wrongdoing and was awarded his commission together with "costs."

The "Subject-to The Sale Of The Buyer's Property" Clause And The "Time Clause"

(I)
If a Client finds a suitable house BEFORE
- his currently owned house is sold and
- he is unable to or not willing to take the risk of carrying 2 houses for a period of time
- then the cautious and only appropriate thing to do is to fashion the proposed purchase on the basis of "I will buy YOUR house provided I can sell MY house."
- In case the Buyer needs new financing or there are other concerns (zoning etc.), then there should be additional covering clauses.

(1) Basically the "subject-to" clause may say:
"This offer is subject to the Buyers entering into an unconditional sale of their property at _____ by _____, 2_____"

(2) Most likely the Seller will refuse to tie up his house (and in effect take it off the market) for a period of time (which could be 60 or 90 days) without some sort of assurance that he is
- not going to waste his time (e.g. the Buyer's house may not sell because it is unrealistically priced) OR
- alternatively the Seller may miss an opportunity to sell his house to another Buyer who is ready, willing and able to deal now. (E.g. he has the cash in the hand).

(3) For the Seller's protection, the Listing Salesperson will insert into the contract a clause saying that the Seller will accept this contract
   (a) provided he can continue marketing his house during the (60 to 90 days) time period.
   (b) If during that time the Seller should obtain another acceptable (firm and subject-free) offer, then he will **give WRITTEN notice**
      - **either directly to the Buyer**
      - or else it could be SPECIFIED that such notice can also be served onto his Realtor

      TO FIRM UP HIS PROPOSED PURCHASE by removing from the contract
      - the condition dealing with the sale of the Buyer's house AND
      - by removing ALL other subject-to clauses (e.g. financing, rezoning, feasibility study etc.).
      - **AND ALL of this MUST be done during a predetermined and specified time period;** depending on market conditions this can be anywhere from 24 to 72 hours either

- chronological time (which includes Sundays and Statutory Holidays)
- OR ELSE Sundays and Statutory Holidays can be extra time.
- THUS the Seller's property is NOT completely OFF the market EXCEPT for the (afore-mentioned) "stipulated number of HOURS" which are
  - between the INVOCATION of the TIME CLAUSE
  - AND ITS SPECIFIED DEADLINE.

NOTE: Instead of a number of "hours," some Realtors make reference to "Banking Days" or "Working Days" or "Business Days."
- The expression of "Banking Days" is vague, because different banks may be open for business on different days.
- "Working Days" and "Business Days" are also to be avoided, because they too are open to interpretation.

(c) It is further preferable that the Sellers should specify in their NOTICE that: the **BUYERS' REPLY** (which is the notification from the Buyers to the Sellers)
- **MUST be in WRITING** and
- **MUST be in the hands of the Sellers** (or their Realtor)
- **WITHIN the specified** (24 to 72 hours) **TIME LIMIT.**

Some Realtors may argue that
- the VERBAL removal of a condition precedent (followed up by a written notice) is in compliance with the industry practice in the area OR that
- the original Contract of Purchase and Sale **itself did not require the PHYSICAL DELIVERY** of the notice **within** the stipulated (24 to 72 hours) time period.

In this connection Realtors may wish to read the B.C. Supreme Court (Victoria), Date 1997-09-11, Docket No. 0987/97 law case of **"Donald McCARTHY v. John AMISS, Barry BOWES AND Ann BLONDEAU"** AND **"Wayne Douglas RANDALL and Joan Mary RANDALL v. John David AMISS"** where 2 sets of Buyers ended up fighting over one house because of the delivery of the notification of the "subject"-removal.

(4) (a) If the Buyers are unable to firm up their agreement, then they should step aside, in order to enable the Sellers to deal with the 2nd offer.
(b) Should the Buyers **fail to remove ALL conditions BEFORE the expiry of the notice period, then the Contract will be terminated (automatically)** and the Buyers' deposit will be returned to the Buyers.

To summarize: the Sellers' acceptance wording may be as follows:

"The Sellers' acceptance of this offer is subject to them being able to continue marketing and selling their property at _____ during the above-mentioned time

period (until_____, 2_____.)
Should the Sellers receive another bona fide (firm, subject-free) acceptable offer any time before _____, 2_____ then the Sellers will give written notice to the Buyers through their Realtor (Mr... of ... Realty Ltd.) **to REMOVE ALL conditions precedent and "subject-to" clauses** from this contract within _____ hours chronological time (to include Sundays and Statutory Holidays) and make it a FIRM and "subject-free" transaction.

Any reply or notification from the Buyers to the Sellers must be in WRITING and such document must be physically in the hands of the Sellers WITHIN the specified time limit.

Should the Buyers fail to remove ALL conditions and subject-to clauses BEFORE the expiry of the notice period then the Contract will terminate and the Buyers' deposit will be returned to the Buyers."

If the Buyers are agreeable, then the Sellers have now
- an accepted conditional offer on their property
- and are waiting for the conditions to be removed.
- **At the same time they can continue marketing their house.**

(II)
WHAT HAPPENS if another offer materializes?
(a) Offer # 2 will be treated as a "back-up offer."
(b) To be on the safe side and in order to prevent any misunderstandings, it may be advisable to write at the top of the 2nd offer: "BACK-UP OFFER"
(c) and the Sellers' ACCEPTANCE of the back-up offer must be "subject to" them being able to cut all (previous) legal ties with the original (first) Buyers.

> E.g.: "The Sellers' acceptance of this BACK-UP offer is subject to them ceasing to be obligated in any way whatsoever under the previous Contract of Purchase and Sale dated _____, 2_____ with the first Buyers Mr. and Mrs. _____ by the expiry of the NOTICE PERIOD which is _____a.m./p.m. on_____, 2_____"

(d) The intent is that the BACK-UP contract will become a firm and binding contract between the Sellers and the second set of Buyers, PROVIDED that Buyers # 1 (under the previous contract) FAIL TO REMOVE all "subject-to" clauses agreed to by the previously agreed-to DEADLINE.

(III)
NEXT the SELLERS' ACCEPTANCE of the "Back-Up" offer will trigger the "TIME CLAUSE NOTICE."
(a) The Sellers must find out if the Buyers of the first contract will

- firm up their deal by the removal of all the subject-to clauses OR
- if they will step aside and thus enable the Sellers to deal with the 2nd set of Buyers.

(b) This is done by the Sellers serving NOTICE IN WRITING to the original first Buyers invoking the TIME CLAUSE:

"NOTICE TO THE BUYERS Mr. and Mrs._____ under the Contract of Purchase and Sale dated _____, 2_____ for the property at _____. This document represents written notice from the Sellers to the Buyers advising them that the Sellers have received another bona fide acceptable offer on their house at _____.
The Buyers are herewith requested to REMOVE all subject-to clauses and conditions precedent from the Contract of Purchase and Sale dated _____, 2_____ within the previously stipulated _____ hours.
Should the Buyers fail to remove all conditions and subject-to clauses from the said Contract of Purchase and Sale dated _____, 2_____ by the expiry of the notice period then the contract shall terminate at the end of the _____ hours AND the Buyers' deposit shall be returned to the Buyers immediately.
The _____ hour notice starts at: _____a.m./p.m._____, 2_____
The _____ hour notice expires at: _____a.m./p.m._____, 2_____

Any notification from the Buyers to the Sellers must be in writing and must be in the hands of the Sellers within the specified time limit. Time is of the essence."

(IV) **Sundry notes:**

(1) The offers from Buyer "A" and Buyer "B" do NOT have to be identical; it is the Seller's decision what price and terms he is willing to accept.

(2) (a) Theoretically, Buyer "B"s offer could be lower in Full Price, but "all cash" with quick completion
   (b) whereas Buyer "A"s offer may be higher in price, but Buyer "A" house (which he is trying to sell) may be overpriced and have little chance of selling in the near future.
   (c) Under these circumstances the Seller could elect to go with Buyer "B" although the price may not be as advantageous. Of course, before serving any notice on Buyer "A," the Seller can try to make a counter offer to Buyer "B" to explore if he can obtain a more favourable price from him.

(3) If the first offer is lower in price than the 2nd offer, then it does not have to "meet and beat" the (higher) full price of the 2nd offer.

(4) **All Buyer "A" is required to do is to make a decision**

- if he is going to "firm up" his sale (by removing all subject clauses) or
- if he will step aside.

(5) Even if a Contract is "firm" (all conditions having been removed), but BEFORE COMPLETION
   - the Sellers may accept additional offers as BACK-UP offers IN SEQUENCE.
   - The Listing Salesperson should NOT discourage other offers from being presented (provided those Buyers are willing to take a chance and wait).

NOTE:
(a) The Realtor must observe his fiduciary duty of OBEDIENCE if his Sellers instruct him that they do not want to consider any further offers (because they have a "firm deal").
(b) However, **a conscientious Salesperson will caution his Clients** that even a firm deal can collapse for a number of reasons:
   - Death of one or both of the Buyers (e.g. car accident).
   - Unforeseen financial disasters: one of the Buyers looses his job and the other Buyer cannot qualify for the new mortgage alone by herself (cannot handle the monthly payments).
   - Unforeseen problems with the property itself.

(6) When are the Sellers totally (100%) protected?
   (a) When all necessary documents have been executed and registered in the Land Titles Office (and the Title transfer is completed)
   (b) AND all of the Sales Proceeds (money) are in the Sellers' bank account.

(7) **A word of CAUTION about "REPUDIATION."**
   (a) Repudiation is one contracting party's
      - unequivocal statement of his intention NOT to be bound by the terms of the original contract
      - OR his unequivocal refusal to perform the terms of the contract.
   (b) In view of the above, the other contracting party then has to make the following decision:
      - he can insist that the "repudiating party" must honour the contract (and go through with it)
      - OR he can decide that "the contract is at an end" and ask for damages (for breach of contract).
   (c) Should he decide to "treat the contract as 'AT AN END' then the procedure is NOT complete until NOTICE IN WRITING of his election (decision) is given to the party which had repudiated.
   (d) As this is a very complicated legal matter, it is best that a **Realtor should NOT get involved in a "repudiation" and he should definitely NOT give any advice in this matter.**

(e) Should this subject come up then the Realtor **MUST URGE HIS CLIENT TO OBTAIN COMPETENT LEGAL ADVICE WITHOUT ANY DELAY.**

(f) If the Client refuses to obtain legal advice, then the Realtor should protect himself by
- confirming in writing the Client's refusal to obtain legal advice AND
- by giving a copy of that memo to the Client (e.g. by FAX, which will show the time and date when it was sent).
- As usual it is good to remember that an ounce of "prevention" is worth a pound of "cure."

Overcoming Objections - Part I

BASIC CONSIDERATIONS FOR THE REALTOR.

Before an athlete competes, he will
a) train vigorously (physical preparation),
b) prepare himself mentally (psychological preparation).

The competition itself will take place in the right location, under the favourable weather conditions and with the use of the right equipment.

In some ways, the Realtor also goes into an arena to compete (to get a listing or make a sale). The outcome of his efforts will depend in part on how well he is prepared and equipped, if the location favours his undertaking etc.

A) **The Realtor's PREPARATION or "Forewarned is Forearmed."**

1) **BEFORE** you meet with your Clients:
    - **VISUALIZE in your mind the ENTIRE interview process** from the moment you meet the Client all the way until you say goodbye.
    - **Prepare in your mind a script of**
        - what you want to say and
        - what you want to achieve.
    - **ANTICIPATE and PREPARE for the worst:** mentally make a list of everything that COULD possibly go wrong, so you won't be caught off guard. Having done that, you will have the satisfaction and peace of mind that you will be able to face and deal with the worst. Everything else should be easier.
    - **Prepare POSITIVE RESPONSES to ALL of the NEGATIVE OBJECTIONS** you have thought of: **think carefully and elaborately through various ways how you may be able to counter or overcome predictable or possible OBSTACLES.** E.g.
        - the offered price is not enough for the Sellers;
        - the Mrs. will not throw in the washer and dryer;
        - when you arrive the TV is on and
        - the kids are not yet in bed;
        - the dog got out of the backyard;
        - husband and wife had a fight;
        - the husband is late coming home from work, he is tired and hungry.
    - **THINK of all the STANDARD and POSSIBLE objections, questions and problems which may arise especially if you are inexperienced.**
    - If you are not agile of mind, prepare yourself in advance for them
        - **by REHEARSING mentally the appropriate answers.**

- Keep on PRACTICING the above UNTIL IT BECOMES SECOND NATURE TO YOU.

There are several very compelling **reasons why a Realtor should rehearse:**
- No athlete would ever compete and no actor would perform without a lot of practice. Even a person giving a speech in front of an audience will attest to the fact that preparation is important.
- **DILIGENT PRACTICE is the best antidote for jittery nerves and sweaty palms.** The saying of **"practice makes perfect"** has been around for a long time. The great Roman poet OVID (whose full name was Publius Ovidius Naso 43 BC - AD 17 or 18 - he died in exile) was reported as saying: **"PRACTICE is the best of all instructions."**
- The public has an uncanny ability to recognize it if you are "winging it" or "playing it by ear."
- The Clients will also judge YOU by the quality of your presentation. (e.g. "Is he a real 'Pro' and are we in good hands with him?")
- It is a lot easier to deal with Customers once you have their confidence.

2) All of us have heard that **"AN OUNCE OF PREVENTION IS WORTH A POUND OF CURE."**
A lot of objections can be avoided if you do your homework by realistically assessing what the Client
- really **NEEDS** (**"needs"** equal **LOGIC,** e.g. we need 3 bedrooms)
- really **WANTS** (**"wants"** are **EMOTIONS** e.g. we want "elbow room")
- and what he can **REALISTICALLY AFFORD.**

It is up to the Realtor to qualify the Client and show him only properties which will fit into these categories. The better a job he does, the less objections he will encounter.

3) The Realtor must realize that objections, stalls, questions and interruptions of all kinds are **perfectly natural components and byproducts** of any serious discussion or negotiation.

4) With time the Realtor will develop **a basically standard PLANNED and "CANNED" presentation** which he will use with **LOGICAL SEQUENCE** during the interview together **with the appropriate variations and amendments to suit the occasion.** With increased and broadened experience the Realtor will not only gain knowledge, but also **develop confidence in himself what to say and how to conduct himself under these circumstances.**

5) Realtors shouldn't be obsessed by the competition from other Realtors.
- Don't allow it to confuse you
- or to shatter your confidence
- and thereby dominate your thinking

- and enslave your mind.

If you consider other Realtors as a threat, then better realize that you yourself - in turn - may appear as such to your competition.

6) Have all your documentation and supporting information neatly organized, so that you will have all material and notes at your fingertips when you need it.

7) **Take great comfort from your thorough preparation. It will boost your confidence for the appointment.**

B) **Choose your LOCATION wisely.**

1) For the Realtor it is very important to have the Client's full and undivided attention. For this purpose, **a comfortable location ensuring privacy** should be chosen where **a relaxed atmosphere** can be created.
   (a) Some Realtors prefer to conduct business in a private office back at the Realty Company.
   (b) The last choice should be public places like a restaurant (no privacy, too many noisy distractions) or a park (no desk to write on; it is awkward to write on your briefcase propped up on your knees).
   (c) If the meeting takes place at the Client's house (e.g. for a listing), then make sure that "the coast is clear": all other competing actions, distractions and non-productive pre-occupations must be eliminated:
   - TV and radio turned off,
   - kids in bed,
   - pets out of the way,
   - pager and cell phone turned to "silent."
   - Choose a comfortable location (e.g. the kitchen) and create a relaxed atmosphere ("At home we always discuss important things around the kitchen table").

2) Right from the beginning of the appointment **the Realtor should take charge in a non-confrontational manner.** To a certain extent
   - it is HE who will write the script for the ensuing conversations and discussions which will take place
   - and thus HE should be able to control the events. E.g. ("May I come in, please?")
   - "Where may I hang my coat?")
   - If the Realtor is able to "guide" the Clients and the events then he must take care to **avoid clashes of personalities.**

POSSIBLE PERSONALITY CLASH BETWEEN THE REALTOR AND HIS CLIENT.

A fundamental problem is that **unknowingly, unintentionally** and **unfortunately** there is often a **PERSONALITY CLASH** between the Realtor and his Client. (e.g. while trying to make a point with an "introvert Client," an "extrovert Realtor" may end up (psychologically speaking) acting like the proverbial bull in the china shop. In order to **SUCCESSFULLY handle objections when they arise**, an astute Realtor will **AVOID ALL PERSONALITY CLASHES.** If there is too great a difference between the Realtor's and the Client's personalities, then the Realtor may have to consider to temporarily adjust and to modify **HIS (the Realtor's) personality STYLE** in order to facilitate and **better achieve positive interaction with the Client.**

Under no circumstances should the Realtor become a chameleon and mimic or become a walking carbon copy of the Client's personality: NO!

But in order **to better achieve a LINK (positive INTERACTION)** with the Client the Realtor should try to **temporarily fit (adjust, modify) himself "TO"** the Client's personality. In other words **the Realtor may have to tune down his own assertiveness and simultaneously increase his responsiveness.**

To better understand this pitfall, various personality categories will be outlined here in very general terms in order to highlight the dangerous personality "OPPOSITES":

PERSONALITY GROUPS:
(1) **Assertive/autocratic**

On the **POSITIVE SIDE** this person is:
- disciplined and competitive.
- He is also direct, thorough, decisive and efficient.
- He drives himself mercilessly.

On the **NEGATIVE SIDE** this person is:
- a risk taker and likes to act fast (" do it now").
- He tends to make snap decisions without thinking first.
- He is dominating, uncompromising and has strong opinions,
- he is pushy, harsh, tough and overconfident.
- He also likes to drive everybody else.

By sheer necessity many Realtors (especially Top Producers) belong to this category.

(2) **Responsive/Amicable**

On the **POSITIVE SIDE** this person is:
- approachable, friendly, emotional, communicative, supportive, willing, dependable, personable, acquiescing

On the **NEGATIVE SIDE** this person is:
- impulsive, illogical, changeable, unorganized, undisciplined

Many Realtors strive to have the "Positive Side" of this category, but suffer especially from the "unorganized."

(3) **Analytical**
On the **POSITIVE SIDE** this person is:
- industrious, disciplined, persistent, orderly, serious, formal, business like

On the **NEGATIVE SIDE** this person is:
- indecisive, exacting, impersonal, cold, often uncommunicative or not communicative enough.

Many "workaholics" fit into this category.
In real life, people often belong to one dominant category, but in addition have a mixture of positive and/or negative elements from several of the other groups.

C) **Strategic PSYCHOLOGY is important.**

(1) Preferably the Realtor should sit face to face with the Clients in order to see
- their **facial expressions,**
- their **mannerisms** and
- their **body language.**

(2) **WHAT WILL HELP** the Realtor to unlock the Client's hesitation and indecision?
 (a) **By asking questions:** "Did we cover everything?" "Is everything clear?"
 (b) **The Realtor should pay attention** to the Client's
  - **voice** (easy, strained, hoarse, agitated, raised tone of voice; this will give him a clue as to the Client's **emotions**).
  - **the spoken words (the speed of talking)**
  - the Realtor should try to **disregard a Client's irritating voice:** e.g. singsong speech, rasping or guttural tone of voice, difficult to understand accent
  - and **understand the real meaning of what the Client is REALLY trying to say.**
  - He should not only **listen attentively, but LISTEN ACTIVELY** by giving non-verbal feedback (e.g. nodding with the head; a little approving smile; a puzzled look).
 (c) The Realtor should also **STOP AND THINK before talking.** Talk less and observe more.
 (d) The Realtor should **NOT OVERWHELM** the Client with a verbal torrent

of incomprehensible details (technical terms, shop talk etc.)

D) IN THE HEAT OF THE BATTLE.

The power of the mind is phenomenal and in the heat of the battle the Realtor will have to **be MENTALLY STRONG in order not to be thrown off course, distracted or discouraged.**

1) The Client should be allowed to vent his objections because **he is thereby expressing his feelings and concerns.**

THE ONLY REASON WHY he is doing that is **because he WANTS HIS PROBLEMS SOLVED.** If he wasn't interested, he wouldn't waste his time making the objection.

2) In order to understand the Client, one of the biggest mistakes a Realtor can make is that he **doesn't HEAR OUT the Client's ENTIRE objection.** Instead of letting the Client finish and hearing out what he has to say, the anxious Realtor jumps right in with a quick answer in order to "overcome the objection."
   - By prematurely interrupting the Client, the Realtor may inadvertently make things worse! By the **Realtor's negative ACTION** of choking off and brushing aside his (the Client's) concerns with (what the Client may perceive) as a pat (glib, contemptuous or inaccurate) answer, the Client will resent (**negative REACTION**) the Realtor and in the end the Realtor will lose.
   - Therefore the Realtor should observe the following:
     - thou shalt not rush the discussion
     - thou shalt not interrupt the Client
     - thou shalt let him finish.

One must wonder why some Realtors would persistently interrupt a Client. The answer to this puzzle is simple: uncontrolled thoughtless babbling is caused by mental constipation:
- stubbornly clinging to outdated methods;
- not "using his head";
- not willing to learn new things and
- not willing to change with the times.

3) **Instead of overpowering domination,** wouldn't it be a lot smarter for the Realtor to hear EVERYTHING the Client has to say and **then evaluate in his mind,** if it is a **VALID concern** or not? **Some objections may turn out to be merely cloaked requests for MORE INFORMATION.**

4) Wouldn't it be better for the Realtor to give the Client some time to think and let

the Client "save face" by appearing concerned and then making his point through diplomatic negotiation?

5) A vital tool in a Realtor's sales arsenal is **EMPATHY**. The Realtor must be able to put himself into his Clients' shoes in order to better understand their feelings and motivations. Under no circumstances should this be confused with **SYMPATHY**, which is moaning and crying along with the Client about some perceived "injustices" or "non-existent and imagined problems."

6) The Realtor should strive to build and establish the Client's confidence and trust in him by discovering exactly what problems the Client has.
He can achieve this by being **SUPPORTIVE** and **listening closely to gain sufficient information** to determine exactly what the Client's doubts, reasons for indecision, fear and worries are.
   - All of this will give the Realtor further **valuable clue**s on how to deal successfully with the Client's objections.
   - If still in doubt, (more) QUESTIONS should be asked which should **FOCUS ON** the Client's **NEEDS, objectives and prime interests/concerns.**

7) Explain to the prospective Client **the BENEFITS which he will gain and the LOSSES which he will avoid** if he follows your suggestions.

8) The Realtor should be ready and willing to answer all questions (objections) **immediately, completely, truthfully and competently.**
   - If necessary he should demonstrate to the Client that he wants to understand the problem. This is called "going the extra mile."
   - If the Realtor doesn't know the answer, then he should admit it and offer to find out and let the Client know by a specified deadline.
   - **The worst thing to do is to bluff or fudge around.** Clients will sense and/or recognize it.
   - **Any lies will invariably come to haunt you.** The trouble with lying is that one has to remember in the afternoon what was lied about in the morning. As time goes by it becomes more and more difficult "to keep the story" straight. On the other hand **the TRUTH is and always stays the same.**

9) When requested, the Realtor should provide specific information and clear-cut solutions.
   - **Suggested solutions should be**
   - sound and concise,
   - logical and well-organized,
   - and above **all clear and easily understandable for a lay-person;** especially for somebody who is under the pressure or stress from negotiating.

E) CONCERNING BODY LANGUAGE:

Generally speaking, Clients' objections come in 2 forms:

(a) If you are lucky, the Client will **"actively" VOICE his objection**. Thus you will know what bothers him and where you stand; and it will be a lot easier to deal with it.

(b) An inexperienced Realtor may not recognize the Client's **"passive" objection SIGNALS**:
- the Client remains (sullenly) silent or
- he may abruptly change the subject to something entirely unrelated (Danger! He may have given up on you … in frustration);
- or possibly even terminate the conversation and the appointment.
- Or else he may wince,
- he may shrug his shoulders or
- wrinkle his brows in a subtle frown.

The Realtor should **BE ALERT** to meaningful glances between husband and wife or for casual but indicative bits of conversation between them. These may give an alert Realtor valuable clues how to proceed!

THE REALTOR in turn SHOULD GUARD HIS OWN BODY LANGUAGE because the Client has eyes too! The following can betray the Realtor's worry that the sale might be slipping away:
- clenched fists or teeth
- wrinkled forehead
- tightly compressed lips,
- inadvertently rubbing a tight neck
- moving (rotating) shoulders in order to relieve aching muscles between the shoulder blades
- twitch in one eye
- twitch around the mouth
- sweating profusely
- rapid-fire idle talk (blabbing "small talk," unrelated nonsense)
- thoughtlessly lighting up a cigarette
- wringing hands or nervous hand gestures.

F) STOP AND THINK!

1) In order to better overcome objections, the Realtor should **STOP AND THINK BEFORE TALKING.**

(a) Is this a valid concern? Yes or no?
When he does start talking, then he should:
- meet any serious objection fair and square
- try to satisfy the Client as much as possible.
- Once he has dealt with the objection, he shouldn't rehash or dwell on it anymore. No "post mortems" please! It's done, settled and FINISHED!

(b) In response to an objection **the Realtor should TALK LESS. This means to QUIT (thoughtless) BABBLING.**
Don't overwhelm the Client with
- a verbal torrent of incomprehensible technical terms
- or an avalanche of unimportant details.

These will only confuse him.

2) The Realtor should **pay attention to the PACE of the conversation** and shouldn't rush the discussion:
- He should monitor the participants' involvement (are they still with him or are their thoughts straying?),
- He should test the amount of comprehension **(how much have the Clients absorbed of what has been said?)**
- and he should be alert to the amount of progress (how near are we to a "Trial Close?").

3) Within a reasonable limit the Realtor should be **PERSISTENT**. "Persistent" does NOT mean doggedly hounding the prospect and high pressuring him.

4) The Realtor should **watch and hold his TEMPER** even if he has heard this specific objection many times before. It is the first time for THIS particular Client. This includes objections which (to the Realtor) appear as ridiculous or insignificant. Always remember that these same objections are certainly NOT ridiculous or insignificant for the Client.
Therefore **"thou shalt let the Client vent,"** because
- by expressing his feelings he is giving you clues about his concerns;
- and the Client is "venting" because he wants his problems solved.

G) OVERCOMING OBJECTIONS IS THE ICING ON THE CAKE OF THE SALE.

1) The Realtor should be a "Gentleman":
- this includes respect and courtesy for the Client.
- All of which is part of being a "Professional."
- **It also helps to retain a sense of humour.**

2) The Realtor is meeting the Client "on business" and is not making a social call;

therefore **he shouldn't take anything personal**. He also should **not confuse a REFUSAL with a personal REJECTION.**

When the Client says "NO" he is merely stating his opinion.
- which could be IN ERROR, or
- could be based on incomplete or wrong information or
- it could be a misunderstanding or miscommunication.
- It may also be just his business decision.
- Don't jump to premature and/or rash conclusions. In this case "NO" could possibly or sometimes mean "MAYBE."

3) The Realtor shouldn't have an inflated or fragile EGO. **Having CONTROL over HIS EMOTIONS will give the Realtor a powerful advantage.**

4) If offering anecdotal evidence of his problem-solving expertise (e.g. "When the Smiths bought a house last year, this is what happened..."):
- don't use an example in poor taste (sarcasm or ridicule) which may cause embarrassment. The Clients could think that they will be next year's example in your repertory.
- Don't become repetitive, because people get bored easily.
- Don't be too short and curt, but not too longwinded either.

5) The best solution to a thorny objection may be to refer **to and enlist the help and protection from experts**. E.g.
- a **Certified Building Inspector** to check the condition of the house.
- **A lawyer** to look over the Contract of Purchase and Sale, or to address some legal matters. E.g.
   - possession before registration,
   - matters concerning **guaranties and warranties**
   - **boundary problems** (Certificate of Non-Encroachment [commonly known as Survey Certificate])
- **A Well Inspector** (testing the quality and quantity of the well water).
- In the sale of a business **an accountant** should review the books and financial statements.
- **An accountant** may also explain income tax ramifications, matters concerning GST etc.
- For the sale of an industrial or commercial property an **"Environmental Impact Inspection"** would ensure that there is no toxic waste on the property.
- Sundry **follow-up services** (e.g. for cleaning, painting, repairs offered by reliable tradesmen).

Overcoming Objections - Part II

In the past Realtors were taught to develop and learn by heart PROVEN FORMULAS to "BYPASS," "TIE DOWN" or "TURN AROUND" objections. For example some of these tactics included standard phraseology like:

(1) **The "Bypass":**
The Realtor may say to an objection: "Why don't we set that aside right now and concentrate on …"
Depending on how skilfully the Realtor is able to present this and depending on the Client's personality and sophistication this approach may or may no longer work nowadays. At any rate, the danger is that the Client will get the impression that his concern may not be important enough for the Realtor to pause in his quest to get him to sign on the dotted line.

(2) **"Tie Downs":**
In the Good Old Days Realtors used to give an Oscar-winning "100% natural" performance with cute "tie downs" like:
"I can almost smell the steaks sizzling on the barbecue out on the patio, CAN'T YOU?....OR **the Inverted Tie Down** ("Don't you think that …" or "wouldn't you want to …")
These were **painfully obvious manipulative attempts** which could lead to an embarrassing silence if the Client replied: "We are vegetarians and don't eat meat."

It may be more diplomatic and effective for the Realtor to say the following: "This patio is about the same size as I have at home. We use ours a lot in summer time for barbecuing and entertaining."
With this kind of statement the Realtor has
- identified himself with the Client.
- He has also painted a mental picture of the patio's use without running the risk of dwelling into what is being cooked.

(3) **The Realtor's CREDIBILITY may be at stake** with some of the following:
Realtor:
- "Based on all the facts you brought up, I think that you may have a point, HOWEVER …"
- "I understand exactly how you feel, BUT …"
- "I couldn't agree with you more, ALTHOUGH …"

The problem with this tactic was always the following: **if the Realtor really understood the facts and how the Client felt, then why would he have to argue differently?**

It is very unlikely that a modern-day Client will buy these thinly veiled tactics.

(4) **Minimizing and ridiculing "The Difference."**
Client: "I am not prepared to go the extra $ 5,000."
Realtor: "Let's keep everything in its proper perspective. Do you realize that the additional $ 5,000 on the full price works out to about $ 2.00 a day over the life time of the mortgage? This amount is what a cup of coffee costs nowadays."

This rejoinder assumes 2 things:
(a) that today's Client is not sophisticated enough to recognize that the act of reducing the $ 5,000 in question to what appears (at least on the surface) as "painless" component fraction (approx. $ 2.00 a day "translates" into the $ 5,000.00) is nothing but a "spiel" based on some spurious math.
(b) Can the Realtor honestly pretend with a straight face that he has rapidly calculated (in his head) the interest on the $ 5,000 over the life time of the mortgage and that the sum total of the principal plus the accrued interest divided by the number of days over the amortization period really works out to $ 2.00 a day? The Realtor may congratulate himself that he has whittled the problem down to a "manageable size" and reduced the $ 5,000 to something ridiculously small, but **what are the chances that today's Client will share his opinion?**

The following are some suggested methods of **diplomatically handling STANDARD OBJECTIONS to BASIC PROBLEMS:**

(1) **THE CONDITION OF THE HOUSE.**
(a) "This property needs A LOT of work."
   "This house needs painting inside and out."
   "The yard is a mess."

Suggested possible **SOLUTIONS**.
- All of these conditions can be remedied with some elbow grease and/or cash.
- This sort of objection **may be merely the Client's OPENING GAMBIT to see how much the Seller is willing to come down**.
- If the Client criticizes every nail and stick of wood in the house don't despair: he must be interested otherwise he wouldn't waste his time criticising. When he is finally finished criticising you may consider asking him with a concerned face if there is ANYTHING which he likes about the house? He might surprise you by saying that he likes the location. To this reply (light-heartedly): "In that case why don't you buy it, provided the price is right?"
In which case you have not only overcome an objection, but have also made (simultaneously) a TRIAL CLOSE!

As far as the painting and messy yard are concerned:
(a) there are always painters and gardeners advertising for work in local papers or students looking for summer employment. They will be happy to paint and clean

up the mess at a reasonable price.

(b) Or the Buyer could have a few friends over for a "work cookout" - everybody helps out and will be rewarded with a barbecue and beer. This should appeal especially to the younger crowd.

(c) And finally the best of all is that the Buyer has a chance **to paint and decorate to suit HIS OWN TASTE.** He doesn't have to accept somebody else's colour scheme and the yard will look just like HE wants it.

(d) **"Before I can make an offer, I need to get first a price on remodelling the kitchen** (or bathroom, finishing the basement, painting the outside etc.)"
Hallelujah! This is no objection or unfounded stall; the Client obviously likes the house, he is willing to do the work and spend some money. **He is merely searching for INFORMATION to substantiate the amount of reduction in price which he will be asking from the Seller.**

(e) **"This property requires TOO MUCH work."**
By saying this the Client may have meant to say:
"Too much work **for US.**"
- He is not a handyman and cannot afford to hire subtrades;
- The amount of deferred maintenance (neglect) appears to him as an overpowering threat: the work which needs to be done is simply too much for him to tackle financially, physically and emotionally.

The sad fact is that this is the wrong house for him, even if he should get it cheaper.

Of course, all Realtors know that **the "RIGHT PRICE" remedies all defects**. If it is cheap enough, then somebody is always willing to clean up the dirt and mess and make the necessary repairs. The Realtor just has to find the right person by **addressing his sales efforts and future advertising to a HANDYMAN or somebody with deep pockets.**

(2) **The pitfalls of dealing with "ADVISERS."**
This can be a real minefield.
  (a) Avoid anything that will cause anxiety, controversy, arguments or frustration.
  (b) **NEVER let the "Adviser" become an adversary.**
  (c) The Realtor's mettle will be put to the test by him trying to **diplomatically maintain control of the situation.**
  (d) To achieve this the Realtor must convince BOTH the Client as well as the Adviser that:
     - he (the Realtor) is earnestly trying to help the Client
     - the Realtor must demonstrate his enthusiastic WILLINGNESS to

cooperate with the Adviser in order to "serve the Client."
- the Realtor must strive to achieve an obvious-to-all "atmosphere of teamwork" with the Adviser. Especially with a lawyer or bank manager or close relative.

"The LAWYER" as adviser.
Client: **"Before we sign this, we want to talk to our lawyer first."**
The Realtor must realize that:
- There is no graceful way out of this one;
- any opposition is hopeless;
- it will only make him look bad and the Client will become apprehensive that the Realtor is trying to hide something.

Suggested SOLUTION:
As soon as possible the Realtor should try and meet with the lawyer but on the basis of an equal professional who has nothing but "the best interests in mind for the COMMON Client."

NOTE: If the Client has to chose between the advice from a lawyer and information given by a Realtor, then the lawyer will win out at all times. Don't be upset by this, because the lawyer (by giving advice) will shoulder a part of the responsibility. No doubt, he will suggest some (hopefully only minor) changes; but once these problems are solved, the Realtor is home free.

Offers drawn up by a lawyer may for various reasons not be acceptable to the Sellers (or else the Sellers in turn will hire a lawyer of their own "to look things over").

"The PARENTS" as advisers.
Clients: **"Before we decide, we want our parents to see the house."**
NOTE: No Realtor should consider even for a moment to fight family ties. The parents naturally want nothing but the best for their children. The young couple is looking for reassurance.

SUGGESTED SOLUTIONS:
(a) **Dealing with the Parents.**
- An astute Realtor will realize that the parents will look at the house from THEIR perspective.
- The parents also have to be sold on the benefits and advantages of the house.
- The parents have to be reassured that it is the best possible bargain for the young couple's financial ability.
- If the parents want a better house for their children, then they can always give the young couple some financial help.

(b) **Dealing with the Young Couple.**
- At the same time the Realtor should tell the young couple in private and as diplomatically as possible, that it is THEY who will be living in the house and

not the parents.
- Under no circumstances should the parents be made to look bad (e.g. old-fashioned).
- Well-meaning relatives are not real estate "experts" even if they have bought and sold before. Therefore, they are going to be EXTRA cautious.
- The final decision must be made by the Young Couple and not by the Parents.

"The FAMILY CONSTRUCTION EXPERT" as adviser.
Clients: **"Before we decide, we want Uncle Joe to look the house over first."**
30 years ago Uncle Joe built a barn/shed/dog house on the Prairies. Ever since that time he has been basking in the position of "Construction Expert of the Family." A big drawing card is that he will do the inspection for nothing.

The problem with this type of adviser is as follows:
- A "No cost" inspection done by a self-proclaimed expert
- who is a long-time pillar of the family.
- Because of simple self-defense, Uncle Joe's role is to be "critical of everything" because he has to cover himself in case something should go wrong later on.
- At the same time because of Uncle Joe's extensive family ties the Realtor (who is a potential stranger in comparison with Uncle Joe) must be careful not to run Uncle Joe's "expertise" down; even if it is painfully obvious that Uncle Joe doesn't know the difference between a hammer and a thumb.

SUGGESTED SOLUTION:
- The Realtor should tactfully explain to his Buyers that they are unwittingly subjecting old Uncle Joe to a terrible burden of responsibility by having him judge the construction and advise them. By all means Uncle Joe should look at the house, but it may be unfair and stressful for everybody in the family to put one of its members under this sort of obligation.
- Wouldn't it be better for everybody, if this matter was put on a business-like basis by hiring an outside party, namely an Accredited Professional Building Inspector? His fee will be more than justified and offset by him discovering and warning about costly future repairs. Some inspectors may even suggest how these repairs can be effected and a ballpark cost for them.
- If the Seller is seriously interested in selling, he might be willing to atone (or at least share) financially some of these costs (by agreeing to lower the selling price).
- At any rate, after a professional inspection there should be no bad surprises in the future. For these reasons it is very important that Realtors should always recommend the services of a professional.

(3) **The age-old problem of "AGE."**
Client: **"This house is too old."**
Realtor: the Realtor's solution is to
(a) discuss "age" in general terms:
- "They don't build them anymore like they used to" OR
- **for practical purposes**, what is the difference between 11 years old and 15 as long as the house is in good shape and there are 3 bedrooms and 2 bathrooms?"
- **emphasize eye-opening facts.** For example:
- clean and in A-1 shape,
- lots of updating was done,
- the price is within the Buyer's budget,
- there is an assumable 1st mortgage with an attractive low interest rate which is good for several more years.
- Proximity to services (bus, schools and shops) and
- amenities (all bedrooms are on the same floor),
- established neighbourhood of other wellkept homes.

(4) **The "mother of all problems."..The PRICE.**
CAUTION: In this connection **Realtors should review their Fiduciary Obligations of confidentiality, care and loyalty.**

(a) The Client says: **"The asking price is too high."**
DISCUSSION:
This can mean one of 3 things:
- The house may be genuinely overpriced or else
- it is their opening salvo, to intimidate you and/or the Sellers during the upcoming negotiations or
- it is really too high for THEM (the house is out of their price range).

(b) The Client says: **"How much less will they take?"**
- The Realtor can safely quote only the Listed Price.
- The Realtor shouldn't assume or try to guess what the Seller will or will not take.
- The Realtor can offer to his Buyer a Market Analysis of the subject property.
- **The Realtor's role is**
  - to write up the offer
  - to present the offer
  - to try to close the offer.
  - If he cannot close the offer, then the Realtor should bring back to his Buyer the best possible counter offer.
  - However, **the final decision concerning the Selling Price will be made by the Buyer and Seller.**

(c) The Client says: **"What? They turned $ X down? That was a good offer and the owners should have grabbed it."**
Obviously the Buyers had in mind to offer less than the previous offer.
Actually, if the Listing Salesperson involved would have observed his fiduciary duties, then nobody else should be aware that there had been a previous offer and for how much (unless he was expressly authorized by the Sellers to do so).

SUGGESTED SOLUTION:
The Realtor should explain to the Clients, that there could still be a chance:
- Perhaps the Sellers have had second thoughts and regretted having rejected the original offer for $ ...
- Perhaps their situation has changed since that first offer, making it more imperative to accept an offer at THIS time.
- Perhaps the Seller has not had anymore showings and offers since that first one; he may have realized that he has made a mistake turning that previous offer down. He might be ready to take the next offer.

(d) The Client says: **"Let us know if the price comes down."**
DISCUSSION:
As far as these Buyers are concerned, this house is either overpriced or priced out of their reach. If it is a Buyer's Market and the Seller has a good reason for selling, then chances are that the Buyers will eventually get their wish.

(5) **"WAITING" can have its hazards:**
The footloose Buyers may
- look around on their own and buy a FSBO or
- talk to another Realtor and buy something else from him.
- In either case you have lost out.

SUGGESTED SOLUTION:
- Contact the Listing Salesperson of the house involved and ask him if there have been any showings or offers recently. He may be able to give you some valuable clues to encourage your Clients to write an offer NOW instead of waiting.
- Tell your Buyers that this house is being actively marketed
    - and that it could be sold to somebody else while they are waiting AND/OR
    - that they may have to compete against another offer at some future date when they finally get around to writing.
    - Reiterate all the benefits and advantages of the home;
    - **remind them that the house suits them in every respect, except for the price.**
    - Right now they don't have to compete against any other offers and thus they may get it at (or close to) "their" (hoped for) price.

- Tell them that you are prepared to go the extra mile for them and present any reasonable offer;
- you are willing to invest YOUR time and YOUR hard work (and YOUR gas) in an effort (to present their offer) - ALL AT NO COST to them. Therefore what have THEY got to lose by writing an offer?

(6) **General EMOTIONAL uncertainty, doubts and indecisions.**
Client: **"We need more time to think it over."**
"We want to sleep over it."
"This is a big step for us."
"We are not in the habit of making snap (quick) decisions."
"We want to talk it over at home"

SUGGESTED SOLUTION:
Generally Clients have 2 reasons for postponing to make a decision (to buy or sell):

(a) the reason they tell to the salesperson and
(b) the REAL reason which they try to hide and keep hidden from the salesperson.

In order to be able to communicate intelligently, the Realtor should find out by diplomatic questioning what is bothering the Client:
The clients may
- genuinely have the habit of not making snap decisions
- be generally uncertain and unsure and/or
- need more information about something.
- Be in the process of getting "cold feet" because they have to make a big decision.
- It might even be **part of the Client's personality** to be unsure of himself.

Client: **"We are not yet ready to buy."**
"We have just started to look; we want to look around some more before making a decision."

SUGGESTED SOLUTION:
Fair enough - valid point.
Find out how many homes they have seen so far.
Find out if they are already working with another Realtor and if not, then make every effort to become THEIR Realtor.

Client: **"We will phone you if we are interested."**

SUGGESTED SOLUTION:
(a) Amongst many other things, this could mean that it wasn't the right house for them.

(b) There might be some **major problem** (which they don't want to talk about) with this particular property:
- too close to some relatives or (former) friends with whom they may not be on the best of terms;
- for some reason they may not like the neighbourhood (e.g. not good enough for them).
- The house is too far from amenities (transportation, schools, shopping) for them (they may have only one car, or one of the parties is not driving).
- They have seen another house with another Realtor and they like that house better.

(7) **It is tough to CLOSE a deal if and when there are NO objections.**

If the prospective Buyer's reaction to a house is consistently and pleasantly non-committal, then he may have no interest in or intention of buying that house. Only when he becomes emotionally involved and develops a keen interest in owning the house, then it suddenly becomes an entirely different ball game: his fears, doubts, concerns and worries will all rise to the surface in the form of **OBJECTIONS**.

A Realtor shouldn't fear them.

Overcoming Objections - Part III

As long as the Realtor and his Client are walking down a path of agreement, the process is no more than **"ORDER TAKING."** The **real SELLING STARTS** when the Client says "NO!" That is where the "overcoming of objections" comes in.

OVERCOMING OBJECTIONS can be defined (in a positive sense) as the efforts of a Realtor to **CONSTRUCTIVELY INFLUENCE the thoughts and perspective of a Client in order to consequently motivate him to action for the Client's ULTIMATE BENEFIT.**

As times have been changing and the public has become more and more sophisticated, selling methods - by necessity - also had to be changing. **Intrusive selling techniques of the past no longer work.** By thoughtlessly rattling off outdated verbal tactics (which the modern Client will recognize as such), a Realtor will run the risk of appearing as a sleazy salesperson (out of the past) who is determined to make the sale at all costs.

The following 2 examples will illustrate this:

(1) In the Good Old Days the Realtor was taught to consider complaints about the size or shape of a room as immaterial and that he should relentlessly press ahead by making the Buyer see the room in a "different" light.

Client: **"This Master Bedroom is too small for us."**
Realtor looking puzzled: "Let me get this straight: you said that the Master Bedroom was smaller than you would like? Would you please elaborate on that for me?"

This question obviously puts the Client on the spot, because he has either too much furniture or his furniture is bulky.

Client: **"Our furniture doesn't fit into this bedroom."**
Realtor: "A few minutes ago you said that the kids' bedrooms were ok. So we only have to worry about this one. Have you ever considered doing without the 2nd dresser or getting a smaller bed? Like trading your king-sized bed for a queen-sized bed?"

This Realtor's suggested solution doesn't sound like it is genuinely in the interests of the Clients. Mrs. Buyer may not appreciate this sort of tactic, because it was she who had picked out the furniture, or she may just have bought it recently. Mr. Buyer - who is over 6 ft. tall and weighs 250 lbs. - will want his nocturnal comfort in the king-sized bed. Therefore, the Realtor's suggestion is insensitive.

(2) Another example:
Worried Client: **"We are concerned if we are doing the right thing by borrowing**

a part of the downpayment."

Uncaring Realtor: "Don't worry about it. It is normal that everybody gets cold feet at one time or another. Come on! We don't want to loose this house. Sign here.

The process of OVERCOMING OBJECTIONS has changed from the crude mentally overpowering of the Client to the subtle art of GENTLE PERSUASION and the use of psychology. Nowadays a Realtor must
- understand people and
- act with honesty and integrity
- the Client and Realtor must literally "fit" together (hand in glove, be on the "same wave length").
- Gentle persuasion will return the Realtor and his Client to **the process of walking down the aforementioned path of agreement**.

The GOOD NEWS is that **modern techniques of overcoming objections CAN BE LEARNED** - albeit with some effort - by ANY Realtor. However, in order to thoroughly master it until it becomes AUTOMATIC requires many hours of practice involving the proverbial "blood, sweat and tears" of failing in the field. The idea is
- **to learn from your mistakes and**
- **polish your performance for the next time.**

Only the untrained salesperson will remain unsure of himself and dread the Client's negative feedback (which is what objections are). The untrained salesperson doesn't understand **how useful and constructive objections** can actually be when communicating with a Client.

Objections can actually be HEALTHY BUYING SIGNALS and therefore, there is **NOTHING TO FEAR about them**.

Here are some **BASIC ideas** on which a Realtor can build his **KNOWLEDGE and EXPERTISE** for overcoming objections.

1) Above all, the Realtor must speak in his own, normal way and use only words which are part of HIS standard vocabulary.

2) **Artificial formulas and high-pressure tactics are to be AVOIDED.**

3) **The Realtor must understand the Client.** All of us have heard it said many times before that Realtors are in the **PEOPLE BUSINESS**. Once the Realtor has fully realized that, he will understand and act accordingly:
   (a) The Clients are just as nervous and apprehensive as the unsure Realtor is - possibly even more so.

(b) Therefore, it is of vital importance (for the achievement of a mutually satisfactory conclusion of the transaction) **that at least ONE of the parties (hopefully the Realtor) should know what is going on and what he is doing.**
(c) It is a human tendency to procrastinate and find excuses to postpone having to make a decision.
(d) People are often **motivated by GREED and FEAR.**

GREED can be defined as **the hope of obtaining an exaggerated and/or unreasonable degree of "more, bigger and better":**
- **more money** (that is one of the reasons for an over-priced listing)
- a bigger house in a better neighbourhood for less money (in the case of a Buyer's low-ball offer).

FEAR (in the commercial sense) **is the foreboding sentiment of dread over the impending regret for a LOSS.** E.g.:
"We should have accepted the first Buyer's offer."
"That house was a good buy; I am sorry that I didn't agree to go up that extra $5,000.00 in the price."

(e) A skilful Realtor will explain to his Clients the reverse side of the afore-mentioned 2 motivators, namely:
- the **BENEFITS** which he will **GAIN** and
- the **LOSSES** which he will **AVOID** if he follows the Realtor's suggestions.
- **The Client must be reassured** that he is making the right decision or getting **the best possible deal**.
- This includes his additional desires of **"SAVING MONEY" and "INVESTING WISELY."**

In every serious sales negotiation **The PRICE** and **TERMS** will be an important and legitimate factor.
The following are some suggestions how to overcome the PRICE DIFFERENCE:
1) The Realtor must prove to and persuade his Buyer that the RESULTS he will get (by accepting the Seller's counter offer) are **WORTH MORE THAN** the (increased) price he will be paying.

2) In other words, **the increased price must be amply offset by an increased degree of BENEFITS and ADVANTAGES to be gained.** E.g.:
- the quality of construction
- the size (floor area) of the house
- the floor plan of the house (no steps to climb, the bedrooms are located away from the living area),
- the enjoyment of the house (comfort, less maintenance)

- the size and condition of the lot (big lot for children to play in; small lot for minimum maintenance).
- the advantages and/or prestige of the neighbourhood,
- the proximity to amenities (schools, transportation, shopping, parks, churches etc.)

3) A Master Salesman will use **powerfully DESCRIPTIVE words** in order to create in the Client's mind flashes of
   - **comfort,**
   - **security,**
   - **leisure time with loved ones** (holidays, family, children and pets)
   - the attractive placement of furniture,
   - **convenience** (floor plan, proximity to amenities)
   - **instant gratification** (they can emulate the success of others who have made the decision to buy).

4) Certain words have a **strong emotional impact**. To become successful, a Realtor must
   - **develop** and then
   - **use a powerful sales VOCABULARY**
   - **AND he MUST fit it in smoothly into HIS normal way of talking.**

   Here are some examples:
   Expressive: luxurious, flawless, elegant, spotless, pristine
   Dynamic: powerful, rugged, breakthrough
   Personal: you, we, ours.

5) The Realtor must also distinguish between **FEATURES and BENEFITS**.
   - **A FEATURE** has no sales impact, because it simply says what is: e.g. 3 bedrooms
   - **A BENEFIT describes what it does:**
     (a) the advantage or satisfaction that each child can have his/her own bedroom.
     (b) OR: "The real benefit to you is that you can move in right away."
     (c) OR: ".... what this means to you, Mr. and Mrs. Buyer is ...."

6) Once **the SPARK of INTEREST has been ignited**, it is only logical to follow through by **fanning the FLAMES of DESIRE**: The modern psychological way of selling the Client (on the benefits which he and his family will enjoy) is by **FLESHING OUT these aforementioned "flashes" into MORE ELABORATE PICTURES of comfort, security etc.**

7) However, the Realtor should guard himself from overdoing it. Don't get carried

away. To literally swoon in raptures of delight can and will come across as phony.

8) The Realtor must pay heed to the Client's certain **OTHER psychological NEEDS:**
   (a) During the interview, there is nothing more important for a Client than **HIS needs**. The Client **NEEDS to FEEL**
      - that **HE** is at all times **"Number 1"** and
      - **"in control"** of the situation.
      - That the Realtor is **listening carefully to his**
      - **WANTS** (desires)
      - **CONCERNS** (problems) and
      - **OBJECTIVES** (e.g. for the Buyer the "best possible deal" is the lowest price; for the Seller the "most amount of money in the shortest possible time with the least amount of inconvenience").
   (b) The Client also wants the Realtor's **full and undivided attention**. Therefore, cell phones and pagers must be turned off or tuned to "silent." To have discussions interrupted by beeping pagers followed by: "Excuse me, I have to phone this person right away" tells the Client, **that somebody else is more important than HE is**.
   (c) **Any interruptions will also take the wind out of the sails of your presentation.** (Where were we? Oh, yes..)
   (d) Nobody likes to feel that he has been wrong. If the Client has been mistaken, then the Realtor must become a World-Class Diplomat in order to avoid hurting the Client's feelings (**negative reaction**) while still trying to get his point across.
   (e) For the Client, an objection is sometimes an **EXCUSE or a DEFENCE MECHANISM to slow down the pace of the selling/listing process**.
      - The Client might need some time (or breathing room) to be able to THINK;
      - He may wish to ponder a certain point which the Realtor has made.
      - Some objections are
         - **nothing more than CLOAKED REQUESTS FOR MORE INFORMATION,**
         - or an indication of or an effort to **obscure the Client's general emotional uncertainty**.
   (f) Under no circumstances should the Realtor show his "superiority" by
      - the excessive use of technical terms,
      - rubbing in the Client's ignorance about real estate (rumours of what the house down the road sold for)
      - somehow ineptly and inadvertently demonstrating to the Client that he (the Realtor) is actually trying to control the situation. The Client will resent being manipulated in an overt way.

At all times the Realtor must make the Client feel COMFORTABLE.

Overcoming Objections - Part IV
Recognizing the Death Knell.

In order to avoid
- wasting his precious time or
- attracting a Client's complaint or worse still
- getting involved in a costly law suit

the Realtor must be able to recognize when the "DEATHKNELL" tolls. When THAT bell tolls, then there is no more point in "overcoming objections."
The following are a few examples of situations where the Realtor may consider to
- cut his losses by dropping certain types of Clients
- and to look for greener pastures elsewhere.

(1) **The reluctant or uncooperative "partner" (Co-Owner).**
   (a) One of the owners doesn't really want to sell the house. There is continuous disagreement between the Sellers: the problems start with the signing of the listing and from there things go steadily downhill.
   (b) For some reason one of the Buyers doesn't want to buy this particular house and makes strenuous objections, most of which are not really warranted.

Regardless of what kind of "silver-tongued selling miracles" you will perform, these types of persons will drag their feet "big time." They will make your life sour by placing every conceivable obstacle in your way. In the end they will invariably win, because the "other" Seller or "other" Buyer will give up. Why? Simply for the sake of domestic peace and tranquility. Too late will you realize that you never had a chance!

(2) **No money.**
   (a) The Sellers have insufficient equity in the house to pay the real estate commission. This should be an obvious "no brainer" unless
      - a relative or friend will pay the commission on their behalf or
      - you are willing to work "pro bono" (provide your services for free).
   (b) Both Buyers work and together they make good money. However, for some reason they are unable to save up a downpayment. Each payday they spend freely and then some. In reality they are poor money managers.
   Recently some lenders have started to consider granting "no-downpayment"-type of financing under certain circumstances. Often this involves a personal "side loan." As the Buyers have no actual equity (in the first few years) there is a good chance that they will eventually end up in financial trouble: inability to keep up the high mortgage payments caused by income interruptions due to various reasons (illness, loss of job, they split up and one alone cannot keep up the monthly payments).

(3) **Bad credit rating.**
People with a marginal credit rating may be better off to rent until such time when their financial affairs are in better order. However, high-risk lenders will provide mortgage financing at high interest rates and/or financing with a built-in "bonus" (in the form of a discounted loan amount. In effect, this "discount" is prepaid interest). This also is a good prescription to put a financially over-extended person into (more) financial trouble. For this type of situation, the Seller should NOT be asked to carry any portion of the mortgage. The reaon should be obvious (eventually they both will end up in trouble).

(4) **A person with many debts:**
Creditors and collection agencies are constantly calling. See above.

(5) **Previous bankruptcy.**
For these unfortunate persons it is difficult if not impossible to get credit. Even after the bankruptcy has been "discharged," there may still be a stigma attached to them.
Often it will be suggested to them to get a "guarantor" or "Co-signer" to help them to qualify for credit. Such guarantors (often a relative or friend) will run the risk of having to make the loan payments, if the prime borrower is unable to do so. This should be explained to them before they sign on the dotted line.

(6) **Insufficient income to service**
- the mortgage payments and/or
- the accumulated total of all other debts.

A Client may qualify for the Gross Debt Service Ratio (the "PIT" Principal, Interest and 1/12 Taxes payment) BUT they may not qualify for the "TOTAL Gross Debt Service Ratio" (which includes all other debts, e.g. credit card balances, car loan etc.). A favourite solution is to amalgamate all other debts and thereby lower the overall total debt payments.
- Another solution may be to buy a house with a "mortgage helper" (income from an illegal basement suite). This type of rental income could be discontinued if the local Municipality shuts down the suite (because it does not conform to the current zoning, fire regulations, building code etc.) This usually happens after a neighbour complains.

Case law:
- **"Burnaby (City) v. Pocrnic,"** B.C. Court of Appeal, Docket CA025530, Date 1999-11-12
- **"Langley (Township) v. Wood"** B.C. Supreme Court, Docket No. A963884, Vancouver, Date 1998-06-24
- **"Tenants' Rights Action Coalition v. Corp. of Delta"** B.C. Supreme Court, Docket A961448, Date 1997-09-19
- **"R. v. Pesti,"** B.C. Supreme Court, Docket CC911000, Date 1991-11-27

In all of the above cases the Defendant Homeowners argued that "everybody else" in the area had basement suites. It didn't do them any good. Their suites were shut down.

(7) **People in distress:**
   The Clients have too much on their plate:
   - insecurity of his job (pending lay-off, cut-back, the employing company has been sold and the staff is being reassigned).
   - Pending break-up of the marriage (buying a house will not cure this problem).
   - Serious problems with children or elderly relatives.
   - Fighting in all directions:
     - law suits (with a bad neighbour)
     - strike action (at work)
     - recuperating from an accident etc.

(8) Going through **a (messy) divorce could be the ONLY exception to this "List of Woes."**
   The simple reason is because **the house will have to be sold eventually** (to partition the assets).
   Although a marriage breakup may result in a saleable listing the Realtor will earn every Cent of his commission by
   - the stressful situation created by the fighting Sellers and
   - their respective lawyers who will try and achieve the best possible settlement for their own Clients. Occasionally this could mean that one of the parties' signature on the Contract of Purchase and Sale may not be readily available or at least not until "certain outstanding items" are settled between the parties. This delay in dealing with the offer will put pressure not only on the Realtor, but also on the prospective Buyer (an innocent bystander) who has made an offer in good faith and wants to have an answer.

   As an outsider, a Realtor may also see with some alarm that often little attention is paid how all of the upheaval surrounding the divorce will affect the children of the torn family.

Overcoming Objections - Part V
Forewarned is forearmed.

Use this **SUMMARY to prepare - in your own words - GOOD ANSWERS** how to overcome the following objections:

When **SELLING**:

1) **CONDITION OF THE HOUSE:**
The house needs a lot of work
The house needs too much work
The house needs cleaning
The house needs painting inside and out
The yard is a mess
There is only one bathroom in the house
The basement is not finished
There are water marks in the basement
The house is too old
The Master Bedroom is too small for us
Our furniture doesn't fit into the living room
The **STIGMATIZED** house: the house was in a fire
                               the basement used to be flooded
Before I can make an offer, I need to get first a price on:
- remodelling the kitchen
- remodelling the bathroom
- finishing the basement

2) **THE LOCATION OF THE HOUSE:**
This house is on a busy street
If you stand in the backyard you can hear the traffic noise from the freeway
There are power lines nearby
The drive-way is too steep

3) **THE ADVISORS:**
Before we make an offer/before we decide …
WE WANT
- our parents to see the house
- Uncle Joe to have a look at it

Before we sign this, we want to talk to our lawyer first

4) **THE STALL:**
We are concerned if we are doing the right thing
This is a big step for us, we need more time to think it over

We have just started to look
We want to look around some more before making a decision
We are in no rush to buy
We want to sleep over it

5) THE PRICE:
The price is too high
How much less will they take?
What? They have turned $ XXX down? They should have grabbed it. Let us know when the price comes down.

When LISTING:

1) The COMMISSION:
The commission is too high/too much
Will you cut/reduce your commission?
Will you settle for a lower commission?
The price of our home will be too high if you add your commission.
By not dealing with you we'll save the commission.
If we don't have to pay a commission then we will be able to sell at a lower price.
You can show my house to your buyers. If you bring me a deal, then I will pay you a commission.
A few days ago Joe Blow came by and seemed to be interested. He might come back and buy our house, in which case your commission will be in the way.

2) The PRICE:
I am not going to sell unless I get my price.
I want to start (list) my house at a high(er) price; I can always come down later on when an offer comes in.
Another Realtor said that he could get us more money.

3) The STALL:
We want to try it by ourselves for another week.
We have a friend/relative in the real estate business.
Your office is too far away.
Your Company is too small/too large.
We have never heard of you/your company.
We want to think it over.
We want to sleep on it first.
We don't want to tie up our house.
We don't want to be tied down to only one real estate.
We don't want to sign anything.
Other salesmen have been showing our house without them having a listing.

The market is good, we don't need to deal with a Realtor to sell our house.
We had it on MLS and it didn't sell.
But you didn't show my house while it was listed.
We are in no hurry to sell.
We must sell quickly and don't have any time to waste.
We have heard bad things about real estate people.
60 days is too long to tie myself up.
I only want a 30-day listing.
I don't want a sign on my property.
This is the wrong time of the year to sell.
I want to wait till the school year is over.
I want to wait till the flowers come out and the yard looks better.
I don't want to end up on the street; therefore I want to find the right house first before I sell.

Overcoming Objections - Part VI
How to overcome 27 OBSTACLES when trying for a LISTING.

Various refusals and objections and a suggested outline of possible rebuttals are given next.

The Reader is encouraged to learn to formulate his answers with words which are part of his natural vocabulary and to talk in the manner in which he is usually accustomed to speak.

That way he will
(a) remember the rebuttals a lot easier and
(b) won't forget something.
(c) On the other hand reciting memorized lines in a sing-song will come across as "artificial" and obviously indoctrinated.

(1) OWNER: "The commission is too much/too high."
"Will you cut/reduce your commission?"
"Will you settle for a lower commission/rate?"

REALTOR:

The owner's basic or ultimate concern is his NET EQUITY, which he wants to guard at all costs. Once the Realtor realizes and understands this, everything else will fall into place.

POSITIVE ARGUMENTS:
(a) **The Realtor must convince the Client that he is worth the full amount of the commission.**
  - "What experience have you had by buying a less expensive product? E.g. Quality shoes (although more expensive) will give you good and long service. Will cheap shoes do the same?"
  - "On the other hand have you ever been sorry for buying a high quality item? Expensive and good quality clothes fit better, look better and surely last a lot longer."
  - **"The bitterness of poor quality lingers a lot longer than the initial sweet taste of its low price."**

(b) **By reiterating the wide range of benefits and advantages his services have to offer.**
  - "No, I won't work for less, but I will explain to you how I will provide you with MORE VALUE for your commission Dollar."
  - "I will do more than just stick a sign on your lawn.
    I have an extensive Sales Program to market your house.
    This will require that I spend my money promoting it.
    My only guaranty for getting my promotion money back is my hard work and confidence in my ability. We are in this together. You can rest assured that I

will work hard to sell your house."

(c) "In the final analysis, **the commission you pay is NOT AN EXPENSE but a WISE INVESTMENT in the ADVANTAGEOUS SALE of your house.**"

(d) A (tempting) **negative argument** would be to say: "Mr. Seller! How would you feel if you were to go to work today and your boss arbitrarily cuts your wages?" NOTE: this sort of argument can turn out to be counterproductive because it could be interpreted as confrontational.

(2) OWNER: **"We want to try it by ourselves for another week."**
REALTOR:
   (a) You have to convince the owner that by waiting, he may miss out on some good Buyers who are RIGHT NOW actively searching in the market, either by themselves (by reading ads, looking for Realtor signs) or with another Realtor.
   (b) You can also use the "urgency close" by outlining that you could schedule an ad and Open House for the next weekend, put the house on the Office Tour and order your sign.

(3) OWNER: **"A few days ago Joe Blow came by and seemed to be interested.** He might come back and buy our house, in which case your commission will be in the way."
REALTOR:
Enquire if the owner can contact Joe Blow to see if he is genuinely interested. If he doesn't have Joe Blow's phone number then suggest that you will take an **Exclusive Listing on which you can incorporate the stipulation that the Seller has the right to sell privately (without paying a commission) to Joe Blow (ONLY) by a certain date.** Once that date has passed and there is no sign of Joe Blow, then the Exclusive Listing can be turned into a Multiple Listing and the owner has not lost (wasted) any time on the start-up formalities. (e.g. sign up, tour, ads etc.)

(4) OWNER: **"We have a friend in the real estate business"**
REALTOR:
No doubt you will ask yourself: "If he has a friend in the real estate business, why then hasn't he already listed with him?"
   (a) Possibly it is because his friend also will charge him a commission. So the underlying problem is not so much the Realtor friend, but the commission.
   (b) You cannot afford to hurt the owner's feelings by running his friend down. In addition it would be unethical to do that to a fellow Realtor.
   (c) Instead offer to compete with the friend on a business like basis for the listing. Cautiously suggest to the owner that friendship and business do not always make the best possible mix.
   (d) As a last resort offer to **co-list** the house with the Realtor friend, **provided he signs a listing with YOU right NOW!**

(e) Maybe he doesn't have a "Realtor friend" after all.

(5) OWNER: **"Your Company is too small."**
"Your Company is too large."
REALTOR:
What has the size of the Real Estate Company got to do with your promotion, marketing and hard work?

(6) OWNER: **"Your office is too far away from my house"**
REALTOR:
What has the distance of the house to the office got to do with the marketing of the house?
(a) Your real estate license is valid anywhere in your Province or State.
(b) This is the age of electronics: FAX, cell phones, pagers, computers etc. tend to shrink distances.
(c) You are hard-working and hungry: you drive a reliable car and are willing to go to the end of the world to sell a house.
(d) By listing the house on the Multiple Listing Service, "nearby" Realtors will not be shut out. In fact MLS is a general invitation to all Realtors - near and far - to bring their prospective Buyers to this house.

(7) OWNER: **"Another Realtor said that he could get us more money."**
REALTOR:
Explain to the owner the importance of listing at or near Market Value and the dangers of overpricing (see the chapters on Market Value and Overpricing in this book).

(8) OWNER: **"This is a big decision: We want to think it over."** "We want to sleep on it."
REALTOR:
With this the Seller says that he can't handle it anymore and that he is backed into a corner. He needs some space to gather his wits. You may have gone too fast.
(a) Ask if there is anything unclear or needs to be explained some more. As you are here now, this would be a good opportunity to do so.
(b) If no, then be gracious and make a little joke.
 - Say that you will be "pillowsophical" about it.
 - You are willing to wait provided he will call you as soon as he has reached a decision.
(c) For more answers read the chapters on "Overcoming Objections" and "Closing Techniques" in this book.

(9) OWNER: **"But you didn't show my house while it was listed."**
REALTOR:
- (a) "I didn't show your house, because I didn't have the right type of buyer for it."
- (b) "I prequalify all potential buyers to ensure that they are financially able to buy and that they want and need your particular type of house."
- (c) "Also, I have an obligation to service first my own Clients. Now if you were listed with me, you - no doubt - would prefer that I give YOU FIRST my undivided attention and good service."

(10) OWNER: **"We don't want to tie up our house."**
REALTOR:
The owner will not "tie up" his house, because you are willing to show your goodwill by offering to cancel the listing anytime **when he has a VALID cause to complain and you fail to remedy such a complaint promptly**. (Obviously you will not give a release for a flimsy pretext, in order to enable the Seller to sell his house behind your back).

(11) OWNER: **"We don't want to be tied down to only one Real Estate Company."**
REALTOR:
The owner's fear is that you will not cooperate with any other Realtor because you want to earn the entire commission yourself. This problem can be solved by putting the house on MLS.

(12) OWNER: **"I don't want to sign anything."**
"You can show my house to your Buyers. If you bring me a deal, then I'll pay you a commission."
"Other salesmen have been showing my house without them having a listing."
REALTOR:
This is the old problem of working an "Open Listing" where there is no written listing contract; the asking price and commission payable are at the whim of the Seller.
- (a) In order to be **legally enforceable**, everything in real estate has to be **in writing**.

  Explain to the owner that you are willing to do business only on a proper, legal basis:
  - Without his written authorization, you cannot represent him in case another Realtor brings an offer.
  - Without a signed listing contract you cannot safely and with any certainty quote to a Buyer an asking price.
  - As the asking price will be at the whim of the Seller it might be higher or lower when you arrive with the Buyer on his door step. It would look pretty silly and embarrassing if you quoted one price and he would quote

another during the showing.
(b) The Listing Contract or a separate Commission or Fee Agreement secures the payment of the commission. If there is nothing in writing to assure you of a certain commission (either a percentage of the Selling Price or a predetermined lump sum) you may find yourself in a real predicament. When you bring such an owner an acceptable offer
- he may offer you a ridiculously low commission or
- no commission at all;
- he may tell you that you are the Buyer's Agent and should, therefore, collect your commission from the Buyer.
- If you write up a counter offer with your commission built into the price, the Buyer will balk.
- If you try to collapse the sale out of frustration, then what are you going to tell the Buyer?
- What will prevent the Buyer and Seller from getting together and making a deal without you?
- As all prior dealings with the Seller were verbal, it is essentially his word against yours.
- This is not exactly a sound basis on which to claim a commission in Court.

(c) Therefore, it is not a good idea to leave such matters on a half hazard basis, unenforceable understanding or uncertain verbal agreement.
(d) If the owner doesn't wish to do business on a proper basis, it may be better for the Realtor to walk away from this situation. **It has the potential of being a law suit magnet.** Even if there is nothing in writing, **the Realtor could attract or incur some liability or Agency Duties by his actions, his words or by merely being "cloaked" in the appearance of the Seller's Agent.**

(13) OWNER: **"We don't want to list with a Real Estate Broker."** TRANSLATION: "We don't want to deal with Realtors because we have heard many bad things and don't trust them."
REALTOR:
This is a 2-fold problem:
(a) You are a potential stranger to them. You have to gain their confidence and trust.
(b) Sellers will try to hide their true feelings (especially fears) because of **learned behaviour**. Learned behaviour starts in childhood when parents caution children about the dangers of crossing a busy street.

In adulthood they hear and read about inept doctors, shady lawyers and sharp salesmen.

Would it therefore be surprising if they may be worried that the Realtor will be tempted to **underlist ("give away")** their house in order to make a quick and easy commission? Or else they may fear that they will be subjected to high pressure tactics, unscrupulous negotiation strategies and the proverbial "snake-oil salesman" manoeuvres.

(14) OWNER: "We don't need to deal with a Realtor to sell our house."
"We can sell our home ourselves."
REALTOR:
(a) Explain the advantages and benefits of dealing with a Realtor, especially in a Buyer's Market.
(b) Outline the pitfalls of a do-it-yourself FSBO. (See the chapter about FSBO in this book).

(15) OWNER: "We had it on MLS and it didn't sell."
REALTOR:
There are only 3 reasons why a property listed on MLS doesn't sell:
(a) The asking **price**.
(b) The physical **condition** of the house.
(c) The **location** of the house.

Even if the Listing Salesperson doesn't do an adequate job, as long as the asking price is realistic and the house is in a reasonable condition and in an acceptable location, then some other Realtor is bound to sell it.

At any rate: The **"RIGHT PRICE" will remedy all defects (condition, cleanliness and location).**

(16) OWNER: "The price of our home will be too high if you add your commission."
REALTOR:
The amount of the commission added to a realistic asking price will usually not deter a serious buyer. A problem arises only if the owner's asking price is too high to start with.

(17) OWNER: "We are in no hurry to sell our house."
REALTOR:
This is good news; this will give us ample/sufficient time to market/promote the house properly/extensively in order to obtain for you the maximum selling price.

(18) OWNER: "We can't afford to waste time. We have to sell our home quickly."
REALTOR:
This is a good reason to use the services of a professional Realtor who can give you maximum exposure in the shortest possible period of time: Multiple Listing and Internet, office tour, MLS tour etc.

Overcoming Objections - Part VI

(19) OWNER: **"By not dealing with you we'll save the commission."**
REALTOR:
Please read the corresponding chapter on FSBO in this book.

(20) OWNER: **"I am not going to sell unless I get my price."**
REALTOR:
Determine the REAL reason why this owner is selling.
(a) His words may just be bravado intended to impress or intimidate you. Sometimes an owner is misguided and temporarily mistaken about the value of his house. If he has a good reason for selling then he will in due course bring his asking price in line with Market Value (provided you have proven to him through good service, that his initial price was unrealistic).
(b) If his reason for selling is **ONLY a PROFIT motive, then such a Seller is poorly motivated.** Regardless of what kind of superb service you will shower him with, he is liable to turn down offers even in excess of Market Value. Such a Seller doesn't really care what the Market Value of his house is. For him selling his house is merely a business venture/past time.
Do you really want to waste your precious time and hard work on somebody like him?

(21) OWNER: **"I want to start/list high/at my price. I can always come down later."**
REALTOR:
Read the chapter on "Overpricing" in this book.

(22) OWNER: **"60 days is too long to tie myself up.** I want to give you only a 30-day listing."
REALTOR:
(a) It is difficult to achieve MAXIMUM MARKET EXPOSURE in only 30 days. Marketing is like launching an ocean liner. It takes some time to achieve maximum speed and effect.
(b) The Multiple Listing Service requires a minimum listing period of 60 days. It is out of my hands. If you want to list on MLS, then we have to obey their rules.
(c) I am going to invest my time, work and advertising money promoting the sale of your house. From past experience and in view of the current market conditions I know that 30 days will be insufficient time to effect a sale.
(d) Your 30 day listing is liable to run out (of time) just before we get an offer.

(23) OWNER: **"We have never heard of you before."**
REALTOR:
"Mr. Seller: the important thing for you to decide is what kind of service you will receive from the Realtor you will eventually hire to market your property."
(a) I am not a highly visible superstar. Fame is fleeting.

- I have been around for a long time.
- I am a good foot soldier who works quietly, efficiently and diligently for his clients.
- I take pride in the quality of my work and the kind of personalized service I give to my Clients.
- That is why I only carry the number of listings which I feel I can service properly.
- That is why you don't see my signs all over the place.

(b) I am new in the business and everybody has to start sometime.
- I am ambitious and intend to make my mark in my chosen profession.
- Therefore, I will TRY HARDER and WORK HARDER for you.
- I am teamed up with a highly experienced senior salesperson who will work together with me on your house.

(24) OWNER: "We have never heard of your Company before."
REALTOR:
- We are a young Company formed about … years ago.
- Our sales crew consists of … enthusiastic and hard working professionals.
- Everybody knows what they are doing.
- The combined number of years of service of our sales staff is … years.
- We have a highly experienced senior Manager/Nominee in charge of the office.
- Our Company's goal is to be in the top 10% of sales production in our Board area.

(25) OWNER: "This is the wrong time of the year to sell."
January and February:
OWNER: RIGHT NOW IS NO GOOD BECAUSE …
- it is too soon after Christmas
- the weather is bad (cold, snow, rain, fog)
- we want to wait till the flowers come out and the place looks better.

REALTOR:
(a) Many buyers (apartment dwellers, first time Buyers) who have postponed buying before the holidays have made New Year's Resolutions to buy this year. They are now out in force looking to buy a house.
(b) For the reasons you have mentioned there are not too many houses on the market right now. **A limited selection of houses for sale means for you reduced competition and your house will fetch top price.**
(c) Many Buyers want to see the yard in its worst condition. Their reasoning is that if they like the yard now then they will surely love it when the weather is better (in summer).

Overcoming Objections - Part VI

March and April:
OWNER: RIGHT NOW IS NO GOOD BECAUSE ...
- (a) income tax time, our car and house insurances are coming up.
- (b) We don't want to pull the kids out of school.
- (c) Before we sell, we will have to paint the house first and right now it is too wet to paint the outside.

REALTOR:
- (a) The spring market always has increased sales activity because more Buyers are out.
- (b) The flowers are coming out and the lawn is looking better.
- (c) People have increased optimism in spring because the days are getting longer and everything starts looking nice.
- (d) Many Sellers are asking for longer possession (close to the end of the school year).
- (e) You can paint the interior of the house right now; you can paint the outside when the weather permits it.
- (f) You can offer a prospective Buyer to paint HIS preferred colour scheme or
- (g) alternatively you can grant him an allowance on the price if he paints himself. Thereby you will save yourself a lot of work and hassle.

May and June:
OWNER: RIGHT NOW IS NO GOOD BECAUSE ...
- (a) People are getting ready for their vacations.
- (b) The house taxes are due at the beginning of July.
- (c) We are busy planting the garden and painting the house.

REALTOR:
- (a) The late spring/early summer market is the best time of the year to sell.
- (b) Due to your efforts, the lawns are in good shape and the house looks great.
- (c) The days are getting longer and people are looking in the evenings.

July and August:
OWNER: RIGHT NOW IS NO GOOD BECAUSE ...
- (a) Everybody is at the beach or away on vacation.
- (b) It's too hot for Buyers to look.
- (c) We will be away on vacation.
- (d) The house is in a mess because we have just come back from vacation.

REALTOR:
- (a) Smart people want to get settled before school starts.
- (b) People are driving around in airconditioned cars.
- (c) Because of long daylight hours, people are looking in the evenings when it is cooler.
- (d) I am bonded and you can leave me a house key. I will personally open up the house and be present whenever it is shown. Wouldn't it be nice if I could FAX

you an offer while you are away on holidays?
(e) It takes several days to process a listing, have a For Sale sign up etc. Would 1 week give you enough time to put your house in order?

September and October:
OWNER: RIGHT NOW IS NO GOOD BECAUSE …
(a) The kids are back in school.
(b) The weather is changing, the leaves are falling etc.
REALTOR:
(a) The weather is still good: not too hot, just comfortable.
(b) Many people who have been on holidays want to buy at the beginning of the school year before the kids get too settled in their school routine.

November and December:
OWNER: RIGHT NOW IS NO GOOD BECAUSE …
(a) We don't want to move before Christmas.
(b) The weather is bad. Who wants to move when it rains or snows?
REALTOR:
(a) There is less competition because many Sellers have taken their homes off the market.
(b) Some people are willing to pay a premium price if they can get settled in their new home in time for Christmas.
(c) Some people want to buy now and move in the new year.
(d) Hire a moving company. They have tarps to protect your furniture while it is being carried from the house to the truck.

(26) OWNER: **"I don't want a sign on my property."**
REALTOR:
(a) First of all find out why the owner doesn't want a sign. Let him give you his reasons. Most likely he is embarrassed by what the neighbours will say if his house doesn't sell.
(b) Convince him that his house WILL be sold. Therefore he should disregard the neighbours. Who cares what they think after he has moved away?
(c) A sign works for the Seller day and night, 24-hours a day, seven days a week. It costs him nothing.
(d) Often Buyers are driving around in a neighbourhood looking for For Sale signs before they phone a Realtor. Unless there is a sign on the front lawn, how are these potential Buyers going to know that the house is for sale?

(27) OWNER:
"I want to find the right house first before I sell."
"I will list my house only after I have bought."
"I don't want to end up on the street. I must know where I am going to move to."

Overcoming Objections - Part VI

REALTOR:

If you BUY FIRST before you sell, it is like going hunting without a gun which is nothing more than a nice sightseeing trip. The following will take place.

(a) When you find the right house, all you can do is to make an offer "subject to the sale of your house" by a certain date (say 60 days).

(b) Because you have no ready cash to complete the purchase, you don't have too much bargaining power.

(c) The Seller will not want to tie down his house and take it off the market for you alone because he has no assurance that your house will sell. To protect himself he will insist that an "escape clause" be put into the contract and he will continue marketing his house. If another acceptable offer materializes during those 60 days he will give you 24 (or 48 or 72) hours notice to remove all subject clauses from your contract and firm up the sale. Failure to do so on your part means that your contract will automatically become null and void at the end of the notice period. The owner is then free to accept the other offer.

(d) If your house isn't sold when you are served with the notice, then you have 2 options:
- you must either step aside or
- arrange for bridge financing in which case you will find yourself carrying 2 houses for a period of time.

(e) The aforementioned **period of 60 days** in which the owner will have to sell his house will be used up as follows:
- 1 day for completing the listing and faxing it to the Board.
- You may just have missed the cut-off for the next catalogue. This means that the house will not appear in a catalogue until the next one comes out, which could be up to 2 weeks hence.
- The Board photographer has to take a picture. Allow 3 days for processing.
- Depending on the time frame, your house could be in the next catalogue but it might be too late for a picture.
- Of course, your house will be on the computer. Some Realtors are still computer illiterate.
- Your Realtor will schedule your house for the Office Tour
- However the next available slot for the Multiple Listing Tour could be some time away.
- The "For Sale" Sign will be up in 2 days.
- Hopefully it is possible to meet the deadline for an ad in next weekend's newspaper.
- As a guesstimate approximately 10 to 14 days will be taken up by the preliminary groundwork.

This leaves the Seller only 45 days to sell.
- A potential Buyer will need 15 days (or a little less) to arrange for his new financing and the conveyancing.

For practical purposes this leaves the Seller only 30 days to sell, which isn't much.
- (f) Due to this time limitation, he is reduced to dealing with a limited number of Buyers.
- (g) With the threat of the escape clause hanging over his head, **the Seller is in no position to hold out for a good price on his present house.** It must go on the block "cheap." ("Sacrifice Price").
- (h) In order to get some quick action going his Realtor will advertise "Owner has bought and must sell." This is liable to **attract some ruthless bargain hunters who will have no qualms to take advantage of the Seller's predicament.**
- (i) Because the owner had little bargaining power (no ready cash) when he bought, he most likely has bought high; or at least higher than he could have if his house was sold and he had the cash.
- (j) Because he is under pressure to sell, **he doesn't have the luxury of being able to wait and will most likely have to take what he can get.** Chances are that he will sell low.
- (k) There is also the possibility that he will receive no offers, but still will be served with the "notice" to remove all subject clauses. The smart thing to do is to step aside. He will be disappointed because he couldn't get the house he wanted, he did a lot of running around and had a good deal of excitement - all for nothing.

WHAT HAPPENS IF HE LISTS FIRST before buying?
- (a) The preliminaries of ordering a sign, pictures, catalogues etc. can be dealt with without being under pressure or wasting precious time.
- (b) The house can be listed a little higher (as long as it is not grossly overpriced).
- (c) There is nothing to stop the Seller from looking around immediately in order to familiarize himself with the Market.
- (d) If he finds the ideal house, he can always make an offer "subject to the sale of his house." This way at least he will not have to waste precious days before the ball gets rolling on his old house; everything will be already well on its way.
- (e) If he gets an offer before he has found a house that is of interest to him, he can afford the luxury of driving a hard bargain and hold out for a good price.
- (f) In order not to end up on the street he can ask for a long possession. He can also put a proviso into his contract that by mutual agreement (between him and his Buyers) the completion, possession and adjustment dates can be adjusted (shortened) in order to coincide with the dates of the Seller's next purchase.
- (g) If he makes an offer after he has a firm sale on his house (with a substantial non-refundable deposit), then he no longer needs the "subject to the sale" clause and can drive a harder bargain than in the previous method where he bought first before selling.

If everything goes as planned, then this way the owner can most likely sell high and buy low. And that is what everybody wants.

Closing Techniques - Part I
A few initial thoughts about CLOSING TECHNIQUES.

Above all, the good news is that closing techniques also can be learned. With some effort involving
- an investment of time,
- diligent practice and
- suitable preparation

everybody can become a Master of Closing Techniques.

Basically the act of closing is persuading the Client to sign on the dotted line. This he will usually do after making first some or various objections. As mentioned before for some unfortunate Realtors "objections" may be an unwelcome adversity. An unskilled Realtor fears OBJECTIONS and will freeze in terror similar to a deer who is caught at night in the headlights of a car. When objections come up Realtors should not be paralyzed by the fear of failure because the exhilaration of a hard-won success cannot be experienced unless there is the looming frustration of failure at the other end of the equation.

Experience and mental strength come from struggling with adversity. An experienced Realtor will view OBJECTIONS as an OPPORTUNITY TO CLOSE because as long as the Client makes objections, he is interested. If he stops making objections then he is either ready to buy or sell or else he has lost interest in the project.

An inept Realtor will memorize and use outdated and manipulative "closing scripts" which he will recite in an grating sing-song tone of voice. Such pushy manoeuvres and pressure tactics will eventually turn out to be not only counter productive, but also ineffective. They may have worked in the past, but they will be resented by today's more sophisticated Clients.

"**Scripts**" may be useful only in so far as they may help us to crystallize in our own minds what it is which stops the Client from picking up the pen and signing.

It should be neither a secret nor a surprise that the things which stop Clients are
- their unvoiced fears,
- their unsolved problems and concerns and
- their unfulfilled needs.

(1)
No doubt, the Reader must have heard it many times before that God gave us one mouth and 2 ears: this alone should indicate to a reasonably alert Realtor that
- **LISTENING** to what the Client **really** has to say
- will **lead us** to **his "problem"**
- which **must be solved**
- before he is willing or able **to make a decision.**

Closing Techniques - Part I

This also is part of the closing process.

(2)
Of course, there are some people who due to their personality are never comfortable in making a quick decision. They need a certain amount of time and space to gather their wits and if the Realtor is not willing to grant it to them, then they will not do business with him.
Recognizing when it is necessary to back off is a further part of the closing process.

(3)
The Realtor's **MENTAL APPROACH** to closing
- his ATTITUDE,
- his CONFIDENCE in himself and
- his EXPECTATIONS to win will largely determine his success or failure rates.

Before you can convince somebody else, you must be able to convince yourself.

(4)
Attitude is often the difference between closing a deal or it falling apart. **Your self-image is situated in your mind**. Whatever information you feed into your subconscious mind, will determine what you end up as.
Positive thoughts and goals will bear good fruit.
The opposite is "garbage in - garbage out."

(5)
An experienced Realtor will trust his **INSTINCTS** (obtained through accumulated experience) when the time and place are right to attempt the "closing." The knowledge of how and when "to close" comes unfortunately only with a lot of work, trials and errors, failures and frustrations and the **LESSONS which you will LEARN FROM THEM.**
But in the end **victory is glorious**.

(6)
It is also the Realtor's job to help the Clients make the decision which is best for them.
During this process **the Realtor must rely on and deal with facts.**
The Clients are involved with emotions (e.g. the enjoyment of living in a fine home).

(7)
Once the Realtor has gone over the financial picture and made sure that everything else fits then it is time for him "to close" by talking about BENEFITS,
- may they be positive or negative ones (e.g. the satisfaction of receiving excellent value for their money or the fear of loosing out on a bargain).

(8)
In the end, **the best closing technique is to simply ask for the order.**

Closing Techniques - Part II
... or "bringing home the bacon through gentle persuasion."

It has been mentioned before that "selling" is walking down a path of agreement. After the last and final objection has been overcome the logical next step is to OBTAIN THE ORDER.

It is a sad fact of real estate life that many salespersons who have mastered
- a flawless listing presentation,
- have given excellent service,
- who have learned to overcome the toughest objections with great skill and tenacity, these same salespersons will regularly fall flat on their faces when the time comes to ask the Client to sign on the dotted line.

For some unfathomable reason they
- either **misjudge the TIMING** for the close or
- they **talk themselves "past closing"** or
- they aren't sure **"how to get AROUND to it"** (namely how to diplomatically guide the conversation to the subject of "writing") or
- due to lack of confidence or knowledge and/or experience they aren't sure **"how to go ABOUT it"** or else
- they are just plain unable to ask for the order because they are either too fearful or embarrassed.

(I) **How to become a MASTER CLOSER.**
   (a) **Closing is the art of gentle persuasion.**
   (b) Just like it was with "overcoming objections," the good news is that **"closing" can be learned by ANYONE who is willing to make the effort.**
   (c) Yes, it does take a lot of **PRACTICE**.
   (d) You should also not be afraid to fail (occasionally), especially while you are still learning. To keep one's sanity, **a defeat must be treated as a LEARNING EXPERIENCE** and NOT as a personal rejection.

The famous baseball player Babe Ruth earned glory because of his record-setting number of home runs. Did you know that he also set another major league record for having struck out some 1,300 times?

Occasionally a Realtor is faced with failure, not because of something he has done or failed to do, but because of an unforeseen situation over which he has little or no control.
Possibly there may be some unresolved family situations, which have been simmering under the surface for along time and which will suddenly erupt with the advent of an offer.
For example:
(a) husband and wife are splitting up and suddenly one of the parties decides that he or she wants a bigger share of the sales proceeds from the sale of the house.

Closing Techniques - Part II

(b) A sale can also balance precariously on the whim of a child; say a teenager who adamantly refuses to move because he is heavily involved with local school activities or doesn't want to leave long-time friends.

(c) Even an entity in a faraway place can create problems; e.g. the Head Office of a private mortgage company is making the refinancing of the house difficult or prohibitively expensive by demanding a huge prepayment penalty.

(II) If you used some common sense, then **there is NO MAGIC to "closing."** General prerequisites are:

(1) The Realtor should **ARRIVE PREPARED**.
As you could be in for a tough time with the Clients, make sure that you have **adequate PHYSICAL and MENTAL REST** before you see them.

(2) You will have to be **MENTALLY STRONG** in order to be confident in
- WHO you are and
- WHAT you are and
- **what you can do:** be proud of the fact that you are a "Salesperson": **a salesperson is somebody who "CAN MAKE THINGS HAPPEN."**
- Resist the temptation of fancying yourself as a "Consultant." (A consultant is somebody who is giving "advice"; giving advice on a subject on which you are not an expert is a short cut into Court!).

(3) Arriving prepared also means that you have with you:
- an adequate supply of Listing Contracts and Contracts of Purchase and Sale (in case you spoil one).
- 2 working ballpoints (in case one of them runs out)
- other necessities are: calculator, ruler, scratch pad etc. If you use a BINDER, then it would be nifty to have a sticker across the front reading "SOLD" or "EXPERIENCE AT WORK." These are (not so) subliminal messages.

(4) **REHEARSE beforehand what you are going to say.**
Essentially the Client must BENEFIT from the transaction.
Have your words down pat in a well rehearsed but nevertheless spontaneously-sounding canned sales talk; but be flexible enough to adjust to a changing situation.

(III) **A FEW WORDS ABOUT "TIME."**

(1) By **ARRIVING ON TIME** for the appointment you are bound to MAKE A GOOD IMPRESSION. This is especially true in the case of a Listing Appointment where you meet the Sellers for the first time.
For the Realtor this may be just another routine appointment - one of many.
For the Client on the other hand this meeting may be
- the first time around and
- of crucial importance and
- something which he may have nervously anticipated (you are a stranger to him

and he has been wondering what to expect).
(2) The Realtor should give himself **ENOUGH TIME** to close. This simply means that he shouldn't make any other appointments for that evening or time period.

If a Realtor schedules a listing appointment and the presentation of 2 offers ALL during THE SAME time period (e.g. an evening), then most likely the following will happen:
  (a) The Realtor will have to rush all Clients in order to get to the next appointment. There will be simply no time for unproductive niceties, unforeseen delays or inconvenient questions.
  (b) In spite of the Realtor's best efforts he is bound to run out of time and be late for at least one of the subsequent appointments.
  (c) Because of the distances between the 3 locations and unforeseen traffic conditions, the Realtor will be tempted to drive more aggressively and faster in order to make up for lost time. Thus on the road he may endanger himself and/or others.
  (d) In HIS mind the Realtor will see himself as a super-busy red-hot Ace. To the Clients he will most likely appear as an insensitive person who doesn't have enough time to spend with THEM because he is "chasing the buck."
  (e) Chances are that the Realtor will end up with 3 sets of dissatisfied Clients.

(IV) A FEW WORDS ABOUT "TIMING."

As the Realtor is seeing his Client "on business" **his closing efforts**
- **MUST start within the first few seconds of the meeting.**
- From then on **EVERYTHING he does and says throughout the entire process MUST FOCUS on the single and sole objective of "closing."**
- If, on the other hand the Realtor is treating this like a social call, then he might as well go home to watch TV or do something else more constructive.

(V) BE COGNISANT of individual DIFFERENCES.

Realtors are dealing with human beings of
- different cultural backgrounds,
- different life experiences,
- different educational and sophistication levels,
- different PERSONALITY TYPES.

In order to increase success in closing and reduce frustration, misunderstandings and resentment, the Realtor must (as much as possible) avoid having HIS personality clash with the characteristics of the Client's personality. E.g.

EXTROVERTS come in a large variety. They often
- loudly monopolize the conversation,
- take the initiative and
- may talk incessantly without thinking.

- Some of them are "bottom-line" people and risk-takers who want results.
- Some others are more forceful, decisive, independent and could be outright rude.
- Some could become disillusioned quickly because they are impatient.
- Some of their better qualities are that they can be friendly, demonstrative, expressive and enthusiastic.
- Many think that INTROVERTS are aloof, cold and detached.

INTROVERTS also come in a large variety.
- Basically they are more private and withdrawn people.
- They think a lot (or at least more) before saying or doing something.
- Some are analytical, methodical, conservative and careful;
- often they are people who are hard(er) to read.
- They will be swayed by logic, but are slower to come around.
- They find EXTROVERTS to be rude, loud and annoying.

In order to survive in a competitive business, a Realtor must by necessity be aggressive. Depending on his personality he can be either vocal and (within certain limits) forthright or more quiet and confident. Whatever the case may be, by using **EMPATHY an experienced Realtor will instinctively tune down some of the negative aspects of his personality when dealing with a Client who is the opposite of his personality type.** The bottom line is that the REALTOR MUST ADJUST HIS APPROACH TO THE CLIENT'S INDIVIDUAL PERSONALITY AND NEEDS.

(VI) SETTING THE STAGE FOR CLOSING.

(1) The Realtor must make sure that there are **NO or at least only a MINIMUM of INTERRUPTIONS.**
The reason for this is that the Realtor must have the Clients'
- undivided attention so that they not only
- HEAR what the Realtor has to say, but also
- have the required UNDISTURBED TIME to fully absorb what they have heard.

THEREFORE
- switch your pager to "silent,"
- turn off you cell phone (set it to take a message) and
- ask the Clients to shut off the TV and/or radio because you "find it difficult to compete with them."
- Hopefully the kids will be in bed by now (or in school) and the cute family dog will chew on something in his basket.

(2) Getting the Client to the stage of signing is an **EMOTIONAL UNDERTAKING.** If the pressure is too great, then it will only cause the Client **anxiety, indecision, frustration and regrets.** There can be no regrets if the transaction is to survive

till the closing day. If the Client signed under pressure he is liable to change his mind.

(VII) During the ACTUAL CLOSING PROCESS.

(1) The Realtor must **CREATE and MAINTAIN a RELAXED ATMOSPHERE** during the closing. The Realtor should become **"CUSTOMER ORIENTED"**:
   (a) while dealing with the Client, the Realtor should forget all of HIS personal troubles and about the entire world around him.
   (b) Instead the Realtor should **concentrate** on
   - the Clients
   - on what is going on
   - on what is being said
   - nothing else matters for the time being until such time when the interview is finished.
   (c) The Realtor shouldn't **argue, be impatient or sarcastic** with the Clients.
   (d) The Realtor should be there to **ASSIST in a PLEASANT MANNER**.
   (e) The Realtor should **be supportive and help the Client** through his anxiety-ridden decision-making process.
   (f) By offering **constructive suggestions**, the Realtor can **become part of the decision-making process**.
   (g) The Client must be looked upon as
   - a PARTNER in the transaction
   - and NOT as an obstacle to be conquered or as an adversary to be hunted down on the way to the commission cheque.
   (h) The Realtor should become **"FUTURE ORIENTED"**; by making sure that in the end EVERYBODY WINS he will enhance his prospects for future referrals and repeat business.
   (I) At the same time the Realtor should strive to **AVOID becoming "CUSTOMER DOMINATED"**: have the courage to tell the Client that it may be impossible to do EVERYTHING he wants or asks for.

(2) **The SPOKEN WORD and BODY LANGUAGE.**
   (a) Getting people to the stage of signing is an **emotional undertaking**: if the pressure is too great, it will cause the Client not only **anxiety and frustration but also it may reinforce his INDECISION.**
   (b) The Realtor must therefore strive to understand the Client's **EMOTIONS**; this is achieved by the Realtor being willing to do the following:
   - he must learn to not only listen to AND
   - reflect on the **CONTENT of the SPOKEN WORDS** the Client is saying when he talks about **his NEEDS and WANTS** but also to
   - the **TONE of VOICE** in which the Client is communicating AND
   - to read between the lines by paying careful attention to the Client's **BODY**

LANGUAGE.
- **This is called "listening between the lines": what is the person FEELING but not saying?**
- Let the Client know that you not only hear his words but also understand the emotional content.

Of course, the same rules apply to the Realtor. The Client will invariably sense it if the Realtor shows
- panic (insecurity),
- his frustration (with the lack of progress) and
- anxiety (about having wasted a lot of time and eventually having to go home empty handed).
- The Client will invariably sense this and he will become doubtful and suspicious.

(3) A FEW TIPS ABOUT "LISTENING."

Attentive listening is an ACTIVE PROCESS which requires a lot of PRACTICE in the field. Amongst others it requires
(a) silence (don't interrupt the Client)
(b) participation (by staying awake and alert, nodding with your head etc.)
(c) openness (trying to understand the Client's side)
(d) empathy (being receptive to the Client's FEELINGS)
(e) occasional intense conversation: when the Realtor is trying to unlock the reasons for the Client's hesitation or indecision by asking **CLARIFYING QUESTIONS:**
- "Is everything clear?"
- "Did we cover everything?"
(f) To become part of the decision making process by offering constructive suggestions.

NOTE: **Be careful "HOW" you ask your questions:**
As some persons feel threatened by what they perceive as "harsh questions" (penetrating interrogation, boxing them in), the Realtor must be diplomatic, cautious, gentle etc.
Instead of saying with irritation or agitation: "Why don't you want to accept this good offer? Why are you holding out for more money?"
… try saying: "Mr. and Mrs. Seller. As we are on the same team, would you please share with me your reasons why you are making a counter offer? As your Agent I am required to bring to your attention that a counter offer can jeopardize the sale; the Buyer has the option to just walk away from this deal if he doesn't accept your counter offer. He can even walk away if we subsequently go back with the same figure which he has offered to us now."

CAUTION: **"LISTENING" does NOT include:**
- daydreaming with a vacant stare in your eyes.

- Your mind wandering to something more interesting,
- eye lids drooping, yawning, scratching your head etc.
- fingers drumming impatiently on the table

(VIII) The following are the **WAYS to "CLOSING."**

(1) The Realtor must present to his Clients
- attractive,
- advantageous,
- profitable and
- painless ways of **achieving his goals (SATISFYING his NEEDS and WANTS)**.
- It should be made abundantly clear **how EASILY the Client can accomplish his objectives** if he would only SIGN on the dotted lined. (E.g. "If you accept this offer, then we won't have to show the house again").

(2) The Realtor must **STICK TO THE FACTS**: words like "always" and "never" seldom describe REALITY and often they result in a defensive reaction from the Client, who - by your obvious exaggerations - will become doubtful and suspicious about your credibility.

(3) Recognize and pay attention to the Client's **DECISION MAKING PROCESS**:
   (a) **Preparation and Presentation:**
   The Realtor systematically submits facts and information to the Client for his consideration.
   (b) **Incubation:**
   The Client intellectually analyses and digests the information; "pro and contra" logical thought patterns are formed in conjunction with and substantiated by emotional considerations.
   (c) **Illumination and Decision:**
   Answers begin to be formed (first possibly only in the subconscious mind) and based on these - **DECISIONS are triggered by EMOTIONS**.
   (d) When is it time to hold your tongue and keep quiet?
   - When husband and wife start discussing the positive aspects and concentrate on the good features of the house: **DON'T INTERRUPT THEM, because they are well on the way of convincing themselves.**
   - When husband and wife talk about their family living in the house, which child will be in which bedroom and how it will fill their needs; **let them talk and don't change the subject, because they are already SOLD.** Any experienced Realtor will confirm that "love of family" is an A-1 home-buying motivator.
   (e) In a nutshell - **"GENTLE PERSUASION"** is to lead the Client GENTLY and not by the use of brute force. Possibly a good comparison would be if you picture in your mind a tug boat nudging an ocean liner safely into its berth at the harbour.

A last word about "emotions" and a strange situation which probably has happened to many a Realtor.

Question:
Why does a family adamantly say that they need a 3 bedroom full basement house on a large treed lot out in the country (for privacy) and then they end up buying a 2 bedroom no-basement rancher on a postage stamp sized lot without one single tree in the middle of the city?

Answer:
Because their decision to **"like"** for some reason the small house is an **emotional** one. In their minds they will then advance all the necessary "logical" reasons to justify what they have already decided on in their hearts.

Recommendation to frustrated Realtors who want to keep their sanity:
Chalk it up to experience and **don't try to make sense out of nonsense ...**

Closing Techniques - Part III
Important Considerations and Strategies.

A) WHO MAKES THE DECISION?

The FINAL decision to accept or reject a Contract of Purchase and Sale is made by the Client and not the Realtor. Just because the Client said "NO" to a certain price or terms yesterday, it doesn't mean that he will say "NO" again at some future time.
NOTE: In the past Realtors have been sued for
   (a) **unilaterally ASSUMING** that an offer was not acceptable to their Sellers because
   - the Sellers had previously rejected similar offers and/or
   - had given "instructions" to the Realtor NOT to present to them offers "under a certain amount."
   (b) **unilaterally DECIDING** on their own to reject the offer without first showing it to and/or consulting with the Client.
   (c) **It is (legally and ethically) important to let the Client make the FINAL decision, because (unknown to the Realtor) the Client's circumstances may have changed in the meantime.**

B) ALL PARTIES MUST AGREE.
(1) When a major decision has to be made all registered owners MUST make it JOINTLY (and ALL must sign in order to make the contract legally enforceable). Unless the husband has a legal Power of Attorney, he cannot legally sign on behalf of his wife (because unknown to everybody else, she may not want to sell).
(2) That way no seeds of discontent are sown and if something should go wrong later on, there can be no resentful finger pointing.
(3) In order to reach a joint decision between husband and wife or sundry partners, the parties may require some privacy so that they can talk. The Realtor should tactfully withdraw even if he considers it to be a (for him) risky manoeuvre (He lost control of the conversation). In a way this situation may be akin to a bullfighter turning his back to a snorting bull in the arena and running the risk of getting gored in the back.
However, if things work out - and chances are that they will (provided that the Realtor has done a good job so far) - then the results can be spectacular. The Clients will appreciate your courtesy and tactful consideration and most likely will consequently recommend you to others.

C) What are the CLIENT'S NEEDS and WANTS?

The **BUYER'S goal** is to put the best possible roof over his family's head at the lowest possible price.

The **SELLER'S goal** is to obtain the most amount of money in the shortest possible time with the least amount of inconvenience.

D) The following are some INGREDIENTS for a successful "closing."
The Realtor should
(1) **Analyze** the Client's NEEDS and WANTS,
(2) **Observe** the Client's reactions (body language) to the Realtor's suggested solutions. They will give to the Realtor valuable clues
  - how to carry on and
  - what to do next.
(3) **Answer** questions to
  - dispel all fears
  - solve all problems
  - eliminate all doubts and
(4) generally **make it easy** for the Client to say "YES!" by ANSWERING ALL QUESTIONS COMPLETELY and TRUTHFULLY.
(5) **Stick to the facts.** "Puffing" may result in the Client's defensive reaction or the Realtor's damaged credibility.
(6) **Reflect** on the CONTENT of the Client's spoken word and reflect on his FEELINGS (empathy).
(7) **LISTEN between the lines.** What is the Client feeling but NOT ACTUALLY SAYING?

E) The TRIAL Close.
Whenever during a presentation the Realtor gets the feeling that the Client is ready to sign, he should make a TRIAL CLOSE as long as the Client is aware of all details and ramifications.
(1) This is especially true during a listing presentation. If the Sellers are satisfied to list with you, then there is little point in belabouring your Sales Achievement Awards etc. Stop your presentation right then and there and start filling out the Listing Contract.
(2) If you are showing houses and the Buyers like the 2nd house they see, stop right then and there, cancel the other appointments and concentrate on getting an offer on this one. If you say: "I know that you like this home, because it suits you to a "T," but I have 6 more lined up to show you" — chances are that you will only confuse the Clients. They will end up buying nothing on that day. Eventually they may even buy from somebody else.

F) CLOSING STRATEGIES.

1) **The ASSUMPTIVE Close.**

In this "close" there is NO ROOM FOR NEGATIVITY: the Realtor must positively assume that the Clients are going to buy or sell or list and that everything is going to go through without a hitch.

The Realtor must remember that it is
- **EMOTIONS that make people act** and that
- their objections often are a mere subterfuge for not having to make a decision.

After all legitimate doubts have been laid to rest, the salesperson ASSUMES that the Client will sign and SILENTLY SHOVES THE CONTRACT AND PEN ACROSS THE TABLE to the Client who is in deep thought. BITE YOUR TONGUE, sit motionless and don't spoil the silence by saying a single word. This is very hard to do, but **the Client must have uninterrupted SILENCE and TIME to THINK**. When he is finished thinking (however long it may take) he WILL eventually SPEAK or ACT. Just simply wait in silence (even if it seems like an eternity to you) till he picks up the ballpoint pen and signs. If you move or say something, it will shatter the rapture and kill the propitious moment. Anybody who has ever witnessed a high-stakes poker game can attest that when it comes to the final "showdown" the first person who moves or grunts something - usually looses.

The Client will win by signing the contract, the Realtor will succeed by remaining silent and motionless.

2) THE URGENCY CLOSE.

This type of "close" must be in the form of **a genuinely concerned and business-like discussion** with a Valued Client.
- Everybody must be on an equal footing.
- **Both the Clients and the Realtor are PARTNERS in the transaction.**
- For obvious reasons, all statements must be 100% true.
- High pressure emotional sneak attacks must be AVOIDED.
- Obviously bald-faced exaggerations can be offensive or misconstrued. E.g.
    - "Don't run the risk of loosing this home, because it is SURE TO GO UP in value."
      (Comment: How does the Realtor know this, unless speculative prices are rising rapidly in an unusually volatile Seller's Market).
    - "Money deteriorates RAPIDLY through inflation - pay off the mortgage with shrinking Dollars."
      (Comment: lending institutions have guarded against this by introducing various expiry terms in their mortgages (e.g. a 3 year renewal term).
      Generally speaking wages also tend to rise and inflation has been low in recent years. This statement is only true if there is galloping inflation over a long period of time. E.g. during the time of Germany's Weimar Republic after WWI when the Mark deteriorated daily and it literally took a suitcase full of cash to buy a loaf of bread.
    - "If you woke up tomorrow morning and found that this home was sold this evening, would you be glad or disappointed that you couldn't make up your

mind to buy it when you had the chance?"
(Comment: This outdated Snake-Oil-Salesman-Close is most likely offensive to the Client).

Because no Clients like to be high pressured by anybody, the Realtor must be very careful when elaborating on ADVANTAGES (or the inducement of a negative benefit) for making a decision right away rather than "later on." E.g.:

3) If it is the right home for them, then the Realtor should
    - **ignite the spark** and
    - **fan the flame by** creating mental flashes of cosy comfort and security. This is called the

    "SELLING THE BENEFITS - CLOSE."
    YOUR conviction will show and YOUR **enthusiasm** will catch on.

(a) Create in the Buyer's mind pictures of
- **COSY COMFORT:**
    - shelter from the elements
    - better facilities and utility
    - less work, upkeep, maintenance
    - more leisure time
    - an easier life
- **SECURITY:**
    - independence
    - children playing in a fenced yard and not on the road
    - financial well-being
    - increasing equity means increasing net worth (wealth)
    - a hedge against creeping inflation (pay off the mortgage with constantly shrinking/devaluing Dollars)
    - freedom from fear ((no landlord raising the rent or selling the house from under you)
    - future profit (from accumulated equity) to be used to upgrade to a bigger, better house
    - the house is a financial vehicle to save for the owner's retirement
- **HAPPINESS:**
    - family gatherings on holidays
    - special occasions
    - children playing
    - pets lounging in their favourite place
    - prestige
    - privacy

(b) **How to "close" with other POSITIVE benefits or advantages.**
Client: "We want to think it over and will call you after the weekend."
Realtor: "I have an ad in the paper for Saturday and I have scheduled an 'Open House' for Sunday. If you make an offer NOW, then the Seller can consider it before the weekend and if he accepts, I will cancel the ad and my Open House."
OR alternatively: "If you make an offer NOW, then you will have a clear shot to get the house because you will NOT have to compete against any other offers."

Client: "We want to wait till the interest rates come down."
Realtor: "It is easier to negotiate on the price TODAY because there aren't enough Buyers around who can qualify for a mortgage at THIS interest rate. Once rates come down, Buyers will come out in droves, flood the market with offers and consequently prices will rise because it will become a Seller's Market. Higher prices will necessitate larger mortgages. Chances are that the monthly payments on such larger mortgages will be HIGHER than what they would be if you were to buy now. **This defeats the purpose for waiting.**
In the long run a lower loan amount also means LESS DEBT to be paid off.

Client: "I think that we will wait with buying until we have saved up a bigger downpayment."
Realtor: "A house is a good investment because OVER A NUMBER OF YEARS its value tends to rise faster than people's wages. Although incomes are higher than what they were 30 years ago, house prices have outstripped financially many a young family's ability to buy."

Client: "We will rent for a while longer, because renting is cheaper than making those high mortgage payments."
Realtor:
(a) "The burden of carrying a mortgage is greatest in the first few years. The good thing is that the monthly payments will remain CONSTANT for the TERM of the mortgage (e.g. 5 years). At least you know where you stand and as long as you keep up your mortgage payments, nobody can evict you.
(b) On the other hand, a landlord can raise the rent every year or he can decide to sell the house and you will have to move.
(c) After renting for 5 years, the tenant has nothing to show for; on the other hand an owner will have accumulated some equity by
   - the constantly reducing principal amount of the mortgage and - hopefully
   - the increasing market value of the house."

(b) **SUGGESTED INDUCEMENTS can also be a NEGATIVE BENEFIT.**
Realtor: "Mr. and Mrs. Seller, if you accept this offer now we won't have to show your house anymore."

- OR:

Realtor: "Mr. and Mrs. Buyer, because this attractive home is well priced, several Realtors from other Companies have shown it to their clients in the last few days. Chances are that sooner or later the Sellers will receive an offer from one of them. At THIS moment, there are no other offers on the table. So if you act now, you will not have to compete against any other offers."

- OR:

Realtor: "Mr. and Mrs. Buyer, we have seen many homes. You have indicated that this one meets all of your requirements. If you make an offer now you will not have to look anymore at other houses." (Translation: they won't have to get a baby-sitter; after seeing a great number of houses, at least one of them if not both husband and wife will be fed up looking).

3) THE MINOR POINTS CLOSE.

Unless the price offered by the Buyers is the Sellers' Asking Price, THE PRICE is often THE GREATEST STUMBLING BLOCK. The strategy in this type of "close" is to **settle first on small/ minor issues** (e.g. possession date, the scheduling of a building inspection, which appliances stay etc.) **before tackling the "big/major" one.**
The Realtor may tactfully suggest that the Sellers should look at the offer in its ENTIRETY. That way **"all of US will have an opportunity to solve the smaller problems first."** With these words, the Realtor puts himself on the side of his Valued Clients (the Sellers) and the implication is:

a) if even the minor points are not acceptable, then there is no doubt that the entire offer is no good. It can be easily disposed of without regrets.
b) On the other hand, **if everything else fits, then perhaps WE can work out some COMPROMISE on the price.**
c) Suggestions for SOLVING MINOR ISSUES.
   - **Coaxing a BUYER:** "Should we try and see if they leave the drapes, washer and dryer?"
   - **Protecting the Buyer and the Seller:** "The Buyer wants a building inspection done. This is for his protection AND is also good for you. The Buyer will pay for the inspection. We can schedule the inspection for a convenient time for you."
   - **Giving the SELLER an ALTERNATIVE CHOICE:** "The Buyers are flexible because they are renting. Would 60 or 90 days possession be better for you?"

4) FINALLY WE HAVE TO TACKLE "THE BIG ONE - THE PRICE."

Once all other (minor) problems have been solved, there is nothing left but to face the music, grab the bull by the horns and eliminate the LAST IMPEDIMENT, which is the PRICE. This is not the time for fancy double-talk or beating around the bush;

instead make a simple straight forward request for a decision.

Client: "This price is too low."
Realtor: "Mr. and Mrs. Seller. We put your house on the market 2 months ago. A total of 50 Realtors have come through on the Office and Multiple Listing Tours. At the time we have discussed the Tour Average Appraisal. I have advertised your house 5 times and we had 3 Open Houses. Some 15 people came through during these Opens. 9 other Realtors have brought their prospective buyers to view your house. In the first month we had a couple of offers for $ X which you turned down. Since then there have been no other offers. **We have come a long way and this is the last hurdle. It would be a shame to quit now.**"

At this point try the "Assumptive Close": shove the offer and your ballpoint pen across the table and keep silent until the Seller picks up the pen and signs.

5) If they are still undecided about the price, try the **"PAD and BALLPOINT CLOSE"** which will ILLUSTRATE THE BENEFITS and reassure the vacillating Sellers through the authority and power of the WRITTEN WORD: **Take out a sheet of paper and write 'YES' in the top left- hand corner and 'NO' in the top right-hand corner.**
   (a) Then suggest that the Sellers should think of all the reasons why they should accept the offer and list them under "YES."
   (b) All the points why they should not accept the offer will appear under "NO."
   (c) You may have to assist them a little in this endeavour because their minds could be in a turmoil trying hard not to forget something.
   (d) Then add up both sides and hopefully the "YES" side will outweigh the "NO" side.

6) **The BUYER wants to make a rough LOW-BALL OFFER:**
   Client: "We want to see what the Sellers will take. So let's try this price first. If they don't like it, they can always make a counter-offer."
   Realtor: "As your Agent I am obliged to tell you that - based on past experience - this strategy may jeopardize getting this house for you. When an offer is considerably less than Market Value, then the Sellers will take it "personally" and may be offended.
   Not only that they will reject your offer, but most likely they won't even make a counter offer. If you subsequently make a higher offer, they may still be turned off and difficult to deal with."

7) **A FEW GENERAL "DON'Ts."**

(1) It is preferable NOT to discuss a Counter Offer over the phone. It is very easy, nay, TOO EASY for the Client to say "No." Your chances of closing the counter offer

are far better if you confront the client in person (he can't just hang up on you) and he **sees the PRINTED WORD. With the offer on the table in front of him, all he has to do is to initial the changes and it is DONE!**

(2) **Don't beg by using the "Last Resort Close":**
Realtor: "My mother told me that when everything else fails, I should BEG. So what do I have to do to get you to go ahead with this?"
(Comment: This is neither cute nor is it funny. In fact it can be downright humiliating, if the Seller suggests to you that you should cut your sweat-soaked commission to bridge the financial gap between him and the Buyer). Of course it is every Realtor's prerogative to decide when to cut his commission. Regrettably, it can become a (bad) habit. Weak Closers will offer to cut their commission at the first sign of resistance or trouble.

(3) **Don't try to make the Client feel guilty:**
Realtor: "Mr. Seller. Even after 20 years in the business, I am still trying to learn and improve myself. What have I done wrong in my presentation?"
(Comment: if you don't know this after having been in the business for 20 years, then you are a slow learner indeed).

(4) **On the use of EUPHEMISMS:**
(a) Some people are apprehensive when they have to "sign a contract." They may be less reluctant to **"okay the offer"** or **"initial"** or **"approve"** the changes. A **"contract"** can be referred to as an **"agreement."**
(b) Speak normally, the way you usually do.
- Don't use fancy double talk or artificialities which are not part of your or the Client's regular vocabulary. E.g. "endorse the paperwork."
- If the Buyer asks: "What is the price of this house?" say:
  - "The owners are asking $ ..." or
  - "The Listing Price of this house is $ ...."

How would you feel if somebody said to you: "Mr. Buyer, when the Sellers allowed me the opportunity to become involved in the marketing of their lovely home they set the TOTAL INVESTMENT at ONLY $ ...."
- The "Deposit" is the deposit and not the "earnest money" (although legally it probably is).
- The "Downpayment" is not the "initial investment," it is the Buyer's equity.
- The "monthly mortgage payments" are not "monthly investments" because a certain chunk thereof is paid out (and lost) as interest.

8) **SUMMARY.**
The most important thing to remember in "closing" is that

(a) **frequent and intelligent COMMUNICATION is the KEY to**
- develop COOPERATIVE CLIENTS and
- to be able to deal with them SUCCESSFULLY.
- The Client should become a PARTNER in the transaction and NOT an adversary.
- By offering CONSTRUCTIVE SUGGESTIONS, the REALTOR will become part of the decision making process.

(b) The Realtor should make sure that in the end EVERYBODY WINS because he (the Realtor) will want the Clients' future repeat business and referrals.

(c) To be a Master Closer, you will have to become the
TOTAL PACKAGE.
- Regardless of your knowledge, skill and experience,
- regardless of the number of hours you put in each day
- regardless of how well you are dressed or what sort of fancy car you drive … **there can be NO SALE unless and until there is a CLOSE.**

(d) RESULTS (financial rewards, prestige, admiration of your peers etc.) are measured ONLY by the number of COMPLETED SALES.

(e) NEAR MISSES or CLOSE CALLS count only in horseshoes and hand grenades.

(f) If in doubt, don't forget to **simply ASK FOR THE ORDER.**

The Contract Of Purchase And Sale

In the course of their business Realtors are expected:
(a) to bring Buyers and Sellers together.
(b) To prepare legally enforceable contracts; e.g. the Contract of Purchase and Sale which sets out the price and terms of the sale and binds the contracting parties together.

In this connection please NOTE:
- The Realtor has the fiduciary duty of CARE.
- The Courts consider Realtors to have the ability and skill to draft a legally enforceable document.

See: "**CHAND v. SABO BROS. REALTY LTD.,**" [1979] 2 W.W.R. 248 14 A.R. 302 (C.A.)

(c) In order to ensure that their Clients understand what they are signing **each item and clause in a contract must be not only CLEAR but also SPECIFIC and in UNDERSTANDABLE LANGUAGE to**
- accurately reflect the intentions of the parties (everybody has to comprehend who will do what and when),
- so that there can be no possibility of misunderstandings and/or miscommunications and
- in order to prevent the loss of the sale and to avoid costly litigation.

Initially the Selling Salesperson prepares the offer to purchase by committing in writing the price, terms and conditions which his Client (the Buyer) has in mind and intends to offer.

To avoid ambiguity, the Realtor may consider
- not to use (incorrectly memorized) complicated legalistic clauses
- but instead **employ language which is simple and straight forward with clear and concise wording.**
- In case of doubt when standard "approved phrases" are employed (e.g. suggested "subject-to" clauses) then they should be explained to the Client, together with the preprinted portions of the contract.

IT BEARS REPEATING: It is of paramount importance for EVERYBODY involved, that the Clients should understand what they are signing.

In "**McKenzie v. Walsh**" 61 SCR 312 (1921) 1 WWR 1017 it was said that there are 3 essential elements to any real estate contract:
(1) The contracting parties
(2) The price
(3) The property

The following are additional important details of a Contract of Purchase and Sale:
(1) **The BUYERS' full names** as they will appear in the Land Titles office records.

Realtors who just write initials in a name (e.g. J. D. Brown) may mistakenly think that it is the conveyancing solicitor's job (after all he gets paid for it, doesn't he?) to find out what the party's full name is. Well, it is his overworked conveyancing secretary who will have to waste her precious time trying to track down the party to ascertain the full name PROVIDED the Realtor has supplied her with a phone number where the party can be contacted during the day. One cannot very well expect the secretary to make phone calls after her regular work hours.

The Buyers' address (including postal code) and work and home telephone numbers. This contact information is also required by the conveyancing secretary.

ALL BUYERS and ALL SELLERS (all registered owners) must sign the contract AND
ALL CONTRACTING PARTIES must receive a complete copy thereof (signed by everybody).

The problems when the Buyer is shown as:
"(Name) **and/or NOMINEE**" … or "(Name) **and/or ASSIGNEE**."

(a) The contract is probably void for uncertainty if the original Buyer only intended that the Seller and a "Third Party to be nominated by the Buyer" were to contract with each other. E.g. in a case when the Buyer merely intends to "flip" the property for a profit.
(b) If the contract mentions that the Buyer has to arrange new financing from an outside source, then the question arises if the subsequently assigned Buyer has the financial strength and ability (employment) to arrange the new financing.
(c) The question of who the actual Buyer eventually is will be of crucial importance when the Seller is carrying a portion of the outstanding debt by way of a mortgage. He may be willing to carry a mortgage for the original Buyer; but why should he do so for a total stranger whose credit worthiness is unknown?
(d) The above difficulties can be overcome provided the original Buyer assures the Seller **in writing by inserting** into the Contract of Purchase and Sale a **clause to the effect that**
- "**The Original Buyer will remain personally liable to the Seller** under this agreement even if a third party is nominated to complete the purchase AND
- **the Buyer will remain liable to the Seller AS A GUARANTOR** for the mortgage the Seller is carrying."

(2) **The SELLERS'** (ALL registered owners) **full names**, address (including postal code) and work and home telephone numbers.

(3) The municipal address and legal description of the property.

(4) The full price offered and accepted. The Selling Price may be crossed out and

changed several times in case of repeated counter offers. To avoid any uncertainty what the finally agreed upon price is, it may be a good idea to find a blank spot somewhere in the contract and confirm: "All contracting parties herewith agree that the finally agreed upon Full Selling Price is $ ..." (Of course, this will have to be initialled by everybody).

(5) **The deposit:**
- the amount of deposit,
- the timing and amounts of staggered deposits,
- who is holding it "in trust,"
- refundable and non-refundable.
- If the deposit is to be held in an interest bearing account;
- who will receive the interest.
- What happens to the deposit?

Example for the refund of the deposit:
"If this condition has not been satisfied by the time therein specified, the Buyer shall by notice in writing to the Seller, at the Buyer's option, either waive such condition and complete the purchase of the property or elect not to complete. **In the latter event, the Buyer shall be entitled to a refund of the deposits paid to such date plus accrued interest.** This Agreement shall then be of no further force and effect and neither party shall have any further obligation hereunder to the other."

(6) **The terms and conditions of the contract.**

(7) **A list of fixtures and chattels** which are staying with the property at no extra charge.

(8) **DATES:**
   (a) The date when the offer is made
   (b) How long the offer (or any counter offer) is open till
   (c) The date of acceptance.
       In the case when negotiations are dragging on over several days **it is important to specify the DATE of the FINAL acceptance.** The reason for this is because **that date is the starting point from which all deadlines** (for staggered deposits and subject removals) are measured from (e.g. "the deposit of $ ... to be made within 24 hours of acceptance").
   (d) **The Completion Date must** be a weekday when the Land Titles Office is open. Land Title Offices are very busy at the end of the month.
   (e) By the end of COMPLETION DAY, the Seller is entitled to have all of his sales proceeds. If the Realtor is holding trust funds in excess of the real estate commission, then he must make the appropriate arrangements to ensure that the Seller will receive the excess funds in a timely manner.

The Completion Date should be a few days before the Possession and Adjustment Dates in order to enable the Seller to COMPLETE THE PURCHASE OF HIS NEXT HOUSE.
(f) **Possession and Adjustment Dates.**

(9) **Representations and Warranties** must be in writing to be enforceable.
The Realtor should ensure that the warranties will survive the closing.

(10) **A counter offer** extinguishes the original offer.
A counter offer is "a brand new ball game."
Don't forget to state how long the counter offer is open till.

(11) **ALL AMENDMENTS** to the original Contract of Purchase and Sale and all "subject"-removals
- must be in writing on an appropriate Amendment Form (issued by the local Real Estate Board);
- all contracting parties must sign and
- everybody is to receive a copy thereof.

(12) **The AMENDMENT** and/or "subject"-removal must
- refer to the original contract and
- should state that "all other terms and conditions remain the same" and
- to reaffirm that "time shall remain of the essence."

(13) Occasionally it is mentioned in a Contract of Purchase and Sale, that the Buyer has the privilege of **removing the subject clause "unilaterally."** This means that he can remove the subject clause by himself and the Seller may not be needed for his input. Whereas this may be so, the Realtor should consider the following points:
   (a) **Simple courtesy and common sense require that the Seller be informed that the subject clause has been removed.**
   (b) If this is done verbally and the Seller did not sign the the subject removal form, then (in case of a dispute later on) it will be difficult to prove that the Seller has been informed of the subject removal.
   (c) Realtors work hard to earn their commissions; why should they take the risk of a possible collapsed sale because of the lack of the Seller's signature?

(14) **ABOUT FAX COPIES.**
   (a) If all contracting parties are locally available, it is preferable to obtain ORIGINAL SIGNATURES on an ORIGINAL DOCUMENT.
   (b) The FAXing of a COMPLETE CONTRACT should be done when one of the parties is not available (out of town).
   (c) Realtors who are sending a contract by FAX must follow up and confirm that all FAXed pages have been received in good and legible condition.

(d) FAXes have a tendency of deteriorating and becoming difficult to read after the same document has been sent back and forth several times. Before it gets to that stage, a photocopy of the contract could be made and used subsequently.
(e) A FAXed contract comes into effect when
- the FAXed contract bearing the signatures of all contracting parties has been received AND
- it was communicated to the offeror.

(15) **ABOUT E-MAILS.**
(a) One of the problems with e-mail is how it can be established with any certainty that the person who has sent the e-mail is actually the person from whom it was supposed to have been received.
(b) As the contracting parties' SIGNATURES are required on the document, the Contract can be "forwarded" by e-mail as an "attachment."

The "Subject-to" Clause - Part I

Generally speaking, many a Realtor is not very interested in what appears to him as legalistic hairsplitting when it comes to subject clauses. Only after they find themselves in Court along with their Clients, does the matter of Conditions Precedent, Options and Subject-to clauses become of more importance to them. In the last few years a number of judicial opinions have been expressed on this matter. For obvious reasons (self-preservation, to avoid huge legal fees) it is important that Realtors should grasp the concepts and understand the general legal principles relating to this matter.

In order to avoid confusions, misunderstandings or "loose ends" it is suggested that "subject to" clauses should contain the following details:

1) **A clear identification** of the purpose of the "subject-to" clause. E.g. obtaining financing, selling his own home, getting subdivision approval etc.
2) **A specific date** by which the "subject to" clause must be removed. A sufficient time frame should be allowed to give the Buyer or Seller a realistic chance to achieve whatever their intentions are.
3) (a) It should be specified that **"Notice must be given in writing to the other party"** (or his agent) when the "subject-to" clause is fulfilled, waived or removed.
   (b) When the "subject-to" clause says that it could be removed "unilaterally" then it means that no acknowledging signature is required from the other party. Of course a cautious Realtor will realize, that there could be trouble when **there is no written evidence** that the other party was notified of the subject removal:
   - even if the other party is given a copy of the document in which the subject clause was unilaterally removed, **this document could be misplaced or lost**.
   - Later on if the other party wants to get out of the deal for some reason, he may claim that he was not aware of the subject removal and/or that he had not been notified.
   - The Realtor is then faced with the difficult task of proving it otherwise.
4) There should be **a provision that the deposit will be increased to a specified amount** when the "subject-to" clause is being removed.
5) Furthermore, there should be **a written acknowledgement that the contract will become binding on all contracting parties**, as soon as the subject-to clause has been removed and the deposit increased.
6) Details should be given **of the future disposition of the deposit monies:**
   (a) All deposit monies together with any interest earned **shall be credited to the account of the Buyer and shall be applied to the purchase price.**
   (b) Alternatively, **what will happen to the Buyer's deposit in case the deal does not complete** due to a default by the Buyer?
   (E.g. the Seller can retain the deposit as liquidated damages and if so accepted by the Seller it will represent the full amount of damages to which he is entitled

under this contract. Depending on the circumstances, some Sellers may not agree to this, because their foreseeable future damages might be higher than what the amount of the deposit is).

7) It would be further helpful if it is indicated in detail
    "What will happen if the subject-to clause is not removed?":
    (a) Upon expiry of the "subject-to" clause the agreement of purchase and sale
        - will become null and void
        - is no longer in force and effect
        - the rights and obligations of the parties to the contract shall be terminated.

In **"HARVEY v. BLACK"** (1993), 3 W.W.R. 527 (Alta. Q.B.) at p. 530 it says that the Agreement contained a provision that the agreement would fail if the conditions were not met.

(b) To be on the safe side the contracting parties should still sign a separate "Mutual Release" which will include instructions for the disposition of the deposit. E.g. the deposit will be returned to the Buyer immediately
    - together with any interest earned
    - and without deductions of any kind.

There are 3 categories of "subject-to" clauses.

(a) Each "condition precedent" case must be considered on its own facts.
(b) A "condition precedent" is an obligation or a right which is suspended until an **objectively identified EVENT happens.** (Cheshire and Fifoot "Law of Contract" (8th ed.) p. 116).
(c) A "condition precedent" may either
    - act as an **ingredient which suspends performance of an otherwise complete contract** OR
    - **alternatively it may NOT create a binding agreement.**
(d) It all depends upon
    - the **intention of the parties** as expressed in the contract itself and
    - as shown by surrounding (subsequent) **events** of the deal.
(e) A faulty "subject-to" clause may be viewed as
    - constituting merely an offer,
    - or else as an unpaid option or
    - alternatively it can be void for uncertainty.

Category # I
In this category the "subject" clause is
- **precisely** expressed
- has a **clear** meaning

- and is **OBJECTIVE**.

As a consequence, the contract between the parties
- **is basically complete** and
- **neither party can withdraw from it.**
- The performance of the contract is held in abeyance (or temporary suspension) until such time when the parties know whether the (objective) "condition precedent" is fulfilled.

Category # II
The "subject" clause is
- imprecise,
- **depends entirely and manifestly upon the SUBJECTIVE state of MIND of the Buyer or Seller.**
- The subject clause **does not create an obligation** for the parties involved to complete the contract until such time when the subject clause is removed.
- **As a consequence the contract is still regarded as being merely an offer and there is NO binding agreement.**

E.g.: "Subject to the Buyer inspecting the inside of the house by ... and him being totally satisfied with it. **This condition is for the sole benefit of the Buyer.**"

In this case the Buyer is attempting to
(a) bind the Seller (**but not himself**) to the Contract of Purchase and Sale
(b) without giving the Seller any valuable consideration in exchange.
(c) The Buyer is trying to give himself
- total flexibility.
- His decision is made at his sole discretion
- so that he has a free and unfettered hand
- in order to be in sole control of the offer,
- while being bound to nothing unless he chooses to be bound.

In **"GRIFFIN v. MARTENS"** (1988) 27 BCLR (2d) 152 (BCCA) at p. 154 the Court held that the clause reading "... subject to the Buyer being able to arrange satisfactory financing on or before ..." was not only **subject to the "WHIM or FANCY" of the Buyer,** but it identified and considered the following problems:

(1) The Contract of Purchase and Sale may be silent about what is the minimum amount of financing needed.
(2) "Financing" must be pursued by the Buyer
- **actively (the Buyer must make his best effort)**
- and financing cannot be rejected unreasonably (or arbitrarily), but only on reasonable specified grounds.

(3) Unless the Contract for Purchase and Sale specified what is meant by "satisfactory financing" a standard is not ascertainable. There are the following 4 possible interpretations:

   (a) **The financing is "satisfactory" to a reasonable Buyer about whom nothing else is known.**

      This alternative does not give sufficient meaning to the word "satisfactory" in the context of the Contract of Purchase and Sale.

   (b) **"Satisfactory" to a reasonable Buyer in the objective circumstances of the Buyer.**

      This combines subjective and objective standards.

   (c) **"Satisfactory" to a reasonable Buyer with all the subjective but reasonable standards of that particular Buyer.**

      In this case the word "satisfactory" has a full and subjective significance, while at the same time the Buyer is committing himself to making his honest and best efforts. He cannot withhold his "satisfaction" unreasonably.

   (d) **"Satisfactory" to this particular, individual Buyer with all of his quirks and prejudices, but acting honestly.**

      This alternative means that the financing has to be satisfactory to him (to that particular purchaser) and that interpretation could turn the Contract of Purchase and Sale into an Option. (However, often there is no mutual intention to support that construction). Such an Option is only enforceable if some ADDITIONAL CONSIDERATION is given to the Seller which he can keep regardless if the Buyer goes through with the transaction or not.

If there is NO additional consideration, then the agreement
- cannot be construed as an OPTION CONTRACT (should the Buyer decide not to proceed, then his original deposit would be returned to him).
- the Contract of Purchase and Sale is only an OFFER from the Seller to sell the property to the prospective Buyer on certain terms
- and that it could be revoked (by the Seller) at any time prior to the unequivocal acceptance by the Buyer.

TO SUMMARIZE: The words **"sole discretion"** and **"satisfaction"** do NOT refer to an EVENT, but refer to a DECISION (one way or the other) which is based on unknown and unspecified "subjective" factors. The Courts can neither TEST nor can they ASCERTAIN exactly WHAT it is which must be satisfied.

Category # III
The "subject-to" clause is **partly subjective and partly objective**.
Example: "subject to the Municipal Planning Department approving the subdivision plan."
In this case the Buyer (or his representative) has to make an application to the Planning Department and he has to take all of the required steps to obtain approval. This may

include some extra effort to expedite the approval process.

"PACTA SUNT SERVANDA" (promises are to be kept).

The DIFFERENCE between the TRUE CONDITION PRECEDENT and the PROMISSORY CONDITION is:

(a) Failure or **non-fulfilment of a CONDITION PRECEDENT TERMINATES** the contractual agreement between the parties.
(b) Failure or **non-fulfilment of a PROMISSORY CONDITION** may not (unless the party **culpably [through his own deliberate action] fails to do so**, because that party cannot take advantage of his own wrong).

Example: "Subject to THE BUYER carrying out PROPERTY FEASIBILITY STUDIES within … days."
This is not a true condition precedent because it requires one of the parties
- to do something to bring about the fulfilment of the condition and
- that requirement of action (namely e.g. to conduct an analysis of the soil conditions) was part of the consideration moving from that party to support the promise of the other party, **hence the condition was PROMISSORY.**
- Failure of a promissory condition may not end the contractual arrangement.
- The major problems with promissory conditions have been **UNCERTAINTY** where the party required to do something has an "option or discretion" about the doing of that something.

LAW CASES dealing with "conditions precedent" etc.

"BLACK GAVIN & Co. Ltd. v. CHEUNG et al" 20 BCLR 21 The Buyer's offer was subject to his inspection and ("whim or fancy") approval of the premises, chattels and accounts. There is no sale nor an obligation to complete unless and until the prospective Buyer gives his approval of the items mentioned above.

"MURRAY McDERMID HOLDINGS LTD. v. THATER" 42 BCLR 119 The Buyer's offer to buy the Seller's property was "subject to the approval of the President of the Corporate Buyer" (the Buyer was a Company). This clause is "subjective" because the human being (namely the corporate President) must attain a certain **state of mind**: to like the property and the terms of the proposed Contract. No contract exists until such time when the subject clause is removed (up to that time the agreement is considered to be merely an offer from the Seller to the Buyer to sell the property).

"KITSILANO ENTERPRISES LTD. v. G & A DEVELOPMENTS LTD." (1990-06-21) 48 BCLR 70 (BCSC Docket # C 885149) elaborates on agreements containing conditions which create binding contracts and those which may be said to

be merely offers. Where a 3rd party has to approve or grant financing it may constitute a "promissory condition" which requires that each party has to do whatever is reasonably necessary so that the condition will be met (fulfilled):
- The **Buyer** must make an active and honest effort to obtain the financing needed
- The **Seller** must grant access to the property
    - for the Appraiser to do the mortgage appraisal for the lending institution,
    - for the Surveyor, if a Certificate of Non-Encroachment (Survey Certificate) is required by the Lender.
    - For the Building Inspector (if the Buyer wants a professional report about the condition of the property).

"Mark 7 Development Ltd. v. Peace Holdings Ltd." (1991-01-29), 53 BCLR (2d) 217 BC Court of Appeal Docket # CA 011107. The Court decided that one of the conditions precedent was **"manifestly dependent upon the subjective state of mind of the plaintiff"** and as a result the interim agreement never became binding on the plaintiff and **remained only an offer until the relevant subjective state of mind had been reached."** The condition precedent was entirely subjective and it was particularly specified that the Buyer could arbitrarily decide whether to accept (the leases) or not.

"WIEBE v. BOBSIEN" (1984) 59 BCLR 183 (BCSC) upheld on appeal (1985) 64 BCLR 194 (C.A.) The condition precedent "subject to the Buyer's satisfactory building inspection" **combined both objective and subjective standards.**

(a) **The objective aspect** was the Buyer's responsibility to obtain a building inspection. For that purpose the Buyer had to
- expend a certain amount of inconvenience ("work" in the form of phoning around and selecting a suitable Building Inspector);
- shoulder the economic risk of having to pay for a Building Inspection Report which could possibly and eventually discourage him from buying the house. (However the cost of an inspection is negligible in comparison with the cost of replacing a leaking roof or having to make expensive foundation repairs).

(b) **The subjective aspect** of the clause is that:
- the "subject clause" had to
    - produce for him **information (advice)** which would put his mind at ease.
    - To grant him sufficient time to reach a considered opinion.
    - It is **ONLY** the Buyer who has to be satisfied by the results of the inspection
    - **before** the agreement would be consummated.
- The Buyer is obliged to:
    - consider the Inspection Report carefully and
    - not to reject it arbitrarily but only on reasonable specified grounds.

"**UT RES MAGIS VALEAT QUAM PEREAT**" (Freely translated: a deed shall never be void where the words may be applied to any extent to make it good).

It has been held that it is not the function of the Courts to set aside a Contract of Purchase and Sale because it contained a clause that is not precisely expressed. It was further held that if a clause has an ascertainable meaning, then the Courts
- should strive to find it,
- they should look at **substance and NOT mere form** and
- they should try to retain and give effect to the agreement which the contracting parties have created.

WHAT can happen, if there is a CONDITIONAL CONTRACT and the condition(s) were not satisfied or waived in writing and in a timely fashion?

"KNIGHT v. EXPLORATION INNOVATIONS INC." (2002-03-01) ABQB Docket # 990119309 Under [48] it says: "The December 16th Agreement did not explicitly provide for failure of the agreement if the conditions were not met… However, the mere fact that a provision of that nature did not exist in the December 16th Agreement is not by itself determinative of its possible failure."

"POSSIBLE ENTERPRISES LTD. v. NEWCOMEN" B.C. Supreme Court (1998-06-02) Docket 5334, Nelson Registry. In this case, the subject-to clause had not been removed. It was held that
- The written contract should be considered first, reading the words in their ordinary and natural sense.
- The Court must construe the contract in accordance with the parties' intentions.
- Matters ought to be determined on their merits rather than on points of procedure.
- The Defendant gave no notice at any time that she was solely relying on this condition [in this case to satisfy herself as to the boundaries of the property].
- Where a term of a contract is unclear, the Court may go outside the document. **The acts of the parties "in pursuance of the instrument may be looked at as a clue to their intentions."** (DiCastri, Law of Vendor and Purchaser (3rd edition) paragraph 395).
- Considering this transaction in that light, the proper construction is that the party concerned [namely the Defendant] had an opportunity to withdraw, but **failing to do so and failing such notice, the EXPECTATIONS OF THE CONTRACTING PARTIES** was that the CONDITION WOULD LAPSE.
- **This is clearly how the parties behaved.**

This case also refers to **"WOELLER v. ORFUS et al,"** Ontario High Court, November 26, 1979) 1106 DLR (3d) 115: In circumstances where
- there has been no effort to satisfy a condition and
- there is no evidence that the condition could not have been satisfied, **a CONTRACT**

WILL NORMALLY BE ENFORCED.
- Reference is also made to **"GILCHRIST v. COMMODORE,"** Court of Appeal, November 23, 1931, 40 O.W.N.577

Appeal by the Plaintiff from the judgment of Kelly, J., dismissing the claim, and in favour of the Defendant on his counterclaim. The Appeal was dismissed with costs.

The "Subject-to" Clause - Part II

Occasionally the enforceability of conditional offers represents problems for many a Realtor. Specifically the difficulty is in recognizing the difference between
- subject clauses which require the approval of somebody else (other than the Buyer and Seller) and
- subject clauses which are subject to the "whim and fancy" of the Buyer or Seller.

Thankfully it is not the function of the Courts to set aside Contracts of Purchase and Sale for uncertainty merely because they contain a clause that is not precisely expressed. See **"GRIFFIN v. MARTENS, TYMAR DEVELOPMENTS AND TD LIMITED,"** (1988) 27 BCLR (2d) 152 BCCA)

(I) Offers which contain a so called **"THIRD PARTY APPROVAL CLAUSE" create a contract which neither the Buyer nor the Seller can revoke during the period the condition remains open to be removed. This type of clause is often referred to as a TRUE CONDITION PRECEDENT.**
A true condition precedent is simply an "external" condition the fulfilment of which depends entirely on the will, actions, cooperation and/or the granting of something by **a third party (who is NOT a party to the contract). See "TURNEY v. ZHILKA,"** [1959] SCR 578 at 583.

As soon as the parties sign the Contract of Purchase and Sale a **BINDING contract is created**, although **its COMPLETION is subject to the removal of the condition precedent**. In other words, the performance of the contract is **HELD IN SUSPENSE** until such time when the parties know whether the OBJECTIVE condition precedent is fulfilled. E.g.: "Subject to the Buyer obtaining a new 1st mortgage from …bank by ….."

In this example (Condition Precedent) **the Buyer has**
- **an obligation to do whatever is reasonably necessary** in order to obtain the new financing.
- The Buyer has an obligation to **PURSUE financing ACTIVELY**
- and **NOT to reject financing arbitrarily or unreasonably.**
- If he does not make his best efforts to meet the condition (and uses it as an excuse to get out of the deal), then the Seller will have his remedy in damages.

(II) **"WHIM AND FANCY"** clauses are **"promissory"** conditions which depend entirely upon the **SUBJECTIVE state of mind** of the Buyer or Seller. The party who makes this condition
- has the right to make an arbitrary decision.
- This subjectivity is such that a Judge couldn't apply any type of test to determine if the Buyer or Seller had used his best efforts to satisfy the condition.

Example:
"The Buyer will examine the list of fixtures and will indicate in writing on or before … whether they are acceptable to him or not. This condition is for the sole benefit of the Buyer and may be waived by him unilaterally at his discretion."

(a) This type of **"subjective-state-of-mind" clause** will not result in a binding contract.
(b) It will remain an offer until **the relevant subjective state of mind has been reached and the subject/problem resolved.**
(c) But it may/will create an OPTION to be exercised within the specified period of time.
This means that one party (e.g. the Seller) is free to revoke his acceptance any time before he receives notice that the Buyer has removed or waived the condition.
(d) This "OPTION"-type of offer is unenforceable **unless the agreement is made under a seal or there is a separate legal consideration.**

Example:
"Subject to the Seller consulting with his accountant about the income tax ramifications resulting from this sale. The income tax advice received must be satisfactory to the Seller at his sole discretion."

Example:
"This agreement is subject to the Seller obtaining legal advice from a lawyer of the Seller's choice on or before … and such advice is to deal with the legal enforceability of the contract. This subject clause is for the sole benefit of the Seller."

In both of the above cases the Seller
- did not give any legal consideration in exchange for trying to bind the Buyer to the contract.
- At the same time he is providing himself a period of time and the flexibility to make an arbitrary decision based on the expert advice and/or information he receives.

FAULTY SUBJECT CLAUSES will result in contracts which are
- merely offers or
- options without consideration or
- they are void for uncertainty.

(III) There is a third variation of conditions, **namely where the condition is partly subjective and partly objective.**

Example:
"The Buyer's obligation to buy the lands is subject to the Buyer advising the Seller in writing that the Buyer has completed and is satisfied as to all legal, physical,

environmental and financial aspects for the development of the lands.

This condition is for the sole benefit of the Buyer and must be satisfied or waived in writing on or before that date occurring ninety (90) days following the acceptance date of this offer or this offer shall terminate and the initial deposit and interest shall be returned to the Buyer forthwith.

The Buyer may extend, at his option, the date for satisfaction or waiver of the above condition precedent for one additional 90-day period upon written notice and payment of $ 15,000.00 as a non-refundable deposit for the extension. The additional deposit is to be applied to the Purchase Price upon completion.

In consideration of the sum of $ 10.00, the receipt and sufficiency of which is hereby acknowledged by the Seller, the Seller hereby agrees not to terminate this agreement during the period stipulated for satisfaction (and/or waive) of the condition precedent set forth above."

In this case the Buyer has
- a free hand (is unrestricted) during the first 90 day time period;
- he is in control and
- **he is not bound to anything unless he chooses to be bound.**
- **The Buyer is trying to bind the Seller, but not himself.**
- **The condition is partly subjective and partly objective.**

Therefore, unless the legal consideration offered is a substantial amount of money,
- there will still be an uneven balance between the contracting parties:
- one party will be locked into the Contract, while the other party still has the luxury of being able to unilaterally decide if he will proceed with the contract or not.

(IV) The meaning of the words "**satisfaction**," "**discretion**," "**feasibility**" are vague, because a Judge cannot test them against something to show what must be satisfied.

Example:
"Subject to the Municipal Planning Dept. approving a satisfactory subdivision plan creating 30 lots."
Although at first blush this seems to be an "objective" third party approval condition, it will require the subjective effort of the Buyer to
- present the proposal in a timely manner to the Municipality
- to try to persuade the Planning Dept. to approve the creation of 30 lots by packaging the proposal in an attractive way (this may be called "persuasion")
- and generally do what is reasonably required to expedite the approval process; to keep things moving instead of letting them bog down in bureaucratic delays.

Example:
"Subject to purchaser's satisfactory building inspection."
This clause combines both objective and subjective standards.

The OBJECTIVE portion is that the Buyer must obtain a building inspection.
The SUBJECTIVE aspect of this clause is that after having received and studied the inspection report, it is the Buyer who has to be satisfied with the condition of the house.
In this case the Buyer has some
- inconvenience (namely finding and choosing an inspector with whom he is comfortable with) and
- a certain economic risk (he has to pay for the inspection report; the cost thereof will be lost if he is not satisfied with the condition of the house and chooses not to proceed with the purchase).

This "subject clause" gives the Buyer sufficient time to reach a considered opinion based upon information and advice received from an expert whom he trusts.
To summarize the Buyer was seeking advice and having received same, by necessary inference will then decide himself.

In the end, **the INTERPRETATION of a contract** depends on
- the INTENTIONS of the contracting parties as expressed in the contract and
- as the Judge can examine them in the contexts of the facts surrounding the case.

The Deposit

When a Realtor drafts an offer to purchase he sets into motion a procedure which hopefully will end up in a firm contract and eventually in a completed sale.
As part of the offer, there must be some sort of **legal consideration**. The Reader may wish to consult "Black's Law Dictionary" for the definitions of various types of "consideration." Legal dictionaries are available at a Public Library or possibly at your local Real Estate Board's library.

The Legal (or "valuable") Consideration is given by the promisor to the promisee and can be either
- the payment of some money (as low as $ 1.00) or
- an act or a promise to do something. In the absence of an immediate monetary deposit accompanying the offer, a binding contract can also be created by the contracting parties' mutual exchange of promises. E.g.: "The deposit of $ ... will be paid after the removal of all 'subject' clauses."

NOTE: Realtors have a Fiduciary Duty to their Clients **to fully disclose all pertinent facts** which may have an influence on
- the saleability and/or
- value of the property.
- The key is PROPER COMMUNICATION.

The following are some of the subjects which should be discussed with SELLERS and BUYERS:

(I) **The REASONS for a deposit are:**
(1) **From a LEGAL point of view, there** has to be VALUABLE CONSIDERATION to make a contract (not under seal) binding. (If a contract is under a seal [the red dot next to the contracting parties' signatures] then the law presumes that "legal consideration" exists, because the parties have apparently **"contracted in a solemn form").**
(2) The presence of the deposit indicates
- **that the Buyer has the serious intention of being legally bound.**
- **A PROMISE** that the Buyer will perform the terms of the contract.
- The deposit is **PART of the PURCHASE PRICE**.
(3) **From a PSYCHOLOGICAL point of view**
- **the size, form and time factor** of the deposit creates in **the SELLER'S mind** an impression of how serious the Buyer is or appears to be.
The average Seller is not familiar with legal technicalities.
Therefore the Buyer's promise
- of a **small** deposit (e.g. $ 1.00, although perfectly legal) or

- a deposit **at some future time** (e.g. after subject removal) **may be misunderstood because**
  (a) **the Seller may think that the Buyer is**
     - not serious or
     - a trifler or else
     - that he is playing games.
  (b) **There appears to be little incentive** for the Seller to enter into meaningful negotiations.
  (c) **There seems to be no valid reason** for the Seller to tie up his house (and possibly take it off the market) for the sake of such a marginal proposition.
  (d) Even some Realtors feel that a "strong" (sizeable) deposit (sufficient to cover their commission) will "keep the Buyer honest" (translation: more committed to completing the deal).

(4) On the other hand **the BUYER may be apprehensive that**
   - he could somehow loose his deposit if his offer is not accepted.
   - Or alternatively that he may have trouble or encounter undue delay in getting the deposit back from the Realtor.
   - Or that the Seller will be reluctant to sign a release of the deposit in case the Buyer is unable to remove the subject clause(s).

(5) Alternatively **some Buyers may be under the erroneous impression** that
   - a Contract of Purchase and Sale is not binding on the parties until all subject clauses have been removed or
   - by not offering an immediate deposit it will be "easier" for them to get out of the deal at a later date if they choose to do so.

   Both of the above are misconceptions.
   - The obligations of the Contract start as soon as the offer (or counteroffer) has been accepted.
   - In fact **all contracting parties must make their best efforts** to satisfy and to remove all subject clauses.

(6) **When the Buyer offers his deposit only AFTER subject removal**
   - then the Seller may think that his property is tied up for a period of time with "nothing concrete up-front,"
   - while all the time one or the other of the contracting parties may also be under the mistaken impression that they don't have a pressing incentive to satisfy the subject clause(s) in a timely fashion.
   - **In a case like that the Listing Broker should**
   - discuss with his Sellers the desirability of an "up-front deposit" v. the potential ramifications of a deposit at a later date (e.g. after subject removals).
   - The Sellers should also be advised that this situation can be remedied by the Seller making a counter offer dealing with the timing of the deposit. Of course, **it should be the Seller's decision** to make such a counter offer.

To put the BUYER'S mind at ease about the deposit it is incumbent upon the Selling Salesperson to discuss with the Buyer the ins-and-outs of the deposit. **The following are some of the points which should be elaborated on:**

(1) **The psychological impact of a "strong" (big) deposit on the Seller's mind** will reassure the Seller that
- "the Buyer means business."
- "The Buyer is serious" (about buying the property) and that he can be relied upon to complete the terms of the accepted contract.
- As a consequence of the Buyer's demonstration of goodwill (in the form of an adequate deposit), chances are that the Seller will reciprocate by negotiating in a more meaningful way.

(2) **The Realtor is required by law** to deposit the Buyer's deposit cheque without undue delay into his Company's Trust Account (especially if offers and counter-offers drag on for an extended period of time). It is also more business like to deposit the cheque, instead of carrying it around in the pocket. Of course, there is also the possibility of misplacing it somehow.

(3) If the offer is not accepted, if negotiations come to an end and no sale results, then the Seller has no valid claim against the deposit; obviously it is refundable to the Buyer.

(4) The Realtor should explain to the Buyer
- **the procedure** and
- **the length of time involved** for the Realty Company to issue a refund cheque to him:
  In case the Buyer gives an uncertified cheque, the Real Estate Company will have to wait for a few days for the deposit cheque to clear through their and the Buyer's bank BEFORE issuing a refund cheque. The reason for this is as follows: if the Buyer issues a "stop-payment" order with his bank and on the other hand the Real Estate Company issues promptly a refund cheque then the Company could be out some money.

(5) If the Buyer can prove that he has honestly made his best efforts to satisfy the subject clause (e.g. to obtain a new mortgage) and failed, then the Seller cannot very well lay claim to the deposit.

(II) **If there is NO DEPOSIT accompanying the offer**, then the Selling Salesperson should, of course,

(1) **NOT COMPLETE** in the Contract of Purchase and Sale the clause reading:
"Receipt of the above mentioned deposit is hereby acknowledged by the undersigned Selling Agent."
Obviously this sentence SHOULD BE CROSSED OUT and initialled.

(2) Some Realtors are reluctant to take a deposit cheque with the initial offer, because they try to avoid
- the "waste of time" and

The Deposit

- the "nuisance of additional paperwork" which is required if a sale doesn't materialize and the deposit has to be returned.
- For that reason they may write in the Contract of Purchase and Sale that **"the Buyer's deposit is payable UPON ACCEPTANCE."** Unfortunately these Realtors do not seem to understand or appreciate that with this particular kind of wording **the deposit becomes due and payable the moment when the offer is ACCEPTED by the Sellers**. This in turn means that the deposit cheque MUST be in the Realtor's possession at the time when the offer is presented.
- If, on the other hand, the intention is
  - to first get the offer accepted and
  - then to meet the Buyer sometime later to obtain the deposit cheque
  - **then the proper wording is that "the deposit will be payable within 24 hours of acceptance."**

(3) If the deposit is made subsequent to acceptance, then **the Selling Broker MUST notify the Listing Broker AND the Sellers that and when the deposit has been made**. The smart thing is to create a paper trail (something IN WRITING). E.g. a phone call followed up by a confirmation by FAX. To FAX a photocopy of the deposit cheque may conceivably require the permission of the Buyer (because the cheque reveals banking details).

(4) **If the Buyer FAILS to pay the deposit** as stipulated in the contract
- then the **Listing Broker and the Seller must be notified immediately**.
- The Seller should obtain legal advice about his option to terminate the contract.

(5) **If there is a DELAY in obtaining the deposit within the specified time**, then
- the Listing Broker and the Sellers MUST be notified accordingly and
- the contracting parties should seek legal advice as to their positions.

(6) **If the deposit cheque is RETURNED as NSF** (refused by the bank due to there being **insufficient funds** in the Buyer's bank account), then
  (a) the Buyer has breached the agreement,
  (b) **the Sellers and Listing Brokers MUST be notified IMMEDIATELY.**
  (c) Simultaneously **the Buyer also should be contacted** to ascertain if
   - he is aware of the problem with the cheque and
   - what (if anything) he intends to do about this situation (e.g. if there was a mistake by the bank and/or if he still wants the property).
  (d) At the SELLER's option and with his express permission, the Buyer may be given an opportunity to immediately replace the old NSF cheque with a new certified cheque or a bank draft.
  (e) **If the deposit is not replaced immediately** then the Seller should be advised to obtain legal advice without delay in order to determine if
   - the Contract is still binding or not (so that he can go ahead and resell the property to somebody else without the danger of the Buyer coming back on the scene at some later date trying to tie up the property in litigation)
   - and if the Seller has any claims against the Buyer. The Realtor should

refrain from mentioning any "liquidated damages" because that is a subject matter best discussed between the Clients and their respective lawyers.

(7) **If the Buyer issues a "stop payment" order at his bank (BEFORE the deposit cheque could be deposited in the Realty Company's Trust Account) then**
- the Listing Broker and the Seller must be notified immediately and
- all contracting parties should be urged to seek without delay legal advice concerning their positions.

(III) STAGGERED DEPOSITS:

A possible compromise solution to appease the various concerns of apprehensive Buyers and Sellers could be that
- several deposits are to be made
- in staggered amounts
- over a period of time.

For example:
- A $ 1,000.00 initial deposit cheque to accompany the offer.
- A further $ 1,500.00 increase in the deposit within 24-hours of acceptance.
- A further $ 2,500.00 increase in the deposit upon removal of all "subject-to" clauses.

This way there will be a $ 5,000 deposit when the contract is firm (subject-free), which should satisfied everybody.

If all parties agree to proceed in this way, then **the Realtor must take great care that ALL DEADLINES for the various deposit increases are promptly met on time** or else the Seller can refuse to complete.

In **"JOHAL v. MAGAT,"** B.C. Supreme Court, Date 1993-03-05, Docket No. S0-7672, the Buyer had contracted that he would tender a $ 5,000.00 deposit within 24 hours of acceptance. For some reason he didn't pay the deposit until 2 days later. The Seller refused to close and the Buyer sued for specific performance. At the trial the Buyer claimed that he "has had some verbal discussions with the Seller that he could pay later," but the Buyer was not able to produce any proof in writing to that effect. The Judge ruled that there was a clear cut contract with an express proviso and that the deposit was not paid within the time fixed by the agreement. The Buyer's allegation of a vague oral extension agreement was rejected and the Buyer lost.

This teaches the following important lessons:

a) **In order to be enforceable, all subsequent and especially any verbal agreements or changes and additions to a contract MUST be in writing and initialled by**

ALL of the contracting parties.

b) If the offer is countered back and forth over a period of time, then it should be obvious that **somewhere in the body of the contract the DATE and TIME of the finally agreed-upon acceptance MUST BE SHOWN** in order to have a written record of the STARTING point from which all deadlines depend.

(IV) IF THE DEPOSIT IS TO BEAR INTEREST.

If there is a sizeable deposit held in Trust for an extended period of time, then the contracting parties may agree IN WRITING to place the deposit monies into an interest bearing Trust A/C with the interest accruing to the benefit of the Buyer.

(V) The TRUST ACCOUNT.

(a) The Real Estate Company is holding the Buyer's **deposit "in Trust" as a "STAKEHOLDER."** This means that NOBODY can touch monies in a Trust Account: neither the Buyer, nor the Seller and certainly not the Realtor.

(b) Through legislation strict guidelines have been established under which monies can be withdrawn from the Trust Account.
The Reader is encouraged to familiarize himself with his local legislation in this respect.

(VI) The COLLAPSED SALE.

Should a sale collapse for some reason, the Realtor is not at liberty to release the deposit from the Trust Account, **unless there is an express written agreement between the Buyers and Sellers directing the Realtor** to pay out the deposit monies according to the specific wishes of the parties.

(a) **A "Collapsed Sale Report"** must be completed for the Office Records and
(b) **a separate "Mutual Release"** has to be signed by all Sellers and Buyers
- releasing each other from all legal obligations and
- directing the disposition of the deposit.

This is the only correct and prudent procedure to be adhered to. To do otherwise may turn out to be highly risky and costly for everybody, especially for the Realtor: time consuming law suits, expensive legal fees, disciplinary action from the Real Estate Board, lots of stress and valuable time lost from work.

(c) **If the parties cannot agree on the disposition of the deposit** which is held "in Trust" by the Real Estate Company and
- if this disagreement has been going on for an unusually long period of time and
- it appears that there is no chance for a resolution or settlement in the near future,
- then the Realtor has the option of paying the disputed monies into Court. Proper advance notice of this must be given to all parties, because retrieving

such deposit monies from the Court may entail extra legal fees.
(d) Even if there is no deposit, a MUTUAL RELEASE should nevertheless be signed by the contracting parties to release each other from any legal obligations which may have been created. The reason for this is that all contracting parties should be able to go their separate ways without fear of some unexpected future legal action.

(VII) Refundable v. Non-Refundable Deposits.

When is the deposit REFUNDABLE?
(a) When the Buyer's offer is not accepted and negotiations have definitely come to an end.
(b) After a Buyer has made his "Best Efforts" to remove all "subject-to clauses" and finds that he cannot. **(Unfulfilled condition precedent).**
(c) **"Uncertainty in the terms of the contract"** entered into could under certain circumstances also result in the refund of a deposit.

On the other hand, it is generally considered that the Buyer's **deposit will become NON-REFUNDABLE** in the following situations:

(a) If the Seller is ready, willing and able to do everything which he is supposed to, but **the Buyer deliberately avoids his contractual obligations**. See **"Lemac Holdings Ltd. v. Paul's Holdings Ltd.,"** (1982) B.C.D. Civ. 2244-05, County Court West. F 800878 New Westminster, 40 B.C.L.R. 241
(b) Once all "subject-to clauses" have been removed from the contract at which time the sale is said to become "firm."

To preclude in advance any possible misunderstandings between the contracting parties what their intentions are, some Realtors prefer to grab the bull by the horn and insert a specific clause into the Contract dealing with the non-refundability of the deposit.
For example a Realtor could attempt to say that
"It is a condition of this contract, that the entire deposit of $... becomes non-refundable from and starting with the day when all "subject-to clauses" have been removed. Specifically this means that in case of non-completion by the Buyer, the entire deposit of $... will be forfeited to the Seller and will be paid out to the Seller on (the contemplated) Completion Date."
Although this may not be a sure fire and legally watertight clause, it should go a long way to convince a Judge what the parties' intentions were.
Obviously **if the Seller doesn't complete**, then the Buyer shouldn't be punished by loosing his deposit.

(VIII) If THE DEPOSIT IS PAID TO SOMEBODY ELSE other than the Realtor.
(1) CAUTION: If the deposit is held by somebody else other than in the Realtor's Trust Account, **then the first order of business is that the Realtor should ensure**

that he does NOT sign the "ACKNOWLEDGMENT OF DEPOSIT" in the Contract. (In the heat of the battle, the Realtor may forget and sign it routinely - big mistake!)

(2) **If the Seller demands that the Buyer pay the deposit directly to him or his (the Seller's) lawyer, then the Buyer should obtain independent legal advice before doing so.** The reason for this is that neither the Seller nor the Seller's lawyer will hold the deposit as a 'Stakeholder'. The Buyer may have to sue to get his deposit back.

It should be understood that the Buyer's lawyer works for the Buyer and the Seller's lawyer for the Seller. Under usual circumstances neither one of them will hold the deposit as a 'Stakeholder'.

(3) Basically the problem to be addressed is, if the Lawyer or Notary Public is holding the deposit money in trust
   (a) **FOR one of the parties to the transaction OR**
   (b) **if he is holding it as a "STAKEHOLDER."**

If the Lawyer or Notary Public is supposed to act as a STAKEHOLDER pursuant to the provisions of the local REAL ESTATE ACT (or other local equivalent legislation), then:

   (a) ALL contracting parties must agree to this IN WRITING.
   (b) The Lawyer or Notary Public must indicate in writing that he is willing and able to act as a "Stakeholder."
   (c) The Lawyer or Notary Public must give his written undertaking that
      - he will hold the deposit as a Stakeholder and NOT in Trust for one of the parties AND
      - that upon completion of the transaction he will disburse the Trust Funds as stipulated in the Contract of Purchase and Sale.
      - Should the sale not complete, then he will - upon the Realtor's request - repay the deposit monies to the Real Estate Company which will continue to act as a 'Stakeholder'.

(IX) **If the Selling Broker is not holding the deposit in his Trust Account**, then he has an **OBLIGATION**
   - to **keep track of the deposit** by **VERIFYING** that the Buyer has indeed paid the deposit to the Lawyer or Notary Public in a timely fashion AND
   - to **INFORM** the Sellers and Listing Broker accordingly.

(X) **If the deposit EXCEEDS the total amount of the real estate commission.**
Any monies in excess of the real estate commission are due to the Seller on completion of the transaction and registration of all necessary documents.
Excess funds can be handled in 2 ways:

(a) On the Completion Date
   - the Real Estate Company has to be in close communication with the Conveyancing Solicitor.

- **As soon as final registration particulars have been received, the excess monies** can be released to the Seller.

  Arrangements will have to be made for the Seller to either pick up the cheque from the Real Estate Office or to have it delivered to him at his house or to his lawyer or any other disposition agreed upon.

(b) The Conveyancing Solicitor may request the excess amount from the Real Estate Company before Completion Date.
- Such request must be in writing and
- **the Lawyer or Notary must give his written undertaking that he will hold such funds as a 'stakeholder'.** (See above).

The Limited Dual Agency

This situation arises when
- a Listing Salesperson finds a Buyer (of his own) who wants to buy the property which is listed with him.
- Another salesperson from the same Company as the Listing Salesperson is acting as a Buyer's Agent for a Client who is interested in the listed property.

In these situations **the following BASIC PROBLEMS will arise:**

(1) There are **conflicting interests between the Buyers and Sellers**.
  (a) The Buyers want to buy the property at the lowest possible price.
  (b) The Sellers want to sell the property at the highest possible price.

(2) The Realtor who is acting as Agent for BOTH the Sellers and the Buyers will obviously end up in **a conflict of interest situation** because the basis of "Single Agency" ("personal representation") requires
  - him to give **his exclusive and total allegiance (LOYALTY) to his Principal** and
  - that he will promote his Principal's interests with single minded purpose for the Principal's BENEFIT.

(3) As already the Bible says that ONE Servant cannot serve TWO Masters at the same time, the Agent's conflict of interest appears to be (almost) insoluble.

(4) The solution to this dilemma is the "Dual Agency" which (in British Columbia) has been modified to limit the duty of disclosure to some degree and for that reason is called the "LIMITED Dual Agency."

(5) The "Limited Dual Agency Agreement" is a separate document and essentially it is a 3-party contract between the Buyers, the Sellers and the Real Estate Company ("Agency" rests with the Company and not the individual Salesperson).
  (a) The Buyers and Sellers consent to a certain limitation of the Realtor's "duty of disclosure" and
  (b) the Agent promises to deal with BOTH of them **impartially** and **to remain neutral and objective** during the transaction.

(6) The Realtor must obtain **IN WRITING** the Clients' **"INFORMED CONSENT"** to the Limited Dual Agency Agreement. For that purpose the following must be disclosed and discussed with the Buyers and Sellers IN A TIMELY MANNER:
  (a) The TERMS of the Realtor's Dual Agency relationship with BOTH Clients:
    - The Agent will **act impartially** with everybody.

- The Realtor **cannot advise or advocate** on behalf of either party **where doing so would enhance the interest of one party over the other.**
- The Realtor has "a duty of disclosure" to both the Buyers and the Sellers **except for the 3 specific non-disclosures** outlined in the Limited Dual Agency Agreement.
- The Realtor **cannot make unilaterally** certain **fundamental and arbitrary decisions** which may affect his Principal. The following example should illustrate this:

Listing Salesperson has an appointment with his Sellers to present an offer from a Buyer of his own. (Limited Dual Agency situation). BEFORE this offer is presented, the Listing Salesperson is contacted by another Realtor who wants to show the property to a qualified and very interested Buyer.

The problem to be considered is as follows:

The Listing Salesperson already has a written offer on hand (namely his own) which may be acceptable to the Sellers. Under these circumstances
- should the Listing Salesperson discourage the Competitor's showing so that he could proceed to present his own offer to the Sellers (after all right now it is the only written offer and "a bird in the hand is worth 2 in the bush" as the saying goes).
- If the Competitor Realtor insists on a showing should he offer him a "Back-up" position in case he manages to get an offer in due course.
- Should the Listing Salesperson inform the Sellers that another Realtor wants to show their house and should he advise the Sellers to wait to see if the showing by the Competitor Realtor produces another and perhaps higher offer?

The correct decision for the Realtor is:
- The Listing Salesperson/Dual Agent MUST inform the Sellers of the pending showing by the Competitor.
- By denying a prospective Buyer and his Agent the opportunity to view the property and to make an offer there could be
  - a "LOSS OF OPPORTUNITY" and
  - possible negligence within the meaning of certain provisions under the B.C. Real Estate Act [now RESA] for the Listing Salesperson's failure to act in the best interest of his Seller.
- The Listing Salesperson/Dual Agent **MUST inform the Sellers of the DEADLINE for acceptance of his existing offer** (which is "on hand" and ready to be presented).
- **The final decision what to do is up to the Sellers to decide.**

(b) **The Realtor CANNOT DISCLOSE to the SELLERS:**
- How high in price the Buyers are willing or able to go. All the Realtor can do is to refer to the price in the Buyers' offer. There can be no discussion of any "counter offer strategies."
- What the **Buyers' motivation to buy** is and

- **other personal information about the Buyers** (unless it is specifically authorized by the Buyers in writing).

(c) **The Realtor CANNOT DISCLOSE to the BUYERS:**
- How low a price the Sellers are willing or able to accept. All the Realtor can do is to point out the Asking Price in the Listing Contract. There can be no discussion of any strategies what price to offer initially.
- What **the Sellers' motivation to sell** is and
- other **personal information about the Sellers** (unless it is specifically authorized by the Sellers in writing).
- **The Agent STILL HAS A DUTY OF DISCLOSING to the Buyers ANY DEFECTS of the property which are known to him.**

(d) Obviously these limitations which are placed on the Realtor's usual fiduciary duties **will curtail useful information** for the Clients. Therefore the Clients should be given an opportunity to make **a fully informed CHOICE of the TYPE of representation** they wish to receive. (Limited Dual Agency or Transaction Brokerage).

(e) A word about the afore-mentioned **"timely manner"**:
- The full implications of presentation by a Dual Agent must be disclosed to the Sellers and Buyers
- AND the Limited Dual Agency Agreement MUST be signed
- **BEFORE** the Realtor starts acting as a Dual Agent and
- **BEFORE** any of the parties discloses confidential information to the Agent.

(7) **THE FOLLOWING are some situations where a Limited Dual Agency is not advisable.**

The Buyers should be given "no agency" and treated as "Customers" where the Listing Broker has a close, long-term and ongoing relationship with the Sellers. E.g.:
- The Seller is a relative (spouse, parent, child etc.) of the Listing Broker.
- The Seller is a long-time close friend or business associate of the Listing Broker.
- The Listing Broker is marketing a project (a subdivision or a condominium complex) for a developer (and thus is involved in an ongoing long-term business relationship).

(8) **WHAT ALTERNATIVES ARE THERE if the Clients do not agree to a LIMITED DUAL AGENCY AGREEMENT?**

(a) The Listing Broker can remain the Sellers' Agent and give "no agency" to the Buyers (treat them as "Customers).

(b) The Realtor can act as a TRANSACTION BROKER by giving both the Sellers and the Buyers "no agency":
- with the Sellers from the time of taking the listing and
- with the Buyers from the time of first substantial contact.

(c) **Designated Agency.**
When a real estate company finds itself in a Dual Agency situation, management can try to solve the cross-advocating problem of the opposing interests of the Buyers and Sellers by appointing one salesperson to represent only the interest of the Seller and another salesperson (from the same company) to represent only the Buyer. The Company itself will be in a "Dual Agency" or "Transaction Broker" position while supervising both salespersons.

Some of the difficulties with Designated Agency are:

(a) The Real Estate Company's interest in using the "Designated Agency" alternative may possibly be perceived as a conflict of interest because of the basic profit motive: The Buyer will not be lost to another competitor and the Company will be able to get both "ends" of the commission.
(b) Managing Brokers in small companies (who are also selling part time in order to augment their income) cannot be a Designated Agent, because most likely they are familiar with some confidential information about either the Buyer or the Seller.
(c) The same goes for Realtors working in small villages, where everybody knows everything about anybody else.
(d) Before anybody can be appointed as a Designated Agent in a LARGE company, the Manager must ensure that this person is not privy to some confidential information which would disqualify him from becoming a Designated Agent. Some of this information could be acquired quite innocently (e.g. through being somebody's holidays relief or during an Open House). From a practical point of view, how can a Manager in a 100 salespersons office keep track of who knows what?
(e) What happens when the Client doesn't want their Realtor's Company to represent the other side by "Designated Agency?"
- Will the Buyer say: "Please find me a home, but don't show me any of your or your company's listings?"
- Will the Seller say: "I will list my house with you provided you promise that neither you nor anybody else from your Company will bring one of your Buyer Clients to see my house."
(f) Problems with Designated Agency have not yet been tested in Court. Theoretically, if a problem arises the Real Estate Company (acting as a Dual Agent or as a Transaction Broker) could try to distance itself from legal liability.
- Could some special degree of liability be shifted to the individual realtor who was acting as the Designated Agent?
- Could a salesperson eventually find himself standing alone in the Court's docket facing legal and financial consequences?
(g) What incentive would a Realtor have

- to spend his after-tax Dollars on advertising or
- to hold an "Open House" or
- to even show the property

WHEN HE KNOWS IN ADVANCE
- that he has no opportunity to double-end his listing because
- he will have to turn over any potential Buyers to somebody else in his Company.

(9) TO SUMMARIZE:

The 3 most important ELEMENTS of correct conduct in a "Dual Agency" situation are:
(a) The **DISCLOSURE** of
- the limitations placed on the Realtor and
- the implications of a Dual Agency.

(b) The **IMPARTIALITY** of the Realtor in his dealings with the contracting parties (neutral and objective).

(c) The **informed CONSENT** of the parties to the Dual Agency Agreement.

(10) Case law involving "Dual Agency."

"LEE v. ROYAL PACIFIC REALTY CORP." B.C. Supreme Court, Date 2003-06-12, Docket No. C 995919
- Duty in contract and in tort not to disclose confidential information.
- A positive duty to disclose material changes.

"TASSY v. BORDERLESS INC." Ontario Superior Court of Justice, Date 2005-01-27, Docket 02-CV-238556SR
82 year old Realtor failed to explain "Agency" and "Dual Agency."

"TKACHUK v. MARTIN" B.C. Supreme Court Date 1997-07-15, Docket 96-2553
Damages for misrepresentation, negligence, breach of fiduciary duty of CARE, breach of contract:
- incorrect market evaluation: the listing price was too low.
- A Buyer bought Lot 2 for $ 35,000.00 and flipped it for $ 65,000.00.

"PAUL v. JUNG" B.C. Supreme Court, Date 1998-06-05, Docket 34289 The Realtor involved preferred to work as a "Buyer's Agent." At [64] "Limited Dual Agency" is discussed. At [65] the Court deals with the Agent's obligation to give written notice of the existence of a fundamental issue of conflict of interest.

"COLUMBUS v. MEHNER" Alaska Superior Court (USA law case) **deals with undisclosed dual agency.**

The Presentation Of Offers - Part I
"Presenting an offer like a Pro."

It has often been said that Realtors are in the "People Business." Therefore, it should come as no surprise that the presentation of an offer is or can be an extremely trying experience for everyone, including the Realtors. And yet, for the Realtor at least the presentation of an offer should be nothing more than routine business. Unfortunately it nevertheless becomes often "personal" (rejection) and/or a dramatic experience (stress).

Why? There are several reasons:

(I) **The PSYCHOLOGICAL CONCERNS** of the various parties.

(1) **The Sellers** may be nervous because they are concerned about what is in store for them.
   (a) Do they have to take the Buyers' offered low price?
   (b) If they make a counteroffer, will the Buyers accept it or will they walk away from the deal?
   (c) The Listing Salesperson may have mentioned that the Selling Salesperson "works ONLY for the Buyer" and that explanation was interpreted (misunderstood) by the Sellers as a "warning" against the other Realtor.
   (c) As a consequence of this "warning" the Sellers may be apprehensive that the Buyer's Agent
   - could be more experienced than their own Realtor and
   - that he may try something underhanded or
   - use high-pressure tactics.

(2) **The Listing Salesperson** doesn't know the Buyer's Agent and wonders how much cooperation there will be between them.
   (a) If the Listing Salesperson is fairly inexperienced or may have heard "something bad" about the Selling Salesperson then (justified or not) alarm bells may be going off in his head.
   (b) What sort of an offer is the Selling Salesperson going to bring? What are the chances of closing it?
   (c) How will his Sellers react to the offer? Has he prepared them enough to consider the offer?

(3) **The Selling Salesperson** knows that this is the moment of truth; if he is lucky and/or plays his cards right, then this will be the beginning of a process at the end of which the cash register will ring.
   His concerns are:
   (a) Personality-wise how difficult is the Seller going to be to deal with?

(b) How motivated is the Seller to accept an offer for less than his asking price?
(c) How much cooperation is he (the Selling Salesperson) going to get from the Listing Salesperson?
- Is the Listing Salesperson going to act as a confrontational "advocate" for the Seller?
- Is he going to be hostile or suspicious and make everybody's life sour?
- Or is he going to be cooperative and pleasantly helpful in closing the sale?

A lot of the worrisome PROBLEMS can be ELIMINATED if:

(a) Both Realtors
- conduct themselves in a professional manner
- and resist the temptation of "posturing" or
- acting in any kind of adversarial/confrontational way
- realize that the offer presentation is nothing "personal"
- cooperate towards the common goal of trying to "make the deal fly."

(b) If the Listing Salesperson has done good preliminary work:
- has he given the Sellers good service?
- Has he educated them about Market Value?
- Has he properly prepared them what to expect during the offer presentation and
- has he lessened the tension by explaining the non-threatening role of the Selling Salesperson?

(c) Because the Selling Salesperson is dealing with 2 or more potential strangers (namely the Sellers and the Listing Salesperson) **the Selling Salesperson should go out of his way to:**
- conduct himself with the utmost COURTESY at all times,
- use COMMON SENSE,
- act PROFESSIONALLY and
- **LISTEN** with his
  - **ears** (hearing the words),
  - **eyes** (observe BODY LANGUAGE),
  - **heart (interpret what is being said)** and with his
  - **INTELLECT to read between the lines what has NOT been said.**

(II) The following are a few COMMON SENSE THINGS to do BEFORE meeting with the Sellers:
(a) There is a lot at stake and you will have to be able to use all of your wits. In order for you to be able **to confront with confidence all eventualities,** you should be PHYSICALLY rested and MENTALLY fresh (have a "clear head").

(b) You should also realize that **the outcome of an offer presentation** depends to a certain extent on
- **How YOU conduct yourself** (see above) and on
- **YOUR control** of events and how **YOU will influence** these events as they unfold and take place.
- You should have a battle plan ready.
- **Rehearse beforehand in your mind** the various steps
  - of what will take place and
  - what you are going to say and do. **This includes preparing sound answers to overcome difficult objections.**

(c) **Leave yourself plenty of time to present the offer.**
- Don't over book yourself with other appointments immediately afterwards. The Sellers may think that
  - you are not willing to spend enough time with them or
  - that they are merely another "number" or "notch on the belt of your success."
- The Listing Salesperson could be frustrated: the Selling Salesperson
  - had presented the offer perfunctorily,
  - had made a hurried attempt at closing it
  - but unfortunately had to rush off to another appointment.
  - If only he would have been able to spend a little more time with the Sellers and him, then this offer could possibly have been closed.

(III) A few COMMON SENSE ITEMS to remember when MEETING with the Sellers.
(a) It is important to **arrive on time**.
- Preferably you should be there a few minutes ahead of the appointed time.
- By not being late you will avoid arriving on the owners' door step all sweaty and out of breath.
- For a few moments sit in your car and calm your nerves. It has been mentioned before: TOBACCO, ALCOHOL and CLIENTS don't mix.
  - In your car you sit in a confined space. Even if you puff out of your partially rolled down car window, the cigarette smoke will cling to and saturate your clothes. The sensitive nose of a non-smoker will find the tobacco stench as revoltingly offensive.
  - Even if you substitute expensive hootch for cheap plonk a furtive swig from the bottle will result in alcohol on your breath instead of creating fire in your belly; it will also dull your senses.
- **A few deep breaths of fresh air will**
  - pump extra oxygen into your system and
  - stop trembling hands and sweaty palms.

- To eliminate unwelcome interruptions,
  - turn off your cell phone and
  - switch your pager to mute.
- After you have composed yourself and while you are walking up to the house **resolve that you will NOT cut your commission** ... regardless of what happens.

(b) **MAKE THE OTHER AGENT YOUR ALLY.**
- You have to set the right tone starting with the first phone call, requesting to set up an appointment to present the offer.
- Let him know that you look forward to working with him.
- This is going to be a good experience for EVERYBODY.

(c) **Be CONSIDERATE of the Listing Salesperson.**
- Preferably both of you should first meet on the street and then go into the house together.
- Ask yourself how the Listing Salesperson will feel if he arrives and finds you sitting with his Clients at the kitchen table having the time of your life.
- Ask yourself how the Sellers are going to feel if you insist on coming in and they don't have their own Salesperson present. Are they going to feel comfortable with you, a stranger?
- What are you going to talk about?
- What will you say if they want to see the offer before their salesperson arrives?
- If the Listing Salesperson doesn't show up within say 15 minutes of the appointed time, then go up to the front door and ask the owners if they have heard from him yet.

This will let them know that:
- at least YOU have been there on time and
- at the same time you will find out if the Listing Salesperson is expected any time soon or if there is going to be a serious delay.
- If there is a considerable delay before his arrival (say 1 or 2 hours), you may consider accepting the owners' invitation to go into the house (especially on a cold, dark winter's night).
- By agreement with everybody you could also reschedule the appointment for a later time.

(d) **The first impression**

We have previously discussed the importance of the "first impression." One or more of the Sellers may have been present when you showed the house to your Buyers. But chances are that not ALL of the Sellers were present. You will enhance your chances of closing your offer if you make a professional, business-like but non-threatening impression.

(e) For strategic reasons suggest to sit around a table for the presentation of the offer
- so that you can show them the offer easily

- and in order to be able to write.
- Try to sit directly across from both Sellers (in such a way as to enable you to see both of them at the same time),
- with the other Realtor being on your left or right side.

(f) **Breaking the ice.**
Small talk can take place while everybody is in the process of sitting down and getting comfortable around a table. This phase shouldn't be more than 5 minutes (10 minutes maximum); if you spend too much time on small talk, then the Sellers will
- become impatient,
- you may loose their undivided attention
- and maybe even their goodwill (they may become annoyed with you for wasting time).

(g) **Get down to business!** As soon as you have created **a relaxed and comfortable atmosphere** present the offer quickly and gently.

(h) **A few sincere words** about anything POSITIVE you can think of:
- Compliment the Sellers that their lovely home was available for showing on short notice.
- In a general way what may have motivated the Buyers to make the offer (cleanliness, updating etc.)

(i) **Humanizing the Buyers** means telling the Sellers in a few short words who the Buyers are and how familiar they are with the market. (e.g. the Buyers are John and Mary "X" and they have 2 children, a boy 10 and a girl 7; he works at … and she is a part-time …They have been pre-qualified by their bank for the new mortgage).

All of the above will set the stage for the formalities to commence.

(j) **At this crucial stage** the following COUNTERPRODUCTIVE THINGS SHOULD BE AVOIDED:
Don't beat around the bush for hours building your case by
- lecturing on the life history of the Buyers' family or
- lamenting about the economy, taxes, the real estate market, the competition, the hot/cold weather or minor details in the offer (what stays and what doesn't) etc.
- Don't antagonize the Sellers and Listing Salesperson by sitting there and clutching the offer in your cramped fists while READING aloud the offer to them. (Actually you may be droning on in a monotonous voice).
  - They may resent having to sit there in silent frustration like school children.
  - Their minds may begin to wander.
  - **Has it occurred to you that the Sellers and the other Realtor are also capable of reading?**

A BETTER STRATEGY is:

- **for the Selling Salesperson to give to EVERYBODY a copy of the offer;** the reason for this is that everybody should be able to go over it together (simultaneously). (Photocopies can easily be made beforehand at the office).
- The original can be given either to the Listing Salesperson or to the Sellers.
- If the Listing Salesperson wants a few minutes to peruse the offer, then keep quiet while EVERYBODY is reading.
- If you give a copy of the offer ONLY to the Listing Salesperson and he is reading it quietly then
    - YOU will be sitting there impatiently and
    - the SELLERS will be wondering what it is all about.
- Both Realtors should realize that
    - **the Sellers are the STARS of this show. They are the most important persons sitting there simply because of the fact that they own the house.**
    - The Realtors are merely supporting cast members.
    - What is of prime interest to the Sellers?
        - The PRICE.
        - Actually it is not so much the PRICE itself,
        - but the NET EQUITY or rather
        - the **NET SALE PROCEEDS** (which is the sum of money which the Seller gets into his hands after the dust has settled, that is after deduction of the existing mortgages, the commission etc.).

(IV) **In the heat of the battle.**
(a) For the Selling Salesperson it is nearly impossible to predict what the Sellers will take, because:
- a lot depends on the **Sellers' MOTIVATION TO SELL.**
- A lot depends on how much money the Seller ends up with (his net sales proceeds).
- A lot also depends on how good a job the Listing Salesperson has done in preparing the Sellers what to expect: offers v. listing price, what the realistic Market Value of the property is etc.

(b) The following are **COMMON OBSTACLES TO AN ACCEPTANCE:**
- the difference of OPINIONS and EMOTIONS between the Sellers and Buyers.
- The price and terms (which the Buyer is able and willing to offer and the Seller is able and willing to accept).
- Possession dates and
- what "stays" with the house (included at no extra charge in the Selling Price).

(c) **Other PSYCHOLOGICAL THINGS TO BE CONSIDERED at this stage are:**
- **NEVER APOLOGIZE for the offer which you are bringing.** If the offer is

so horribly low-ball that you are ashamed then you shouldn't have written it up in the first place. Apologizing for an offer is not only unprofessional, but it may also be a breach of your fiduciary duties to your client, the Buyer.
You may also appear to the others present as a defeatist.
- Don't jump the gun and assume that the Seller will not like the offer. Only the OWNERS make that DECISION and NOT you.
- Therefore let the Seller tell you how he feels about the offer. Give him an opportunity to get things off his chest.
- As long as he is commenting and complaining about various items in the offer, it means that he is still interested in making a deal.

(d) **Shut up and let the Sellers THINK.**
Quit talking because a torrent of your words will
- prevent the owners from thinking constructively
- create the impression that you are
- anxious or
- lack confidence or
- that you are high pressuring.

(e) **You are in trouble only** when the Sellers quit talking, say nothing further and just sit there in stone faced silence and/or with a grim, disapproving look.

The Presentation Of Offers - Part II

"How to BECOME a MASTER NEGOTIATOR."

(I) In order to NEGOTIATE like a Pro you must know that:
- Every transaction is unique and negotiations can sometimes become complex.
- Good negotiation skills are people skills.

  (a) A MASTER NEGOTIATOR will have **learned to SENSE**
- when to speak,
- what to ask and
- when to back off tactfully.

  (b) **He will let the Clients talk;** he will let them vent their objections all of which HE may have heard many times before; but HE understands that **for the CLIENTS it is the first time around**.

  (c) **So simply sit back and listen,** because what is going on is important for THEM as well as YOU. Be sure that you also create an impression of being interested:
- Take notes, but don't argue.
- If asked a question answer it briefly and be concise.
- Point out again the positive items in your offer.
- The Clients need reassurance that they are doing the right thing.

  (d) **It is essential to determine:**
- what is a "must" for the Clients
- what is important
- what is negotiable
- and what is of little importance.

  (e) **Resist the temptation** of ridiculing or belittling something. It may turn out to be counter productive.

  (f) A Master Negotiator understands that the negotiating tactics of Sellers sometimes involve **"STALLING"** which **is a decision NOT to make a decision.**

  (g) It is good to remind the Clients that **meeting the other party halfway** is
- easier to accomplish and
- in addition it will probably be more productive in the long run.

(II) **What takes place during the bargaining process?**

(1) **Everybody WANTS to be a winner** in the bargaining process. In real life there is usually some bluffing, some give-and-take and chances are that neither party will get everything they want.

(2) **Everybody SHOULD be a winner if:** the Realtors involved in the transaction
- act like professionals and use common sense.
- Are courteous, observe their fiduciary duties

- and make sure that there are no "loose ends."
(3) **Everybody WILL be a winner when:**
  - the Sellers manage to sell their house,
  - the Buyers succeed in buying a roof over their heads
  - and the Realtors will have earned their commission.

(III) ACCEPTANCE AND TERMINOLOGY.
(1)
- In case of an ACCEPTANCE all parties to the contract are legally bound to perform the terms of the contract.
- **Acceptance should be communicated IMMEDIATELY** to the other party
- for **legal** reasons and
- for **psychological** reasons (the Clients are anxious to hear about the outcome).

(2)
- In contract law the OFFEROR is the person or party who is making the offer. By signing the offer this party indicates that it is willing to enter into a legal relationship. Customarily the OFFEROR is a Buyer.
- The OFFEREE is the person or party to whom the offer is made to. This is customarily the Seller who will be bound to the offer by his acceptance thereof.

(IV) The COUNTER OFFER.
(a) A counter offer should be the last resort AFTER all possibilities of closing the initial offer have been exhausted.

(b) The Listing Broker may explain to his Sellers that the first offer is often the BEST offer which the Sellers may get. After refusing a good initial offer and subsequently wasting precious time, many an owner ended up accepting a lower price at a later date.

(c) Before making a counter-offer the Client should carefully weigh the pros and cons and the risks.
It should be explained to the Sellers TACTFULLY that the Buyer has the option of walking away from a counter offer. When making a counter-offer all previous bets are off and the parties are back to square one in the negotiation process.

(e) **Any "cautioning" about turning down an offer** should be done
  - in an intelligent way and
  - in a non-threatening manner.

The following is A SUMMARY of points which you could use to dissuade a Seller from making a Counter Offer:

- These Buyers are serious Clients and
- they have not rushed lightly into making this offer.
- They have been pre-approved for their new financing.
- They have looked around a lot and
- are thoroughly familiar with what is available on the market.
- The Buyers also like another house and it was a toss-up on which property they

would make an offer first.
- The reason why they have made an offer on your house is ….
- No doubt, your Realtor has already discussed with you the Market Value of your property and the current market conditions for this area.
- When making a counter offer all previous bets are off and the parties are back to square one in the negotiation process.
- Before making a counter offer you may wish to carefully weigh the pros and cons and be prepared to accept the consequences if the other party decides to walk away from the deal.
- As I am not totally sure what my Buyers will do if you make a counter offer, I would respectfully suggest to you not to take any chances and to give the offer in front of you your serious consideration.
- If you accept the offer on the table in front of you, then your house is sold. Is it worth your while to gamble with a counter offer?
- If you accept this offer then you will not have to have any more Open Houses and showings.
- If you accept this offer then you will be able to go on with your plans, e.g. finding another house.

(V) **Two or more simultaneous COUNTER OFFERS.**

It is not recommended to let the Seller make 2 or more counter offers SIMULTANEOUSLY. Especially vulnerable to making mistakes are unseasoned Realtors. The risk of selling one house at the same time to several different Buyers is simply too great. Misunderstandings and errors can easily happen.

Only very experienced Realtors may consider to attempt making simultaneous counter offers, but only
- under some unusual circumstances and/or
- for very important and/or unavoidable reasons.
- **Even then it is strongly recommended that the Clients should be urged to obtain proper legal advice BEFORE they sign anything.**

HOW IT COULD BE ATTEMPTED.
(a) Each Counter Offer should be separately and distinctively enumerated at the top of the Contract for Purchase and Sale; e.g. Counter Offer # 1, Counter Offer # 2 etc.
(b) Also there MUST be a specific clause in the contract that
- "the Sellers' acceptance of Counter Offer # 2 is subject to the collapse of the prior Counter Offer # 1 to (name of Buyer # 1) by (time and date when the acceptance of Counter Offer # 1 is open till)."
- Also it MUST be specifically mentioned that the Seller will and can no longer be obligated in any way to Buyer # 1 ("cease to have any legal obligations under Counter Offer # 1").

(c) A sufficient time period must be allowed for Counter Offer #2 to be accepted AFTER the time period when Counter Offer #1 had elapsed.

(d) It should be made clear that Counter Offer # 2 will become automatically null and void should there be "unqualified acceptance" of Counter Offer # 1. Provided he doesn't mind waiting to see if Deal # 1 does complete, Buyer # 2 may or may not decide at a later time to make a new offer as a "back-up offer."
(e) It should also be fully understood (by everybody) that Buyer # 1 who receives Counter Offer # 1 can
- only make an "unqualified acceptance" (if there is "unqualified acceptance" on Counter Offer # 2).
- If Buyer # 1 wants to counter (change something) in the Counter Offer # 1 and there is "unqualified acceptance" on Counter Offer # 2 then Buyer # 1's counter-counter offer comes AFTER the accepted Counter Offer # 2.

(VI) THERE SHOULD BE "NO LOOSE ENDS."

"BUBURUZ v. CREIGHTON et al" Docket # 01/4236 and **"CHUNG v. CREIGHTON et al,"** Docket S070960, B.C. Supreme Court, Date 2003-02-27. In these 2 confusing and most likely expensive law suits 2 separate Buyers competed for a waterfront property in Crescent Beach, B.C.

In case # 1, one of the Sellers accepted the offer in writing, the other one verbally. Then they purportedly attempted to revoke the written acceptance, possibly because the wife of Buyer # 2 had made a no-subject offer 2 days later and had assigned the Contract to her husband. Caveats were filed against the property, Buyer # 1 sued in Victoria, Buyer # 2 in the New Westminster Registry. Everybody sued for specific performance, damages for breach of contract and the Realtors were third-partied. The Judge ruled that the 2 law suits could NOT be heard together: the Buburuz action must proceed to trial ahead of the Chung action.

Some of the lessons which can be learned from the above are that **at ALL times it is very IMPORTANT**
(a) Not to take any "short cuts."
(b) Everything should be spelled out clearly in the Contract of Purchase and Sale,
(c) Everybody must understand and know "what" is expected of him and "when."
(d) Verbal acceptance and/or verbal Counter Offers or
Vague verbal additional promises or
Imprecise and/or evasive "solutions" to UNSOLVED PROBLEMS ARE ALL SURE-FIRE WAYS to ending up in Court.
- To re-open some or all negotiations at a future date will result in
    - either further whittling and Nickel-and-Diming
    - which in turn can lead to more or less undisguised threats of non-completion by one or the other of the parties if they don't get their way.

(VII) The actual PROCEDURE of presenting offers.

FOR YOUR OWN PROTECTION:

It is very important that you should familiarize yourself with your local Real Estate Board's rules regarding the presentation of offers. Many of these are simply a matter of courtesy and common sense; e.g.
- There should be no undue delay in the presentation of an offer. If a Listing Salesperson receives a message from another Realtor that he has an offer to present on one of his listings then
  - the call should be returned promptly.
  - An appointment to present the offer should be made with the Sellers at their earliest convenience.
- **If the Listing Salesperson is for some reason unable or not available to present the offer, then a substitute must be appointed.** This can be either another salesperson from the same office or the Manager.
- The presentation of an offer should not be unduly delayed in anticipation of receiving other not yet written future offers. E.g. A Selling Salesperson notifies the Listing Salesperson on a Friday that he would like to present a written offer.

The Listing Salesperson says: "I have an ad in the paper and have an Open House scheduled for Sunday. I hope to receive an offer from somebody who may come to my "OPEN." We will present all offers on Monday evening." The Reader may decide if the Listing Salesperson is putting his own interests ahead of those of his Clients. (Breach of the fiduciary duty of LOYALTY).

In the above case, the Seller should see this offer right away. Technically speaking it is then his decision to deal with the offer on the spot or to wait till after the weekend. Provided, of course, that the Buyer is willing to wait till Monday evening for an answer.
- ALL offers must be presented to the Sellers for their consideration. The Listing Salesperson cannot make any unilateral decisions to accept or reject an offer.
- A Salesperson can be sued by his Clients
  - for blindly following "previously received instructions" and
  - based on such previous instructions to subsequently
    - discourage other Realtors from writing an allegedly inferior offer or
    - for refusing to present certain offers.
  E.g. The owners may have told their Realtor: "We don't want to see any offers under $ 200,000." The Listing Salesperson should realize that the owner's circumstances could change after some time and that at a later date he may very well entertain an offer under $ 200,000.

MULTIPLE OFFERS.

Real Estate Boards usually have specific rules and recommended procedures how to present Multiple Offers and the Reader is encouraged to familiarize himself with them.

Again it is a matter of courtesy and common sense:
(a) The presentation of all offers takes place simultaneously at a time and place agreeable to everybody (the Sellers and all Realtors).
   - If one of the Realtors is unable to attend, then he must find a substitute for himself.
   - It is not a good idea for a Selling Salesperson to just hand over his Buyer's offer to the Listing Salesperson for presentation because:
      - The offer given to him by the other Realtor may create (for the Listing Salesperson) a conflict of interest.
      The Listing Salesperson may have an offer of his own; armed with the knowledge of what the other offer is, he can improve or enhance his own offer (e.g. by persuading his own Buyer to offer a higher price).
      - The L.S. knows most likely nothing about the other Realtor's Buyers (qualification, motivation to buy).
(b) All offers must be presented in chronological order in which the Listing Salesperson has received notice of the individual offers.
(c) The Sellers will not make a decision until such time when they have seen all offers.
(d) **Each Selling Salesperson must have a fair opportunity to present his offer to the Seller**
   - in the presence of the Listing Salesperson
   - but without having any of the other competing Selling Salespersons present during that time.
(e) After presenting his offer, the individual Selling Salesperson will withdraw and await the Sellers' decision in a neutral place. (E.g. downstairs in the recreation room, outside in his car etc.)
(f) If the Listing Salesperson has an offer of his own, he cannot favour (and "improve") his own offer unfairly over those from other Realtors (e.g. by secretly offering the Seller an inducement in the form of a furtive cut of his commission).

Unethical argument:
"Mr. and Mrs. Seller. If you will accept my offer over everybody else's, then I will kick back to you $ 2,000.00 from my selling commission. I am not greedy. By accepting my offer with the commission cut both of us will win. You will have your house sold and I will still end up with more money than on a sale where you would accept an offer from one of the other guys. But let's keep our private arrangement confidential. The other guys do not need to know about it."

(g) After all offers have been presented, the Sellers will discuss with the Listing

Salesperson each individual offer — all at the same time.
(h) At this stage all offers compete only on the basis of price, terms, conditions etc. The sequence in which individual offers had been received is no longer of importance.
(i) The Sellers will select the most appealing offer and either accept it or make a counter offer.
(j) After the Sellers have made their decision, the Listing Salesperson should
- thank each attending Realtor for his interest and effort
- and return all rejected offers to the individual Realtors.
- He cannot disclose what the property sold for.
- The customary procedure is to discuss with the Realtor whose offer was successful, some of the finalizing details: access for the appraiser, subject removals etc.

(VIII) "THOU SHALT NOT CUT THY COMMISSION."

The real estate commission is paid:

(1) **For the WORK DONE by the Realtor.** Regardless of what the AMOUNT of work is or how quickly the property was sold, the Seller had contracted that he will either pay
- a certain percentage (of the Selling Price) or
- a predetermined lump sum

  as commission to the Realtor for successfully effecting a SALE.
(2) **For The Realtor's:**
- years of accumulated experience,
- knowledge of the current real estate market,
- appraisal ability,
- marketing efforts (which include reimbursement of advertising and promotional expenses, car repairs, gas, insurance, licensing fees etc.) and
- his investment of time.
- Tenacious negotiations,
- skilful performance (this includes connections with Lending Institutions, appraisers, surveyors and lawyers)

To cut the real estate commission is often:
- unnecessary,
- a result of bad work habits,
- a result of poor closing techniques,
- due to a lack of confidence in one's abilities,
- accompanied by the Client's loss of respect for the Realtor.

Cutting the commission is always unprofessional.

Thoughtless Clients (e.g. the Sellers from Hell) should be made tactfully aware that chiselling on the commission and cutting somebody's earnings

- tends to discourage a person from making his best efforts.
- It also festers doubt and promotes suspicion and resentment.

When is it time for "STRATEGIC SILENCE?"
When the situation arises that the Sellers and Buyers are a few hundred or even thousand Dollars apart and nobody wants to move any more on the price.
Then it is like playing poker. The first person who speaks up and/or caves in ... looses.

Most of the time it is NOT true that "half a loaf of bread is better than nothing."
The only possible exception may be the presentation of an offer
- during the dying hours of the last day of the listing and
- you are positive that there is absolutely no chance that the Sellers are going to extend your listing.
- Under these circumstances you may decide to rescue whatever portion of the commission you can. If you don't then you may find that the Buyers and Sellers will eventually get together and do the transaction without you and without the commission.

All of the time it is true that the real estate commission is a BARGAIN.

The Presentation Of Offers - Part III

Reasons why a Selling Salesperson should be able to present his own offer to the Seller.

(1) Occasionally some Realtors misunderstand the "personal representation" aspect of agency. Under a mistaken notion of "advocacy" they act in a deplorably confrontational manner and place uncalled for stumbling blocks in the way of the Selling Broker and consequently make a sale difficult.

(2) "Agency" is also misused occasionally. For example when the Listing Salesperson tells the Selling Salesperson: "The Seller doesn't want to meet with you because YOU are working for the Buyer. Just FAX your offer over to me and I will present it to the Seller."

As the public is not familiar with "agency," this sort of idea most likely originates from a Listing Salesperson who wants to be in total control.

(a) In the By-Laws of Real Estate Boards there is usually a section which says that a member should not speak ill of his competition. Whereas there is nothing wrong with disclosing that the Selling Broker works for the Buyer one is left to wonder why it would be necessary to "demonize" a fellow Realtor to the extent that the Seller is apprehensive to meet with the Selling Salesperson.

(b) There is another problem: who is to know if the Seller really and actually refused to meet with the Selling Salesperson. Who is to know if this is nothing more than a barefaced lie by the Listing Salesperson who merely wants to have a free hand while simultaneously ingratiating himself with his Client? One way of finding out would be to ask for a written note from the Seller confirming that he indeed doesn't wish to see the Selling Salesperson.

(c) Regrettably it gets worse!
- This faxing-the-offer request forces the Selling Broker to abrogate his right to present his own offer (which is outlined in the Real Estate Boards' aforementioned By-laws).
- One fine day an intrepid lawyer may suggest in Court that the Selling Salesperson's acquiescence to the "just-fax-the-offer" request may be an (albeit involuntary) breach of the Buyer's Agent's fiduciary duty to his client: to wit that
- the Selling Realtor didn't make his best effort of rendering "personal representation" when presenting his Client's offer.
- By faxing the offer he took the easy way out
- and this action was tantamount to quitting in the home stretch.

(d) The practice of "just faxing the offer to the Listing Broker" is further **eminently UNFAIR to**
- **a Buyer's Agent and to his BUYER.**

The Listing Broker now knows what the Buyer's Agent's offer is; should the Listing Salesperson have an offer of his own, then this information will enable him to make sure that his own Buyer's offer is more attractive to the Seller
- by either getting a slightly higher price or
- by cutting his commission.

As a consequence of this advance knowledge there can be no "level playing field" between the 2 Realtors because the Selling Broker in turn is not given an opportunity to improve his offer.

- **The SELLERS are deprived of the benefit of receiving the Selling Broker's input. The SELLERS WILL NEVER KNOW what sort of FINAL SELLING PRICE could have been achieved.** The Seller is reduced to simply having to choose between the 2 offers in front of him:
- namely the faxed offer from the absent Buyer's Agent
- and the Listing Salesperson's offer.
- **The LISTING SALESPERSON may be in breach of his Fiduciary Duty of Care to his Clients (the Sellers)** because the Sellers have thus been deprived of the opportunity of maximizing their Selling Price. Of course the average consumer isn't aware of all of this. Possibly many a Realtor isn't either.

Alternatively some Realtors simply don't care and are just concerned with wanting to double-end the sale. Such a Listing Realtor is putting **his own selfish interests over and above those of his Client: and that is called a breach of the Realtor's Fiduciary Obligation of Loyalty.**

(3) The practice of having the offer FAXED is also shortsighted on the part of the Listing Salesperson. Actually it is to the Listing Salesperson's ADVANTAGE to let the Buyer's Agent be physically present during the offer presentation.
   (a) **The Buyer's Agent can "humanize the Buyer";** because of his first-hand knowledge he can assure the Seller that
   - the Buyer is serious (he has looked around, knows the market and has decided on making an offer).
   - The Buyer is qualified (preapproved for the mortgage).
   - It may also be easier, more expedient and psychologically important to let the Selling Salesperson draft any counter offer. When the Buyer sees the counter offer he will recognize his Agent's handwriting; consequently he will be more comfortable knowing that HIS Agent had made his BEST EFFORTS on HIS behalf by bringing back a counter offer with the lowest possible price and best available terms. **This will increase the chances of closing such a counter offer.**
   (b) The following will make it MORE DIFFICULT to close a counter offer:
   - If the counter offer is just faxed back to the Selling Salesperson and
   - the changes appear in somebody else's handwriting

- and the document is a deteriorating (hard to read) FAX copy instead of being an original document with original changes, then
- the Buyer will realize that HIS Agent wasn't there when HIS offer was presented. In fact his offer was at the whim of strangers (the Seller and Listing Salesperson who was working for the Seller). There was nobody there to speak up and fight for him, the Buyer. (Advocacy, personal representation).
- Having been absent from the proceedings, the Buyer's Agent will be of little practical help: he has no first hand knowledge or background information for some of the reasons of the counter offer.

(c) During the offer presentation the Listing Salesperson can tactfully ask the Buyer's Agent how the Buyer arrived at his offered price. If the Buyer's Agent is worth his salt (meaning experienced enough) then he will produce an up-to-date market analysis (which he had originally prepared for the benefit of his Buyer). **The Seller will then hear from somebody else (other than from his own Realtor) that his house is overpriced.** Believe it or not, but that carries often a lot of weight!

(d) **The Listing Salesperson together with his Sellers should then peruse carefully the Market Analysis;** by discussing it in detail with his Clients the chances of the Listing Salesperson being able
- to close the offer will increase
- or else he will get a realistic counter offer and
- if everything else fails, he will be able to reduce the Listing Price later on.

(e) The Sellers will probably think that their Realtor is not only conscientious but also concerned about their welfare.

In the end the Listing Salesperson will come out smelling like roses while the Selling Salesperson will be the "bad guy" (because he is the last and therefore the best remembered bearer of the bad news that the asking price was too high). Just like the "good cop v. bad cop" routine in the movies.

(f) **To summarize:** as a consequence of the judicious use of the Selling Salesperson the property will
- either be sold
- or else the Sellers will be more receptive for a price reduction (counter offer, Listing Price reduction) and
- in the end EVERYBODY will be a winner.

The Perils Of Revoking A Counter-offer

"Revocation" and its consequences can be dry legal topics peppered with technicalities. In order to make the subject matter more meaningful an effort has been made to deal with it in a concise and practical manner.

The long-suffering Salesperson who will most likely find himself in the epicentre of an emotional turmoil (generated by the intricacies of a revocation)
- **must learn how to protect his health** and
- he must also **educate himself how to avoid mistakes** in the legal quicksand which will surround him.

Both "Offers" and "counter offers" can be revoked.

(I)
Incredibly enough a BUYER sometimes changes his mind and withdraws his offer PRIOR to its acceptance by the Seller. As there is no contract, not much can happen "legally."

- **The SELLER and the Listing Salesperson** no doubt will be
  - surprised about the Buyer's last minute change of heart,
  - perhaps even somewhat annoyed about the inconvenience and
  - occasionally maybe even be disappointed.

  UNDER THE CIRCUMSTANCES they should be grateful that a shaky Buyer didn't waste any more of their time.

- **DAMAGE CONTROL for the BUYER'S AGENT:**
(1) PRACTICAL CONSIDERATIONS.
The Realtor should quickly find out why the Buyer is vacillating. What has changed his mind during the relatively short time period between the signing of the offer and its attempted presentation?
  - (a) **Problems which can be solved:**
    - Has the Realtor addressed all of the Buyers' concerns?
    - Did the Buyer see or hear about another house which could be of interest to him?
    - Did the Buyer hear something "bad" about the property after talking to a neighbour?
    - **"Buyer's Remorse."** This is an irrational emotional reaction which some Buyers suddenly have because they think that they may have acted hastily.
  - (b) **Problems which cannot be solved:**
    - The sudden loss of employment,
    - an unexpected job transfer.

- The onset of sudden illness or an injury (car accident).
- A serious change in the fabric of the family.

(2) To protect the Realtor's MENTAL HEALTH:
   (a) Most likely the Selling Salesperson will be embarrassed and frustrated. After having done a lot of work he is now back to square one. It is normal to feel that way.
   (b) • WARNING: A lot of accumulated and unresolved frustration can cause illness (ulcers, headaches).
       • It is preferable to dispose of frustrations discretely (in private and not to or in front of others at the office).
   (c) The Realtor may wish to reevaluate the Buyer:
       • **Is the Buyer sufficiently motivated** and in a position **to buy in the near future?**
       • Is it worth while to start again the arduous process of showing houses to somebody who is nearly impossible to please and a time waster?
         In the long run, is it preferable to cut one's losses and drop the "lookeeloo?"

(II) **When the SELLER is revoking HIS counter offer.**
REVOCATION becomes more complicated when the OFFEROR is the SELLER.

(1) **The Seller (offeror) can revoke his counter offer at any**
   • time PRIOR to the acceptance (of the counter offer) by the Buyer (offeree)
   • **PROVIDED that the revocation has been communicated to the Offeree (Buyer) PRIOR to acceptance.**

(2) Revocation can be given to
   • the BUYER or
   • the Buyer's AGENT.
   The Agent is "more than a mere messenger boy and the scope of his authority extends to the receipt of notice" on behalf of the Buyer. See **"B. Zar Enterprises Corporation v. Hitchen"** [1982], 34 B.C.L.R. 87 (BCSC) and similarly **"Lloyd v. Howard"** [1942] 3 D.L.R. 443 Ontario High Court.

(3) **Revocation can be given either VERBALLY or IN WRITING.**
   (a) **VERBAL revocation** can be given personally to the Buyer's Agent. **It is too risky and probably NOT ENOUGH to just leave a message on the Buyer's Agent's**
       • voice mail or
       • his answering machine at his home or
       • with the answering service at his office.
   (b) **WRITTEN revocation.**
       To protect the Sellers and the Listing Broker from getting involved in a messy law suit, it is important to be able **to PROVE that the revocation was effective. Revocation is best achieved IN WRITING by means of "BEYOND-DISPUTE-DOCUMENTATION."**

- By FAX (the FAX will show the time and date sent) or
- By hand-delivery of the revocation document to the Buyer's Agent himself.
- If it is not possible to meet with him and the Listing Salesperson has to leave the revocation with the receptionist at the Buyer's Agent's office, then a "receipt" (showing time and date of delivery) should be obtained which acknowledges that an urgent (time sensitive) and important document has been delivered for Buyer "A"s Agent.

- For ADDITIONAL PROTECTION the Listing Salesperson should endeavour to obtain (through the Buyer's Agent) **the Buyers' WRITTEN CONFIRMATION that the revocation has been successfully communicated.** To obtain such a document will depend on the goodwill and cooperation of Buyer "A" and his Agent. In case of resistance the Listing Salesperson should explain that
  - a lot is at stake and therefore all "T"s should be crossed and all "i" should be dotted.
  - Alternatively, people who fail to create a proper paper trail because they are either sloppy or in a rush may have an occasion to repent at their leisure later on in Court.
  - If there is still no positive response, then the Listing Salesperson should enter into his work diary detailed notations describing his efforts in this respect.

(4) **The revocation is valid, if**
- the intention to revoke is clear and
- if notice of revocation is given (to the Buyer) BEFORE the Buyer's acceptance of the counter offer is communicated to the Sellers. See **"Hahn v. Hanson"** B.C. Supreme Court, Docket 940710, Date 1994-06-01 (there was no contract between the parties because the Seller was not given notice of the Buyer's acceptance of the counter offer).

Revocations of Sellers' counter offers happen in times when the real estate market becomes superheated and prices escalate rapidly in a "Seller's Market." Listing Salespersons will phone the Selling Salesperson and before the hapless Realtor at the other end of the line can even grunt "hello," the Listing Salesperson trumpets into the phone: "My Sellers herewith revoke their counter offer." Occasionally a Buyer may claim to have accepted the Sellers' counter offer prior to receiving the revocation. In that case a displeased Seller may decide to avail himself of the services of a lawyer.

(5) **There is one EXCEPTION to revocation:**
If the Seller is willing to BIND himself to keep his counter offer open for acceptance for a certain period of time
- by a **separate SPECIFIC contract**
- with an **ADDITIONAL** (token) **CONSIDERATION** which is given by the Buyer to the Seller specifically for **keeping the counter offer "OPEN FOR ACCEPTANCE for a certain period of time."**

This can be achieved by inserting into the Contract of Purchase and Sale a suitably worded clause. E.g.: "The Buyer herewith pays $ 25.00 to the Seller AS CONSIDERATION for the Seller keeping his counter offer open for acceptance until (time), (date)."

This clause may be used in the sale of
- subdivision land or
- commercial and industrial properties.
- "Unique" residential properties: waterfront homes, expensive mansions, the sale of an island etc.

Lawyers are often involved in the drafting of these type of contracts.

(III) The following scenario describes

HOW A REVOCATION CAN GO WRONG.

(1) The Seller receives an offer from Buyer "A" on Monday evening;
(2) The Seller does not accept the offer but makes a counter offer which is left open for the Buyer's acceptance until Thursday noon.
(3) On Tuesday evening the Seller receives another and better offer from Buyer "B."
(4) Of course, the Seller immediately wants to
- accept the (higher priced) offer from Buyer "B" and to
- discontinue all dealings with Buyer "A."
(5) **To achieve this, the Seller must successfully revoke his counter offer to Buyer "A."**
(6) The Listing Salesperson attempts to revoke his Seller's counter offer by phoning the Agent for Buyer "A." For some reason Buyer "A"s Agent does not respond to repeated pages. As the Listing Salesperson is unable to talk to him in person, he leaves messages revoking the counter offer
- on Buyer "A"s Agent's answering machine at his home and
- with the answering service at the Buyer "A"s Agent's office.
(7) On the strength of these efforts (repeated pages plus 2 phone messages) the Listing Salesperson then
- advises the Seller that the counter offer has been revoked and
- that the Seller can now accept "unconditionally" the offer from Buyer "B."
- **The Listing Salesperson has just made A SERIOUS MISTAKE!**
(8) Shortly after the Seller had accepted the 2nd offer, the Listing Salesperson receives a phone call from the Agent of Buyer "A" advising him that
- Buyer "A" had accepted the Seller's counter offer.
- When the Listing Salesperson enquires why he hadn't phoned back following the repeated pages and phone messages, Buyer "A"s Agent claims
  - that he didn't get the Listing Salesperson's pages and messages
  - and that he had not been at home to check his answering machine.
- Consequently he was not aware of the attempted (verbal) revocation.

(NOTE: Occasionally it is possible that an Answering Service runs behind in the processing and paging out of messages. Reasons for this can be the sudden onset of a high volume of incoming calls combined with a shortage of staff).

(9) At this stage the Seller has sold his house to 2 different Buyers. In the ensuing orgy of litigation the Listing Salesperson will play a prominent role in several law suits.

(10) Both Buyers immediately sue the Seller and the Listing Broker. In due course 4 law firms will become involved.
(Lawyers for Buyers "A" and "B," the Seller and the Listing Salesperson).

(11) On the strength of selling his house, the Seller had made an offer to buy a new house under construction. This has the potential of additional damages.

(12) Eventually one of the Buyers is bought off and the other Buyer completes.

(13) The Seller arranges for bridge financing and is thus able to complete his new house purchase.

(14) Settlement costs and legal fees are considerable.

(IV) HOW COULD THIS SITUATION HAVE BEEN AVOIDED?

(1) The BEST WAY to avoid this problem would have been to **persuade the Sellers NOT to sign anything** (namely NOT to formally accept [in writing] the offer from Buyer "B") **UNTIL such time when**
   (a) revocation has been successfully communicated to Buyer "A" by means of "BEYOND-DISPUTE-DOCUMENTATION IN WRITING"
   (b) AND **Buyer "A" had confirmed in writing** that he had received the revocation in a timely fashion.

(2) If the Listing Salesperson is NOT able to convince his Sellers of the wisdom of delaying their acceptance of Buyer "B"s offer, then the Listing Salesperson **must insert a clause** into the Contract of Purchase and Sale, saying that **"the Sellers' acceptance of Buyer "B"s offer is 'subject-to' the Sellers receiving written confirmation from Buyer "A" that the revocation had been successfully achieved and that all legal ties with Buyer "A" have been severed."**

(3) A relatively simple alternative solution is, **NOT to hold counter offers open for a long period of time.** Whereas the Buyer should be given a reasonable period of time to make a decision, there is no reason to tie up a house (and to effectively take it off the market) for several days.

(V) During the revocation process, the Listing Salesperson will encounter the following **practical and psychological pressures:**

(1) (a) **The SELLERS** wish to discontinue quickly all dealings with the (previous) Buyer "A."
   (b) For obvious reasons they are eager to accept the better offer from Buyer "B."
   (c) The Sellers may be under pressure to sell (e.g. job transfer and the husband has to leave town shortly). If asked to wait with their acceptance of the better offer they may find it emotionally difficult to deal with the delay.
   (d) **It is important that the Listing Salesperson**

- appreciates the emotional state his Sellers are in (e.g. why they may be impatient).
- **Suitable counter measures to resolve problems are:**
  - proper COMMUNICATION and
  - a detailed EXPLANATION of what has to take place
  - and a candid discussion of the possible CONSEQUENCES should something go wrong.

(e) Reasonable Clients will then understand and appreciate what the Listing Salesperson is trying to do for them. The pressure should be off.

(2) **If Buyer "A" (LOWER offer) has his own Realtor and Buyer "B" (HIGHER offer) has his own Realtor:**

(a) Buyer "B" and his Realtor must be informed that there is a counter-offer in place to a previous Buyer "A." No details of the original offer or the counter offer can be revealed.

(b) Buyer "B"'s Realtor may exert a certain amount of pressure on the Listing Salesperson
- to obtain "some sort of commitment" from the Seller that he will accept Buyer "B"'s offer and
- to effect a speedy resolution of the situation with Buyer "A."

(c) The Listing Salesperson must obtain Buyer "A"'s Agent's full cooperation in order to achieve the successful revocation of the counter offer.

(3) **If Buyer "A" (LOWER offer) is dealing with another Broker and Buyer "B" (HIGHER offer) has made his offer through the Listing Salesperson.**

(a) Because of the potential of "double-ending" (not having to share the commission with another Realtor) the Listing Salesperson has a powerful personal financial incentive to successfully revoke the counter offer to Buyer "A."

(b) Such revocation must proceed in the normal fashion.

(c) Under no circumstances should this tempt the Listing Salesperson to cut corners and/or not to act scrupulously correct and ethical with ALL parties. (E.g. Buyer "B" cannot be told what Buyer "A"'s offer was, nor details about the counter offer).

(d) As far as Buyer "B" is concerned, the Listing Salesperson has 2 choices.
- He can offer "no agency" to Buyer "B" (and act as a Transaction Broker) or
- He can become a "Limited Dual Agent" acting for the Seller and Buyer "B" under the provisions set out in the "Limited Dual Agency" Agreement which all parties must sign before entering into a Contract of Purchase and Sale.

(4) **If both Buyer "A" (LOWER offer) and Buyer "B" (HIGHER offer) have made their respective offers through the Listing Salesperson then it is recommended to proceed with extreme caution:**

(a) The Salesperson should first discuss the entire matter with his Manager and/or the Owner/Nominee of the Company

(b) who in turn may wish to obtain independent legal advice.

Areas of concern are:
(a) What is the Listing Salesperson's agency relationship with each individual Buyer?
(b) Both Buyers must be dealt with fairly and ethically.
(c) Neither Buyer "A"s original offer nor the Seller's counter offer can be disclosed to Buyer "B." Buyer "B" must decide independently what his best offer is.
(d) The Seller should be advised to obtain independent legal advice.
(e) Revocation of Buyer "A"s lower offer will take place in the prescribed manner.

(5) **If the Buyer "B" has made his offer through a Realtor who is working in the same office as the Listing Salesperson.**
As far as the 2 Salespersons are concerned, there could be the option of **"Designated Agency"** as an alternative to the "Limited Dual Agency" option.
(a) If Buyer "A" is an outside Realtor's Client, then the revocation can proceed in the normal fashion.
(b) If Buyer "A" is the Client of the Listing Salesperson or the Client of another Salesperson (who is also working in the same office as the Listing Salesperson) then proceed with caution. See No. (4) above.

(6) **If on the other hand Buyer "A" has made his (lower) offer through the Listing Salesperson and Buyer "B"s (better) offer comes through an outside Realtor then** the Listing Salesperson will find himself
- in the unenviable position of having to kiss his own sale (and double-ender) goodbye;
- simultaneously he must walk the fine line of having to be fair and ethical to all of his Clients (namely both his Seller and his Buyer "A"). It is recommended to proceed with caution.

Case law:
(1) **"HUGHES v. GRYRATRON DEVELOPMENTS LTD."** B.C. Supreme Court, Vancouver Registry C883072
(2) **"BUBURUZ v. CREIGHTON et al"** and **"CHUNG v. CREIGHTON et al,"** Third party "Re/Max Colonial Pacific Realty." B.C. Supreme Court, Docket # 01/4236, Date 2003-02-27. Two buyers have conflicting claims against a waterfront property in Crescent Beach, B.C. Each plaintiff seeks an order for specific performance or alternatively damages in lieu of specific performance and damages for breach of contract.

Commission Cutting And Selling Bonus

(I)
The real estate commission is the financial remuneration which a Realtor earns for the successful sale of a property. The commission can be either
- a percentage of the Selling Price or
- a predetermined lump sum.

Because of the provisions of the Competition Act the commission payable is negotiable. Commission structures may vary from one Company to another. Real Estate Companies whose sales staff is working as "Independent Contractors" (they get 100% of the commission and pay for their own expenses) often leave the decision of how much commission will be charged up to their salespersons.

A real estate commission is charged for:
(a) The Realtor's **services rendered** (his time commitment, efforts and diligence).
(b) The Realtor's **experience, expertise and ability**.
(c) The Realtor's **cost of doing business:**
   - Office rent
   - Franchise fees, license fees, membership dues
   - signs and business cards, stationary etc.
   - promotional items and advertising
   - car expenses (repair and maintenance, gas, insurance)
   - clothing, computers, pagers etc.
   - income tax payable

Realtors work on the "success principle":
- if they sell something, then they get paid.
- Regardless of how hard they may work, if they don't succeed, then they will earn nothing.
- If a Realtor has spent a lot of money promoting a property and that property doesn't sell, then the Realtor must absorb the cost. The Client owes him nothing.
- In view of the above the services of a Realtor must be one of the biggest bargains around.

(II)
This brings us to the philosophical problem of **WHO pays the commission?** The Seller or the Buyer?
  (a) Technically the cash for the commission flows from the Seller; but in reality it is the Buyer who enables the Seller to pay out the cash. Why? Because **the Seller looks to his NET EQUITY:** to wit, his prime concern is what he gets into his hands after the discharge of all existing mortgages, debts and the payment of the commission.
  (b) **The Buyer** on the other hand **is mainly concerned with the**

AFFORDABILITY of the FULL (PURCHASE) PRICE: at the end of the negotiation process his available downpayment plus the maximum mortgage which he can afford (to service) have to add up to the proposed Purchase Price. The Buyer's CASH FLOW is of critical importance to him. He also has to scratch together some cash for legal fees, taxes, moving costs etc. That is why the average Buyer is usually unable to dig into his pockets to pay for any portion of the commission.

(III)
Commission "CUTTING" occurs when - as a result of being unable to close an offer - the Listing Salesperson and/or the Selling Salesperson or both - offer to forego a portion of the originally stipulated commission due to them, in order to bridge the final and apparently unresolvable gap between what the Buyer is able and willing to pay and what the Seller is able and/or willing to accept.

(IV)
When commission cutting takes place practical, ethical and legal problems can arise.
(a) **The cutting of the commission can become a bad habit.** A Realtor who is a weak "closer" will tend to offer to cut his commission at the first hint of the Seller's or Buyer's resistance to signing on the dotted line. In the long run this bad habit will
  • damage the Realtor's self esteem and
  • undermine his confidence.
  • Ironically his (ungrateful) Client may not respect him.
(b) From a courtesy point of view it is imperative that both Realtors should discuss any proposed commission cutting in private and out of sight and hearing of the Seller. Under no circumstances should one of the Realtors bring up the subject in front of the Client without having first checked discreetly with the other Realtor. Failure to do so may put the other Realtor (in front of his Client) into an untenable position of economic duress.
(c) The Reader is encouraged to consult the MLS Rules and Regulations of his local Real Estate Board: most likely there are some provisions saying that any change of the commission from its originally agreed upon structure
  • must be "mutually agreed" to by everybody involved,
  • must be in writing and
  • may not be prejudicial to any of the Realtors involved.
(d) Sometimes a Listing Salesperson will refuse to participate in the commission cutting because he reasons: "I have a good and saleable listing. Why should I cut my commission just to help finance a total stranger (namely somebody else's Buyer) who means nothing to me? If I decide to cut my share of the commission then it should be done only for a Buyer of my own."
(e) At this stage some Realtors will no doubt feel that the interests of the Client/Seller come before the welfare of the Realtor and therefore, the Realtor has some sort of

obligation (fiduciary or otherwise) to cut his commission. These Realtors should realize that **commission cutting is a CONCESSION**, a variation from the originally agreed upon commission payable. The Listing Contract says nothing about having to cut the commission in order to make a sale possible. This is backed up by the Courts:

In **"Western Mortgage (Realty) Corp. v. Small World Holdings Inc.,"** B.C. Supreme Court (1992-01-10) BCSC C915156 and B.C. Court of Appeal (1993-01-22) CA015069, 77 BCLR (2d) 324 the Court of Appeal notes:

"… there is no evidence that the parties intended to amend the listing agreement and there is nothing in the agreement of purchase and sale to warrant that conclusion."

In **"H.W. Liebig Co. v. Leading Investments Ltd."** Supreme Court of Canada [1986] 1 S.C.R. 70, 65 N.R., 209 the Judges said:

"The Listing Agreement governed. The bargain between vendor and broker was struck when the listing agreement was signed and its meaning was not altered by reading it with the agreement of purchase and sale." It says further at [31]:

"… The contract between the Vendor and the Real Estate Broker cannot be changed by the subsequent dealings between the Vendor and his intended Purchaser… **Otherwise the Vendor would be unjustly enriched from the efforts of the Broker at the Vendor's request."**

(f) Many a Seller may not have the necessary understanding or sympathy that he shouldn't take it for granted that a Realtor will or should work for less than was originally agreed upon.

Occasionally even a certain amount of bitterness may result between the Selling and the Listing Broker if one of them refuses to reduce his share of the commission just to make the other Realtor's deal fly.

It is a personal decision if somebody decides that due to some pressing circumstances (e.g. the worry of loosing a disloyal Buyer) he will settle for less; a Realtor who is willing to sacrifice a portion of his commission has no right to assume that his fellow Realtor will feel the same way.

It would be damaging to the Listing Salesperson's relationship with his Seller, if the Buyer's Agent were to inform the Seller that the property could have been sold, except for the refusal of the Listing Salesperson to cut his share of the commission.

(g) If no sale results because the amount of commission cutting is not sufficient to bridge the gap between what the Seller wants and the Buyer can pay then it is best to merely inform both Clients that the sale was not possible.

This thought may just shock them into reevaluating their individual positions.

(h) In case of multiple offers it is only the Listing Salesperson who is familiar with each and every offer. It is up to him to **ensure that all offers (including his own) compete on a level playing field.**

If the Listing Broker secretly cuts his commission on his own deal then he would have **an unfair advantage over the other salespersons**. The **other competing salespersons must be given an opportunity to match** or beat the Listing Broker's offer with the reduced commission.

(V)
WHEN IS IT ok TO CUT THE COMMISSION?
(a) Half a loaf of bread is better than nothing whenever you present an offer in the dying hours (between 8 p.m. and midnight) of the LAST day of your listing and you know for sure that your Sellers will NOT give you an extension of the listing.
(b) Other good times for commission cutting are the 32nd day of the month, but only during a leap year.

(VI)
WHO MUST BE NOTIFIED if there is a reduction of the commission?
(1) **The Lending Institution** (bank, credit union etc.), in case the Buyer is arranging new financing. Loan amounts are based on the Selling Price or Appraised Value, whichever is lower. By cutting the commission, the Realtor is giving a BENEFIT to the Buyer. **The subsidy will either**
   - **boost the Buyer's downpayment or else**
   - **it may be viewed as a reduction of the Selling Price.**
(2) **The SELLER** must know about the commission cut/kick-back to the Buyer, in order to be able to make one of the following decisions:
   (a) to either approve the kick-back arrangement between the Realtor(s) and the Buyer(s) OR
   (b) the Seller could reduce the Selling Price and pay a lower commission OR
   (c) alternatively the Seller could choose not to proceed with the sale.
   Refer to **"Ocean City Realty Ltd. v. A & M Holdings Ltd. et al"** (March 6, 1987), B.C. Court of Appeal, 36 DLR (4th) 94

For everybody's PROTECTION the commission cutting arrangement should be well DOCUMENTED IN WRITING. It should show
- the total amount of COMMISSION payable and
- separately the amount of the GST payable by the Seller.

The reason for this is as follows: if everybody agrees to "reduce the commission to $9,000.00" then
- the REALTOR will think that it is "$ 9,000.00 PLUS GST" and
- the SELLER may think $ 9,000.00 in total (INCLUDING GST)."

This misunderstanding can become a real problem (last minute needless excitement) when the Seller signs the Statement of Adjustment in the lawyer's office shortly before registration of documents.

(3) **The Conveyancing Solicitor** must be given written instructions exactly what the commission is. Once the Statement of Adjustment has been typed, the lawyer's office will be reluctant to make changes to accommodate a previously (to him) unreported change in commission: additional work costs extra money which neither the Buyer nor the Seller will be prepared to pay.

(VII) INCENTIVES TO PROMOTE THE SALE OF A PROPERTY.
(1) **Will a HIGHER commission make a house sell faster?**

In competition with other commissions offered on similar houses situated in the area, the Seller may decide to offer a higher total commission in order to entice a Buyer's Agent to sell his house in preference over others. The Listing Salesperson may not defeat his Seller's intention by pocketing the "bonus" under the guise of "extra-ordinary" selling efforts. To demonstrate: the commission offered on similar homes is 7% with the Selling Broker and Listing Broker each receiving 3.5%. Supposing a Seller offers a total commission of 10%: his intention is to give to the Selling Broker 6.5%.

On circulated Multiple Listings often only the Selling Broker's share of the commission is shown (and not the total commission). If the Listing Broker offers a Cooperating Broker 3.5% then that Broker will (mistakenly) think that the total commission is 7%. It will be a bad surprise when he finds out later on that the total commission is actually 10% and the Listing Broker will pocket 6.5% thereof under the guise of putting on a "special sales campaign."

This sort of action not only completely defeats the Seller's intentions but also the Listing Broker is putting his own welfare ahead of the interests of his Client.

(2) **Alternatively a SELLING BONUS can be an extra lump sum of money offered directly to the Selling Broker** in addition to the agreed upon (shared with the Listing Broker) commission. This situation is similar to a "finder's fee" paid to a Realtor by some lending institutions.

The Buyer's Agent must make full and timely disclosure of any extraordinary benefits and obtain his Client's (the Buyer's) consent.

For those who think that it is not the Client's business what "extra money" the Realtor might get, it is respectfully recommended that they familiarize themselves with certain sections of the Criminal Code of Canada dealing with "Secret Commissions." Surprisingly enough the "Payer of the extra benefit" may be equally as culpable as the "Recipient" thereof. By failing to make full disclosure to the Client, the Realtor runs the additional risk of invalidating (breaching) his agency relationship with him.

From a more immediate and practical point of view it may occur to the Buyer that
- his Agent may have deliberately "steered" him to the property because of the Selling Bonus.
- Possibly other properties (with a lower commission structure and/or no bonus) could have been more suitable to him - but hadn't been shown to him.

(3) Instead of paying a Selling Bonus or an increased commission **a Seller will get MORE mileage and LESS problems if he will SIMPLY REDUCE HIS ASKING PRICE.**

If his asking price is a shade below those of competing properties in the area, chances are that his house will sell next.

ADDENDUM TO (Page No._____ of _____) Contract of Purchase and Sale
dated _____ for the sale of the property at

_____

COMMISSION AGREEMENT

The Total Gross Commission payable by the Seller is _____% of the first $100,000.00 plus _____% on the balance of the Selling Price of $ _____

PLUS APPLICABLE GST ON THE COMMISSION
OR
the predetermined lump sum of $ _____ PLUS APPLICABLE GST.

COMMISSION SPLIT

Listing Broker _____ % plus GST ... OR $ _____ plus GST

Selling Broker _____ % plus GST ... OR $ _____ plus GST

Acknowledged, understood and approved
this _____ day of _____ , 2_____

In case the Buyer is arranging new financing, then the Lending Institution must be informed of this Commission Agreement

_____   _____
Signature (Seller)   Witness

_____   _____
Signature (Seller)   Witness

_____   _____
Signature (Buyer)   Witness

_____   _____
Signature (Buyer)   Witness

Listing Broker Company Name _____

_____
Listing Salesperson's signature

Selling Broker Company Name _____

_____
Selling Salesperson's signature

"After Sale" Service

"After Sale" Service is the service which is rendered between
- the time of the acceptance of an offer and
- the completion of the transaction. (Registration of all documents and disbursement of the sales proceeds).

The OBJECTIVE of the "After Sale" service is
- to ensure that everything will run smoothly and to the Clients' satisfaction.
- To avoid "loose ends" meaning generally bad surprises which
  - result in complaints and/or law suits
  - and/or jeopardize the sale.
- A smoothly running "end-phase" of the transaction will make the Clients happy. Many of them may have heard from friends and relatives "horror stories of last minute disasters." They will appreciate it if their thorough Realtor "runs interference" for them and protects them from unwelcome "rough edges." In gratitude they in turn will eventually recommend their Realtor to others and they will deal with him again in the future.

A) THE PAPERWORK.

Realtors who hate doing paperwork should be reminded that
- **"The job isn't complete until the paperwork is done!"**
- If for no other reason they should protect their hard earned commission out of sheer self-preservation. A lot of time, work, effort and money have gone into making a deal possible; there is no justifiable reason to jeopardize everything in the home stretch.

Here is **a suggested list of what needs to be done:**

(1) Promptly turn into the office the Buyer's DEPOSIT together with
(2) • copies of the **Contract of Purchase and Sale and**
  - copies of **all addendums**.
  - A copy of the **Property Condition Disclosure Statement** signed by the Sellers and the Buyers
  - a properly completed **SALES RECORD SHEET** or **TRANSACTION RECORD** containing **full conveyancing particulars**.

PLEASE NOTE: "KWOK v. GRIFFITHS," B.C. Supreme Court, Vancouver Registry No. C936487 (January 19, 1996). **A Realtor was found to be negligent for his failure to provide accurate documentation to the Conveyancer.**

(3) Find out the names, addresses, phone and FAX numbers of the lawyers involved who will act
  - for the **Buyers**,
  - for the **Lender** who is granting the new financing and

- for the **Sellers**.
(4) Enquire if the Seller has a recent Survey Certificate (Certificate of non-encroachment). This may save the Buyer some money. A Survey Certificate is often required by the Lending Institution who is granting the new financing.

B) OTHER JOBS.

(1) Enter into your work diary **the DATES for each "subject" removal**.
(2) Make sure that all "subject-to" clauses are fulfilled and removed in writing within the time limit stipulated in the contract. Even if the original subject clause said that it can be removed "unilaterally" **it is still preferable that all subject removal documents and/or amendments be signed by ALL contracting parties**. This is merely **a safety precaution** to avoid future problems or misunderstandings. If a subject clause is removed "unilaterally" it means that only one of the parties is signing it and the other party is given a copy thereof. In case of a future problem the Realtor will find it difficult to prove that the party who didn't sign had been given a copy of the subject removal. Nobody should be able to say later on "I wasn't told" or "I didn't know that…."
(3) EVERYBODY must be given a copy of the signed subject removal document: Sellers, Buyers, Listing Broker and Selling Broker.
(4) The Realtors in turn should give these documents to their Conveyancing Co-Ordinator as soon as possible. By this time the Conveyancing Co-Ordinator will have assigned a DEAL NUMBER for the sale. This number should always be referred to in order to ensure that documents end up in the right office file.
(5) Meet the Mortgage Appraiser at the house and ask him if he would be interested in receiving
  - print-outs of recent sales of similar houses in the area.
  - Information about the lot size, property taxes, age, easements etc.
  (If he is overworked he may appreciate your help; otherwise he may decline).
(6) A mutually suitable appointment should be made between the Sellers, the Certified Home Inspector and the Buyers (who may want to be present during the inspection).
(7) When the sale becomes "FIRM" (all subject clauses having been removed and/or deposits increased) then
  (a) a SOLD sign should be placed on the property.
  (b) It is a nice touch if you let the Seller's children put up the SOLD sign; they will find it exciting.
  (c) You may even end up having your picture taken while shaking hands with the happily smiling Sellers (and their children) in front of the SOLD sign.
  (d) Such a picture should be incorporated into your Listing Presentation Folder.
  (e) After 2 to 3 weeks arrange to have the sign removed. There is nothing as sad looking as an abandoned Real Estate sign leaning against the side of a house.
  (f) If the property was on the MLS then the "firm" sale should be reported to the

local Real Estate Board for publication.
(8) The Clients should be reminded to contact their respective **Insurance Agents:**
- **For the Buyer** the Insurance Agent will have to issue a "binder" to the Lending Institution who is granting the new financing; otherwise the lender will not release the mortgage funds to the conveyancing lawyer.
- **The Sellers** should keep their house insurance in place until the Buyer is moving in. There may be a small overlap of coverage, which is preferable to no coverage.

(9) **Write a CLOSING LETTER** to your Clients and give them a **"list of things to do and people to notify when moving."** You will find a suggested sample letter together with the list referred to at the end of this Chapter.

(10) **As an extra SERVICE** offer to accompany the Clients when they are signing the final documents in the lawyer's office. Some lawyers or Notaries explain in detail the various documents and the Statement of Adjustment; others may hand everything to the Clients for their perusal with a minimum of explanation; in that case you can be of valuable assistance to the (more or less apprehensive) Clients, especially if they are "First Time Buyers." For various reasons Clients often don't ask questions when they are in the lawyer's office. Some popular, but unfortunate misconceptions are:
- they don't want to appear to be 'ignorant';
- the lawyer might charge them more money if they ask too many questions and take up too much of his time.

(11) It may be a good idea to have a final **"walk-through-inspection"** of the house BEFORE the Buyers move in. This is especially important **in the sale of a new house:**
- **the final inspection** should be done together with the Builder and the Buyers.
- The Realtor should prepare a list of all deficiencies and
- fix a deadline (agreed to by all parties) by when the repairs should be completed.
- This deficiency list should be dated and signed by all parties. Everybody should receive a copy thereof (including all Realtors involved).

(12) The transfer of the house keys.

(13) **As a PRACTICAL CLOSING GIFT** (which is income tax deductible as a selling expense) have a locksmith phone your Clients and inform them that he wants to come over "with the compliments of your Realtor Mr..." to change the tumblers in all locks and to cut new keys. All locks will be "keyed alike" which means that the same key will fit all locks. THIS SHOULD IMPRESS YOUR CLIENTS.

Who knows who is running around with an old house key; even on a new house various subtrades may still have a key. This Closing Gift may cost you a few Dollars but it will pay big dividends: it is more permanent than flowers, more practical than a fancy door knocker and there is not much difference in the cost.

CLOSING LETTER TO THE SELLERS (on letterhead)

Dear Mr. and Mrs. ...

Further in connection with the sale of your property at .....

I am writing to you now in order to ensure that the final steps in the completion of this transaction will run smoothly. The CONVEYANCING SOLICITOR who will prepare the final documents on your behalf is:

Name
Address
Phone number
No doubt, he will contact you in due course. However, if you haven't heard from him by ...month/date (select a date about 10 days before Completion Date) then may I suggest that you phone him directly and arrange for an appointment to see him at your convenience. If it is agreeable to you, then I will be pleased to attend with you at the lawyer's office to assist you in reviewing the Statement of Adjustment and all other documents.

For your perusal I am enclosing herewith a check list of "THINGS TO DO and PEOPLE TO NOTIFY WHEN MOVING." (Please do not forget to have the address on your Driver's Licence changed; the Motor Vehicle Branch levies a fine in case you fail to do so).

Please keep your present house insurance in force until noon of the POSSESSION DATE. When the time comes, I will arrange for the transfer of the house keys.

Should you at any time (before completion of the conveyancing) have any questions or problems, please feel free to phone me. Please do not be concerned if you do not hear from me frequently, because a great part of the finalizing work will have to wait until the days immediately preceding the closing date set forth in the contract and many of the steps will go on quietly and efficiently within the lawyer's office and the Land Titles Office.

It was a pleasure working for you and if at any time in the future I can assist you further, or if you have any relatives, neighbours or friends who require realty service of any kind then I do hope that you and they will call on me.

Once again warmest thanks and good wishes for the future.

Sincerely,

MEMO FROM THE DESK OF

Attach your business card here

THINGS TO DO and PEOPLE TO NOTIFY WHEN MOVING.

(1) Obtain ESTIMATES from several moving companies.
   - Find out about their insurance coverage in case of damage or breakage.
   - Check with the Better Business Bureau (there is no charge)
     - if there have been complaints and
     - if they were resolved or not.

(2) Unless you get a "full-pack move," obtain boxes etc.

(3) Obtain CHANGE OF ADDRESS forms from the Post Office.

(4) Using these forms notify all your friends, relatives and/or business associates, clubs and associations etc. where you are a member.

(5) **Make arrangements with the local MOTOR VEHICLE BRANCH to CHANGE THE ADDRESS ON YOUR DRIVER'S LICENSE.**

(6) Notify businesses who make deliveries to your house: e.g. **newspapers, magazines** etc.

(7) **Notify your bank, credit union, credit card companies (VISA, Mastercard, department stores, oil companies etc.)** of your new address.

(8) Arrange for a **"final reading"** for the electricity and gas service.

   Arrange for the transfer of the telephone service to the new location.

(9) Notify all **Government Agencies** which you are dealing with

   (e.g. medical coverage, Pension cheques etc.)

(10) Talk to your insurance agent, especially when the house is going to be vacant for a period of time.

(11) Co-ordinate the timing of your move with the Buyer or Seller.

(12) OPTIONAL: line up a cleaning crew, house painter etc.

Conveyancing Instructions

Realtors invest a lot of time, work hard for long hours and spend a considerable amount of after-tax Dollars on advertising a property. When the property is finally sold logic would demand that they **PROTECT their hard-earned commission** by doing a good job in the final stage of the transaction, which is mostly PAPERWORK. The major report which Realtors are required to complete is known as a

"SALES RECORD SHEET" or "TRANSACTION RECORD" or "DEAL SHEET." This is the equivalent of a BLUEPRINT and shows important details of the sale.

For Realtors who hate paperwork the completion of the "DEAL SHEET" it is NOT exactly a "Labour of Love." In fact it often contains hardly any worthwhile information. **Their attitude is** that they have done their job and it is now **"up to the office"** to do the rest. After all the office gets a Deal Fee or a portion of the commission, don't they? Alternatively they feel that **"the details of the LEGAL END are UP TO THE LAWYER" and HE may as well earn HIS keep!**

What a sad misunderstanding and what a huge mistake all of that is! Here is a reality check of what actually happens to the deal after the Realtor has turned it into the office.

(1)
For the overworked Conveyancing Co-Ordinator or Office Secretary your sale is merely one of many others. She is not a school teacher to grade or correct your paper. Nor does she have the time to track down various missing details. She is merely required to process your deal to the conveyancing lawyer. For that purpose she
- types up a form letter (inserting your Clients' names and the property address),
- attaches a copy of the Contract of Purchase and Sale and
- encloses the "addendums" and "subject removals" which the Salesperson has given to her.
- To the above she adds a copy of the Transaction Record (the way the Salesperson has completed it). This means that **the conveyancing instructions which the lawyer receives stand and fall with the completeness of the "Sales Record Sheet."**
- Then the Office Secretary sends everything off to the lawyer and SHE has done HER job!

NOTE: **Realtors have been sued for NEGLIGENCE because of their failure to provide ACCURATE DOCUMENTATION to the conveyancing Notary.** See **"KWOK v. GRIFFITHS,"** B.C. Supreme Court, Reasons for Judgment January 19, 1996, Docket No. C936487
The Realtor and his office failed to send all of the relevant documentation including a

fully and properly executed AMENDMENT agreement to the conveyancing notary. The Court considered this to be conduct below the standard of care which is expected from a conscientious Realtor. The Realtor was held to be liable to the Buyers for damages resulting from this act of negligence.

(2)
The next stop is **"The Lawyer's Office."**
(a) It is very unlikely that the Lawyer himself will see the fruits of your PAPERWORK when they arrive.
(b) It is his overworked Conveyancing Secretary who opens the mail or receives the FAX.
(c) Few Realtors realize that she is working under heavy time pressure because at all times she has anywhere up to 30 different files on the go.
(d) With stomach-churning frustration she beholds the bare-bones Sales Record Sheet (what the Realtor considered to be the "annoying paperwork.")
(e) Like a Triage Doctor in an emergency situation she classifies the Deal Sheet as an abomination which requires a lot of work by her (for which she doesn't have the time right now).
(f) The file goes to the bottom of the pile of her files. She will work on the missing items when she has more time.
(g) Hoping that the legal description is correct she may decide to order a Title Search.

(3)
The objective of detailed conveyancing instructions is to prevent anything going wrong in the final stage of the deal. The MORE information you give to the conveyancing solicitor the LESS chance is there that the sale may run into some unforeseen difficulties.

(4)
(a) It is a nice touch to phone the conveyancing solicitor's office a few days after your deal has arrived.
(b) Find out which secretary is handling your file.
(c) Introduce yourself to her and ask her if
   - she has received your file and
   - if she needs anything else from you at this time.
   - Tell her that if she needs anything in the future, to call you anytime.
(d) At this stage you now know HER name and phone number and she knows YOUR name and phone number. The chances of your deal completing on time and without a hitch have improved considerably.
(e) **This phone call is important and will pay big future dividends because:**
   - You have exercised your fiduciary duty of CARE vis-a-vis your Clients.
   - You have peace of mind knowing that your conveyancing instructions have

arrived in the lawyer's office. You are one step closer to getting paid. If nothing else, you have acted out of sheer self-preservation.
- **You now know the name of the secretary who is in charge of this file. In case of a problem, she and you both know whom to phone.**
- **You have created goodwill:** the conveyancing secretary will remember you in the future. When she receives your next sale it will most likely go to the top of the pile of files.

(5)
Some of the information which the lawyer (actually his secretary) will appreciate receiving are:
(a) • **The Buyers' and Sellers' full names** (including middle names), occupations and their addresses (including postal codes). Why should the lawyer's secretary waste her precious time tracking down middle names and occupations?
- **An absolute MUST are residence and work phone numbers.** If there is no daytime (work) phone number, then how can the secretary contact the parties to come in and sign the documents? **Secretaries are not required to make phone calls after their working hours.**

b) **At the time when the Salesperson is dealing with the clients, it is easy for him to get everybody's full names, occupations, postal codes, phone numbers etc.:**
- from the BUYER when he writes the offer;
- from the SELLERS after they have accepted the offer.

Thus the Realtor is in a unique position to easily secure this important information. AS AN ADDED BONUS and without having to go out of his way, the Realtor will impress EVERYBODY (the clients as well as his fellow Realtors) that he is thorough and professional.

(c) **The correct postal address of the property sold,** including the postal code. The Buyer will appreciate receiving his future postal code; it will save him time phoning the Post Office.

(d) **The complete and correct legal description.** The Listing Broker most likely has a Title Search and he should give a copy thereof to the Selling Broker.

Addresses and legal descriptions are especially important when selling land: bare acreage or a subdivided lot.

(e) **The Tax Roll Number and the current gross taxes**. These are available from your Real Estate Board's computer under "Municipal Statistics." A call to the City Hall Tax Department will tell you if the taxes are paid or if there are any outstanding balances due together with interest and penalties. When preparing the Statement of Adjustment the Seller's as well as the Buyer's lawyers will independently verify the tax situation. Nevertheless both lawyers will view your advance information about the taxes as a professional gesture.

Conveyancing Instructions

(6)

The correct selling price: Contracts eventually become rather messy because of the various changes taking place in case of offers and counter offers. To an outsider it may not always be clear what the finally agreed upon price is. Many Realtors do make the extra effort of reiterating (in a clear spot somewhere in the Contract) the final selling price (which, of course, must also be initialled by all of the contracting parties).

(7)

The amount of the deposit and who is holding it.
The Office will issue a receipt to the Realtor.

(8)

Existing financial encumbrances which will have to be discharged:
(a) Name, address, phone number, FAX number of who is holding the mortgage. If it is a financial institution, then there might be a special Mortgage Department at the Head Office.
(b) **The Mortgage Loan Number** should be quoted to enable the Lending Institution to locate the information easier.
(c) At the time of listing, the Listing Broker hopefully has alerted the Seller of any prepayment penalties, discharge fees and administration fees charged by the Lender.
(d) **These are in addition to the "legal fees"** (the lawyer's fees and Land Title costs) required to discharge a mortgage.
(e) The Seller must pay all of these and if he is not properly prepared for them, then there will arise a "bad surprise" situation in the lawyer's office when he signs the final papers. In the worst case scenario, the Seller may not have enough money (proceeds from the sale of his old house) to buy his next house. He may refuse to close.

(9)

Non-financial encumbrances like a Right-of-Way or Easement (in favour of a Municipality or a Public Utility)
(a) cannot be discharged and
(b) **should be brought to the Buyer's attention before** he enters into a binding Contract of Purchase and Sale.
(c) **Worst case scenario:** because of an easement the Buyer cannot build a swimming pool in the back yard or make an addition to the house. Lawyers customarily discuss these matters with the Clients.

(10)

Details about the Buyers' NEW financing:
(a) Name and address of the Lending Institution.
(b) To prevent any misunderstandings or miscommunications: the Name, address and phone number of the person whom the conveyancing solicitor should contact to

obtain details of the new loan. (E.g. the loan amount, interest rate etc.)
(c) In addition to an appraisal many lending institutions require a Survey Certificate (Certificate of Non-encroachment).
- It takes a few days to order and obtain a new one from a Surveyor.
- The Seller may have an old one which the Lender may accept provided the Seller makes a Statutory Declaration that there have been no new additions or alterations to the house. That way the Buyer could save himself the cost of a new survey.

(11)
The name, address and phone number of the Buyers' INSURANCE AGENT who has to supply to the lawyer a copy of the "insurance binder" with "loss payable firstly to the new 1st mortgagee."
Freestanding cast iron fireplaces or woodburning stoves (if not professionally installed with the appropriate Municipal Permits and inspections) may cause insurance problems: they could be regarded as an uninsurable fire hazard.
In order to avoid last minute anxious scrambling, a prudent Listing Broker will tackle this problem at the beginning of his marketing efforts.

(12)
(a) **The correct amount of the real estate commission plus GST.**
(b) In case the commission is reduced, then there should be a clear-cut written agreement signed by all effected parties including the Realtors. In this regard misunderstandings commonly happen due to IMPRECISE LANGUAGE. E.g.: everybody agrees to reduce the commission to $ 8,000.00.
- The Realtors' understanding is $ 8,000.00 PLUS GST
- The Seller's understanding is $ 8,000.00 in total (which means including GST).
(c) Once the Statement of Adjustment is typed (showing an incorrect amount of commission) there could be additional costs to recalculate and retype the Statement of Adjustment. Most likely both the Buyers as well as the Sellers will refuse to pay those additional costs.
(d) In order to avoid arbitration at the Real Estate Board the Realtors between themselves should have a properly written understanding **what the commission split is**.

(13)
Attention should be paid to **the timing of the Completion, Possession and Adjustment Dates:** if the sale on hand is one of several in a chain, then all COMPLETION DATES must be carefully synchronized with the subsequent sales. Care should be taken that each of the Sellers-turned-Buyer have their Sales Proceeds in hand in sufficient time to be able to complete their next purchase. Theoretically it may be possible to have 2 transactions complete on the same day but chances of success are slim. It is merely asking for trouble.

Analysis of THE PROBLEM OF "BACK-TO-BACK CLOSINGS" on the same day.

(1) Consider the following scenario: your Client is selling his house and buying another one. You try to have his SALE AND his PURCHASE BOTH COMPLETE on the same day.

(2) **The following PEOPLE are involved:**
   (a) Your Client "The SELLER # 1" plus his "Lawyer"
   (b) The "BUYER" (of your Seller's house) and his "Lawyer."
   (c) This Buyer's lawyer may or may not be able to act also for the Lending Institution which is granting the new financing. Sometimes a Lender insists that a separate lawyer should act only for them in the preparation of the new mortgage documents.
   (d) "SELLER # 2" (whose house Seller # 1 is buying) and his own lawyer.
   (e) Various Clerks in the Land Titles Office, who are checking the submitted documents for errors.
   (f) It is very unlikely that the conveyancing lawyers themselves will attend in the Land Titles Office. Instead many lawyers use the services of Independent Filing Clerks who pick up the documents from the various lawyers' offices and bring them to the Land Titles Office, where they submit all documents for registration.
   (g) Clerks in the Lending Institution (who will release the new mortgage funds to the Buyer's lawyer upon the registration of the new mortgage).
   (h) This transfer of the mortgage funds from the Lender to the Buyer's lawyer could be done
   - either electronically or else
   - a cheque will be couriered to the lawyer. The courier could be delayed by traffic.
   (i) Upon registration of the sale of "SELLER # 1's" house, a courier will bring the "sales proceeds" from the Buyer's lawyer to the Seller's lawyer who uses a portion of the money to discharge any existing financial encumbrances. See **"NORFOLK v. AIKENS"** (1989), 41 B.C.L.R. (2d) 145 and **"GROSS v. COTTIER"** B.C. Court of Appeal, Date 1992-08-27, Docket No. CA013135
   The courier could be delayed in traffic.
   (j) The lawyer acting for Seller # 1 cannot register the title transfer documents for **Seller's # 1 PURCHASE of the next house** until the SALE of Seller # 1's house is complete and all funds are in his possession. Usually by that time the Land Titles Office is just about to close for the day.
   (k) Seller # 2 (whose house Seller # 1 is BUYING) is entitled to receive HIS SALES PROCEEDS ON COMPLETION DAY and that is very unlikely to happen under the circumstances.

In the above example, there seem to be about a dozen people involved expediting documents and money. Any delays will cause serious ramifications all the way down the line.

Ideally there should be 1 or 2 "rest days" between closings or else the Seller-turned-Buyer should arrange for interim or bridge financing, so that his purchase can occur independently from his sale.

(14)
If at all possible you should AVOID choosing as "Closing Date"
- a FRIDAY or
- the day immediately BEFORE or AFTER a statutory holiday or
- the FIRST or LAST day of the month.

The reason for this is that Lending Institutions, the Land Titles Office, lawyers and notaries are especially busy on those days. Of course, these days can be chosen to be POSSESSION and ADJUSTMENT DATES.

(15)
The sale of businesses, revenue and industrial properties pose special problems and will require additional, more elaborate and specialized documentation. (e.g. financial statements, environmental impact statements and hazard test reports etc.)

(16)
(a) Both Sellers and Buyers owe to each other a duty to act in good faith to honestly perform the terms of the contract and to take all reasonable steps necessary to complete on time the contract entered into.
(b) The Realtor must contribute his share of careful work to enable both parties to do so.

Getting Along With Lawyers

In the course of business Realtors and Lawyers often serve the same Clients. There is the potential that they can be very valuable to each other. Sadly however, occasionally less than an ideal degree of cooperation results through useless misunderstandings, poor communication and lack of consideration. This is inevitably blamed on the alleged incompatibility between Realtors and Lawyers. What should be a profitable and efficient professional relationship between experts in separate fields, is instead frustrated into counter-productive and totally unnecessary posturing. At one time or another, both parties may be guilty of contributing to this problem. If Realtors and Lawyers would only make the extra effort and take a careful look at the other's point of view, many of these petty differences would disappear. Each party has their own responsibilities and obligations and is competent in his area of endeavour and the other should understand and respect that.

Admittedly, there are some fundamental differences in their backgrounds. A Lawyer must study for many years and pass difficult examinations. Even after he is finished with his University education, he has to serve an internship (practicum) before he can strike out on his own. **His destiny is to act as his Client's ADVOCATE (champion) and for that reason he is trained to conduct his business in a more confrontational manner.**

On the other hand a Realtor's initial pre-licensing education is a lot shorter and can often be taken by correspondence. However many Realtors spend a lifetime improving their selling skills and enhancing their continued education. **Realtors are trained to be "Brokers or Go-betweens."** In order to succeed for their clients they have
- **to be conciliatory and**
- **able to negotiate compromises.**
- **They have to come up with solutions** and
- **build bridges of understanding.**

There are 2 basic areas of concern when Realtors are dealing with Lawyers. The first one has to do with **"giving advice."** Realtors must have a basic working knowledge of real estate law, but are not allowed to give "legal advice." If they do, then they will find themselves in trouble because they would be practicing law. In reality very few Realtors, if any, would want to give legal advice. The burden of responsibility is just too great. But what burns many Realtors up is that Lawyers without qualified first-hand knowledge of the real estate market and values, often appear to "recommend" acceptance or rejection of an offer. This is viewed by many Realtors as giving "real estate advice." If a lawyer is not qualified like a Realtor, then he should be no more justified in giving real estate advice than a Realtor is for giving legal advice.

A lawyer, of course, has the right and responsibility to give whatever advice he believes to be of benefit to his client. The more important question is if a lawyer would really take the risk and responsibility of making an arbitrary decision on behalf of his client without having adequate back-up information to substantiate his recommendation. More likely he may be merely exploring with his Client how the Client feels about the offered price and discuss with him the pros and cons and legal ramifications of the offer. Lawyers employ a special jargon and often express themselves in guarded language; e.g. they may say something without admitting that they have actually said it. Therefore, when a Lawyer tells a Realtor that he has "recommended" the rejection of the offer, it may be merely his way of speaking and the decision was basically made by the Client.

The 2nd area of a Realtor's concern arises, when the Client says that before he is signing, he wants his lawyer to look over the contract first. Realtors sometimes accuse lawyers for being "too technical," they "cross all t's and dot all i's" and they make "insignificant changes" just to be obstinate or to justify their fee. Also they are said to be "too cautious, conservative or pessimistic."

Let's look at the other side of the coin. Because of the continuously increasing complexities of today's real estate transactions, competent legal advice is not only advisable, but often essential. It also shifts a certain amount of the responsibility from the Realtor onto the Lawyer. The Lawyer has his livelihood (licence) at stake, therefore, he cannot take any chances and tolerate or approve a sloppily written contract. He has no choice but to cross all "t's" and dot all "i's." If the contract is ambiguous (difficult to determine the intent of the parties), then the contract may be unenforceable (voidable) for uncertainty. Thus it is only natural if lawyers are critical or cautious when they have to protect their Clients and themselves. Truly they are the last line of defence against mistakes. Taking everything into consideration this represents a great deal of responsibility. Realtors will have nothing to fear if they use care, diligence and skill in drafting enforceable contracts.

Another area which will help to establish friendly working relations with Lawyers is for Realtors to give them proper, detailed and complete conveyancing instructions. The Sales Transaction Sheets should include everything: full names, occupations and phone numbers of the parties, correct address and legal description of the property sold, all details about any existing encumbrances which will have to be discharged, details whom to contact for the new financing, signed copies of all subject removals, a Survey Certificate (Certificate of Non-encroachment) if available and last, but not least, the correct amount of the real estate commission and deposit. Neither the lawyer nor his secretary are detectives; they often work under time pressure. Valuable time is wasted trying to track down somebody's middle name or occupation or which branch of the bank holds the mortgage etc.

At any given time, a conveyancing secretary may have 20 or more files on the go. If for no other reason than to protect his hard-earned commission, it is imperative for a Realtor to ensure that the paperwork runs smoothly in the home stretch. This is only common sense.

NEVER ARGUE WITH A LAWYER. Even if you win, you will loose in the long run. If a Client has to choose between the advice of a lawyer and that of a Realtor, he will invariably take the advice of the Lawyer. So what happens if there is a serious disagreement between a Realtor and a Lawyer? The last thing that should take place is a heated verbal exchange in front of the Client. Similar to parents fighting in front of their children, the situation is untenable. There is no justification to compete as opponents. Preferably, any discussion should be conducted on a dignified level and out of earshot of the Client. **The Realtor as Natural Negotiator has the advantage and should attempt a "friendly persuasion"** (to diplomatically let the other side "save face") by making a calm, courteous, confident and convincing presentation of his side of the argument. And this certainly shouldn't be misunderstood to mean "making nice" in order to court the goodwill of the Lawyer.

A few words about finding the right lawyer. In Canada, the legal profession seems to frown on aggressive advertising, therefore, you may have to shop around. Keep in mind that we all are only people. If your personality clashes with that of a particular lawyer and you suspect that the he graduated in the bottom half of his class, then find somebody else. If you are not comfortable with that person, then chances are that your Client will be neither. Established lawyers often have full schedules, big offices with a number of secretaries and their conveyancing work is humming along highly efficiently like a well-oiled machine. Young lawyers fresh out of law school are eager for business, energetic and enthusiastic. They also brim with new ideas and give excellent personalized service.

The Land Titles Office fees are set in stone. What the lawyer charges for his work may or may not be flexible. Whatever his fees are, the client should view them as a wise investment in peace of mind: the protection as a result of a well-done job is worth every Cent.

A Realtor has every reason to be proud of his Herculean achievement of bringing Buyer and Seller together. In the home stretch **the Realtor and Lawyer should work together as equals in a team effort atmosphere.** Only then will everybody win and benefit: The Realtor, the Lawyer and above all the Client.

Selling A Rented Property

Selling a rented property can be a difficult task at the best of times. For the sake of their Clients (the Seller/Landlord) hard working Realtors will have to be very patient and courteous with (uncooperative) tenants. Besides such emotional challenges, Realtors may also have to face legal ones.

(I) **The PARTIES involved in the sale of a rented property are:**

(1) **The OWNER/SELLER/LANDLORD.**
The SELLER can have various reasons for selling:
 (a) **The NEED:** He needs the cash (the proceeds from the sale of the house) for something else.
 (b) **The TIMING:** A hot Seller's Market may be the ideal time to obtain a very advantageous price.
 (c) **EMOTIONAL:**
  - He may be fed up dealing with the current tenants.
  - He may be generally fed up dealing with tenants.
 (d) Changes in **local TENANCY LEGISLATION** can make the selection process of tenants more onerous and/or the business relationship between Landlord and Tenants more complicated.
 (e) Changes in **INCOME TAX LAWS** for rental properties can make such investments less attractive.

SUNDRY PROBLEMS FOR A LANDLORD.
 (a) To begin with a cautious Landlord will minimize some of his problems by choosing the tenants carefully: credit check, confirmation of employment, references.
 (b) The reason why he must be thorough and do his "due diligence" BEFORE entering into a rental contract is simply this: in case of a dispute later on the Landlord may find it difficult to get rid of a bad tenant. An uncooperative tenant could choose to ignore a Tenancy Office Arbitrator's decision (ordering him to move out) and make various time consuming appeals. Tenancy legislation may vary with location.
 (c) Wilful damage to the rented premises is difficult to prove. As a bad tenant is surely not going to admit it, the Landlord may have to seek redress in Court.
 (d) **Unpaid rent is NOT a criminal offence.** Technically it is a breach of contract between the Landlord and the Tenants and as such the Courts consider it to be a **civil matter.** Such **law suits usually turn out to be lengthy, frustrating and expensive exercises in futility** (even if the Landlord wins his case it may be difficult to collect from the Defendant Tenant).
 (e) To boot, the outcome of any law suit is by no means a foregone conclusion.

After the Seller has listed the house for sale, he is usually EMOTIONALLY "finished with it" and is looking impatiently forward to receiving his money.

When the sale of the rented house becomes "firm" the Buyers may require that the Seller/Landlord give to the tenants the proper notice to vacate the premises. In this regard the Seller may ask for help from his Realtor.

(2) **The BUYERS.**

Many Buyers who end up buying a tenant occupied property will stipulate in their offer that they want to have **"vacant possession."** Their reasons for this may be:
 (a) PRIVACY: they don't want to share the house with strangers.
 (b) CONVENIENCE:
  - they want to have a free hand to do some painting and/or repairs;
  - they want to occupy the entire house and place their furniture.
 (c) CAUTION: They do not wish to become a Landlord (not even for a short period of time) because
  - they don't want any hassle with potentially difficult strangers who may refuse to move out.
  - They have heard horror stories about tenants who are noisy and messy.
  - The cost of cleaning up the property can exceed the amount of the security deposit.
 (d) EMOTIONALLY the Buyers may be somewhat apprehensive about what the tenants will do (or not do). However, they generally have confidence in the ability of their Realtor (the Buyer's Agent) to protect them from and to solve all potential problems.

(3) **The TENANTS.**

Most likely the tenants
 (a) will not be overly happy about having to move.
 (b) If they are militant by nature, then they also will know "THEIR RIGHTS" (length of notice for showings, length of notice for possession etc.)
 (c) They may procrastinate in their search for other accommodation or
 (d) they may have a problem finding suitable other accommodation (limited selection; landlords may refuse to take pets or they will charge a higher rent than what the tenants are currently paying).
 (e) The tenants don't want to pay rent twice by partially overlapping tenancies.
 (f) Consequently the tenants may literally move out in the last minute (e.g. in the late evening of the last rental day instead of at noon). When they are finished moving out, they may be too exhausted or unwilling to clean up after themselves. If their security deposit is for only a small amount they may choose to forfeit it and leave the place in a mess.
 g) Some uncaring or vindictive tenants may even view (in their minds) the leaving-of-the-mess-behind as an indirect punishment of the Landlord who "deserves" to be punished for causing them the inconvenience of having to move.

(II) **The REALTORS involved in the sale of a rented property are:**

(1) **The LISTING Salesperson.**
He is relieved and glad that he doesn't have to deal anymore with those pesky tenants who had made his life sour whenever the house had to be shown. Based on his past dealings with the tenants he may have some uneasy foreboding of coming trouble. In the meantime all he can do is to wait and see and not to rock the boat for the time being.

(2) **The SELLING Salesperson (the BUYER's AGENT).**
He is relieved that he has finally managed to sell something to these footloose and disloyal Buyers. In fact he was in such a hurry to get the Buyers "on paper" that he didn't even have time to check with the Listing Broker to find out to whom the drapes and appliances belonged to (to the Tenants or to the Landlord). He decided that he would ask the Sellers when the offer was being presented. (**Wrong decision:** the Buyers will be disappointed when they find out that they cannot have the appliances because they belonged to the tenants. They may be reluctant to accept a counter offer).

(3) **The DUTIES and responsibilities of the Realtors involved.**
When selling a rented property, the cooperation and concerted effort of both Realtors involved are required to
- (a) anticipate and diplomatically preclude looming problems from happening.
- (b) Minimize unnecessary expenses (to prevent disagreements from escalating into law suits) and
- (c) to smooth over ruffled feelings.
- (d) **To ensure that the Contract of Purchase and Sale is**
  - (A) **LEGALLY ENFORCEABLE.**
    In the past the Courts have found that Realtors hold themselves out to have special skills. One of those skills is their ability to draft legally enforceable contracts. For JUDGMENTS dealing with Realtors' special skills to write enforceable contracts see:
    "**RUSSELL et al v. WISPINSKI et al,**" B.C. Supreme Court, 13 B.C.L.R. (2d), Date May 13, 1987. This judgment in turn mentions the following 2 other cases:
    "**CHAND v. SABO BROS. REALTY LTD.**" (1979) 2 W.W.R. 248, 14 A.R. 302 (C.A.) and
    "**HAWRYLUK v. KORSAKOFF**" (1956) 20 W.W.R. 394 (Man.C.A.)
  - (B) **That the Contract of Purchase and Sale is NOT ambiguous** about some of its details: e.g.
    - the exact time and date for possession.
    - If it is to be "possession subject to the following tenancies ..." or "vacant possession."
    - If it is a month-to-month rental or a lease (in which case the term of

- its expiry is needed).
- The amount of monthly rent paid and what it includes (e.g. heat and light),
- the date of the last rent increase and
- the amount of security deposit lodged.
- Who is responsible for what (repairs).
- Identify what belongs to the Tenants and what belongs to the Landlord/Seller.
- If the appliances belong to the Tenants, then they have the right to take these with them.
- If the appliances belong to the Landlord/Seller and he is willing to leave them with the house, then it should be stipulated in the Contract of Purchase and Sale that the appliances must be "in good working condition and clean ON the Possession Date. But the Seller will NOT give to the Buyer any future warranties or guarantees." (Merely because they are USED appliances and the Seller is not an Appliance Dealer).

(e) **"THE PROBLEM."**

On a Friday night at supper time the Buyer's Agent (the Selling Salesperson) receives the following frantic phone call from his Clients (the Buyers): "The tenants have left the house in a frightful mess; there is garbage all over the place. Come on down and see for yourself. We have already taken 2 truck loads of junk to the dump. It is costing us a lot of money. Also they have taken the fridge and stove with them. There is a hole in the back door and it wasn't there before when we saw the house. They have even taken the towel racks, all the light bulbs and the fancy toilet seat from the bathroom, you know the one with the coins floating in the clear plastic seat."

Possible solutions to "THE PROBLEM."

(A) Realtors should be aware that a section of the Criminal Code of Canada makes it an offence to vandalize a house on the way out the door or to strip it of its fixtures. Besides tenants, this is occasionally done by a vindictive ex-spouse or a bitter former home owner who has lost his house through foreclosure.

(B) The Buyer may wish to insert a clause into the Contract of Purchase and Sale to the effect that "The Seller warrants that all garbage and debris will be removed from the premises by the Possession Date and that the house and yard will be left in a clean state and good condition."

The Seller may object to this clause, but at least he has been made aware of what is expected of him.

(C) In order to give the Seller/Landlord some time to clean up the house and to repair any damages, **the Buyer's POSSESSION DATE should NOT coincide with the Tenants' moving-out-date.**

(D) The Seller/Landlord is presumably holding a substantial DAMAGE DEPOSIT from the tenants which shouldn't be refunded to them until such time when
- the tenants have moved out and
- he (the Landlord) had inspected the house and
- found it to be in acceptable condition.

(E) **If the Seller fails to clean up the premises and effect the necessary repairs, then the Buyer**
- should not panic and start hauling out the garbage.
- Instead he should take picture of the mess and damages (as future proof in a Small Claims Court action).
- With the assistance of his Realtor he should give **written notice to the Seller** that unless he will remedy the outstanding items within a specified period of time, then the Buyer will arrange for the clean-up etc. and then present him the bill for it. Yes, it can end up in Small Claims Court or Mediation. Of course, the difficulty with this is that in real life the Buyer and his furniture have to go somewhere eventually. Staying with relatives or friends or in a motel is only a temporary solution.

(F) Alternatively the Buyer may try to hold back some money from the Seller's Sales Proceeds (he will succeed only **if this "hold-back" was part of and included in his original offer and was accepted by the Seller** as part and parcel of all other terms and conditions. Even if the Seller had struck out this clause, the Buyer will have nevertheless succeeded in putting the Seller on notice of what will be expected of him on Possession Date.

(G) **WHAT HAPPENS if the Landlord/Seller will list his house for sale only AFTER the tenants have moved out?**
- Unfortunately the Seller will have to make 2 or 3 mortgage payments while the house is vacant.
- However **the following are ADVANTAGES:**
  There will be no problems with the tenants
  - making showings difficult or
  - moving out late and
  - leaving a mess behind.
  - **As the house will be vacant**
    - it can be shown at any time (even on short or no notice),
    - and a Buyer can have QUICK POSSESSION.
    - The Landlord will have a chance to improve the appearance of the property by
    - cleaning up the premises
    - effecting repairs and painting where needed.
    - As a result the house will sell
    - quicker,

- with less hassle and
- **most likely for a better price because the house will show better.**

The mortgage payments which will have to be made while the house is vacant should be viewed as an "investment" in the trouble free, smart and speedy sale of the property.

CASE LAW:

"BEACOCK v. WETTER" B.C. Supreme Court, New Westminster Registry, Date 2005-07-11, Docket No. L88987 The chronic late payment of the rent is not a variation (amendment) of the rental contract. Notice to move.

"COVEY v. St. DENIS" B.C. Supreme Court, Date 2003-07-22, Docket No. 13260 Standard of review of an Arbitrator's decision. The tenant may elect to treat the tenancy as ended
- if the Landlord has breached a material term of the agreement
- and if the tenant advises the Landlord accordingly.

"Al STOBER CONSTRUCTION LTD. v. LONG" B.C. Supreme Court, Date 2001-05-25, Docket No. 52219 Reasonableness and materiality of a "No Pets" clause. Notice of rent increase. Grounds for judicial review: alleged breach by the Arbitrator of procedural fairness or natural justice. The legislature's intent is that Courts should not interfere with an Arbitrator's decision except where it is patently unreasonable.

In **"Re MILLER and ZUCHEK"** (1982), 132 D.L.R. (3d) 142 (B.C.C.A.) the Court held that "reasonableness and materiality" of a "no pets clause" in a residential tenancy agreement was a question of "mixed law and fact."

"CAESAR & ELLIOT GROUP et al v. SHERWOOD et al" [2000] B.C.J. No. 1445 (S.C.) The issue: whether an arbitrator erred in finding that a Notice of Rent Increase was invalid.

Selling A Property With Unauthorized Accommodation

For many years neither the private sector nor the 3 levels of Government (municipal, provincial and federal) have been able to solve adequately the growing problem of low cost rental accommodation. This shortage of affordable rental housing is most apparent in the regions of major urban areas. There local politicians seem to have decided that unauthorized secondary suites in single family residences are an expedient way out of the dilemma where to "warehouse" the multitude of people who are flocking to the "big cities" in ever increasing numbers.

Originally the idea of an "In-Law Suite" was to give loving accommodation in the family home to a close blood relative (e.g. an elderly parent, a handicapped child) or somebody related by marriage or adoption to the principal (occupant) owners of the dwelling. Unfortunately over the years there has been a lot of bending of some of the rules and as a consequence the public is now divided about the issue of secondary suites. For the last few years many of the former revenue generating properties like duplexes, triplexes and small (up to 10 suites) apartment blocks have not been built. Instead of these type of properties, contractors seem to have concentrated on building - what is often called- huge "Monster Houses" with 2 or 3 basement or "side" suites. Usually its occupants are total strangers to each other. Houses with 3 suites are preferred, because of the expectation that the rental income from 2 of the suites will subsidize the mortgage and the income from the 3rd suite buys the Landlord's groceries.

Frequently the Landlord insists that the rent is paid in (untraceable) cash and therefore he has little incentive to declare the rental income for tax purposes. Unless somebody reports the Landlord, Revenue Canada appears to be unable to collect millions of potential tax Dollars.

Obviously the tenants are vulnerable to landlord abuse.

Because of the sheer number of suites there is little or no effective municipal supervision possible to ensure that these accommodations adhere to basic health, safety, building codes (ceiling height, electrical, plumbing and soundproofing) or fire codes or meet smoke and ventilation regulations.

Public opinion pro and contra the suites is often emotional and uncompromising on both sides of the fence.

Those who favour the traditional single-family neighbourhood are concerned with
(a) the loss of the neighbourhood's character; for them it is a "quality of life" issue. Frequently moving transient tenants have little or no pride in the neighbourhood.
(b) However, these tenants will cause the inevitable increase in traffic, noise, pollution and congestion (on-street parking problems are especially bad in a cul-de-sac).

(c) People also feel that the tenants do not contribute (by way of taxation) their fair share of the community's costs for roads, utilities (water, sewer and garbage), police, schools and the maintenance of parks and playgrounds.

Advocates for the secondary suites say that
- the suites will accommodate the rapid population growth
- without creating further urban sprawl or loss of precious farmland to new subdivisions.
- It is also argued that secondary suites are the most cost effective and efficient method of producing cheap and almost instant rental housing in sufficient volume
- without the 3 levels of government having to spend any money.
- Because of the recent huge increases in property values many new homeowner can no longer afford to live in a house unless they have a "mortgage helper" (revenue from an illegal suite).

Throughout B.C. there is no consistent municipal policy on secondary suites. About 25% of the municipalities do not permit secondary suites in any area. The remaining local governments have a bewildering range of approaches from
- outright "closing their eyes and doing nothing" because of the (political) fear of antagonizing a large block of voters
- to "acting only if an immediate neighbour is complaining"
- or alternatively to permitting suites not only in 2-family zones and through site-specific rezoning, but also tolerate illegal suites in single family residences zones.
- In 1995 the then B.C. Minister of Housing, Recreation and Consumer Services had a report published entitled "Rental Housing Trends in B.C."

(I) **The Municipality v. Owners of properties with illegal accommodation.**

(1) Reduced to its essentials, the matter of illegal suites (the politically correct expression is "unauthorized accommodation") is a case of an owner deliberately flouting the Municipal By-Laws for his own benefit and in the hope of not being detected.

(2) Although many municipalities may observe a silent or temporary moratorium on the question of permitting suites or not, it should be understood that local governments do have the right to make and enforce By-Laws. The general rules in that respect have been summarized in **"MONTREAL (City) v. ARCADE AMUSEMENTS INC.,"** [1985] 1 S.C.R. 368 at p. 404 based on the decision of Lord Russell of Killowen in **"KRUSE v. JOHNSON"** [1898] 2 Q.B. 91 (H.L.).

(3) In B.C. Section 963 (now section 903) of the MUNICIPAL ACT, RSBC 1979, c. 290 sets out a local government's authority with respect to zoning by-laws.

(4) The principle of municipal law is that By-Laws must affect everybody equally.

Municipal legislation must be impartial and cannot discriminate and/or show favouritism to certain sections of the population.

(5) Unauthorized accommodation has triggered legal action by various municipalities against numerous owners. A review of a number of law cases showed that in all cases the defendant homeowners have lost and had to discontinue the illegal suite.

The following are some examples:

(a) **"BURNABY (City) v. POCRNIC,"** B.C. Court of Appeal, Docket CA025530, Date 1999-11-12 A case of persistent and defiant infringement of the By-Laws; the defence was a claim for immunity "because everybody else is having illegal suites."

(b) **"LANGLEY (Township) v. WOOD,"** B.C. Supreme Court, Docket A963884, Vancouver 1998-06-24 Breach of the Township's zoning By-Laws because of the continued rental of 2 units on the property.

(c) **"TENANTS' RIGHTS ACTION COALITION v. CORP. OF DELTA"** B.C. Supreme Court, Docket A961448, Date 1997-09-19 The Defendant owners had bought a house in Delta which was situated in an area zoned RS4 (Single Family Dwelling). A suite was already located in the house and it was rented. The new owners installed a half wall to divide the basement into 2 suites. Delta relied on the decision in **"FAMINOW v. NORTH VANCOUVER (District),"** (1988), 24 BCLR (2d) 49, 61 DLR (4th) 747 (BCAA). By invoking the definition of "FAMILY" used in Delta's By-Law, it appears to be a valid zoning device to regulate the "USE" and "CHARACTER" of residential premises and to control (within its authority) additional uses of single family dwellings.

(d) **"R. v. PESTI,"** B.C. Supreme Court, Docket CC911000, Date 1991-11-27 Prior to February 1990 the respondent's property in North Vancouver contained 3 dwelling units. Under the City zoning By-Law only one dwelling unit was allowed. As directed by the City the lower floor unit was removed in May 1990. Sometime later Council passed a resolution regarding the "Illegal Suite Enforcement Issue," which said that during the period of the moratorium, the City of North Vancouver would not permit the construction of illegal suites nor would it permit the re-establishment of suites which had been previously removed. Nevertheless the Respondents re-established the illegal lower floor suite by reinstating the cooking facilities and by removing stairs which had been installed between the lower floor and the main floor in order to comply with the City's original directive. The Respondents' defence of accusing the City of exercising bad faith and (discriminatory) conduct failed. Pursuant to s. 686(4) of the Criminal Code a verdict of guilty with respect to the offence was entered against both Respondents (owners).

(e) **"THE CORPORATION OF THE CITY OF NORTH VANCOUVER v. JOHN AND EILEEN VANNECK,"** B.C. Supreme Court (Vancouver), Date 1997-06-09, Docket No. A970081 In spite of the fact that the subject property had for many years 2 house numbers and 2 meters, it was in a single family zoning. The owners strenuously argued that the building was "legally non-conforming" or alternatively the City was barred by operation of the doctrines of laches, acquiescence or estoppel. The owners lost and had to remove the illegal accommodation within a specified time limit.

(II) **What is a REALTOR'S LIABILITY when selling a property with UNAUTHORIZED accommodation?**

(1) For a Realtor to conspire to work with a Seller or counselling a Buyer to contravene municipal By-Laws is not only inappropriate, but probably also illegal because it may have serious repercussions:
- namely the loss of the (illegal) rental income (when the suite is shut down) and subsequent financial hardship for the homeowner (no more "mortgage helper").
- Negation of an insurance claim in case of extensive (fire) damage, because the property is/was or has become "non-conforming" when the municipality changed the calculation of buildable house floor areas.

(2) In **"MALPASS v. MORRISON,"** Ontario Superior Court of Justice, Docket 19781A/A0, Date 2004-11-09 the Court found that the Realtor owed to the Buyer both an equitable duty and a legal duty to tell him that the basement bedroom was not in compliance with the municipal By-Law. For not fully disclosing this information regarding the property (which might have affected the Buyer's decision-making process) the Realtor had to pay about $ 62,000.00 in damages.

(3) **"ECK v. MONTREAL TRUST COMPANY OF CANADA,"** B.C. Supreme Court, Docket 89/989, Date 1991-02-18. This case dealt with the illegal rental of a cottage [being a 2nd building on the land]. The Realtors were assessed $ 20,872.50 in damages (for fraudulent misrepresentation, special damages for moving expenses and lawyer's fees).

(4) In **"MURRAY v. TILLEY and OWEN GRIMES REALTY (2000) INC."** Supreme Court of Newfoundland and Labrador, Date 2005-01-06, Docket 200203T0200 under section [82] the Court analyses a Realtor's "duty to inquire and disclose." Liability flows not from the untruth of a representation, but from the breach of a Realtor's legal obligation to obtain certain information and in turn to disclose such information to his Client. The Defendant Realtors were liable for damages in the amount of $ 23,525.00 for the diminution in the fair market value of the subject property, as well as for mental distress (one of the Plaintiffs was

expecting a child).

(5) In order to be able to give "INFORMED CONSENT" when entering into an Agency relationship with a Realtor, a "Customer" is entitled to have a reasonable expectation of being told EVERYTHING he needs to know even during pre-contractual negotiations. See **"HODGKINSON v. SIMMS,"** B.C. Court of Appeal CA 011048 and Supreme Court of Canada [1994] 3 S.C.R. 377 (honesty in bargaining during precontractual representations: one party must make to the other party proper disclosure of material facts even if they are adverse to the other party. Liability in tort).

(6) Once an agency relationship has been established, then the Realtor has Fiduciary Duties to his Clients:
- Standard of Care
- Full disclosure of all pertinent facts etc.

(7) Also see Part # 1 of "The PROPERTY CONDITION DISCLOSURE STATEMENT" in this book.

Selling Renovated Properties And Owner Built Houses

Extra caution should be taken when dealing with a renovated property, **especially when the Realtor is emphasizing the various renovations as a selling feature.**

The following are commonly done renovations which could add value to the property or at least may make it more saleable:

Remodelling the kitchen
Remodelling the bathroom
Exterior painting
Interior painting
Finishing the basement (recreation room, extra bedroom, extra bathroom, home office)
Well kept landscaping; a property fence
A new energy efficient heating system
New double glazed windows

The Listing Salesperson should:
(1) Verify with the local Municipality that
    (a) the required permits have been taken out for the work done.
    (b) The required inspections (including the final inspections) have been made.
(2) Investigate any "warranties" (e.g. for the roof)
    (a) Verify that the warranty actually exists (and obtain a copy thereof).
    (b) Investigate if the company or individual who has given the warranty is still in business.
    (c) Investigate if the warranty is transferable.
    (d) Verify the conditions and terms of the transfer of the warranty (e.g. obtain a written assignment of the warranty from the Roofing Company).
(3) Investigate if the remodelled end product (e.g. finished basement suite) meets current local Zoning and Building By-Laws and fire regulations.
(4) Investigate if the building and/or its use has become "legally non-conforming" due to municipal changes in zoning or due to other changes, e.g.:
    (a) Changes in the side yard setbacks for gross-density half acre lots can create legal non-conforming status for existing homes built out and up to the previous smaller setback.
    (b) An existing "over-sized" or "mega" home may become legally non-conforming when by-law amendments are adopted calling for a reduction in the buildable floor area ratio. This may mean that the owner:
        - cannot legally add a detached garage.
        - Cannot add onto the house.
        - If 75% of the building is damaged (e.g. by fire) then the new building must meet all then current By-Law provisions as of the date of the fire occurrence. In other words, it cannot be rebuilt to its former size.

"JAKUBKE v. SUSSEX GROUP SRC REALTY CORP.," Supreme Court of B.C., May 7, 1993, Docket No. 891795

The Seller had added a West Wing (bedroom and bathroom) which contravened the Municipal Building Code and Bylaws. The Seller was found to be liable for fraudulent misrepresentation because he suppressed the truth about his remodelling work. The Realtors were found liable for negligent misrepresentation (they failed to realize that a problem existed and didn't inform the Buyer so that the Buyer could investigate further).

"ECK v. MONTREAL TRUST COMPANY OF CANADA," B.C. Supreme Court, [1991-02-18], Docket No. 89/989

The Buyer had been searching for a property which could produce a certain income. Eventually the Buyer bought a property which had been converted into 3 suites and a separate new cottage which had 2 floors. The rental from the cottage was suggested to be $ 550.00 and she was led to believe that the total annual income from the 3 suites and the cottage was approx. $ 24,000.00. After taking possession, the City informed the Buyer that the cottage was in contravention of a zoning By-Law. The Realtor never informed the Buyer that the cottage could not legally be rented. When she discovered that it would not produce the income expected, she sold the property and sued for damages. She was successful.

The following is a suggested wording when selling a property with accommodation which is or could be illegal (e.g.: advertised as "Mortgage Helper," "In-law suite," "Nanny's Accommodation," "Grandma's quarters" etc.):

"The Buyer hereby acknowledges that he has been advised that this property contains or may contain unauthorized accommodation; consequently there is a possibility that the rental income thereof could be discontinued."

The Selling Salesperson:
(1) Should obtain for the Buyer all pertinent information in order to enable the Buyer to make an "informed decision" about
   - buying or not and
   - about the property's value.
(2) Should suggest to the Buyer to **obtain a written report from a Certified Home Inspector.** If the Client declines to do so, a prudent Realtor will insert a clause into the Contract of Purchase and Sale that the Buyer has declined to hire an Inspector.

AMATEUR BUILDERS and HANDYMAN CONTRACTORS.

Sometimes people build a home for their own use; they may do this either entirely by themselves or with the help of various subtrades or a contractor. When they sell the house (even after they have lived in it for a number of years) they then become liable to a subsequent owner for any unsafe conditions or hidden dangers. Consumer protection requires that subsequent owner/occupants should be entitled to rely on the skill of the original builder.

Even an amateur builder is expected to have built the house to be reasonably fit for its intended use.
Subsequent owners may also have a potential claim for
- negligently completed construction
- negligently supervised construction
- construction below the standard of care reasonably required.

"SWEENEY v. BREEDVELD" (2003-04-14) Provincial Court of B.C., Docket No. S13153 Deals with the risks encountered when buying a used home from an owner/builder who had no previous construction experience.

"PATON v. LITTLE" (2003-01-28), Saskatchewan Court of Queen's Bench, Docket No. QB03040; QB 182/01JCMJ The Defendant Little was his own general contractor when he built the house in 1983. On the building permit application it was specified that the house will be on a concrete foundation. Attached to the permit issued by the Municipal Engineering Department was the proviso: "If a preserved wood foundation is to be used, plans shall be submitted to the undersigned [Engineering Department] for approval. Such plans must bear the seal of a professional engineer registered in Saskatchewan." Little decided to build with the wood substitute, but he did not obtain or submit the required plans or engineering certification. The consequences were dire. The Defendants sold the house to the Plaintiff in January 2001 and after moving in the Buyer discovered that the elevation of the house was such that the wooden foundations walls were quite badly deflected inward, because they were not standing up to the pressure from the backfill. There was also dampness and moisture in the basement. As the defects were actively concealed by the Defendants, the Plaintiff Buyers received judgement.

"MARIANI v. LEMSTRA" (2003-02-14) Ontario Superior Court of Justice, Docket 5635-93. John Lemstra acted as General Contractor and built a home with the help of some subtrades. The Lemstra family moved into the house without obtaining a final inspection and occupancy permit. They continued working on the house while living in it. After 3 years they sold the house to Mrs. Mariani who discovered a number of serious defects after having moved in (e.g. the centre load-bearing wall was structurally unsound [it shifted and cracked and was dangerous within the meaning of the Provincial Building Code]. The basement leaked and mould appeared). **The Court found that a Seller/Builder knows a lot more about the state of the house and quality of its construction than does another Seller.**

In the above the following other law case was considered: **"WINNIPEG CONDOMINIUM CORPORATION No. 36 v. BIRD CONSTRUCTION CO.,"** Supreme Court of Canada, (1995-01-26) Docket No.. 23624 A newly constructed building is sold by the developer; however subsequently a dangerous defect was discovered. The contractor is responsible to subsequent buyers for the cost of repairs of latent defects which render the building dangerous.

How To Avoid A Law Suit

The law is not always perfect and due to the vagaries of litigation the outcome of a law suit is often uncertain.

Whenever possible the **best course of action is to avoid law suits altogether.**

If you have the misfortune of ending up in Court you should keep in mind that you must have the following:
- a good cause,
- good evidence (seamless records),
- a good deal of money
- to hire a good lawyer.
- A good deal of patience: law suits are very time consuming because of "legal manoeuvres" and "scheduling."
- When you finally manage to get into Court you may have to suffer through a good deal of complicated legal arguments.
- Of course, you also need a good judge.
- But above all you need a lot of GOOD LUCK.
  No wonder that the French Emperor Napoleon said that law suits are an absolute leprosy and a social cancer.

(I) THE FOLLOWING TAKES PLACE DURING THE PROCESS OF A TRIAL.

(1) The feuding parties present **EVIDENCE and ARGUMENTS.**
There is also the **BURDEN OF PROOF.**
EVIDENCE can be open to interpretation and sometimes is affected by the demeanour of the individual who is giving the evidence.

(2) **A JUDGE** presides at the trial and
- **assesses the CREDIBILITY** of those who give evidence.
- **He decides which evidence to accept and which to reject.** [See "FARNYA v. CHORNY" (1951), (B.C.C.A.) 4 W.W.R. (NS)171]. Justice cannot depend on who is the best actor in the witness box.

(3) **The CREDIBILITY** of a person giving evidence depends on
- his knowledge and ability to describe clearly what he has seen and heard.
- His powers of observation and memory (what he truthfully remembers) and
- on being confident and quick-minded.

(4) On the other hand some persons giving evidence may
- get caught in a clumsy lie or
- worse still might be shrewd and adept in the half-lie combining skilfully exaggeration with partial suppression of the truth.

(5) As evidence is open to interpretation, a Judge may occasionally focus on a small or specific portion of the evidence and give it more importance than it was intended to receive.

(6) At the end of the trial the **Judge applies the law to the facts of the case and renders his decision (judgment).**

(II) Unfortunately Realtors are being sued by dissatisfied clients with ever increasing aggressiveness.

WHAT MOTIVATES A CLIENT TO SUE?
For some reason Buyers often assume that
- the Realtor knows literally everything about the property.
- Some may even think that the Realtor is a "guarantor" of the condition of the house.
- Regardless of what the Seller's "Property Condition Disclosure Statement" says if something bad happens after the Buyers move in they automatically assume that somebody (the Seller or the Realtor) failed to disclose the fault.

The favourite accusations against Realtors are
- negligence,
- misrepresentation and
- the ultimate catch-all of "Breach of Fiduciary Duty."
- The Business Practices or Ethics Committee of the local real estate board also adds the old standby of "Breach of the Golden Rule."

Here are a few suggestions how a Realtor can protect himself:

(1) **Learn** everything you can about the real estate business:
- especially about (patent and latent) defects,
- the various kinds of "representations" (what is puffing; what is the difference between innocent, negligent and fraudulent misrepresentations).

(2) **Watch** what you say to your clients: are you merely passing on information or are you giving "advice" on subjects which you are not qualified for?

(3) Whenever possible, **try to shift the liability onto an expert**. For independent legal advice always suggest that Clients should consult a lawyer. Point out to the Client that even if it costs him some money now, he may save himself a lot of money and grief later on. To protect yourself, **you may have to document your suggestion as a "subject" clause** in the Contract of Purchase and Sale.
Alternatively make a suitable notation in your Deal File or Work Diary (note both the time and date of the occasion).

(4) Always suggest that **the property be checked over by a qualified licensed Home Inspector.** Sometimes it may be necessary to go one step further:
To check the presence or absence of sundry **PESTS (e.g. wood deteriorating bugs)**

suggest to consult a **Certified Pest Control Specialist**.

Where serious soil stability and foundation problems are suspected an ENGINEERING REPORT should be obtained.

   (a) Whatever type of inspector the Buyer decides on, don't just suggest the name of one particular Inspector because you could somehow attract liability if he overlooks something. Instead let the Client choose from a list of Inspectors.

   (b) If the client should decline, then be sure to **DOCUMENT his refusal** in your work diary or the Deal File (date, time, location: your thoroughness may impress a Judge some day).

(5) **Are you making promises** which you are not able or willing to keep? "Mr. Seller: I will work my fingers to the bone for you!" or "I will advertise your house in the newspaper every week."

(6) When you are making your **Agency Disclosure** are you disclosing your services or are you inadvertently giving the (incorrect) impression that you are telling the Client all about the duties and liabilities which **AGENCY confers on BOTH of you?** (Remember that the Principal is vicariously responsible for the wrongful actions of his Agent).

(7) (a) **Information obtained from the Seller should be verified by the Listing Broker** regardless of how sincere or sophisticated the Seller appears to be.

   (b) If there is any doubt then **information obtained from the Listing Broker should be verified by the Selling Broker.**

   (c) **The independent verification of specific information is an absolute "MUST" if a certain item is of paramount IMPORTANCE to the Buyer and he has told you so** (e.g. a low interest rate with a long renewal date on an assumable mortgage).

(8) Get into the habit of keeping for each client **a detailed and accurate communications log**. You can either scribble onto the back of your file or else you can set something up on your computer. If you are too lazy or in a rush to keep good records then some day you may have a chance to repent it at leisure in Court.

(9) Judges have the difficult task of deciding **"on the balance of probabilities"** who is to be believed. When you give evidence in Court, are you going to make a good and strong impression? **Are you able to back up your facts with proof? On the other hand** - even if you are innocent - you can still loose if you waffle and your story is full of holes. **Lousy record keeping may come back to haunt you with a vengeance.**

(10) **Keep all FAX communications in** your file. The FAX will document and corroborate the date and time it was sent.

(11) **Make print copies of all e-mail communications.** Same as with the FAXES, printed e-mail copies show the time and date and thus can be used to determine and prove the timeline of events, namely who knew and did what and when.

(12) **Be very careful when you prepare "Hand-out Brochures"** (accurate room sizes, floor area, age of house, sewer connection, zoning, correct lot size, easements etc.)

(13) If you are giving out **financial statements** (e.g. in the sale of a business), inventories, Statements of Assets and Liabilities etc. make sure that they are **prepared by an accountant and that they are up-to-date**. If the year-end reports are not available, then obtain the latest one, together with an interim report prepared by the Seller's accountant (and not the Seller).

(14) And finally **learn to part company with the Clients-from-hell**. These are the petulant, reluctant and belligerent Clients who make sarcastic remarks about your commission and that your built-in instincts warn you about. Regardless of how much time, money and effort you are willing to spend on these people, regardless of how many concessions you are making in the vain hope of trying to make this difficult-to-please person happy, you will never succeed.

After you have cut your commission to the bone, they may still sue you (to pay for any repairs) or may complain about you at the Real Estate Board. (What have they got to loose? Even if you are found to be innocent, the complaining member of the public will not have to pay any hearing costs, nor will they be required to apologize to you).

Serving these kind of clients will never be worth what it may cost you:
- the bad experience will mercilessly sap your strength, health and enthusiasm and waste your time.
- If you don't dump them in time then chances are that in the end you will invariably feel that you have been taken to the cleaners.

Judging from the perusal of many law cases brought on by dissatisfied Clients one is left to wonder why it would almost appear that a Realtor is not entitled to make an honest or innocent mistake.

By way of a comparison here are some interesting examples of the Standard of Care in cases of alleged Solicitor Negligence.

"Jacobson Ford-Mercury Sales Ltd. v. Sivertz" (1980) 1 WWR 141 It was stated: "A lawyer is obliged to act as a 'prudent solicitor' and must 'bring to the exercise of his profession a reasonable amount of knowledge, skill and care in connection with the business of his client'.

There is no liability for mere errors in judgment because a solicitor does NOT untertake NOT TO MAKE MISTAKES but only NOT to make NEGLIGENT mistakes.

The determination is said to be a question of degree and there is a borderline between negligence and no negligence." See "Linden Canadian Tort Law" 1977, pp. 108 - 109.

In **"Marbel Developments Ltd. v. Pirani"** (1994-01-24) BCSC Vancouver Registry No. C925970 it was held that: "A solicitor's duty is determined by the work undertaken rather than by his or her circumstances - **the standard is only one of reasonable competence: it is NOT a standard of perfection - or of strict liability."**

A solicitor's standard of care was also considered by the Supreme Court of Canada in **"Central and Eastern Trust Company v. Rafuse"** (1986), 2 SCR 147.

"When A Deal Goes Sour"

"Subject-to" clauses are inserted into a contract for the protection of the contracting parties. E.g. with the "subject to financing clause" the Buyer protects himself by saying that he will buy the house only if he can obtain the necessary financing.

It is important that in all cases the Clients' subsequent actions will match their originally professed intentions. For that purpose the parties must make an honest effort to satisfy each "subject" clause. E.g. if a Buyer changes his mind he cannot use the "subject to financing" clause as an excuse to back out of the sale. He would have to supply written proof to demonstrate that he had made his "BEST EFFORT" to obtain financing and that his application had been declined by several Lending Institutions.

(I)
If a sale collapses because one or several of the "subject-to" clauses couldn't be removed, then it may be disappointing to the people involved, but there should be no serious legal repercussions. If everybody is agreeable to collapse the sale then the contracting parties
- will sign a **MUTUAL RELEASE** and
- will jointly give written instructions to the Real Estate Company about the disposition of the deposit which is being held "in Trust" by them.

(II)
If on the other hand a deal goes sour after all of the "subject-to" clauses had been removed and the sale has become "FIRM," then matters can quickly deteriorate into a situation with serious consequences. E.g. relying on the strength of his "firm" sale the Seller may have bought another property and consequently will find himself in a precarious legal and financial position. Tempers will flare and stress levels will sharply escalate when the lawyers start making phone calls and write "position letters" to each other.

(1) **IF THE BUYER reneges on the contract**, then the SELLER has the following choices:
    (a) He can refuse to accept the Buyer's refusal to complete and **sue for "Specific Performance"** in an attempt to force the Buyer to go through with the deal. From a practical point of view the problem with that is that
- it often takes a long time to get into Court.
- During that waiting period the legal fees will continue to grow.
- If the real estate market declines and values should drop while the parties are waiting for their Court date,
  - then the reluctant Buyer may find that he will not be able to complete even if he is ordered to.
  - The reason for this is that Lending Institutions will base their loan amounts on the "Then-Current-Value" and not on an "outdated-and-too-high" Selling Price of the past. Unless the Buyer can come up

with the extra cash to cover the mortgage shortfall, then everybody will realize that going to Court was a waste of time and money. It would have been far better to negotiate some sort of compromise/settlement in the beginning.
(b) To mitigate his losses before prices drop again, the Seller would have to try to resell the house fairly quickly.
(c) As Court procedures take a long time the real estate company could pay the deposit into Court after having given the required notice to everybody. The "notice" is required because eventually it will cost some legal fees to get the money out of Court.
(d) If the Seller resells the house (at a loss) then he can **sue for DAMAGES or "loss of bargain"**: the "loss" would be the **difference** between the **originally** contracted Selling Price and the "Then-Current-Value" (namely the eventually achieved Selling Price) **at a subsequent date chosen by the Court**.
(e) In certain circumstances, the Seller could also try to **sue for "consequential damages"** as a result of and flowing from the Buyer's breach of contract.

(2) **WHEN THE SELLER reneges on the contract**, then the BUYER also has legal remedies (e.g. specific performance).

Provided that the Buyer is ready, willing and able to complete in a timely manner on a firm and subject-free contract, there is the additional interesting issue of the **Realtors' entitlement to their commission.**
The commission entitlement is based on
- the wording of the Listing Contract and
- the principle that the Realtors have done all that was required of them, namely produce a Buyer who is ready, willing and able to complete on Completion Date.

WHAT should a REALTOR DO when A DEAL GOES SOUR?

(1) **NEGATIVE CONDUCT IS COUNTER PRODUCTIVE:**
(a) The Realtor should NOT become emotionally involved in this toxic affair.
(b) He should also NOT adopt an uncooperative, resentful or adversarial attitude against the other Realtor and that Realtor's Client. **(Bad public relations)**.
(c) He should avoid becoming actively involved in the legal dispute between the Seller and the Buyer by giving well meaning but possibly poor legal advice. Whereas the temptation might be great to save his Client some legal fees this misguided action could cost the Realtor dearly: he can be sued for negligence.
(d) The Realtor should avoid to lament publicly and bitterly about his lost commission. Whereas he has every right to be upset about his misfortune a public display of his emotions could have negative effects on his business relationships.

(2) **The following are POSITIVE SURVIVAL STRATEGIES.**
   (a) If the situation warrants it then the Realtor should **recommend to his Client to obtain competent legal advice without delay.**
   (b) The Realtor should discuss the collapsed sale immediately with his Sales Manager. His supervisor not only needs to know what is going on but he may have some constructive ideas or suggestions how to save the deal or at least how to minimize the damage. After all **Realtors are "idea people" and "problem solvers."**
   (c) Considering that the Realtor is supposed to be the not-emotionally-involved "Professional" he should be sympathetic to and supportive of his Client without loosing sight of his objectivity.
   (d) In conjunction with all parties and their respective lawyers the Realtor should make himself available for any "damage control" action. He should offer to the lawyers his willingness to assist in exploring all possibilities of salvaging whatever can be saved of the deal.
   (e) This requires the wholehearted and unreserved cooperation of all Realtors involved.
   (f) A smart Realtor will PROFIT by turning this unhappy affair into a **LEARNING EXPERIENCE** in order to protect himself and any of his Clients in the future.
(3) **If the deal CANNOT be saved**, then the Realtor should:
   (a) Complete a "Collapsed Sales Report" for the Office records.
   (b) Obtain from all contracting parties
      - **a written RELEASE** (releasing each other of all legal liabilities which may have been created).
      - **Specific WRITTEN instructions about the disposition of the Deposit.** Occasionally this can become a contentious issue. Any negotiations between the feuding parties about the deposit (who gets what and how much) is best left to their respective lawyers. As STAKEHOLDER of the deposit the Realtor should NOT get involved in this.
   (c) Above all, the Realtor should not become distracted or discouraged by the slow pace of the unfolding legal action; the worst thing which he could do is to become paralyzed into inaction by anxiously waiting on the sidelines for the mess to be resolved.
   (d) Having done all he could for the parties involved he should devote himself to more profitable endeavours by CONTINUING UNDETERRED in his sales efforts with OTHER Clients.
   (e) In due course when the Clients from the collapsed sale have settled their differences, he can always go back and find another Buyer for the Seller's house or find another house for his former Buyer.

A Realtor's Right To Commission When The Transaction Is Not Completed

Every Realtor has the right to protect his commissions to the best of his ability. Of course he can see a lawyer but the lawyer's fees may exceed the total amount of the commission. For those who may wish to go to Small Claims Court, here are a few helpful hints for your consideration.

Go to your local Court House Law Library and ask the librarian for assistance to find for you the following:

- "Topical Law Reports by CCH Canadian Limited,"
- DiCastri "Law of Vendor & Purchaser" 3rd edition and
- JOWITT's Dictionary of English Law, 2nd edition by John BURKE.

These will lead you to numerous law cases of interest. The information is available to the public at any Law Library (most likely at no cost except for photocopying).

The **"Right to Commission"** is determined by the **WORDING of the LISTING CONTRACT**. This wording is of prime importance and will override a general rule derived from the case law. The Listing Contract often says that the commission is earned by the Realtor when there is a valid, subject-free, firm contract of Purchase and Sale between the Seller and Buyer. Of course, the Buyer must be ready, willing and able to complete on Completion Date. In case there is a conflict between the terms of the Listing Contract and those of the Contract of Purchase & Sale as to the payment of commission, the terms of the Listing Contract will prevail, since there is no consideration for any new contract (between the Realtors and the Seller) arising out of the Contract for Purchase & Sale.

See **"Leading Investments Ltd. v. New Forest Investments Ltd."** (1982), 126 D.L.R. (3d) 75. (I am quoting the codes, so that any interested reader will be able to locate the case in the law library).

(1) **If the BUYER fails to complete:**
"**Howell v. Kenton Agencies Ltd.**" (1953) 1 D.L.R. 821 (Ont. H.C.): the commission was not contingent on completion of the sale nor payable out of the proceeds, the agent was entitled to recover, even though the default was that of the Buyer.
2) The Realtor stands a better chance to recover commission **when the failure to complete is the fault of the SELLER.**
   (a) "**Advantage Homes Ltd. v. Jones**" Surrey Small Claims Court file # 29682
   The agent has been held to be entitled to commission upon **refusal of the owner to proceed**. This decision was on the grounds that the agent had done all he was required to do namely produce a subject-free firm sale from a buyer ready, willing and able to proceed on the date set for completion.

(b) **"Western Mortgage (Realty) Corp. v. Small World Holdings Inc."** (1993), 77 B.C.L.R. (2d) 324 (C.A.) The Listing Contract provided that a commission was to be payable "upon a binding contract of sale being entered into." The express terms of the contract made the commission payable.

(c) **"Bolohan v. John R. Marsh & Co"** (1979) 11 R 1, Ont.H.C. Commission is payable, **even where the transaction is aborted through no fault of the Seller;** whether the commission is payable will be determined by the general law of contract and also by the wording of the Listing agreement.

(d) **"Professional Realty Corporation Ltd. v. H. Y. Louie Co. Limited."** B.C.S.C., November 1, 1989, Court File No. C 883597 The agreement (between the parties) was not ambiguous; but even if it were ambiguous, the Court would imply the term that commission is payable once the agent had done all required of it, based on extrinsic evidence as to universal custom in the real estate industry and behaviour of the defendant.

(e) **"Robert D. Berto Ltd. v. Cushley et al"** (1977), 78 D.L.R. (3d) 713 (Ont. Dist. Ct.) Where, in an agreement for the purchase and sale of land, the Seller agrees to pay a commission to a real estate company for procuring the offer, the commission is payable **even though the sale is, owing to defects in the title, not completed**.

(f) **"Lewis Realty Ltd. v. Skalbania"** (1980)23 B.C.L.R.336 (C.A.) The Seller could not give good title because it was held in trust for himself and another who would not agree to the sale. The listing on the standard Vancouver Real Estate Board form provided that the commission was to be payable, inter alia, on a binding contract of sale being brought into being. This having been done **(the failure of the Seller to make title was only a mistake in expectations)**, the agent was entitled to the commission. The decision was on the grounds that the agent had done all he was required to do, namely find a buyer ready, willing and able to proceed on the date set for completion.

(g) **"United Real Estate Inc. v. Headrick"** (1987) 65 Sask. R.118 (Q.B.); aff. (1988), 69 Sask. R. 310 (C.A.) Privity of contract between the Seller and Selling Agent. As a general rule, the Selling Agent and the Seller have no privity of contract, **unless the evidence was that the parties intended to create it**; e.g. a "Buyer's Agent Commission Protection Agreement." In "Headrick," the agreement to pay the Selling Agent his portion of the commission was found in the agreement between the Selling Agent and the Listing Agent, because they were fellow members of the Multiple Listing Service.

For further discussion please read the appropriate chapter in Sales Meeting # 52 of this book.

However, before you unleash the forces of the Small Claims Court it might be a good idea to **first discuss the merits of your case with your Manager and a Lawyer:**

Remember that:
- you cannot sue in your own name;
- the Plaintiff must be the employer real estate company (even if you are an independent contractor).
- With your case you must file a photocopy of your real estate license (to prove to the Court that you are a licensed Realtor).
- And some Realtors, keeping good public relations in mind, will wish to chalk up a collapsed sale as the price of doing business.

Dealing With Disappointments

The insidious minefield of disappointments is littered with the bodies of hurt Realtors. Any Realtor who is pitching for a listing or who is presenting a good offer is naturally optimistic that things will pan out in his favour. If for some unfathomable reason the hoped for results subsequently don't materialise, a human being is liable to experience

- **that "pang" of disappointment and**
- **that sudden empty feeling of frustration and intense helplessness.**
- Other emotions which could be experienced are: **shock, disbelief, anger, anxiety and the "laying-of-blame."**

Depending on the individual Realtor's personality the extent of the crisis he might find himself experiencing may range from

- absolutely nothing (a few lucky ones are able to just shrug this kind of incident off)
- to a certain degree of annoyance which requires some sort of **CLOSURE** to heal the hurt: "to be done with it" or "to be finished with it."

Don't play the "BLAME"-game.
The hurt caused by a disappointment can be compounded by the **additional belief of having been "rejected."** Many a Realtor jumps to the conclusion that any rejection means **"personal rejection"** and **"personal failure."** This sort of progression reminds one of the inscription on the lintel over the Gate to Hell: "Through me the road to the City of Desolation (goes) … lay down all hope, you that go in by me." (Dante's "Divine Comedy," book "Inferno," Canto III).

The gurus who grind out inspirational books and positive message tapes tell us

- to have **"a positive mental attitude"** and
- to learn to **"view a defeat as an opportunity"** or as a **"stepping stone to bigger and better things."**

These lofty revelations are true, of course. But on the other hand a Realtor works on a "commission only" basis and on many an occasion for him this "positive" business will sound hollow if he suddenly comes to **the sickening realization of having just missed out** on the possibility of earning a $ 15,000 commission.

The "guilt" crisis can take on more serious proportions if we think that in the final analysis we have also let down our loved ones. To exacerbate this situation some only too human Realtors may experience:

(1) **USELESS and HARMFUL "FLASH BACKS":**
   These are **recurrent and distressing recollections** of the "event," especially if it is the latest one in a series of "bad things" which have happened to him.
   (a) **A negative outlook on life is brought about when the Realtor is**

ENDLESSLY and OBSESSIVELY REHASHING in his mind his "many failures."
(b) This sort of CIRCULAR THINKING amounts to a concentrated REHEARSING of UNHAPPINESS.

(2) **THE POWER OF THE MIND is phenomenal** and it can either make or break you.
  (a) **NEGATIVE THOUGHTS** will only produce
   - constant and habitual **NEGATIVE TALK** and eventually
   - all of it will lead to a **MISERABLE LIFE.**
  (b) **SADNESS feeds FEAR and CONFUSION.**
  FEAR can be a mind twister and as a result the killer of good fortune. Fear of danger results in the fight-or-flight response. In Real Estate **FEAR** may alert you to take action to protect yourself from being rejected and failing again. After the atrocious emotional bashing received from several consecutive failures, some Realtors may feel more or less apprehensive and reluctant to put themselves AGAIN into harms way. (Remember the old saying: "You are cruising for a bruising"). For that reason they invent all sorts of **excuses for NOT doing constructive work**; e.g.
   - "I have no talent for prospecting."
   - "Listing isn't my strong point."
   - "Interest rates are too high right now."
   - "I'll buckle down and get to work right after the holidays."

  Such feeble excuses
   - **are DISTORTED thinking and**
   - **are merely a pretext for PROCRASTINATION.**
   - With that sort of attitude the salesperson is already defeated (and bound to fail) **before** he even picks up the phone or walks into the customer's house.

(3) **Common symptoms of this state of mind are:**
   - a feeling of vague **SADNESS,**
   - a feeling of general **helplessness,**
   - **hopelessness and**
   - **worthlessness.**

(4) **ALL** of these feelings are **INGREDIENTS for**
   - acquiring a LOW SELF-ESTEEM and
   - a NEGATIVE MENTAL ATTITUDE.

This unhealthy and counter productive frame of mind is usually obvious to everybody else except, of course, for the person so effected and afflicted. Alternatively, in many cases such a person simply refuses to admit that he has a problem or closes his mind to

it. **To just drift along in a rut is**
- a lot more comfortable and
- a lot less work and
- a lot safer than going out again to face a harsh world.

ANALYSIS and CONSEQUENCES OF THE "DOOMSDAY SCENARIO."

Realtors who persist in this sort of doomsday scenario will
- invariably end up in a **SALES SLUMP.**
- The inevitable consequence of a sales slump is an **unsatisfactory cash flow situation:** bills have the sickening habit of coming in regardless if one has the money to pay for them or not.
- The continuously **increasing FINANCIAL PRESSURE will result in additional burdens in the Realtor's life.**
- When the **accumulated misery becomes too prolonged,** then some people may have **trouble falling or staying asleep.**
- The "body" is the vehicle which carts the "mind" around.
  If the body is constantly tired (and doesn't get adequate rest), then eventually it will go on strike (which is called "illness": such illness may be either physical or emotional).
- **As a consequence** of getting an insufficient amount of good rest people may become **miserable, irritable and could even be prone to outbursts of anger.**
  Because of possible (social and financial) repercussions such anger will NOT be vented against "strangers" (customers or people at work). Instead it will be let out with impunity in the privacy of your home against family members and friends. Remember the song: "You always hurt the ones you love?"

- Anybody unable to control his emotions because of his **reality-distorted way of thinking may require PROFESSIONAL HELP:**
  - For personal problems talk to your doctor, clergyman or a counsellor.
  - To put you on the right track for real estate talk to your Manager or perhaps a kindly disposed senior sales associate.

2 WARNINGS:
(a) Would it be too facetious to say that in the long run rearranging one's sock drawer may be more constructive and productive for one's real estate career than seeking solace in a bottle or other "recreational" drugs? Instead of relaxing you, these 2 particular "solutions" are liable to make matters only worse. They have the potential of creating new and additional problems.
(b) Sales Managers should be alert to the fact that **negativity is contagious** and one vocal defeatist's extensive broadcasting of his "bad luck" can cause an epidemic of frayed nerves in any office.

DAMAGE CONTROL.

(1) **BE REALISTIC but not pessimistic.**
   (a) We live in an imperfect world with imperfect people. Chances are that sooner or later we will be rejected by somebody or disappointed by something.
   (b) Realtors are in the PEOPLE BUSINESS. If a Realtor is active, then the law of average says that he can expect to have his share of FAILURE EXPERIENCES.
   (c) It is best to **face failure experiences WITH COURAGE and NOT with submissive resignation.**

(2) **Make a REALITY CHECK of what REALLY happened.**
   Logic says that
   (a) the Realtor and the Customer are meeting **on business.**
   (b) Most likely on that occasion the Realtor and the Customer are relative **strangers** to each other.
   (c) For reasons of his own this stranger (the Customer) decides not to do business with the Realtor: e.g. he refuses to list with him. At that point in time the Realtor obviously doesn't know why the Customer refused to do business (and possibly ended up doing business with somebody else).
   (d) Unless the Realtor knows for sure what those reasons were, he has **no logical justification** to feel that he was **rejected as a PERSON** (as a father, brother, husband etc.)
   (e) Of course, there is always the theoretical possibility that the Customer didn't like something the Realtor said or did: e.g. his suggested listing price, the extent of his service, the amount of the commission.
   (f) **The GOOD news is that the Realtor can salvage something from this debacle:**
      - he can **LEARN FROM HIS MISTAKES** and
      - with **INCREASING EXPERIENCE** he should have **LESS FAILURES** in the future.

(3) **ANALYZE how the disappointment came about** in the first place.
   Investigate impartially and solve the problem once and for all time. You have **nothing to fear and much to gain** by going over the "episode" **(but only ONCE, please!) to review if you have made any mistakes.**
   (a) Were you yourself the cause by lack of discipline, knowledge or lack of follow-through?
   (b) Have you set your expectations too high? Were they unrealistic?
   (c) Or was it through the aggressive or competitive or thoughtless behaviour of others?
   (d) **If you have come to the conclusion that YOU have made the mistake,** then learn from it for the next time!

(e) **If the answer is "NO,"** then you have nothing to blame yourself for. As there is no need for recrimination, logic demands that there is no point in continuing to punish yourself for something you had no control over or didn't cause.
(f) **If there is no ready answer and the whole thing makes no sense,** then don't waste your time trying to make sense out of nonsense.

(4) The basic premise therefore is:
 (a) **"Learn to LEARN."**
  For his mental and physical health and financial salvation it is important that a Realtor should
  - **hone his Selling skills** by accumulating knowledge and experience.
  - **Learn to live WITH the emotions of his Clients.**
  - **BRING his OWN EMOTIONS UNDER CONTROL.**
 (b) To achieve **CONTROL over his own emotions**, the Realtor must
  - **engage in a more LOGICAL and**
  - **consequently more REWARDING way of THINKING.**
  - The good news is that **AN INDIVIDUAL can actually CHOOSE THE WAY he is THINKING.** It will take some effort, but it can be done by **monitoring your self-talk** (another word for "thinking").
  - Catch yourself when you begin to have negative thoughts and feelings.
  - Instead of indulging in them, say **"STOP! END PROGRAM and DELETE!"**
 (c) In the final analysis the Realtor must either **learn to adapt or else he will perish as a Realtor and leave the business.**

(5) The following are some **SUGGESTIONS** how a Realtor can put himself back on the right track. Take what you think may be useful for you, discard the rest.
 (a) **To repeatedly dwell on negative things** can bring about nothing but undesirable problems, including health problems. **No client, no deal and no amount of money (commission Dollars) are worth getting sick over. If you don't have your health, then "you've got NOTHING."**
 (b) **Let your feelings out.**
  To keep your emotional equilibrium, don't bottle up your feelings: carrying a hurt around is tantamount to labouring under the crushing weight of a boulder.
  - Resolve to get rid of this excess baggage.
  - If you feel the need to let off steam, then do so. As soon as practically possible find a private place where you can vent/release your anger, hurt and frustration without making a spectacle of yourself in front of other people.
  - Scream, punch a pillow, lament to your heart's content and **grieve for your loss, but EVENTUALLY you MUST be done with it.**
  - **Alternatively try to whack a few balls at the golf driving range.** It might

improve your golf game and get rid of some accumulated hostility.
(c) A cornerstone of sanity is **the distinction between REALITY** and **ILLUSION.** If somebody has caused you a hurt, then try **NOT to hold a grudge.** (Easier said than done!).
- **Holding a grudge is handling anger destructively.**
- **The ONLY person you will hurt is YOURSELF.**
- The other party may not even realize what he has done to you or worse, he may not even care!
- Alternatively, he may have long forgotten about you and the hurtful incident while you are still tearing yourself apart about it.

(d) **Don't jump to any premature conclusions.**
Postpone doing or saying anything rash until
- you have had an opportunity to think through the situation
- and have calmed down sufficiently to where you have gained control of yourself.
- Analyze how important this matter (which caused the disappointment) REALLY was for you.
- Ask yourself if you are possibly exaggerating the situation and are just feeling sorry for yourself.

(e) **As a BONUS this reflection will enable you to RESUME operating from a POSITION of STRENGTH.**

(6) **HOW to face FAILURE EXPERIENCES with COURAGE.**
(a) By having a total commitment to your profession: constantly learn your trade and improve your skills.
(b) If you have the inner stimulus and are properly motivated you will find that you can do almost anything.
(c) You must be willing to **pay the price for success**; the occasional disappointment and rejection are unfortunately part of doing business.
(d) **Turn a stumbling block into an opportunity.**
There is no use crying over spilled milk. What's done is done! You cannot change the past. **Forget about the mistakes,** but **remember the LESSONS they taught you.**
(e) Drown your troubles in **new work** ... and work tirelessly.
(f) A good portion of your daily conversation is with yourself. It is called **"thinking."**
Your mind is a powerful thing: **If you let your thinking be NEGATIVE then you will literally BRAINWASH yourself into failure.**
Have you ever heard the saying that "there are no **born** losers, you have to **train** to become one?" Why would anybody have the ambition to become a loser?
(g) **POSITIVE THINKING is also powerful.**
- It will determine how you feel about yourself and
- how other people will see you.

- Try to associate mostly with happy and successful people.
- Pay sincere compliments and
- try to make other people feel important.
- Good things are bound to rub off on you.

(h) Realize that **the emotional low is ONLY TEMPORARY.**
If necessary, repeat to yourself a mantra:
- This, too, will pass.
- **FAILURES don't have to be FINAL.**
- Before the light of dawn comes, it has to get really dark first.

(7) **For relief try a dose of OPTIMISM.**
Remember the old saying that "The best defence is an offence?"
Optimism is that strange and logic-defying but wonderful human habit of hoping for or expecting something good to happen, even in defiance of all of the odds.

WHAT ADVANTAGES does OPTIMISM OFFER YOU?
- For some reason people actually seem to BENEFIT from unbounded optimism.
- Optimists seem to
  - respond better to stress
  - suffer from less illnesses and less depression,
  - achieve more goals and
  - seem to live happier and longer.
- Possibly part of the answer is that they have discovered certain **desirable qualities that make life worth living.** Like e.g.
  - contentment with their lot in life and
  - personal fulfilment,
  - strength of character and a healthy life.
- **Optimists count their BLESSINGS and not their troubles.**

(8) **LIVE IN THE PRESENT and commit yourself to a course of action.**
(a) **Focus less on the misery** and more on ensuring that things will go right the next time around.
(b) Don't become paralyzed into inactivity by refusing to do business unless ALL conditions are perfect: they never will be.
(c) So pick yourself up off the floor and get going! If you muddle through as best as you can you will find that **ACTIVITY WILL MAKE THE MISERY DISAPPEAR.**
(d) **Stick to your original plan.** Reconfirm what you have decided to achieve and never take your eyes off your goals.
(e) Do ONE thing EACH day to help you move toward your goal.
Remember NOAH (from the Bible). While he was busy working on his ship in the middle of dry land, Noah had to endure a lot of sarcasm and ridicule from his

neighbours. Of course, it wasn't raining while he was building the Ark.

(9) **VISUALIZE YOUR SUCCESS.**
   - Tack on a corkboard a picture of the car you want to buy or a picture of a desired holiday destination.
   - Fabricate little cards with positive affirmations:
     - "I can change"
     - "I have the power to change"
     - "I will change"
     - "Good things will happen to me"
     - "My future will be great"
     - "I enjoy my friends"
     - "I get along with people"
     - "I can fall asleep easily"
     - "I will wake up refreshed"
     - "Nothing can or will upset me."

(10) Good things don't just happen by themselves, one has to make them happen. One of the best ways of being able to cope with a setback is by **KEEPING BUSY.** Picture yourself juggling 10 balls in the air. If you drop one, it is no big deal, because you have 9 others left. However, if you have only 3 balls in the air and you drop one of them, then you have lost 1/3 of your act (production). If you juggle only with one ball and drop it, then there is nothing left to work with. In plain words: if your entire future hangs on the outcome of one listing appointment or one sale, then you are headed for BIG trouble.

A good way to keep busy is by having a **LISTING PROGRAM in place** whereby you keep busy systematically by trying daily to get a listing. In that case **the odd failure will become a LEARNING experience and nothing more.** By having the strength to go on to the next one, you will be too busy to dwell on any negative feelings.

(11) Use a **distraction strategy to take your mind off the pain.** Guide your thoughts away from the disappointment or perceived rejection by using some technique like **meditation or self-hypnosis.** The deep concentration required for these techniques will serve to distract the mind.

(12) **Keep busy with pleasant activities.**
Loose yourself in a hobby (remember the song "... a few of my favourite things?") Doing something you enjoy means you are more likely to stick with it. Any **"feel-good" activity** which can divert your attention will help you to get over your disappointment. Quiet hobbies can be reading, stamp collecting, listening to music, going to a movie or concert etc. Invite friends over for dinner and to play cards.

Also physical activities like gardening, jogging, walking, dancing and exercising fall into these beneficial categories.

(13) Try **smiling**.
Greet people with a smile. Smiling is infectious. As an added bonus it will also make YOU feel better. Have you ever tried to be miserable or grumpy with a genuine and warm smile on your face? It is impossible. **The LESS you laugh … the less OCCASION you will have to laugh!**

(14) Remember that your judgement (of the hurt) is coloured by YOUR accumulated personal experiences and perceptions. **Emotional upsets and fear reactions CAN be conquered by**
- **clear thinking,**
- **logical thought processes and**
- **deliberate actions.**
- You will improve the quality of your life and those around you by leading a life of healthy analysis (reality check) and reasoned decision making.

(15) **Forgive** the person (and that includes yourself!) who has caused your hurt and pain. Refusing to forgive is like licking your emotional wounds: somehow and subconsciously it may be enjoyable but it will prolong the suffering. **By the act of forgiveness you ACTIVELY CHOOSE to let go of an ugly situation.**
Sometimes and for some of us IT IS NOT EASY TO FORGIVE.
To help yourself to achieve this difficult goal ask yourself the following questions:
(a) What will I profit by NOT forgiving?
(b) Is there any good reason why I shouldn't be done with it?
(c) Isn't it time to move on to something better, more promising and more constructive?

The reward will be great if you manage to jettison the bone-crushing burden of hurt, hate, guilt and recrimination:
- With the burden gone, an immense sense of relief will engulf you.
- You will be able to put your life back together again and enjoy it.
- **Time is precious so don't waste it.** Once again you will be able to face the rest of your life with confidence.

(16) **Loving support** is the glue which holds life together.
Hopefully there is a kind-hearted person in your life whose hand will reach out periodically and gently touch your cheek and carefully wipe away all searing tears of pain. Be kind to that person: he or she deserves the best YOU and life can offer.

Are You Living In A Citadel Of S-T-R-E-S-S ?

Scientists theorize that at the dawn of mankind there must have been a period of human evolution that was extremely difficult and tumultuous; somehow the lesson (instinct for self-preservation and survival) and memory of that period was distilled in human beings as the "fight-or-flight" reaction. This has been passed on ever since from one generation to the next: possibly in the form of an imprint on the genes.

Medical interest in the phenomenon of "STRESS" began on the battlefield, where the devastating effects of chronic stress are unmistakable. During the U.S. Civil War, palpitations were so common that they became known as **"soldier's heart."** During World War I soldiers' crippling anxiety was called **"shell shock"** which was attributed to the vibrations from heavy artillery, which - doctors believed — caused damage to blood vessels in the brain. During World War II this theory was abandoned and the problem was renamed **"battle fatigue."** Current thought is that in battle the fight-or-flight response to constant danger becomes chronic and long-term chemical changes occur in the body, leading to depression of the immune system and a cascade of problems.

According to the late Dr. Hans Selye, the Austrian-born founding father of stress research, **stress is the rate of wear and tear on the human body and is a silent destroyer** often resulting in internal damage. Stress is known to be a major contributor, either directly or indirectly, to
- coronary heart disease,
- high blood pressure,
- heavy drinking resulting in cirrhosis of the liver,
- all sorts of ulcers ranging from a nervous stomach (frequent diarrhea) to ulcerative colitis (a painful chronic inflammation of the colon).

All of these debilitating illnesses in turn result in absenteeism and lost productivity.

Stress usually causes that extra burst of adrenaline to prime muscles, focus your attention and get your nerves ready for that sudden "fight-or-flight" reaction. This was great for a caveman confronting a sabre-tooth tiger, but in today's modern times, this response to many perceived threats is often inappropriate behaviour: e.g.
- **road rage,** which is the name of a modern phenomenon describing various degrees of hostile confrontations between car drivers (especially on a freeway).
- When airlines stopped allowing people to smoke on planes, a new form of stress (dubbed **"air rage"**) appeared: fuelled by alcoholic drinks, nicotine deprivation now occasionally results in unruly passenger behaviour.

Realtors are living in a world of uncertainties and what used to be an occasional calamity is now a chronic, relentless psychological situation:
- sales are lost because of Clients' job insecurity (downsizing).
- Due to tidal waves of new technology Realtors are nearly overwhelmed by a constant

onslaught of rapid changes in the way the real estate business is conducted.
- Even on holidays, workaholics can now remain slaves to stress by pounding away at their lap-tops and babbling into their cell phones.
- Many Realtors and their employing Companies are financially threatened by a reduction of net income as a result of dropping commissions and rising expenses.
- For the breed of thrill seekers, there is life in the fast lane: hectic schedules, too many commitments and time constraints, all wonderful stress substitutes for extreme sports.
- **Managers often suffer from a combination of high demands and lots of responsibility, but little personal control and independent authority.**
- However stress can also be caused by less mundane things: **"hassles"** (the trials and tribulations and petty annoyances of everyday life):
  - a shoelace that snaps when you are late for an appointment.
  - Driving across town in heavy traffic or in a snow storm.
  - A sense of panic over a deadline: the market is slow and nobody is coming to your Open Houses and your client says: "I must have my house sold by the end of the month."
  - The old day-to-day frictions of dealing with uncaring bureaucrats, careless fellow Realtors and possibly unfair or perceived-as-unethical competitors.

Realtors know only too well what some of **the symptoms of stress** are:
- stomach churning,
- back and neck muscles knotting,
- tension in the facial muscles (twitching),
- heart racing or pounding,
- teeth on edge,
- rapid breath, sweating profusely and/or a nervous cough.

It is a sorry sign of our times, that the 3 best selling drugs in the country are:
- an ulcer medication (Tagamet),
- a hypertension (high blood pressure) drug (Inderal) and
- a tranquilizer (Valium).

Cardiologists Meyer Friedman and Ray Rosenman have identified 2 classes of behaviour in human beings:

The "Type A" person has 2 main components:
(a) **they operate under the illusion that pressure improves performance,** without realizing that this may be true only up to a certain point: after that, efficiency drops off sharply.
(b) They have a tendency to **try to accomplish too many things in too little time.** Even on holidays over-programmed job frenzy leaves Type A's so hyper that the prospect of a few days of **unstructured leisure** is unbearable. Therefore, they maintain a furious pace of "leisure activities" and families that go with them

often need a vacation after "THE VACATION."

As all of this stress results in free-floating hostility, **"Type A" people are irritated by trivial things.** They respond constantly as though they were in an emergency or threatening situation (like the caveman used to be). As a result they are aggressive and combative and will take on the nearest person, which unfortunately often is the wife or some other member of the family.

The **"Type B"** are calmer people who accept a certain amount of stress as a positive and pleasurable thing, maybe even as the spice of life.

What measures can a busy Salesperson realistically adopt as INTELLIGENT COPING BEHAVIOUR to keep stress at bay?

(a) **You have to achieve a sense of "being in control of your life."** As a Realtor you are in the enviable position of being able to dictate the pace and style of your work. You must learn to say "NO" occasionally.
(b) **Diagnose the SOURCE of your stress problem.** If necessary chop the problem up into smaller more manageable pieces. If you still cannot deal with them, then **remove yourself from the situation:** avoid them for a while, remain polite, but not as involved or invested. A Seller who repeatedly refuses to accept offers at fair market value (because he "is in no rush to sell") will become - psychologically speaking - **your JAILER in your CITADEL OF STRESS.**
(c) Realize that lining your coffin with gold will do your corpse no good. If you think that "you can take it with you" then ask yourself: "Have you ever seen a hearse with luggage racks?"
(d) We are constantly admonished to **"exercise regularly and eat sensibly."** To reduce cumulative stress, everybody (except for thee and me) seems to be massaging, jogging, hot-tubbing, twisting himself into a pretzel (Yoga) or dieting (starving themselves in various ways).

As each day is different in the life of a Realtor, we often eat on the run and many of us don't have the time or the inclination to have a daily 60 minute workout. But **everybody should be able to spare time for a 15-minute low-effort-high-return energy and emotion power-boost: LEARN HOW TO RELAX!**

No single approach to relaxation is right for everyone.

Meditation or self-hypnosis activate a built-in mechanism which acts as the opposite of the fight-and-flight response. Find a quiet place, pull off the road, close your eyes, sit comfortably and
- progressively relax one by one all of the muscles in your body.
- Shut your mouth and breathe through your nose SLOWLY, EVENLY

(without pauses), SMOOTHLY and SILENTLY. (Have you noticed that mouth breathing occurs at high levels of anxiety?)
- Don't try to clear or empty your mind (that takes many years of disciplined learning). **Just STILL your mind by letting it wander to a pleasant place or topic.**
- Unless you want to imitate a gerbil running around on a revolving wheel, **avoid rehashing worrisome problems or engaging in circular arguments.**

(e) If you are not up to the rigours of **Yoga or Tai Chi,** simply **stretch or do a posture check throughout the day** to combat your tendency to hunch your shoulders forward. Stand perfectly straight, relax the hands down at your sides (your hands should come to a natural rest directly underneath the hips with the thumbs pointing forward - if not, then you are slouching.)

(f) **Restore your strength and perspective**
- by taking a few days off;
- if you are overtired, have a good night's sleep.

(g) **Give your poor abused stomach a break**
- do NOT devour junk food,
- eat (slowly) some nourishing meals,
- chew your food well,
- don't gulp air.

(h) **Pay attention to other areas of your life:**
- a network of friends and family will provide social support for a single parent with the dual stresses of financial pressure (to stave off poverty) and the loneliness of a ghetto life.
- Consider joining a club, a service organization, a church or temple of your choice; they usually have a social program. You might be surprised by the many benefits of attending some of their social functions. You may even like it — if nothing else, company alleviates misery.

Between the extremes of fight-or-flight battle-field-like spasms of too much tension and the stupefying dullness of a boringly uneventful life, **the challenge is to find the level of MANAGEABLE stress that will invigorate your life instead of ravaging it. The object is NOT to escape the EFFECTS of stress** (which are inescapable in any event), but to **CONTROL them intelligently and to CHANNEL them** onto a constructive and beneficial level.

How To Snap Out Of A Sales Slump - Part I
Concise and practical help how to put out the fires.

When a person feels sick, he goes to see his family doctor. The physician will:
- listen to the patient's complaints,
- examine the patient and
- if necessary, various tests will be conducted.
- The doctor will then evaluate the symptoms,
- consider the results of the tests
- and the healing treatment will be based on his comprehensive diagnosis.

On the other hand when the average Realtor finds himself to be in a sales slump, nobody wants to talk about it. Not only is there generally little sympathy around for a salesperson in a slump, but such a Realtor is even embarrassed to mention his problems to others because he may be shunned by everybody similarly to what lepers used to be in biblical times. Many Realtors who are in a slump may not be sure about the cause or extent of their predicament. Vaguely they are puzzled that "there is something wrong" and painfully they are aware that as a result there is "no commission money coming in."

What help can a Realtor "patient" look for? For one there are all the books and tapes about Positive Mental Attitude, self-esteem, goals, time management etc. With many of these one has to plough through pages and pages of anecdotal reminiscences of the authors. All the while the poor "slump-sufferer" needs and urgently wants **CONCISE and PRACTICAL step-by-step HELP how to put out the fires. Well, here is an attempt to help you.**

(I) **To conduct a SELF-DIAGNOSIS,** ask yourself if you are suffering from any of the following symptoms:
  (a) Business is slow for you (and yet everybody else seems to be quite busy).
  (b) You have come to the conclusion that
      - the business is overrun with more and more Realtors.
      - In fact there are just too many Realtors around for an individual like you to be able to earn a decent living.
  (c) Your competitors seem to be younger, more aggressive and sharper than you.
  (d) "New technology" frightens and confuses you.
  (e) The real estate business is changing and not necessarily for the better.
  (f) Your competitors are also changing.
  (g) YOU are NOT changing or you are not willing to change.
  (h) For quite some time you have dreaded answering the telephone.
  (i) Lately the telephone has actually almost stopped ringing for you.
  (j) You are fed up having to deal with unreasonable Customers.
  (k) Even former Clients are disloyal and are leaving you for the competition.
  (l) As your business disappears, it can no longer support your lifestyle.

(m) More and more you are considering getting a "real job."

Do these complaints sound familiar? At the office they usually can be heard from an individual who is letting off steam while standing around idly and nursing a cup of coffee.

(II) The following are some practical suggestions of how you can extricate yourself out of a slump. As always, take what appeals to you and ignore the rest.

LESSON # 1
(a) This may sound stupid, but if you find yourself in a hole, then the first thing to do is to quit digging yourself deeper into the hole. In other words: **DISCONTINUE WHATEVER YOU WERE DOING and reassess your situation, possibly with the help of your Manager.**
(b) **There is NO point in passively WISHING for something to happen.** E.g. Chances are poor that a Buyer or Seller will magically materialize out of the thin air, asking for you.
(c) **ACKNOWLEDGE TO YOURSELF that YOU and ONLY you are the one and only person who can MAKE something POSITIVE to HAPPEN.**
(d) To help you out, tape on your bathroom mirror the following Latin Proverb: **"TUUM EST"** (translation: **"It is up to you"**). It should give you a reminder every morning.

LESSON # 2
If you are paralyzed into inaction by any sort of imaginary pain then it is similar to squatting low to the ground with your spurs on: a painful experience which should be avoided or at least discontinued and definitely not to be repeated.
This means that **YOU have to make an all-out EFFORT** to:
(a) **GET GOING TODAY** (and NOT tomorrow!) **with some sort of self-designed program to suit your needs and your personality.** If you are stuck, ask your Manager for help. He knows your strengths and weaknesses and will be able to assist you.
Part of this program should be that:
(b) To stay **COMPETITIVE** you must become **BETTER INFORMED.**
(c) To get a listing or to make a sale you must **talk to MORE PEOPLE.** This endeavour is called **"prospecting."**
(d) **Never miss a good chance to SHUT UP.** Quit broadcasting (and lamenting about) your "misfortunes." Feeling sorry for yourself is counter-productive.

LESSON # 3
If you are in a slump, the problem is
(A) **Partly PHYSICAL.**
Success in sales requires high levels of energy and vitality. So take care of

yourself. After each success (a sale, a listing, a price reduction etc.) pamper (reward) yourself a little.

Your BODY is the vehicle which carries around your mind.

If the body is down and out, it will go on strike. This condition is commonly referred to as "illness." If the body is sick then the mind will be unable to go anywhere.

In order to function properly **the body requires:**
- an adequate amount of **rest and sleep.**
- **Nutritious food** and
- **some physical activity.**
  Greasy fast food doesn't exactly qualify as "nutritious" and raising a bottle of beer to your lips cannot be considered as a "workout."
- **Accept yourself as you are.** Some of us are overweighed by nature. We will never become gaunt hard bodies even if we were to mortify ourselves in an austere Shaolin Temple on top of the Himalayas and eat only weeds and grasshoppers.

(B) **Partly PSYCHOLOGICAL:**

Decide to make an enormous **INVESTMENT IN YOURSELF! Your MIND also has NEEDS which must be met.** E.g.
- **rest** (diversion) and
- the **right** type of **sustenance** (see below):
  Develop a magnificent curiosity to **LEARN HOW TO GET THINGS DONE.**

(a) As mentioned before, you have to become **better informed.** This cannot happen overnight.
- You must feed your mind by beginning **a long-range do-it-yourself project of PERSONAL DEVELOPMENT.**
- The **OBJECTIVE** is to give yourself the training you require to become the VERY BEST salesperson YOU can be.

(b) **UPGRADE your MIND** with
- **knowledge,**
- **descriptive language,**
- **communications skills,**
- **closing techniques,**
- **accumulated experience and**
- **good judgment.**
  PLEASE NOTE:
  *** **GOOD judgment comes from EXPERIENCE. Unfortunately a lot of experience comes from previous BAD judgment.** ***

The more you upgrade **YOURSELF** (namely the TOTAL YOU) …
- the more it will result in **YOU gaining increased confidence in your abilities**.
- Surprisingly even the people around you (including your Clients!) will experience increased confidence in you as well. The simple reason for this is that **YOU will be able to deal with them on a higher, more professional level.**

(c) **WORRY is the most useless of all emotions.**
- An excessive amount of it can paralyse you into inaction.
- By itself, no amount of worrying will make a bit of a difference or change a thing. Only ACTION will.
- Few people are immune to worry, so you are not alone fighting it.

(d) When you go to bed, **stop your mind from fretting** over things which **you cannot change while it is still night time.** Worrying while you are laying in bed is utterly counter productive, unless you enjoy tossing around aimlessly during a sleepless night. Remind yourself that your body will feel poorly next morning if your mind prevents it from getting adequate rest.

PSYCHOLOGICALLY learn

(1) **How to be mentally strong.**

(a) When you find that things generally are at the worst, then that is the very moment in time when you need to be at your best.

(b) You must resolve **NOT to be harmed by rejections and disappointments;** God knows there will be many of them in any kind of real estate market.

(c) **Adopt Counter Measures:**
- For some people an effective armour against the searing emotional pain caused by rejections and disappointments (usually from thoughtless and uncaring people) is **the stoic intellectual acceptance of the unalterable reality,** that
    - rejections and disappointments HAVE taken place. (As the saying goes: there is no point in crying over spilled milk. It has taken place and there is nothing that you can do about it any longer.)
    - The only constructive thing which you can do, however, is to wipe up the mess (put it out of your mind) and go on living - hopefully WISER.
    - On the other hand some people may need the healing experience of "venting" (in a non-destructive manner) their emotions of anger and frustration. Do your "venting" in private. It should not take any longer than 1/2 hour. There is no constructive or valid reason for prolonging "the mourning."

ON THE POSITIVE SIDE: all of you can take heart that **progress IS possible: you CAN change the future** (and thereby feel better)
- by deciding to learn from these temporary setbacks and
- by applying the lessons of your experience in the future. This, by the way, is called

gaining experience in the School of Hard Knocks.

(d) A poor market is a universal level playing field: all of your associates in the office as well as all of your competitors are in the same boat as you are. If nothing else, this should be a comforting thought, because misery likes company.

Psst! Don't tell anybody, but there is a positive side even to this; in fact it could be a golden opportunity for you: if your competitors are discouraged, then chances are that they will either stop working or leave the business altogether. **In either case there will be less competition against you.**

(e) Out of sheer self-preservation you should **associate only with "winners"**: these are positive, optimistic but also realistic people who have charted the right direction in their lives. Besides rubbing shoulders with them **you should actively promote your listings to these type of salespersons.**

(f) Keep in mind the Realtors' old proverb that it is difficult to "soar like an eagle" if you continuously hang around with a bunch of turkeys. It is sad but true: if you make it a habit to associate only with bottom feeders then don't be surprised if eventually you become one of them.

(g) Instead of perpetuating fear and bad news during a difficult real estate market each Realtor (without ignoring reality) has an unique opportunity to become an "Ambassador of Reason" spreading confidence and calm to his associates and the public (his Clients). Realistically speaking, what can the average person do anyway about the ups and downs of interest rates and the country's economy?

(h) Sales Managers should remind their staff to go on with the normal routine of their daily lives. There is little or nothing to be gained by becoming mesmerized by the "bad news" propagated in the media.

(i) Count your blessings! In comparison with what has happened to some other people you know of, your occasional rejections and disappointments may (on due reflection) appear as trivial and insignificant. (Although they still can be vexing on a personal level).

(III) FROM A PRACTICAL POINT OF VIEW: "what can or should you do when there is nothing to do?" (In this respect you may also consult other Chapters in this book).

(1) If you are in a slump or in a slow market, **everything you do must have at least a 50/50 chance of making you some money IN THE NEAR FUTURE.** For that purpose you must **obtain a complete UNDERSTANDING of your business:**

(a) **What type** of real estate (which kind of house, condos, land etc.) **will most likely sell in the CURRENT real estate market?** Concentrate your efforts on whatever sells best and easiest.

(b) What is the price range in which there is the best and most active sales activity? (In a slow market: what is the price range in which there is STILL some SALES activity?)

(c) What type of clientele (Buyers or Sellers) is most likely to be profitable for you? First-time Buyers, trade-ups (they need more space) or trade-downs (empty nesters).

(d) Accept that **the public's buying and selling BEHAVIOUR will change.** Basically real estate transactions are driven by physical and emotional needs.

"Physical" means the need for a bigger or a smaller house; in other words, there is a **practical or a functional component involved.**

"Emotional" means a discretionary motive which requires not only a sufficient amount money but also emotional "justification" to overcome possible barriers of some sort of guilt; in other words, a posh luxury house is not necessarily needed, but it will make the Clients' private and/or business life more enjoyable or meaningful.

(e) Tape the following sentence onto your fridge door and/or the bathroom mirror:
LEARN TO QUALIFY and select EVERY Buyer and Seller for:
- **"urgency"**
- **"need"**
- **"financial ability."**

To ensure your own personal survival it will be absolutely necessary that you become objective about these 3 items. There is simply no room for any misplaced sentiments. Reality will catch up with you and in the end the only person you will have fooled is yourself.

(f) WORK ONLY WITH THE BEST!
- Avoid like the plague hard-core grinding and habitually criticising Buyers with little money and no credit.
- The same goes for unreasonably greedy Sellers who boast that they "are in no rush to sell." They are well known to demand an unusually high level of service while paying only a minimal commission.

These type of "Clients" will
- ruthlessly waste your precious time,
- frustrate you mentally and
- exhaust you physically and
- in the end will crush you financially (no sale = no commission income).

(g) Observe and analyze your competition.
- Learn from them.
- Emulate the good things they do and avoid the unproductive ones.

How To Snap Out Of A Slump - Part II

About POLISHING UP YOUR ENTHUSIASM and maintaining a POSITIVE MENTAL ATTITUDE.

Suppose you find yourself in the following situation:

(a) You are physically exhausted and you have hit an emotional "low" **and don't know "WHY."**
(b) Your "significant other" confided in you that you "have to get a grip on yourself," **but you are not sure "HOW."**
(c) Your Sales Manager keeps on harping about goal-setting and all the while **you are "WORRIED" sick about your cash-flow and the poor state of your finances.**
(d) You attend a seminar where somebody lectures about **"maintaining a POSITIVE MENTAL ATTITUDE" without going into any details how to acquire it in the first place.**
(e) The lucky new salesperson sitting next to you in the bull pen (you know, the one who is so new that he couldn't possibly know anything worthwhile about real estate); well he somehow managed to get 2 new listings and make 1 sale so far this month - and only half of the month is over!

Under such circumstances it can be difficult to put on a "Happy Face" and "Maintain a Positive Mental Attitude."

Well, let me help you out with some thoughts about **how to polish up your enthusiasm and the formula how to acquire a POSITIVE MENTAL ATTITUDE.**

(1) **CIVILITY is a sign of strength and not of weakness.**
   (a) Pretending that you are in a state of glorious euphoria when you actually are not, is a **delusion.** And yet, if you honestly confide that you may have some problems, nobody seems to be interested. To boot people will jump to the conclusion that you like to whine or wallow in self-pity or negativity.
   (b) No matter what amount of misery lurks inside you, the whole world nowadays expects you to say that you are "fine" when they greet you with the standard "How're ya today?" Don't delude yourself into thinking that this question is **an actual enquiry about your health and well being. No,** it is merely a routine opening formula, similar to chanting the "California Goodbye Mantra" of "Have a nice day."
   (c) If you don't feel like participating in these everyday formula-type greetings then you can be civil when you meet somebody by greeting him with
      • **a warm "HELLO" combined with a pleasant SMILE**
      • **and make it a point of addressing him by his name.**

      According to "Dear Abby" the shortest distance between 2 people is a smile.

By mentioning his name you acknowledge him directly as a (to you) important individual person.

(2) "ATTITUDE" is neither a natural talent, nor is it an accident. It is **merely GOOD HABITS** which means that it can be **acquired**.

  (a) **Learn how to "live with CHANGE":**

It is unrealistic for you to expect to be able to change over night, merely because you have decided to do so. For change to last you have to TAKE SMALL STEPS. One of these small steps is to **learn something. How can you hope to achieve a better life without improving yourself?**

  (b) **Learn how to "SURVIVE":**

To successfully survive anything
- You must be determined to **persevere.**
- You cannot afford to quit until your goal is achieved.
- **Without any hesitation** you must decide to "stay the course."
- **Without any reservation** (you cannot hold anything back) you must REFUSE to give in.
- If it is necessary then you may have to start all over again and try harder the next time around.

  (c) **Learn how to "PROFIT" from it:**

If you are successful, then the pay-off will be glorious for you:
- a better life,
- a harmonious family,
- loyal friends and customers,
- financial success, peace of mind, prestige etc.

  (d) The **ALTITUDE (height) of your success,** will be determined by
- your **Aptitude** (which means HOW SKILFULLY you apply your knowledge and experience in your business) AND
- your **Attitude (ACTIVITY ABSORBS ANXIETY).**

(3) **SPEAK SOFTLY,** because people tend to tune out loud or shrill voices.

(4) **RESOLVE** to make a **CONSCIOUS EFFORT** to be
- **genuinely pleasant**)
- **kind and**)   **TO EVERYBODY**
- **courteous**)

As a DIRECT CONSEQUENCE
- **this will make them and YOU feel good.**
- **PEOPLE will LIKE to DEAL with YOU.**
- For YOU it will be EASIER to deal with Clients and others.
- **People** in turn **WILL SMILE AT YOU** and
- **they will REMEMBER YOU as a nice person to have around.**
- As an added bonus you will notice that **your GENERAL ATTITUDE will gradually change for the better.**

(5) **Your emotional age, maturity and a good sense of humour** are of considerable importance. All of us have encountered 65 year old "teenagers" and 25 year old "senior citizens." The reason for this is because **your BRAIN** is a powerful machine which can either make or break you.

(a) **Carefully MONITOR your self-talk** (which is commonly known as your "THOUGHTS").
Habitual NEGATIVE thoughts will produce
- **habitual negative TALK** (what else is going to come out of your mouth?)
- As a result such a person **will lead a MISERABLE life.**

Therefore, each time you catch yourself thinking something **NEGATIVE**, **you must say to yourself IMMEDIATELY:**
STOP! CANCEL! DELETE PROGRAM!

(b) Even if you have managed to brainwash yourself into continued negativity **there is still hope** because
- **you have the POWER to change**
- and create for yourself **your own personalized and pleasant life script.**

This is because **you can CHOOSE** to replace depressing negative thoughts with more beneficial and positive ones.

(c) **Look at the switch** (from being currently a PESSIMIST to becoming an OPTIMIST) **as an ADVENTURE** or better still as an **INVESTMENT in your life.**

(A) Perhaps because a person's attitude affects the biochemistry of his brain, **Optimists seem to**
- live longer,
- be healthier,
- have a better home life and
- succeed more in business.

(B) Can YOU think of any valid reasons why you should not live a life based on **VALUES which are admired by all?**
- Honesty and integrity,
- compassion, empathy and patience.
- The willingness to work hard and for long hours.
- **The courage to endure** ("I can do it, no matter how difficult it may be and no matter what it takes to achieve it").

(6) **YOU can REACT to BAD news in 2 ways:**

(a) **EMOTIONALLY:**
In the PRESENT: the emotional reaction to something bad is typified by

the all-too-common knee-jerk response of **panicking** and **PAIN** (hurt).

In the PAST: Something painful which happened in the past, is often remembered with **ANGER**.

If this anger from the past
- has not been dealt with (forgiven)
- and if it is redirected against yourself then it is called **"GUILT."** GUILT can cause "stress" which in turn can hurt your body by producing "illness." It is a vicious cycle.

In the FUTURE: If you anticipate something **painful in the future, it will cause you ANXIETY and WORRY** (these are useless emotions "in the present").

From all of this it should be obvious that reacting only **emotionally** is not too good for you.

(b) INTELLECTUALLY: The intellectual reaction, on the other hand, can be summarized in 2 simple words: **"sit tight"** until you have had a chance to evaluate, consider, reconsider, reflect, decide and finally to act decisively.

(7) Understand and **accept that your chronological age will impose on you SOME LIMITATIONS:** it is unreasonable to expect that a 65 year old person has the same stamina as a 25 year old. **AGE** is often the defining reason why a person's goals change over time; and so is **HEALTH**. If your arthritic knees can accurately predict every drop of rain, then you will have to **learn to CONSERVE your strength for good days.**

(8) A word **about money:** (this is covered more extensively in another Chapter of this book).
 (a) It may sound dumb, but if you don't manage your "stash" properly, then you will suffer from "Pennies Envy" or worse: most people live up to their current income when they are flush and then hope that the next commission cheque will come through on time. That is a good way to fall behind because eventually you will have to put every Cent you make into catching up (e.g. especially for unpaid income tax).
 (b) **When income is unpredictable you must discipline yourself to budget for week-to-week rock-bottom fixed cash-flow survival needs** (absolute necessities to live on).
 (c) **Financial security and freedom from pressure** will automatically improve
  - your quality of life,
  - your zest for life,
  - your outlook on life,

- your general attitude
- and most likely your sales production. Many people can sell better if they are under no pressures of any kind.

(9) **Decide to be a "VICTOR" and not a "Victim."**
   (a) Quit blaming outside situations (bad weather, the world economy etc.) for your misfortunes. **You are the ONLY person** who decides whether you will be hurt, depressed, angry, worried, afraid or feel guilty.
   (b) Understand that **NEGATIVITY** is something that
   - resides in you permanently (and to different degrees in everybody else also)
   - and that **it must be defeated daily.**
   (c) **People respect strength** and therefore, it should be obvious that **you must operate from a position of strength.** How can you do that?
   - **By accumulating KNOWLEDGE and EXPERIENCE,**
   - **by summoning up COURAGE and**
   - **by working SMARTLY:**
   - Looking for Buyers and Sellers in places where they are not likely to be - is a lot like seeking the living among the dead.
   - If you work in areas where there will be little or no results, then you will succeed only in exhausting yourself physically and mentally and poison the well of your enthusiasm (and your PMA).
   - If you continually loiter with losers, seek the negative and absorb trash, then eventually you will mirror your environment.
   (d) **It will be FAR MORE VALUABLE FOR YOU if you decide to**
   - **cultivate your "WILL,"**
   - **develop your "MIND" and**
   - **educate your "HEART."**
   If you succeed in this then your rewards will be stunning.

(10) And now I can no longer postpone my sermon on **"PROCRASTINATION."**
   (a) Procrastination is to postpone something for tomorrow, what you should have done last year. E.g.:
   "We have to get organized"
   "Starting tomorrow, I am going to phone 50 expired MLS every day"
   "One of these days I am going to wash my car."
   (b) Fiddling aimlessly for hours on the computer is a pleasant way of passing an afternoon. As an "added bonus" you will be able to avoid talking to prospective Customers. By "sunset" it will "dawn" on you that you have wasted unproductively precious selling hours.
   As a result you may have a guilty conscience during the late afternoon which in turn will be a good excuse to do nothing in real estate for the rest of the evening. Ah well, as they used to say: "The slowest Christian was lunch for the hungry lions in the Roman Coliseum."

(c) Misguided procrastination is doing a lot of **unproductive paperwork** instead of talking to somebody about selling or buying. E.g. **traditional ways of goal-setting teach that**
- **you must write down** what you want to achieve and to **review it frequently** (because nebulous, ambitious goals are merely an unguided, never-ending search for an elusive meaning).
- Regretfully, for many this can result in a condition called **paralysis-by-analysis.** They are so busy reviewing constantly what the state of their goals is that they don't get around to listing or selling.

(11) **Life begins today: "Carpe diem" (seize the day).**
   (a) Don't keep planning on how you are going to decorate your tomorrows.
   (b) No one controls your destiny but YOU.
   (c) YOU must take responsibility for yourself.
   (d) Go out into the world and see the people. That's where the action is.

(12) **List and sell as if your life depended on it:** not only YOUR life, but also the lives of everyone who means anything to you.

Keep 2 more things in mind:
- **"perseverance" is another name for "success"** and
- God gives nothing to those who keep their arms crossed while they are sitting comfortably on their behinds.

How To Snap Out Of A Slump - Part III
Analysis of what a "NEGATIVE MENTAL ATTITUDE" is.

In real estate circles it is not fashionable to talk candidly about the daily emotional problems which the average Realtor may encounter. Instead of trying to diagnose what is wrong we take short-cuts:
- we either ignore and/or try to bury our psychological problems or
- we deal with them as best as we can. After all everybody in our business wants to appear to radiate a **Positive Mental Attitude,** don't they?
- However the fundamental question is this: HOW does the average Realtor know how to select and apply **the right panacea to the corresponding emotional sore?** Especially if he is not really sure what it is that is getting him down?

To tackle this dilemma we will have to do the unspeakable and identify and discuss — ugghh! - **"NEGATIVE MENTAL ATTITUDES."** Not the run-of-the-mill ones like greed, being irritable, rude or destructively critical, **but the more insidious ones which effect directly a Realtor's work, income and health.**

(I) We have talked about this before but **have you noticed some of the following additional SYMPTOMS in yourself?**
- Your interests are out of sync with the NEW (= CURRENT) way in which business is done.
- Everybody (and especially your Competition) is obsessed with "technology."
- The business is changing so rapidly that you long for the "good old days."
- Yes, you used to say it many times before that "selling real estate was fun"; but lately all of the joy seems to have gone out of it. All you have is a few overpriced listings and no pending sales.
- You dread going to the office. You feel uncomfortable in the "hustle and bustle" of the excited new salespersons the Manager has hired recently.
- Actually the real estate business in general is overrun with too many young eager beavers.
- Customers have become "unreasonable, aggressive and stubborn" and you are fed up having to deal with them. Buyers only make low-ball offers and Sellers are no longer embarrassed to ask you to cut your commission.
- Even former clients are becoming disloyal and have started dealing with your competitors.
- You wince in exasperation when your telephone rings.
- You used to make good money selling real estate. Lately you are merely eking out a poor living.

STOP! Before you decide to turn in your license and get "a real job," let me tell you that I have heard these gripes ever since I have started in real estate in 1962.

Incidentally, the "new technology" in the early '60s was the Multiple Listing Service. For a long time Sellers resisted paying a 7% commission and were reluctant to open up their homes to hoards of Realtors who came from different companies.

They preferred to do business "discretely": list "Exclusive," pay a 5% commission and there were no "For Sale" signs on front lawns. Many Realtors cooperated only with Realtor "friends" who were "in the loop" (translation: they cooperated with a few select Realtors with whom they were used to do business with and who in turn reciprocated, of course). Under these circumstances why should established Realtors give away half a commission to somebody who is new in the business? Or, worse still, a Realtor who is a total stranger and who came from (or worked in) another part of town and now is trying to break into their protected territory? Times have changed, haven't they? Can you imagine selling real estate today without MLS?

(II) Next we should consider a **list of some festering PROBLEMS** each one of which can bring about **a poor quality of life.**

(1) We have touched on **"WORRY"** before but here are **a few MORE words about this particular subject.**

Worry is probably the most useless of all emotions, because by itself it does not and cannot change anything regardless of how much worrying you are prepared to do. If you genuinely want to avoid some disaster and change something, then somewhere along the line you must stop worrying and **DO SOMETHING** about the situation. **ACTION is the sole effective antidote to worry.** E.g. "list" yourself out of a slump.

Senseless, uncontrolled **worry can achieve** the following:
- it will **literally paint pictures of fear into your mind**
- and it will literally paralyse you into **doing nothing.**
- Worry can also become a **BAD HABIT.**
- If worry becomes a bad habit, it will lead to **PESSIMISM**
- and both together can result in **HEALTH PROBLEMS**: indigestion, bad breath, a facial twitch, a nervous cough, a wide variety of painful ulcers, anxiety etc.

(2) **PESSIMISM is**
- seeing the HOLE in the doughnut and fearing to taste the good product.
- Have you noticed that pessimistic people always seem to be in a bad mood and sometimes have some bizarre notions?
- People with negative personalities tend to repel other people (turn them off). A constantly pessimistic Realtor may find himself shunned by his fellow Realtors.
- Pessimistic people are **lonely in their misery** because nobody wants to be around them.

- Who in his right mind wants to cultivate an association with unpleasantness?

(3) One more time we will have to return to **PROCRASTINATION.**
Procrastination is the unfortunate and **hard-to-break habit** of putting off until "later" that which you should have done a long time ago.
People who procrastinate are **COMPROMISING with** or **POSTPONING DIFFICULTIES** instead of **HARNESSING** and **using** them as **STEPPING STONES to OPPORTUNITIES and advancement.**
E.g. some Realtors can't sell because "the time isn't right": in winter it snows, in summer everybody goes on holidays. The list is endless.
As **the time will NEVER be "just perfect"** you will
- have to make up your mind to start wherever you are right now and
- work with whatever tools and circumstances you have at your command.
- Trust in yourself that you will find BETTER TOOLS (experience) as you go along.
- **Warning: waiting for the right time can become a PERMANENT HABIT and you will MISS OUT on a lot of business.**

(4) **LACK OF PERSISTENCE.**
Many of us are GOOD STARTERS but POOR FINISHERS. Some people are prone to giving up at the first signs of resistance or difficulty; e.g. it is NOT a good closing technique to offer to cut the commission as soon as the Seller says "no" for the first time.
This type of **FAILURE can be OVERCOME by**
- **self-discipline,**
- **accumulated knowledge and**
- **increased confidence.**
- Occasionally you may be "lucky" by being at the right time in the right place. ** But only PERSISTENT hard work will succeed in making you CONSISTENTLY and FREQUENTLY "lucky"**.

(5) **LACK OF AMBITION.**
In the hierarchy of salespersons a "mediocre producer" is
- one of the highest of the bottom half and
- one of the lowest of the top half of the crowd.

Many people without ambition hope to get "a freebie." Regrettably there is no such thing as a "free lunch." Every day you must overcome the uncontrolled desire of wanting something for nothing. If you want to get ahead in life, you must be **willing to PAY THE PRICE.**
One of the ways of "paying the price" is by **increasing your EDUCATION.**

*** **Education consists not only of**
- the **ACCUMULATION of knowledge,**
- but also of **knowing how to effectively and persistently APPLYING that knowledge** to get what you want, without walking over or stepping on others.***

It is good to remember that Realtors are not merely paid for
- their hard work, but also for
- their knowledge and accumulated experience,
- **but more particularly for WHAT THEY can DO with THAT which they KNOW.**

On the other hand many of us know of some over-educated "Professors of Real Estate" who know every sales technique, every Board By-law and all legal judgments and yet they are unable to SELL anything. Often they are not even able to give away free peanuts to the monkeys in the zoo. They have book knowledge but no business sense how to use that knowledge.

(6) MENTAL LAZINESS.
- Mental laziness goes hand in hand with lack of ambition.
- Other characteristics are lack of imagination and lack of enthusiasm.
- It also includes **INDIFFERENCE** towards the plight of others and - strangely enough - **of oneself.**
- Mentally lazy people are willing to accept without protest whatever compensation life may offer them.
- They are satisfied to bargaining with life for mere PENNIES instead of demanding prosperity, happiness and "all the trimmings."
- They are also comfortable to associate with marginal producers who are willing to tolerate poverty (and accept it with resignation).
- A well-defined central purpose of life (a definite goal) is too much work and bother for them.
- For mentally lazy people "guessing" is less troublesome than "thinking."
- Why should they subject themselves to the inconvenience of making efforts to acquire facts or knowledge — all of THAT just so that they can THINK accurately?
- They prefer to act on "opinions" created by "guesswork" which is based on "snap-judgments."

(7) INDECISION:
- **He who hesitates is lost - "always" and "in all ways."**
- Indecision resembles slow death on the time payment plan.
- Through over-caution many people are paralysed by FEAR into inaction.
- They know all the roads leading to disaster, but it doesn't even occur to

them to search for any paths which may avoid failure.
- Life is full of chances. The person who is not willing to take some reasonable chances and moderate risks, will have to be satisfied with and will have to settle for whatever is left over when the others (the rest of mankind) are finished choosing.

(8) REGRETS:
The unfortunate person who lives in the past and has many regrets is haunted
- by failure and
- by missed opportunities.

What a nightmarish way of living.

(III) THE CURE:
Fellow Realtor! **GUARD YOURSELF** against these emotional curses of your life. It goes without saying that people who are suffering from serious, prolonged and life-destroying emotional distress may wish to consider getting professional help.

For others, who merely want a better understanding of how to successfully cope with daily aggravations, I would suggest to get more information by reading good self-help books and attending seminars, workshops etc.

Eventually you should be able to **find your own personalized, made-to-order "relief from head to toe." The rewards for your persistent efforts will be plentiful.**

How To Keep Busy And Sell In A Slow Market

A slow market is usually a BUYERS' MARKET. There are many properties for sale who are competing against each other for the attention of the few qualified Buyers which are in the market. Buyers shop around and are more difficult to deal with because they are looking for bargains. Consequently prices tend to drop. The majority of Realtors are concentrating on latching onto a Buyer.

On the other hand, there are a lot of prospective Sellers around and therefore they are easier to deal with. Well here is a twisted thought: **"LIST" YOURSELF out of a slump and your listings will KEEP YOU BUSY in a slow market.** In fact if you have realistically priced listings of attractive homes, then the Buyers will come **to you.** **"PRICED RIGHT" means** properties which are
- listed a little lower than competing properties and
- a little higher than recent sales of similar properties in the area.

Here is how to do it:

(1) **You must become** not just good and not even outstanding, but **absolutely brilliant in "THE BASICS."** Much has been said and written about "The Basics" and we all should know them. (See another Chapter in this book).

(2) **But in a slow market all of that is not enough.**
  (a) Concentrate your efforts on getting listings.
  (b) Through trial and error you must become **a Champion Lister**.
  (c) "Qualify" the Sellers' reasons for selling. Take the listing only if the Seller MUST SELL.
  (d) Don't forget to negotiate price reductions and extensions.
  (e) Write descriptive ads that will draw calls.
  (f) If you have enough **GOOD LISTINGS then Buyers will come to you sooner or later.**
  (g) **Show only "priced-right" properties.**
  If you **frustrate Buyers in a slow market by showing them mostly overpriced properties then you are liable to loose them.**
  (h) You will have to **learn to BETTER interpret your clients' body language.** With every fibre of your being you have to constantly
    - **look out for BUYING SIGNALS or**
    - **the Client's unspoken "DECISION SIGNALS."**
  (i) You have to master **the subtle art of "sure-fire closing."**
  (j) **WORK HARD(er) and WORK SMART(er).**
  (k) **Start early and finish late.** This is the time in your life to "work long hours" and have few days off. That is the price you will have to pay for success.

"The Basics" also mean 1,001 other things:
(a) Make sure that your **signs are clean and in good shape** (in a Buyer's eye they may form a first impression of you).
(b) Prepare a thorough **feature sheet** with lot size, taxes, floor area, **room sizes** (so people know if their furniture will fit).
(c) **A map** showing schools, parks, churches, bus lines and the proximity to shopping will be helpful to influence a Client's buying decision.
(d) Do a **"Just Listed" mail out** and phone home owners in a 1 or 2 block radius around your listing and ask them if they have a friend or relative wanting to live nearby.
(e) While you are at it, also don't forget to **enquire if THEY** or one of their neighbours **are thinking of selling or buying** in the near future; then call on them and/or diarize them for a follow-up.
(f) 2 things which will help "closing" the Buyer:
- Line up **financing** (a pre-approved mortgage) and
- possibly even a **house inspection report** (which should give the Buyers increased confidence in their decision making process).

(g) By asking the current owners why they bought this house in the first place, you may be able to **determine who the most likely future Buyer for your listing might be.** Then aim all of your advertising towards that kind of person.
(h) **Take 2 or 3 photographs of your listing from different angles;** and then alternate the pictures in your ads; also periodically rewrite the wording and heading of your ads. Because the market is slow it will take a while to sell the house. By changing pictures and rewriting the ad you will "camouflage" the fact that you are still advertising the same house.
(i) When Realtors look through a MLS catalogue or browse on the computer, many of them just look at the picture and peruse the "comments." Change both of them at least once during the life time of your listing.
(j) **GOOD SERVICE = GOOD PUBLIC RELATIONS = and as a bonus some day you will have less problems closing an offer.** (Because by then the Sellers "will know the score.")
- **After each showing, follow up** with a phone call to the Realtor who has shown your listing; thank him or her for the showing (good public relations) and ask for their Buyers' comments; **these should be passed along to the Sellers:** you may not realize it, but your Sellers are sitting there day in and day out wondering what is going on. They may ask themselves: "Why isn't anybody making an offer on our home?"
- **Put your listing on the MLS Tour** and discuss with your Sellers the Tour Average Appraisal; ditto for the Office Tour.

(k) **Preview every listing in your area.** You and your Seller should know what your competition is. Moreover, if a Buyer doesn't like your listing, then you can show and sell him into one of the other properties which are for sale in the neighbourhood.
(l) **Keep track of all "solds" in your area,** so that you will have "ammunition" (meaning the correct information) when you present an offer on your own listing.

(m) **Keep your Seller informed of the market** and review/reduce the asking price periodically.

(n) After your listing is sold, **do a "Just Sold" mail out** and phone AGAIN home owners in a 1 or 2 block radius. Somebody may have changed his mind since your last phone call and he may NOW be ready to sell.

(o) "The Basics" also mean that you must **develop a daily routine** (from which you cannot deviate) **of worthwhile activities** (namely the ones which have at least a 50/50 chance of making you some money IN THE NEAR FUTURE, remember?).

You must stick to this routine with stubborn and consistent perseverance.

(p) As you are your own boss, you have the luxury of deciding how many hours a day and how many days a week you want to work the "50/50-chance-stuff." To keep yourself on track, it might be a good idea to **prepare a Weekly Activity Sheet,** setting out the days from Monday to Sunday. Then make rubrics for your basic daily routine activities and set aside a couple of minutes at the end of your working day to complete this daily report. Alternatively you can use your daily appointment calendar.

(q) **At the end of your work day** ask yourself:
- Did I have a plan for today and did I adhere to it?
- What do I plan to do tomorrow?

(r) **At the end of your work week,** review with yourself:
This week:
- on how many days did I get out of bed at a REGULAR time and go to work?
- How much **CONSTRUCTIVE WORK** did I do? (In case you forgot, the definition of "constructive work" is anything which has at least a 50/50 chance of resulting in a commission during the next 30 days or sooner). **In a slow market anything else is at best a long shot or at worst a waste of time or wishful thinking.**
- How much time did I spend at the office, drinking coffee and gossiping while my significant other, my children and friends etc. thought that I was out in the field working hard selling real estate?

Be honest, because the only person you will fool is yourself.

If the answer is not to your liking, then you have to review if you are prepared to pay the admittedly steep price for success. I have read somewhere that it is only in the dictionary that SUCCESS comes before WORK.

About The Personal Safety Of Realtors

At first blush selling real estate doesn't appear to be a very dangerous occupation. Certainly not when compared to a construction worker balancing himself precariously on slippery steel girders some 20 stories up in the air; or a mechanic working around dangerous machinery.

And yet, what other profession (other than real estate) can you think of as **so vulnerable to the threat of a physical assault?**

- Who else takes a lone male who is a complete stranger into her car and drives him to a vacant new house in the isolation of a subdivision of unoccupied homes under construction?
- How many of you have met Customers after hours at the office and there was nobody else around and the people became agitated or hostile?
- Have you ever gone to a stranger's house in the dark of the night to get a listing or make a sale?
- Have you ever spent hours alone in a house and put a sign on the front lawn inviting all strangers to walk in? (That is what is happening at an "Open House").

The reality is that male and female Realtors have been attacked, robbed and beaten severely in some of these situations.

Assaults can also be
(a) **verbal** (sarcastic remarks about commissions and "rich" Realtors; suggestive innuendos).
(b) **Sexual** (ranging from unwelcome advances, "accidental" touching or brushing up against etc.) and
(c) then there is a plethora of other things like **harassment** and **stalking** (when Realtors get involved with Clients on a more personal and private level resulting in somebody's jealousy, anger etc.).
(d) **financial** (a "Buyer" borrowing a small amount of money "temporarily" from a trusting Realtor).
(e) **On the road:**
When you let your emotions get the better of you then **ROAD RAGE can rear its ugly head.** A 3,000 lbs. car in the hands of a reckless or viciously aggressive driver can become a lethal weapon.
- Did you ever prevent another car from passing you or switching lanes?
- Do you stare at another driver with open hostility or shake your head disapprovingly when he shouts obscenities or makes certain hand gestures?
- Do you honk your horn excessively and with confrontational displeasure at an aggressive driver?

Violence in a Realtor's workplace should be recognized as a serious occupational hazard and not just as something that comes with the territory (acceptable "cost of doing business" or the price of "earning a good living").

The costs and consequences of any type of assault can be frightening and devastating to your personal well-being and enormous:
- the physical pain,
- the emotional trauma,
- the financial loss (time lost from work) and finally
- the possibility of subsequent physical or mental long-term disabilities.

Realtors are mistaken if they think that they have no control over their personal security. Here are some **suggestions to PREVENT or deal with VIOLENCE:**

(1) Recognize that **a violent assault can happen to ANYONE (including you!) ... ANYWHERE ... ANYTIME.**
- **Learn to assess** the various degrees of security risks which you will encounter in different situations.
- **Listen to your instincts** and
- **avoid** getting yourself into a precarious situation in the first place.

(2) Don't fluctuate between paranoic terror and recklessness. **Safe practices must become an instinctive, automatic part of a Realtor's life, both on and off the job.**

(3) When you are **on the road** try to remember the 3 basic safety precautions:
  (a) **Don't drink and drive.**
  (b) **Always wear your seat belt** and insist that your passengers do also.
  (c) **Think and drive defensively.**
  This simply means that as soon as you start the engine of your car you should always be on the alert that somebody might do something stupid — unexpectedly!
  (d) While driving, continuously observe, search and scan your surroundings.
  (e) Be courteous to other drivers.
  - If you are not sure who has the right-of-way, then yield to the other driver.
  - Pull over if somebody is persistently tailgating you.
  (f) Don't be aggressive. Instead learn to forgive. Let him change lanes, let him pass. He may be in a hurry to get a speeding ticket. Speed also kills. He might be searching impatiently for the next available accident.
  (g) Alcohol and speed are the ingredients for a fatal cocktail.
  (h) Keep to a minimum all distractions while driving.
  - Paying attention to the traffic around you is an absolute necessity for your self-preservation.
  - "Multi-tasking" is not a required activity to drive a car: E.g.
  - Talking on the cell phone for a long period of time.
  - Listening to and concentrating on inspirational sales seminar tapes.
  (i) Schedule your appointments in such a way as to leave yourself sufficient time to get there. It is not good fighting rush hour traffic while you are stressed.
  (j) Always lock your doors when driving, especially if there are children in the car.

(k) When you get out of your car, even if it is only for a few minutes, **turn off the motor,** shift to "park," set the hand brake and lock the doors.
(l) At night, if possible park in a well-lit area and observe the surroundings as you leave and return to your car.
(m) Should you car brake down for some reason, especially at night, remain in your car with the doors locked and windows up. Hopefully you have a cell phone to call for help. Other methods of drawing attention to your stalled vehicle are to put the hood up and turn on the emergency flashers. Wait for the police or ask people who do stop to send a tow truck to your location. It may not be wise to accept help from a stranger by getting into his car to drive to the next gas station.
(n) Unless you are a mechanic, common sense says never to tinker around on a hot or running engine: keep long hair, loose clothing (shirt sleeves etc.) and jewelry (e.g. dangling bracelets) away from the rotating engine fan or other moving components (like the engine belts). A burning cigarette may drop a hot spark onto some grease-soaked fuel-related part of the engine and start a fire.
(o) **We age at different rates** and physical and mental decline are unfortunately inevitable. Short of the sudden onset of some sort of catastrophic event (e.g. a stroke), this decline takes place at an imperceptible rate: it is something like watching paint dry. As we get older brain cells die, muscle mass drops, tissues and organs age and as a result we are **slower processing information: we have a REDUCED REACTION TIME and our NIGHT VISION, colour contrasts and spatial integration get to be compromised.** Young people have a **larger peripheral visual field** than older persons. If you have problems turning your head to look over your shoulder when checking traffic then buy an **auxiliary wide-angle mirror.**
You may have to get used to bi-focal or tri-focal glasses.
Those of us who are taking prescription medications should **read the labels because some of these medications may cause DROWSINESS.** Discuss the side effects with your doctor.
(p) If you find that you have more and more close calls and/or fender benders, if cars and pedestrians suddenly appear out of "nowhere" or "out of thin air," if you find traffic becoming intimidating, then it may be time to review your driving skills. By taking a **refresher Safe Driving Course you will upgrade not only your PERFORMANCE but also your CONFIDENCE.**

(4) **There is no magic shield against violence.**
(a) When showing a vacant house in a remote location, always let the prospective Buyer **walk AHEAD of you. Stay in the hall or doorway, instead of entering into a vacant room (confined area) with him.**
(b) A cell phone prominently displayed on a clip-on holder may serve as a deterrent and give you an illusion of security. But in the case of a sudden, unexpected and determined physical attack, you probably will have no chance to get to it anyway.

(c) Pepper spray may backfire.
(d) Some Realtors have taken a self-defence course. Rather than forcing yourself into rigid techniques which you may forget or not be able to use in a crisis situation
   - learn to react without thinking.
   - Learn to make your defensive moves become a natural part of your body movements.

(5) **In a true emergency the objective should be to get away.**
A violent 6 ft. 230 lbs. attacker has the element of surprise and the size and bulk of his body on his side. If you find yourself thrown to the ground and pinned on your back before you have a chance to run away, then by all means fight back to the best of your ability. Flail your arms and legs wildly; but don't try to overpower the assailant. Scream into his ear.
Your sole objective should be to get away, so that you can call for help (on your cell phone or from a neighbour). If the Pepper Spray or the piercing alarm whistle are in your car or in your purse on the kitchen counter, if your arms are pinned to your sides, then all you have left to defend yourself with is **STREET SMARTS which means dirty fighting.** Understand that in **this** situation you are no longer required to be friendly, helpful and nice.
   (a) A head butt against his nose or a good kick between his legs may give you just enough of an opening to get your arms free.
   (b) Don't scratch his face, because it will only make him madder. Instead rake or gouge his eyes. Primitive, but effective even with football-player-sized professional wrestlers.

(6) **Adopt a "buddy system."**
   - Somebody should always know where you are and for how long.
   - Keep periodic contact by phone.
   - Maintain and share information about suspicious clients.
   - For your mutual benefit learn to work together with others.

(7) When the front desk receptionist goes home
   - **the front door should have a lock which locks itself automatically,** so that nobody can open it from the outside, unless they have a key.
   - For the use by Clients who come after office hours, **there should be a buzzer besides the door** to alert you (waiting inside) that they have arrived.
   - It would also be desirable to install a monitored alarm system with a **"panic button."**

(8) **Security is everyone's business.**
   (a) Many real estate companies do not have a comprehensive Security Action Plan or policy in place.
   (b) The subject of a Realtor's personal safety should be discussed at least once a

year during a sales meeting.
(c) There should be periodic updates.
(d) These measures will result in a decrease in stress for everybody and an improvement in staff morale. If Salespersons feel secure in their knowledge that their Manager and Company care about their physical safety and emotional well-being, then **they are more likely to perform better. It will also build loyalty.**

THUS EVERYBODY WILL WIN IN THE END.

Footnotes On Your Aching Feet

Because human beings are bipeds they depend for locomotion on their legs and feet. Each foot contains 26 bones and is a little marvel of engineering. Did you know that the bones in your feet represent about 25% of your skeleton?

The public often pictures in their minds a Realtor sitting in a comfortable chair behind a big executive desk in an airconditioned luxurious office. Contrary to this popular myth selling real estate is not a sedentary office job. An active Realtor spends the major portion of his working life on his feet.

Therefore, if your feet hurt atrociously at the end of the day after having shown many houses to Clients, you should not ignore the warning signals. It is not normal for feet to hurt excruciatingly. **Pain, tenderness, excessive itching and blisters are the body's way of telling us that something is wrong.** Regrettably, many Realtors end up as Walking Wounded because
- they either routinely ignore these warning signs
- or else they reason that foot pain is merely one more price which they have to pay for success or
- they are forced to continue working in order to earn a badly needed commission cheque.

If your feet hurt, you may hurt all over.

For minor aches and pains, a comforting foot bath and/or massage may do the trick; soothing powder may alleviate minor itching.

Foot disorders and/or continuous serious foot pain can lead to more serious problems which should be discussed without delay with the family doctor or a podiatrist.

Abnormalities of the foot affect a large percentage of the population but in some cases it can be corrected with orthotics, properly fitting shoes or even other simple means. For example:

Ingrown toenails: it is NOT a cosmetic problem, when the corners of your toenails dig painfully into the flesh and skin. This condition is often caused by improper nail trimming, but also by pressure from poorly fitting shoes. Cut your nails straight across; don't cut down the sides or round them off.

SORE, CRACKING HEELS: the skin around your heels dries out and turns into thick and tough callous in which eventually deep and painful cracks appear. If it is a mild case, use a pumice stone. Alternatively a daily application of a little cream after a warm foot bath may work for you. If you can't solve the problem, you should see a podiatrist.

Bunions: these are misaligned big toe joints, which can become swollen and tender, causing the first joint of the big toe to slant outward and the second joint to angle toward the other toes. This condition often starts with fallen arches or a pronating foot, which will cause the joint to become unstable. It is aggravated by narrow shoes.

Hammertoes: the toes are bent in a claw-like position, usually because of a muscle imbalance or possibly from arthritis.

Heel pain: this could be either from a Heel Spur (a growth of bone in the heel) or possibly plantar fasciitis (an inflammation of connective tissue which runs along the bottom of the foot and is attached to the heel). See your doctor SAP.

CORNS: layers of dead thick skin are formed on toes from rubbing the foot inside of improperly fitting shoes.

CALLUS: this is a thickening of the skin on the ball of the foot.

Athlete's foot: is caused by a fungus which thrives in hot, moist environments, like e.g. locker rooms, public showers etc. It manifests itself as itching and discoloration between the toes; but it can also be on the arch as a white, itchy discoloration.

WARTS: are a viral infection usually found on the feet or hands. They should be treated by a doctor.

BLISTERS: are caused by friction of the foot inside a tight shoe, usually over a long period of time. The tender spot can be cushioned with a small pad of cotton batten; of course, properly sized shoes are a must.

A very personal and embarrassing foot problem is **sweaty, unpleasantly smelling feet and yellow toe nails.** A family doctor, podiatrist or dermatologist should investigate for a fungus or skin infection. Your feet could also be allergic to the dye in your shoes.

In less serious cases, you can pamper your feet with a soothing foot bath; many stores carry various medicated refreshing bath salts. Talcum powder or an antiperspirant spray may alleviate some of the foot odour.

And this brings us to the subject of S H O E S .
For many reasons (e.g. fashion, style, poorly trained sales clerks) many people wear improperly fitting shoes. Therefore
RULE # 1 is: IF THE SHOE DOESN'T FIT, DON'T WEAR IT.
(a) Don't let a sales clerk talk you into wearing anything on your feet that doesn't fit the best for you or that wouldn't be comfortable on a good, long walk.
(b) **Contrary to popular belief there is no such thing as a "breaking-in" period.**

The following is a simple test, which everybody can do. LOOK AT YOUR SHOES:
(a) **if the heel of your shoe is worn more on the inside than the outside,** then you are a **PRONATOR**.
That means that when you walk you roll your feet inward each time your heel strikes the ground. You need a control shoe specially built for you to counteract this tendency.
(b) **If your heel is worn more on the outside,** then you are an **UNDERPRONATOR**, which means you ought to wear a shoe with more cushioning.

When CHOOSING shoes you should ask yourself the following questions:
- How much time do you spend on your feet each day?
- How old are you and how much do you weigh?
- Do you have foot or ankle pain when walking?
- Do you have flat feet, very high arches or a high instep?
- Do you have arthritis or joint pain in your feet?
- Do you have poor circulation (constantly ice-cold feet) or leg cramps, numbness or burning in your feet?

When BUYING shoes you may wish to keep in mind the following:

(1) Shoes come in different shapes and sizes and **are not uniformly manufactured:** slight variations from one brand to another could mean that the same size shoe in one brand may not fit you as well as in another.

(2) **Shop for shoes in the late afternoon** when your feet have expanded (become larger or swollen slightly) and adjusted to your walking pattern after you have been on your feet all day.

(3) **Make sure that you are getting a proper fit.** Ill-fitting or worn-out shoes cause undue stress on your feet and ankles and thus could be the origins of many of your problems. Clerks in good shoe stores have a measuring device, **which not only measures the LENGTH of your foot, but also the WIDTH.** Every time you buy new shoes have the clerk measure BOTH feet. Many people have one foot slightly larger than the other; also your foot size may increase or change as you grow older.

(4) Shoes must fit your heels as well as your toes. **Shoes fit properly if** the heel is snug and does not slip or slide and if there is a thumb's width (or about 1/2 inch) space between the longest toe and the tip of the toe box (the front end of the shoe). You should be able to wiggle all of your toes freely.

(5) Try on both shoes and walk around in them to ensure that they feel comfortable. If the shoes feel too tight or not just right, then don't buy them.

(6) **Shoes should provide good and effective cushioning (built into the sole) for shock absorption.**

The sole of the shoe should be constructed from material which is ideal for security (grip the ground to prevent slipping). The ideal walking shoe is stable from side to side and ought to fully bend at the ball of the foot.

(7) **Don't cut corners when buying shoes.** Expensive shoes fit and look better and with proper care they will last longer. Treat your shoes as an investment in your health and work.

(8) Instead of ill-conceived fashion considerations, **choose shoes based**
  - **on your weight,**
  - **on your foot structure (high instep, arches etc.) and**
  - **on your walking requirements and habits.**

(9) Shoes with **very high heels and pointy toes and comfort don't mix.** When your foot is elevated in the heel, then the law of gravity will shift a large portion of your body weight from your heel forward towards the front of your foot. Stiletto heels may be gorgeous and sexy, but they are hardly the right footwear for an arduous task like showing a dozen properties on a hot summer afternoon. There are times when walking in "sensible shoes" may avoid a lot of needless foot pain, knee and lower back pain.

(10) **During inclement weather,** thoughtful salespersons will protect their precious tootsies by wearing appropriate footwear. Whereas winter shoes should be warm and water repellant, they don't necessarily have to resemble Godzilla's combat boots. The soles should provide traction and stability on a variety of winter surfaces (ice, Matterhorn-sized snow banks, lake-sized rain puddles).

Happy walking!

Realtors, Marriage And Divorce - Part I

In my 35-year real estate career, I have had many times the sad occasion to observe the destruction of a family by divorce. It is something like open-heart surgery with a chain saw. Sometimes Clients were involved, sometimes it was the family of a fellow Realtor.

Only a few split-ups were amicable; most of them involved bitter, protracted and costly Court battles fought over children and money. The ones who suffered most from this sorry experience were the children. While the parents were busy wrangling, some of the children harboured **GUILT** because of divided loyalties. Consequently many of the children did badly in school or developed behavioral problems.

I have no hard statistics to cite the percentage of Realtors getting divorced, but my general impression over the years was that our business produced more than its fair share of broken homes.

The reasons for this are many:

(1) Realtors lead a high-octane life in a cruel world filled with savage frustrations and a multitude of pressures:
   - living on "commissions" only means irregularity of income and often entails financial uncertainty.
   - Working long hours 7 days a week in a highly competitive business.
   - Always being "on call" and at the mercy of a ringing telephone.
   - Trying to please and appease relentlessly demanding Clients (unreasonable Sellers and disloyal Buyers).
   - Endeavouring to accomplish too much in too little time.
   - The effects of constant stress on mind and body.

(2) Many Realtors suffer from a deep-down nagging bad conscience that due to their work (the number of hours which **THEY control to a certain extent**), they are NOT spending enough quality time with their families.

(3) Somebody with a penchant for philandering may find that the grass is greener on the other side of the fence. A Realtor certainly has the perfect excuse (and opportunity) to be out at all hours of the day and night. When he comes home empty handed, there is an iron-clad alibi: "Honey, I was working hard on this listing/deal, but the stupid Client wouldn't budge/sign it."

(4) The wife also is super busy trying to hold up her end of the bargain: driving the kids to school, Little League, PTA, shopping, housekeeping, cooking, looking after an elderly or sick relative. In addition she may also have a (part-time) job.

(5) Quality time and conjugal bliss are in short supply because both partners are

- physically too tired and
- emotionally too stressed out.

(6) As a result, sooner or later husband and wife become like 2 ships passing each other in the night.

(7) When things gang up, one of the parties may discover the restorative powers of a stiff drink; or two, or more.
Too late does he/she realize that there is no numbing relief, no solace or no solution (for problems) to be found at the bottom of a bottle. Excessive drinking will only create more and/or some new problems.

(8) Alcohol and drugs can set suppressed emotions free, resulting in mental and occasionally in physical violence.

(9) Children will learn from and imitate their parents (who- for better and for worse - are their role models). Many social ills stem from dysfunctional families.

(10) All of these things will destroy the unity of a marriage and family and fracture the relationship of its members.

The interesting question is, **how do people get themselves into this sort of predicament?**

IN THE BEGINNING ...
Honeymooners believe (and rightly so)
- that there has never been such a love as theirs and
- that their love will never end. Maybe somebody else's will, but not theirs.
- That there will be no misunderstandings because they will "communicate with each other."
- That they will always share their innermost thoughts.
- No problems, disappointments, tragedies and illnesses (physical and mental) will be too great that they cannot cope with them and/or overcome them.
- In the contrary! Problems of any kind will only serve to cement their relationship more firmly. After all they married "for better or for worse."
- Poverty and financial adversity will have no effect.
- There will be no quarrels over money (the filthy lucre).
- They will be eternally faithful to each other and nothing and nobody will or can ever come between them.
- Temptations leading to infidelity will be simply ignored.

WHEN THE HONEYMOON IS OVER ...
- Reality sets in with a vengeance - warts and all: bills, dirty diapers, job worries etc.

- "Cash flow" is a difficult-to-ignore aspect of "money."
- Prolonged illness and suffering can demean a person and corrode a marriage.
- Blind romance will be tempered by the monotony of daily life: do this, don't do that, nag, nag, the phone rings continuously, "I don't have any more time for myself."
- Yes, we have closed our eyes to the fact that things can or will happen that were neither planned nor could they be anticipated.
- For a brief period of time we have ignored
  - the pressures of life and
  - the weakness of human nature.
  - Reluctantly we come to the sober conclusion that "the road to hell is paved with good intentions" … after all.

On the other hand we BEHOLD THE OLD COUPLE, white-haired and with deeply lined faces. Shaking hands crippled by arthritis. One in a wheel chair, the other with a hunched-over back from years of hard work. Both have experienced many trials and sorrows. And yet they have become so much a part of each other that it is difficult to discern where one leaves off and the other one begins. They seem to have the ability to read each other's thoughts and to anticipate each other's wishes. How can they do that? How did they learn to cope with the ravages of life?

Here are some ideas which were gleaned from people who have been married for a long time.

1) **Be considerate and generous** with ALL members of your family.
   - When **your partner** is too tired to cook, take the family out for dinner.
   - Take time to **talk to your wife ALONE and AFTER the kids have gone to bed.** She might be starved for some adult conversation. Also there just might be something constructive to talk about between husband and wife.
2) Because you can control your appointments, make a serious effort to **have supper with your family.** A daily common meal will **build unity.**
   - Listen to what the others have to tell you — it is important to them.
   - **Don't talk real estate at the table.**
   - **Don't bring home your job stress.** (Doing that are signs of ignorant self-absorption).
   - Make an effort to smile, but don't grin.
3) **Good manners and courtesy:** all members of your family deserve these just as much if not more than your Clients and fellow Realtors. You will also want to teach good manners to your children.
4) As a matter of courtesy all serious decisions which will profoundly influence the entire family should be discussed jointly with your partner, because
   - 2 brains can cover more territory than one and
   - decisions made by **mutual agreement carry mutual responsibility.** The reason for this should be self-evident.

5) Pay **little unexpected compliments** to your wife: "My Dear, the supper you cooked tonight was especially tasty."
   - Open a door for her (e.g. when entering a restaurant).
   - Hold hands with her when walking.
   - Occasionally send her flowers or bring home an unexpected little gift.

6) **Your kindness to your wife will bear great dividends.**
   - If you are nice to her then she will be nice back to you **PLUS a little interest** in the form of kindness. Being grateful for the good feelings which have been generated and possibly somewhat surprised about the extra interest of kindness you may gratefully feel that it is only right to continue the exchange of kindness with a bonus of double interest. Thus both of you are on your way to wonderful domestic harmony.
   - On the other hand if you are mean and ill tempered, she is liable to reciprocate in kind - and most likely also with some "mean" interest. You, of course, cannot let her get away with that and answer in kind plus triple interest in the form of verbal abuse. If you both manage to keep this up over a period of time, you will eventually make 2 lawyers happy … in Divorce Court.

7) **If you have a disagreement,** remain civilized. Don't be disagreeable, abrasive or abusive.
   - Shouting at the top of your lungs will win no argument.
   - Hurtful words spoken in haste or anger can be forgiven, but regrettably they can never be forgotten.

8) Don't go to sleep before you have reconciled. **Learn how to ask for forgiveness.**
   - This is the start of the healing process after the melt-down.
   - There should be no room for false or stubbornly misplaced pride.

9) You will have to **learn to make allowances** for any weakness your partner may have. As a true help-mate, you should discreetly compensate with your strength for the other's shortcomings. **And vice versa.**

10) Develop a sense of being a couple. Don't think of yourselves any longer as 2 separate individuals: you are a TEAM now (the 2 of you against the world). It is essential that both of you should pull in the same direction.

11) It is an asset to have and **maintain a good sense of humour.** Life is serious enough, so learn to laugh at yourself and at yourselves. E.g.:
    As head of the household you may consider yourself to be in charge of the "Big Decisions": e.g. an in-depth analysis of the Federal Government's fiscal policy. Or should the UN send troops to a particular trouble spot.

Seeing that in addition to having to make the "Big Decisions" you are also always very busy selling real estate. Therefore your wife should preside over the many "small decisions":
- when and where we go on holidays.
- What kind of new fridge we are buying.
- The family budget (most likely you have neither the time nor the interest for it).

12) Take a **yearly holiday with your family.** For a month if the family budget can stand it. It will renew and solidify everybody's relationship with everybody. It will also result in beautiful memories for later years. Your cell phone should be used only for emergencies (e.g. flat tire, out of gas etc.). Your lap top should be used only for games for the kids.

13) **Control your anger and frustrations.** Vent them somewhere else but not on the members of your family. If you must let off steam,
   - then indulge your primal scream while flailing at the punching bag in the privacy of your basement (at least you won't make a public spectacle of yourself).
   - Go to the gym to work off whatever bothers you. After a while there may be the added bonus of you becoming quite slim and muscular.
   - Whack some balls at the driving range and picture in your mind a hateful face on each of the golf balls. As an added bonus this may improve your golf game.

14) Instead of doing something around the house or with your children, don't spend your entire weekend unshaven, lounging in your underwear on the chesterfield drinking beer while watching the hockey/baseball/football games all day long.
   - It will antagonize your wife.
   - It will embarrass your teenage daughter(s).
   - It will be a poor example for your teenage son(s).
   - After years of neglect, can you really expect your grown-up children to spend "quality time" with you in your old age?

15) **TRUST and RESPECT have to be earned;** once lost, they are difficult to replace/regain.

16) Those of you who are bringing up children will appreciate that they must be taught **the difference between good and evil.** Basically all religions are doing just that and thus they have a civilising effect on mankind.

17) What harm is there if all of you together **visit HIM at HIS HOUSE for an hour once a week and hear HIS teachings?** What harm is there if a Little One gives "thanks" for the food before all of you start to eat?

18) At one end of the spectrum, there are people who feel that if they pray together, they will stay together. At the other end of the spectrum there will be those who say: "Thank God that I am an Atheist."

Like the Prussian King Frederick the Great said: "Everybody has permission to go to his type of heaven in his own fashion."

19) Gather invaluable ideas to
    - strengthen your relationship with your family
    - and to protect yourself against divorce.
    - Every day ask yourself: "Can I spare and invest a few minutes today to save (improve) my marriage?"

20) With **DOMESTIC PEACE reigning at the Home Front there will be an additional huge bonus for you: you will be able to SELL REAL ESTATE a lot BETTER:**
    - You will have a good outlook on life (the old "Positive Mental Attitude").
    - You will be able to concentrate better on the job at hand (because you have one thing less to worry about)
    - and **at the end of your work day you will have a warm refuge to come home to** where you will encounter nothing but friendly faces. After parking your car, leave all of your worries out in the garage because inside the house you will have a wonderful opportunity to recharge your batteries.

Realtors, Marriage And Divorce - Part II

A few thoughts about the meaning of a "marriage."

In some ways a marriage is like a building. Buildings sitting on a properly constructed concrete foundation or when they are anchored solidly on rock formations will remain solid regardless of high winds, bad weather or earthquakes.

In a marriage **LOVE,** of course, is the foundation. In order to endure LOVE must be diligently maintained and bonded throughout a lifetime by **TENDERNESS.** This can take many forms:
- a thoughtful little compliment here or there,
- a quick encouraging smile,
- an understanding glance,
- a quick little kiss or a pat on the cheek.

All of these will cost you absolutely nothing and yet they will yield for your marriage an enormous amount of goodwill, contentment and reciprocal love. **And finally tenderness will also help you to grow old together gracefully.**

The structure above the foundation will also have to be built with care and maintained lovingly over a life time. Sufficient time, care and effort must be spent on details of utility, comfort and safety. Please remember that especially **children value safety and security.**

On the other hand a building slapped up in a hurry with little thought given to its quality will result in a shabby and uncomfortable edifice. Often such buildings will receive carelessly little or no upkeep and over time they will become dilapidated.

Hand in hand with LOVE and TENDERNESS come **RESPECT** and **TRUST.** Each partner must **respect** the other. You may not always agree on everything, but it is essential that you respect the other person's point of view. Yes, there are bound to be differences of opinion in your future; but at all times and in all situations it is preferable to talk it over instead of fighting. Always be aware that during a fight you are liable to say things which will or are intended to hurt the other person. Afterwards the other person will hopefully "forgive" you, but the hurtful words can never be forgotten. And the wounds from them can fester secretly for years like dryrot. If you had a fight, never go to sleep mad. Make up and both of you will sleep better.

TRUST merely means that you don't have to look constantly over your shoulder. You can unflinchingly rely on your partner. It is the 2 of you against the world! Support with your strength the other person's weak points and the 2 of you will become an invincible unit.

In a good marriage there must also be **PRUDENCE.** Prudence means many things:
- to run a household in an economically efficient way,
- do not throw money out of the window needlessly.
- Conduct yourselves in daily life in such a way as to enhance the marriage-partnership on its road of life.
- Always be generous to each other in spirit and in all ways.

And finally there is **HOPE.** In fact, there MUST be hope, because without it life would be hopeless in more ways than one.

Regardless of how bad things might be today, there is always a TOMORROW. Instead of dwelling on and revisiting in your mind the failures of yesterday, realize that just around the corner there is a glorious sunrise coming up for a new day. This particular feature is always a tough one and only through the mutual steadfast support will your marriage team be able to prevail. Both partners should remind each other many times that the trials and tribulations of life can turn out to be a stepping stone to bigger and better things. You will find that they were and that they are.

If you believe in a Supreme Being, than pray that God may protect you and yours and keep you all safely in the palm of his hand.

May your marriage turn out to be as harmonious and successful as you envisioned it on the day you said "I DO."

Common Sense Tips On Money Matters

Why is it that some Realtors feel that financial planning is:
- too tedious or
- too time consuming or
- complicated rocket science?

As a result they procrastinate and end up doing nothing.

Others again are too preoccupied with chasing their next commission to give much thought to handling their money prudently (commonly referred to as **"budgeting"**). With a "laissez-fair" attitude they prefer to fly by the seat of their pants.
Realtors in these 2 categories live from cheque to cheque, which often is a bumpy and chaotic roller coaster ride of feast or famine.

Others again feel that they are simply not good money managers and decide to take the elegant but expensive way out by hiring a Financial Adviser.

And finally there are those who refuse to turn over their hard-earned cash to any stranger; instead they go to seminars and read everything they can lay their hands on to educate themselves to **become self-sufficient Masters Of Their Own Fate.** If you want to be one of those, then read on because you may wish to learn about and consider

The 7 pillars of a Realtor's FINANCIAL structure:

1) Instead of procrastinating, **take the time to**
   - **EXAMINE** and **EVALUATE** honestly and **periodically the STATE of your PERSONAL** and business **FINANCES.**
   - **Assessing once a year your "THEN-current" situation and**
   - **formulating your goals** (because what you want to achieve will probably change from time to time) **MUST** be one of the **constant monetary pillars** at every stage of your life. **The result is CONTROL and FREEDOM.**
   - **By constantly and regularly putting your financial house in order** and restating your goals, **you will be able to obtain** a certain amount of **financial CONTROL over YOUR LIFE** and consequently relative **FREEDOM from FINANCIAL WORRY.**

2) **Budgeting:** this is hard, because **it requires ...**
   S E L F - D I S C I P L I N E .

(a) **Buy only what you need and not what you want.** By making initially small sacrifices (and by not giving in to foolish temptations to splurge) you will, in due course, enjoy big long-term benefits.

(b) **Expense bills have the bad habit of coming in with sickening punctuality and regularity.** Because a Realtor's commission income is irregular and largely unpredictable, he must constantly watch his **CASH FLOW**.

*** You must discipline yourself to **budget for week-to-week rock-bottom fixed cash-flow survival needs** (these are the absolute necessities to live on and to stay in business).

Set up 2 bank accounts:

- a **"WORKING Account"** in the form of an interest-bearing checking account on which you can write an unlimited number of free cheques. (This is often available from a Credit Union). **From THIS account you pay all of your bills:**
  - your "living expenses" (e.g. food, hydro, house mortgage payment etc.)
  - your "business expenses" (e.g. office rent, advertising, membership fees, income tax etc.)

When you get a commission cheque you **MUST deposit it into a**
- **separate "SAVINGS Account"** which you will access only once a month to transfer to your "Working Account" a predetermined lump sum of money for your living and business expenses. **In effect YOU PAY YOURSELF A MONTHLY WAGE.** For the rest of the time you must pretend that the money accumulating in the **"SAVINGS ACCOUNT" is NOT your money** and therefore, cannot be touched, regardless what sort of temptations and good deals come up (except, of course, in case of a genuine emergency).

3) **Saving:**
Many big producers make lots of money and yet have nothing to show for in the end. Why? Because **they spend it all** - and often more! Therefore, "saving" starts with:

(a) **"Don't spend more than you earn."** Try to live a little BELOW your means. In other words, **SPEND the "INTEREST" portion only and avoid dipping into your CAPITAL.**

(b) **"Don't make debts on which you pay a high interest rate."** E.g. credit card debts should be paid off quickly. If you are in the habit of maxing out your credit cards, you may wish to consider switching to a DEBIT CARD or simply to pay cash in order to break the bad cycle. If you pay cash, then you are forced to stop buying when the cash runs out.

(c) **"SAVING"** also requires that you REGULARLY set aside a certain amount of money for a rainy day, your future (e.g. holidays, a new car, a new TV, your **retirement**) and your **child's education** (into a Registered Educational Savings

Plan). While contributions to RESP's are at the present time not income tax deductible (for the contributor),
- the earnings will accumulate on a tax-deferred basis,
- the Government makes a certain contribution and
- some day all of it will assist with the payment of your child's University education costs.

If you are a "poor saver" then you will have nothing to invest with.

4) **Investing:** the purpose of investing is the accumulation and growth of assets. There are **"liquid assets"** (cash, Canada Savings Bonds etc.), and **"semi-liquid assets"** (these cannot be instantly or readily turned into cash and may require variable amounts of time to liquidate, e.g. property). Different people are willing to assume **different levels of risk.** Obviously, the higher the risk, the higher the return (e.g. mutual funds).

There is no such thing as a "free lunch." Don't be desperate and give in to the temptation of making some "hot money fast." If it is too good to be true, then it usually is. **A fool and his money are soon parted.** Whenever somebody is pressuring you to rush into an investment decision (so you will not "miss the boat" and "get in on the ground floor"), you run the risk of making a mistake in which case you eventually will have the opportunity of repenting at your leisure. Always remember that **the pain of losing money far outweighs the pleasure of gaining it.** Do your homework (research) and in due course make a sober decision based on facts. And then don't forget to **ACT**.

Common sense says that no amount of information and research can eliminate all uncertainty. Take the long-range view and recognize the fact that mistakes can be part of the game.

Unless you are a born gambler or are able to tolerate a lot of stress, stay away from "leveraging" (borrowing money to the maximum in order to finance some risky venture).

When gauging if an investment is good for you, remember that **it is preferable to be "approximately" right, rather than to be "precisely" wrong.**

NEVER PUT ALL OF YOUR EGGS INTO ONE BASKET. It is prudent to have a reasonable mix of liquid and semi-liquid assets.

Furthermore you must also be at ease with the various risk factors. The answer to the dilemma of choosing between High Risk and No Risk is to DIVERSIFY. Better still is to **stick to what you know best** which is **REAL ESTATE.** Consider buying a house to rent out (the tenant will pay off your mortgage).

- Buy an older but basically sound house which needs some cleaning and painting. Many people nowadays don't like to clean up somebody else's dirt. For that reason and because you will have to spend some money putting the house in shape, you must try to buy it **BELOW market value.**
- If the Seller won't cooperate and you are unable to get it for **your price,** then just walk away: he might change his mind later on and/or at any rate there are plenty more fish in the ocean.
- Make sure that the house is on a full-sized serviced lot in a good area. While the value of the structure will go down with time (physical and functional depreciation), **the value of the land will increase** (provided it is not an oddball, irregular or substandard lot).
- Set the monthly rent just a shade below "market rent." This strategy should attract a good tenant who will stay for a long time (because he can't get cheaper rent anywhere else) and who will pay the rent regularly and punctually.
- Have a written month-to-month rental contract which sets out who is responsible for what.
- From a practical point of view a lease is enforceable only against the landlord (because the house is there). On the other hand if the tenant disappears into the night and without a trace, then you will be unable to sue him regardless of the legality of your lease. Therefore, a lease will not give you the security you want. Treating your tenant fairly - will!

5) **Reduce your tax burden:**
   (a) **TAX PLANNING** should be a year-round affair and not just a frantic last minute effort just before income tax filing time.
   (b) Because tax laws are complicated and changing frequently do yourself a favour and **have your income tax return done by a good tax accountant** — his fees are tax deductible.
   (c) **Keep good records.**
   (d) **Keep a receipt for everything.**
   (e) **Keep extensive business expense records: if you wine and dine a client, be sure to write his name on the receipt.** (Income tax auditors wish to see that there is an actual connection between the expense incurred and business done).
   (f) **Keep a daily car mileage log together with receipts for gas and repairs and maintenance.** (In this connection Credit Card receipts will come in handy).
   (g) You must keep all of your business income tax records for a minimum of 7 years. If you want to destroy some records (receipts for paid bills, bank statements etc.) in the 8th year, you should apply in writing for permission to do so by writing to the local director of the CCRA (Canada Customs and Revenue Agency) - the former Revenue Canada.
   (h) Bite the bullet and pay your income tax in full and all instalments on time. Falling behind is an almost insurmountable curse.

(i) Be sure to make your maximum RRSP contribution. It is a good way to defer taxes and save money for your retirement.

(j) Whenever possible make your interest expenses tax deductible. Generally interest on money borrowed for investments or business is tax deductible. But **before you sign the loan agreement, it is always prudent to check first with Revenue Canada (CCRA) or your accountant.**

(k) Consider the advantages and disadvantages between **owning and leasing.** Some people lease cars, office equipment and everything else, just in order to be able to write the cost off income tax. Before you go overboard with leasing, **remember your cash flow** and what can happen to you if there is a downturn in business.

(l) Leasing a car for 2 years with an option of buying the car at a predetermined price may be of interest to some people. By prepaying the 2 year lease in one lump sum payment, you will most likely get a considerable reduction (in interest) over what it would cost you if you were to make monthly lease payments over the 2 years. At the end of the lease period you know the car and how it was maintained; this beats buying a used car and somebody else's troubles. Also, the predetermined buy-out price could be lower than the then-current price of a similar used car.

(m) If your spouse has a real estate sales license, then you can try to split your income.

(n) **Don't borrow money needlessly or recklessly.** The road to financial perdition is paved with the broken dreams of many bankrupts.

6) **Plan for your retirement:**
   (a) During your working years **your constant long range plan must be to pay down and eliminate all debts** (where the interest expense cannot be deducted from income tax). Being totally debt-free when retirement comes around is a wonderful feeling and will eliminate a lot of pressure.
   (b) If you have your RRSP's and investments properly lined up, you should be able to face with confidence the autumn of your life.
   Start building your RRSPs early in life: it is a wonderful way of saving, accumulating assets over many years and reducing your tax burden during high-income years.
   (c) If you are in your 60's and you decide to make up for lost time by gambling wildly on the stock market or buying lottery tickets in the hope of creating a last minute windfall profit, keep in mind that at best these are long shots.

7) **Security: In case of illness or long-term disability,** you may be just a pay cheque away from the poor house. Especially if you have a family to support, short-term and long-term disability insurance and/or **income replacement insurance** are obviously of great importance. A word of caution: this kind of insurance is initially available only when you are young and/or in good health. After a heart attack

many insurance companies will most likely decline you.

For business travel (e.g. conventions) or holidays out of your province or to another country, **additional travel insurance** (medical insurance coverage for illness or accident) is a must. The cost of hospitalization in a foreign country can be astronomical and financially crippling. If you have a preexisting long-term illness, then you may have to shop around for travel insurance. A good place to start is with your local Automobile Association or Travel Agents.

In closing I would like to share with you 2 lines which I have read somewhere and which have made an impression on me:

"If your **outflow** exceeds your **income**
then your **upkeep** will be your **downfall**."

MONTHLY RENTAL CONTRACT

MADE this _____ day of _____, _____.

BETWEEN: _____

                                                  hereinafter called the LANDLORDS

AND: _____

                                                  hereinafter called the TENANTS

WITNESSETH, that in consideration of the monthly rents, covenants and conditions hereinafter respectively reserved and contained, the said Landlords do demise and rent onto the said Tenants

THE PROPERTY AT _____, _____
FROM the _____ day of _____, _____.
YIELDING AND PAYING to the said Landlords, the **clear monthly rent or sum of** $ _____ (_____) DOLLARS
of lawful money of Canada.

Heat, light, cablevision and telephone will be paid by the tenants. The Tenants will also be responsible for any expenses incurred in the daily operation of the house (e.g. furnace filter, change of any water faucet washers etc.)

THERE WILL BE _____ adults _____ children _____ pets occupying the property.

ONE CLEAR MONTH's NOTICE IN WRITING, from the date of rental, IS REQUIRED FROM ALL PARTIES TO TERMINATE THIS RENTAL CONTRACT.

AS A CONDITION OF THIS MONTHLY RENTAL CONTRACT it is agreed to by all parties that there will be **NO INTEREST PAYABLE** by the Landlords on the **SECURITY DEPOSIT** which will be kept in a non-interest-bearing current account.

AND THE said TENANTS PROMISE TO THE LANDLORDS:
(1) To pay the rent on time and as stipulated above.
(2) The tenants will not assign or sublet the premises, or increase the number of occupants or pets without the Landlords' permission.
(3) The Tenants will report to the Landlords **IMMEDIATELY** any damage or urgent repairs needed to the premises.
(4) It is the Tenants' responsibility (and NOT the Landlords') to place adequate **RENTER's INSURANCE** on his/her/their contents (belongings) in the house. A photocopy of this insurance policy will be delivered to the Landlords within 30 days after commencement of rental.
    If the Tenants do not have contents insurance, then any loss or damage (in case of a fire or break-in) is the responsibility of the Tenants.

(5) The Tenants will not do anything on the premises which will increase the premium rate of the Landlords' fire insurance or invalidate any of the Landlords' insurance policies for the said premises.

(6) The Tenants will not carry on any business or deeds on the said premises that are illegal or shall be deemed as a nuisance.

(7) The Tenants are responsible for any damage caused by them; reasonable wear and tear and damage by fire and tempest or "Acts of God" (e.g. flood, earthquake) are excepted.

The Landlord does not have Earthquake Insurance on this house and in case of destruction of the premises, this Monthly Rental Contract is at an end and the Tenants must find alternative accommodation at their own expense.

(8) The Tenants will keep the premises in a clean condition and good repair. Any alterations, remodelling and painting (choice of colour and quality of paint) must be approved by the Landlords.

(9) The Tenants will keep the lawn cut and the yard in a condition acceptable to the By-Law Enforcement Officer of the local municipal authority.

(10) **IN CASE OF VACATING THE PROPERTY, it is expressly understood and agreed upon that the TENANTS**
- Will leave the premises in GOOD REPAIR and GOOD CONDITION acceptable to the Landlords (e.g. same condition as the premises were when the tenants first moved in).
- Will leave the premises in a clean condition (which means floors vacuumed, swept and washed; the house is empty of all furniture, belongings, debris etc. AND all garbage is disposed of and not merely left at or near the backlane.

(11) The Landlords are NOT responsible for any unpaid Hydro, cablevision, telephone bills or unauthorized repairs.

FAILURE TO COMPLY WITH THE ABOVE WILL MEAN FORFEITURE OF THE SECURITY DEPOSIT.

By affixing their signatures, the undersigned herewith accept the above conditions.

_____   _____
Tenant   Tenant

_____   _____
Landlord   Landlord

Thoughts For The New Year

ON TIMING
The marvellous thing is that you don't have to wait for January 1st to come around to resolve to make a fresh start. **The best time** to decide to improve something **is ... "NOW."**

ON MAKING DECISIONS
With the accumulation of experience you tend to make good decisions. Regrettably, experience is often gained by making a number of bad decisions.

ON MISTAKES
It is fatuous to think that you will never make a mistake somewhere along the way, much less a costly one. Many avoidable errors are the result of overconfidence or carelessness. Don't rehash in your mind your past mistakes - forget them! But **always remember the LESSONS they have taught you.**

ON HURTS
A harsh word spoken in haste and possibly even unthinkingly, can be very hurtful. The hurt may be forgiven, but the episode can never be forgotten. This goes for family, friends and strangers. Pay-back time could come many years later.

ON YOUR INTELLECTUAL DEVELOPMENT
It is delusionary to think that at the present time you know everything that you need to know now and in the future. The moment you stop exercising the muscles between your ears, intellectual stagnation will start you on the proverbial slippery slope to being "left behind" or becoming "out of date."

ON EDUCATION
Have you **learned** your trade?
Do you **understand** the real estate business?
Do you lack up-to-date education in the latest developments in your trade and as a result do you lack **the requisite marketing skills and attributes necessary for survival** in a highly competitive business?
"Ditto" for a tough market?

ON PROSPECTS, CUSTOMERS AND CLIENTS
Do you fail to recognize and/or concentrate on **REAL Clients who are ready to buy and sell NOW?**
Are you familiar with the current market?
Do you know what is for sale?
Have you gone on Tours or inspected properties on your own? Are you showing a multitude of houses (which you have never previewed before) to Buyers before you really understand what your Prospective Clients want?

ON SERVICE
Have you mastered the necessary elements of **CLIENT-CENTRED SERVICE?**
Are you interested in solving the clients' individual and particular problems?
Do you really want to help these people to reach their real estate goals which- simply put - is obtaining the most value for their money regardless if they are selling or buying?
In your rush to get your Clients to sign on the dotted line, are you an "impatient closer?" In other words, do you give them too little time and choice to make a considered decision? Or are you the opposite and talk yourself right past closing by confusing your Clients with an avalanche of trivial particulars?

ON THE ART OF COMMUNICATION
Are you in the habit of using a multitude of technical terms in order to impress people?
Are your communications with your clients too complicated?
Are you communicating too much of the wrong thing at the wrong time?
Are you more interested in showing off your eloquence, wit and wisdom rather than listening to what your Clients want, need and can afford?
God gave you one mouth and 2 ears; **this should tell you that "CAREFUL LISTENING" is not only an excellent CLOSING TOOL, but also a time-saving device.**

ON COMPLAINTS
A complaint is a person's communication to you that something has gone wrong in your business relationship.
Are you in the habit of taking care of unhappy customers promptly and graciously?
Do you realize that satisfying a complaint can be the beginning of a beautiful friendship?
That once the problem is solved, **a formerly unhappy Client** can become **a loyal Client for life** who in turn may refer to you many more Clients?
In view of this, do you see a complaint as a Golden Opportunity for future business or as a nuisance to be ignored?

ON USING COMMON SENSE
Have you studied your Competitors and learned from them?
Do you keep records of the results of your marketing procedures, so you know **what to do again (because it worked) and what to avoid (because it didn't)?**
Do you leave your FULL name when you leave a message for somebody to call you? (If there are 4 "Johns" working in your office, which one will get the call when the other party calls back?)
Do you think before you speak?
Do you ponder the consequences of your actions?

ON THE VALUE OF TIME
After your health, your time is your most valuable asset.
Have you mastered Time Management techniques? e.g. doing the most important

things FIRST?

Are you returning calls from your Prospects, Customers, Clients and fellow Realtors promptly?

Do you waste precious time by deliberately playing telephone tag? By having yourself paged through the office instead of leaving the number where you can be reached at that moment in time?

Are you using labour saving devices to make your life easier?

ON AVOIDING LAW SUITS

In your dealings with clients, do you realize what is the **dividing line between giving "information" and giving "advice?"**

In order to close a sale, will you recklessly give advice on a subject in which you are not really qualified to do so?

Did you verify and research all data on your listings or the property on which you are writing an offer on?

Did you protect your Clients with "subject to" clauses?

Like the saying goes: an ounce of prevention is worth a pound of cure. That is also the reason why Noah built the ark BEFORE it started to rain.

ON YOUR LIFE AND FUTURE

Have you developed an investment program (with an Annual Dollar Objective) for financial independence?

Is selling real estate your vehicle of choice for achieving financial independence?

Is it your goal to give your loved ones a relatively worry-free and good life?

Do you periodically take time out to enjoy with them the wondrous journey of life?

Or are you a workaholic for whom work is the sole source of joy?

If you postpone your major leisure time projects (e.g. a trip around the world) until your retirement, then you could be in for a bad surprise. The "Golden Age" may not quite be what you expected it to be; to your dismay you may discover that everything hurts and what doesn't hurt - doesn't work.

Worthwhile New Year's Resolutions

Every December 31st we make a wish list of what great things we will accomplish in the New Year. Come January we then throw ourselves enthusiastically into an - alas only short-lived - orgy of "being organized" and earnestly try to "attain goals." Unfortunately most of it will fizzle out after the next full moon.

New Year's Resolutions like goals must be
- simple and worthwhile,
- precisely formulated
- and attainable.

An old cliche says that "today is the first day of the rest of your life." Therefore, (New Year's) **RESOLUTIONS can be made on ANY DAY during the year** and you do not have to wait till December 31st.

The following are a few suggestions for worthwhile resolutions which will **lead to good working habits.**

(1) Although every day is different in a salesperson's life, try to make an effort to
- **start your working day at the office.**
- **Whenever possible your working day should start at a REGULAR TIME.**

(2) Do not march turkeys up and down the airport runway trying to teach them to fly. Similarly **do not waste your time with**
- undecided and/or unqualified Buyers
- and stubbornly unreasonable Sellers.

(3) It is vital that you keep up-to-date with new developments in the real estate business. Therefore, make a serious effort to attend
- the Office Sales Meetings
- and a few seminars put on by your Real Estate Board.

(4) To find out what is new "for sale" and to familiarize yourself with the current market, attend whenever possible
- the Office Tour
- and the Multiple Listing Tour.

(5) Make an ironclad contract with yourself, that **every day you will make ONE LISTING EFFORT** before your weary head hits the pillow at bedtime. This daily listing effort (which incidentally is not easy to keep up over a long period of time) should translate into 365 listing efforts for the year. There are only 2 exceptions allowed:

(a) If you were showing homes to a hot Buyer all day long and present his offer in the evening
  (b) or if you are in the hospital under the knife.

(6) Domestic peace and harmony are the bedrock of life. To strengthen your family bonds spend **more time with your wife and children.**
   - We will eat supper **together.**
   - We will go on a holiday **together.**
   - After the children have gone to bed, I will **talk to my wife/husband/partner and spend more time with her/him.**

(7) Make an effort to bring your **financial affairs in order.**
   Amongst others, this can mean:
   - **pay off some debts.**
   - Put some money aside **for a rainy day.**
   - Put some money aside **for your retirement.**
   - For **THIS YEAR try to live BELOW your means.**
     This definitely doesn't mean that you cut back on food, car, house upkeep etc. It simply means to keep your **discretionary spending under control:**
     - Before you thoughtlessly spend (waste) a loonie, turn it over twice.
     - DO NOT BUY
       - appealing, but basically unnecessary gizmos or gadgets, electronic or otherwise.
       - Luxury holidays to far away places which you can ill afford.

     You get the drift…

More New Year's Resolutions And 12 Ways How To Keep Them

Well it is that time of the year again when we say: "Out with the old and in with the new." We are determined to "turn over a new leaf" and "improve ourselves" somehow in the New Year.

The New Year's Eve celebrations (even if you are only watching them on TV) bring on both a sense of renewal as well as an old malaise: the guilt that last year's resolutions were short lived. By January 3rd some of us were smoking again, by the end of January we kissed our diet goodbye because we had lost only 1 pound instead of the hoped for 10. By the middle of February we gave up on phone canvassing, because we couldn't stand the many rejections. As usual we then lamely consoled ourselves that the road to hell is paved with good intentions.

I hate to disappoint those of you who are under the illusion that "this year is going to be different." It is not. The one and only thing which we can be fairly certain of is that we will have to keep on breathing. Everything else is negotiable and variable regardless of how sincere your resolves were or are. As a lay person I am not qualified to lecture about human behaviour modification, but here are **a few tips on how you may possibly increase your chances of keeping some of your New Year's Resolutions:**

(1) Recognize that **BIG changes are made by taking SMALL steps.**

(2) Don't overwhelm yourself by making too many resolutions; one or two will do.

(3) **Commitment is a major issue.** Are you prepared to make the necessary sacrifices? Are you really willing and able to invest the required effort and time which is required to keep your resolution? It takes a lot of energy and self-discipline to live up to whatever you have resolved to do ... especially when nobody is watching.

(4) Much has been said about **setting goals.** A New Year's Party is neither the time nor the place to make last-minute, rash and ill-defined resolutions; after you have had a few drinks don't puff out your chest and announce to the world that you will adopt a "healthy lifestyle": lose weight, eat better, relax more, get more sleep, exercise, quit smoking and/or drinking etc. If subsequently you fail to deliver on your promises, you will feel not only guilty but it will also be a humiliating and ego-draining experience.

(5) You may be better off **making quietly a resolution about something which you have been thinking about for a while.** A positive and worthwhile objective which you have been kicking around in your mind, but somehow never got around to doing it.

(6) **It takes a solid strategy to reach and surpass realistic goals.** Instead of setting high and noble goals (which are tough to keep), **make New Year's Resolutions which are ridiculously easy to keep.** E.g. I want to lose one pound. As soon as you have achieved that goal (whenever it may be) and maintained your new weight for a while, then renegotiate with yourself that you will lose "another pound" and so on. But please don't cheat by
- wearing loose and ill-fitting clothes or
- by weighing yourself one day fully clothed (including your heavy mud boots) and the next day by weighing yourself in the nude. You won't fool anybody.

To quit smoking cold turkey may be too much of a shock to your system. If you can't do it, then smoke one cigarette less a day for a week or two and keep on reducing the total number of cigarettes until you have smoked your last one. **That way you will be able to celebrate nothing but positive achievements and successes throughout the year.**

(7) If at first you don't succeed then try and try again.
To give up is a sure-fire formula for failure.

(8) Sooner or later we had to come around to the subject of **work: increased productivity** is not achieved by eating more fibre, but by getting off your duff. So take your vitamins, put on some comfortable shoes and find the stamina to work, work, work.
  (a) In the daily grind of real estate, a lot of it is **"repetitive work."**
  (b) For those of you who feel the need of doing only **"meaningful work"** I will let you in on a little secret: **a lot of "repetitive work" will eventually "MEAN" that you get paid.**
  (c) E.g. resolve that "Every day I will make ONE listing effort during which I will actually talk to a potential seller." This isn't as easy as it looks, because the operative words are "every day" and the fact that you actually have to speak to a live person. Leaving a message on an answering machine doesn't count.

(9) It will be helpful if you try to pay attention to your thinking: whenever possible counter negative ideas with positive thoughts.
Instead of reproaching yourself for failing during a listing presentation, say: "Today I have made some progress. I have learned another thing what not to say/do when pitching for a listing."

(10) It goes without saying that many of us will resolve to **spend more quality time with our families.** This is difficult to do when the market is hot and you are working 12-plus hour days.
But there are many little things which you can do consistently every day. Please note that the key word is "persistence":
- even if everything has gone wrong for you during your workday, don't arrive

home by kicking the front door open with the wrath of Zeus.
- Instead make a concerted effort to greet your spouse and your children pleasantly.
- A simple hello with a little smile will do.
- Giving a little kiss on somebody's cheek is an added bonus.
- From the lines in your tired face everybody will anyway recognize what sort of a day you have had.
- Your effort to be civilized under trying circumstances will be appreciated by all.
- Don't be severely critical if dinner doesn't resemble a candle-lit culinary triumph; your wife may also have had a bad day.
- All of these little things are relatively easy to do and yet will go a long way in solidifying your family relationships.

(11) Whatever your resolutions are, try to make them a regular part of your daily life.

(12) The general idea is to get through the year feeling good and to finish it happily satisfied.

HAPPY NEW YEAR TO YOU ALL!

"Vigilantibus Non Dormientibus Scripta Est Lex"
(The Law is written for the wide-awake ... not for the sleepy)

It should only be fair that every Realtor should have the right to protect his commission to the best of his ability.

Up to a certain financial limit the Small Claims Court will provide a speedy and inexpensive resolution of a commission dispute; the parties involved do not need a lawyer.

Disputes for commission amounts exceeding the Small Claims Court limit can be settled in a higher Court where the services of a lawyer are advisable. For obvious reasons the amount of his fees must be taken into consideration when the decision to sue is made.

However, before you unleash the forces of the Courts, it might be a good idea to **first discuss the merits of the case with your Manager and/or a Lawyer.**
Remember that:
- you cannot sue in your own name; the Plaintiff must be the employing Real Estate Company (even if you are an Independent Contractor).
- The Court may require proof of licensing (See "Real Estate Act"; also **"Coldwell Banker Powder Country v. Smith,"** BCSC [2000-10-27] Docket No. 3615)
- Some Realtors, keeping good public relations in mind, may decide to chalk up a Seller's refusal to pay the commission as the price of doing business. By all means it is every Realtor's right to let the defaulting Client "get away with commission."

The following CLOSING ARGUMENTS have been used successfully when a real estate company sued for a commission. (**"Sutton Group - Medallion Realty v. Bouwman,"** Provincial Court of B.C., Surrey Small Claims Court File # 52354, Judgment February 1, 2005).

The Realtor's RIGHT TO COMMISSION is based on the Listing Contract.
The contracting parties of the Listing Contract are
- the Sellers and
- the Real Estate Company.

The legitimate expectation of these contracting parties
    (a) at the time of the **signing** of the Listing Contract AND
    (b) at the time that the Real Estate Company's
- services,
- material efforts and
- expertise

were PROVIDED to and ACCEPTED by the Sellers WAS THAT

THE Real Estate Company would have earned an entitlement to compensation IF a BUYER was INTRODUCED and/or CONTRACTED WITH who is ready, willing and able to complete the sale on Completion Date.

(1) The Real Estate Company says that it was
   - the **"EFFECTIVE CAUSE OF SALE"** and
   - that the Sellers have a legal obligation to pay for those services.

(2) The Real Estate Company further says that there is no evidence that
   - the Realtor's services were to be provided gratuitously
   - or that these services were imposed on the Sellers.
   - **This is NOT a case of gratuitous services being foisted upon an unwilling recipient.**

(3) By refusing to pay the real estate commission as claimed, the Sellers have
   - **breached** the terms of the Listing Contract and
   - **have taken the BENEFITS** of the Real Estate Company's services **while committing the INJUSTICE OF ENRICHMENT** in the context of the relationship of the parties.

(4) The Real Estate Company claims that
   - it has **suffered a corresponding DEPRIVATION** and
   - that there is **NO JURISTIC REASON** entitling the Sellers to that **UNJUST ENRICHMENT.**
   - The keeping of the enrichment or benefit without recompense would be **"against conscience."**

(5) Alternatively the Real Estate Company claims **DAMAGES on a "QUANTUM MERUIT" basis.**

DISCUSSION and CASE LAW:

(I) **The Right to commission BASED on the LISTING CONTRACT.**

Basically the **"RIGHT TO COMMISSION"** is determined by the **WORDING of the LISTING CONTRACT.** This wording is of prime importance and will override a general rule derived from the case law. The Listing Contract often says that the commission is earned by the Realtor **when there is a valid, subject-free, firm contract of Purchase and Sale achieved between the Seller and Buyer.** Of course, the Buyer must be ready, willing and able to complete on Completion Date.

In case there is a conflict (as to the payment of the commission) between the terms of the Listing Contract and those mentioned in the Contract of Purchase and Sale, **the terms of the Listing Contract will prevail,** since there is no (legal) consideration for any new contract (between the Realtors and the Sellers) arising out of the Contract for Purchase and Sale. The Contract of Purchase and Sale is a contract between the Sellers and the Buyers.

(1) **"Western Mortgage (Realty) Corp. v. Small World Holdings Inc."**
    BC. Supreme Court (1992-01-10) BCSC C915156 and
    B.C. Court of Appeal (1993-01-22), CA015069, 77 BCLR (2d) 324

Highlights (supplied for the convenience of the Reader):
  (a) The Listing Agreement contained the term that there will be a commission paid **"upon a binding contract of sale of the said property being entered into during the term of this Exclusive Listing Agreement."**
  (b) The Purchaser Bay River Development did not perform in accordance with the Contract of Purchase and Sale on the completion date. The deposit was forfeit to the Seller.
  (c) "When the efforts of the Realtor result in a binding contract being entered into and the express terms of the contract make commission payable on that event, then ... the Realtor will have earned his commission."
  (d) **As the Court of Appeal also notes** "there is no evidence that the parties intended to amend the listing agreement and there is nothing in the Agreement of Purchase and Sale to warrant that conclusion.... Reading the two documents in harmony ... the Agreement of Purchase and Sale merely confirms the bargain struck in the Listing Agreement."

A Law Case cited in #1:

"H. W. Liebig Co. v. Leading Investments Ltd."
Supreme Court of Canada, [1986] 1 S.C.R.70, 65 N.R. 209

Highlights (supplied for the convenience of the Reader):

  (a) As outlined **per** Dickson C.M. and Lamer and LaForest JJ.: **"The LISTING AGREEMENT governed.** The bargain between vendor and broker was struck when the Listing Agreement was signed and its meaning was not altered by reading it with the Agreement of Purchase and Sale.... The vendor, by signing the Agreement of Purchase and Sale, intended to accept the buyer's offer; **the clause in that agreement concerning the broker's commission merely confirmed the bargain struck in the Listing Agreement."**
  (b) "... The contract between the vendor and the real estate broker **cannot be changed by the subsequent dealings between the vendor and his intended purchaser."**

(c) "... The broker could recover for his services to the vendor on a quantum meruit …in restitution. Otherwise **the vendor would be unjustly enriched** from the efforts of the broker at the vendor's request."

Another Law Case cited in #1:
"Luxor (Eastbourne) Ltd. v. Cooper"
[1941] 1 All E.R. 33 (H.L.)

Highlights (supplied for the convenience of the Reader):

At page 124 it says regarding contracts for real estate commissions:
(1) Commission contracts are subject to no peculiar rules or principles of their own; the law which governs them is the law which governs all contracts and all questions of agency.
(2) No general rule can be laid down by which the rights of the agent or the liability of the principal under commission contracts are to be determined.
In each case …[the rights of the agent or the liability of the principal under commission contracts] must depend upon the exact terms of the contract in question, and upon the true construction of those terms.
It says further: "It is agreed on all sides that the presumption is **against the adding to contracts of terms which the parties have not expressed.** The general presumption is that the **parties have expressed every material term which they have intended should govern their agreement**, whether oral or in writing."

Another Law Case cited in # 1

"Realtech Realty Corp. v. Dancorp Developments Ltd."
B.C. Court of Appeal (1991-10-18) BCCA CA013239)

Highlights (supplied for the convenience of the Reader):

(a) … Realtech had performed in accordance with these provisions and was therefore entitled to the agreed commission.
(b) … the Plaintiff had done what it was retained to do, namely find lenders ready, willing and able to lend…
(c) … the Plaintiff was not responsible for the increased costs… **the advent of increased costs did not relieve Dancorp from the commission obligation.**

(II) The Right to commission BASED ON THE CONCEPT of "THE UNBROKEN CHAIN of events."

(2) "Re/Max Centre City Realty v. Friesen"
Provincial Court of B.C., (2002-06-19) Prince George, Docket No. SM 14266

Highlights (supplied for the convenience of the Reader):

Same Sellers plus Same Buyers in Sale # 1 and Sale # 2
(a) Listing Agent's Remuneration is based on the terms of the Listing Contract.
(b) Due to the Realtor's sales efforts the Buyer was introduced to the property and a First Sale resulted.
(c) For various reasons this First Sale did not complete.
(d) **The Defendant Sellers claim that "the eventual sale of the property was the result of a 'new sales arrangement' made after the expiry of the listing contract** and that prior to the date of sale, the Buyers were not ready, willing and able to complete the sale."
(e) The Judge noted the "similarity of contract terms"
(f) **HELD:**
- the Realtor was the **"effective cause of sale"**
- there was an UNBROKEN CHAIN OF EVENTS
- the arrangements between the Buyers and Sellers were not (completely) broken.

The Plaintiff REALTORS had judgment.

(3) "Homelife Okanagan Realty Inc. v. Galvagno"
B.C. Supreme Court (1994-11-07) BCSC 9242

Highlights (supplied for the convenience of the Reader):

Same Seller + Same Buyers
(a) The Realtor introduced the Buyers to the property
(b) The Realtor assisted in the initial negotiations between the parties and thus laid the foundation upon which the sale was eventually based.
(c) The Realtor is entitled to the commission pursuant to the Listing Contract.

The Plaintiff Realtors had judgment against the Defendants Sellers.

52 Sales Meetings

(III) The Right to commission when the Realtor was the "Effective Cause of Sale" ALTHOUGH the Realtor was NOT FULLY INVOLVED in all details of a SUBSEQUENT SALE.

(4) **"Murray Goldman Real Estate Ltd. v. Captain Developments Ltd. et al" Ontario Court of Appeal (February 21, 1978)**

Highlights (supplied for the convenience of the Reader):

(a) A Seller of land agreed to pay a commission to a Realtor on the completion of the transaction.
(b) The transaction was not completed on time and a new agreement was substituted with a different company named as Buyer but under the SAME CONTROL as the original purchaser.
(c) The 2nd agreement contained no promise to pay commission.

IT WAS HELD that the new agreement was in effect an EXTENSION and amendment of the old, and consequently the commission was payable as agreed.

(5) **"Century 21 Creston Valley Realty Ltd. v. Farm Credit Corp." B.C. County Court of Kootenay, Creston Registry No. 67, (June 18, 1990), BCJ # 1461**

Highlights (supplied for the convenience of the Reader):

(a) The Defendant Seller sought to by-pass the Realtor.
(b) The Court decided that the Agent was the "effective cause of sale" even though it had nothing to do with the final contract.
(c) It was sufficient that it brought the parties together and that the introduction of the buyer resulted in the completed sale.
(d) There was an implied agreement that the Seller would pay a commission.
(e) **The Judge would also have awarded damages on the grounds of preventing UNJUST ENRICHMENT.**
The commission would have been $ 9,500.00. On the grounds of unjust enrichment $ 9,800 was found to be the appropriate remuneration due to the Plaintiff Realtor.

LAW CASES referred to in this (# 5) law suit:

(a) **"West Park Realty Ltd. v. Ector Developments Ltd."**
[1990] B.C.J. No. 1038, No. 2286/87 County Court of Cariboo:

Highlights (supplied for the convenience of the Reader):

The Court held that
- to be the "effective cause of sale," it is not necessary that the Agent effect the final contract of sale.
- If he brings the vendor and purchaser together and creates a contractual relationship between them resulting in a completed sale, he has ... earned his commission... **The transaction was NOT at an end.**
- **(The Seller's) CONDUCT amounted to a continuous effort to bring this transaction to a successful closing.** The agreement of ..., **as modified ...later, was never abandoned.** There was a continuous course of dealings to bring it to a conclusion. It was the agreement which closed on ... **with a variation. There was NO new interim agreement.**

The Plaintiff Realtor received judgment.

(b) **Fridman's "Law of Agency" 5th ed. at p. 166** quoting Erle, C.J. in **"Green v. Bartlett (1863),** 14 C.B.N.S. 681 at 685 it is said: "If the relation of buyer and seller is really brought about by the act of the agent he is entitled to commission although the actual sale has not been effected by him."

(c) **"Park Lane Ranch v. Fleetwood Village Holdings Ltd."**
(1980) 17 R.P.R. 35 (B.C.S.C.) UNJUST ENRICHMENT

(IV) **The Right to commission on the basis of**
- **QUANTUM MERUIT (payment [or damages] for work done)**
- **and the principles of UNJUST ENRICHMENT**

(6) **"Century 21 Gold Team Realty Ltd. v. 443979 B.C. Ltd."**
B.C. Supreme Court, (January 10, 1996), Docket No. A933924

Highlights (supplied for the convenience of the Reader):

The Seller refused to pay commission for various reasons.

The Honourable Mr. Justice H. A. Callaghan said:
At 21
The test is whether the services provided by the Realtor either caused or materially contributed ...(to the sale).
It is not necessary that the Agent be the sole effective cause of the agreement in order to demonstrate a benefit to the Defendant. See "Bancorp Mortgage Limited v. Sicon Group Inc." B.C. Supreme Court (1990-06-25), Docket No. C882795,
At 22
... it was the Plaintiff, Pirie (the Realtor), who solidified that interest in the property and brought (the Buyer) Molnar to the negotiating table with the Defendant (Seller).

The Plaintiffs (Realtors) did the very thing they were hired to do -canvass the market and bring an interested party to the table.
At 23
Since a contract was concluded the Plaintiff (Realtor) is entitled to be paid.

(7) **"Bedaux Real Estate Inc. v. Real Land Developments Ltd."**
Alberta Provincial Court (2005-01-14), Docket P0390103811

Highlights (supplied for the convenience of the Reader):

The Judge awarded compensation for the Real Estate Company's services rendered on a "quantum meruit by way of damages."

(V) The Right to commission on the basis of UNJUST ENRICHMENT.

(8) **"Prospero International Realty Inc. d.b.a. Profile Leasing Group v. TBGC Leasing Limited"**
B.C. Supreme Court [1999-05-28] Docket No. C952572

Highlights (supplied for the convenience of the Reader):

DISCUSSION of UNJUST ENRICHMENT:

(a) **An enrichment or a benefit**: an enrichment without recompense is "against conscience." See "**Bancorp Mortgage Ltd. v. Sicon Group Inc.**" [1990-06-25] BCSC 2 BLR (2d) 161

(b) **A corresponding deprivation:** the Plaintiff did suffer a corresponding deprivation as he was not compensated for his services which were provided to the Defendant. There is no evidence that these services were to be provided gratuitously or that these services were imposed on the Defendant.

(c) **The absence of any juristic reason for the enrichment.** There is no juristic reason entitling the Defendant to that enrichment. See "**Pettkus v. Becker**" **(1980), 117 D.L.R. (3d) 257 (S.C.C.).**
Please **refer to [61]** in Prospero v. TBGC "**It is the injustice of the enrichment or benefit in the context of the relationship of the parties** that is of primary importance. See "**National Trust Co. v. Atlas Cabinets & Furniture Ltd.**" [1990], 38 C.L.R. 106 (BCCA).
At [62] it says in "Prospero": "…it must be evident that the retention of the benefit would be unjust in the circumstances of the case or that keeping of the enrichment or benefit without recompense would be "**against conscience.**"

(d) **"Effective Cause of Sale"**: the Plaintiff Realtor not only materially contributed to the sale, but his introduction of the Buyer was **the foundation upon which the negotiations which resulted in the purchase and sale proceeded and without which they would NOT have proceeded.** At [65} in "Prospero" it says: "There is no evidence that the (Realtor's) services were to be provided gratuitously or that these services were imposed on the Defendants."

(e) At [67] in "Prospero" it says: "... **the payment of the commission was an ONGOING OBLIGATION, regardless of the amount of the final purchase (price).** Also see [69] and [70] in "Prospero International Realty Inc. v. TBGC Leasing"

JUDGMENT was granted to the Plaintiffs.

(9) **"Colony Park Enterprises Inc. v. Screpnechuk"**
Alberta Court of Queen's Bench, Action No. 9903-08402, Date: 2002-01-16

Highlights (supplied for the convenience of the Reader):

- At [26] **Quantum Meruit**: Law case referred to is: **"Royal LePage Real Estate Services Ltd. v. Frederick Church"** (May 3, 1991) Queen's Bench 80 Alta. L.R. (2d) 122
- At [27] to [30] = **Unjust enrichment** with several cases
- At [31] "...there is a **variation in the price ultimately arrived at between the vendor and the purchaser** from that proposed by the Plaintiff, ... the deal proposed in August and the one made in November are virtually the same."

The Realtor was awarded his commission.

(10) **"West Coast Engineering Ltd. v. Homelife Benchmark Realty Corp."**
B.C.Supreme Court (1994-08-25) Docket No. C907369

Highlights (supplied for the convenience of the Reader):

- The Plaintiff Seller claims damages arising from the sale of acreage; the Plaintiff alleges it sold the property at substantially less than fair market value as the result of the Defendant Realtor's breaches of (fiduciary) duty and negligence.
- The Defendant Realtor counterclaimed for unpaid commission.
- Research to establish Market Value (different sale prices)
- Realtor's sales efforts
- The Plaintiff's action is dismissed

The Realtor's counterclaim succeeded: judgment was granted for the commission.

(VI) The Right to commission when the TRANSACTION IS NOT COMPLETED.

(11) If the BUYER fails to complete:
   (a) "Howell v. Kenton Agencies Ltd."
   (1953) 1 D.L.R. 821 (Ont. H.C.)

Highlights (supplied for the convenience of the Reader):

The payment of the commission was not contingent on the completion of the sale nor payable out of the proceeds; the agent was entitled to recover, even though the default was that of the Buyer.

   (b) "Kellner v. Stickland" [16 R.P.R. (3d), p.125]
   B.C. Supreme Court (May 16, 1997), Docket NW SO-35434
   B.C. Court of Appeal (1998-09-25), Docket CA023249

Highlights (supplied for the convenience of the Reader):

Depending on the wording (terms) of the Listing Contract, the Realtor may be entitled to commission **even in case of default, whether by the Seller or by the Buyer.**
The Honourable Judge Taylor J. said at 39:
"Having fulfilled the terms of its obligation under the listing agreement in my view the Plaintiff (Realtor) is entitled to a commission."
The Purchaser had defaulted.
The Realtor received his commission.

   (c) "Bolohan v. John R. Marsh & Co."
   (1979) 11 R 1, Ont. H.C.

   Highlights (supplied for the convenience of the Reader):

   Commission is payable, even where **the transaction is aborted through no fault of the Seller;** whether the commission is payable will be determined by the general law of contract and also by the wording of the Listing Agreement.

(12) The Realtor stands a better chance to recover the commission when **the failure to complete is the fault of the SELLER.**

   (a) "Advantage Homes Ltd. v. Jones"
   Surrey B.C. Small Claims Court file # 29682

   Highlights (supplied for the convenience of the Reader):

The agent has been held to be entitled to commission upon the **refusal of the owner to proceed.** This decision was on the grounds that the agent had done all he was required to do, namely produce a subject-free firm sale from a Buyer ready, willing and able to proceed on the date set for completion.

(b) "Professional Realty Corporation Ltd. v. H. Y. Louie Co. Ltd." BCSC (November 1, 1989) Docket No. C883597

Highlights (supplied for the convenience of the Reader):

The agreement between the parties was not ambiguous; **but even if it were ambiguous,** the Court would imply the term that commission is payable once the agent had done all required of it, based on extrinsic evidence as to universal custom in the real estate industry and the behaviour of the Defendant.

(c) "Robert D. Berto Ltd. v. Cushley et al" (1977), 78 D.L.R. (3d) 713 (Ont. Dist. Ct.)

Highlights (supplied for the convenience of the Reader):

Where, in an agreement for the purchase and sale of land, the Seller agrees to pay a commission to a real estate company for procuring the offer, the commission is payable even though the sale is, **owing to defects in the title, not completed.**

(d) "Lewis Realty Ltd. v. Skalbania" (1980) 23 B.C.L.R. 336 (C.A.)

Highlights (supplied for the convenience of the Reader):

The Seller could not give good title because it was held in trust for himself and another who would not agree to the sale. The listing on the standard Vancouver Real Estate Board form provided that the commission was to be payable, inter alia, on a binding contract of sale being brought into being. This having been done **(the failure of the Seller to make title was only a mistake in expectations)**, the Agent was entitled to the commission. The decision was on the grounds that the agent had done all he was required to do, namely find a Buyer ready, willing and able to proceed on the date set for completion.

(VII) SUNDRY OTHER ISSUES which a Realtor may be faced with.

(A) THE DUTIES OF AN AGENT

(13) "D'ATRI v. CHILCOTT"
(1975), 7 O.R. (2d) 249 at 258 (H.C.)

Highlights (supplied for the convenience of the Reader):

(a) The relationship between a real estate agent and his Client (Seller) is a **fiduciary and confidential** one.
(b) The Agent has a duty to make full disclosure of all facts **(within his knowledge)** which may affect the value of the property.
(c) **The transaction must be a "righteous one"** and the Selling Price achieved must be not only adequate, but also as advantageous to the Principal as any other price which the Agent could have, by him exercising diligence, obtained from a third party.
(d) The onus is on the Realtor to prove that those duties have been fully complied with.

(B) Sundry Issues:
- The LISTING PRICE,
- FAIR MARKET VALUE,
- APPRAISALS,
- THE "RIGHTEOUS PRICE"

(14) "Phelan v. Realty World Empire Realty Ltd."
(1994-04-05), BCSC C913326 …. 38 R.P.R.(2nd)

Highlights (supplied for the convenience of the Reader):

(a) A Realtor is not a certified appraiser.
(b) The Realtor does not make the final decision about the listing price; the Realtor makes a recommendation for the Seller to consider.
(c) There is no contractual duty between the Seller and the Realtor when the listing price is discussed based on the Realtor's market research.
(d) The Listing agreement is signed AFTER this discussion; any liability for advice given about the listing price must lie in tort and not in contract.
(e) **A Realtor must disclose all material facts which might affect the value of the property.**
(f) **QUOTE OF JUDGE W. G. BAKER:** "In my view, Chief Justice Nemetz did not say, and did not intend to say, that a real estate agent will be found to have breached his fiduciary duty, or to have been negligent, merely because the

price obtained was not the "best possible price" which might have been obtained for the property. How could the "best possible price" be determined? It is not synonymous with fair market value, since some purchaser might be found who, for reasons peculiar to it, might be prepared to pay more, even much more, for a property than its fair market value."

(g) **THE JUDGE SAYS FURTHER:** "I do not think that the law is that a fiduciary has an absolute obligation to be right. Of course, a fiduciary is **not permitted to be wrong because**
- of a conflict of interest
- he has acted fraudulently or behaved in a grossly incompetent fashion
- or failed to make full disclosure of all facts **WITHIN HIS KNOWLEDGE** which might affect the value of the principal's property.

(h) **Real estate appraisal is an inexact science.** Variations in the opinions of real estate agents, and in the opinions of real estate appraisers, are common. A 5% variation between the opinions of different appraisers concerning the value of this type of property is reasonable and not unusual.

(C) Allegation of BREACH OF FIDUCIARY DUTY: Standard of Care and Professional Negligence

(15) A discussion of "Standard of Care" can be found in
"**Deane v. Tapestry Realty Ltd.**"
(2001-03-21) B.C. Provincial Court, New Westminster Registry, File No. C009678

Highlights (supplied for the convenience of the Reader):

(a) In order to prove his case, the Claimant (dissatisfied Client) must show that the Defendant's (Realtor's) work and actions have fallen below the standard of a reasonably prudent real estate agent in the performance of his duty of care. See **"Haag v. Marshall" (1989) 61 D.L.R. (4th) 371 at 382 [BCCA].**

(b) In order to accomplish that, the Claimant (dissatisfied Client) must provide to the Court **some evidence what the "Standard of Care" is.** See "**Snijders et al v. Morgan et al**" **(unreported), October 9, 1996, B.C. Supreme Court, Nelson Registry No. 4747.**

(c) One way of doing that would be to bring to Court an "expert" (independent real estate professional) to explain and testify what the standard of care in this particular regard would be.

(16) "Barker v. 100 Mile Realty Ltd.,"
BCSC (2000-02-23) Kamloops, B.C. Docket No. 23302

Highlights (supplied for the convenience of the Reader):

(a) **Discussion of the Listing Price.** The Realtor doesn't make the decision, he merely explains his recommendation. The Seller makes the decision what the Listing Price will be.
(b) Discussion of duty owed by a Real Estate Agent.
(c) The Seller's claims for damages and complaints of Realtor's negligence and breach of fiduciary duty were dismissed, because the Seller has failed to provide satisfactory proof.

(17) "Fraser v. Powell River Real Estate Ltd."
B.C. Supreme Court (1997-03-27) BCSC S0431

Highlights (supplied for the convenience of the Reader):

(a) Realtor's standard of care
NOTE…IMPORTANT:
(b) **All allegations against the Realtor must be substantiated.**
(c) **Any damages must be proven.**
At [35] it says: "With respect to all of these complaints, there is no evidence that (the Realtor) knew of the problems or ought to have known of them. The Plaintiffs have not satisfied the onus of showing that they relied upon his representations…"
At [37] it says: "I conclude that the Plaintiffs **have not established that (the Realtor's) conduct fell short of the standard of care expected of** a realtor in the circumstances and their action against the Defendants (Real Estate Company and Salesman) is dismissed."

(18) "NIXON v. EDEN"
B.C. Supreme Court (1998-08-11) Docket # 31857

Highlights (supplied for the convenience of the Reader):

The Seller must establish that in the preparation of a CMA the defendant Realtor was negligent, i.e. failed to meet the requisite standard of reasonable skill, care and diligence expected of a professional real estate salesman.

(19) "HAAG v. MARSHALL"
(1989) 61 D.L.R. 4th 371 (BCCA)

Highlights (supplied for the convenience of the Reader):

Mr. Justice Lambert said at p. 382 "…in cases of **professional negligence** above all, with the many difficult and varied situations met, it must be fairly demonstrated that it has fallen below an established standard or practice in the profession."

(20) "REIDY MOTORS LTD. v. GRIMM"
Alberta Queeen's Bench (January 3, 1996)
Alberta Court of Appeal, Calgary Civil Sittings (June 13, 1997)

Highlights (supplied for the convenience of the Reader):

Agent's duty to make full disclosure to his principal. By flipping the property and not disclosing the increase in value before closing, the Defendant Realtor had breached his fiduciary duty to his Client. The Defendant Realtor was required to disgorge himself of the profit made on sale, including the commission paid by the Plaintiff (Seller).

The Alberta Court of Appeal held that notwithstanding the breach of fiduciary relationship the **REALTOR WAS ENTITLED TO HIS COMMISSION.** If a Real Estate Broker is entitled to his commission when there has been a breach of fiduciary relationship, a fortiori, he is so entitled when he has acted in good faith, albeit negligently.

(D) THE CREDIBILITY OF WITNESSES IN COURT

(21) "FARNYA v. CHORNY"
(1951) 4 WWR (NS) 171 (BCCA)

Highlights (supplied for the convenience of the Reader):

(a) Justice does not depend on who is the best actor in the witness box.
(b) The presiding Judge in Court must take into consideration:
- if the personal demeanour of a witness carries the conviction of truth and the appearance of sincerity.
- "Credibility" is a combination of may factors; e.g. knowledge, powers of observation, accurate memory, judgment and the ability to describe clearly and concisely what the witness has seen and heard.
- If (the truth of) the story of the witness is in harmony with the preponderance of the probabilities which a practical and informed person

would recognize as "reasonable."
(c) In case of conflict of evidence, the Judge must also examine and weigh the credibility of
- a quick-minded, experienced and confident witness **versus**
- the testimony of a shrewd person adept in the half-lie and who is experienced in combining skilful exaggeration with the partial suppression of the truth.

(E) FAILURE TO REMOVE A "SUBJECT-TO" CLAUSE.

(22) "Possible Enterprises Ltd. v. Newcomen"
B.C. Supreme Court, (1998-06-02) Docket 5334, Nelson Registry

Highlights (supplied for the convenience of the Reader):

- The written contract should be considered first, reading the words in their ordinary and natural sense.
- The Court must construe the contract in accordance with the parties' intentions.
- Matters ought to be determined on their merits rather than on points of procedure.
- The Defendant gave no notice at any time that she was solely relying on this condition (in this case to satisfy herself as to the boundaries of the property).
- It was not clear what form of notice was required, if any.
- Where a term of a contract is unclear, the Court may go outside the document. **The acts of the parties "in pursuance of the instrument may be looked at as a clue to their intentions."** [DiCastri, Law of Vendor and Purchaser (3d edition) paragraph 395].
- Considering this transaction in that light, the proper construction is that the Defendant had an opportunity to withdraw, but **failing to do so and failing such notice, the EXPECTATIONS OF THE PARTIES was that the CONDITION WOULD LAPSE.** This is clearly how the Defendant behaved.

This law case also refers to
"WOELLER v. ORFUS et al,"
Ontario Hight Court of Justice, November 26, 1979, 1106 D.L.R. (3d)115
In circumstances where
- there has been no effort to satisfy a condition and
- there is no evidence that the condition could not have been satisfied, a **CONTRACT WILL NORMALLY BE ENFORCED.**

Another law case referred to in this connection is:
"Gilchrist v. Commodore"
Court of Appeal, November 23, 1931, 40 O.W.N. 577
Appeal by the Plaintiff from the judgment of Kelly, J., dismissing the claim, and in favour of the defendant on his counterclaim.
The Appeal was dismissed with costs.